Finding Birds
The Complete Guide

Eric Dempsey & Michael O'Clery

Gill & Macmillan

Find a Region or County

The book is organised by region and county.

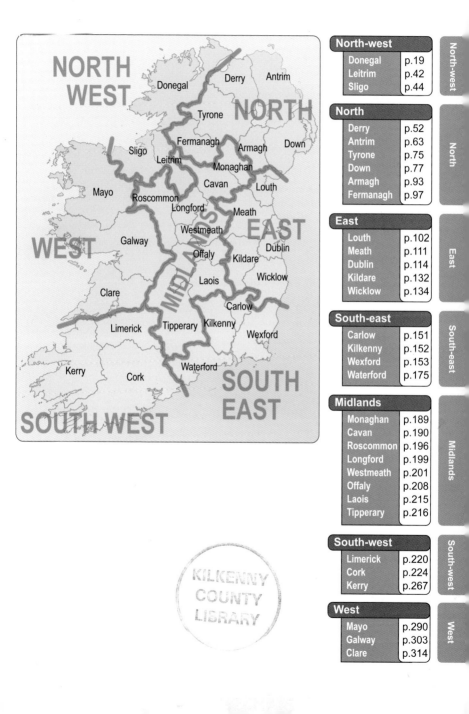

Gill & Macmillan Ltd
Hume Avenue, Park West, Dublin 12
with associated companies throughout the world
www.gillmacmillan.ie
© Text: Eric Dempsey and Michael O'Clery, 2007
© Paintings and Maps: Michael O'Clery, 2007
978 07171 3916 3
Index compiled by Cover To Cover
Design and print origination by Michael O'Clery
Printed in Malaysia

The paper used in this book comes from wood pulp of managed forests. For every tree felled, at least one tree is planted, thereby renewing natural resources.

A CIP catalogue record for this book is available from the British Library.

5 4 3 2 1

Contents

vi

Acknowledgments

There are many people who have assisted us during the course of producing this book. Without them, it could not have been completed. We would especially like to thank Joe Adamson, Pat Brennan, Ed Carty, Derek Charles, Tom Cuffe, Fergus Fitzgerald, Dara Fitzpatrick, Colum Flynn, Kieran Grace, Joe Hobbs, Harry Hussey, Andrea Kelly, Paul Kelly, Anthony McGeehan, Esther Murphy, Bobbie Reeners, Brad Robson, Jim Wilson, Steve Wing and Peter Wolstenholme for a combination of their time, assistance, advice and encouragement.

Special thanks also to Dave Allen, Lorraine Benson, Dermot Breen, Victor Caschera, Alex Copland, Kevin Cronin, Tony Culley, Phil Davies, Ursula Desmond, Jim Dowdall, Ian Enlander, Sean Farrell, Wilton Farrelly, Jim Fitzharris, Owen Foley, Ian Forsyth, Tom Gittings, Nick Gray, John Hammond, Niall Hatch, Aidan Kelly, Pat Lonergan, John Lovatt, John Lynch, Breffni Martin, Paul Moore, Killian Mullarney, Bert Murphy, John Murphy, Kevin Murphy, Tony Murray, Tony Nagle, Eanna ní Lamhna, Alan O'Brien, Dennis O'Sullivan, Mick O'Sullivan, Oran O'Sullivan, Chris Peppiatt, Sean Pierce, John Power, Ian Rippey, Julie Roe, Neil Sharkey, Robert Vaughan, Paul Walsh and Jerry Wray for their support and assistance.

For technical assistance, many thanks to Owen Barry, Devin Doyle and Scott Fairweather.

Finally, we would like to thank our parents and families for their continued support and encouragement.

Eric Dempsey & Michael O'Clery
May 2007

How to use this book

The book is divided into three main parts:

• Introduction

• 60 Common Species. A summary of the commonest birds which you are likely to encounter

• Sites. The best and most productive sites in Ireland for finding birds

Introduction
Includes a brief introduction to birdwatching in Ireland, as well as information on currency, driving in Ireland, accommodation, the phone system and transport infrastructure.

60 Common Species
A summary and map of the occurrence of the 60 commonest species, showing where and when you can expect to see them. These 60 common species are generally NOT included in the species lists for each site, to avoid unnecessary repetition. They are only mentioned in the main text if there is a particular reason to do so. You can expect to see these species on any birdwatching trip in Ireland, in the relevant season and habitat.

Sites
To find a particular site, refer to 'Find a Region or County' at the front of the book. If you wish to locate the birdwatching sites in a particular county, see the Contents pages.

At the top of each main site account is the site heading, showing name, site number, the grid reference, the best time to visit, a location map (national) and a location map (regional). See below for an example.

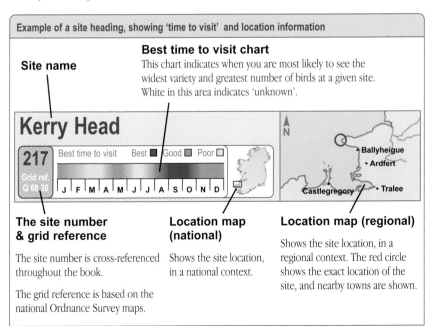

Example of a site heading, showing 'time to visit' and location information

Site name

Best time to visit chart
This chart indicates when you are most likely to see the widest variety and greatest number of birds at a given site. White in this area indicates 'unknown'.

Kerry Head

217

Grid ref. Q 68 30

Best time to visit   Best ■ Good ■ Poor □

J F M A M J J A S O N D

Ballyheigue
Ardfert
Castlegregory   Tralee

The site number & grid reference
The site number is cross-referenced throughout the book.

The grid reference is based on the national Ordnance Survey maps.

Location map (national)
Shows the site location, in a national context.

Location map (regional)
Shows the site location, in a regional context. The red circle shows the exact location of the site, and nearby towns are shown.

1

The first paragraph of each main site account gives a summary of the area and notable species which might be seen.

In the 'Directions' section, compass points are abbreviated to N, S, E and W. Directions and distances are given from the nearest town, where applicable, and road numbers given where possible. All major and many minor sites are mapped. All distances are given in metres (m) and kilometres (km). For a Kilometre/Mileage conversion chart, see page 4.

In the 'Species' section, it should be emphasised that the 60 commonest species are generally not included (unless particularly noteworthy numbers or concentrations occur). In this section, the following abbreviations are used: (O) Occasional – This species can be expected to occur at this site occasionally, though may not be seen on each visit; (R) Rare – This species is seen only rarely.

In the 'Rarities' section, a list of rare birds which have been seen at that site is included. These are generally species which have occurred in the past decade or so (some particularly noteworthy older records are included) and, while not intended to be comprehensive, it should give an indication of what unusual species have occurred at that site.

Minor sites are given much the same treatment, though the information is given in summary form. Most counties have an 'Other sites' section where further details are given of sites which perhaps lack large numbers or variety of birds, or are difficult to access or poorly known, but which warrant attention. These are also listed in the Index.

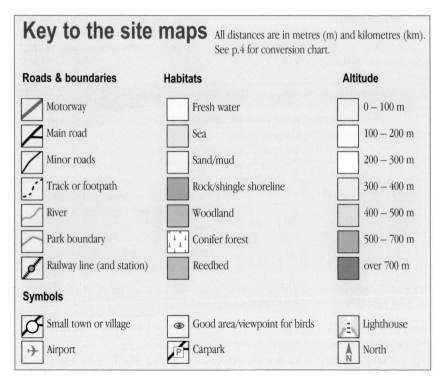

Key to the site maps
All distances are in metres (m) and kilometres (km). See p.4 for conversion chart.

Roads & boundaries

- Motorway
- Main road
- Minor roads
- Track or footpath
- River
- Park boundary
- Railway line (and station)

Symbols

- Small town or village
- Airport

Habitats

- Fresh water
- Sea
- Sand/mud
- Rock/shingle shoreline
- Woodland
- Conifer forest
- Reedbed

- Good area/viewpoint for birds
- Carpark

Altitude

- 0 – 100 m
- 100 – 200 m
- 200 – 300 m
- 300 – 400 m
- 400 – 500 m
- 500 – 700 m
- over 700 m

- Lighthouse
- North

Introduction

Birdwatching in Ireland

In recent years, the interest in birds and birdwatching in Ireland has grown significantly... and for good reason. For the birdwatcher, Ireland has much to offer. It has some of the largest breeding seabird colonies in the world, huge flocks of wintering shorebirds and wildfowl, and is excellently situated for autumn seabird passage. In spring and autumn, there is also the possibility of seeing a host of rare and unusual migrant species. In addition, the Shannon Callows of the midland counties and the remote islands of north Donegal are the last strongholds of the globally threatened Corncrake. Dublin and Wexford also hold large breeding colonies of the rare and exquisite Roseate Tern.

There have been up to 430 different species of birds recorded so far in Ireland. Of these, approximately 100 are considered as resident species. Up to 90 species are either summer or winter visitors (such as Swallows and Brent Geese respectively) while another 30 are passage migrants using Ireland as a mere stopover on their migration (such as Whimbrels and Arctic Skuas). The other 210 species recorded are scarce, rare or extremely rare migrants and vagrants.

Ireland is unique in that, by comparison to most European countries, it has been isolated as an island for approximately 8,000 years. As a result, Ireland has three distinct subspecies of breeding birds, Coal Tit, Jay and Dipper, while the Irish Red Grouse is also considered by some to be distinct from those found elsewhere in Europe. Such early isolation also explains why many non-migratory species such as Tawny Owl and Nuthatch failed to reach Ireland and so do not occur here.

In winter, Ireland, lying on the western edge of Europe, is ideally located to attract waders, wildfowl and passerines from breeding grounds in Arctic Canada, Greenland, Iceland, northern Europe and Siberia. Our climate is dominated by the mild Atlantic weather systems and, because of this, we rarely suffer the harsh winter weather that grips our European neighbours each year. Our comparatively mild winters and the extensive areas of intertidal mudflats provide rich, soft feeding for thousands of waders, while our wet climate creates the necessary wetlands for countless wildfowl. Each year 'northern' gulls such as Iceland and Glaucous Gulls arrive in northern and western counties, while American Herring Gulls are now annual visitors. For many, Ireland offers a rare opportunity to gain experience of these species that rarely venture into mainland Europe. As well as that, our relatively snow-free weather provides ideal wintering grounds for migrant thrushes and finches, while our resident species enjoy a lower winter mortality rate than those on mainland Europe.

Shaped by the power of the sea, the rugged Irish coastline varies from the low, rocky shorelines of the east coast to the high cliffs of the headlands and islands of southern and western regions. Surrounded by food-rich waters, such habitat is ideal for breeding seabirds in summer, and few European countries can surpass the variety and sheer numbers found along our coastline. Birds like Razorbills, Guillemots and Kittiwakes nest on the steepest cliffs, while on the islands off Kerry, the largest breeding numbers of Storm Petrels in the world can be found. The dramatic Skellig Islands are home to over 28,000 pairs of Gannets.

In autumn, the annual passage of seabirds off the western seaboard is unsurpassed. Shearwaters, petrels and skuas pass headlands like Ramore Head in Antrim, Kilcummin in Mayo, the Bridges of Ross in Clare, as well as the headlands and islands off the south-western counties of Kerry and Cork in suitable weather conditions (see p.356 for further information on Seawatching). In recent years, Ireland has become *the* destination for a chance encounter with Fea's (soft-plumaged) Petrel. Breeding in the Cape Verde Islands and Madeira, this species was virtually unknown in Irish waters before the 1990s but is now seen annually.

Deciduous forests make up a small proportion of Ireland's woodlands, with coniferous plantations dominating many upland regions. True Oak forests are confined to small areas in Wicklow and Kerry. However, Ireland's hedgerows are a unique feature of our countryside. With up to 70% of the Irish countryside consisting of farmland, hedgerows still act as natural borders to land and Ireland provides some of the best examples of such habitat to be found anywhere in Europe. Thousands of kilometres of hedgerows meander across the landscape and, in summer, these ancient land boundaries are alive with songs of resident and visiting species alike.

Ireland holds one last superb attraction to the visiting birdwatcher – solitude. Birdwatching is still in its youth in Ireland and it's not unusual to spend a midweek day at one of Europe's birdwatching hotspots in perfect weather conditions, at the right time of the year, and not meet another person. The opportunity of discovering your own birds is immense and this makes birdwatching in Ireland a very special experience indeed.

Facts for the visitor

Political System The Republic of Ireland is an independent republic with its own government and legislature. The six counties that make up Northern Ireland are part of the United Kingdom of Great Britain and Northern Ireland.

Currency The currency in the Republic of Ireland is the Euro (€) while in Northern Ireland the currency is the pound sterling (£). Exchange rates vary and currencies can be exchanged at banks throughout the country.

Driving in Ireland Driving is on the left-hand side of the road both in the Republic of Ireland and Northern Ireland. However, it should be noted that all distance signs and speed limits are given in kilometres (km) in the Republic of Ireland, while those in Northern Ireland are given in miles. In order to drive in the Republic of Ireland or Northern Ireland, a current EU driving licence is required. For drivers from non-EU countries, an International Driving Permit is required. These can be obtained from motoring organi-

Conversion chart

Distance

Km	Km/Miles	Miles
1.60	1	0.62
3.21	2	1.24
4.82	3	1.86
6.43	4	2.48
8.04	5	3.10
16.09	10	6.21
32.18	20	12.42
48.28	30	18.64
64.37	40	24.85
80.46	50	31.06

Speed

Km per hour	Miles per hour
30	19
40	25
50	31
60	37
80	50
100	62
120	75

sations in your home country. If driving your own car, it is also advisable to carry the vehicle registration as well as having adequate insurance cover.

Car Hire Cars can be hired on-line in advance from all of the major car hire companies or directly at car ferry terminals and airports.

Accommodation There is a wide variety of accommodation available in Ireland ranging from the most expensive hotels, to guest-houses, Bed & Breakfasts (B&Bs) and hostels. The peak tourist season is July and August and advance booking is advisable for this period. Many small B&Bs and hostels close for the winter period (October to February). The tourist boards can advise you on the availability of accommodation.

Telephone System The telephone systems of the Republic of Ireland and that of Northern Ireland are slightly different. The international dialling code for the Republic of Ireland is 00353, followed by the telephone number (but drop the first digit '0' of the local code). For Northern Ireland, the code is 0044, followed by the telephone number (but drop the first digit '0' from the local code). There is now mobile phone coverage throughout Ireland but the technology may differ from other countries. It is worth checking in advance to learn if your mobile phone can operate successfully in Ireland before travelling.

Bird Information Lines The Birds of Ireland News Service provides up-to-date reports of rare bird sightings throughout Ireland. The hotline numbers are as follows:
Republic of Ireland: 1550 111 700
Northern Ireland: 0901 063 0600
Calls to these numbers are charged at premium rates.

To report rare bird sightings, call 00353/01 8307364. In Northern Ireland, local news is available from Flightlines at 0044/ 048 91 467 408.

Useful websites

Irish Birdwatching
- www.birdsireland.com – The Birds of Ireland News Service website. Hire a guide, plan a trip. Recent rarity photos.
- www.birdwatchireland.ie – Ireland's leading bird conservation organisation. Join online, conservation projects, online shop.
- www.countynaturetrust.tripod.com – Irish wildlife conservation.
- www.rspb.org.uk – Bird conservation in Northern Ireland.
- www.wwt.org.uk – Wildfowl and Wetlands Trust, with reserves in Northern Ireland.
- www.ispca.ie – Local contacts for care of sick or injured birds in Ireland.
- www.cr-birding.be – Database of colour-ringing schemes around the world.
- www.mikebrownphotography.com – Bird and wildlife photography from Mike Brown.
- www.irishbirdimages.com – Bird photography by Paul Kelly.
- www.wildlifesnaps.com – Bird photography by Tom Shevlin.

Weather
- www.met.ie – Weather forecasts from Met Éireann, the Irish Meteorological Office.

Tourism & Travel
- www.discovernorthernireland.com – The official site of the Northern Ireland Tourist Board. Extensive information on travel and accommodation. Many useful links.
- www.ireland.travel.ie – The official site of the Republic of Ireland Tourist Board, Fáilte Ireland. Extensive information on travel and accommodation. Many useful links.

Transport
- www.buseireann.ie – The bus company in the Republic of Ireland. Timetables, prices and online booking.
- www.irishrail.ie – Iarnród Éireann, the rail company in the Republic of Ireland. Timetables, prices and online booking.
- www.translink.co.uk – Combined rail and bus service for Northern Ireland.

Principal towns & road networks of Ireland

Motorways are named with the prefix 'M', e.g. M1 in the Republic of Ireland and Northern Ireland.
National routes are named with the prefix 'N', e.g. N17. In Northern Ireland with the prefix 'A', e.g. A6.
Regional routes are named with the prefix 'R', e.g. R759. In Northern Ireland with the prefix 'B', e.g. B51.

Rail, air & car ferry networks of Ireland

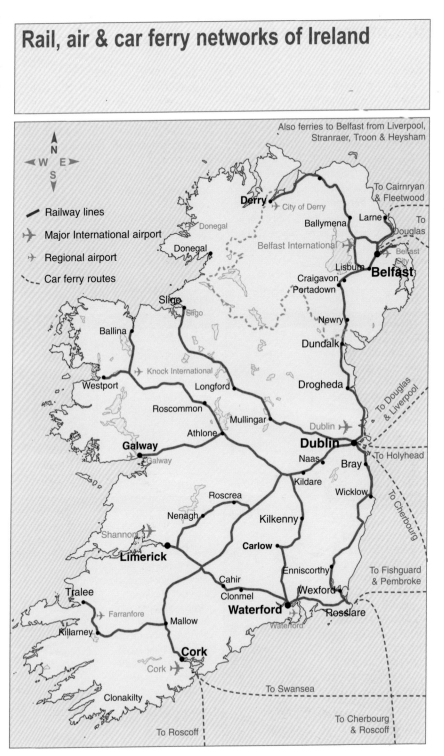

Also ferries to Belfast from Liverpool, Stranraer, Troon & Heysham

N
W **E**
S

— Railway lines
✈ Major International airport
✈ Regional airport
- - - Car ferry routes

To Cairnryan & Fleetwood

Derry • City of Derry
Donegal
Donegal
Ballymena
Larne
To Douglas
Belfast International ✈
Lisburn
Belfast City
Belfast
Craigavon
Portadown
Sligo
Sligo
Newry
Ballina
Dundalk
Knock International ✈
Westport
Longford
Drogheda
To Douglas & Liverpool
Roscommon
Mullingar
Athlone
Dublin ✈
Galway
Galway
Dublin
Naas
Bray
To Holyhead
Kildare
Roscrea
Wicklow
Nenagh
Kilkenny
Shannon ✈
To Cherbourg
Limerick
Carlow
Tralee
Enniscorthy
To Fishguard & Pembroke
Cahir
Wexford
Farranfore ✈
Clonmel
Waterford
Rosslare
Killarney
Mallow
Waterford
Cork
Cork ✈
To Swansea
Clonakilty

To Roscoff

To Cherbourg & Roscoff

7

60 Common Species

The following is a summary of the 60 commonest species to be found in Ireland, with a short note on each about season and habitat. To avoid repetition and unwieldy long lists of birds, these species are generally *not* mentioned throughout the main site accounts. They are only mentioned in the site accounts in certain cases, where unusual concentrations or high numbers of one of these common species occur.

These are the species which a beginner would be largely familiar with, and which any visitor to the country, seeing Ireland's birds for the first time, would certainly see within a few days of his or her trip.

| Time of year | Very common ■ | Common ■ | Rare □ |
| Map | | Summer □ | Winter ■ | All year ■ |

Mute Swan

Time of year

| J | F | M | A | M | J | J | A | S | O | N | D |

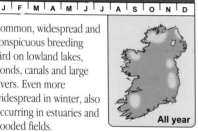

Common, widespread and conspicuous breeding bird on lowland lakes, ponds, canals and large rivers. Even more widespread in winter, also occurring in estuaries and flooded fields.

All year

Mallard

Time of year

| J | F | M | A | M | J | J | A | S | O | N | D |

Found very commonly on virtually all freshwater and estuarine habitats at all times of the year. Numbers highest in winter.

All year

Shelduck

Time of year

| J | F | M | A | M | J | J | A | S | O | N | D |

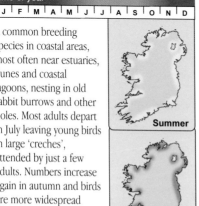

A common breeding species in coastal areas, most often near estuaries, dunes and coastal lagoons, nesting in old rabbit burrows and other holes. Most adults depart in July leaving young birds in large 'creches', attended by just a few adults. Numbers increase again in autumn and birds are more widespread throughout the winter months.

Summer

Winter

Gannet

Time of year

| J | F | M | A | M | J | J | A | S | O | N | D |

Common throughout the year, nesting in considerable numbers in five colonies (marked red on the map). Numbers highest in summer with birds seen offshore from all coasts, but particularly common on the south and west coasts. Much less common in late winter.

Summer

Winter

Pheasant

Time of year

J F M A M J J A S O N D

Common resident of farmland, rough pasture, field margins, woodland, upland scrub and marsh edges. Scarce in parts of the far western coastal fringes.

All year

Sparrowhawk

Time of year

J F M A M J J A S O N D

Widespread resident, in woodland, farmland, hedgerows and large gardens, only avoiding open habitats such as moorland.

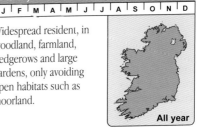

All year

Grey Heron

Time of year

J F M A M J J A S O N D

Common and widespread on estuaries, rocky and sandy coastlines, lagoons, rivers, lakes and marshes throughout the year. Slightly more common and widespread in winter.

All year

Kestrel

Time of year

J F M A M J J A S O N D

Widespread in virtually all habitats, including offshore islands, high mountains and even town centres. Frequently seen hovering along roadside verges.

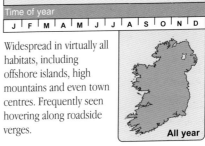

All year

Moorhen

Time of year

J F M A M J J A S O N D

A widespread and common bird of streams, rivers, canals, marshes, lakes and ponds. Fewer in western coastal fringes.

All year

Coot

Time of year

J F M A M J J A S O N D

Common resident, usually on larger, more open bodies of fresh water than Moorhen, such as lakes and reservoirs. Numbers increase in winter.

All year

Grey Heron

Oystercatcher

Time of year

| J | F | M | A | M | J | J | A | S | O | N | D |

Common winter visitor to estuaries, and rocky and sandy coasts, occasionally on farmland and open grassy areas. Less numerous but still widespread in summer on E, W and N coasts, breeding in small numbers on isolated shingle beaches. Rare far inland at any season.

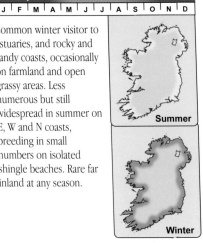

Summer

Winter

Oystercatchers

Ringed Plover

Time of year

| J | F | M | A | M | J | J | A | S | O | N | D |

A common bird in coastal areas, breeding on quiet shingle and stony beaches. A small number breed inland, on flood meadows and lake edges. Greater numbers occur in winter, when it is widespread and common in all coastal and estuarine habitats.

Summer

Winter

Sanderling

Time of year

| J | F | M | A | M | J | J | A | S | O | N | D |

Common winter visitor to estuaries and sandy shorelines, though mostly absent from mid-May to early August.

Winter

Curlew

Time of year

| J | F | M | A | M | J | J | A | S | O | N | D |

Scarce breeding bird in upland areas in summer, though non-breeding birds can often be found on estuaries. Much commoner in autumn, winter and early spring, when flocks are widespread and common in all coastal and many inland areas, on estuaries, mudflats and coastal grasslands, and around freshwater lakes and marshes.

Summer

Winter

Snipe

Time of year

| J | F | M | A | M | J | J | A | S | O | N | D |

Widespread, uncommon breeding bird in marshes and wetlands. Much commoner in winter, when it can be found in virtually any open wet or marshy habitat.

All year

Time of year   Very common ■   Common ▨   Rare ☐

Redshank

Time of year

| J | F | M | A | M | J | J | A | S | O | N | D |

Common winter visitor to estuaries and sandy coasts, occasionally on rocky coasts and flooded grassland near the coast. Less numerous but still widespread in summer. Breeds mainly in the north-west and west in small numbers on the midland lakes, turloughs and pools.

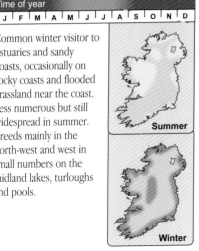
Summer

Winter

Redshank

Greenshank

Time of year

| J | F | M | A | M | J | J | A | S | O | N | D |

Common and widespread winter visitor to estuaries, creeks and muddy pools by the coast. Uncommon or absent from late May to the end of July. Rare inland.

Winter

Turnstone

Time of year

| J | F | M | A | M | J | J | A | S | O | N | D |

A common coastal bird in winter wherever there is rocky shoreline, including piers and seawalls. A small number of non-breeding birds remain throughout the summer.

Winter

Black-headed Gull

Time of year

| J | F | M | A | M | J | J | A | S | O | N | D |

Nests colonially on small islands on freshwater lakes and marshes, occasionally in coastal areas. Far commoner and more widespread outside the breeding season when it can be found in virtually all lowland and coastal areas of the country, including wet fields, lakes and pools well inland, as well as town centres.

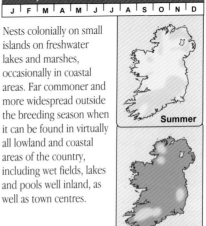
Summer

Winter

Common Gull

Time of year

| J | F | M | A | M | J | J | A | S | O | N | D |

Locally common in summer, generally near their breeding colonies in the N and W, though non-breeding birds can be found in most coastal areas. In winter, widespread and common on estuaries, marshes, rocky and sandy shore-lines and fields near coasts, less common inland.

Summer

Winter

Map   Summer ☐   Winter ■   All year ▨

KK321175

11

Common Gull

Great Black-backed Gull

Common in small numbers at coastal sites throughout the year, breeding in small colonies or singly on coastal cliffs or islands. In winter slightly more widespread including well inland, gathering with other gulls at favoured sites such as rubbish dumps, harbours and estuaries.

Summer

Winter

Lesser Black-backed Gull

In summer, breeds in loose colonies on freshwater and coastal islands, often with other gull species. Although formally a summer visitor, it can be found in small numbers at many coastal and inland areas throughout the winter. It is often found wherever other gull species congregate, such as rubbish dumps, harbours, gull roosts and estuaries.

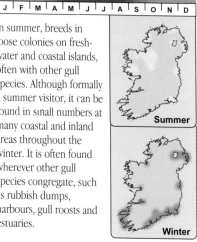

Summer

Winter

Rock Dove & Feral Pigeon

Rock Doves are uncommon throughout the year, along coastal cliffs, offshore islands and nearby agricultural areas.

The Feral Pigeon is common in virtually all large towns, near mills and large farms, particularly in grain-growing areas in the east and south, but can be found virtually anywhere.

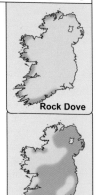

Rock Dove

Feral Pigeon

Herring Gull

Common and widespread in summer (though has recently declined), at estuaries, coastal cliffs and islands throughout the year. Recently nesting on rooftops in major cities. In winter more widespread and common in all coastal areas and often well inland, wherever other gull species congregate.

Summer

Winter

Rock Dove

Time of year   Very common ■   Common ▨   Rare ☐

Woodpigeon

Time of year

| J | F | M | A | M | J | J | A | S | O | N | D |

Very common and conspicuous breeding resident in farmland, woodland, parks and suburbs. Even more numerous in winter.

All year

Collared Dove

Time of year

| J | F | M | A | M | J | J | A | S | O | N | D |

Common and widespread in suburbs, parks and farmland throughout Ireland, often nesting in isolated conifers. A regular visitor to bird tables.

All year

Swift

Time of year

| J | F | M | A | M | J | J | A | S | O | N | D |

Common in towns and cities from May to early September. Seen in screaming flocks, low over rooftops on summer evenings. Otherwise frequents a wide variety of habitats, often feeding over lakes, reedbeds and woodland.

Summer

Skylark

Time of year

| J | F | M | A | M | J | J | A | S | O | N | D |

Common resident in rough grassland, dunes and meadows up to about 300m. Even commoner in winter and found in a wider variety of habitats, including estuary margins and moorland areas.

All year

Sand Martin

Time of year

| J | F | M | A | M | J | J | A | S | O | N | D |

Common summer visitor, particularly in the west, nesting in holes in sandy cliffs, gravel pits and quarries. Less numerous in the north and east. Often feeds over lakes.

Summer

Sand Martin

Swallow

Time of year

| J | F | M | A | M | J | J | A | S | O | N | D |

Abundant widespread summer visitor, nesting in farm sheds, outbuildings and ruins throughout the country, even on offshore islands and in some suburbs.

Summer

House Martin

Time of year

| J | F | M | A | M | J | J | A | S | O | N | D |

Common and widespread summer visitor, though thinly distributed in parts of the north-western coastal fringe. Nests under house eaves, occasionally on cliffs or under bridges.

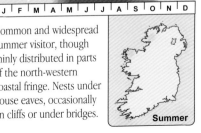

Summer

Map   Summer ☐   Winter ■   All year ■

13

Meadow Pipit

Time of year

J	F	M	A	M	J	J	A	S	O	N	D

Abundant in all rough grassland areas, dunes, and meadows, including high mountain moorland and offshore islands, throughout the year.

All year

Dunnock

Time of year

J	F	M	A	M	J	J	A	S	O	N	D

Often inconspicuous but very common in hedgerows, gardens, woodland edges and scrub throughout the country at all times of the year.

All year

Rock Pipit

Time of year

J	F	M	A	M	J	J	A	S	O	N	D

Very common all year along rocky shores and beaches throughout the country, though rarely seen more than a few hundred metres inland.

All year

Robin

Time of year

J	F	M	A	M	J	J	A	S	O	N	D

Abundant resident in virtually all habitats throughout Ireland, only avoiding open moorland and mountain tops. Often tame and inquisitive.

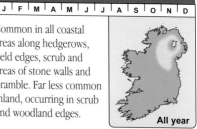

All year

Pied Wagtail

Time of year

J	F	M	A	M	J	J	A	S	O	N	D

Common and widespread all year on farmland, shorelines, on tracks, on river and shore margins and in towns throughout the year.

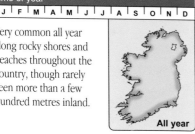

All year

Stonechat

Time of year

J	F	M	A	M	J	J	A	S	O	N	D

Common in all coastal areas along hedgerows, field edges, scrub and areas of stone walls and bramble. Far less common inland, occurring in scrub and woodland edges.

All year

Wren

Time of year

J	F	M	A	M	J	J	A	S	O	N	D

Very common in virtually all habitats. Commonest in gardens, hedgerow and woodland edges, but also found near the highest peaks and on remote offshore islands.

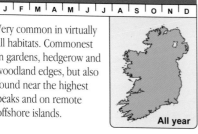

All year

Wren

Time of year   Very common ■   Common ▨   Rare ☐

Blackbird

Time of year

| J | F | M | A | M | J | J | A | S | O | N | D |

Very common throughout the year in gardens, parks, hedgerow and woodland. Even more numerous in winter.

All year

Fieldfare

Time of year

| J | F | M | A | M | J | J | A | S | O | N | D |

Common and widespread in hedgerows and fields, arriving with the first frosty nights in mid-October. Numerous throughout winter, particularly during very cold weather, with numbers dwindling by March.

Winter

Song Thrush

Time of year

| J | F | M | A | M | J | J | A | S | O | N | D |

Common throughout the year in gardens, hedgerow, scrub and woodland.

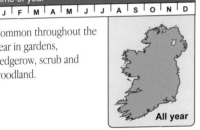

All year

Redwing

Time of year

| J | F | M | A | M | J | J | A | S | O | N | D |

Common and widespread winter visitor, in hedgerows, fields, parks and gardens, arriving during frosty nights in mid-October. Numerous throughout winter, though uncommon by March and often absent by April. Large numbers occur during spells of particularly cold weather.

Winter

Mistle Thrush

Time of year

| J | F | M | A | M | J | J | A | S | O | N | D |

Reasonably common on farmland, hedgerows and forest edges, usually in more open areas than Song Thrush, and occasionally high on mountainsides. Less common in the extreme west.

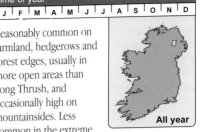

All year

Goldcrest

Time of year

| J | F | M | A | M | J | J | A | S | O | N | D |

Common throughout the year in woodland areas, especially favouring conifers. Also found in mature gardens, woodland scrub, and well-grown hedgerows.

All year

Coal Tit

Time of year

| J | F | M | A | M | J | J | A | S | O | N | D |

Common throughout the year in woodland areas, especially conifers, mature gardens and well-grown hedgerows, though less common in the far western coastal fringes.

All year

Redwing

Map   Summer ☐   Winter ■   All year ■

Blue Tit

Time of year

| J | F | M | A | M | J | J | A | S | O | N | D |

Common in nearly all lowland habitats wherever there is some cover, from farmland, hedgerow and woodland, to gardens and in towns.

All year

Great Tit

Time of year

| J | F | M | A | M | J | J | A | S | O | N | D |

Common on farmland, hedgerows, forest, woodland edges and gardens throughout the country.

All year

Magpie

Time of year

| J | F | M | A | M | J | J | A | S | O | N | D |

Very common and conspicuous resident throughout the year in all habitats except high mountains, open moorland and offshore islands.

All year

Jackdaw

Time of year

| J | F | M | A | M | J | J | A | S | O | N | D |

Abundant on open farmland, gardens and suburbs at all times of the year. Forms large flocks in winter on grassland and fields. Often nests on chimney pots in towns and villages.

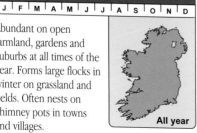

All year

Rook

Time of year

| J | F | M | A | M | J | J | A | S | O | N | D |

One of the most abundant species in Ireland, resident on farmland and open grassland throughout the country. Nests in large, noisy colonies called rookeries, high in the treetops. Even greater numbers in winter.

All year

Hooded Crow

Time of year

| J | F | M | A | M | J | J | A | S | O | N | D |

Widespread and common resident throughout the year in virtually all areas, including islands, mountain areas and towns.

All year

Hooded Crow

Raven

Time of year

| J | F | M | A | M | J | J | A | S | O | N | D |

Thinly distributed but widespread, commonest in northern and western areas. Typically seen around coastal and inland cliffs, uplands and mountain areas. Less common inland, usually near hills and woodland, occasionally farmland.

All year

Time of year   Very common ■   Common ▨   Rare ☐

Starling

Time of year

| J | F | M | A | M | J | J | A | S | O | N | D |

Common in summer throughout the country on farmland, towns and open grassy areas. Abundant in winter, often forming large flocks on farmland and in coastal areas.

All year

Goldfinch

Time of year

| J | F | M | A | M | J | J | A | S | O | N | D |

Common throughout the year on overgrown fields, scrub, farmland areas, hedgerows and woodland edges. Increasingly visiting gardens in winter.

All year

House Sparrow

Time of year

| J | F | M | A | M | J | J | A | S | O | N | D |

Common near houses, often in small flocks in towns and villages and around farmyards.

All year

Linnet

Time of year

| J | F | M | A | M | J | J | A | S | O | N | D |

Common throughout the year in fields, on hedgerows, rough grassland, stubble fields and scrub. Occasionally seen in large winter flocks.

All year

Chaffinch

Time of year

| J | F | M | A | M | J | J | A | S | O | N | D |

Common all year in woodland, gardens, scrub and mature hedgerows.

All year

Bullfinch

Time of year

| J | F | M | A | M | J | J | A | S | O | N | D |

Inconspicuous but reasonably common all year wherever there are hedgrows, scrub, mature gardens and woodland edges. Less common on the northern and western coastal fringes.

All year

Greenfinch

Time of year

| J | F | M | A | M | J | J | A | S | O | N | D |

Common all year near woodland edges, gardens, scrub and mature hedgerows.

All year

Reed Bunting

Time of year

| J | F | M | A | M | J | J | A | S | O | N | D |

Common in reedbeds, scrub, vegetated wetlands and rough field edges throughout the year.

All year

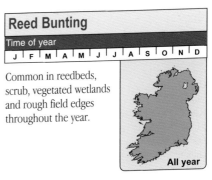

Map   Summer ☐   Winter ■   All year ▨

17

Sites

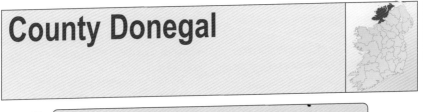

County Donegal

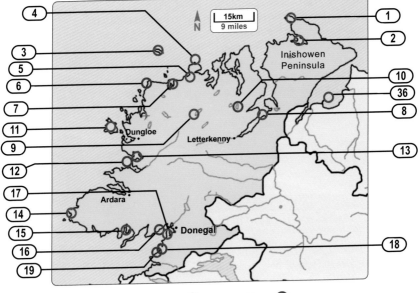

Main Sites ⭕ Minor Sites ⭕

Donegal is the second largest county in Ireland, after Cork, and its deeply indented coastline, islands, moorland and high mountains provide a diverse mix of habitats and spectacular scenery.

Many of the larger Donegal offshore islands are inhabited, with relatively easy access, and feature a number of interesting breeding species, such as Eider, terns, seabirds and Chough. The Corncrake still holds on in the NW extremities of the county, particularly Tory Island.

Situated so far north, there is a distinctly 'Scottish' flavour to the breeding avifauna, with Eider quite common on coasts, Buzzard, Golden Plover and Grouse in the mountains, and a few pairs of Whooper Swan, Goosander and Red-throated Diver breeding in the remoter areas. Ospreys have been lingering in early summer and may soon breed, and Glenveagh National Park is the centre of the

Golden Eagle reintroduction project, with many free-flying birds establishing territories in and around the park.

Autumn migration has been paid a lot of attention of late, particularly at Tory Island (Site 3) and Rocky Point (Site 14), and the list of unusual migrants is growing. The migrants seen are often of Greenland and Icelandic origin, but some extreme rarities have been recorded with their origins in eastern Europe and beyond.

Autumn seawatching is also good at several headlands, with a good mix of shearwaters, skuas and terns in suitable conditions, from July to the end of October.

In winter the numerous estuaries and lakes hold large numbers of swans, geese, wildfowl and waders, with Lough Swilly outstanding in this respect. Barnacle Geese, Eider and Long-tailed Duck are just some of the winter specialities.

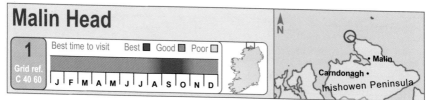

Malin Head

1

Grid ref.
C 40 60

| Best time to visit | Best ■ Good ▨ Poor ☐ |
| J | F | M | A | M | J | J | A | S | O | N | D |

The most northerly site on mainland Ireland, good for migrants and seawatching, especially in autumn.

The area is rather flat and bleak, with little cover, but the area is particularly good for Eider offshore, and Buzzard. Although a Bird Observatory operated successfully on Malin Head in the 1960s, it has been seldom watched in autumn since. There is obviously great potential for further interesting discoveries.

Directions Map 1, right. From Carndonagh, drive N through Malin on the R242, and continue N, following the road around the headland, stopping at suitable vantage points.

Species
All year Eider, Buzzard, Cormorant, Shag, Chough.

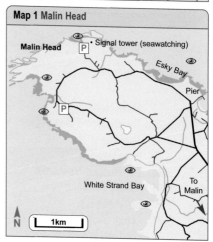

Map 1 Malin Head

Spring & summer Corncrake (R), Sedge Warbler, Wheatear.

Autumn & winter Whooper Swan (autumn), Greylag Goose (autumn), White-fronted Goose (O autumn), Barnacle Goose (common autumn, up to 800), Red-throated Diver, Great Northern Diver, Hen Harrier (O), Merlin, Golden Plover, Lapwing, Purple Sandpiper (rocky coasts, winter), Snipe, Redwing (occasionally 1000s in autumn), Siskin (O), Redpoll (O), Lapland Bunting (O Sept & Oct), Snow Bunting (O autumn).

Seawatching (best late July to end Oct, from just N of the signal tower). Red-throated Diver, Great Northern Diver, Fulmar, 'Blue' Fulmar (O), Great Shearwater (R), Sooty Shearwater, Manx Shearwater, Balearic Shearwater (O), Storm Petrel, Leach's Petrel, Cormorant, Shag, Pomarine Skua (O), Arctic Skua, Great Skua, Sabine's Gull (R), Iceland Gull (R), Glaucous Gull (R), Sandwich Tern (O), Common Tern (O), Arctic Tern, Guillemot, Razorbill, Black Guillemot, Puffin (small numbers). See SEAWATCHING, p.356.

Rarities Black-browed Albatross, Cory's Shearwater, Black Tern, Little Auk, Hoopoe, Red-breasted Flycatcher, Yellow-browed Warbler, Rose-coloured Starling.

A large bay with small numbers, but a good variety of waterfowl and waders in winter, and an area of dunes and machair which has a sizeable flock of Barnacle Geese.

Directions Map 2, below. Trawbreaga Bay has numerous access points on all sides. Doagh Isle (actually a peninsula) has access by road on the E side, and it is possible to walk NE from the carpark at Ballyliffin, behind the golf course.

The Barnacle Geese are often found at Doagh Isle, but are highly mobile, occasionally feeding on the mudflats or on adjacent farmland. If disturbance is

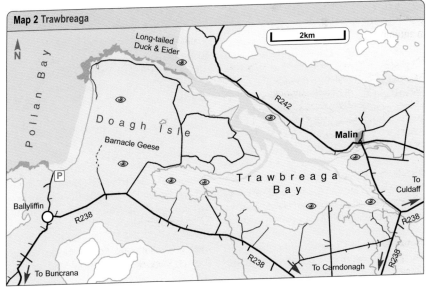

high, they may be located at Glashedy Island 2km offshore.

Species
All year Eider, Lapwing, Chough.

Autumn & winter Whooper Swan (O), Barnacle Goose (Doagh Isle, often 600+). Brent Goose (300+), Greylag Goose, Wigeon, Teal, Shoveler (O), Long-tailed Duck (entrance to Trawbreaga Bay), Eider, Goldeneye, Great Crested Grebe (O), Red-throated and Great Northern Diver (entrance to Trawbreaga Bay), Golden Plover, Grey Plover, Lapwing, Dunlin, Bar-tailed Godwit, gulls (often 100s of regular species).

Spring & summer Common, Arctic and Little Terns used to nest to the NW of Doagh Isle, and may still be seen in the area.

Rarities Pink-footed Goose, Iceland Gull, Snow Bunting.

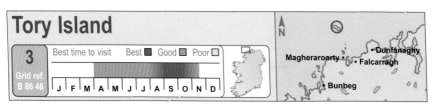

Tory is Ireland's most remote inhabited island, 12km N of the Donegal mainland. It is one of the best sites in Ireland for rare autumn migrants, and for Corncrake in summer.

Tory also has a good selection of breeding seabirds, including a sizeable colony of Puffins, reasonable seawatching possibilities, and with a café, hostel, B&Bs, hotel, pubs and shop, it makes an excellent base for a birdwatching holiday.

Directions Map 3, next page. Daily sailings with Turasmara Teo (+353 74 9531320), leave Bunbeg and Magheraroarty, departure times varying according to tide. Another faster boat operates from Magheraroarty. Call +353 74 9135920 or +353 86 8108411. Tickets can be bought at both piers before sailing, though booking is advisable. Sailings can be cancelled at any time due to adverse weather. Winter sailings are Monday to Friday only and are frequently cancelled.

In autumn, the best areas for passerine migrants are the small gardens, stone walls and overgrown fields around the two villages and lighthouse. The best conditions are during a NE, E, SE or S wind with rain, though migrants can arrive at any time and from any direction. A strong NW wind in late Sept or Oct will often bring geese and swans from the Arctic, along with perhaps Snow and Lapland Buntings. Of the three small lakes, Lough Ayes attracts most of the waders and wildfowl.

Although the list of birds recorded is impressive, it should be borne in mind that there are relatively few resident birds on Tory – no Blackbirds, Dunnocks or Robins, for example – and unless suitable conditions prevail, the island can hold only a handful of species. A little luck and patience may be needed.

Seawatching is good from August to October, although numbers are generally less than at nearby headlands (see Bloody Foreland, Site 6). The best area to watch from is just N of the lighthouse at the W end of the island where shelter is afforded by stone walls.

Species
All year Eider, Fulmar, Manx Shearwater (though R winter), Gannet, Peregrine, Chough, Tree Sparrow.

Tree Sparrows are very common on Tory, with only a few House Sparrows (and occasional hybrids).

Autumn Whooper Swan, Pink-footed Goose (R), Greylag Goose (O), Barnacle Goose (especially October), Wigeon, Teal, Red-throated Diver, Great Northern Diver, 'Blue' Fulmar (O), Sooty Shearwater (O), Storm Petrel (O), Leach's Petrel (O), Hen Harrier (R), Merlin, Golden Plover, Lapwing, Little Stint (R), Curlew Sandpiper (R), Ruff (R), Purple Sandpiper (O), Black-tailed

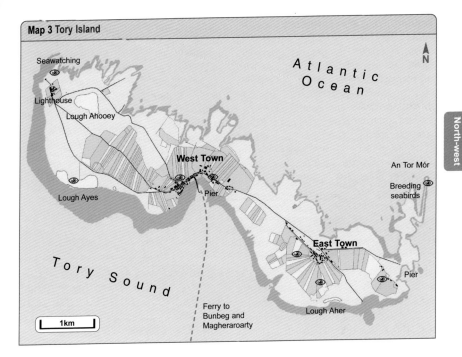

Map 3 Tory Island

Seawatching

Lighthouse

Lough Ahooey

West Town

Lough Ayes

Pier

Atlantic Ocean

An Tor Mór

Breeding seabirds

East Town

Pier

Tory Sound

1km

Ferry to Bunbeg and Magheraroarty

Lough Aher

N

Godwit (O), Bar-tailed Godwit, Curlew, Whimbrel, Pomarine Skua (O), Arctic Skua, Great Skua, Iceland Gull (R), Glaucous Gull (R), terns, auks, Redstart (R), Whinchat (R), Reed Warbler (R), Lesser Whitethroat (R), Whitethroat (O), Garden Warbler (O), Blackcap, Yellow-browed Warbler (R), Spotted Flycatcher (O), Pied Flycatcher (O), Brambling (R), Lapland Bunting (O), Snow Bunting (O).

Redwing (and lesser numbers of Fieldfare) occasionally arrive on Tory in hundreds, sometimes thousands, in late September and October, often during N or E winds.

Winter The ferry is regularly cancelled during storms and, with much reduced daylight, little birdwatching has been carried out on the island in winter. However, Snow Bunting and Gyr Falcon have been noted.

Spring & summer Whooper Swan (O), Storm Petrel (O from ferry), Corncrake, Lapwing, Arctic Tern, Little Tern, Guillemot, Razorbill, Black Guillemot, Puffin, Wheatear, Sedge Warbler.

Corncrakes can be seen in and around the fields and stone walls around East and West Town. They

are fully protected by law, so you must not try to flush birds by walking through fields. In any case, you are far more likely to see a Corncrake by sitting patiently in an area overlooking several fields from which birds are calling, and waiting. Birds will often fly short distances and occasionally perch on walls, or in the open, if left alone. Trying to flush a bird usually drives it deeper into cover. *Do not use tape lures.*

Little Tern

23

Rarities Although a bird observatory was established on Tory from 1958 to 1964, it was only in the late 80s and early 90s that birders again began regular visits in autumn. Their efforts have been well rewarded. Along with numerous Greenland and Icelandic wildfowl and passerines, large 'falls' of thrushes, pipits and buntings are often recorded in autumn. Some recent rarities include Great Shearwater, Garganey, Semipalmated Sandpiper, Pectoral Sandpiper, Long-tailed Skua, Sabine's Gull, Little Auk, Turtle Dove, Richard's Pipit, Tree Pipit, Pechora Pipit, Yellow Wagtail, Paddyfield Warbler, Reed Warbler, Melodious Warbler, Barred Warbler, Lesser Whitethroat, Radde's Warbler, Rose-coloured Starling, Arctic Redpoll, Common Rosefinch, Crossbill, Yellow-breasted Bunting, Black-headed Bunting, Little Bunting and Ortolan Bunting.

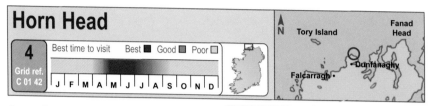

Horn Head

4

Grid ref.
C 01 42

Best time to visit   Best ■ Good ■ Poor □

J F M A M J J A S O N D

N Tory Island   Fanad Head
Dunfanaghy
Falcarragh

Some of the most spectacular coastal scenery in Ireland with huge numbers of nesting seabirds to be seen in spring and summer.

Directions Map 4, right. Signposted from Dunfanaghy. As you leave Dunfanaghy, the road curves around and down to the bay, before rising steeply along the E flanks of the enormous cliffs. There are numerous vantage points, though a telescope is recommended for good views of the huge auk colonies.

Species
Summer 6000+ pairs of Fulmar, Guillemot and Razorbill, 5000 pairs of Kittiwake and lesser numbers of Shag, Cormorant, Black Guillemot and Puffin. Peregrine, Rock Dove, Twite (O).

Other times of year The area is likely to attract autumn migrants, probably similar to Malin Head (Site 1). Ring Ouzel and Crossbill have been noted.

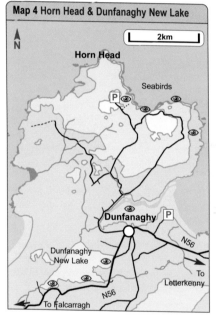

Map 4 Horn Head & Dunfanaghy New Lake

2km

N

Horn Head

Seabirds

P

Dunfanaghy P

N56

Dunfanaghy
New Lake

To
Letterkenny

To Falcarragh   N56

Dunfanaghy New Lake

5

Grid ref.
O 02 38

Best time to visit   Best ■ Good ■ Poor □

J F M A M J J A S O N D

N Tory Island   Fanad Head
Dunfanaghy
Falcarragh

A large, shallow lake with a good variety of duck in winter, and flocks of both Barnacle and White-fronted Geese.

Directions Map 4, above. Easily viewed from the N56 road just 1km SW of Dunfanaghy.

The 200 or so White-fronted Geese are often found on the grass fields around the lake, but if disturbed may be closer to Horn Head. The Barnacle Geese, if disturbed from these fields, will often be found on nearby offshore islands.

Species
Autumn, winter & spring Whooper Swan (more often in autumn and spring), Pink-footed Goose (R), White-fronted Goose, Greylag Goose (O), Barnacle Goose, Wigeon, Gadwall (O), Teal, Pintail, Shoveler, Pochard, Tufted Duck, Scaup (O), Goldeneye, Red-breasted Merganser, Merlin, Peregrine, Golden Plover, Lapwing, Snipe, Curlew, gulls.

Rarities Canada Goose, American Wigeon, Blue-winged Teal, Ring-necked Duck, Little Egret.

Dunfanaghy Estuary is easily explored from the town. Typical species here include Red-throated Diver, Little Egret (R), Brent Goose, Shelduck, Wigeon, Eider (O), Long-tailed Duck (O), Red-breasted Merganser, Grey Plover, Knot (O), Dunlin, Bar-tailed Godwit and Curlew.

6 Bloody Foreland Grid ref. B 81 35

A good seawatching spot in autumn, and the possibility of some unusual migrants, also in autumn.

Bloody Foreland is the extreme NW corner of the Donegal mainland. It has long been known as a good seawatching location, especially during W or NW gales in autumn. More recently, it has been shown to attract some rare migrant passerines in autumn, particularly the gardens along the R257 (Map 5, right).

For **seawatching**, driving from Gortahork to Bunbeg on the R257, the headland is obvious across bleak moorland to your right. The road takes a sharp left, but continuing on right will bring you to a small settlement of houses, overlooking Alliwinny Bay. Park here and walk out along the clifftop to your right. This is a very exposed site in high winds, so bring good water-proof clothing. In good conditions in autumn, likely species include Red-throated Diver, Great

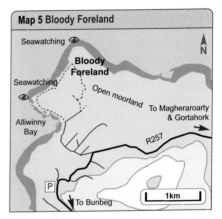

Map 5 Bloody Foreland

Long-tailed Skua

Northern Diver, Fulmar, Sooty Shearwater, Manx Shearwater, Balearic Shearwater (R), Storm Petrel (O), Leach's Petrel (mainly Sept & Oct), Gannet, Shag, Grey Phalarope (R), Pomarine Skua (O), Arctic Skua, Great Skua, Kittiwake, Sabine's Gull (R), Common Tern (R), Arctic Tern, Black Tern (R), Guillemot, Razorbill, Black Guillemot, Puffin (O), Little Auk (R). See SEAWATCHING, p.356.

Other species include Barnacle Goose (passage, Oct), Peregrine (O all year), Golden Plover (passage), Purple Sandpiper (winter), Wheatear (spring & summer), Chough (O, all year). Passerine migrants have been found in Sept and Oct in the gardens, including Lesser Whitethroat, Arctic Warbler and Yellow-browed Warbler.

Rarities seen in recent years include White-billed Diver, Cory's Shearwater, Great Shearwater, Long-tailed Skua, Snow Bunting and Lapland Bunting.

7 Ballyness Bay Grid ref. B 91 33

An estuary which attracts small numbers of wildfowl and waders in winter.

See Map 6, right. Ballyness Bay is just W of Falcarragh and is easily viewed from a number of points. On the E side, several side roads lead to the estuary, the easiest to access on the N56 between Falcarragh and Gortahork. As this road continues to Magheraroarty, there are more views to your right, and from Magheraroarty, it is possible to walk the coastal path along the dunes, which also allows views over the estuary. 1 to 2 hours before and after high tide are the best times

The massive sand dunes at the mouth of the estuary are impressive but hold few birds.

Ballyness Bay supports nationally important numbers of Ringed Plover and Sanderling. It also supports a relatively high diversity of waterbird species.

Regular species include Whooper Swan (O), Barnacle Goose (O), Brent Goose, Wigeon, Teal, Pintail (O), Eider (O), Common Scoter (O, Magheraroarty), Red-breasted Merganser, Red-

throated Diver, Great Northern Diver (both divers near Magheraroarty), Little Grebe, Merlin (O), Peregrine, Golden Plover, Grey Plover, Dunlin, Bar-tailed Godwit, gulls, Chough.

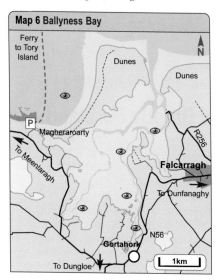

Map 6 Ballyness Bay

Lough Swilly

8	Best time to visit	Best ■ Good ■ Poor ☐											
Grid ref. C 30 25	J	F	M	A	M	J	J	A	S	O	N	D	

An enormous estuary complex with several outstanding sites for swans, geese, waterfowl, waders and gulls in winter. Terns, wildfowl and some waders nest in summer.

Directions Map 7, p.28. Although almost 43km long, N to S, most of the better birdwatching sites are in the southern half. Directions and descriptions of each of the main sites are treated separately, below.

Rathmullan (C 29 27) Map 7, p.28 The sandy beach here holds good numbers of Ringed Plover, Bar-tailed Godwit and gulls, all easily viewed from the village seafront. The area offshore of Rathmullan is one of the best areas for Great

Crested Grebe and Slavonian Grebe, diving duck and divers. Turnstone and Purple Sandpiper are generally found on rocky shores N from here. Try just N of Kinnegar Strand, 2km N of Rathmelton, on the R247. A small flock of Scaup is often present well offshore. Another good area for Slavonian Grebe is offshore from Ray, 4km SW of Rathmullan. Easily viewed from several places along the R247. High tide is best.

Leannan Estuary (C 23 22) Map 7, p.28. The upper part of the estuary is easily viewed from the town of Ramelton (or Ramelton), and Goldeneye can often be seen in that area. There are several other viewpoints: Leaving Ramelton N to Rathmullan on the R247, take 2 right turns to the shoreline, after 300m and 1km respectively, and again from the main road after 1.2km. The S side of the estuary can be viewed by leaving Ramelton E along the town seafront, and taking the first left on the edge of town. The estuary is easily viewed along this road. Mid tide is best.

Big Isle (C 23 13) Map 7, next page. Like Inch Levels and Blanket Nook, Big Isle has extensive areas of polder and thus holds many of the wintering Whooper Swans, White-fronted Geese and Greylag Geese along with good numbers of Lapwing and Golden Plover. A variety of other wildfowl and some waders is usually present. Big Isle can be explored from Manorcunningham. Two roads, immediately N and S of the village, lead W along narrow roads to the polders and small lake of Big Isle.

Blanket Nook (C 30 19) Map 7a, next page. A polder and man-made lake created by a dyke along its NW edge. In winter, holds Whooper Swan (100s), Greylag Geese, many wildfowl, including 100s each of Wigeon and Teal, and a range of other waterbirds. When water levels are low, a good variety of waders can be present. Slavonian Grebe is occasionally present offshore, as are grebes, divers and some diving duck, while Oystercatcher and Curlews often number well into the 100s.

Newton Cunningham is the nearest village. From there, take the N13 to Buncrana and take a left after 2km. Follow this road and take a right at Castle Hill. Continue until the lake is visible ahead. Good views can be obtained by crossing the small bridge to the pumping station.

Inch Lake & Levels (C 35 22) Map 7, next page and 7b, p.29. The 850ha of polder and reclaimed farmland (Inch Levels) S of Inch Lake is one of the main areas for swans, White-fronted Goose and Greylag Goose, wildfowl, Coot (400+) and waders. The geese and swans are quite mobile around the SE of Lough Swilly, but generally feed on the Inch Levels farmland by day, and roost on the lake. Divers and grebes can be found seaward of the two dykes, W and N of the lake.

Inch Lake is also an excellent site for breeding birds in summer, including Little Grebe, Great Crested Grebe, Tufted Duck, Water Rail, Dunlin

(O), Black-headed Gull (100s), Sandwich Tern (100s), Common Tern and Sedge Warbler.

The nearest town is Bridgend. From there, take the N13 W toward Newton Cunningham and take a right after 2km. Continue straight at the cross-roads to the lake shore. The N end of the Lake can be viewed by driving from Bridgend to Burnfoot and continuing on the R238 to Buncrana and taking a left after 2km. After 1km, the lake becomes visible on your left. Immediately on the right at this spot is Fahan Creek.

Fahan Creek (C 34 25) Map 7b, p.29. Can be viewed from several places along the R238, or from the causeway to Inch Island. Further views can be had by taking the first left, then left again, after crossing the causeway onto Inch Island. Brent Geese frequent the mudflats on the E side of Inch Island with smaller numbers of Teal and Dunlin. Small numbers of grebes, divers and some diving duck are usually present.

Buncrana (C 34 31) Map 7, next page. Small numbers of divers are regular offshore, as are Great Crested Grebe, Slavonian Grebe and Red-breasted Mergansers. Purple Sandpiper can be found in small numbers along rocky shores.

Species
Summer (Inch Lake) Mute Swan (100+), Little Grebe, Great Crested Grebe, Tufted Duck, Water Rail, Corncrake (R), Dunlin (O), Black-headed Gull (100s), Sandwich Tern (100s), Common Tern, Sedge Warbler.

Spring, autumn & winter Lough Swilly is one of the most important waterbird sites in Ireland. It holds internationally important numbers of Mute Swan, Whooper Swan (1500+), White-fronted Goose (1000+) and Greylag Goose (2000+).

Other species include Bewick's Swan, Pink-footed Goose, Barnacle Goose (O), Canada Goose (O, most are introduced birds), Brent Goose, Shelduck (700+), Wigeon (1500+), Gadwall (O), Teal (1500+), Pintail (O), Shoveler, Pochard, Tufted Duck, Scaup, Eider (O, outer Bay), Long-tailed Duck (O), Common Scoter (small numbers, outer bay), Goldeneye (150+), Red-breasted Merganser, Red-throated Diver, Black-throated Diver (R), Great Northern Diver (all divers, outer

Bay),. Great Crested Grebe (often 250+, outer bay), Slavonian Grebe, Hen Harrier, Buzzard (O), Merlin (O), Peregrine, Coot (500+), Water Rail, Oystercatcher (1500+), Golden Plover (2000+), Grey Plover, Lapwing (often 1500+), Knot, Little Stint (O autumn), Curlew Sandpiper (O autumn), Purple Sandpiper (O, outer bay), Dunlin (7000+), Ruff (O autumn & winter), Jack Snipe (R), Snipe, Black-tailed Godwit, Bar-tailed Godwit, Green Sandpiper (O autumn, R winter), Curlew (1700+), Redshank (1400), Greenshank, gulls (see below), Turnstone (outer estuary), Sandwich Tern (O

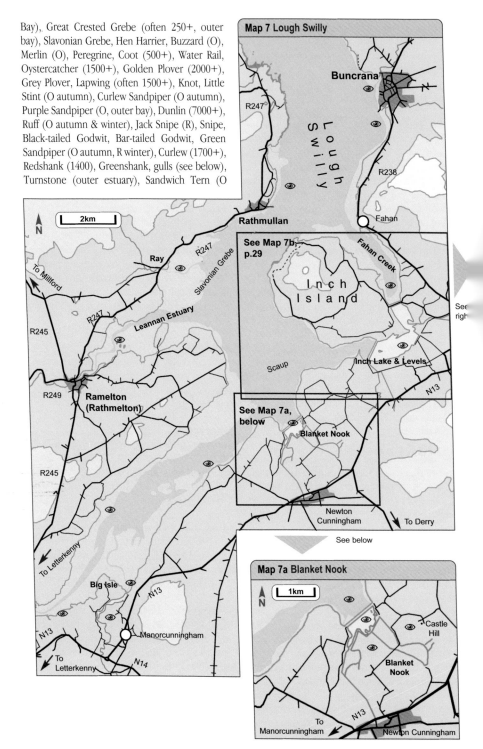

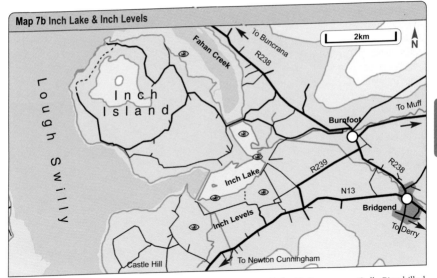

Map 7b Inch Lake & Inch Levels

2km

autumn & winter), Black Tern (R autumn), Short-eared Owl (O winter), Kingfisher (R), Twite (R), Lapland Bunting (R), Snow Bunting (R).

Gulls can be particularly numerous, with 1500+ Black-headed Gull, 3000+ Common Gull, 600+ Herring Gull and small numbers of Lesser Black-backed Gull & Great Black-backed Gull. Rarer species include Mediterranean Gull, Ring-billed Gull, Iceland Gull and Glaucous Gull.

Rarities Bean Goose, Snow Goose, Canada Goose (genuine vagrants have been recorded), American Wigeon, Ring-necked Duck, Ferruginous Duck, Lesser Scaup, Velvet Scoter, Smew, Ruddy Duck, Quail, Gyr Falcon, American Golden Plover, Semipalmated Sandpiper.

Glenveagh National Park

9

Grid ref.
C 03 23

Best time to visit   Best ■ Good ■ Poor □

J F M A M J J A S O N D

The largest National Park in Ireland (140km²), with large areas of upland wilderness. Particularly good in spring, with a wide variety of lake, mountain and woodland birds, and the centre of the Golden Eagle reintroduction project.

Directions Map 8, next page. From Letterkenny, take the N56 through Kilmacrenan, and turn left on to the Gweedore road (R255), or alternatively via Church Hill, and past Gartan and Akibbon lakes on the R251. Access from the N of Donegal is via Creeslough or Falcarragh and from the W via Gweedore and Dunlewy. The park is well signposted from all directions.

The park is open throughout the year. The Visitor Centre and Castle are open daily from March to early November, 10:00am to 18:30pm. The tearooms at the Castle are open daily from mid-March until November and then every weekend through the winter. Admission to the park, Visitor Centre and gardens is free, though there is an admission charge for the Castle.

The **Visitor Centre**, at the N end of Lough Beagh, provides displays and exhibits of the park's natural history and a small restuarant provides meals and snacks. Detailed maps of the park and a full bird list are also available. Cars are not allowed beyond the Visitor Centre carpark but a

29

Map 8 Glenveagh National Park

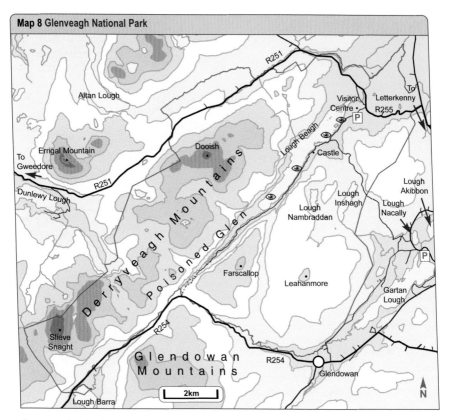

frequent shuttle bus service runs the 3km between the Visitor Centre and the Castle (weekends only in winter).

For further information, contact +353 74 37090.

Most of the park is remote wilderness, and all precautions should be taken if venturing away from the Visitor Centre and Castle areas.

Short walks of interest to birdwatcher are:
• A 2km Nature Trail starts near the Visitor Centre and passes through both planted and native woods, with excellent views over the lake.
• A track leads S from the Castle, along the shore through oak woodland. A longer walk along this path leads to the top of the Glen and further, to open mountain and moorland.
• There is a short walk of 1km just beyond the Castle (from the old sawmill), leading to a vantage point above the Castle. This goes through mature oak woodland.
• Guided nature walks are held once a week in

July and August and there is a 6-hour guided hill walk every month from May to October. Enquire at the Visitor Centre, phone +353 74 37090.

Lough Barra on the S edge of the park has large areas of intact peat bog, where White-fronted Geese may be found in winter (though numbers have declined in recent years), and Curlew and Dunlin breed in summer.

Species
All year Hen Harrier (O), Buzzard (O), Golden Eagle (see below), Merlin (O), Peregrine, Red Grouse (heather moorland), Snipe, Curlew, Woodcock, Long-eared Owl (R), Kingfisher (R), Grey Wagtail (rivers), Dipper (rivers), Long-tailed Tit, Treecreeper, Jay, Raven, Siskin (conifers), Redpoll (conifers), Crossbill (R, conifers).

The **Golden Eagle** reintroduction project is centred in Glenveagh National Park, and over 40 eagles have been released in the area to date. Birds can occasionally be seen in the upland areas

Golden Eagle

of the park, with several territories established within the park boundaries. Others have spread into nearby mountain ranges. The survival rate of the released birds has been high and the first breeding attempt took place in 2005. Further releases are planned over the coming years, the aim being to establish a viable population. It is estimated that County Donegal could potentially support 7-10 breeding pairs of Golden Eagles, the north-west of Ireland (Galway to Donegal) 22-30 pairs, and Ireland may eventually hold 50-100 pairs. For the latest information, see www.goldeneagle.ie.

Spring & summer Goosander (O), Red-throated Diver (O), Golden Plover (high plateau), Dunlin, Curlew, Common Sandpiper, Cuckoo (O), Redstart (R), Whinchat (O), Wheatear (open, rocky areas), Ring Ouzel (R, high peaks), Grasshopper Warbler (O), Blackcap (O), Wood Warbler (R), Chiffchaff, Willow Warbler, Spotted Flycatcher.

Winter Whooper Swan (R), Wigeon (O), Teal, Pochard (O), Jack Snipe (R), Fieldfare, Redwing, Snow Bunting (O, high mountain).

Rarities Red-throated Diver, Great Northern Diver, Snowy Owl, Osprey, Tree Pipit, Pied Flycatcher, Twite.

10 Lough Fern Grid ref. C 18 23

A shallow freshwater lake which holds reasonable numbers of waterfowl in the winter, notably Pochard.

See Map 9, right. Lough Fern, located 10km N of Letterkenny and 2km SSW of Millford, is easily viewed from the minor road between Millford and Kilmacrenan, which runs the length of the W side of the lake. Further views are possible by walking through the pine forest in the NE corner to the E side of the lake. More distant views are possible from the S side, along the R249.

In winter, regular waterbirds include Little Grebe, Great Crested Grebe (O), Whooper Swan, Greylag Goose, Wigeon, Teal (O), Pochard (usually several hundred, occasionally up to 1000), Tufted Duck, Scaup (R), and Goldeneye (O).

Rare species include Pink-footed Goose, and there have been several mid-winter sightings of Goosander.

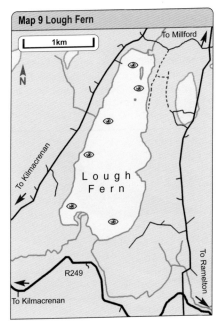

Map 9 Lough Fern

1km

To Millford

N

To Kilmacrenan

L o u g h
F e r n

To Ramelton

R249

To Kilmacrenan

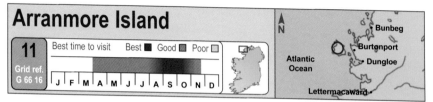

Arranmore Island

11
Grid ref.
G 66 16

Best time to visit   Best ■ Good ▨ Poor ☐

J F M A M J J A S O N D

N

Atlantic Ocean

Bunbeg
Burtonport
Dungloe
Lettermacaward

A large, inhabited island 2km off the NW coast of Donegal, good for migrants and seawatching, especially in the autumn.

Directions Map 10, next page. Arranmore is reached by car ferry from Burtonport (see p.40). Burtonport is signposted locally as 'Ailt an Chorráin'. The ferry operates all year, with between five and eight sailings daily, and is only rarely cancelled due to weather. Phone +353 74 9520532 for further details and bookings. The ferry docks at the main village, Leabgarrow, where there is a hotel, hostel, restuarant, pub and shops.

Most of the islands 800 inhabitants live on the E and SE side of the island, and much of the remainder is high moorland, small lakes and cliffs. The small beaches on the E side and at Rannagh have small numbers of the regular waders, while most of the tree and hedgerow cover for migrants is on the E side, around Leabgarrow and on the sheltered NE side N of Leabgarrow. Migrants are also noted regularly around the lighthouse buildings.

There is a small seabird colony on Illanaran, off the SW coast, with Fulmar, Shag and Kittiwake, and small numbers of Guillemot and Black Guillemot. Common Tern and Arctic Tern are

seen in summer and autumn, though they don't breed in the area.

There are huge tracts of upland moorland covering most of the centre, SW, W and N of the island, the central part of which is served by a metalled road and easily explored by car and on foot. The lakes area around Cluidaniller Mountain is good for Merlin, Golden Plover and Wheatear. Dotterel and Snowy Owl have also been recorded in this area. Lough Shore can hold small numbers of wildfowl in autumn and winter, and Common Sandpiper breeds commonly around these lakes in summer.

Seawatching is best from the low clifftop just below the lighthouse where there is some shelter from the lighthouse walls. The best conditions in autumn are during strong W or NW winds, though SSW through to NNW can also be good. This may also prove to be a good site for recording northward skua passage in May. See SEAWATCHING, p.356.

Species
All year Merlin (O), Peregrine, Golden Plover (upland areas), Black Guillemot, Chough.

Spring & summer Whooper Swan (R), Red-breasted Merganser, Manx Shearwater, Common Sandpiper (upland lakes), Common Tern (O), Arctic Tern (O), Black Guillemot, Corncrake (R), Cuckoo, Wheatear, Sedge Warbler, Willow Warbler.

Autumn Whooper Swan, Barnacle Goose, Pink-footed Goose (R), Wigeon, Common Scoter (O), Red-throated Diver, Great Northern Diver, 'Blue' Fulmar (O), Manx Shearwater, Sooty Shearwater, Balearic Shearwater, Storm Petrel, Leach's Petrel, Hen Harrier (R), Grey Phalarope (O), Pomarine Skua, Arctic Skua, Great Skua, Long-tailed Skua (R), Sabine's Gull (O), Ring-billed Gull (O), Iceland Gull (O), Glaucous Gull (O), Sandwich

Common Sandpiper

32

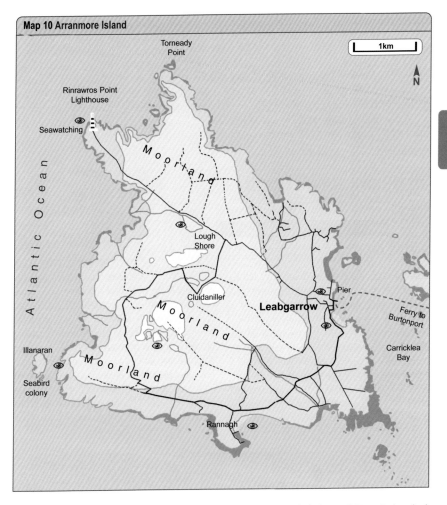

Map 10 Arranmore Island

Torneady Point

1km

N

Rinrawros Point
Lighthouse

Seawatching

Moorland

Atlantic Ocean

Lough
Shore

Cluidaniller

Leabgarrow

Pier

Ferry to
Burtonport

Moorland

Illanaran

Carricklea
Bay

Moorland

Seabird
colony

Rannagh

Tern, Arctic Tern, Common Tern (O), Little Tern (O), Guillemot, Razorbill, Puffin, Black Redstart (O), Fieldfare, Redwing, Whitethroat (O), Garden Warbler (O), Blackcap, Yellow-browed Warbler (R), Wood Warbler (R), Chiffchaff, Willow Warbler, Spotted Flycatcher, Pied Flycatcher (O), Brambling (O), Twite (R), Crossbill (R), Lapland Bunting (O), Snow Bunting (O).

Rarities Eider, Black-throated Diver, Red-necked Grebe, Great Shearwater, Cory's Shearwater, Semipalmated Plover, Jack Snipe, Dotterel, Mediterranean Gull, Little Gull, Little Auk, Snowy Owl, Wryneck, Citrine Wagtail, Bluethroat, Lesser Whitethroat, Ortolan Bunting.

12 Gweebarra Bay Grid ref. G 78 99

A large sea bay, fringed by rocky coast and sand dunes. A good location for Long-tailed Duck and Barnacle Goose in winter.

Gweebarra Bay is an 8km wide bay, stretching from Crohy Head in the N to Dunmore Head in the S.

33

Inland from Gweebarra Bay is Trawenagh Bay (see p.40), with a variety of wintering wildfowl and waders.

The Barnacle Goose flock regularly occurs on Inishkeel Island which is just offshore from Portnoo. Tramore Strand, just to the W of Portnoo, holds divers and Long-tailed Duck.

Another site for Long-tailed Duck is Dooey Beach which runs for 2km S of Dooey Point, best reached via Lettermacaward. Small numbers of Common Scoter also occur.

Other typical species here throughout winter include Brent Goose, Wigeon, Eider (small numbers), Red-breasted Merganser, Red-throated Diver, Great Northern Diver, Lapwing, Dunlin, Curlew, gulls, including Iceland Gull (R).

Sheskinmore Lough

13
Grid ref.
G 69 95

Best time to visit   Best ■ Good ▧ Poor ☐

J F M A M J J A S O N D

A shallow lake, backed by dunes and reeds, with occasional goose flocks in winter and breeding waders in summer.

Directions Map 11, below. Travelling N on the R261, between Ardara and Portnoo, take the left, signposted for Rosbeg. After 1.5km there is a signpost for Sheskinmore Lough Hide to the left. Go down the narrow road and the small concrete, unscreened hide is reached after 200m. There are good if distant views over the lake.

The W side of the lake can be reached by returning to the main road and turning left, onto the road to Rosbeg. After 1.5km, a caravan park behind a beach is apparent on the left. It is possible to park here and explore further on foot, though permission should be sought before entering any farmland. Divers and occasional Eider and Long-tailed Duck can be seen offshore in winter. The S and SE sides of the lake can also be reached on foot from several side roads off the main R261, between Ardara and Portnoo, but

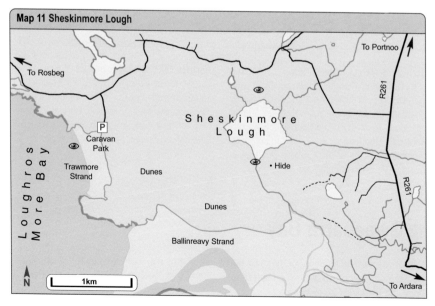

Map 11 Sheskinmore Lough

permission should be sought, and disturbance of any wildfowl on the lake should be avoided.

Species
All year Teal, Water Rail, Chough, Twite (R).

Autumn, winter & spring Whooper Swan (O), Pink-footed Goose (O), White-fronted Goose (usually 30+), Greylag Goose (O), Barnacle Goose (O, 50+), Wigeon, Teal, Shoveler (O), Tufted Duck (O), Eider (O offshore), Long-tailed Duck (O offshore), Red-throated Diver (offshore), Great Northern Diver (offshore), Great Crested Grebe (O), Cormorant, Hen Harrier, Buzzard (R), Merlin, Golden Plover, Lapwing (100s), Dunlin, Jack Snipe (O), Snipe.

The Barnacle Goose flock used to number 800+ but they are now seldom seen around the lake. Instead, smaller numbers usually frequent the grassy fields just S of the lake, at Loughros Point. White-fronted Geese use the lake area mainly as a roost, and only feed there when disturbance is low. If not at the lake, the geese will be feeding at small and often inaccessible bog lakes in the surrounding area.

Summer Corncrake (R), Lapwing, Dunlin, Snipe, Common Sandiper, Grasshopper Warbler, Sedge Warbler, Wheatear.

Rarities Marsh Harrier, Dotterel.

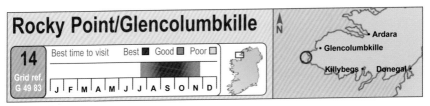

Rocky Point/Glencolumbkille

14

Grid ref. G 49 83

Best time to visit   Best ■ Good ■ Poor ☐

J F M A M J J A S O N D

Ardara
• Glencolumbkille
Killybegs   Donegal

In recent autumns, a well-watched area, shown to have potential for rare migrants and with good seawatching nearby.

Directions Map 12, next page. 'Rocky Point' refers to the area from Glencolumbkille to Malin More and Malin Beg, in the far SW of Donegal. Rocky Point itself, to the NW of Malin More, is the main seawatching point, and is, in fact, part of the larger headland, Rossan Point. The three main villages are easily explored from the R263. Many migrants have been found in and around the gardens and hedgerows in these area, and many open country species have been found on Rocky Point, but the whole area is worthy of exploration.

The uninhabited Rathlin O'Birne island is 3km offshore and has no local ferry services, but it is possible, with a telescope, to see wildfowl, gulls and other species on the island from the coast at Malin Beg.

Like many migration headlands, weather plays an important role in the occurrence of migrants. Passerine migration is best in autumn with E or NE winds, although calm conditions, with a large area of high pressure over Ireland, have also produced good numbers of migrants.

Seawatching is best in strong NW winds, though WSW through to WNW can be good, and this has proven to be the best seawatching site in NW Ireland (though actual numbers and variety are generally less than at sites further S such as Kilcummin Head, Site 241).

Species
All year Fulmar, Cormorant, Shag, Kittiwake, Chough, Long-tailed Tit (O), Treecreeper (O), Twite (O).

Autumn Whooper Swan, Pink-footed Goose (R), White-fronted Goose (R), Barnacle Goose (late Sept onward), Brent Goose (O), Greylag Goose (O), Wigeon, Teal, Gadwall (O), Shoveler (R), Pintail, (R), Tufted Duck (R), Scaup (R), Long-tailed Duck (R), Eider, Common Scoter (O), Red-breasted Merganser (O), Red-throated Diver, Great Northern Diver, 'Blue' Fulmar, Manx Shearwater, Mediterranean Shearwater (O), Sooty

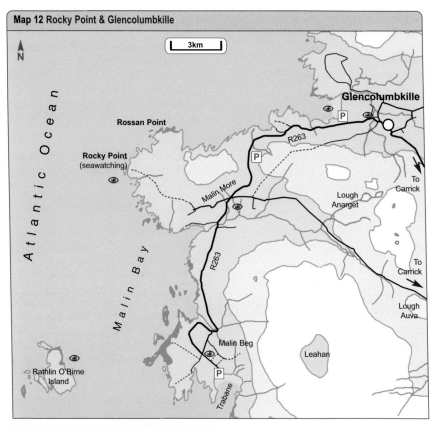

Map 12 Rocky Point & Glencolumbkille

N

3km

Atlantic Ocean

Rossan Point

Glencolumbkille

R263

Rocky Point
(seawatching)

Malin More

To
Carrick

Lough
Anarget

R263

To
Carrick

Lough
Auva

Malin Bay

Malin Beg

Leahan

Rathlin O'Birne
Island

Trabane

Citrine Wagtail

Gull (R), Iceland Gull (R), Glaucous Gull (R), Sandwich Tern, Arctic Tern, Black Tern (R), Guillemot, Razorbill, Black Guillemot (R), Little Auk (R), Puffin, Turtle Dove (R), Grey Wagail, Yellow Wagtail (R), Waxwing (R), Dipper, Wheatear, Whinchat (R), Black Redstart (R), Redstart (R), Ring Ouzel (R), Fieldfare, Redwing, Grasshopper Warbler (R), Reed Warbler (R), Blackcap, Garden Warbler (O), Yellow-browed Warbler (R), Willow Warbler, Chiffchaff, Spotted Flycatcher (O), Long-tailed Tit (R), Brambling (O), Siskin, Snow Bunting (O), Lapland Bunting (O).

Shearwater, Great Shearwater (O, mainly Sept), Leach's Petrel, Storm Petrel, Hen Harrier (O), Merlin (O), Peregrine, Water Rail (R), Golden Plover, Purple Sandpiper (O), Dunlin (O), Jack Snipe (R), Snipe, Woodcock (R), Black-tailed Godwit (R), Bar-tailed Godwit (O), Whimbrel, Grey Phalarope (O), Great Skua, Arctic Skua, Pomarine Skua, Long-tailed Skua (R), Sabine's

Spring Grey Plover (R), Whimbrel, Common Sandpiper, Cuckoo (O), Wheatear, Grasshopper Warbler (O), Sedge Warbler (O), Whitethroat (O), Willow Warbler, Spotted Flycatcher (O), Pied Flycatcher (O).

Rarities Green-winged Teal, Black-throated Diver, Cory's Shearwater, Buzzard, Osprey, Red-footed Falcon, Hobby, Corncrake, Dotterel

36

(including a flock of 18 in May 1992), White-rumped Sandpiper, Buff-breasted Sandpiper, Ruff, Little Gull, Yellow-legged Gull, Kumlien's Gull, Wryneck, Short-toed Lark, Richard's Pipit, Tree Pipit, Scandinavian Rock Pipit, Citrine Wagtail, Red-backed Shrike, Melodious Warbler, Lesser Whitethroat, Barred Warbler, Firecrest, Red-breasted Flycatcher, Rose-coloured Starling, Scarlet Rosefinch (R), Ortolan Bunting.

Killybegs

15

Grid ref.
G 71 76

Best time to visit   Best ■ Good ■ Poor □

J F M A M J J A S O N D

North-west

The largest fishing port in Ireland and one of the best sites in Ireland for 'northern' and other rare gulls in winter.

Directions Map 13, below. 20km W of Donegal. Take the N56 from Donegal to Ardara, turning left after 20km, signposted for Killybegs on the R263. Just before arriving at the town, the estuary left and right of the road is worth checking for gulls, particularly at low tide. A good view of this area can be had by crossing the causeway and pulling into the left, just as the road ascends into Killybegs town. Gulls are numerous around the rooftops in the town and all around the port area, but Gallagher's factory, with a blue corrugated roof, on the left as you enter the town from the N, is a particularly good spot. The harbour area will also have many gulls present (though numbers are dependent on trawler activity). Access to some of the piers has been restricted recently. The Rough Point area is good for roosting gulls, as well as some sea duck and auks.

The W side of Killybegs Harbour is another good area for gulls. Drive to the slipway, to the SE of Rough Point, and scan the beach and adjacent shoreline.

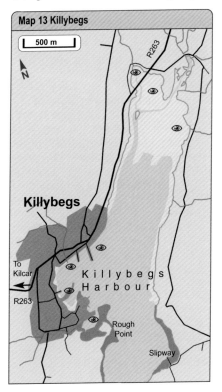

Species

Spring, autumn & winter Brent Goose (small numbers), Wigeon (small numbers), Teal (small numbers), Red-breasted Merganser, Eider (R), Whimbrel (May, R in winter), Curlew, Mediterranean Gull, Little Gull (O), Ring-billed Gull (O), Iceland Gull (O), Glaucous Gull (O), Kittiwake (O), Sandwich Tern (Spring, R winter), Twite (R winter).

Summer Sandwich Tern (O), occasionally some of the gulls mentioned above.

Rarities Velvet Scoter, Slavonian Grebe, 'Blue' Fulmar, Grey Phalarope, Caspian Gull, Yellow-legged Gull, American Herring Gull, Kumlien's Gull (almost annual), Thayer's Gull, Ross's Gull.

37

16 Mountcharles Grid ref. G 87 76

The large bay just south of the village of Mountcharles is one of the most reliable spots in the NW of Ireland for Black-throated Diver in winter.

Map 14, next page. Mountcharles is 6km W from Donegal town on the N56 Donegal to Killybegs road. Travelling from Donegal, as the road enters the town of Mountcharles it swings right. Just after this, take the first left, then left again, and a right when you come to the mouth of the estuary directly ahead. This stretch of road runs along the shore for 1.5km as far as a small pier, and it is here that Black-throated Divers are regular in winter. A telescope is recommended, as birds can often be distant. High tide is usually best, and can bring them closer to the shore. Calm conditions are also helpful.

Other species include Brent Goose (O), Eider (small numbers), Red-breasted Merganser, Red-throated Diver, Great Northern Diver (often 50+) and Slavonian Grebe (R). Rare species include Velvet Scoter and Pomarine Skua (autumn).

A large, shallow bay, with high numbers of divers, wildfowl and waders in winter.

Directions Map 14, next page. The best areas, in winter, are as follows.

Mountcharles See Site 16, above.

Inner Donegal Bay The N side of Inner Donegal Bay can be explored by leaving Donegal town centre W on the N56. On the edge of town, take a left and explore the shoreline around Rossylongan Strand for waders and some wildfowl. Return to the N56, take a left, and another left after 1km for more views along a road which ends at a carpark just behind a sandy beach.

The N15 which leaves Donegal town S, follows the coast for about 4km, and offers further views of the Inner Bay.

10km S of Donegal on the N15, take a right, signposted for **Murvagh** (G 89 72). The road leads to two carparks behind the 3.5km long beach. This area is good for divers, Common Scoter, and small numbers of Eider, Long-tailed Duck and Red-breasted Merganser.

Durnish Lough See Site 18, next page.

Species
Autumn, winter & spring Whooper Swan (O), Brent Goose, Wigeon, Teal, Pintail (R), Shoveler (O), Eider (O), Long-tailed Duck, Common Scoter (up to 1000), Velvet Scoter (O), Goldeneye, Red-breasted Merganser, Red-throated Diver, Black-throated Diver (O), Great Northern Diver (often 100+), Great Crested Grebe, Slavonian Grebe (O), Water Rail (R), Golden Plover, Grey Plover, Lapwing, Knot, Sanderling, Purple Sandpiper (rocky coasts), Dunlin, Snipe, Bar-tailed Godwit, Whimbrel (autumn & spring, R winter), Curlew, Spotted Redshank (R), gulls, Sandwich Tern (O autumn, R winter), Kingfisher (O).

Surf Scoter and Velvet Scoter occur almost every winter, with the main scoter flocks on the outer bay, along with Eider and Long-tailed Duck, both in small numbers.

Rarities Surf Scoter, Iceland Gull, Snow Bunting.

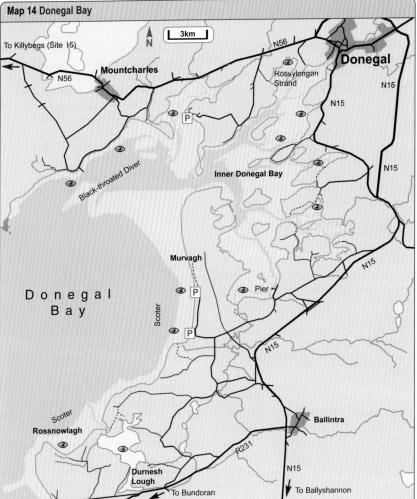

Map 14 Donegal Bay

3km

N

To Killybegs (Site 15)

N56

Mountcharles

N56

Rossylongan Strand

Donegal

N15

N15

N15

Black-throated Diver

Inner Donegal Bay

N15

Donegal Bay

Murvagh

P

Scoter

P

Pier

N15

N15

Scoter

Ballintra

Rossnowlagh

R231

Durnesh Lough

N15

To Bundoran

To Ballyshannon

18 Durnesh Lough Grid ref. G 87 69

A shallow freshwater lake, good for Whooper Swan and other wildfowl in winter.

Durnesh Lough is a shallow, slightly brackish lagoon, located 1km E of Rossnowlagh (see Map 14, above). It has a stony and muddy shoreline and extensive reedbeds.

The S end of the Lough can be reached by taking the first right after passing the lake on the R231 from Ballintra to Rossnowlagh. Good views can be had from the R231 itself. For the N end, take the second right after passing the lake on the

R231 from Ballintra to Rossnowlagh. Park near the caravan park and explore the shoreline N of here, with views over the lake to the E.

Bewick's Swan used to be regular at this site, but is now R, though Whooper Swan still occur in good numbers (often 100+), and Teal, Wigeon, Pochard, Tufted Duck and the occasional Scaup are winter visitors. White-fronted Goose has occurred.

In summer, Sedge Warbler is common in the reedbeds and Cuckoo is sometimes seen in May and June.

19 Rossnowlagh Grid ref. G 85 66

A large scoter flock and other sea duck in winter.

See Map 14, p.39. From Bundoran, travelling N on the N15 to Donegal town, Rossnowlagh is signposted to the left at Ballyshannon, on the R231. The bay becomes visible from this road, from the clifftop at the Smuggler's Creek Bar, just S of the main Rossnowlagh beach area. The views from here are excellent, especially in calm weather, though a telescope is recommended.

The Common Scoter flocks often number into the 100s throughout winter and usually has small numbers of Velvet and occasionally Surf Scoter, while Great Northern and Red-throated Diver are regular. Long-tailed Duck and Eider can also be found, as can auks, some gulls and small numbers of Purple Sandpiper along the rocky shores. Black-throated Diver and Slavonian Grebe have occurred, though they are more frequently recorded further N in Donegal Bay (Site 17) and Mountcharles (Site 16).

Other sites

Inishtrahull (C 49 65). This small island, 7km offshore, 8km NE of Malin Head, is uninhabited but was manned as a Bird Observatory in autumn during the 1960s. Migration proved interesting, and no doubt many of the species seen since on Tory Island (Site 3) must occur. However, there are only occasional ferries to the island in summer and no facilities. Any prolonged stay on the island would have to be largely self sufficiant. Enquire at the pier at Bulbinbeg for day trips to the island.

Fanad Head (C 18 44) offers good autumn seawatching, with the same conditions and seabird species as Malin Head (Site 1). Eider and Long-tailed Duck are frequent along the coast in winter, particularly to the SW, and other species include Red-throated Diver, Great Northern Diver, Buzzard and Purple Sandpiper.

Greencastle (C 64 40) is a small harbour at the W side of the entrance to Lough Foyle (Site 36) and directly opposite Magilligan Point (Site 34). It attracts small numbers of gulls in winter, and Iceland and Glaucous Gull are seen each winter. Purple Sandpipers can also be found in small numbers along rocky coasts in this area.

Burtonport (G 72 15) If travelling to Arranmore Island (Site 11), it is worth allowing a little time to check the gulls at Burtonport. Iceland, Glaucous and Ring-billed Gull have all been seen in the harbour, with numbers of gulls largely dependent on local trawler activity. Long-tailed Skua has been seen.

Inishfree Bay (B 76 22) is located on the NW coast of Donegal, between Burtonport and Bunbeg. This site is particularly good for Long-tailed Duck and Great Northern Diver, with up to 50 of each and both regular offshore in winter. The R259 is the main road to Donegal Airport, and Inishfree Bay can be explored by taking side roads to the left as you approach the airport. A telescope is recommended.

Other species usually present in winter include Brent Goose, Teal, Eider, Common Scoter (small numbers), Red-throated Diver, Black-throated Diver (R), Golden Plover, Purple Sandpiper, Curlew and gulls.

Trawenagh Bay (B78 04), 10km S of Dunglow and 8km N of Lettermacaward, is a large, shallow estuary which holds a number of wildfowl and waders in winter. The N56 Glenties to Dunglow road passes the E end of the estuary and exploring the N and S sides is straightforward, with minor roads around much of the edge of the estuary.

Species include Barnacle Goose (W side of estuary), Brent Goose, Wigeon (small numbers), Long-tailed Duck (O, mouth of the estuary), Red-breasted Merganser, Ringed Plover (up to 200), Golden Plover and Curlew.

Loughs Akibbon & Nacally (C 06 18) are two freshwater lakes just outside the E boundariy of Glenveagh National Park (Site 9), good in winter for small numbers of wildfowl, particularly Pochard. They are located 2km NW of Church Hill, 12km NW of Letterkenny. See Map 8, p.30.

Other regularly occurring species are Whooper Swan, Teal, Pochard and Tufted Duck.

Slieve League (G 57 77). The highest marine cliffs in Europe are worth a trip in their own right, but it is also a good site for seabirds, Peregrine, Kestrel and Chough. Ring Ouzel occurs occasionally on passage. The cliffs are best approached from the E and they are well signposted from Killybegs via Carrick and Teelin. Boat trips to the cliffs run from Teelin in summer, phone +353 74 9739365 or +353 74 9739327.

Ballyshannon (G 85 62). The Erne estuary to the W of the town is best explored from the N side of the main river. Leaving Ballyshannon on the R231 to Rossnowlagh, take a left just after leaving the town and after crossing a small river. Views of the estuary can be had from along this road, and it is possible to walk, at low tide, to the outer estuary. The S side is a military camp with no access.

Some Brent Geese and small numbers of the regular waders and duck frequent the inner estuary in winter. In late summer each year, a large moulting flock of Red-breasted Mergansers gathers near the mouth of the bay, numbering 500 in the past, though somewhat reduced these days. Smaller numbers remain through the winter, when Long-tailed Duck can also be found.

Bundoran (G 82 59). This popular seaside town has gatherings of gulls, Brent Geese and waders in the main bay in front of the town. To the N of town, heading N, take a left turn, signposted for Fairy Bridges. This is a good clifftop vantage point to scan the huge, sandy bay to your right. Eider, Red-throated Diver and Great Northern Diver are frequent here, and occasional Long-tailed Duck and Velvet Scoter can be found among the Common Scoter, and King Eider, Surf Scoter and Black-throated Diver have been seen. Purple Sandpiper are present here in small numbers along rocky shores. The rough ground below the Great Northern Hotel has been a regular wintering site for Twite, with up to 30 present, though numbers have been declining.

Swifts and Grey Wagtail

County Leitrim

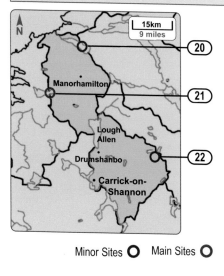

| 15km |
| 9 miles |

N

Manorhamilton

Lough Allen

Drumshanbo

Carrick-on-Shannon

20

21

22

Minor Sites O   Main Sites O

Leitrim has the smallest population of any county in Ireland, and a mere 4km of coastline, the least of any coastal county.

It is also one of the least known ornithologically, and despite the lack of notable sites listed here, there may well be rewards for those willing to explore the interior, where beautiful, rolling hills hide a multitude of lakes, particularly in the S and E of the county. Small areas of native woodland can hold breeding Garden Warbler in summer.

Glencar Lake, on the Sligo/Leitrim border, is one of the better known and accessible lakes, and Lough Melvin the largest, but both have relatively low densities of birds. Lough Allen, which divides the county in two, is deep and relatively poor for birds.

20 Lough Melvin Grid ref. G 86 54

A large lake which attracts small numbers of waterbirds in winter.

Lough Melvin is located 4km SE of Bundoran and 6km S of Ballyshannon, with the NE corner lying in County Fermanagh. Wildfowl numbers are generally low, but a thorough search of the lake should reveal a selection of birds.

The lake can be viewed from a number of parking and picnic areas, particularly in the E half of the lake. The Derrynaseer Amenity Area is located just on the Leitrim side of the border, while further E into Northern Ireland there is another sheltered bay at Bilberry Island (G 92 52). 1km to the E, around the town of Garrison, are two carparks and a small woodland area which holds many of the regular woodland species. On the S side of the lake, there are more lakeside carparks and viewpoints along the R282.

The main species encountered in winter are Whooper Swan (O), Wigeon, Teal, Pochard (O), Tufted Duck, Scaup (R), Goldeneye, Lapwing, Snipe, Cormorant, and small numbers of gulls.

Osprey has also been recorded here recently.

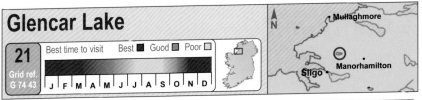

Glencar Lake

21	Best time to visit	Best ■ Good ■ Poor □
Grid ref. G 74 43	J F M A M J J A S O N D	

A freshwater lake in a beautiful setting, on the Sligo/Leitrim border, with a variety of water-birds in winter and good general woodland birdwatching in the vicinity.

Directions Map 15, right. From Sligo town, take the N16 to Manorhamilton/Enniskillen. After 6km take a left, which after a further 2km will bring you to the lake, visible on your right. Although the entire lake is easily viewed from this road, most of the waterbirds gather at the E end, near the Glencar Waterfall carpark. There is also a carpark and viewpoint on the N16 on the hillside above the lake, though views are more distant.

Species
All year Cormorant, Peregrine (O), Grey Wagtail, Dipper (rivers up to and around Glencar Waterfall), Long-tailed Tit, Treecreeper, Jay (O), Chough.

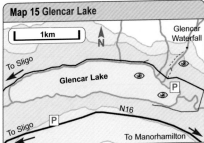
Map 15 Glencar Lake

Late autumn & winter Whooper Swan (R), Teal (O), Wigeon (O), Pochard, Tufted Duck, Goldeneye, Curlew (O).

Other species Peregrine and Chough occur on the slopes above the Glencar Waterfall and there are several interesting walks nearby with a good variety of regular woodland species.

22 Ballinamore area Grid ref. H 16 19

A number of small to medium-sized fresh-water lakes, good for wildfowl and some waders.

Around Ballinamore town, on the Cavan/Leitrim border, and from Ballinamore S to Carrick-on-Shannon, are around 70 small freshwater lakes. In winter each of these hold small numbers of birds, but cumulatively, a day spent searching these lakes should reveal small numbers of Whooper and Mute Swans, Wigeon, Teal and a few Pochard, Goldeneye and Tufted Duck. Waders are repre-sented by small numbers of Golden Plover, Lapwing and Curlew. Rare species are occasionally found, such as Common Scoter, Slavonian Grebe and Black-necked Grebe. Water Rail and Kingfisher are occasionally seen.

Other sites

Rinn Lough Lakes (N 10 94). The Rinn Lough Lakes are a cluster of lakes, turloughs and surrounding flooded farmland on the County Leitrim side of the River Shannon. Each lake supports small numbers of waterfowl in winter, and a thorough search of the area should reveal Whooper Swan, White-fronted Goose (O), Wigeon, Teal, Pochard, Tufted Duck, Goldeneye, Great Crested Grebe, Water Rail, Golden Plover, Lapwing, Snipe, Curlew and Kingfisher (O). Smew has been found in this area.

County Sligo

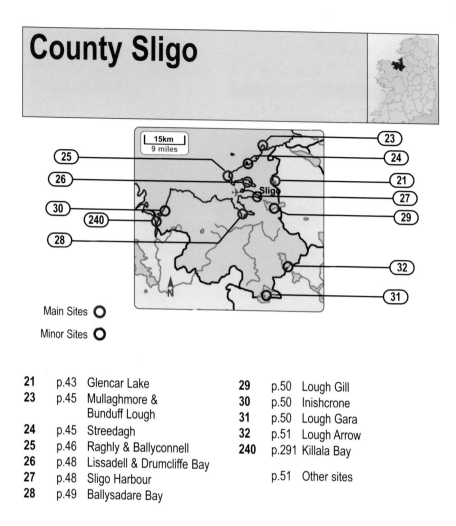

15km
9 miles

23
24
25
26
21
30
27
240
29
28

Sligo

32
31

Main Sites **O**

Minor Sites **O**

The dominant landscape feature of much of County Sligo is Benbulben. This impressive tabletop mountain overlooks the main birdwatching areas of Sligo, Drumcliffe Bay, Sligo Harbour and Ballysadare Bay, and the Goose Fields at Lissadell and Raghly. The latter two are best known for their large flocks of Barnacle Geese in winter.

The coast north from Raghly is particularly good for Eider, Purple Sandpiper and occasionally Long-tailed Duck, while Mullaghmore and Bunduff Lough are excellent areas for a variety of species, particu-

larly in autumn and winter. Seawatching in autumn at Mullaghmore (and to a lesser extent at Ballyconnell) has also produced some good seabird records.

Inland there are many lakes worthy of exploration. The best of these are Lough Gara and Lough Arrow in the south of the county, and Lough Gill, close to Sligo town. Though most sites are primarily autumn and winter birdwatching areas, the extensive forests around Lough Gill offer good opportunities in spring and summer to see a variety of woodland species.

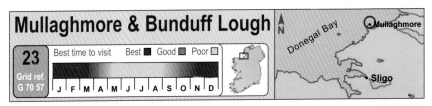

Mullaghmore & Bunduff Lough

23
Grid ref.
G 70 57

Best time to visit   Best ■ Good ■ Poor □

J F M A M J J A S O N D

A headland and large bay, good for seaduck, divers and gulls, and a series of shallow, reed-fringed lakes, good for Whooper Swan and some wildfowl in winter.

Directions Map 16, right. From Sligo, take the N15 to Donegal. After 20km, the road passes through Cliffony. Take the left here, signposted for Mullaghmore, or continue for another 1.5km before again taking a left off the N15, also signposted for Mullaghmore. The first turn off the N15 will bring you direct to Mullaghmore, the second to Mullaghmore via Bunduff Lough (actually three lakes). These lakes are easily viewed from the roadside. The bay at Mullaghmore is easily viewed from the road just before the harbour.

Species

Autumn, winter & spring Whooper Swan (autumn, less often in winter), Brent Goose, Wigeon, Gadwall (R), Teal, Pintail (R), Shoveler (O), Pochard (O), Tufted Duck, Scaup (O), Red-breasted Merganser, Eider (O, off Mullaghmore), Long-tailed Duck (O), Common Scoter, Red-throated Diver, Great Northern Diver, Black-throated Diver (R), Golden Plover, Lapwing, Purple Sandpiper (rocky shores), Dunlin (beach), Ruff (O autumn), Black-tailed Godwit (O), Glaucous Gull (R), auks, Short-eared Owl (R), Chough, Snow Bunting (R).

Summer Around the lakes, Whooper Swan (R), Cuckoo, Grasshopper Warbler, Sedge Warbler, Whitethroat.

Map 16 Mullaghmore & Bunduff Lough

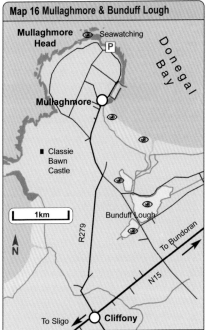

Seawatching In strong NW or W gales in Sept and Oct, reasonable seawatching can be had from Mullaghmore Head. Gannet, Fulmar and Kittiwake are often numerous, while Manx Shearwater, Sooty Shearwater, Storm Petrel, Leach's Petrel and Arctic, Pomarine and Great Skua can be seen in small numbers. See also SEAWATCHING, p.356.

Rarities Goosander, Great Shearwater, Marsh Harrier, Buzzard, Long-tailed Skua, Sabine's Gull, Whiskered Tern.

24 Streedagh Grid ref. G 63 50

In winter, a good site for Eider and Purple Sandpiper and occasional Long-tailed Duck. The estuary here has small numbers of waders, mainly in autumn.

From Sligo, take the N15 to Donegal and after 15km, the road reaches the village of Grange. Take the left, signposted for Streedagh, just before entering the village, and a right after 1km. Ignore a left fork up to a small housing estate and continue straight, reaching a carpark just behind the beach, with the estuary on your right.

In winter, the best area for birds is on the seaward side at the SW end of the beach. Purple Sandpiper are regular around the rocky shore, especially at low tide. Eider are often present just offshore, occasionally further out into the bay. Small numbers of Common Scoter, divers and auks can also be seen. Velvet Scoter have been seen here, and Arctic and Great Skua may be found in autumn, particularly during westerly gales.

The inner estuary has small numbers of Dunlin and other waders, especially in autumn and early winter. The first Great White Egret for Ireland was recorded here in 1984.

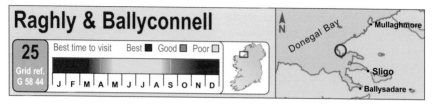

Raghly & Ballyconnell

25

Grid ref.
G 58 44

Best time to visit   Best ■ Good ▨ Poor ☐

| J | F | M | A | M | J | J | A | S | O | N | D |

Donegal Bay   Mullaghmore   Sligo   Ballysadare

One of the best mainland sites in Ireland to see wintering Barnacle Geese.

Directions Map 17, next page. The area known as Ballintemple, between Raghly and Ballyconnell, is where Barnacle Geese are most regularly seen, from October to April.

To get to Raghly from Sligo, head N on the N15 to Donegal and 200m past Yeats' Grave, turn left for Carney. At Carney village, take a left and continue for 7km and take another left. **Raghly Harbour** is 5km at the end of this road. To get to the fields at **Ballintemple**, leave Raghly, heading N, and take the first left, continue for 1km and the Barnacle Geese are often present in the fields downhill to your left. Another spot which they frequent is the fields on your left as you drive about 1 to 2km from Raghly on the road to Lissadell. If the birds are not present here, they may be at Lissadell (Site 26) or in coastal fields just N of Ballyconnell. The Barnacle Geese roost most nights on Inishmurray island, about 9km offshore (see p.51) and dramatic dawn and dusk flights to and from the island can be seen, most often from Ballyconnell.

Trawbane is a small bay which attracts waders in autumn and winter. Leaving the shop/pub at Ballyconnell, take the main road back toward Sligo and take a left after 1km. After 1km, the road then sweeps right, parallel to the coast, and ends at the bay. Small numbers of Dunlin and occasional Curlew Sandpiper and Little Stint are seen here most autumns, and Eider are usually present offshore outside the summer months.

Species
Autumn & winter Whooper Swan (O), Pink-footed Goose (R), White-fronted Goose (R), Brent Goose, Canada Goose (1 or 2 each winter with the Barnacle Geese), Barnacle Goose (100s), Eider, Long-tailed Duck, Common Scoter, Red-breasted

Barnacle Geese

Merganser, Red-throated Diver, Great Northern Diver, Hen Harrier (O), Merlin (O), Peregrine (O), Little Stint (R Trawbane), Curlew Sandpiper (O Trawbane), Purple Sandpiper (O), Dunlin, Arctic Skua (usually several present in Sligo Bay, Aug & Sept), auks, Chough.

Seawatching In strong NW or W gales in September and October, there can be reasonable seawatching from Ballyconnell. Leach's Petrels are regular in such conditions, and Grey Phalarope, Pomarine, Arctic, Long-tailed and Great Skua have been recorded. See also SEAWATCHING, p.356.

Raghly is a reasonably good site for seeing Storm Petrel, which occasionally venture into Sligo Bay on summer evenings. A telescope is recommended.

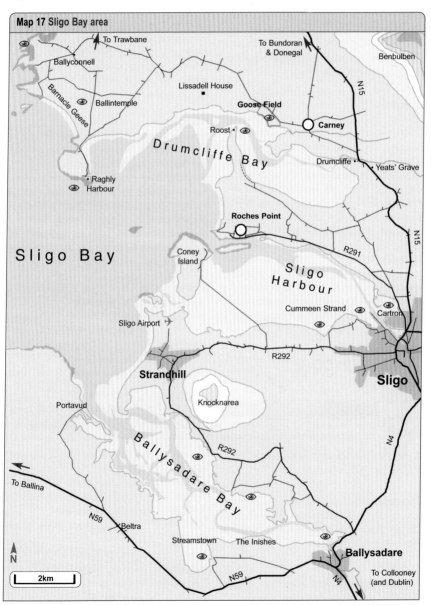

Map 17 Sligo Bay area

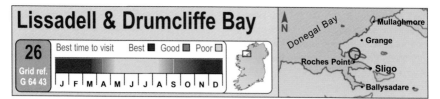

Lissadell & Drumcliffe Bay

26

Grid ref.
G 64 43

Best time to visit   Best ■ Good ■ Poor □

J F M A M J J A S O N D

Donegal Bay · Mullaghmore · Grange · Roches Point · Sligo · Ballysadare

The Goose Field at Lissadell has long been known as a haunt of Barnacle Geese in winter, though the birds are only sometimes present here. Nearby Drumcliffe Bay has a high tide roost for waders, particularly good in autumn. The channel between the two areas is particularly good for Long-tailed Duck.

Directions Map 17, previous page. The northernmost of the three bays comprising Sligo Bay. For the Goose Field, from Sligo, take the main N15 Sligo to Donegal road for 6km. Just after 'Yeats' Grave', turn left at Yeats Tavern for Carney and Lissadell. At Carney village, take a left, and the Goose Field is on the left side of the road after 1km. The Goose Field usually has a few Wigeon and Teal, but if the Barnacle Geese are not present, try Ballintemple near Raghly (Site 25).

Drumcliffe Bay doesn't hold many birds, but has a very good wader roost at the tip of the large sandy spit at the entrance to Drumcliffe Bay. There are often good numbers of waders at high tide, particularly if this is in the evening. Numbers and variety

are greatest in autumn. From Roches Point, take the R291 to Sligo. After 1.5km, take a left and go another 1km along a narrow twisting road, before taking another left. This narrow, straight road ends after about 2km, so park and walk along the shore for 1km to the sandy spit. The roost is prone to disturbance, so approach cautiously. The channels between the spit and the Goose Field are also good for Long-tailed Duck at high tide.

Species

Autumn & winter Whooper Swan (O), Brent Goose, Barnacle Goose (100s), Wigeon, Teal, Shoveler, Long-tailed Duck, Red-throated Diver, Great Northern Diver, Grey Plover, Golden Plover, Lapwing, Knot, Curlew Sandpiper (O autumn), Dunlin, Ruff (R), Snipe, Black-tailed Godwit, Whimbrel (autumn & spring), Common Sandpiper (O autumn), Sandwich Tern (autumn), Arctic Skua (usually several present in the outer bay, Aug & Sept).

Rarities Canada Goose (with Barnacle Geese), Little Gull, Black Tern, Brambling.

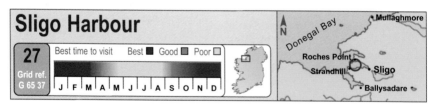

Sligo Harbour

27

Grid ref.
G 65 37

Best time to visit   Best ■ Good ■ Poor □

J F M A M J J A S O N D

Donegal Bay · Mullaghmore · Roches Point · Strandhill · Sligo · Ballysadare

A large muddy estuary, good for wildfowl, waders and gulls, mainly in winter.

Directions Map 17, previous page. The best areas for birds are close to Sligo town, NW of the main bridge. The N side of the bay, as far as Roches Point, is largely rocky, and holds relatively few birds.

For **Cartron Marsh**, leave Sligo town N, on the N15 Sligo to Donegal road, and cross the main

road bridge. After 100m, take a left onto the R291, signposted for Roches Point. Just 200m along this road is a housing estate on the left, with an obvious left turn onto a road which follows the shoreline of a tidal bay – Cartron Marsh. It is easily viewed from the road and is best at low or mid tide.

The estuary beside the **Sligo Docks**, close to Sligo town, W to **Cummeen Strand** is good for waders, some waterfowl and gulls in winter. To the NW of Sligo town, locate the road bridge for the N15 Sligo to Donegal road. The docks and a large industrial area are obvious downriver and to the SW, as is the long, straight road which follows the shoreline. Excellent views over the estuary and bay can be had along this road. Low to mid tide is best, as most birds are absent at high tide. The last left turn along this road, after 1km, goes roughly parallel to the shoreline, eventually to **Cummeen Strand** and gives further views over the bay before joining the R292 to Strandhill. Brent Geese and Wigeon can be numerous at Cummeen Strand in early autumn.

Species
Autumn & winter Whooper Swan (O), Brent Goose (250+), Wigeon, Gadwall (O), Teal, Pintail (O), Scaup (O), Goldeneye, Red-breasted Merganser, Red-throated Diver, Great Northern Diver, Great Crested Grebe (O), Cormorant, Little Egret (O), Hen Harrier (R), Merlin (O), Peregrine (O), Oystercatcher (800+), Ringed Plover (150+), Golden Plover, Grey Plover, Lapwing, Knot, Curlew Sandpiper (O autumn), Purple Sandpiper (O), Dunlin, Ruff (R autumn), Snipe, Black-tailed Godwit (small numbers), Bar-tailed Godwit, Redshank (800+), Greenshank (40+), gulls, Iceland Gull (O winter), Glaucous Gull (O winter), Arctic Skua, (O outer bay, autumn), Mediterranean Gull (R), Ring-billed Gull (O), Sandwich Tern (outer bay, summer & autumn, R winter), Black Guillemot (outer bay).

Rarities Black Brant, Forster's Tern.

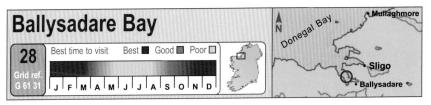

Ballysadare Bay

28
Grid ref.
G 61 31

Best time to visit   Best ■ Good ■ Poor □

| J | F | M | A | M | J | J | A | S | O | N | D |

Waders and duck, mainly in autumn, and large numbers of Brent Geese in winter. From early autumn to early spring a good variety of waders and some duck can also be seen. Small numbers of Black-tailed Godwit winter here.

Directions Map 17, p.47. The southernmost of the three bays of Sligo Bay, reached from Sligo by taking the main N4 Sligo to Dublin road. Follow the signposts to Ballysadare, and just before reaching the town, the estuary is visible to your right. *Be wary of traffic on this narrow, winding road and park carefully.* Mid to close to high tide is best.

The N side of the estuary can be explored by leaving Ballysadare N, as if returning to Sligo. Just 700m after leaving Ballysadare, take a left, onto the R292, signposted for Strandhill. Several side roads to the left, and this road itself, skirt the northern edge of the estuary.

The best site on the southern side of the estuary is **Streamstown**, and Brent Geese and other wildfowl and waders can be found here. Leaving Ballysadare W on the N59 to Ballina, take a right turn after 1km, signposted for Streamstown. This road leads to the shoreline and good views of the estuary. Another area worthy of attention is **Portavud**, at the entrance to Ballysadare Bay. Gulls and terns can gather here, and occasionally Arctic Skuas are seen in autumn. To reach it, return to the N59 and continue on toward Ballina, through Beltra, then take the first turn to the right signposted for Aughris Head (see p.51). Continue for 3km and take a right at the junction.

Species
Autumn & winter Whooper Swan (O), Brent Goose (300+), Wigeon, Teal, Shoveler (O), Pochard (O), Eider (O), Long-tailed Duck (outer bay), Common Scoter (O), Goldeneye, Red-breasted Merganser, Red-throated Diver, Great Northern Diver, Slavonian Grebe (R), Great Crested Grebe, Cormorant, Little Egret (O), Merlin (O winter), Peregrine (O), Golden Plover, Grey Plover, Lapwing, Knot, Little Stint (O autumn), Curlew Sandpiper (O autumn), Dunlin (1500+), Ruff (O autumn), Jack Snipe (O), Snipe, Black-tailed Godwit, Bar-tailed Godwit, Green

Sandpiper (O autumn, R winter), gulls. The large river running through Ballysadare town has Kingfisher, Grey Wagtail and Dipper.

Rarities Green-winged Teal, Baird's Sandpiper, Lesser Yellowlegs, Black Tern.

29 Lough Gill Grid ref. G 75 33

A large, deep lake just 2km E of Sligo town, which has a limited variety of waterbirds, but good broadleaf woodland habitat around it. A spring visit is highly recommended

Three roads, the R286, R288 and R287, circle the lake, with several viewpoints and carparks. The best woodland areas are Slishwood on the S shore, and Hazelwood on the N side, off the R286. Access and carparking are straightforward, and there are numerous trails.

All the regular woodland species can be found at these two sites (best in spring), including Blackcap, Chiffchaff, Willow Warbler, Spotted Flycatcher, Long-tailed Tit, Treecreeper and Jay. Rarer woodland birds have been found, such as Redstart and Wood Warbler, and Common Crossbill can be found in coniferous forest.

The lake usually has little but Mute Swan, Cormorant and Mallard, though Whooper Swan, Wigeon, Teal, Pochard, Tufted Duck and Goldeneye have been seen in winter, albeit in small numbers.

30 Inishcrone Grid ref. G 28 30

A small town on the E side of Killala Bay (Site 240) and a good place from which to explore Outer Killala Bay.

See Map146, p.291. From Sligo, take the N59 to Ballina, but take the R297 at Dromore West for an interesting coastal route to Inishcrone. From Ballina, Inishcrone is well signposted from the town, via Castleconor on the R297.

There are several spots on the seafront from which to scan the bay, though a telescope is

recommended. In winter, Eider, Long-tailed Duck, Common Scoter, Red-throated Diver, Great Northern Diver, Great Crested Grebe and auks can all be found offshore, while small numbers of Purple Sandpiper can be found on the shore to the N of the town. During autumn gales, skuas can sometimes be seen sheltering in the bay.

Rarer birds seen here include Black-throated Diver, Slavonian Grebe and Buzzard.

31 Lough Gara Grid ref. M 70 98

A freshwater lake, good for waterbirds in winter, with a large flock of both Whooper Swans and White-fronted Geese.

Lough Gara is 7km W of Boyle and 7km NE of Ballaghadreen.

The Whooper Swans are usually found on the S shore of the lower lake or on the upper lakes, while the White-fronted Geese are either present there, or can be found feeding on Inchmore,

Derrymore and Inch Islands, and on the tip of the Derrybeg peninsula. 300-400 of each are present most winters, though the Whitefront numbers have been falling.

There is a good variety of other waterbirds present, such as Barnacle Goose (R), Wigeon, Teal, Pintail (O), Shoveler, Pochard, Tufted Duck, Goldeneye, Great Crested Grebe, Water Rail (O), Golden Plover, Lapwing, Snipe, and small numbers of gulls.

32 **Lough Arrow** Grid ref. G 79 11

A large freshwater lake, about 30km S of Sligo town, good for waterbirds in winter.

The lake straddles the Sligo/Roscommon border in the S of County Sligo. From Sligo town, take the N4 to Castlebaldwin, and there are a few signposted viewpoints between there and Ballinafad, though access is limited and there is no one outstanding viewpoint over the lake. It is possible to travel around the lake on backroads, and there are other signposted picnic spots and laybys to view the lake. A telescope is recommended.

There is good forest habitat around the lake, where all the regular woodland species can be found in spring, including Cuckoo (O), Blackcap, Garden Warbler (O), Chiffchaff, Willow Warbler and Spotted Flycatcher. Throughout the year, Water Rail, Woodcock, Long-tailed Tit, Treecreeper and Jay can be found, while in summer, Sedge Warbler and Grasshopper Warbler are common (the latter difficult to see). Small numbers of Common Scoter used to occur, but are rare now.

In winter, there are good numbers of waterbirds, especially Little Grebe (often 100+), Whooper Swan (O), Wigeon, Teal, Pochard, Tufted Duck, Scaup (O), Goldeneye, Redbreasted Merganser, Great Crested Grebe and Cormorant.

Rare birds seen include Ring-necked Duck and Smew.

Other sites

Inishmurray (G 57 54) is an unihabited island 13km W of Mullaghmore (Site 23), where it is possible to book a boat trip with local boat operators. Enquire locally for times and prices but bear in mind that access is limited by bad weather. Trips generally run from June to September. The island has good numbers of nesting Eider, Arctic and Common Tern, while Storm Petrels nest in the walls of the sixth-century monastery.

Benbulben & Kings Mountain (G 70 45), 9km N of Sligo town, are spectacular mountain walks in their own right, and have several pairs of Chough, one of the few regular inland nesting sites in the country. Golden Plover occur, especially in spring.

Ballygawley Lough (G 69 28) is located 2.5km E of Ballysadare, and holds small numbers of wildfowl in winter. There is a small carpark and picnic area from where the lake can be viewed. Species include Cormorant, Whooper Swan, Wigeon, Teal, Pochard (O), Tufted Duck, Scaup and Goldeneye.

Colgagh Lough (G 74 36) is 4km E of Sligo town, on the main R286, and 1 km N of Lough Arrow (Site 32, above). Leaving Sligo on the R286 (following signs for Parke's Castle), Colgagh Lough is the first lake, visible on your left, downhill from the road. There is a small carpark above the lake which offers excellent views. Regular species in winter include Whooper Swan (O), Wigeon, Teal, Pochard (O), Tufted Duck and Goldeneye, while occasional waders, such as Redshank (O), Greenshank (O) and Curlew (O), can also be seen.

Lenadoon Point (G 31 38), in the far W of County Sligo, can have good seawatching from late August to the end of October. Many seabirds are pushed into Donegal Bay by strong W or NW winds and pass close to Lenadoon Point on their way back out into the Atlantic. However, if time and transport permit, it would be better to go to Kilcummin Head (Site 241) across the bay. Not only will there be even more birds, but they will pass much closer. See Kilcummin Head for likely species.

Like Lenadoon Point above, **Aughris Head** (G 50 37) can have good seabirds in the same conditions in autumn. Leach's Petrel, Grey Phalarope, Sabine's Gull, Arctic Skua, Pomarine Skua and Great Skua have all been recorded. It is well signposted at several points between Templeboy and Dromard, on the main N59 road from Ballysadare to Ballina.

County Derry

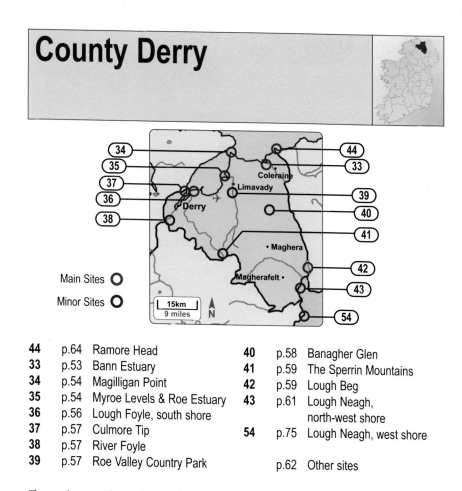

Main Sites ○

Minor Sites ○

| 15km |
| 9 miles |

The north coast of Derry has a rich variety of habitats, which hold large numbers of birds, mainly in winter. Lough Foyle is a huge estuary, bisected by the border with Donegal, but all the best sites for birds lie on the Derry side. The mudflats, grasslands and polders along its south shore are the winter home to hundreds of Whooper Swans and geese, with a supporting cast of thousands of other waterbirds and waders. The Bann Estuary also offers large wintering waterbird populations.

Two other sites in Lough Foyle, Magilligan Point and Culmore Tip, offer identification challenges for birders with more specialised species; skuas at the former, and wintering gulls at the latter.

Derry also has good areas of broadleaved woodland and Roe Valley Country Park and Banagher Glen are perhaps the two best, with all the regular woodland species and frequent sightings of more unusual woodland species such as Redstart and Wood Warbler. Coniferous woodland dominates areas of the Sperrin Mountains in the centre of the county, and many upland species can be seen there.

One of the outstanding birdwatching sites in Northern Ireland is Lough Beg, at the north end of Lough Neagh. This wetland has one of the largest species list of any site in the North and includes not only all the common and most of the scarce wildfowl and waders, but also many rare species, including North American and European waders. Osprey is seen here most years, and a visit at any time of year can be most rewarding.

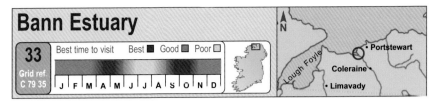

Bann Estuary

33
Grid ref.
C 79 35

Best time to visit   Best ■ Good ■ Poor □

J F M A M J J A S O N D

Portstewart
Lough Foyle
Coleraine
Limavady

A large river estuary, with sand dunes and a large, shallow coastal bay, good for wildfowl and waders in spring and particularly in autumn.

Directions Map 18 below. The river mouth extends approximately 10km from Coleraine to Castlerock, but the 2km stretch from The Barmouth is the best for birds. Travelling from Coleraine to Castlerock on the A2, take a right at Articlave. After 1.5km, turn left at the T-junction, cross the bridge and take a right. There is a carpark just before the railway line. Continue on foot from here. There is a hide by the water's edge, although it is usually locked. The key may be obtained by enquiring at the nearest row of cottages by the river.

Castlerock and **The Barmouth**, 1km E of Castlerock, can be good seawatching sites in autumn, with much the same (though more distant views) of seabirds which pass Ramore Head. Some seaduck, divers and grebes can also be seen offshore, outside the summer months. The Barmouth can be reached on foot (1km distance) by walking the shoreline E of Castlerock, or a 3km walk W along the shore from Portstewart.

The estuary can also be explored on foot from the Portstewart side, but involves a long walk.

Most waders and wildfowl feed on the mudflats of the river mouth at low tide. Eider and divers can be found on the sea around Castlerock and The Barmouth.

Species
Autumn, winter & spring Bewick's Swan (O), Whooper Swan, White-fronted Goose (O), Greylag Goose (feral), Brent Goose (O), Wigeon, Gadwall (O), Teal, Pintail (O), Pochard (O), Tufted Duck (O), Eider (coast), Long-tailed Duck (O, coast), Goldeneye, Red-breasted Merganser, Red-throated Diver (O), Great Northern Diver (O), Little Grebe (O), Great Crested Grebe (O), Slavonian Grebe (R), Cormorant, Golden Plover, Grey Plover, Lapwing (1000+), Knot, Little Stint (O autumn), Curlew Sandpiper (O autumn), Dunlin (up to 1000), Ruff (O autumn), Jack-Snipe (R), Snipe, Black-tailed Godwit, Bar-tailed Godwit, Whimbrel (autumn & spring, R winter), Spotted Redshank (O), Mediterranean Gull (R), Little Gull (O), gulls, terns (autumn), Snow Bunting (occasionally 50+).

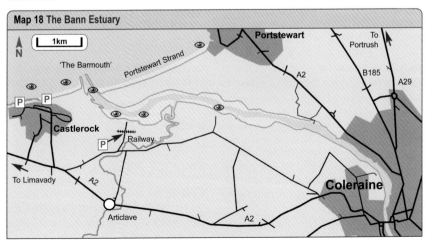

Map 18 The Bann Estuary

1km
N
'The Barmouth'   Portstewart Strand   Portstewart   To Portrush
A2   B185   A29
P P
Castlerock   Railway
P
To Limavady   A2
Articlave   A2   Coleraine

North

53

Seawatching See Ramore Head (Site 44) for species list and suitable conditions. Many of the birds which pass Ramore Head can be seen here also, though most are much further out.

Rarities Garganey, Goosander, Black-throated Diver, Leach's Petrel, Osprey, Semipalmated Sandpiper, White-rumped Sandpiper, Pectoral Sandpiper, Lesser Yellowlegs, Wilson's Phalarope, Ring-billed Gull, Yellow-legged Gull, Iceland Gull, Glaucous Gull, Black Tern.

34 Magilligan Point Grid ref. C 66 38

A low-lying headland backed by dunes, which can be good for divers, seabirds and some seaduck in autumn and winter.

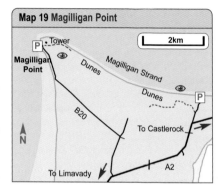

Map 19 Magilligan Point

Magilligan Point lies at the eastern entrance to Lough Foyle, see Map 19, right. It is reached by taking the B20 off the main A2 Limavady to Castlerock road.

Red-throated Diver and Great Northern Diver are regular offshore, and Black-throated Diver is seen most winters. Great Crested Grebes can also be seen, and small numbers of Eider, Long-tailed Duck and Slavonian Grebe occur, more often along the stretch of beach running S of Magilligan Point.

Sited at the entrance to Lough Foyle, the Point is a good area from which to see birds moving along the coast, and various wildfowl and waders which use the Lough can often be seen flying by. During NW gales in autumn, this has proved to be an outstanding area for skua passage, with

Pomarine Skua, Arctic Skua and Great Skua all regular, and even Long-tailed Skua on occasion. Some birds can be seen sheltering on the beaches and harassing other seabirds, most eventually flying into Lough Foyle rather than braving the gales to round the Inishowen Peninsula to the N.

Rarer species seen here include Goosander, Curlew Sandpiper, Sabine's Gull and Black tern.

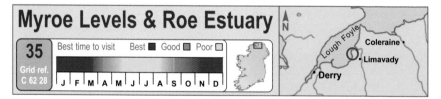

Myroe Levels & Roe Estuary

35	Best time to visit	Best ■ Good ■ Poor □
Grid ref. C 62 28		

J	F	M	A	M	J	J	A	S	O	N	D

An area of estuary, mudflats and grassland which attracts large numbers of Whooper Swan, geese, wildfowl and waders in winter.

Lough Foyle is an internationally important site for Whooper Swan, Brent Goose and Bar-tailed Godwit, and holds nationally important numbers of a further 20 species. Most of the waterfowl and waders frequent the Myroe Levels and Roe Estuary on the E side, though the S shore (Site 36) also holds good numbers of birds.

Directions Map 20, next page.

The area referred to as the **Myroe Levels**, 4km NW of Limavady, actually includes several distinct sites, as follows.

Ballykelly (C 61 23) has a major high tide roost of waders on the mussel ridge opposite the shoreline. From Limavady, take the A2 to Derry, taking a right after passing through Ballykelly. Continue to the railway embankment, park just before the bridge and continue on foot. Waders can be present in the marsh just behind the embankment, including Little Stint and Curlew Sandpiper in autumn.

The open fields at **Burnfoot Drain** (C 63 25) are an excellent spot for Whooper Swan and Greylag Geese. From Ballykelly, head E, toward Limavady on the A2, and take a left after 1.5km. 1km along this road, go straight through the crossroads, and continue straight, on the Broighter Road, for another 2km. Then take a left, and another left, then a right, to the shoreline. Scan the fields at any likely spot for goose and swan flocks, and offshore for waders and waterfowl.

The **Myroe Levels** (C 62 28) are just N of Burnfoot Drain. Again, scan the fields for any flocks of geese and swans. The steps in the seawall at this point offer good views over Lough Foyle, and is one of the best spots for divers and Slavonian Grebe, best at high tide.

The **Roe Estuary** (C 64 29) is located 6km N of Limavady. From Limavady, take the A2 W toward Derry, and at the roundabout on the outskirts of the town, take the right onto the B69. Continue straight for 5km, ignoring all turns, and then take a left. After another 2km, you reach the estuary, where it is possible to park and explore the estuary to the W, under the railway track. Brent Geese are usually present in large numbers, with many other duck and waders offshore.

The N side of the Roe Estuary, **Balls Point** (C 64 29), can be accessed by travelling from Limavady to Coleraine on the A2, turning left after 9km (there is a school on the left just before this turn). Continue for 2.5km to the shore, park, and walk S along the shoreline.

Species

Lough Foyle is one of the most important sites in Ireland for Brent Geese, which arrive into Ireland in early autumn. At that time, up to 3500+ gather along the Myroe shoreline, gradually dispersing to other sites in Ireland as winter progresses. Whooper Swan numbers are highest in autumn and spring, after and before migrating to Iceland, and over 1000 have been recorded at peak times, though 600-800 is more typical in winter. Occasionally, small numbers of White-fronted Geese are recorded.

Autumn, winter & spring Bewick's Swan (small numbers), Whooper Swan (100s), Pink-footed Goose (O), White-fronted Goose, Greylag Goose (100s), Barnacle Goose (R), Dark-Bellied Brent

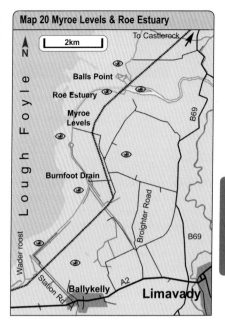

Map 20 Myroe Levels & Roe Estuary

2km

To Castlerock

N

Balls Point

Roe Estuary

Myroe Levels

Burnfoot Drain

Broighter Road

B69

B69

Wader roost

Station Rd

Ballykelly

A2

Limavady

Lough Foyle

North

Goose (R), Brent Goose (1000s), Shelduck (100s), Wigeon (5000+), Gadwall (R), Teal (1000+), Mallard (1000+), Pintail, Shoveler (O), Pochard, Tufted Duck (O), Scaup (small numbers), Eider, Long-tailed Duck, Common Scoter (O), Velvet Scoter (R), Goldeneye, Red-breasted Merganser, Red-throated Diver, Great Northern Diver, Little Grebe, Great Crested Grebe, Slavonian Grebe, Cormorant, Little Egret (R), Hen Harrier, Buzzard, Merlin, Peregrine, Water Rail, Oystercatcher (1000+), Golden Plover (1000s), Grey Plover, Lapwing (1000s), Knot (often 500+), Little Stint (autumn), Curlew Sandpiper (autumn), Dunlin (1000s), Ruff (autumn), Snipe, Black-tailed Godwit, Bar-tailed Godwit (1000+), Whimbrel (100s autumn & spring, O winter), Curlew (1000+), Spotted Redshank (O autumn), Redshank (500+), Greenshank (40+), Common Sandpiper (O spring & autumn, R winter), Mediterranean Gull, Black-headed Gull (1000+), Common Gull (1500+), gulls (many 100s of the regular species), Short-eared Owl (R), Twite (small flocks still regular), Snow Bunting (O winter, up to 200 recorded on occasion).

Rarities Bean Goose, Black Brant, Smew, Gyr Falcon, American Golden Plover, Buff-breasted Sandpiper, Lesser Yellowlegs, Bonaparte's Gull, Iceland Gull, Glaucous Gull, Lapland Bunting.

Lough Foyle, south shore

36

Grid ref.
C 56 22

Best time to visit   Best ■ Good ▨ Poor □

J F M A M J J A S O N D

Coleraine •
Lough Foyle
• Limavady
• Derry

Mudflat and grassland, with large numbers of swans, waterbirds and waders in winter.

Directions Map 21, below.

Donnybrewer Levels (C 51 23) is good for duck and some waders, as well as flocks of Whooper Swan and geese. Leaving Derry on the A2 to Limavady, take a left at the White Horse Hotel. Take the second left, which will lead to a level crossing with an auto barrier. Donnybrewer Levels are just beyond this crossing.

Longfield Levels (C 54 23) is at the E end of Donnybrewer Levels and is good for more duck, and seaduck, divers, grebes and gulls offshore. Travelling from Derry to Limavady on the A2, there is a right turn onto the B118 to Eglinton. Ignore this right turn, instead taking the left turn almost immediately after it onto Station Road. Take the third right onto Lower Airfield Road and *take care crossing the level crossing, which has no barrier.* Beyond the railway line, take the unsurfaced road straight ahead, and then right at the embankment. Continue for another 1km, stop and scan the entire area.

Further views over the mudflats can be had at **Faughanvale** (C 58 22) by going E on the A2 from

Greysteel to Limavady. Take a left, 1.5km from Greysteel to the shore, taking care when crossing the railway tracks. Stop and park before the railway – *do not drive across it.* Brent Goose, Wigeon, waders and gulls can be particularly numerous at this spot.

Species
Autumn, winter & spring Bewick's Swan (O), Whooper Swan, Pink-footed Goose (O), White-fronted Goose (R), Greylag Goose, Brent Goose, Wigeon, Teal, Pintail, Shoveler (R), Pochard, Tufted Duck (O), Scaup (small numbers), Red-breasted Merganser, Red-throated Diver, Great Northern Diver, Great Crested Grebe, Slavonian Grebe (O), Cormorant, Hen Harrier, Buzzard, Merlin, Peregrine, Water Rail, Golden Plover, Grey Plover, Lapwing (1000s), Dunlin, Ruff (O autumn), Snipe, Black-tailed Godwit, Bar-tailed Godwit, Whimbrel (autumn & spring, R winter), Curlew, Common Sandpiper (O spring & autumn, R winter), gulls (many 100s of the regular species), Short-eared Owl (R), Snow Bunting (O).

Rarities Barnacle Goose, Iceland Gull, Glaucous Gull, Ring-billed Gull, Mediterranean Gull, Twite, Lapland Bunting.

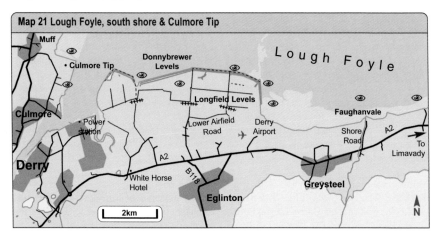

Map 21 Lough Foyle, south shore & Culmore Tip

37 Culmore Tip <small>Grid ref. C 48 24</small>

A landfill site which attracts large numbers of gulls in autumn, winter and spring, including many scarce and rare species.

See Map 21, previous page. The Tip is located on the N outskirts of Derry. Take the A2 N out of Derry, toward Muff and Moville. Take a right just before Muff and the Tip is visible on the left after 500m. Hundreds of gulls frequent the dump, but are more easily viewed on the mudflats and channels immediately to the N of the dump.

All the regular gull species are present, often in considerable numbers, and Mediterranean Gull, Ring-billed Gull, Iceland Gull and Glaucous Gull are often seen. Rarer species include Bonaparte's Gull, Kumlien's Gull, American Herring Gull, Caspian Gull and Yellow-legged Gull. Great Skua, Snow Bunting and Twite have also been seen. The dump is due to close in 2007.

38 River Foyle <small>Grid ref. C 35 10</small>

Grasslands adjacent to the River Foyle which hold numerous swans and duck in winter.

See Map 22, right. The areas for seeing swans and geese are about 13km SSW of Derry city, on either the E or W side of the river. Best are the grasslands around Porthall (C 34 03), Carrickmore (C 34 05) and around the Swilly Burn River. This latter spot can be viewed from the R265, 5km S of Saint Johnstown. Another good area for geese and swans is just W and N of Drumenny (C 36 05), directly across the River Foyle from Carrickmore. Also try Magheraboy (C 35 11), midway between Carrigans and Saint Johnstown. This area is viewable from the R236.

Most of the Wigeon, Teal and other duck are found on the River Foyle itself, with the majority of birds found at and around Saint Johnstown.

Species found in autumn, winter & spring include Great Crested Grebe, Slavonian Grebe (R), Bewick's Swan (O), Whooper Swan (500+), White-fronted Goose (O), Greylag Goose (often 300+), Barnacle Goose (O), Wigeon, Teal, Pintail (O), Shoveler (O), Pochard (O), Tufted Duck, Scaup (O), Goldeneye, Red-breasted Merganser, Golden Plover, Lapwing, Dunlin, Snipe, Curlew, gulls, Kingfisher (O).

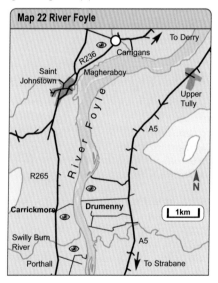

Map 22 River Foyle

39 Roe Valley Country Park <small>Grid ref. C 67 20</small>

One of the best broadleaved woodlands in Northern Ireland which contains a wide variety of woodland species throughout the year, and is particularly good in May and June.

The Park runs along a deep river gorge for 4km, with mature native oak forest along both banks . It has a Visitor Centre, museum, café, audio-visual theatre and a wildlife trail for disabled visitors.

See Map 23, next page. The park is located 500m S of Limavady on the B192 to Dungiven. The Visitor Centre is best approached from the Drumrane Road, off the B192 Limavady to Dungiven road. The park is well signposted on all roads around the town.

There is another access point at the Ballyquinn Road, off the B68 Limavady to

Dungiven road, though access here is via a very narrow bridge.

The Centre is open Mon to Fri from 1st Oct to 1st April, 9am to 5pm (closed weekends), and daily from 30th March to 30th September, 9am to 6pm. Tel: (028) 7772 2074 for further information.

Over 60 species have been seen in the park and include all the regular woodland species. The best and most extensive woodland lies N of the Visitor Centre. Typical woodland birds throughout the year include Woodpigeon, Wren, Dunnock, Robin, Blackbird, Song Thrush, Chiffchaff (R winter), Goldcrest, Long-tailed Tit, Coal Tit, Blue Tit, Great Tit, Treecreeper, Jay (O), Chaffinch and Greenfinch. Fieldfare and Redwing are regular in winter and Buzzard is regular in this area. In spring, Blackcap, Willow Warbler, Chiffchaff and Spotted Flycatcher breed, and this is one of the better sites in Northern Ireland to find Wood Warbler, though they are not recorded every year. Other species include Peregrine, Woodcock (O), Long-eared Owl (R), Grey Wagtail (rivers), Dipper (rivers) and Raven.

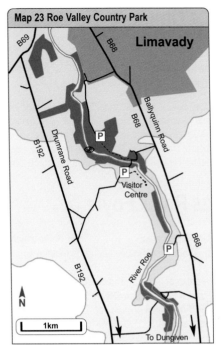

Map 23 Roe Valley Country Park

40 Banagher Glen Grid ref. C 67 45

Banagher Glen is a National Nature Reserve and comprises a large area of semi-natural upland deciduous forest and mixed woodland, with a good selection of woodland birds. Particularly good in May and June.

Map 24, right. The Reserve is located 4km SW of Dungiven, and can be reached by leaving Dungiven via the B74 to Feeny. The Reserve is signposted at the left turn after 3km. It can also be reached by a minor road, from Dungiven town centre via the Castle Environmental Park. The Reserve itself is situated in the three glens of Altnaheglish, Cushcapel and Glenadra rivers, which meet in the middle of the Reserve to form the Owenrigh River. There are two carparks, from which a number of well-maintained trails start. The park is open at all times, though there is no manned information centre.

The birds occurring here are essentially the same as at Roe Valley Country Park (Site 39). Dipper and Grey Wagtail are relatively common along the three rivers higher up the valley.

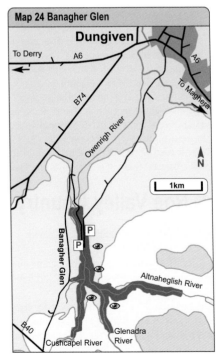

Map 24 Banagher Glen

41 The Sperrin Mountains Grid ref. H 50 90

A large area of upland blanket bog and extensive coniferous forest, good in spring and summer for upland breeding birds.

The Sperrins straddle the border of counties Derry and Tyrone, roughly 15km S of Derry, 5km E of Strabane and 10km NE of Omagh. There are no particular hotspots for birds, though exploration is facilitated by many minor roads crisscrossing the entire area. Large tracts of forestry land have numerous tracks open to the public, which are best cycled or walked.

Peregrine, Wheatear (summer) and Raven are often encountered in the more open areas, while the conifers hold Siskin, Redpoll and small numbers of Treecreeper. Crossbill can occur in these coniferous plantations, mainly from late summer into autumn, though they can be recorded at any time of year.

Hen Harrier do not usually breed in this area, though the occasional non-breeding bird might be seen. Red Grouse and Merlin are only present in very low densities but walking any flat, heather moorland expanse might be productive.

There are generally many fewer birds in winter, though Peregrine is still present.

North

A large lake and wetland area which attracts large numbers of wildfowl and waders in winter, many migrants in spring and autumn, and a varied selection of breeding birds in summer. An outstanding birdwatching location at any time of year.

Lough Beg attracts large numbers of waterbirds each winter, with regular counts in excess of 10,000 birds, with Teal, Wigeon, Lapwing and Golden Plover among the commonest. Whooper Swan occurs mainly around the Creagh in the SW corner.

The Lough's location, between Lough Neagh and the coast to the N, combined with the variety and quality of the habitats, make it one of the best inland sites in Ireland for rare American wildfowl and waders each autumn. Many unusual European species are also seen, especially in spring, and the growing list of unusual species recorded at this site makes it one of Northern Ireland's premier sites for rare birds.

This is one of the best places to see Osprey in Ireland, with one, or sometimes up to three birds frequenting the Lough each spring and/or early

autumn. They are most often seen perching on posts in the middle of the Lough.

Directions Map 25, next page. Lough Beg is 5km long and just over 1km at its widest, and is located to the N of Lough Neagh, 2km N of the village of Toombe and 10km NE of Magherafelt. The lake straddles the Derry/Antrim border, with most of the accessible areas just on the Derry side. See also Map 31, p.71.

Water levels can vary at any time of year and flooding may limit access to some areas. Wildfowling is a popular pastime, particularly on Saturdays, and can affect the local distribution of birds.

The W side of the lake offers the best opportunities for seeing birds. Leaving Toome NW toward Castledawson on the A6, go for 3km, before turning right at McNally's Inn onto the B182, signposted for Bellaghy. After 3km, take a right at the crossroads onto a minor road, passing some bungalows, until the road ends at **Annagh Farm**. *Park carefully.* Walking 1km to the SE will bring you to **Paddy's Dub**, a marshy area which dries out somewhat in spring and is particularly good for waders.

Map 25 Lough Beg

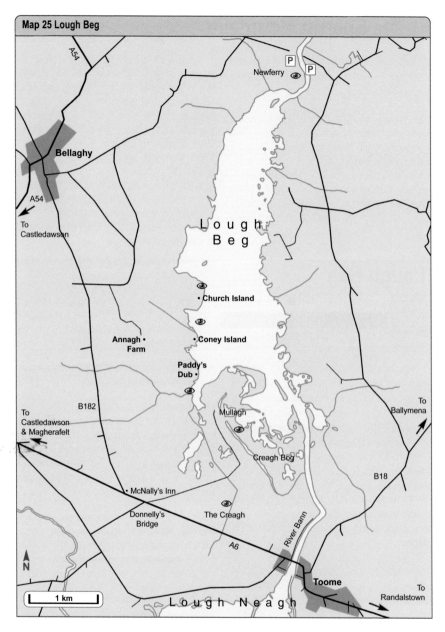

By turning left (N) on the shoreline below Annagh Farm, you will come to an area of raised ground with scattered bushes known as **Coney Island**, which offers extensive views over the lake and a muddy shoreline which is very good for waders in spring and autumn. Gulls and terns can be seen offshore, and there is a good chance of seeing Osprey from here in August and September.

By continuing N along this shoreline to **Church Island**, it is possible to view more muddy shoreline and marsh, with further opportunities for seeing more waders and duck.

For the S side of Lough Beg, leave Toome W, heading for Castledawson, and take a sharp right at Donnelly's Bridge after 2km, and drive to the

60

end of the road. This area, known as **Mullagh**, allows views over a sheltered bay, pools and inlets, and holds many wildfowl and waders, particularly in winter. Whooper Swan favours this corner of Lough Beg, particularly N and E of The Creagh. *Much of this area is private farmland, and permission must be sought for access.* The area to the SE of Mullagh is **Creagh Bog** where more pools and channels offer a multitude of birds at any time of year, though again, this area is private farmland and permission must be sought.

The northernmost shore of the lough can be reached by going N from Bellaghy on the A54 and turning right after 1.2km and right again after 1.2km. Continue straight for 2km to a picnic area at **Newferry** (H 98 98). This spot is best in spring and autumn when waders and duck can occasionally be seen flying along the River Bann on migration.

Views of the E side of Lough Beg are much more limited, though several minor roads can offer distant views. *Take care to seek permission from landowners before crossing private land.*

Species

All year Great Crested Grebe, Little Grebe, Cormorant, Water Rail (O), Peregrine, Teal, Shoveler, Tufted Duck, Red-breasted Merganser, Snipe, Lapwing, Dunlin, Curlew, Kingfisher.

Autumn, winter & spring Whooper Swan, Bewick's Swan (O), White-fronted Goose (O), Greylag Goose, Pink-footed Goose (O), Wigeon

(1000s) Gadwall, Teal (1000+), Pintail (small numbers), Garganey (R, mainly spring), Shoveler, Pochard (100s), Tufted Duck, Goldeneye, Red-breasted Merganser, Ruddy Duck (O), Little Egret (R), Hen Harrier (O), Osprey (R spring & autumn), Merlin (O), Buzzard (O), Coot (100s), Golden Plover (100s), Grey Plover (small numbers), Lapwing (100s), Little Stint (O autumn), Curlew Sandpiper (O autumn), Dunlin, Ruff (O), Jack Snipe (O), Snipe, Black-tailed Godwit (small numbers), Whimbrel (mainly spring), Curlew (100s), Spotted Redshank (O), Green Sandpiper (O), Wood Sandpiper (R autumn), Common Sandpiper (mainly autumn & spring), gulls, Short-eared Owl (O), White Wagtail (spring & autumn).

Summer Common Sandpiper, Black-headed Gulls breed, Common Tern, Cuckoo (O), 1000s of hirundines gather to roost each evening in August and early September. Sedge Warbler, Willow Warbler.

Rarities Snow Goose, American Wigeon, Green-winged Teal, Blue-winged Teal, Red-crested Pochard, Lesser Scaup, Smew, Goosander, Quail, Black-necked Grebe, Corncrake, Crane, Little Ringed Plover, Temminck's Stint, White-rumped Sandpiper, Baird's Sandpiper, Pectoral Sandpiper, Broad-billed Sandpiper, Stilt Sandpiper, Long-billed Dowitcher, Lesser Yellowlegs, Greater Yellowlegs, Wilson's Phalarope, Red-necked Phalarope, Bonaparte's Gull, Black Tern, White-winged Black Tern, Yellow Wagtail, Richard's Pipit, Lapland Bunting.

43 Lough Neagh, north-west shore Grid ref. C 95 85

Large numbers of diving duck in winter.

See Map 31, p.71. See also Site 54, Lough Neagh, west shore, p.75.

The stretch of shoreline between Toome and Ballyronan offers some good views over Lough Neagh, with good numbers of Pochard, Tufted Duck and Goldeneye, and this is one of the better places on Lough Neagh for Scaup. Some Whooper Swans are usually present, though Bewick's Swans are now rare in the area. Other duck usually present throughout winter include Wigeon and Teal, while Great Crested Grebe, Curlew, Lapwing and Golden Plover are usually easily found.

The best area to view this section of the Lough is from Ballyronan (C 94 85), as the road follows the shoreline for 1.5 km, N and S of the small harbour. There are also excellent views from the marina piers. In summer there are breeding Great Crested Grebe and Tufted Duck.

3km N of Ballyronan, take a right at Ballymaguigan, for further views of the Lough and shoreline, from a small pier. Just N from Ballymaguigan, toward Toome on the B18, there are two right turns, each of which offers further views of the Lough and some pools and channels. A telescope is recommended.

Other sites

The 6km of spectacular cliffs to the SW of **Downhill** (C 73 35) provide excellent views of Fulmar, Buzzard, Peregrine and Raven. From Downhill, take the road inland, by the hotel. After 3.5km, a viewpoint is on your right. Other views can be had from below the cliff W of Downhill by pulling over on the main A2 Coleraine to Derry road.

Ness Wood Country Park (C 51 11) and nearby **Ervey Wood** (C 52 11) comprise of 70 hectares of remnant oak and mixed woodland in the steep-sided Burntollet Valley.

Ness Wood is 4.5km NW of Claudy and 13km SE of Derry, and is signposted off the A6 Derry to Belfast road. Ervey Wood is 5.5km NW of Claudy and 12km SE of Derry. It is also signposted off the A6, via Birch Road onto Ervey Road to a carpark. Both parks are open all year and have carparks, paths and information panels.

Species for both sites include most of the regular woodland species, including Buzzard, Long-tailed Tit and Treecreeper. Dippers frequent parts of the Burntollet River and Blackcaps breed. The best time for a visit is spring and early summer.

County Antrim

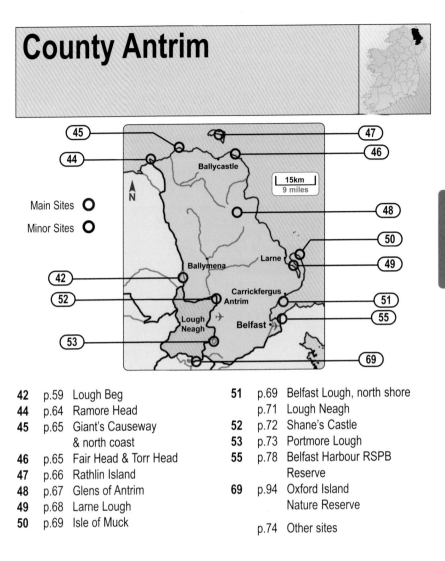

The scenic and rugged north coast of County Antrim has a number of spectacular sites of interest to birdwatchers. The huge cliffs along the north coast in particular are home to large numbers of breeding seabirds, while Eider and various raptors are often seen. The coastline near the world-famous Giant's Causeway has a number of seabird colonies nearby and from there, clifftop walks allow further exploration to Fair Head, Torr Head and beyond. Rathlin Island is equally spectacular and home to one of the largest auk colonies in Ireland.

Ramore Head, close to the border with Derry, is one of Northern Ireland's best seawatching sites and in autumn can produce large movements of seabirds during NW winds. Leach's Petrel, skuas and Sabine's Gull are among the regularly seen species and some very rare seabirds have been recorded passing the headland.

The east coast of Antrim is just as rugged as the north coast, but here there is also a series of sheltered valleys, or glens, each of which has extensive forest cover and abundant birdlife. Early summer birdwatching in this region should reveal all the regular woodland species, plus offer the chance to find some rarer woodland breeders such as Redstart, Wood Warbler and Crossbill. Some of the upland areas still have small populations of moorland species such as Red Grouse.

Also on the east coast are Larne Lough and Belfast Lough which host thousands of wildfowl, waders and gulls in winter, and nesting terns in summer.

Lough Neagh is an outstanding site for waterbirds, and Antrim claims the majority of coastline of the five counties which border the Lough. Particularly good birdwatching sites include Shane's Castle, Portmore Lough and Oxford Island, all of which provide easy access to the shore and views of thousands of wintering duck, waders and gulls. These sites also have breeding reedbed and waterbird species in summer and migrants in spring and autumn, thus providing year-round interest.

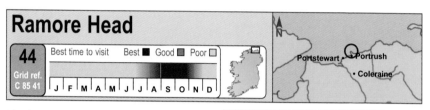

Ramore Head

44	Best time to visit	Best ■ Good ▨ Poor ☐
Grid ref. **C 85 41**	J F M A M J J A S O N D	

The best seawatching site on the north coast, particularly good in autumn.

Directions Map 26, right. The best seawatching spot is the carpark on NE tip of the headland, just to the N of Portrush town. It is possible to walk NNW along the clifftop for even better views, but you will be more exposed to the elements.

An onshore wind is important to drive the birds against the N coast and close to Ramore Head. The best conditions are a strong NW wind, with showers or overcast, though N or W winds can sometimes produce high numbers of seabirds. Birds approach from the NE, often inside the line of small islands known as The Skerries. The best seawatches often occur in the worst weather, so bring rain gear. See also SEAWATCHING, p. 356.

Species

Autumn Red-throated Diver, Great Northern Diver, Fulmar, 'Blue' Fulmar (R), Cory's Shearwater (R), Great Shearwater (R), Sooty Shearwater, Manx Shearwater, Balearic Shearwater (O), Storm Petrel, Leach's Petrel (mainly Sept & Oct), Gannet (often 100s), Cormorant, Shag, Grey Phalarope (O), Pomarine Skua (O), Arctic Skua, Long-tailed Skua (R), Great Skua, Little Gull (R), Sabine's Gull (O), Kittiwake (often 100s), Common Tern (O), Arctic Tern, Black Tern (R), Guillemot, Razorbill, Black Guillemot, Little Auk (R), Puffin (O).

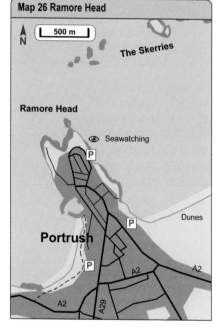

Map 26 Ramore Head

Other species Barnacle Goose (on The Skerries, winter), Wheatear (spring, summer), Peregrine (O all year), Snow Bunting (R), Lapland Bunting (R).

Rarities Velvet Scoter, Goosander, Black-throated Diver, Little Shearwater, Osprey, Black-browed Albatross, Fea's/Zino's Petrel and Wilson's Petrel.

45 Giant's Causeway & north coast Grid ref. C 94 44

Antrim's rugged north coast offers much spectacular scenery, and a variety of seabirds, raptors and other specialities such as Eider.

The unusual rock formations at the Giant's Causeway are internationally renowned and attract hundreds of thousands of visitors each year. The busy area (and expensive carpark) immediately around the Visitor Centre (C 44 94) is perhaps best avoided by the birdwatcher, but there are extensive coastal walks in this area which offer a good variety of seabirds, raptors and Eider.

The coastal path begins at Portballintrae, passes the Giant's Causeway and Benbane Head,

and continues as far as Ballintoy (D 04 44) before heading inland. It would take two days to walk this route, though there are several spots on the B146 W of Portballintrae from which shorter excursions are possible.

All along this route, seabirds such as Fulmar, Kittiwake and auks are apparent, and Manx Shearwater, Gannet, gulls and terns are usually visible offshore. Small parties of Eider gather in the more sheltered bays, and Buzzard and Peregrine are frequently encountered along the cliffs. Rock Dove, Wheatear and Raven can be expected, with Cuckoo possible in early summer. Unfortunately, Twite and Chough no longer occur.

46 Fair Head & Torr Head Grid ref. D 17 43 & D 23 40

The spectacular cliffs at Fair Head and the coast to the E, as far as Torr Head, are worth exploring for raptors and seabirds in summer.

See Map 27, below. Fair Head is 8km E of Ballycastle on the NE corner of Antrim. Torr Head is a further 6km E, and both are well signposted locally. From Ballycastle, take the A2 to Cushendun, turning left after 3.5km, signposted for Murlough and Fair Head. There are obvious carparks along this road, and various paths along the clifftop. The series of small lakes just S of Fair Head can hold Tufted Duck and nesting Black-headed Gulls.

The area is very good for raptors, with Buzzard and Peregrine encountered regularly, and Sparrowhawk and Kestrel also relatively common. Rock Dove, Cuckoo and Raven are also present, although Chough no longer occur (and are now rare anywhere in Northern Ireland).

Seabirds can be seen throughout the area, with many Fulmar and Kittiwake, and at Murlough Bay and Port-aleen Bay, Eider, gulls and auks can usually be seen. Torr Head offers opportunities for seawatching, with Gannet, auks and Manx Shearwater common and the chance of something more unusual.

Golden Eagle, Alpine Swift, Hoopoe, Lapland Bunting and Snow Bunting have all been recorded.

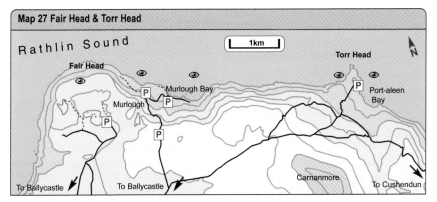

Map 27 Fair Head & Torr Head

Rathlin Island

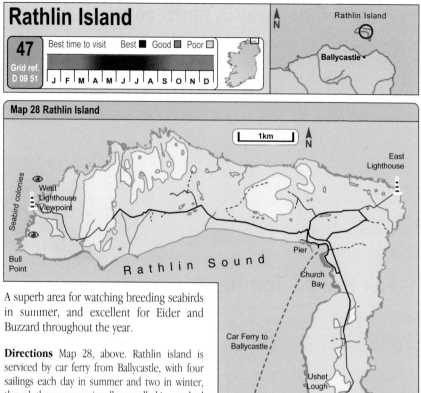

Ballycastle

47

Grid ref.
D 09 51

Best time to visit   Best ■ Good ▨ Poor ☐

J F M A M J J A S O N D

Map 28 Rathlin Island

1km

East
Lighthouse

West
Lighthouse
Viewpoint

Seabird colonies

Bull
Point

R a t h l i n   S o u n d

Pier

Church
Bay

Car Ferry to
Ballycastle

Ushet
Lough

South
Lighthouse

A superb area for watching breeding seabirds in summer, and excellent for Eider and Buzzard throughout the year.

Directions Map 28, above. Rathlin island is serviced by car ferry from Ballycastle, with four sailings each day in summer and two in winter, though they are occasionally cancelled in very bad weather. Journey time is 45 minutes. See www.calmac.co.uk or phone +44 (0)28 20769299 for further details. There are several B&Bs, campsite, a bar and bike hire available at Church Bay.

The largest seabird colonies in Northern Ireland can be viewed from the West Light Viewpoint, open from April to August (best in May and June). Guillemots, Razorbills, Kittiwakes and Fulmars are present in large numbers, and Puffins are easily seen. Access is only allowed under RSPB staff supervision who are not always available, so it is recommended to contact the warden before your visit, at +44 (0)28 20763948.

The Viewpoint is situated at the West Lighthouse, 6km W of the harbour. There is a minibus service operating between the harbour and the West Light Viewpoint for a small charge. Enquire locally.

Eider are numerous throughout the year, often in Church Bay and in small flocks offshore all around

the island, and Buzzard can be encountered almost anywhere, sometimes in small flocks.

Migrants are occasionally noted in spring and autumn, and some waterbirds visit the small lakes on Rathlin in the winter months. Golden Eagle has been seen in most years. Corncrake, Chough and Twite formerly bred on the island, but do so no longer.

Species
All year Teal, Tufted Duck, Eider, Buzzard, Peregrine, gulls, Curlew.

Spring & summer Fulmar (100s), Storm Petrel (R, from the ferry), Manx Shearwater (regular offshore & from the ferry), Gannet (offshore), Shag, Corncrake (R), Whimbrel (mainly May),

Guillemot, Razorbill, Black Guillemot, Puffin, Cuckoo (O), Wheatear, Sedge Warbler, Chiffchaff, Willow Warbler

Autumn Pomarine Skua (O), Arctic Skua (O), Great Skua (O), Redpoll, Siskin.

Winter Whooper Swan, Wigeon, Merlin.

Rarities White-fronted Goose, Pink-footed Goose, Leach's Petrel, King Eider, Red Kite, Marsh Harrier, Golden Eagle, Osprey, Gyr Falcon, Yellow Wagtail, Lesser Whitethroat, Twite (formerly brcd), Rustic Bunting.

48 Glens of Antrim Grid ref. D 20 30

Sheltered and wooded valleys in central and eastern Antrim hold many woodland birds, and are one of the best areas in Ireland for the rare woodland specialities such as Wood Warbler.

This is also one of the areas in Ireland where the persistent birdwatcher might find nesting Pied Flycatcher and Redstart, though they are both very rare and are not seen every year. Crossbill is often present at these sites, in coniferous woodland, most often in late summer into early autumn, though they can occur at any time.

The best time of year for the broadest range of species is mid May to early June, though the number of resident species makes a visit to these woodlands worthwhile at any time.

Some (by no means all) of the best areas are:

Breen Forest (D 12 33) is in the Glenshesk valley, 8km S of Ballycastle on the B15. Deciduous woodland covers the lower slope S of the road, with conifer plantations higher up. Wood Warbler has bred almost every summer at this site, and Pied Flycatcher were occasionally noted and occasionally bred in the past.

Crossbills

Craigagh Wood (D 20 32) is a mainly beech woodland 4km W of Cushendun in the Glendun valley. Wood Warbler breed here in summer with usually one, sometimes two pairs present. From Craigagh Wood, the road goes uphill and on to the Antrim plateau, where Hen Harrier might be found.

The **Glenarriff Valley** (D 22 21) and the broad-leaved woodland at Craignagat have Wood Warbler singing in most summers, along with many other woodland species. Further up the valley, coniferous forest dominates.

The **Glenarm Forest** (D 30 12) in the Glenarm valley has extensive broad-leaved forest which holds all the regular woodland species. Up to five pairs of Wood Warbler nest in summer, though one to three is more typical.

The **Antrim Plateau** (D 15 25) includes all the upland areas in the eastern half of Antrim. Unfortunately, some of the specialities of this area are now much rarer, and only a handful of Red Grouse and Golden Plover can be found nowadays. Hen Harrier is still present, and Buzzard, Raven and Wheatear can usually be found, while Crossbill is sometimes encountered in some of the huge coniferous plantations.

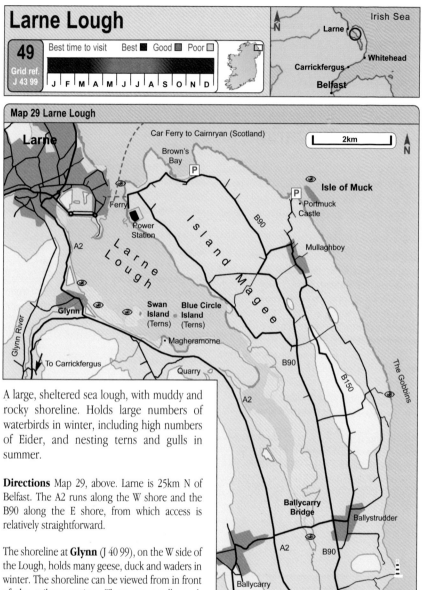

Larne Lough

49
Grid ref.
J 43 99

Best time to visit   Best ■ Good ■ Poor □

J F M A M J J A S O N D

Irish Sea
Larne
Whitehead
Carrickfergus
Belfast

Map 29 Larne Lough

Larne

Car Ferry to Cairnryan (Scotland)

Brown's Bay [P]

Isle of Muck [P]
Portmuck Castle

Ferry
Power Station

B90

A2

Island Magee

Mullaghboy

Larne Lough

Glynn

Swan Island (Terns)   Blue Circle Island (Terns)

Magheramorne

2km

Glynn River

To Carrickfergus

Quarry

B90

A2

B150

The Gobbins

Ballycarry Bridge

Ballystrudder

A2   B90

Ballycarry

To Carrickfergus

Whitehead

A large, sheltered sea lough, with muddy and rocky shoreline. Holds large numbers of waterbirds in winter, including high numbers of Eider, and nesting terns and gulls in summer.

Directions Map 29, above. Larne is 25km N of Belfast. The A2 runs along the W shore and the B90 along the E shore, from which access is relatively straightforward.

The shoreline at **Glynn** (J 40 99), on the W side of the Lough, holds many geese, duck and waders in winter. The shoreline can be viewed from in front of the railway station. There are small, reed-fringed lagoons immediatley N and S of the village. The Glynn River W of the town holds Kingfisher, Grey Wagtail and Dipper.

For 2km N and 3km E of Glynn along the A2, there is good broadleaved woodland habitat, with all the regular woodland species present.

Swan Island (J 42 99) and nearby **Blue Circle Island** (J 43 99, an artificial island) lie just

offshore, 1.5km E of of Glynn. Although it is not possible to visit the tern colonies here, they can be viewed somewhat distantly from Magheramorne, though a telescope is recommended. Red-breasted Merganser, Common Tern and Arctic Tern nest here in summer, and Roseate

68

Tern is usually present and sometimes breeds. Waders use the islands as a high tide roost outside the summer months.

The entrance to Larne Lough (D 41 02), either on the Larne or Island Magee side, and from the vicinity of the Power Station, are the best areas in summer to watch terns as they commute out of Larne Lough to feed. Brown's Bay just to the E of Larne, on the Island Magee side, is also a good area for feeding terns in summer, and a few Eider are usually present.

Ballycarry Bridge (J 46 94) at the S end of the Lough offers the best views over the mudflats and is a good spot for waders and some wildfowl. It is possible to park at the railway station.

Species
All year Greylag Goose (feral birds), Cormorant.

Autumn, winter & spring Whooper Swan (small numbers), Brent Goose, Shelduck (100s), Wigeon, Teal, Pochard (small numbers), Tufted Duck (O), Scaup (O), Eider, Long-tailed Duck (O), Common Scoter (R), Goldeneye, Red-breasted Merganser (often 150+), Red-throated Diver, Great Northern Diver, Little Grebe, Great Crested Grebe, Slavonian Grebe (1-2 most winters), Golden Plover (small numbers), Grey Plover, Lapwing, Little Stint (O autumn), Curlew Sandpiper (O autumn), Purple Sandpiper (rocky shores), Dunlin, Ruff (O autumn & winter), Jack Snipe (O), Snipe, Black-tailed Godwit (small numbers), Bar-tailed Godwit (small numbers), Whimbrel (spring, otherwise R winter), Curlew, Spotted Redshank (R autumn & winter), Green Sandpiper (autumn, R winter), Common Sandpiper (spring & autumn, R winter), gulls, auks (outer bay).

Summer Sandwich Tern, Roseate Tern (O), Common Tern, Arctic Tern, Sedge Warbler.

Rarities Green-winged Teal, Smew, Little Egret, Spoonbill, Marsh Harrier, Wilson's Phalarope, Iceland Gull, Glaucous Gull, Turtle Dove.

50 Isle of Muck Grid ref. D 46 02

A small offshore island with a good selection of breeding seabirds in summer.

See Map 29, previous page. The Isle of Muck is 1.25km N of Mullaghboy, on Island Magee, just to the E of Larne. The Isle of Muck is only 100m offshore, thus views of the seabirds are very good.

A small carpark overlooks the area. Follow signs N from Mullaghboy to Portmuck Caslte.
   Species include Fulmar, Cormorant, Shag, Kittiwake, Guillemot, Razorbill, Black Guillemot and Puffin. Gannet and Manx Shearwater are regular offshore. The best time to visit is from late April to late July.

Belfast Lough, north shore

51	Best time to visit	Best ■ Good ■ Poor ☐
Grid ref. J 35 81	J F M A M J J A S O N D	

Irish Sea

Whitehead
Carrickfergus
Belfast Lough
Belfast

A long, sheltered stretch of coastline with rocky shore and mudflats which attract large numbers of duck, Great Crested Grebe and gulls in winter.

Directions Map 30, next page. The best areas for birds occur along the N shore of Belfast Lough, stretching from the docks area in Belfast city centre, NE to Newtownabbey, Carrickfergus and Whitehead.

From Belfast city centre, leave the city N on the M2. This becomes the M5 for 2km, then the A2 just before Newtownabbey and the following sites are all accessed from the A2, NE to Whitehead.

For the **Whitehouse Lagoon** (J 35 80), take the M2 N out of Belfast, towards Carrickfergus. The M2 becomes the M5 and, shortly after, the Lagoon becomes visible on the left. Take the next left (where the motorway ends) at the roundabout and take another left after 300m, along the side of the church, to a small carpark. The Lagoon can be viewed from the carpark. Many gulls can be present here, including Iceland and Glaucous Gulls in winter. **Macedon Point** (J 35 81) can be reached from Whitehouse Lagoon by walking the path N from the Lagoon under the tunnel. Macedon Point is on the left, about 300m along the shoreline. This coastal path can also be walked S for 3km, as far as the former site of Belfast Dump. This whole area has many waders and wildfowl at low tide, and many thousands of gulls can congregate. Iceland Gull and Glaucous Gull are regular in small numbers most winters.

Green Island (J 38 85) offers further views over the Lough, with more waders, and Red-breasted Merganser and Eider usually present offshore.

The castle and marina on the seafront at **Carrickfergus** (J 41 87) is a good vantage point to scan the outer Lough. Long-tailed Duck, Eider and Red-breasted Merganser favour this area. These species can also be present further NE at **Whitehead** (J 47 91), and Purple Sandpiper is usually seen along the rocky coast. Some seabirds can also be seen here, and Manx Shearwater, Fulmar, Gannet and auks are regular.

Species

Autumn, winter & spring Brent Goose (small numbers), Wigeon, Teal, Tufted Duck, Scaup, Goldeneye, Red-breasted Merganser, Eider, Long-tailed Duck (generally N of Green Island), Common Scoter, Red-throated Diver, Great Northern Diver, Great Crested Grebe (100s, 2200+ have been recorded), Slavonian Grebe (R), Golden Plover, Lapwing, Dunlin, Purple Sandpiper (rocky coasts), Bar-tailed Godwit, Curlew, Guillemot, Razorbill, Black Guillemot.

Gulls are numerous, especially in winter, and Mediterranean Gull, Little Gull, Ring-billed Gull, Iceland Gull and Glaucous Gull are often present with the common species.

Rarities King Eider, Velvet Scoter, Goosander, Red-necked Grebe, Franklin's Gull, Caspian Gull, American Herring Gull, Yellow-legged Gull, Ross's Gull, Black Tern, Little Auk, Alpine Swift, Waxwing, Yellow Wagtail, Eastern Jackdaw.

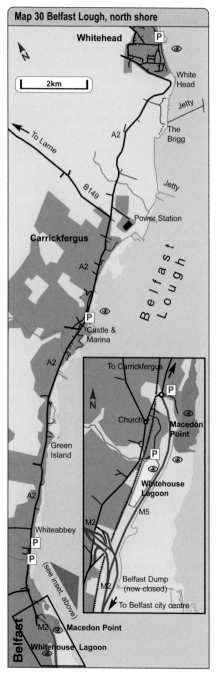

Map 30 Belfast Lough, north shore

Lough Neagh

Lough Neagh is the largest lake in Ireland, with 125km of shoreline. Five counties border Lough Neagh: Antrim, Armagh, Down, Tyrone and Derry.

The lake is relatively shallow, averaging only 9m, and as a result attracts an average of 95,000 water-birds in winter. It is internationally important for seven species and nationally important for a further 15. Main sites are shown here, Map 31.

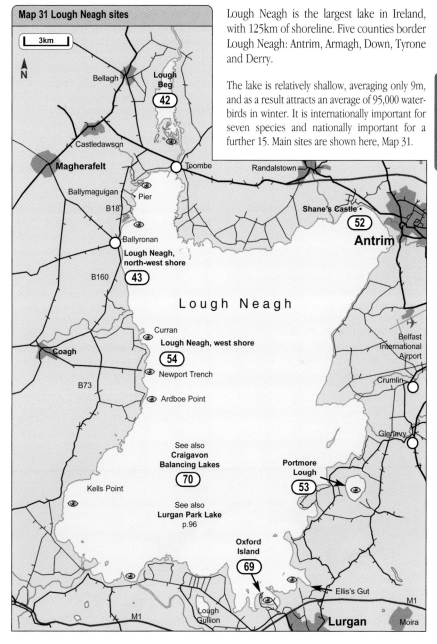

Map 31 Lough Neagh sites

3km

N

Bellagh
Lough Beg (42)
Castledawson
Magherafelt
Ballymaguigan
Pier
B18
Toombe
Randalstown
Shane's Castle
(52)
Antrim
Ballyronan
Lough Neagh, north-west shore (43)
B160
Lough Neagh
Curran
Lough Neagh, west shore (54)
Coagh
Newport Trench
B73
Ardboe Point
Belfast International Airport
Crumlin
Glenavy
See also Craigavon Balancing Lakes (70)
Kells Point
See also Lurgan Park Lake p.96
Portmore Lough (53)
Oxford Island (69)
Lough Gullion
M1
Ellis's Gut
M1
Lurgan
Moira

71

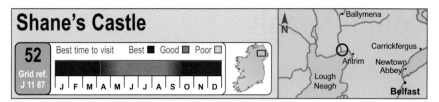

Shane's Castle

52

Grid ref.
J 11 87

Best time to visit   Best ■ Good ■ Poor □

| J | F | M | A | M | J | J | A | S | O | N | D |

Ballymena

Carrickfergus

Antrim   Newtown Abbey

Lough Neagh

Belfast

Good views of large numbers of wildfowl on Lough Neagh, and an excellent area for woodland species in summer.

Directions Map 32, below. Located just W of the outskirts of Antrim town. From Antrim town centre, take the Randalstown Road for 4km, taking a left into the Castle. There is an admission charge for entry. From the M22, take Exit 2 and follow the signs to Antrim. Shane's Castle is on the right after 1.5km. Locally, the Park is well signposted, with a train emblem (for the nearby Miniature Railway).

Some large concentrations of diving duck and grebes occur immediately offshore from Shane's Castle, and S as far as Rea's Wood. Good views can be had from the battlements of the castle itself, from the path which parallels the Miniature Railway, and from the coastal path at Rea's Wood. A telescope is recommended.

Randalstown Forest (J 09 87) to the W of Shane's Castle and **Rea's Woods** (J 14 85), just SW of Antrim town centre, are both excellent woodland areas which hold all the regular woodland species. They are best in May and early June. There are extensive nature trails and marked paths through both.

In winter, large numbers of gulls use this section of Lough Neagh as a roost. Many hundreds of the regular gulls congregate, and some rare species might be expected from time to time.

Species

All year Little Grebe, Great Crested Grebe, Tufted Duck, Water Rail. **Milburn Stream** Kingfisher, Grey Wagtail, Dipper.

Autumn, winter & spring Whooper Swan (O), Wigeon, Teal, Gadwall (O), Shoveler (O), Pochard, Scaup, Goldeneye, Red-breasted Merganser, Lapwing, Curlew, gulls, Siskin, Redpoll.

Summer Common Tern, Sedge Warbler, woodland species, including Blackcap, Willow Warbler, Chiffchaff, Spotted Flycatcher.

Rarities Bewick's Swan, American Wigeon, Red-crested Pochard, Goosander, Smew, Ruddy Duck, Osprey, Little Gull, Ring-billed Gull.

Map 32 Shane's Castle

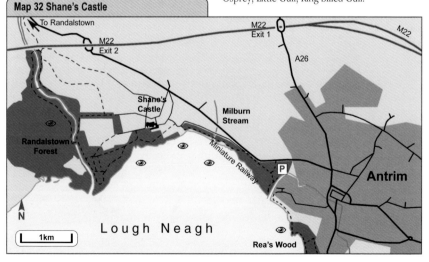

Portmore Lough

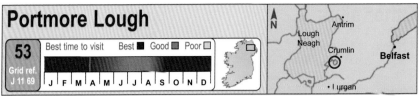

53
Grid ref.
J 11 69

Best time to visit   Best ■ Good ▦ Poor □

J F M A M J J A S O N D

A large, reed-fringed, freshwater lake which attracts large numbers of waterbirds in winter and a good variety of breeding birds.

Portmore Lough is an RSPB Reserve and has a hide, information board and public toilets.

Opening times Open all year, at all times, except the Christmas holiday period. Good boots are needed in winter, when conditions underfoot can be wet. Contact the warden to arrange group visits or for information. Tel: 028 9265 2406.

Directions Map 33, right. Located 18km S of Antrim and 10km N of Lurgan. Leave the M1 at J9, taking the B105 for 5km to Aghalee. From there, follow the Ballycairn Road to Gawley's Gate and turn right onto the B156. George's Island Road is about 1.6km on the right and leads to the Reserve.

Map 33 Portmore Lough

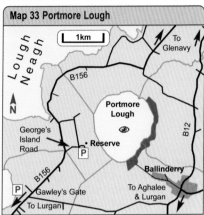

Species
All year Ruddy Duck, Cormorant, Lapwing, Snipe.

Autumn, winter & spring Whooper Swan, Greylag Goose (feral birds), Wigeon, Gadwall, Teal, Pintail (O), Shoveler (O), Pochard, Tufted Duck, Scaup, Goldeneye, Little Grebe, Great Crested Grebe, Hen Harrier, Buzzard (O), Merlin (O), Peregrine, Golden Plover, Little Stint (R autumn), Dunlin, Ruff (O autumn), Curlew, Green Sandpiper (O autumn), gulls.

Summer Some waders breed on the wet meadows fringing the lake, such as Snipe, Redshank and Lapwing. Also Cuckoo (O), Sedge Warbler, Reed Warbler (O), Willow Warbler.

Rarities Pink-footed Goose, White-fronted Goose, Marsh Harrier, Goshawk.

Black-headed Gull

Other sites

Ballyboley Forest (J 31 98) is a reasonably accessible coniferous forest, with a representative selection of birds for the area. It is best reached from Larne, leaving the town on the A8 to Belfast, and taking a right onto the A36 to Kells after 4km. The road climbs steadily and after 6km, shortly after entering the forest, there is a carpark on the left. Another carpark can be reached by continuing on the main road for a further 3km, taking a left shortly after emerging from the trees onto moorland. Public toilets and a small reservoir can be found at this spot. There are trails through the forest.

Typical species to be found in the forest all year include Treecreeper, Redpoll and Siskin and Willow Warbler in summer. The moorland surrounding the forest has breeding Curlew, Raven, occasional sightings of Red Grouse and Hen Harrier. Buzzard has also been seen and Crossbill sometimes occur.

Muckamore (J 16 85) lies on the Six Mile Water River on the southern outskirts of Antrim town. Downriver from the bridge, the riverside path goes through woodland and scrub where many typical woodland species can be seen, including Spotted Flycatcher, Willow Warbler, Chiffchaff and Blackcap in summer. The river is shallow and fast-flowing, and Dipper and Grey Wagtail can usually be seen.

Antrim Road Waterworks (J 32 76), formerly known as Belfast Waterworks, is a large reservoir and a small pool in an inner city site which holds a good variety of species. Dipper, Grey Wagtail and Kingfisher are present, as is a resident flock of Tufted Duck and Mute Swan. The main lake is also used as a roosting and washing area by many gulls. Smew, Iceland Gull, Glaucous Gull and Ring-billed Gull have been recorded. Unfortunately, the area suffers from sectarian tensions, vandalism and even car theft and is now rarely visited by birdwatchers. The reservoir is accessed by exiting the Westlink motorway for Glengormley and continuing up the Antrim Road for 1.3km. Turning left at the junction with Cavehill Road, there are two entrances to the Waterworks on the left.

Dargan Bay (J 35 78) is 4km N of Belfast city centre, and is a good site in winter for large numbers of gulls, with a chance for some of the scarcer species such as Iceland Gull and Glaucous Gull. Good numbers of waders are present at low tide, including Black-tailed Godwit and Dunlin. Large numbers of Great Crested Grebe and a large flock of Scaup can also be seen offshore in winter. From the city centre, leave the M2 at the Fortwilliam Roundabout (the first exit, heading N). Take a right, along the southern edge of Belfast Dump (now closed), and continue E for 600m until the bay becomes visible on your left. Continue along this road to explore the outer bay.

County Tyrone

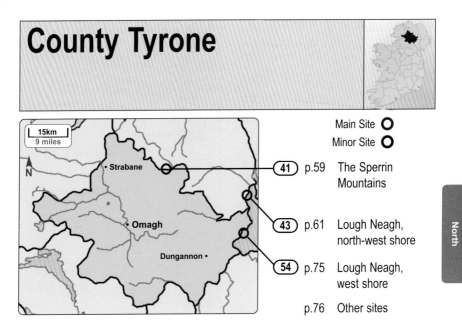

Main Site ◯
Minor Site ◯

North

Although Tyrone is one of the largest counties, the main birdwatching interest is on the 15km stretch of shore along its far eastern edge. This has some good vantage points over Lough Neagh and is excellent for wildfowl in the winter months.

Elsewhere in the county, the sparsely populated rural areas have good general birdwatching, but few outstanding sites. The north of the county has some good upland species in the Sperrin Mountains (Site 41).

Lough Neagh, west shore

54	Best time to visit	Best ■ Good ■ Poor □

Grid ref.
H 96 76

J F M A M J J A S O N D

A section of the Lough Neagh shoreline which holds many wildfowl and some waders in winter.

Directions Map 34, next page. See also Site 43, Lough Neagh, north-west shore, which covers the shoreline immediately N of this area, and an overview of Lough Neagh sites on p.71

Some of the best areas to view this section of the Lough are listed below. Throughout winter, each will hold a small selection of waterbirds, and birds often move between sites.

Kinturk Flat (H 96 79) is 6km E of Coagh. Leave Coagh E on the B160 to Ballyronan and turn right after 3km, and left after 400m. Continue for 2.5km on this road to the shoreline.

Kiltagh Point (H 95 73) can be reached by leaving Coagh SE on the B73 and turning right after 4.5km. Continue on this road (the B161) for 2.2km and turn left. After a further 1.5km there is a junction. At this point, straight on will bring you to Kiltagh Point, a left will take you to nearby **Ardboe Point** (H 96 75).

Newport Trench (H 96 77) is an excellent vantage point. To reach it, leave Coagh on the B73, ignoring all turnoffs. The Lough is visible directly ahead after 6km.

Kells Point (H 93 70) is S of Kiltagh Point (previous page) on the B161 to Coalisland. From Coalisland, go E on the B161 to Brockagh. 1 km after Brockagh, the Lough is visible on the right and by taking the next right, it is possible to view the shoreline at various points.

At all these sites, a telescope is recommended.

Species
All year Tufted Duck, Great Crested Grebe, Cormorant.

Autumn, winter & spring Whooper Swan (O), Wigeon, Gadwall (O), Teal, Shoveler (O), Goldeneye, Pochard, Scaup (O), Hen Harrier (R), Merlin (O), Peregrine (O), Golden Plover, Lapwing, Snipe, Curlew, Common Sandpiper (mainly spring), gulls.

Rarities Bewick's Swan, American Wigeon, Garganey, Lesser Scaup, Smew, Turtle Dove, Eastern Jackdaw.

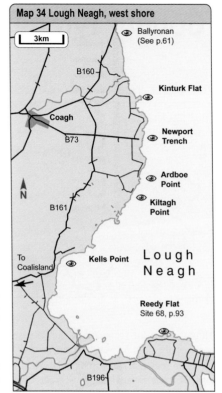

Map 34 Lough Neagh, west shore

3km

B160

Ballyronan (See p.61)

Kinturk Flat

Coagh

B73

Newport Trench

N

B161

Ardboe Point

Kiltagh Point

To Coalisland

Kells Point

Lough Neagh

Reedy Flat Site 68, p.93

B196

Other sites

Annaghroe (H 73 44) is a wintering area for White-fronted Geese, though they have been steadily decling at this and other sites in Northern Ireland. Whooper Swan is usually present in small numbers, and Lapwing, Golden Plover, Snipe and Curlew can be numerous.

From Armagh, take the A28 W to Caledon and after passing Caledon, take a left onto the B45, signposted for Monaghan. This road runs along the N side of the Caledon Estate, and between here and the bridge over the Blackwater River, scan the flooded meadows to the W.

County Down

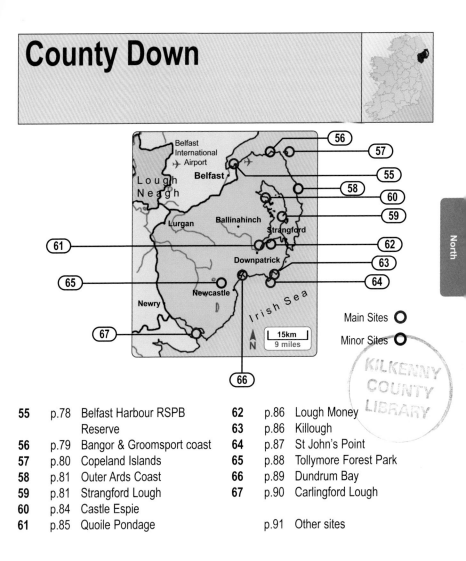

County Down has three major wetland sites of outstanding interest to the birdwatcher. Along the northern edge of the county, Belfast Lough has a rich profusion of coastal sites which attract thousands of waterbirds in winter. The RSPB Reserve at the Belfast Harbour Estate is one of the best such areas and boasts a long list of unusual species.

On the southern edge of the county is Carlingford Lough, another outstanding wetland for wildfowl and waders in winter, and large numbers of nesting terns in summer.

Strangford Lough is the third such wetland, and much the largest in Northern Ireland. 240km of coastline encompass $150km^2$ of superb estuarine habitat. Tens of thousands of wildfowl and waders visit each winter, including up to 80% of the world's population of Pale-bellied Brent Geese each autumn. The Castle Espie Reserve and the Quoile Pondage are two reserves within the Strangford Lough area which are also excellent for attracting a wide variety of lake, marsh and woodland birds, as well as wildfowl and waders.

But there is even more to County Down for the birdwatcher. Other outstanding areas include the estuaries at Killough and Dundrum, and the varied coastline of the Ards Peninsula. Throughout the county are scattered small and medium-sized freshwater lakes which also attract a mix of wintering duck species, and several forest parks which hold a good variety of breeding woodland species, including the only site for Mandarin Duck in Ireland at Tollymore Forest Park.

Finally, two migration hotspots feature prominently. The Copeland Islands off the Bangor coast, which also has a good variety of breeding seabirds, and St John's Point, which is much the best seawatching site on the east coast of Ireland. Betweeen them, these sites have attracted many scarce and rare species in spring and autumn migration, and added many new species to the Northern Ireland list.

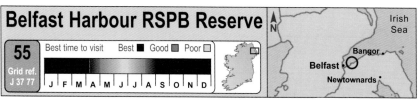

Belfast Harbour RSPB Reserve

55
Grid ref.
J 37 77

Best time to visit   Best ■ Good ■ Poor □

J F M A M J J A S O N D

N

Irish Sea

Bangor
Belfast
Newtownards

A shallow, freshwater wetland attracting wildfowl and shorebirds throughout the year.

During summer, two specially constructed islands hold up to 200 breeding pairs of Common Terns (and some Arctic Terns). In the winter months, large numbers of gulls congregate on the lagoon. Although the lagoon is not tidal, it is used as a high tide roost by shorebirds and wildfowl feeding on nearby inter-tidal mudflats.

Opening times The Reserve's Observation Room (a small Visitor Centre) is open Tues to Sun, 9am to 5pm. Closed Sunday mornings, Mondays, Christmas Day and New Year's Day. Admission is free. Two roadside viewpoints (hides) are always open, even when the Observation Room is closed. Visit www.rspb.org.uk for further information.

Directions Map 35, right. The reserve is situated within the Belfast Harbour Estate on the County Down shore of Belfast Lough, 6km NE of Belfast city centre.

From Belfast city centre, travel onto the M3, heading for Holywood and Bangor. Once on the M3, you will see the Odyssey Arena on the left. Take the next exit for the Arena and turn right at the next set of traffic lights. Follow this road and take a left onto Dee Street at the first set of traffic lights. At the roundabout, take the exit past the

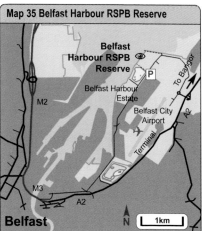

Map 35 Belfast Harbour RSPB Reserve

Belfast Harbour RSPB Reserve
P
To Bangor
Belfast Harbour Estate
M2
Belfast City Airport
A2
Terminal
M3
A2
Belfast
N
1km

checkpoint and follow this road for 3km to the Reserve. Alternatively, continue toward Belfast City Airport on the A2 and just after passing the airport on your left, take the next exit left and turn left again. This road continues right on a round-about (only one exit) and past a shopping centre. Continue past the Tillysburn checkpoint (closed at weekends) and continue 1.5km to the Reserve. A small beach close to this checkpoint is excellent for gulls and waders at high tide.

Species
All year Cormorant, Water Rail, Lapwing, Black-tailed Godwit.

Autumn, winter & spring Wigeon, Gadwall (O), Teal, Pintail (O), Shoveler (O), Pochard (O), Tufted Duck, Scaup (O), Goldeneye, Little Egret (R), Buzzard, Golden Plover, Grey Plover, Little Stint (R autumn), Curlew Sandpiper (O autumn), Dunlin, Ruff (O autumn), Jack Snipe (R), Snipe, Black-tailed Godwit, Bar-tailed Godwit, Whimbrel (spring, R winter), Curlew, Spotted Redshank (R), Green Sandpiper (O autumn), Wood Sandpiper (R autumn), Common Sandpiper (spring & autumn, R winter), Mediterranean Gull (O), Little Gull (O), Ring-billed Gull (O), Yellow-legged Gull (R), Iceland Gull (O), Glaucous Gull (O).

Summer 200 pairs of Common Tern and small numbers of Arctic Tern nest on the lagoon.

Rarities American Wigeon, Green-winged Teal, Baikal Teal, Garganey, Blue-winged Teal, Red-crested Pochard, Smew, Goosander, Velvet Scoter, Spoonbill, Marsh Harrier, Montagu's Harrier, Spotted Crake, Black-winged Stilt, Avocet, Little Ringed Plover, Kentish Plover, Temminck's Stint, Semipalmated Sandpiper, White-rumped Sandpiper, Pectoral Sandpiper, Buff-breasted Sandpiper, Lesser Yellowlegs, Long-billed Dowitcher, Wilson's Phalarope, Arctic Skua, Great Skua, Sabine's Gull, Bonaparte's Gull, Laughing Gull, Caspian Gull, Yellow-legged Gull, White-winged Black Tern, Forster's Tern, Yellow Wagtail, Tree Pipit, Redstart, Pied Flycatcher, Garden Warbler, Waxwing, Eastern Jackdaw, Carrion Crow, Brambling, Twite.

56 Bangor & Groomsport coast Grid ref. J 53 45

A varied stretch of coast with many coastal and wetland birds throughout the year, nesting terns in summer and good seawatching in autumn.

See Map 36, below. The main harbour in the centre of Bangor is well known for the Black Guillemots which nest in the harbour walls. They can be seen in the general vicinity throughout the year.

NE of Bangor, **Ballyholme Bay** holds divers and some duck in winter, and foraging terns in summer. Cockle Island is a tiny island, just offshore from the small town of Groomsport. Arctic Tern nest, as do Red-breasted Merganser, Eider and Ringed Plover. In fact, Eider is reasonably common all along this stretch of coast throughout the year. Sandwich and Common

Tern have nested on Cockle Island in the past, and are regularly seen in the vicinity of the colony.

All along this stretch of coast, seabirds can be seen offshore, including many Manx Shearwater throughout the summer and autumn. Skuas occur in autumn, especially during gales, and occasional rarer seabirds may pass, including Storm Petrel, Leach's Petrel, Sooty Shearwater, Little Gull and Sabine's Gull. **Ballymacormick Point** and **Brigg's Rock** are the two best vantage points.

Brigg's Rocks is also attractive to large numbers of gulls, and Mediterranean Gull is regular, with Iceland and Glaucous Gull occasionally seen each winter, and Ross's Gull, Velvet Scoter, King Eider and Yellow Wagtail have all been recorded here.

Other species recorded in the area include good numbers of Dunlin, Lapwing and Golden

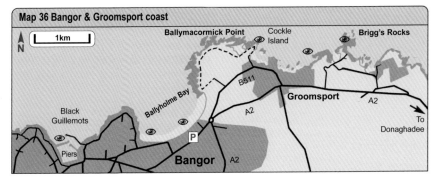

Map 36 Bangor & Groomsport coast

Plover in winter, with small numbers of Purple Sandpiper along rocky coasts. Other waders occur on passage, including some scarce species such as Ruff and Green Sandpiper. In winter, the stubble fields can hold large numbers of finches and regular Tree Sparrow, with Brambling and Lapland Bunting occasionally present.

Rare species recorded here include Black-bellied Brent Goose, Black-throated Diver, Red-necked Grebe, White Stork, Little Tern, Forster's tern, Black Tern, White-winged Black Tern, Scandinavian Rock Pipit, Black Redstart, Waxwing, Eastern Jackdaw, Carrion Crow and Snow Bunting. A Sooty Tern attracted much attention during its stay at the Cockle Island tern colony in 2006.

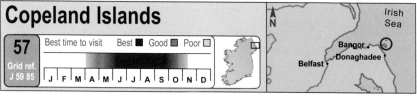

Copeland Islands

57

Grid ref. J 59 85

Best time to visit   Best ■ Good ▨ Poor □

J F M A M J J A S O N D

Three uninhabited islands, one with a Bird Observatory, good for seabirds in summer and migrants in spring and autumn.

Directions Map 37, right. The three islands are all reached by boat from the pier at Donaghadee, 9km E of Bangor. The RSPB arrange trips to John's Island (Lighthouse Island on Ordnance Survey maps), where they manage the Bird Observatory – contact 028 9049 1547. The two other islands are serviced by Nelson's Boats in Donaghadee – contact 028 9188 3403. Boats generally run from May to September.

Copeland Bird Observatory, located in the old lighthouse building on John's Island, has a long and distinguished history, and has been manned on most weekends and some weeks during April to October (sporadically in winter). Numbers of migrants are generally higher in spring than in autumn. Visits to the island are best arranged through the Bookings Secretary, Neville McKee, 67 Temple Rise, Templepatrick, Antrim BT39 OAG. Phone 08494 33068.

Additional information can be obtained from the Secretary, Peter Munro, Talisker Lodge, 54b Templepatrick Road, Ballyclare, County Antrim BT39 9TX. Phone 028 9332 3421 or e-mail talisker.lodge@btopenworld.com.

The Bird Observatory also conducts ringing projects on the breeding Manx Shearwaters. For further information see www.cbo.org.uk.

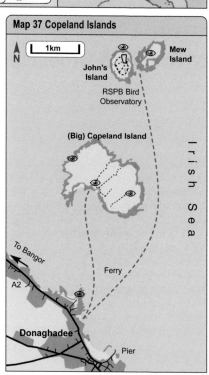

Map 37 Copeland Islands

Species
All year Eider, Black Guillemot, Stock Dove (breeds on Copeland Island – the common dove of the islands).

Spring & autumn Whooper Swan (O), Red-breasted Merganser, Red-throated Diver (O), Great Northern Diver (O), Sooty Shearwater (R), Manx Shearwater (often from ferry), Storm Petrel (O from ferry), Water Rail, gulls, skuas (O), Black

Guillemot, Tree Pipit (R), Wheatear, Black Redstart, Redstart (R), Whinchat, Willow Warbler, Chiffchaff, Grasshopper Warbler, Blackcap (O), Garden Warbler (R), Whitethroat (O), Pied Flycatcher (R), Spotted Flycatcher (O).

Rarities Bewick's Swan, Velvet Scoter, Balearic Shearwater, Marsh Harrier, Rough-legged Buzzard, Sabine's Gull, Little Auk, Red-throated Pipit, Yellow Wagtail, Ring Ouzel, White's Thrush, Reed Warbler, Carrion Crow.

The two first Irish records of Scarlet Tanager and Fox Sparrow have ocurred on Copeland.

Black Guillemot

58 Outer Ards coast Grid ref. J 66 60

A long and varied stretch of coast with many coastal species, large numbers of gulls and some wildfowl in winter.

The E coast of the Ards Peninsula runs almost 45km from Donaghadee to the S tip near Portaferry and comprises of rocky shore, sandy bays and rocky offshore islets. The main birdwatching interest is in the wintering birds. In particular, Eider are quite numerous all along this coast, as are Brent Geese, with smaller numbers of divers, Great Crested Grebe, Goldeneye and Red-breasted Merganser offshore. Rarer waterfowl include Long-tailed Duck and Common Scoter.

Waders include Purple Sandpiper, Golden Plover, Lapwing, Dunlin, Curlew and scarcer species such as Black-tailed and Bar-tailed Godwit, Knot and Snipe. Gulls, particularly Black-headed Gull, are numerous throughout winter, with occasional Mediterranean Gull and Little Gull.

Access to much of the coast is straightforward. The A2 runs S from Donaghadee, hugging the coastline as far as Ballyhalbert, from where it is still possible to follow the coast on minor roads. Particularly productive areas include Ballywalter, Portavogie harbour and Cloghy Bay 3km S of Portavogie, but many bays and beaches are worth a look.

In summer, some seabirds can be seen offshore, including Manx Shearwater, Guillemot, Razorbill and Black Guillemot. Common, Arctic and Sandwich Terns can often be seen foraging offshore.

Strangford Lough

59	Best time to visit	Best ■ Good ■ Poor ☐

Grid ref. J 55 59

J	F	M	A	M	J	J	A	S	O	N	D

A vast inlet of mudflats, sand, saltmarsh, rocky islands and shoreline which attracts some 25,000 wildfowl and 50,000 waders each winter. Three species of tern nest in the summer.

Two other sites, while part of the Strangford Lough area, are of different character, and are treated elsewhere. See Site 60, Castle Espie and Site 61, Quoile Pondage.

Strangford Lough is perhaps best known for large numbers of Brent Goose, which can number 10,000+ (80% of the world population) in early autumn, then dropping throughout mid to late winter as birds disperse S. Numbers rise again in March and April, before the birds depart for the Arctic. It is internatioanally important for a further four species: Shelduck, Knot, Bar-tailed Godwit and Redshank, and nationally important numbers of a further 23 waterbird species.

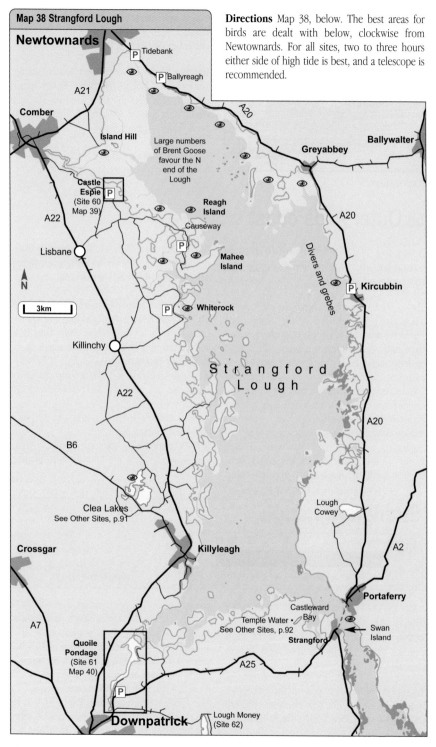

Map 38 Strangford Lough

Newtowntards

Directions Map 38, below. The best areas for birds are dealt with below, clockwise from Newtownards. For all sites, two to three hours either side of high tide is best, and a telescope is recommended.

P Tidebank

P Ballyreagh

A21

Comber

A20

Island Hill

Large numbers of Brent Goose favour the N end of the Lough

Ballywalter

Greyabbey

Castle Espie (Site 60 Map 39) P

A22

A20

Reagh Island

Causeway

Lisbane

P

Mahee Island

N

3km

Killinchy

P **Whiterock**

Divers and grebes

P **Kircubbin**

A22

S t r a n g f o r d L o u g h

A20

B6

Clea Lakes
See Other Sites, p.91

Lough Cowey

A2

Crossgar

Killyleagh

Portaferry

Castleward Bay

Temple Water •
See Other Sites, p.92

Swan Island

Strangford

A7

Quoile Pondage (Site 61 Map 40)

P

A25

Downpatrick

Lough Money (Site 62)

Newtownards to Greyabbey The A20 follows the coast between these two towns. Leaving Newtownards, the estuary comes into view almost immediately at Tidebank, where there is a carpark. This area holds large numbers of Brent Goose and other wildfowl and waders in winter. Just to the S, at Ballyreagh, another layby offers extensive views, and this area is good for large numbers of Golden Plover and Knot in winter. Brent Goose is also found here and Whooper Swan is sometimes present. There are other opportunities to scan the shoreline from this point toward Greyabbey, 12km SE of Newtownards. Here, more Brent Geese and waders can be found.

Kircubbin has deeper water offshore than many other sites, and as a result attracts species such as Slavonian Grebe and divers in winter. This is also the most likely spot for Red-necked Grebe and Black-throated Diver, though both are very rare.

Portaferry & Strangford area Swan Island, close to the ferry terminal at Strangford, provides good views of nesting gulls and terns. In winter, Castleward Bay, just to the W of Strangford, holds some wildfowl and waders. From Portaferry, occasional seabirds and duck can be seen. See also Temple Water, in Other Sites, p.92.

Quoile Pondage See Site 61.

Killyleagh, and minor roads to the N as far as Whiterock, lead to a number of small sheltered bays which hold small numbers of wildfowl and waders in winter.

Whiterock Bay is 3km NE of Killinchy. Follow the signposts from the centre of Killinchy. The coast road around and N of the Bay has many wildfowl and waders throughout winter, and offshore there are Goldeneye and occasional Slavonian Grebe.

Mahee Island & Reagh Island are reached by taking the A21 Comber to Killyleagh road and taking a left after 5km, at Lisbane village. Follow signposts until after 5km you cross a causeway onto Reagh Island. There is a hide and carpark here. Mahee Island is 3km further, on the same road. Throughout this area are extensive and varied views over bays and mudflats. This section

of Strangford Lough holds Brent Goose, Pintail, Shoveler and Black-tailed Godwit.

Castle Espie See Site 60.

Island Hill is reached by taking the A21 Comber to Newtonards road. After 1.5km, take the first right onto the Ringcreevy Road. From here it is 2km to the shoreline, with extensive views over the mudflats. Brent Geese and other wildfowl, as well as many waders, occur throughout this area in winter.

Species
All year Shelduck (2000+ in winter), Cormorant, Peregrine, Water Rail (O), Stock Dove (scarce), Tree Sparrow (O).

Seabirds occasionally venture into the S half of the Lough, with Gannet, Fulmar, Shag, Guillemot, Razorbill and Kittiwake occasionally seen. Even Manx Shearwater, Storm Petrel and Pomarine Skua occur on occasion.

Autumn, winter & spring Whooper Swan (small numbers), Pink-footed Goose (O), White-fronted Goose (O), Greylag Goose (feral birds), Canada Goose (feral birds), Barnacle Goose (mainly feral birds), Brent Goose 1000s (late Aug onwards), Dark-bellied Brent Goose (R), Black Brant (R), Wigeon (1000s), Gadwall, Teal (1000s), Pintail, Shoveler, Scaup, Eider, Goldeneye, Red-breasted Merganser, Black-throated Diver (O), Red-throated Diver, Great Northern Diver, Great Crested Grebe, Slavonian Grebe, Little Egret (O), Hen Harrier (R), Buzzard, Merlin (O), Golden Plover (1000s), Grey Plover, Lapwing (1000s), Dunlin (1000s), Snipe, Black-tailed Godwit, Bar-tailed Godwit, Whimbrel (mainly spring), Curlew, Spotted Redshank (O autumn), Green Sandpiper (O autumn), Common Sandpiper (autumn, R winter), gulls, Short-eared Owl (O).

Summer Some of the waders listed above can over-summer in the Lough. Red-breasted Merganser and a few Eider nest. Common Sandpiper, Black-headed Gull (5000 pairs), Sandwich Tern, Roseate Tern (R), Common Tern, Arctic Tern, Black Guillemot, Cuckoo (O).

Rarities Grey-bellied Brent Goose, Green-winged Teal, American Wigeon, Red-necked Grebe, Great White Egret, Carrion Crow, Snow Bunting.

Castle Espie

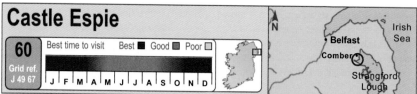

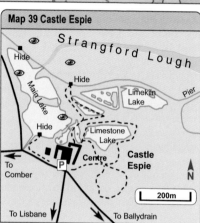

Map 39 Castle Espie

A Wildfowl and Wetlands Trust Reserve, with an impressive wildfowl collection, but also with a series of small lagoons which attracts some migrant waders. There are excellent views over nearby Strangford Lough for large numbers of wildfowl and waders in winter.

The Reserve has a carpark, picnic site, coffee shop, gift and bookshop, and exhibition area, and hosts various events and activities throughout the year.

Opening times Nov to Feb, 11am to 4pm weekdays. 11am to 4.30pm on weekends. March to June, 10.30am to 5.30pm weekdays, 11am to 5.30pm on weekends. July to Aug, 10.30am to 5.30pm weekdays. 11am to 5.30pm weekends. Sept to Oct, 10.30am to 5pm weekdays, 11am to 5.30pm weekends. Parking is free, though there is an admission charge into the Reserve.

Just beyond the main Centre lie various ponds and pens which hold large numbers of captive wildfowl. Beyond, the Main Lake holds many more (wild) birds, and there are hides overlooking the Main Lake and the extensive mudflats of Strangford Lough, though time your visit here to two hours either side of high tide; otherwise birds will be very distant. A woodland walk holds many of the regular woodland species.

Guided walks for groups are possible by prior arrangement. For this, and any other information, telephone 028 9187 4146, or visit www.wwt.org.uk/visit/castleespie/.

Directions Map 39, above. See also Map 38, p.82. Located 18km SE of Belfast and 5km S of Comber, on the NW shore of Strangford Lough. From Comber, take the A22 S toward Killyleagh and Downpatrick. After 500m, take the left signposted for Mahee Island. The reserve is 4km further, on the left, and is well signposted locally.

Species

Autumn, winter & spring Brent Goose, Greylag Goose (feral birds), Canada Goose (feral birds), Wigeon, Gadwall (O), Teal, Pintail (O), Pochard, Tufted Duck, Scaup (O), Goldeneye, Red-breasted Merganser, Little Egret (O), Buzzard (O), Merlin (O), Peregrine, Water Rail, Golden Plover, Grey Plover, Lapwing, Little Stint (R autumn), Curlew Sandpiper (R autumn), Dunlin, Ruff (O autumn), Snipe, Bar-tailed Godwit, Black-tailed Godwit, Whimbrel (mainly spring, R winter), Curlew, Spotted Redshank (R), Green Sandpiper (R autumn), Common Sandpiper (O autumn & spring, R winter), gulls, Kingfisher (O), Wheatear (O spring), Redpoll (O), Siskin (O).

Summer Sedge Warbler, Willow Warbler, Chiffchaff, Blackcap, Spotted Flycatcher.

Rarities Pink-footed Goose, Dark-bellied Brent Goose, Garganey.

Snipe

61
Grid ref.
J 50 48

Best time to visit   Best ■ Good ▨ Poor □

J F M A M J J A S O N D

Map 40 Quoile Pondage

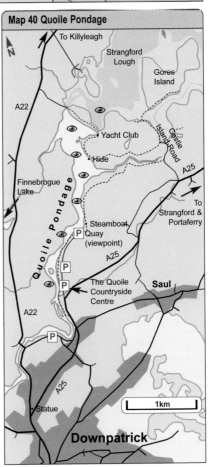

To Killyleagh
Strangford Lough
Gores Island
A22
Yacht Club
Hide
Finnebrogue Lake
Steamboat Quay (viewpoint)
The Quoile Countryside Centre
Saul
A25
To Strangford & Portaferry
A22
Statue
1km
Downpatrick

Quoile Pondage National Nature Reserve is an outstanding site for wildfowl and waders ,particularly in winter but also throughout the year. Good hide, trails and access.

Directions Map 40, right. 1km N of the Downpatrick suburbs. Leave Downpatrick N on the A25, turning right off the roundabout by the large garage. 100m further, take a right, by the statue at the fork in the road. The Quoile Countryside Centre is 2km on the left, on Quay Road, and two carparks are located further along this road, with views and walks along the main river.

To get to the **Hide**, continue along the A25 for another 2km, turning left onto Castle Island Road. The hide is on your left after 1.5km, and more views over the lake can be had by continuing as far as the yacht club.

Further views over the pondage can be had from the A22 to Killyleagh, 1km N of the roundabout and again, 4km N of the roundabout. **Finnebrogue Lake** is also visible to the left on this route, with smaller numbers of much the same species.

Admission to the Reserve is free. The Hide is open from 10am to 4pm daily, though the trail along the river is open at all times. Occasional birdwatching events are held. Tel: 028 4461 5520 for details. The Visitor Centre is open daily from 1st April to 31st August, 11am to 5pm, and from 1st September to 31st March on Saturday and Sunday only, 1pm to 5pm. Website: www.fjiord-lands.org.

Birds, especially wildfowl, are at their most numerous throughout the winter months. Waders are also present throughout winter, but the area is also noted for spring and autumn passage of both wildfowl and waders. At these times, many unusual species have been recorded. In summer, many wildfowl and some waders stay to breed.

Species
All year Gadwall, Tufted Duck, Little Grebe, Great Crested Grebe, Cormorant, Little Egret (O), Hen Harrier (R), Buzzard (O), Water Rail, Woodcock, Curlew, Common Sandpiper (passage, R winter & summer), Long-eared Owl (R), Kingfisher, Long-tailed Tit, Treecreeper.

Spring & summer Garganey (R spring), Wigeon (R summer), Marsh Harrier (R spring), Whimbrel (spring), Common Tern, Cockoo (O), Grasshopper Warbler (O), Sedge Warbler, Reed

85

Warbler (R), Blackcap, Willow Warbler, Chiffchaff, Spotted Flycatcher (O).

Autumn & winter Whooper Swan (O), Pink-footed Goose (O), White-fronted Goose (R), Brent Goose (outer bays), Greylag Goose (mostly feral), Wigeon, Teal, Green-winged Teal (R), Pintail, Garganey (R autumn), Shoveler, Pochard, Pintail, Scaup, Goldeneye, Red-breasted Merganser (outer bay), Goosander (R), Long-tailed Duck (R), Merlin (R), Peregrine, Golden Plover, Lapwing, Little Stint (O autumn), Curlew

Sandpiper (O autumn), Dunlin, Ruff, Jack Snipe (R), Snipe, Black-tailed Godwit, Spotted Redshank, Green Sandpiper (O autumn), Wood Sandpiper (O autumn), Common Sandpiper, gulls, Short-eared Owl (R), Siskin, Redpoll.

Rarities American Wigeon, Ring-necked Duck, Smew, Barrow's Goldeneye, Ruddy Duck, Spoonbill, Osprey, Rough-legged Buzzard, Pectoral Sandpiper, Greater Yellowlegs, Mediterranean Gull, Little Gull, White-winged Black Tern, Great Spotted Woodpecker.

62 Lough Money Grid ref. J 53 45

A freshwater lake, good for wildfowl in winter.

See Map 41, right. Lough Money (marked 'Lough Maney' on Ordnance Survey maps) is a 1km long narrow lake situated to the south of Strangford Lough and approximately 4km east of Downpatrick. From Downpatrick, it is best approached by leaving Downpatrick N on the A25, and turning right off the roundabout by the large garage (still on the A25). 100m further, take a right, by the statue at the fork in the road. The Quoile Countryside Centre (Site 61) is 2km on the left, on Quay Road, but 400m before the Centre, take a right for Saul. By continuing straight, ignoring all turns for the next 3km, you will arrive at the shore of Lough Money. Continue left and follow the road which almost encircles the lake.

This lake is particularly good for Little Grebe, as well as Coot. Other species present in winter

include Whooper Swan (R), Gadwall (O), Pochard, Tufted Duck, Scaup (O), Goldeneye, Great Crested Grebe (O) and Curlew.

Rare birds recorded include Ferruginous Duck, Smew and Mediterranean Gull.

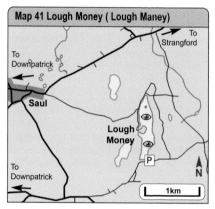

Map 41 Lough Money (Lough Maney)

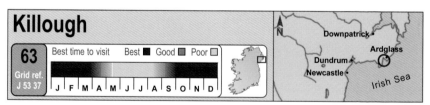

Killough

63	Best time to visit	Best ■ Good ▨ Poor □										
Grid ref. J 53 37	J	F	M	A	M	J	J	A	S	O	N	D

Estuary, mudflat, and a small wetland and reedbed, good in winter for wildfowl, especially Brent Goose, waders and gulls.

Directions Map 42, p.88. Killough lies 9km SE of Downpatrick. Access to the estuary is straightforward, from the town itself, and from the A2 to Ardglass for 2km. The road follows the coast along

much of this stretch and views over the bay are excellent. From Killough Bridge, 1km N of Killough, a small lagoon (part of Strand Lough) is visible on the left, and this area can hold small numbers of waders. S of Killough, the coast is rocky and views over the outer bay can produce Red-breasted Merganser, divers, gulls, and feeding terns in summer.

Strand Lough is a series of small freshwater pools, just 1km N of Killough. Turn left onto the B176 to Downpatrick, and the redbeds of the pools become visible on your right after 500m. Views of the water are restricted, and the habitat generally has been somewhat degraded recently, but this is still a good spot for hearing (and with luck, seeing) Reed Warbler, and many Sedge Warbler, from May to August.

Ardglass is 2km E of Killough and has a tiny bay to the E, enclosed by a rocky shoreline, which holds small numbers of waders and wildfowl in winter. The bay is easily viewed from the A2, which follows the shoreline

Species
Autumn, winter & spring Whooper Swan (O), Brent Goose (300+), Wigeon, Gadwall (O), Teal, Pintail (O), Shoveler (O), Pochard, Tufted Duck, Scaup (O), Goldeneye (O), Red-breasted Merganser, Great Northern Diver (O), Little Grebe, Great Crested Grebe, Cormorant, Little Egret (O), Peregrine, Merlin (O), Golden Plover (100s), Grey Plover, Lapwing, Knot (O), Purple Sandpiper (O rocky coasts), Dunlin, Ruff (O), Snipe, Bar-tailed Godwit (O), Curlew, gulls (particularly Herring Gull), Kingfisher (O).

Summer Water Rail, terns (small numbers), Sedge Warbler, Reed Warbler (reedbeds around Strand Lough), Willow Warbler.

Rarities Bewick's Swan, Dark-Bellied Brent Goose, Spoonbill, Osprey, Long-billed Dowitcher, Green Sandpiper, Glaucous Gull, White-winged Black Tern.

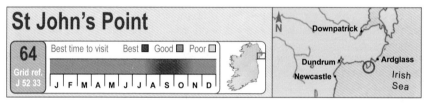

St John's Point

64
Grid ref.
J 52 33

Best time to visit   Best ■ Good ▦ Poor □

| J | F | M | A | M | J | J | A | S | O | N | D |

N   Downpatrick
Dundrum   Ardglass
Newcastle   Irish Sea

The best seawatching and migration headland on the east coast, particularly good in autumn.

Directions Map 42, next page. 3km S of Killough (Site 63, previous page). From Killough, follow the minor coast road S , which after 150m swings inland. Continue for 2km and take a left, which after 1.5km will bring you to the lighthouse. The Point is well signposted locally.

Migrants are generally present after E, SE or S winds in autumn (fewer in spring), particularly if there has been accompanying rain. They are best searched for around the lighthouse complex and back N along the road, where walls and ditches provide some shelter.

Species
Autumn & winter Brent Goose, Wigeon (O), Teal (O), Eider (O), Buzzard (R), Merlin (O), Peregrine, Purple Sandpiper, Snipe, Curlew, gulls, pipits, Black Redstart (R), Chiffchaff, Willow Warbler.

Spring & summer Whimbrel, Wheatear, warblers.

Seawatching is possible year-round, though is best from late July to late Oct. SE winds are much the best, though S or E can occasionally be good.

In autumn, the following species are possible. Red-throated Diver, Great Northern Diver, Black-throated Diver (R), Common Scoter (O), Fulmar, 'Blue' Fulmar (R), Great Shearwater (R), Sooty Shearwater (O), Manx Shearwater (often 100s), Balearic Shearwater (R), Storm Petrel (O), Gannet (often 100s), Cormorant, Shag, Pomarine Skua (R), Arctic Skua (O), Great Skua (O), Long-tailed Skua (R), Sabine's Gull (R), Sandwich Tern, Common Tern, Arctic Tern, Black Tern (R), Guillemot, Razorbill, Black Guillemot (O), Little Auk (R), Puffin (O).

Leach's Petrel & Fea's/Zino's Petrel have been recorded. See also SEAWATCHING, p.356.

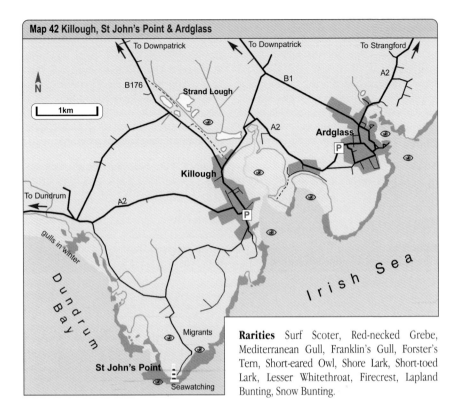

Map 42 Killough, St John's Point & Ardglass

To Downpatrick

To Downpatrick

To Strangford

A2

B1

B176

Strand Lough

N

1km

A2

Ardglass

P

Killough

To Dundrum

A2

P

gulls in winter

Dundrum Bay

Irish Sea

Migrants

St John's Point

Seawatching

Rarities Surf Scoter, Red-necked Grebe, Mediterranean Gull, Franklin's Gull, Forster's Tern, Short-eared Owl, Shore Lark, Short-toed Lark, Lesser Whitethroat, Firecrest, Lapland Bunting, Snow Bunting.

65 Tollymore Forest Park Grid ref. J 34 32

Mature deciduous woodland, large tracts of coniferous forest, and the main area in Ireland for a small population of Mandarin Duck.

3km W of Newcastle. Take the B180 Bryansford Road, leaving Newcastle. Follow signs to the main park entrance, where an admission fee is paid. Open daily, 10a.m. to sunset. There is a café and information centre with maps of the park.

The best woodland areas are in and around the main carpark, and downhill toward the Shimna River. Long walks through mainly coniferous forest on the facing slopes are well marked.

Mandarin Duck are established on the main pools below and S of the carpark area and can occasionally be seen on slower moving stretches of the main river. Another occasional site for Mandarin Duck, mainly outside the breeding season, is the boating pond, downriver, in Newcastle itself.

Other species all year include Long-eared Owl (R), Kingfisher (O), Dipper (O), Long-tailed Tit, Treecreeper, Jay (O), Siskin, Redpoll, Crossbill (O). In summer, Blackcap, Chiffchaff, Willow Warbler and Spotted Flycatcher all breed, while rarer species in recent years include Red Kite, Redstart and Wood Warbler.

Mandarin Duck

Dundrum Bay

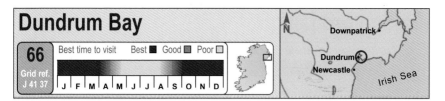

66	Best time to visit	Best ■ Good ▦ Poor ☐
Grid ref. J 41 37	J F M A M J J A S O N D	

An estuary with high numbers of wintering waders, gulls and wildfowl, and a large Common Scoter flock offshore.

Directions Map 43, right. The estuary is 8 km N of Newcastle on the main A2 Newcastle to Belfast road. Most of the bay can be scanned from this road, either side of Dundrum, and from Dundrum itself. The N and E sides can be explored by going from Dundrum, N to Clough, and taking a right onto the A2. Several side roads to the right, off this Clough to Ballykinler road, lead to the shoreline. Mid tide is usually best.

The **Murlough Nature Reserve** is signposted to the left, 2km S of Dundrum. It is mostly sand dune and heath habitat. There is a carpark and information on the Reserve. Take the path through the Reserve which leads to the shore where, in winter, there is a large Common Scoter flock out in the bay, often with a few Velvet Scoter present, and Surf Scoter in some years. Divers, Great Crested Grebe, Goldeneye, auks and occasional Scaup and Long-tailed Duck can also be found. High tide is best, and a telescope is recommended.

Species
Autumn, winter & spring Whooper Swan (O), Dark-Bellied Brent Goose (O), Brent Goose, Mandarin (O), Wigeon, Gadwall (R), Teal, Pintail (O), Shoveler, Scaup (O), Long-tailed Duck, (O), Common Scoter (600+), Surf Scoter (R), Velvet Scoter (O), Goldeneye, Eider (O), Red-breasted Merganser, Little Egret (O), Red-throated Diver, Great Northern Diver, Great Crested Grebe, Oystercatcher (often 2000+), Merlin (O), Peregrine (O), Golden Plover, Grey Plover, Lapwing (2000+), Knot, Little Stint (R autumn), Curlew Sandpiper (R autumn), Purple Sandpiper, Dunlin, Ruff (O), Jack Snipe (O), Snipe, Black-tailed Godwit, Bar-tailed Godwit, Whimbrel (O), Curlew, Spotted Redshank (O), Redshank (800+), Green Sandpiper (R), Common Sandpiper (autumn, R winter), Kingfisher.

Good numbers of gulls are often present, particularly Black-headed Gull (sometimes 1000+) and Common Gull.

Summer The Murlough Nature Reserve has breeding Cuckoo, Grasshopper Warbler, Whitethroat, Blackcap and Spotted Flycatcher.

Rarities Goosander, Black-throated Diver, Red-necked Grebe, Goshawk, Lesser Yellowlegs, Ring-billed Gull, Franklin's Gull.

North

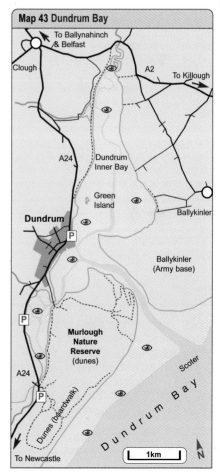

Map 43 Dundrum Bay

89

Carlingford Lough

67

Grid ref.
J 20 13

Best time to visit   Best ■ Good ■ Poor □

J F M A M J J A S O N D

Newry •

Warrenpoint •

Dundalk •

• Kilkeel

Irish Sea

A large sea lough with large numbers of waterfowl, waders and gulls in winter and many nesting terns in summer.

Directions Map 44, below. Roads run along most of the N and S shores of Carlingford Lough, making access relatively straightforward. The N side, particularly around Greencastle, offers the best birdwatching opportunities. From Omeath to Warrenpoint and Rostrevor in winter, Scaup, Long-tailed Duck, Red-breasted Merganser and gulls can be seen offshore, with the occasional Slavonian Grebe. Continue along the A2 to Kilkeel and 5km after Killowen, take a right signposted for Greencastle. **Mill Bay** is on your right and it is possible to scan the bay from several spots along the road, including a picnic site. This is a good area for wildfowl, waders and gulls, best about two hours either side of high tide.

Continue, taking another right after the bridge, also signposted for Greencastle, and further on, the Lough is again visible on your left. The small offshore islands and sandy beaches have many terns in summer, and Brent Geese, some wildfowl, waders and gulls in winter.

On the S shore (most of which is in County Louth), the best area is the sandy bay between Carlingford and Greenore, and again, two hours either side of high tide is best. From Newry, take the B79 to Omeath and Carlingford. This becomes the R173 once over the border into the Republic of Ireland. The Lough is continuously in view to the left along this route. From Dundalk, leave Dundalk N on the N52 and after 2km, take a right at the large roundabout onto the R173 and then NE on the R175, following signs for Carlingford. Just before Greenore, take a left on the R176 to Carlingford. Alternatively, continue on the R175 to Greenore. It is possible to walk much of the coastline between Greenore and Carlingford.

There are often Red-breasted Merganser and Great Northern Diver just offshore from Greenore, and a few pairs of Black Guillemot nest in the quay walls, and can be seen in that area all year. Brent Goose, Wigeon, Teal, Scaup, Black-tailed Godwit, Bar-tailed Godwit and other common waders can be seen, and Kingfisher is regularly seen at Shilties Lough.

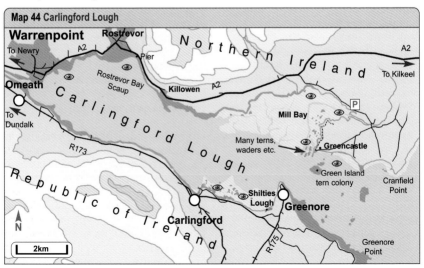

Map 44 Carlingford Lough

Greenshank

Species

Autumn & winter Whooper Swan (O), Greylag Goose (O), Brent Goose, Wigeon, Teal, Scaup, Long-tailed Duck (O Rostrevor Bay to Killowen), Goldeneye, Common Scoter (R), Red-breasted Merganser, Red-throated Diver, Great Northern Diver, Great Crested Grebe, Slavonian Grebe (R), Little Egret (O), Buzzard (hills above & N of Rostrevor), Merlin (O), Peregrine, Golden Plover, Grey Plover, Lapwing, Knot, Dunlin, Jack Snipe (R), Snipe, Purple Sandpiper (O), Black-tailed Godwit, Bar-tailed Godwit, Whimbrel (O), Curlew, gulls, Black Guillemot, Kingfisher (O).

Spring & summer Whimbrel, Common Sandpiper (O), Sandwich Tern, Roseate Tern (O), Common Tern, Arctic Tern.

Most terns nest on Green Island, 300m offshore, S of Greencastle, though small rocky islets 50m W of the trawler pier at Greencastle have smaller numbers which can be viewed more easily.

Rarities Black-throated Diver, Eider, Surf Scoter, Red-necked Grebe, Mediterranean Gull, Forster's Tern, Elegant Tern, Shore Lark.

Other sites

Belfast Lough, south side (J 42 81). The most productive site on the S side of Belfast Lough is Site 55, Belfast Harbour RSPB Reserve. Further E, there are a number of other sites which hold many similar species to Site 51, Belfast Lough, north shore, though in smaller numbers. The stretch of coast from Holywood (J 39 79) to Helen's Bay (J 44 82) has areas of mudflat (mostly near Holywood) which hold many duck and waders in winter.

Kiltonga (J 47 74), nine miles E of Belfast on the W edge of Newtonards, is a small lake with aquatic vegetation, with many of the commoner water-birds, especially in winter. The A20 from Belfast to Newtonards ends in a roundabout. From here, take the first exit, travel 300m to the next junction. Go left here and the lake is visible on your left after 300m.

Belvoir Park (J 33 69) is an excellent area of woodland, just 5km S of Belfast city centre. The park is reached from the A55 outer ring road, between Shaw's Bridge and Newtonbreda. There are carparks and extensive paths through the woodland which contains good broadleaved and coniferous forest. All the regular woodland species occur, though as always, Long-eared Owl and Jay are very elusive. Waxwing is recorded in most winters.

Hillsborough Forest Lake (J 24 58) is adjacent to and just S of Hillsborough town centre, 17km SW of Belfast. The lake holds a good number of wildfowl in winter, including Wigeon, Gadwall, Teal, Pochard and Tufted Duck, and Ruddy Duck is regular. Little Grebe, Great Crested Grebe and Cormorant are also present, and large numbers of Black-headed Gull can be present.

The surrounding mixed woodland has many of the regular woodland species, including Jay and Long-eared Owl. Blackcaps are reasonably common in spring and summer.

Clea Lakes (J 50 55) are 3km from Killyleagh and about 25km SE of Belfast (see Map 38, p.82). The B6 between Killyleagh and Saintfield bisects the lakes and viewing is best from this road and the nearby side roads. The lakes are on private land.

In winter, Wigeon, Gadwall, Teal, Pochard and Goldeneye are usually present, while in summer breeding birds include Great Crested Grebe, Little Grebe and Tufted Duck. Feral Greylag Geese and Canada Geese are usually present, and Kingfisher is an occasional visitor. Some waders occur, but in small numbers, and Lesser Scaup and Smew have been recorded.

Temple Water (J 57 50) is within the Castle Ward Estate 1.5km W of Strangford and is well signposted locally. It is a small, elongated lake which attracts small numbers of waterbirds, mainly in winter. Feral Greylag Geese are present, along with small numbers of Little Grebe, Cormorant and Tufted Duck, while Gadwall, Pochard and Goldeneye are occasionally seen. See Map 38, p.82.

Tyrella Beach (J 47 35) lies 5km W of St John's Point (Site 64). Brent Goose is common here in winter, with many other waders and waterbirds, including Common Scoter, Red-breasted Merganser, Cormorant and divers. Golden Plover can number in the 100s, while Grey Plover, Lapwing, Dunlin, Curlew and gulls can be seen, and Tree Sparrow are occasionally seen in small flocks. Franklin's Gull and Shore Lark have been recorded.

Newcastle (J 37 31) is a large resort town with an extensive sandy beach. In winter, Common Scoter are often present offshore, along with Red-throated and Great Northern Divers, Red-breasted Merganser and small numbers of Great Crested Grebe. Dark-bellied Brent and Black Brant have been seen with the Brent Goose flocks. Long-tailed Duck and Ring-billed Gull have also been recorded.

Inch Abbey (J 47 45) lies just NW of Downpatrick. Take the A7 from the town towards Belfast. After 1km, take the left turn signposted for Inch Abbey. Follow this minor road for 200m and take the next left to reach the carpark.

The tall trees around the churchyard attract many finches in winter, with Hawfinch recorded here. A lakeside walk can produce small numbers of Goldeneye and other diving duck in winter.

County Armagh

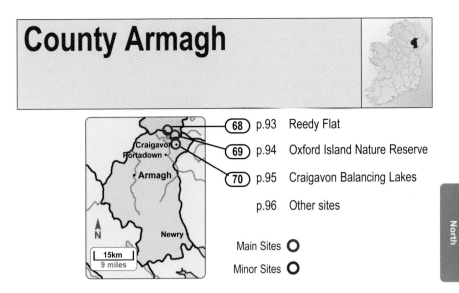

68	p.93	Reedy Flat
69	p.94	Oxford Island Nature Reserve
70	p.95	Craigavon Balancing Lakes
	p.96	Other sites

Main Sites ○

Minor Sites ○

Armagh is a small, inland county with Lough Neagh as its northern boundary. As a result, the main areas for birds are concentrated on, or close to, Lough Neagh which attracts large numbers of wildfowl each winter. Oxford Island Nature Reserve is one of the best locations to visit, with a series of hides and a 'Discovery Centre'. The 'Balancing Lakes' of Craigavon, close to Oxford Island, is also excellent for diving ducks. Lough Neagh is also good for waders, and the Reedy Flat to the west of Oxford Island is one of the best inland sites for rare waders in Northern Ireland. There are also several small lakes south of Lough Neagh that are good for ducks and grebes in winter.

Reedy Flat

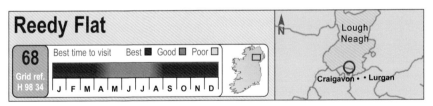

68

Grid ref. H 98 34

Best time to visit   Best ■ Good ■ Poor ☐

J F M A M J J A S O N D

An area of open water and shoreline along the southern edge of Lough Neagh which attracts good numbers of wildfowl and grebes in winter and waders in autumn.

Directions Located to the W of Oxford Island (Site 69), on the S side of Lough Neagh. From Belfast, follow the M1 SW, following signs for Lurgan and Craigavon. Leave the M1 at Exit 10, signposted for Oxford Island. Follow the signs for Oxford Island. Go past the entrance sign to Oxford Island, and at the next T-junction, go right onto the B2. Continue on this road for almost 5km until you reach the village of Derrytrasna. In the village, there is a large church on the right. Take the right turn approximately 500m past the church and close to where the B2 swings left. Follow this narrow road and take the next right and continue for over 1.5km until you see Lough Neagh. This area is known as Reedy Flat and can be viewed from many points along this road.

Species
All year Water Rail, Kingfisher.

Autumn, winter & spring Whooper Swan, Pink-footed Goose (R winter), Wigeon, Gadwall, Teal, Shoveler, Pochard, Tufted Duck, Goldeneye, Hen

Harrier, Merlin, Buzzard, Golden Plover, Lapwing, Knot, Little Stint (R autumn), Curlew Sandpiper (autumn), Dunlin, Ruff (autumn), Jack Snipe (R winter), Snipe, Green Sandpiper (autumn), Wood Sandpiper (R autumn), Short-eared Owl (O winter), Brambling (R winter).

Summer Common Sandpiper, gulls, Common Tern, Sedge Warbler.

Rarities American Wigeon, Garganey, Quail, Red-necked Grebe, Slavonian Grebe, Marsh Harrier, Osprey, Pectoral Sandpiper, Buff-breasted Sandpiper, Black Tern.

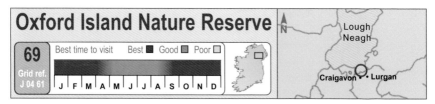

Oxford Island Nature Reserve

A series of shallow, reed-fringed bays that attract large numbers of wildfowl each winter. The Lough Neagh Discovery Centre is situated on the reserve and there are paths and hides throughout.

The Reserve is open daily, except Christmas day. The Discovery Centre is open 10am to 7pm, Mon to Sat, 10am to 7pm Sun, April to Sept. From Oct to March, it is open 10am to 5pm daily. It has a restuarant, Information Office, craft shop and conference rooms.

Directions Map 69, next page. Located on the SE shore of Lough Neagh, 5km NW of Lurgan and 6km N of Craigavon. From Belfast, follow the M1 SW, following signs for Lurgan and Craigavon. Leave the M1 at Exit 10, signposted for Oxford Island. Following the signs for Oxford Island, take a right turn, following the entrance sign for Oxford Island Nature Reserve. The road brings you onto the reserve where, just past Waterside House, is the Waterside Hide. This is the first of a series of five hides on the reserve and this gives good views over Kinnego Bay.

Further W is the Kinnego Hide which again gives excellent views of duck in winter. Follow the road on to the Discovery Centre, where the Discovery Hide lies close by. On the W side of the Discovery Centre is Closet Bay. The first hide, which lies to the E of the Discovery Centre, is Croaghan Hide. This is a good location for seeing terns in summer. The area of woodlands near the Discovery Centre and Croaghan Hide is good for Siskin and Redpoll in winter.

Finally, the Closet Hide, which lies SW of the centre, gives excellent views over Closet Bay. The numerous pathways throughout the reserve are worth walking as the scrub and trees attract finches and buntings in winter, and common warblers in summer. It should be noted that the reserve can attract large numbers of visitors at weekends and the hides can be quite busy.

Species
All year Cormorant, Water Rail, Kingfisher.

Autumn, winter & spring Bewick's Swan (O), Whooper Swan, Greylag Goose (O), White-fronted Goose (R), Wigeon, Gadwall, Teal, Shoveler, Pochard, Tufted Duck, Scaup, Goldeneye, Long-tailed Duck (R), Red-breasted Merganser (O), Hen Harrier, Merlin, Buzzard, Golden Plover, Lapwing, Knot, Little Stint (R autumn), Curlew Sandpiper (autumn), Dunlin, Ruff (autumn), Jack Snipe (R winter), Snipe, Grey Phalarope (R autumn), Mediterranean Gull (R winter), Short-eared Owl (O winter), Reed Warbler (O autumn), Brambling (R winter), Siskin (autumn & winter), Redpoll (O autumn & winter).

Summer Common Sandpiper, gulls, Common Tern, Grasshopper Warbler, Sedge Warbler, Reed Warbler (R), Chiffchaff, Willow Warbler.

Rarities Green-winged Teal, Garganey, Red-crested Pochard, Ring-necked Duck, Ferruginous Duck, Lesser Scaup, Smew, Goosander, Ruddy Duck, Slavonian Grebe, Manx Shearwater, Sooty Shearwater, Storm Petrel, Leach's Petrel, Osprey, Great Skua, Black Tern, White-winged Black Tern, Carrion Crow, Crossbill.

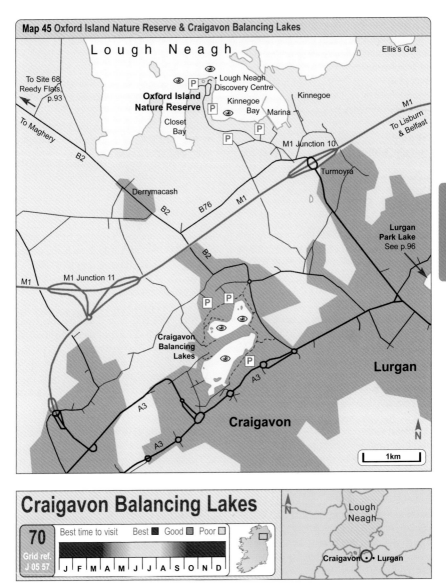

Map 45 Oxford Island Nature Reserve & Craigavon Balancing Lakes

L o u g h   N e a g h

Ellis's Gut

To Site 68
Reedy Flats
p.93

To Maghery

Oxford Island
Nature Reserve

Lough Neagh
Discovery Centre

Kinnegoe

Kinnegoe
Bay

Marina

Closet
Bay

M1

To Lisburn
& Belfast

M1 Junction 10

Turmoyra

B2

Derrymacash

B2

B76

M1

B2

Lurgan
Park Lake
See p.96

M1

M1 Junction 11

P   P

Craigavon
Balancing
Lakes

P

Lurgan

A3

A3

Craigavon

A3

N

1km

Craigavon Balancing Lakes

N

Lough
Neagh

70

Grid ref.
J 05 57

Best time to visit   Best ■ Good ■ Poor □

J F M A M J J A S O N D

Craigavon •• Lurgan

Two artificial lakes that attract good numbers of diving ducks each winter. The lakes are within a park setting and have pathways around them. This provides excellent viewing of the duck flocks which are tamer here than at most other locations.

Directions Map 45, above. From Belfast, follow the M1 SW, following signs for Lurgan and Craigavon. Leave the M1 at Junction 10, signposted for Oxford Island. Follow the signs for Oxford Island. Go past the entrance sign for Oxford Island, staying on the B76, and at the next T-junction go left onto the B2. This then brings you back over the M1 and is signed for Lurgan. From here, follow the signs for Tannaghmore Gardens. At the roundabout, take the right exit, following signs for Tannaghmore Gardens. Follow this small road in and take the first left turn and park at the end. From here, you can see the North Lake. There are pathways around the lake and the ducks can be seen well from many points. A path

95

continues under a flyover at the SE corner and brings you onto the South Lake. Alternatively, at the roundabout, continue straight (ignoring the turn for Tannaghmore Gardens) and continue for approximately 1km until you see North Lake on the right side. A small pathway leads down from the road to the pathways around the lake.

Species

Autumn, winter & spring Teal, Pochard, Tufted Duck, Scaup (O), Goldeneye, Blackcap (winter), Brambling (R winter), Siskin, (winter), Redpoll (winter).

Summer Sedge Warbler, Chiffchaff, Willow Warbler.

Rarities Red-crested Pochard, Ring-necked Duck, Ferruginous Duck, Smew, Goosander, Waxwing, 'Mealy' Redpoll, Crossbill.

Other sites

Lurgan Park Lake (J 08 58) lies in the centre of the town of Lurgan. The large lake within the park attracts small numbers of diving ducks in winter, while the reed-fringed edges are good for Little Grebes.

From Belfast, follow the M1 SW, following signs for Lurgan and Craigavon. Leave the M1 at Exit 10 and follow the signs for Lurgan. As you approach the centre of the town, take a left onto Windsor Avenue. Follow the road down to the entrance to the park. From here, follow the paths around the lake.

Common species found in winter include Tufted Duck and Pochard, while Great Crested and Little Grebes are also present. Lurgan Park also holds a small resident population of Ruddy Ducks. The park is also good for common woodland species such as Treecreeper, Siskin and Redpoll in winter. Rare species that have been recorded here include Ferruginous Duck, Ring-necked Duck, Ring-billed Gull and Waxwing.

Lough Shark/Acton Lake (J 06 42) Lying close to the small villages of Poyntz Pass and Acton on the Armagh/Down border, Lough Shark (sometimes referred to as Acton Lake) is a small freshwater lake that attracts small numbers of diving duck in winter.

From Newry, follow the A27 N until you reach the village of Poyntz Pass. Continue N on the A27 for over 1.6km and take a right turn onto a minor road. Follow this minor road down to the railway crossing. Park here and cross the railway lines.

The lake is partly obscured by trees and the best viewing area is at the S end of the lake. Follow the wide path right at the T-junction and follow to the S end of the lake. The lake holds diving duck such as Pochard and Tufted Duck as well as Whooper Swan in winter. The trees in the area are also good for Treecreeper, Redpoll, Siskin and, occasionally, Crossbill.

Rarities recorded here include Green-winged Teal, Red-crested Pochard and Smew.

Peatlands Park (H 90 61) is 600 acres of mixed woodland, scrubland and peatland 9km to the E of Dungannon. The park has pathways and an educational centre. At weekends, it can be quite busy and has a miniature railway that takes people on guided trips through the park.

From Belfast, follow the M1 SW and take Exit 13. Follow the signs from here for Peatlands Park. In summer, it holds breeding Woodcock and Long-eared Owl, while in winter, Merlin and Hen Harrier are frequently seen. The woodlands also hold common resident species such as Treecreeper, while in summer, common warblers like Blackcap, Chiffchaff and Willow Warbler are found. In winter, Siskin and Redpoll can occur.

County Fermanagh

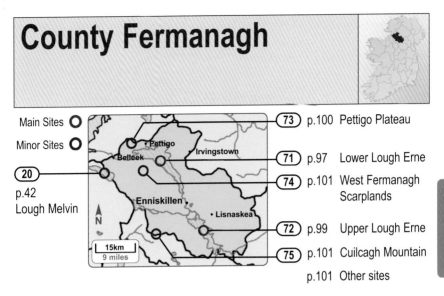

North

Upper and Lower Lough Erne are very much the focus for birdwatching in County Fermanagh. With numerous islands, inlets, bays, rivers and loughs, the two areas provide much habitat for wildfowl and waders in winter, while in summer, some interesting species breed. The many areas of broad-leaved woodland around the lakes are the strongholds of Garden Warbler in Ireland.

Higher areas, such as the Pettigo Plateau and Cuilcagh Mountain, are particularly interesting in summer, when many upland species can be found. The large and often remote coniferous plantations in the county are particularly good for Crossbill. Fermanagh is a county where few birdwatchers venture, yet the range and extent of habitat is excellent and will reward any birdwatcher willing to explore further.

Lower Lough Erne

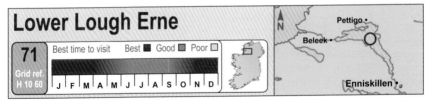

71

Grid ref.
H 10 60

Best time to visit   Best ■ Good ■ Poor □

J F M A M J J A S O N D

Pettigo
Beleek
Enniskillen
N

A very large lake, good for a variety of water-birds in winter, and a good selection of breeding birds in summer.

Lough Erne is famous for being the former centre of the Irish breeding Common Scoter population which peaked at 152 pairs in the late 1960s, though numbers have since declined, with the last breeding record in 1992 and the last sighting in 1998. During those years, both Velvet and Surf Scoter were recorded in summer on the Lough. Birdwatching along much of the Lower Lough is difficult, as there are few concentrations of birds

and where there are, access can be difficult. Particularly good areas include:

Drumgay Lough (H 24 47) Map 46, next page. Located on the N outskirts of Enniskillen. Follow the A32 NE out of Enniskillen for 1.5km and take the minor road right at the Agricultural College. The Lough can be viewed from the roadside, just past the college. Great Crested Grebe, Tufted Duck, Pochard and Goldeneye are common, Shoveler and Scaup are occasionally seen, and a number of other scarce species have been recorded, including White-fronted Goose,

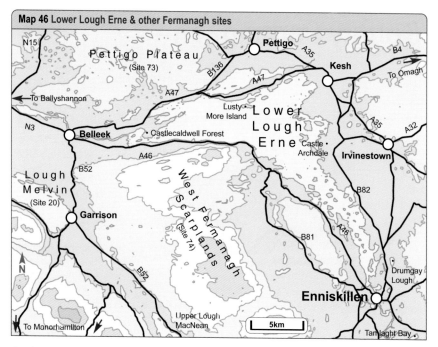

Map 46 Lower Lough Erne & other Fermanagh sites

Greylag Goose, Pink-footed Goose, Ring-necked Duck and Long-tailed Duck. This is possibly Fermanagh's most reliable site for Smew, with up to 5 birds present in some winters. There is a large feral Canada Goose flock, and Whooper Swans are often present in winter. Other species include Buzzard (O), Peregrine, Raven, Water Rail (O), Kingfisher (O) and there is much potential for other unusual species.

Lower Lough Erne Islands RSPB Reserve
The Royal Society for Protection of Birds (RSPB) manages 39 islands on the Lower Lough, many of which are shown on Map 46, above. Ten of these islands are specifically managed for breeding waders and support a third of all Northern Ireland's breeding Redshank and increasing populations of breeding Lapwing, Curlew and Snipe. In addition, Sandwich Terns nest on one island, at the only consistently occupied inland site in Europe (156 pairs in 2005).

Other breeding species include Dunlin, Common Tern, Garden warbler, five gull species and, in recent years, a Yellow-legged Gull has paired with a Lesser Black-backed Gull. Unfortunately, public access is very limited. There is a short footpath on **Lusty More Island** (H 11 61), accessible only by

private boat and a ferry to White Island, near **Castle Archdale** (H 17 59).

Castelcaldwell Forest (H 01 59) is located S of the A47, 8km W of Belleek, and also forms part of the Reserve. It holds all the regular woodland species, as well as occasional Crossbill, and has had singing Wood Warbler in some springs. There are views over the lough but no particular concentrations of waterbirds, though Scaup and Wigeon are regular. In spring and summer, gulls, Common Tern and Sandwich Tern can be seen offshore. Spring wader passage is light but can include Black-tailed Godwit, Whimbrel, Ruff and Greenshank.

Over the years, some very rare species have been recorded at Lower Lough Erne, including Ireland's first Wilson's Petrel in October 1891, breeding Black Tern and summering Red-necked Grebe (still an occasional visitor). Others include American Wigeon, Red-throated Diver, Black-throated Diver, Great Northern Diver, Leach's Petrel, Little Egret, Bittern, Crane, Hobby, Marsh Harrier, Grey Phalarope, Red-necked Phalarope, Mediterranean Gull, Little Gull and Arctic Skua. There is undoubtedly much potential for further exciting discoveries in this underwatched area.

Upper Lough Erne

72

Grid ref.
H 30 20

Best time to visit   Best ■ Good ▦ Poor □

J F M A M J J A S O N D

North

A vast area of lake, forest and wetland, holding reasonable numbers of wildfowl in winter and some interesting breeding species in summer.

Directions Map 46a, right. S of Enniskillen.

The Lough is a complex mix of inlets, islands and bays, and access can be difficult and limited. In winter, there are many wildfowl and waders present, often scattered throughout the lake, but with few major concentrations. Many areas are only accessible by boat, but the main (and easiest) areas for birdwatching are as follows:

Main sites and species

Knockninny Refuge (H 31 27) Map 46a, right. Located 15km S of Enniskillen. From the main A509 Enniskillen to Cavan road, follow a minor road signposted for Knockninny Quay. To the E, Knockninny is the large, obvious hill next to the Lough with a large quarry cut into the N face. View from the minor road before and after the pier. This is a haven for waterfowl during the shooting season (1st September to 31st January), with peak numbers in January, when up to 1000 birds can be present. At such times, it represents the most accessible large concentration of waterfowl in Fermanagh.

Species include large numbers of Whooper Swan, Wigeon, Tufted Duck and Pochard, and some locally scarce species, including Pintail, Shoveler, Gadwall and Scaup. Ring-necked Duck has been recorded here, and there is the potential for other vagrant waterfowl. Numbers from Feb onward are less predictable, as birds can disperse once the shooting season ends.

Colebrook Rivermouth (H 32 31). Take the B127 between Derrylin and Lisnaskea and turn N towards Kilmore Quay at the signpost, 2.5km S of Lisnaskea. Bear right onto a dirt track towards the holiday village. Continue to the end of the road. This road is private and is occasionally closed, in which case you will need to park and walk. Fields

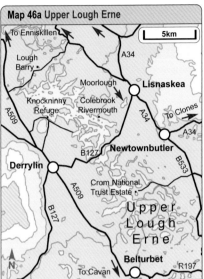

Map 46a Upper Lough Erne

along these roads often hold flocks of Whooper Swans and occasional Bewick's Swan (though much rarer recently).

The area where the Colebrook River enters Upper Lough Erne can have large concentrations of waterfowl, especially after the end of the shooting season (31st January). This area is heavily shot over from 1st September to 31st January and it is usually not worth a visit before early February. Species include Whooper Swan, Bewick's Swan (R), Teal (100s), Green-winged Teal (R), Wigeon, Gadwall, Pintail, Peregrine, Merlin, Golden Plover (100s), Lapwing and Curlew.

In spring, there is potential for passage waders, and Wood Sandpiper and Ruff have been recorded, as has Garganey. Kilmore Lough to the E of the approach road can have high numbers of Wigeon, Pochard and Tufted Duck and small numbers of Whooper Swan, Shoveler, Pintail and Gadwall.

Crom National Trust Estate (H 36 24), 9 km SW of Lisnaskea, is a good woodland area. It is well

99

Garden Warbler

signposted locally and is open to the public from late March to the end of Sept. There is a fee for parking. This is the best site for Garden Warbler in County Fermanagh – look for regenerating coppiced woodland along the many footpaths, in May and June. All the regular woodland species also occur here, including Blackcap (song is very similar to Garden Warbler), and Wood Warbler is occasionally recorded singing in May or June. Osprey has been recorded here in spring on several occasions.

Lakes near Crom National Trust Estate
When approaching Crom Castle from Newtownbutler, check **Kilturk Lough** (H 37 25), just before the entrance to the castle. This lough has large numbers of diving duck in winter, mostly Tufted Duck, Pochard and Goldeneye, but has also been a regular site for Smew in recent winters. Ring-necked Duck and Ruddy Duck have also been seen. The land loughs in this area all have potential for more wildfowl, but birds often

move between them, so any of the lakes in this vicinity are worth a look if you have time. **Cornabrass Lough** (H 40 24), 3km SW of Newtownbutler, and **Sand Lough** (H 37 26) have been particularly productive in recent winters. The occurrence of a Killdeer at nearby **Ports Lough** (H 36 26) demonstrates how there is an abundance of suitable habitat for wildfowl and waders in this whole region.

Moorlough (H 38 29), W of the main A34 road between Newtownbutler and Lisnaskea, has a Black-headed Gull and Common Tern colony on the small islet to the S of the lake, the birds present between May and August.

Tamlaght Bay (H 26 40) is on the W side of the A4 Enniskillen to Belfast road and is best viewed from Derryvullan Church (H 27 40). Currently the easiest site to see the gulls that use the nearby Enniskillen Tip, but this is due to close, and the number of gulls will inevitably decrease. Best from Dec to Apr with Iceland Gull (O) and Glaucous Gull (O), and has had Mediterranean Gull, Little Gull, Yellow-legged Gull and Kumlien's Gull. Lapwing is common in winter and Buzzard is regularly seen overhead, and occasionally, Whooper Swan, Merlin and Peregrine. Drumcullion Lough, to the S, holds a flock of Wigeon.

Lough Barry (H 27 36) is located 4km along the minor road that runs from the A509, across to Inishmore and to Carry Bridge at the N end of Upper Lough Erne. It holds a flock of Tufted Duck in winter and Lesser Scaup has been recorded here recently.

73 Pettigo Plateau Grid ref. H 04 69

A large area of blanket bog and coniferous forest, good in spring and summer for upland breeding birds.

Map 46, p.98. Access is from minor roads approximately midway between Belleek and Pettigo, N of the A47. The habitat extends into Donegal, and numerous mountain tracks are best explored on foot or by bike.

As with similar sites throughout the country, densities of birds are low but the species interesting. Breeding species include Hen Harrier, Merlin, Golden Plover, Red Grouse, Dunlin, Raven, Common Sandpiper and Crossbill. Numbers of the latter vary from year to year. Peregrine can be seen throughout the year.

White-fronted Goose and Whooper Swan are occasionally encountered in this area in winter, and rarer species in recent years include Goosander, Smew and Gyr Falcon. Common Buzzard has increased in this general area in recent years, and Goshawk may breed in the vast coniferous forests of this region.

74 West Fermanagh Scarplands Grid ref. H 05 50

A large area of upland blanket bog and extensive coniferous forest, good in spring and summer for upland breeding birds.

Map 46, p.98. The Scarplands lie W and SW of Lower Lough Erne and extend W to the B52 Garrison to Belcoo road and S to the A4 Enniskillen to Sligo road. The forestry land has numerous tracks open to the public, a few of which can be driven but most of which are better cycled or walked. There are no particular hotspots, and see Pettigo Plateau (Site 73) above for possible species (though Red Grouse and Golden Plover don't breed here). Crossbills are more numerous at this site, although numbers vary year to year.

Winter is a less interesting time, though birds of prey, including Peregrine, are still present. Garrison is the site where Ireland's first Bald Eagle was recorded – shot in 1973.

75 Cuilcagh Mountain Grid ref. H 12 28

A high mountain with extensive blanket bog, very good for upland breeding species in spring and summer.

At 665m, Cuilcagh Mountain is Fermanagh's highest point and dominates the SW Fermanagh skyline on the border with County Cavan.

The mountain lies to the S of the minor road from Blacklion in the W of County Fermanagh, along the S shore of Lower Lough MacNean (see Other Sites, below). Access is possible from three points. There are show caves at Marble Arch and a roadway here goes two-thirds of the way to the summit. Access above the caves is on foot only, from the carpark (H 11 33), and takes approximately 2 hours 30 minutes to the summit.

A second access point is the Hiker's Trail, which leaves Florencecourt National Trust Estate (H 17 34, see Other Sites, below). There is a charge for parking here and the route to the summit takes approximately 3 hours of steady walking on wet ground via the Aghatirourke RSPB Reserve.

The third access point is from the 'parking', signposted at Gortalughany (H 16 30). From here a track leads on to the Aghatirourke RSPB Reserve and joins the Hiker's Trail, taking approximately 3 hours to the summit.

Breeding species include Golden Plover, Merlin, Peregrine, Red Grouse, Wheatear, Raven and Dipper. Hen Harrier regularly hunt across the open landscape.

The flat summit looks ideal for a spring 'trip' of Dotterel and the species has been recorded here on one previous occasion.

Other sites

Florencecourt National Trust Estate (H 17 34), 10km SW of Enniskillen, occasionally holds singing Wood Warbler in spring, in the broadleaved woodland along the lower slopes.

The shores of **Lower Lough MacNean** (H 12 37) near Gortatole have a wintering flock of White-fronted Geese numbering around 100 birds, as well as Whooper Swan, Canada Goose (feral), Great Crested Grebe, Cormorant, Wigeon, Teal, Shoveler (O), Pochard (O), Tufted Duck, Goldeneye, Water Rail (O), Hen Harrier (O), Peregrine, Merlin (O), Lapwing, Snipe and Curlew.

County Louth

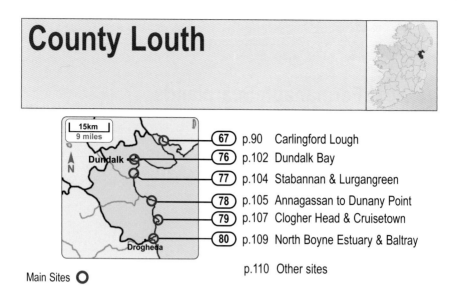

Site	Page	Name
67	p.90	Carlingford Lough
76	p.102	Dundalk Bay
77	p.104	Stabannan & Lurgangreen
78	p.105	Annagassan to Dunany Point
79	p.107	Clogher Head & Cruisetown
80	p.109	North Boyne Estuary & Baltray
	p.110	Other sites

Main Sites O

Louth is the northernmost county in Leinster and has a long coastline stretching from Carlingford Lough and the high hills of the Cooley Peninsula in the north, to where the River Boyne enters the sea at Baltray in the south. In between lie the extensive mudflats of Dundalk Bay, the sandflats of Cruisetown Strand and the estuary of Baltray. There are also several headlands that attract migrants in spring and autumn, including Ballagan Point, Dunany Point and Clogher Head, while the rich pastures just in from the coast attract large numbers of Greylag Geese each winter.

Dundalk Bay

76

Grid ref.
J 09 07

Best time to visit   Best ■ Good ■ Poor □

J F M A M J J A S O N D

Dundalk Bay is an enormous bay with extensive intertidal mudflats, saltmarshes and open water. In winter it holds large numbers of wildfowl, waders and gulls, while the open water is excellent for divers and grebes.

The bay stretches to Annagassan in the S and to Giles' Quay on the N rim. The best areas include Dundalk Docks which gives excellent views over the inner estuary, Soldiers Point, which lies at the eastern end of the southern side of the mouth of the Dundalk Harbour, and Ballymascanlan which is a small inlet on the N side. Further E along the N rim of the bay is Giles' Quay which is excellent for divers and grebes in winter.

Directions Map 47, next page. Heading N on the M1, take the exit signposted for Dundalk South. Follow this road to the major crossroads and continue straight onto the N52 for the docks (the N52 bypasses the town). Alternatively, from Castlebellingham, follow the N1 N, and then turn right onto the N52.

For **Dundalk Docks**, follow the N52 past the shopping centres and continue for approximately 3.5km. Go through the last set of traffic lights and take the small right turn following signs for the docks. This small road leads onto the docks, and the mudflats directly across from the pub can be seen well from the quay wall. This area is excellent

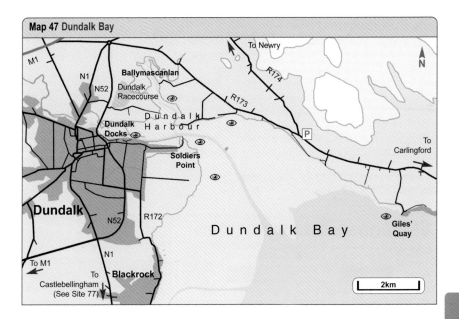

Map 47 Dundalk Bay

To Newry

M1

N1

N52

Ballymascanlan

Dundalk Racecourse

Dundalk Docks

D u n d a l k   H a r b o u r

Soldiers Point

R174

R173

P

To Carlingford

Dundalk

N52   R172

N1

To M1

To Castlebellingham (See Site 77)

Blackrock

D u n d a l k   B a y

Giles' Quay

N

2km

for waders in autumn and winter, with passage birds such as Curlew Sandpiper and Little Stint regularly seen in autumn. Ruff are known to winter at this site. The area is also good for ducks and gulls in winter.

For **Soldiers Point**, from Dundalk Docks, return to the N52 and go left. At the traffic lights, follow left and continue out this road for over 1.5km to where it swings sharp right. At this point, go straight and follow the road to the row of houses at the end. This area is Soldiers Point. The mudflats and the saltmarsh behind the houses can be viewed well from many points by following the path to the left of the last house on the left. In winter, Twite are often seen with the Linnet flocks in this area. The saltmarsh to the S of Soldiers Point is known as South Marsh. This can be reached by walking S from the point, or, if coming from Dundalk, by following the road sharp right (ignoring the road for Soldiers Point) and taking the next left turn. This road then continues S to meet the R172 which will bring you onto the coast road around Blackrock. The mudflats and open water S of Dundalk can be seen from many parking areas along this road.

For **Ballymascanlan**, from Dundalk Docks, return to the N52 and go right. Continue on the N52 over the bridge that crosses the Castletown

River. Approximately 500m N, a small road to the right leads you to a point where the W and outer side of Ballymascanlan can be seen. To view the inner part, continue on the N52 to the major roundabout and take a right onto the R173, signposted for Carlingford. Follow this road for over 3km, going past the village of Ballymascanlan, and take a right turn. This narrow road brings you to the inner section of the mudflats at Ballymascanlan.

For **Giles' Quay**, from the village of Ballymascanlan, continue ESE on the R173 for over 7km and take the right turn down to the coast, signposted for Giles' Quay. Follow this road S for almost 1.5km to the point where the quay wall is visible. In winter, divers and grebes are seen well offshore from this point, with Slavonian Grebe recorded annually. The rocky beach to the W is also good for roosting waders and gulls.

Species
Autumn, winter & spring Brent Goose, Wigeon, Teal, Shoveler (O), Scaup (O), Eider (O), Long-tailed Duck (O), Red-breasted Merganser (O), Red-throated Diver, Great Northern Diver, Little Egret (O winter), Merlin, Buzzard, Golden Plover (1000s), Grey Plover, Lapwing (1000s), Knot, Little Stint (autumn), Curlew Sandpiper (autumn), Dunlin, Ruff (autumn & winter), Jack

103

Snipe (R winter), Snipe, Black-tailed Godwit, Bar-tailed Godwit, Whimbrel (autumn & spring), Spotted Redshank (R autumn & winter), Common Sandpiper (O winter), Green Sandpiper (R autumn), Wood Sandpiper (R autumn), Grey Phalarope (R autumn), Little Gull, Mediterranean Gull (R autumn & winter), Ring-billed Gull (R winter), Iceland Gull (O winter), Glaucous Gull (O winter), Short-eared Owl (winter), Black Redstart (R winter), Brambling (R winter).

Summer Common Sandpiper, gulls, terns, Wheatear.

Some non-breeding waders occur throughout summer, including Curlew and Black-tailed Godwit.

Rarities Goosander, Black-throated Diver, Red-necked Grebe, Slavonian Grebe, Osprey, Long-billed Dowitcher, Lesser Yellowlegs, Wilson's Phalarope, Yellow-legged Gull, Little Auk, Pallid Swift, Scandinavian Rock Pipit, Twite, Lapland Bunting, Snow Bunting.

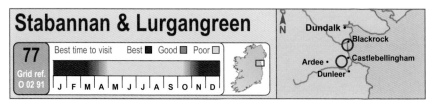

Stabannan & Lurgangreen

77	Best time to visit	Best ■ Good ■ Poor □

Grid ref. O 02 91

| J | F | M | A | M | J | J | A | S | O | N | D |

The open pastures of Stabannan and Braganstown attract large numbers of Greylag Geese and Whooper Swans, and small numbers of White-fronted Goose and Pink-footed Goose each winter.

Many of these birds commute to Lurgangreen which lies on the western side of Dundalk Bay.

Directions Map 48, right. The Stabannan and Braganstown areas lie inland about 3km SW of Castlebellingham. Lurgangreen is located between Blackrock and Castlebellingham, adjacent to the coast.

Stabannan & Braganstown From Castlebellingham, follow the N1 S for almost 4.5km and, at the staggered crossroads, take a right turn. Follow this narrow road W for over 2km, going under the railway bridge, until you reach a T-junction. At this junction, go right. This road continues N for over 3km to the Braganstown area, and fields on either side of the road can hold the geese flocks. *It should be noted that the fields in this area are all on private property so viewing can only be done from the road.* At the T-junction at Braganstown, you can go right and follow this road as it circles the area. At the next T-junction, a right turn will bring you back to the Stabannan Road, while taking a left turn will bring you back to the N1, just S of

Castlebellingham. Again, any of the fields can hold geese in winter.

Many of these birds commute to the open fields at **Lurgangreen** that lie 1km S of Blackrock and

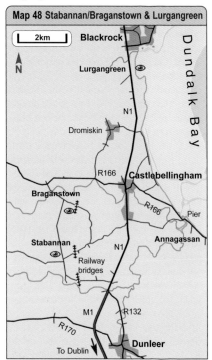

Map 48 Stabannan/Braganstown & Lurgangreen

4km N of Castlebellingham. Waders are also found on the nearby mudflats and roosting on the saltmarshes at Lurgangreen in winter.

From Castlebellingham, take the N1 N for over 4km. The road veers slightly to the left and, from this point onwards, the fields on the right for the next 2km can hold large numbers of geese. However, one of the best areas is the field behind the 'Truck Centre'. These fields and the saltmarsh along the coast can be seen well by following the road N from the Truck Centre and taking the small road on the right, just before the small bridge over the Fane River. Follow this narrow road down to the coast and from here, walk S along the top end of the saltmarsh. The geese regularly move from the fields onto the saltmarsh and can be seen feeding anywhere from this small road, S for over 1.5km. Birds can move inland from Lurgangreen, and also commute to Stabannan/Braganstown.

Species

Autumn, winter & spring Whooper Swan (O), Pink-footed Goose (R), White-fronted Goose (O), Greylag Goose (1000+), Barnacle Goose (R), Brent Goose, Wigeon, Teal, Shoveler (O), Little Egret (O winter), Merlin, Buzzard, Peregrine, Golden Plover (1000s), Grey Plover, Lapwing, Knot, Little Stint (R autumn), Curlew Sandpiper (R autumn), Dunlin, Jack Snipe (R winter), Snipe, Black-tailed Godwit, Bar-tailed Godwit, Whimbrel (spring), Spotted Redshank (R autumn & winter), Green Sandpiper (R autumn), Little Gull, Mediterranean Gull (R autumn & winter), Iceland Gull (R winter), Glaucous Gull (R winter), Short-eared Owl (winter), Brambling (R winter).

Rarities 'Taiga' Bean Goose, 'Tundra' Bean Goose, Canada Goose, Dark-bellied Brent, Garganey, Osprey, Franklin's Gull, Sabine's Gull, Black Tern.

A headland which can attract migrants in spring and autumn, and the southern part of Dundalk Bay, good for wildfowl and waders, mainly in winter.

Lying north of Clogher Head, Dunany Point is a small headland that can attract migrants in spring and autumn. In winter, large flocks of Common Scoter, as well as grebes and divers, can be seen well from the Point. Just to the west of Dunany is Hermitage, a small area of wetland that can attract waders and scarce migrants in autumn. The sea off Hermitage can also be excellent for divers, grebes and duck in winter. Further west, the circular road around Salterstown, and the main coast road to Annagassan, allow excellent views over the southern rim of Dundalk Bay where grebes, divers and ducks can be found in winter.

Directions Map 49, next page. From Clogherhead village, follow NW on the R166 for over 1.2km and, at the church, take the minor road to the right which brings you down to Cruisetown Strand. This coast road continues for over 2km.

Dunany Point At the N end of the coast road, just past the public toilets, the road swings left and inland. 500m further on the main road swings right at a minor T-junction. At this point, continue right and follow this road NE for approximately 2km. At the point where the road turns right, you will see a minor road to the left (straight). Follow this minor road for over 600m and park at the end of this road. To the right, a rough track runs for almost 1km to the coast. This tracks runs to a stony beach where, offshore, divers and large flocks of scoters can gather in winter. The area can be viewed from the end of the track or by following N along the top of the small cliffs. This extra height can give better views of the scoter flocks. A small area of woodland lies 500m N and can hold migrants in spring and autumn.

Map 49 Annagassan to Dunany Point

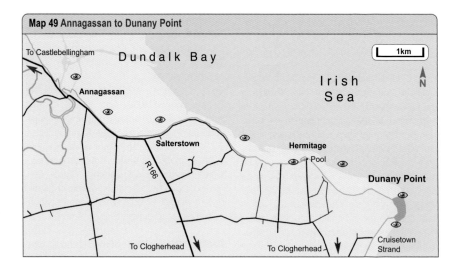

Hermitage At the N end of the coast road, just past the public toilets, the road swings left and inland. 500m further on, the main road swings right at a minor T-junction. At this point, continue right and follow this road NE for approximately 1.2km and take the left turn (straight will bring you to Dunany Point). Follow this road NW for over 1.3km to where it swings sharp left. Follow left and take an immediate right turn onto a minor road. Follow this minor road to the end where a small pool close to the road has attracted many waders and migrants in autumn and spring. The sea directly to the N and E of the end of the road can also hold good numbers of divers, grebes and scoters in winter.

Salterstown, to the W of Hermitage, is also a good place to watch for grebes, divers and scoter and is reached by returning to the main road from Hermitage, taking a right turn and continuing W for almost 3km. At the main crossroads, take a right onto the R166 and take a right turn less than 1km out this road. Follow this minor road down to the coast, and follow W along the shore for almost 2km until it then meets the R166. Any point along this coastal road can hold grebes, divers, ducks, geese and waders in winter.

At the point where the Salterstown circular coast road meets the R166, follow the R166 W along the coast. This is the coastal road to the village of **Annagassan**. Follow this road for over 1.5km, and, like the circular coastal road around Salterstown, this road offers excellent opportunities for seeing grebes, divers, ducks, geese and waders in winter. The R166 continues NW into the village of Castlebellingham.

Species
All year Cormorant, Shag.

Autumn, winter & spring Barnacle Goose (R), Brent Goose, Common Scoter, Eider (O), Long-tailed Duck (O), Red-breasted Merganser, Red-throated Diver, Great Northern Diver, Hen Harrier, Merlin, Buzzard, Peregrine, Golden Plover, Grey Plover, Lapwing, Knot, Little Stint (R autumn), Curlew Sandpiper (autumn), Dunlin, Whimbrel (spring), Spotted Redshank (R autumn & winter), Green Sandpiper (R autumn), Grey Phalarope (R autumn), Little Gull, Mediterranean Gull (R winter), Iceland Gull (R winter), Glaucous Gull (R winter), Short-eared Owl (winter), Whinchat (R autumn), Blackcap (R spring, O autumn), Whitethroat (O autumn), Reed Warbler (R autumn), Grasshopper Warbler (O spring) Brambling (R winter), Siskin, (O autumn & winter), Redpoll (O autumn).

Summer gulls, terns.

Rarities Dark-bellied Brent, King Eider, Surf Scoter, Velvet Scoter, Black-throated Diver, Red-necked Grebe, Slavonian Grebe, Red Kite, Little Ringed Plover, Long-tailed Skua, Water Pipit, Yellow Wagtail, Redstart, Twite, Snow Bunting.

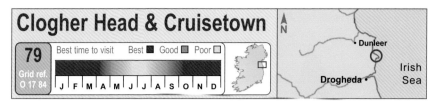

Clogher Head & Cruisetown

79

Grid ref.
O 17 84

Best time to visit   Best ■   Good ■   Poor □

J F M A M J J A S O N D

Dunleer

Drogheda •

Irish
Sea

A headland which can attract migrants in spring and autumn, and a nearby beach, good for gulls and other species, mainly in winter.

Clogher Head is a small headland with dense cover and several gardens that can attract small numbers of migrants in spring and autumn. A small fishing harbour can also attract gulls in winter while the headland itself offers good seawatching opportunities.

Just to the N are the long intertidal sandflats of **Cruisetown Strand**. This is excellent for gulls in winter. The Strand also attracts large numbers of Brent Geese and waders, especially Golden Plover, in autumn and winter, while the fields just inland from the Strand can hold Greylag Goose and Pink-footed Goose.

Offshore, divers, grebes and seaduck are present from the S end of the strand N to Dunany Point.

Togher Pond holds small numbers of ducks and waders in autumn and winter.

Directions Map 50, right. From Drogheda, follow the R167 E along the quays on N side of the Boyne River. The road swings left and then right, away from the quays and passes under the Boyne Viaduct. Approximately 3.5km out this road is a left turn, signposted for Clogher Head. At this point, you can take this left turn and, at the major crossroads over 1km along this road, take a right onto the R166 to Termonfeckin. Alternatively, you can continue along the coast road, past Baltray and follow the R167 inland from the coast until it meets the R166 at Termonfeckin. At the N end of Termonfeckin village, the R166 swings sharply right. From here follow the R166 for over 4km until you reach the village of Clogherhead.

Clogher Head From Clogherhead village, take the right turn half way up the hill in the village. Follow this winding road to the end and park in the large carpark to the right. The gardens close

to the carpark can hold migrants in spring and autumn, while a dense hedgerow from the W side of the carpark down to the road can also hold skulking migrants. At the S end of the carpark, there are several paths out across the headland.

Seawatching is best in autumn and winter, during NE, E or SE winds with rain, and can be done from the low rocky points just S of the carpark (see also SEAWATCHING, p.356). The harbour can sometimes attract Black Redstart in winter, while gulls can be found in small numbers along the

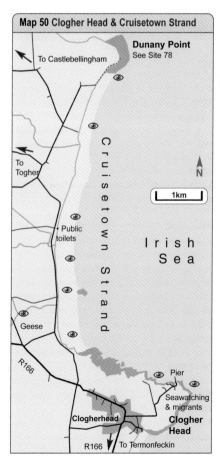

Map 50 Clogher Head & Cruisetown Strand

Dunany Point
See Site 78

To Castlebellingham

To Togher

Public toilets

Geese

R166

C r u i s e t o w n   S t r a n d

I r i s h
S e a

1km

Pier

Seawatching
& migrants

Clogherhead

**Clogher
Head**

R166   To Termonfeckin

East

107

Lapland Bunting

rocky beach under the factory just to W of the slipway below the carpark. The public toilet buildings above the harbour can also provide some shelter for seawatching in bad weather. Ireland's first Rock Thrush was found on Clogher Head in 1974.

Cruisetown Strand From Clogherhead village, go NW on the R166 for over 1.2km and, at the church, take the minor road to the right. This travels N to the strand. Just past the point where the beach comes into view on the right, a small stream enters the sea. This area is an excellent starting point when looking for gulls. Anywhere from this point N to the area past the public toilets almost 2.5km further on, affords excellent views of the beach. In autumn and winter, large numbers of Brent Geese, waders and gulls can be found anywhere along the strand. Offshore, divers, grebes, Common Scoter and Red-breasted Merganser are also found in winter. Greylag Geese can also be found in winter on the pastures just inland from the coast road. These flocks can move over a wide area. To check for these geese, take either the first or second left turns off the coast road. In recent years, Pink-footed Geese have been found with the geese flocks in this area.

In late summer and autumn, large numbers of terns can be found along the strand.

Togher Pond At the N end of the coast road, just past the public toilets, the road swings left and inland. 500m further on, the main road swings right at a minor T-junction. At this point, take a left turn and follow this road out for over 2km. At the next crossroads, take a left turn onto the R166. The small pond is visible on the left side. The area can be difficult to see well from the road. In winter, it holds small numbers of dabbling duck.

Species
All year Cormorant, Shag.

Autumn, winter & spring Whooper Swan (O), Pink-footed Goose (O), White-fronted Goose (R), Barnacle Goose (R), Brent Goose, Common Scoter, Eider (O), Long-tailed Duck (O), Red-breasted Merganser, Red-throated Diver, Great Northern Diver, Hen Harrier, Merlin, Buzzard, Peregrine, Golden Plover (1000s), Grey Plover, Lapwing, Knot, Little Stint (autumn), Curlew Sandpiper (autumn), Dunlin, Ruff (autumn), Jack Snipe (R winter), Whimbrel (O spring), Spotted Redshank (R autumn & winter), Green Sandpiper (R autumn), Wood Sandpiper (R autumn), Grey Phalarope (R autumn), Little Gull, Mediterranean Gull (autumn & winter), Ring-billed Gull (R winter), Iceland Gull (R winter), Glaucous Gull (R winter), Short-eared Owl (winter), Black Redstart (R winter), Redstart (R autumn), Whinchat (R autumn), Ring Ouzel (R autumn), Garden Warbler (R autumn), Blackcap (R spring, O autumn), Whitethroat (O autumn), Reed Warbler (R autumn), Spotted Flycatcher (autumn), Pied Flycatcher (R autumn), Brambling (R winter), Siskin, (O autumn & winter), Redpoll (O autumn).

Summer gulls, terns, Sedge Warbler, Chiffchaff, Willow Warbler, Wheatear.

Rarities Canada Goose, Dark-bellied Brent, Black Brant, Surf Scoter, Velvet Scoter, Black-throated Diver, Red-necked Grebe, Slavonian Grebe, Great Shearwater, Balearic Shearwater, Red Kite, American Golden Plover Long-tailed Skua, Franklin's Gull, Sabine's Gull, Yellow-legged Gull, Forster's Tern, Little Auk, Turtle Dove, Rock Thrush, Yellow-browed Warbler, Twite, Lapland Bunting, Snow Bunting.

Seawatching, autumn & winter Red-throated Diver, Great Northern Diver, Fulmar, Great Shearwater (R autumn), Sooty Shearwater (R autumn), Manx Shearwater, Balearic Shearwater (R autumn), Storm Petrel (O autumn), Gannet, Cormorant, Shag, Grey Phalarope (O autumn), Pomarine Skua, Arctic Skua, Long-tailed Skua (R autumn), Great Skua, Little Gull (R), Sabine's Gull (O Sept), Sandwich Tern (O autumn), Common Tern (O autumn), Arctic Tern (autumn), Guillemot, Razorbill, Black Guillemot (small numbers), Little Auk (R Oct onward).

North Boyne Estuary & Baltray

80
O 15 77

Best time to visit   Best ■ Good ▦ Poor ☐

J F M A M J J A S O N D

Drogheda •

An extensive intertidal mudflat that attracts large numbers of wildfowl and waders in autumn and winter. Birds move between Baltray and Mornington on the Meath side of the Boyne (see Site 81).

Directions Map 51, below. From Drogheda, follow the R167 E along the quays on north side of the Boyne River. The road swings left and then right, away from the quays and passes under the Boyne Viaduct. The estuary can be seen on the right at many points along this road, but note it is a very narrow and busy road, so parking can be difficult. Approximately 3.5km out this road is a left turn, signposted for Clogher Head. Ignore this turn and continue along the coast road for another 1.5km until you see a large parking area on the right opposite a row of houses. The estuary can be checked very well from this point. Continue along the road and take the right turn at the small bridge following signs for the golf course. There are several parking areas along this road where the mudflats are very easily watched. The small river that enters the estuary close to the bridge at the turn can be good for Little Egret. This small road becomes a track at the S end where the mouth of the estuary can be seen.

Species
Autumn, winter & spring Brent Goose, Red-breasted Merganser, Little Egret, Buzzard, Peregrine, Golden Plover (1000s), Grey Plover, Lapwing (1000s), Knot (1000s), Curlew Sandpiper (regular Sept), Dunlin (100s), Ruff (regular Sept), Jack Snipe (O winter), Black-tailed Godwit (100s), Whimbrel (regular spring), Curlew (100s), Spotted Redshank (R autumn & winter), Mediterranean Gull (O winter) Ring-billed Gull (R winter), Glaucous Gull (R winter), Kingfisher.

Rarities Dark-bellied Brent Goose, Green-winged Teal, Osprey, Avocet, American Golden Plover, Pectoral Sandpiper, Long-billed Dowitcher, Lesser Yellowlegs, Laughing Gull, Franklin's Gull, Yellow-legged Gull.

East

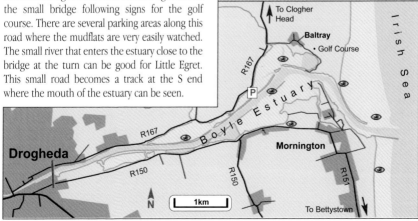

Map 51 The Boyne Estuary

To Clogher Head

Baltray
• Golf Course

R167

P

Boyle Estuary

Irish Sea

Drogheda

R167

R150

Mornington

R150

R151

N

1km

To Bettystown

109

Other sites

Just to the W of Drogheda, **Mell Quarry** (O 07 76) is a working quarry with a large pond that attracts small numbers of diving ducks such as Tufted Duck and Pochard each winter. Ring-necked Duck has been recorded on several occasions and Twite has also been seen. There are two smaller, inaccessible ponds further back in the quarry.

From Drogheda, follow the N1 over Boyle Bridge and continue up the hill, before taking a left turn onto the N51 at the traffic lights. Follow the N51 W for approximately 1km and Mell Quarry is on the right, surrounded by a high metal railing. The area can be quite muddy so boots may be required. The main pond is just inside the main gate and a path around the top gives views to the area below. A steep path runs down to the pond shore. At the time of writing, building works are encroaching on the area, so disturbance and development may result in birds moving to other wintering areas in the future.

Lying to the SE of Carlingford Lough, **Ballagan Point** (J 24 07) is a low-lying headland that juts out into the Irish Sea. In winter, the mudflats around the area are excellent for Brent Geese and waders, while the deeper waters offshore are good for divers and grebes. The area is also good for migrants in autumn and spring with common warblers, Wheatear and White Wagtail regularly seen. There are several gardens and small hedgerows that have, in the past, attracted rarities such as Ireland's second Radde's Warbler. Other birds seen here include Black Tern and Firecrest.

Ballagan Point is reached by taking the R173 from Dundalk, and then travelling NE on the R175 following signs for Carlingford. Less than 100m before the main left turn for Carlingford (R176) is a small turn to the right. Take this turn and then take the second right. This small road brings you into Ballytrasna and then follows the coast for almost 2km to Ballagan Point itself. The gardens and hedgerows anywhere along this road can hold migrants. Sedge Warbler are also found around the small ponds in summer. This area is under-watched and has excellent potential for producing more rare birds in the future.

In late summer, feeding flocks of Storm Petrel and Manx Shearwater are present offshore, while the Point also has excellent potential as a seawatching location in suitable conditions (see also SEAWATCHING, p.356).

County Meath

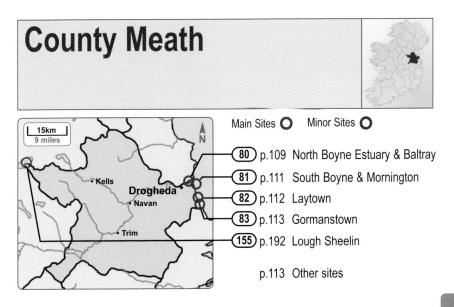

```
15km
9 miles
```

Kells
Drogheda
Navan
Trim

Main Sites ○   Minor Sites ○

(80) p.109 North Boyne Estuary & Baltray
(81) p.111 South Boyne & Mornington
(82) p.112 Laytown
(83) p.113 Gormanstown
(155) p.192 Lough Sheelin

p.113 Other sites

East

County Meath is a large and relatively flat county, bordered by counties Cavan, Monaghan, Louth, Dublin, Kildare, Offaly and Westmeath. It has a short coastline of approximately 10km, from the Boyne Estuary south to the Delvin River mouth. It is there that the most interesting birdwatching areas are concentrated.

There are also some small lakes of interest, distributed chiefly in the west and northwest of the county.

South Boyne & Mornington

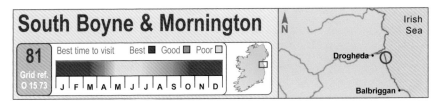

81

Grid ref.
O 15 73

Best time to visit   Best ■ Good ■ Poor □

J F M A M J J A S O N D

Drogheda

Balbriggan

Irish Sea

A tidal estuary which holds large numbers of waders, gulls and wildfowl in winter.

Directions Map 52, next page. From Drogheda, take the R150 E along the S side of the Boyne River. Continue for over 1.5km, under the Boyne Viaduct and pass the industrial buildings and gas holding station on the left. Immediately past the gas station is a large open pond which holds roosting gulls during high tide. Continue E on the R150 for another 2km until you reach Mornington. The tidal estuary can be viewed on the left side.

To view the outer sections of the estuary, continue E, taking the R151 for over 1.5km and take the first minor left turn. Follow this track for approximately 800m to the end. To view the S side of the mouth of the estuary, retrace your steps back to the R151 and continue E for another 400m and take the next left turn. Continue over the small river and either view from the tower immediately ahead or follow the road left to the end.

Species
Autumn, winter & spring Brent Goose, Redbreasted Merganser, Little Egret, Golden Plover (1000s), Grey Plover, Lapwing (1000s), Knot (1000s), Curlew Sandpiper (O Sept), Dunlin (100s), Ruff (O Sept), Jack Snipe (O winter), Black-tailed Godwit (100s), Whimbrel (spring),

111

Curlew (100s), Spotted Redshank (R autumn & winter), Mediterranean Gull (O winter) Ring-billed Gull (R winter), Iceland Gull (R winter), Glaucous Gull (R winter).

Rarities Dark-bellied Brent Goose, Green-winged Teal, Osprey, Avocet, American Golden Plover, Pectoral Sandpiper, Long-billed Dowitcher, Short-billed Dowitcher, Lesser Yellowlegs, Laughing Gull, Yellow-legged Gull.

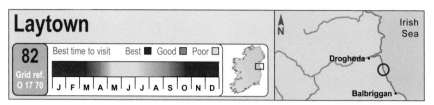

Laytown

82
Grid ref.
O 17 70

Best time to visit   Best ■ Good ▨ Poor ☐

J F M A M J J A S O N D

Irish Sea

Drogheda •

Balbriggan •

A beach and intertidal sandflats which hold good numbers of waders and Brent Geese in winter. Also attracts large numbers of Common Scoter offshore.

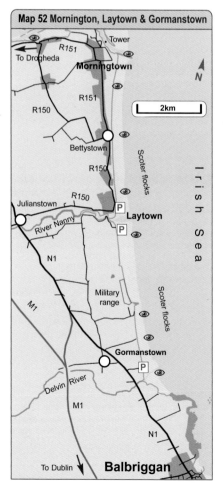

Map 52 Mornington, Laytown & Gormanstown

Tower
To Drogheda
R151
Morningtown
R151
R150
2km
Bettystown
R150
Scoter flocks
Irish Sea
Julianstown
R150
P
Laytown
River Nanny
P
N1
Military range
Scoter flocks
Gormanstown
P
Delvin River
M1
N1
To Dublin
Balbriggan

Directions Map 52, left. Situated 7km SE of Drogheda and 3km E of Julianstown on the R150. Follow the R150 from Julianstown along the River Nanny. Pass under the viaduct and park in the carpark of the public house on the right, just where the road swings left and N along the coast. The flocks of scoter can be checked from the small dunes just behind the public house.

To view the mudflats, continue N on the R150 checking the coastline for 1.8km as far as Bettystown. Scoter flocks also gather offshore and are best viewed from the parking area 400m N of Laytown.

Species
Autumn, winter & spring Brent Goose, Eider (R winter), Common Scoter (1000s), Velvet Scoter (O winter) Golden Plover (1000s), Lapwing (1000s), Knot (1000s), Curlew Sandpiper (R Sept), Dunlin (100s), Mediterranean Gull (R winter), Little Gull (R).

Rarities Dark-bellied Brent Goose, Surf Scoter.

Pied Wagtail

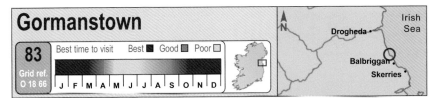

Gormanstown

83	Best time to visit	Best ■ Good ■ Poor □

Grid ref. O 18 66

J F M A M J J A S O N D

Drogheda • Irish Sea

Balbriggan • Skerries

A beach and intertidal sandflats which hold large numbers of gulls in winter. Also hold many terns, including small numbers of Roseate Terns in August and September, and large numbers of Common Scoter offshore in winter. There is a constant movement of birds along the coastal stretch from Laytown (Site 82) south to Gormanstown.

Directions Map 52, previous page. Situated on the Meath/Dublin border, 4.5km S of Laytown and 2.3km N of Balbriggan on the N1. From Balbriggan, head N for 2.3km and, as you cross the Delvin River, take an immediate right turn. Follow this road for 300m, pass under the viaduct and view the beach from the parking area. The Devlin River flows into the sea at this point and this area is excellent for gulls in winter. This point is also the best viewing area for flocks of terns, including Roseate Tern, in August and September.

To view the scoter flocks, return to the N1, and continue N for 500m and take the right turn signposted for the railway station. Follow this road over the railway bridge and view the sea from the dunes. Another good viewing point is reached by returning to the N1 and continuing N for 1km and taking the first right turn. Follow this road down for over 1.5km, under the viaduct, and follow the rough track down to the coast. A telescope is recommended. *It should be noted that the fields inside the dunes are used for military practice and are strictly private.*

Yellowhammer

Species

Autumn, winter & spring Brent Goose, Eider (R winter), Common Scoter (1000s), Velvet Scoter (O winter), Red-throated Diver, Curlew Sandpiper (R Sept), Dunlin (100s), Mediterranean Gull (regular autumn & winter), Little Gull (O), Roseate Tern (regular Aug & Sept), Yellowhammer (stubble fields).

Rarities Dark-bellied Brent Goose, Surf Scoter, Black-throated Diver, Red-necked Grebe, Grey Phalarope, Pomarine Skua, Arctic Skua, Franklin's Gull, Yellow-legged Gull, Elegant Tern.

Other sites

Donore Bog (O 04 70) is a small wetland lying approximately 1km S of Donore village on the Donore-Duleek road. The area can be viewed from a gate on the left side of the road. It has resident Water Rail and attracts small numbers of ducks and waders in winter. Quail has been recorded in the immediate area.

County Dublin

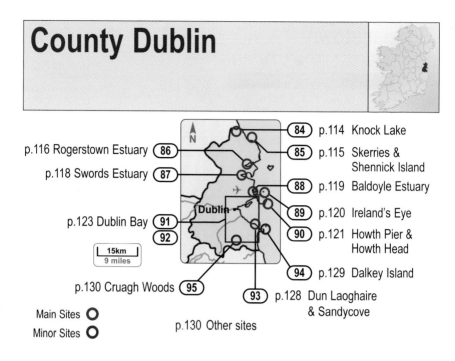

p.116 Rogerstown Estuary **86**

p.118 Swords Estuary **87**

p.123 Dublin Bay **91**
92

15km
9 miles

p.130 Cruagh Woods **95**

Main Sites **O**

Minor Sites **O**

p.130 Other sites

84 p.114 Knock Lake

85 p.115 Skerries & Shennick Island

88 p.119 Baldoyle Estuary

89 p.120 Ireland's Eye

90 p.121 Howth Pier & Howth Head

94 p.129 Dalkey Island

93 p.128 Dun Laoghaire & Sandycove

Situated on the east coast, County Dublin is one of the most productive birding counties in Ireland. Habitats vary from headlands and islands, to coastal estuaries and upland bog. While the suburbs of Dublin city (Ireland's capital city) are growing and spreading inland and north and south along the coast, green belts include the Phoenix Park and the National Botanic Gardens. Various rivers run down to the coast and these, along with the Royal and Grand Canals, provide good habitats for freshwater species such as Dipper and Kingfisher.

The wide estuaries of the North and South Dublin Bays hold large numbers of wildfowl, waders and gulls each winter, while the sea cliffs and islands of north County Dublin are important for breeding seabirds. Small islands off Skerries and Dalkey also have breeding terns, including Roseate Tern, each summer.

Knock Lake

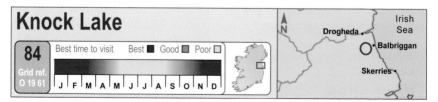

84

Grid ref. O 19 61

Best time to visit   Best ■ Good ■ Poor □

J F M A M J J A S O N D

Drogheda

Balbriggan

Skerries

Irish Sea

A small freshwater lake that holds small numbers of grebes and diving duck in winter.

Directions Map 53, next page. Knock Lake (also known as Knock Reservoir) is situated over 3km S of Balbriggan, and lies between the M1 and the

N1. From Dublin, take M1 N and take the first exit signposted for Balbriggan. Go over the M1 and follow the N1 for Balbriggan. Go straight through the small roundabout and take the next left turn, signposted for Bog of Ring. Continue for 100m and take the first right turn (the main road swings left). Continue for 250 m until you see the lake on the right side. The best viewing point is the gap in the trees at the bottom of the hill. The hide, situated on the S side of the lake, is open on occasions but a key is required to gain access if closed.

Species

Autumn, winter & spring Whooper Swan (R winter), Gadwall (R), Pochard, Tufted Duck, Scaup (O winter), Goldeneye (O winter), Little Grebe, Cormorant, Great Crested Grebe, Buzzard, Water Rail, Lapwing, Curlew, gulls, Redpoll (winter), Brambling (R winter).

Rarities Garganey, Lesser Scaup, Ring-necked Duck, Smew, Goosander, Ruddy Duck, Marsh Harrier, Montagu's Harrier, Osprey, Hobby.

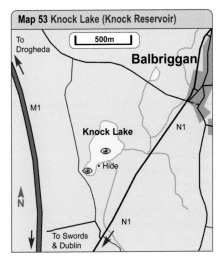

Map 53 Knock Lake (Knock Reservoir)

Skerries & Shennick Island

85
Grid ref.
O 25 60

Best time to visit   Best ■ Good ■ Poor □

J F M A M J J A S O N D

East

Irish Sea
Balbriggan •
• Skerries
Lusk •
• Rush
Swords •
• Malahide

A small coastal town with a stony, intertidal sandflat and small islands offshore. Attracts gulls in winter and large numbers of terns in summer and early autumn. Also good for seawatching in autumn.

Directions Map 54, right. Situated approximately 7km NE of Lusk. From the N1, take a right onto R127 signposted for Skerries, Rush and Lusk. Continue through Lusk, following the signs for Skerries and follow the R127 until the road goes under a narrow railway bridge. Immediately after the bridge is a small roundabout. To reach Skerries harbour, take the first exit. To view the South Beach, take the second exit and follow for 500m until you reach a small crossroads. Continue straight and follow this road for a further 500m until you meet the R128. Take a left and the beach can be viewed on the right.

Directly across from the South Beach is **Shennick Island**. At low tide this can be reached on foot. To reach Skerries Harbour, follow the R128 for 1km. To view the seaward side of Skerries, follow the road along the harbour, take a

Map 54 Skerries & Shennick Island

right at the end of the road and continue to the carpark near the Martello Tower on Red Island. From here, Colt Island and St Patrick's Island are offshore, while further out, the island of Rockabill is clearly visible. Red Island provides good seawatching during onshore winds, while the rocky area near the start of the beach is a site for Purple Sandpiper and Black Redstart in winter.

The small rocky islands N of Skerries are also worth checking for roosting gulls and terns. Follow the R127 N along the coast road to Balbriggan, checking the small islands on the right side. Approximately 3.5km N of Skerries is a large rocky area (an island at high tide), locally named Long Leg. In late summer and autumn, this attracts large numbers of roosting terns (including small numbers of Roseate Tern) and gulls.

Species

All year Fulmar, Cormorant, Shag, Peregrine, Kittiwake.

Autumn, winter & spring White-fronted Goose (R), Barnacle Goose (O), Brent Goose, Scaup (O), Common Scoter, Eider (O), Red-breasted Merganser, Red-throated Diver, Great Northern Diver, Merlin, Buzzard, Golden Plover (100s), Grey Plover, Lapwing, Knot, Purple Sandpiper, Dunlin, Jack Snipe (R winter), Snipe, Black-tailed Godwit, Bar-tailed Godwit, Whimbrel (O spring and autumn), Grey Phalarope (R autumn), Mediterranean Gull (autumn & winter), Ring-billed Gull (R winter), Iceland Gull (O winter), Glaucous Gull (O winter), Short-eared Owl (winter), Black Redstart (winter), Redstart (R autumn), Blackcap (winter), Whitethroat (O autumn),

Summer Sandwich, Common Tern, Arctic Tern, Roseate Tern.

Rarities Pink-footed Goose, Dark-bellied Brent, Surf Scoter, Velvet Scoter, White-billed Diver, Black-throated Diver, Red-necked Grebe, Balearic Shearwater, Great White Egret, Spoonbill, Osprey, Long-tailed Skua, Sabine's Gull, Bonaparte's Gull, Kumlien's Gull, Forster's Tern, Black Tern, Sooty Tern, Little Auk, Hoopoe, Yellow Wagtail, Carrion Crow, Rose-coloured Starling, Lapland Bunting, Snow Bunting, Balck-headed Bunting (Rockabill).

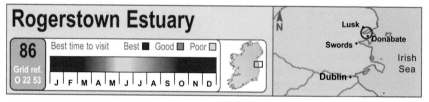

Rogerstown Estuary

86

Grid ref.
O 22 53

Best time to visit   Best ■ Good ■ Poor □

J F M A M J J A S O N D

N

Lusk

Swords •   Donabate

Dublin •

Irish Sea

A tidal estuary which holds large numbers of waders and wildfowl in winter. One of the best Irish sites for Green Sandpiper in autumn, and also attracts rare waders, wildfowl and gulls in autumn and winter.

Directions Map 55, next page. For the **S side** of the estuary, from Dublin, take the M1 N and take the exit signposted for Skerries, Donabate and Rush. At double roundabouts, follow signs for Skerries and Donabate. Continue N on the N1 for 1km and 500m after the end of the dual carriageway, take the second right turn signposted R126, Portrane and Donabate. At the T-junction take a left and head E for approx 600m. Take a left turn after the sign indicating 'Rogerstown Estuary Hide'. Follow the track past the tall trees on right and continue for 200m before taking a right turn. Continue on main track for approx 1km, past the allotments on the left and then open farmland on right. The track

swings sharp left. Continue for 200m to reach the South Hide. The hide is open at weekends from October to March. Good views of the **inner estuary** can be had from the hide area. The 'Flooded Field' directly across from the hide is also worth checking for wildfowl, waders and for roosting gulls.

Green Sandpipers are regularly found from August to October on the inner channels W of the hide. Backtrack to the point where you took the right turn, having passed the tall trees near the entrance. Take a right and continue for 100m to the gate. Continue along the track to an area of open rough ground and head N until the river is visible. Green Sandpipers are found on the exposed mud at low tide and on the small pool to the W of the rough ground.

The **outer estuary** is reached by returning to the R126, turning left, and continuing for 2km to

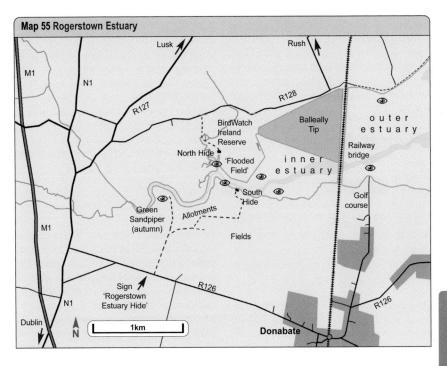

Map 55 Rogerstown Estuary

Lusk

Rush

M1

N1

R127

R128

BirdWatch
Ireland
Reserve

Balleally
Tip

o u t e r
e s t u a r y

North Hide

'Flooded
Field'

i n n e r
e s t u a r y

Railway
bridge

Green
Sandpiper
(autumn)

Allotments

South
Hide

Golf
course

M1

Fields

Sign
'Rogerstown
Estuary Hide'

R126

N1

R126

Dublin

N

1km

Donabate

Donabate. On the far side of Donabate village is a left turn signposted for Beaverstown Golf Course. Take this road for 1.5km, pass the entrance to the golf course and continue until the road ends at a barrier. Continue for 300m down the track where the estuary can be viewed.

For the N side, from the N1, take a right onto R127 signposted for Skerries, Rush and Lusk. Continue for 400m and take the first right turn signposted for Balleally. Continue for approx 1.4km until you reach a row of bungalows on the right. Park at the gate on the right, marked Birdwatch Ireland Reserve. Follow the track for 500m through the trees and across the open fields to reach the North Hide, which remains open at all times. Look SE from the hide to view the 'Flooded Field'. The channels in front of the hide are also good for Green Sandpiper and Kingfisher.

The outer estuary can also be reached by returning to the R128 and continuing on for a further 1.5km until you reach the entrance to Balleally Tip. Continue past the entrance and follow the rough track under the railway bridge (note this track can be flooded in winter). The outer estuary can be viewed from here and by

following the track for a further 500m. Alternatively, return to the R127 and continue for 2.5km to Lusk. Take the R128 to Rush. After approximately 2.5km you will see a large old mill on the left. 100m past this is a right turn onto Spout Road. Take this right turn and continue for 500m until you reach the estuary. Follow the track right to view the estuary or continue a further 300m along the road to the pier to view the mouth of the estuary.

Species

Autumn, winter & spring Greylag Goose, Brent Goose, Pintail, Shoveler, Goldeneye, Red-breasted Merganser, Little Egret, Buzzard, Golden Plover (1000s), Grey Plover, Lapwing (1000s), Knot (1000s), Curlew Sandpiper (Sept), Dunlin (1000s), Ruff (Sept), Jack Snipe (O winter), Black-tailed Godwit (100s), Whimbrel (spring), Curlew (1000s), Spotted Redshank (R autumn & winter), Green Sandpiper (autumn), Wood Sandpiper (R autumn), Mediterranean Gull (O winter) Ring-billed Gull (R winter), Glaucous Gull (O winter), Short-eared Owl (winter), Kingfisher, Blackcap (spring, breeds in woodland near S Hide), Brambling (O winter), Yellowhammer.

117

Rarities Dark-bellied Brent, Black Brant, American Wigeon, Green-winged Teal, American Black Duck, Blue-winged Teal, Red Kite, Goshawk, Osprey, Gyr Falcon, Corncrake, Avocet, American Golden Plover, Semipalmated Sandpiper, Least Sandpiper, White-rumped Sandpiper, Baird's Sandpiper, Pectoral Sandpiper (annual), Buff-breasted Sandpiper, Long-billed Dowitcher, Lesser Yellowlegs, Laughing Gull, American Herring Gull, Yellow-legged Gull, Caspian Gull, Red-throated Pipit, Water Pipit, Lapland Bunting.

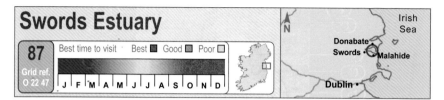

Swords Estuary

87

Grid ref.
O 22 47

Best time to visit · Best ■ Good ■ Poor □

J F M A M J J A S O N D

N

Irish Sea

Donabate
Swords • Malahide

Dublin •

A large estuary which holds important numbers of waders and Brent Geese in winter. Also attracts rare waders, wildfowl and gulls in spring, autumn and winter.

Directions Map 56, below. From Dublin, take the M1 N and the exit signposted for Skerries, Donabate and Rush. At the roundabout go left, signposted for Swords. Continue SW on N1 for 1km and go left at Estuary Roundabout. To view the S side of the estuary, follow the road for 300m and take a right turn at Estuary Road. Continue for 600m, under the M1 bridge. At the small roundabout, continue E for less than 50m and park in to

the right near the Dog Kennels. Note: parking is very restricted in this area so an alternative option would be to continue E for 600m and park in the first layby on left. From Dublin Airport, go N on N1 and take a right at Seatown Road Roundabout. Continue for 500m and take the second exit (straight) at the next roundabout. Continue for 300m to reach the small roundabout near the Dog Kennels as above. To view the open water, continue E and park at any of the laybys on the left.

To view the N side of the estuary, do not take the right at Estuary Road but continue over a small

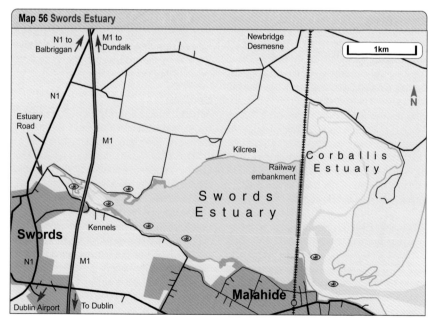

Map 56 Swords Estuary

N1 to Balbriggan
M1 to Dundalk
Newbridge Desmesne
1km
N1
N
Estuary Road
M1
Kilcrea
Railway embankment
Corballis Estuary
Swords
Kennels
Swords Estuary
N1
M1
Malahide
Dublin Airport   To Dublin

bridge and follow the road right. Continue along this road and under the M1 bridge. The tidal estuary can be checked on the right side. To view the open estuary, continue for 1km to the end of the road and check the open water from the slipway. At low tide, a track continues E for 2km from the slipway to the railway embankment. Alternatively, backtrack to the N1 and from the Estuary Roundabout, continue N for 1km. At the double roundabouts, take the exit signposted for Donabate. Follow this road for 200m and take the first right turn. Follow this winding road for 300m, continuing right on the T-junction. Continue on this road for 1.5km to reach a viewing point. To view the area further E, backtrack to main road and continue for 2.4km past the entrance to Newbridge Demesne and take the next right turn signposted Kilcrea. Continue for 1km to reach viewing point.

The **Corballis Estuary** can be checked by returning to the main road and continue E for 100m and take a right turn following the signs for the golf courses. Continue on the road for 750m, going under the railway bridge and viewing the estuary on the right side. The mudflats can be viewed from this road for over 1.5km.

Species
All year Kingfisher, Tree Sparrow.

Autumn, winter & spring Brent Goose, Pochard (100s), Goldeneye (100s), Red-breasted Merganser, Great Crested Grebe, Slavonian Grebe (R winter), Little Egret, Buzzard, Golden Plover (1000s), Grey Plover, Lapwing (1000s), Knot (1000s), Little Stint (Sept), Curlew Sandpiper (Sept), Dunlin (1000s), Ruff (Sept), Black-tailed Godwit (100s), Whimbrel (spring), Spotted Redshank (R autumn & winter), Green Sandpiper (O autumn), Wood Sandpiper (R autumn), Mediterranean Gull (O winter), Little Gull (O).

Summer Black-tailed Godwit, gulls.

Rarities Dark-bellied Brent, Black Brant, Green-winged Teal, Garganey, Ring-necked Duck, Smew, Goosander, Leach's Petrel, Osprey, Avocet, Little Ringed Plover, American Golden Plover, Pacific Golden Plover, Semipalmated Sandpiper, White-rumped Sandpiper, Pectoral Sandpiper, Buff-breasted Sandpiper, Long-billed Dowitcher, Short-billed Dowitcher, Lesser Yellowlegs, Wilson's Phalarope, Laughing Gull, Franklin's Gull, Bonaparte's Gull, Yellow-legged Gull, White-winged Black Tern, Bee-eater, Pine Bunting.

East

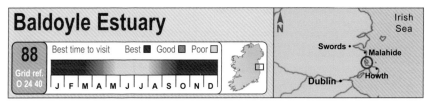

A large, narrow tidal estuary, protected from the sea by a sand-dune system. The area holds good numbers of Brent Geese and waders each winter.

Directions Map 88, next page. Situated S of Portmarnock, Baldoyle Estuary stretches S to Sutton and E to the West Pier at Howth. From Portmarnock, follow the R106 SW until the small roundabout. Take a left at this roundabout and continue on the R106 for approximately 1km. The road goes over a small bridge where the Mayne River flows into the estuary. The muddy banks of the river often attract Green Sandpipers in

autumn and winter. This area also affords good views of the mudflats at low tide.

Continue on the R106 to Baldoyle village, and just after the church, take a left along the R106 coast road to Sutton. The walkway that runs along the estuary continues onto Cush Point at Sutton. To view the outer part of the estuary, continue on the R106 for over 1km to the major crossroads where the R106 meets the R105. Take a left and follow the R105 for 2.5km to Howth village. Along this route there are limited viewing locations due to the railway tracks that run parallel to the road. Take a left onto the West Pier at Howth and view

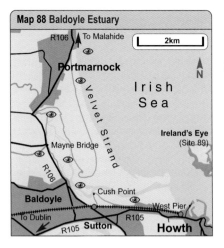

Map 88 Baldoyle Estuary

Irish Sea

To Malahide

Portmarnock

Velvet Strand

Mayne Bridge

R106

R105

Baldoyle

To Dublin

Sutton

Cush Point

West Pier

Howth

Ireland's Eye
(Site 89)

2km

N

from the open area at the base of the pier and also from the back of the wall at the top end of the pier.

The seaward side of Baldoyle can be viewed by walking the Velvet Strand from Portmarnock.

Species

All year Cormorant, Shag, Kingfisher.

Autumn, winter & spring Brent Goose (1000s), Wigeon, Teal, Shoveler, Eider (R winter), Common Scoter, Red-breasted Merganser, Red-throated Diver, Great Northern Diver, Little Egret (O winter), Golden Plover (1000s), Grey Plover (100s), Lapwing, Knot, Sanderling, Little Stint (R autumn) Curlew Sandpiper (R autumn), Dunlin (1000s), Ruff (R autumn), Jack Snipe (winter), Snipe, Black-tailed Godwit, Bar-tailed Godwit, Whimbrel (spring & autumn), Spotted Redshank (R autumn & winter), Green Sandpiper (O autumn & winter), Mediterranean Gull (R autumn & winter), Ring-billed Gull (R winter), Iceland Gull (R winter), Glaucous Gull (R winter), Short-eared Owl (winter), Black Redstart (R winter).

Summer Common Sandpiper, terns.

Rarities Dark-bellied Brent, Black Brant, Velvet Scoter, Goosander, Black-throated Diver, Red-necked Grebe, Slavonian Grebe, Black-winged Stilt, Avocet, Lapland Bunting, Snow Bunting.

Ireland's Eye

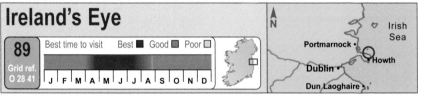

89	Best time to visit	Best ■ Good ▨ Poor ☐												
Grid ref. O 28 41	J	F	M	A	M	J	J	A	S	O	N	D		

Portmarnock •

Irish Sea

Dublin •

Howth

Dun Laoghaire •

N

A small island with grassy slopes, steep cliffs and a sea stack just offshore, which holds large numbers of breeding seabirds in summer, including a Gannet colony. In winter, Brent and occasionally Greylag Geese can be seen from the mainland.

Directions Map 58, right. Lying just N of Howth, the only access to Ireland's Eye is by boat. A regular small boat service runs during the summer months from the East Pier in Howth Harbour. The landing point is on the NW corner of the island, close to the Martello Tower. From here, follow the narrow, rough path E along the N end of the island. As the path climbs, several vantage points afford good view over the cliffs. The area just E of the Martello Tower is the best area to see Puffin in summer. *Care should be taken to avoid walking*

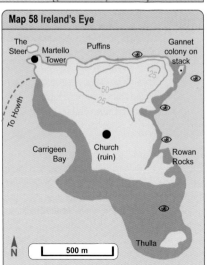

Map 58 Ireland's Eye

The Steer

Martello Tower

Puffins

Gannet colony on stack

To Howth

Carrigeen Bay

Church (ruin)

Rowan Rocks

Thulla

500 m

N

on eggs and chicks as this path leads through a colony of Great Black-backed Gulls and Herring Gulls. Continue to the NE corner (and the highest point of the island) where a sea stack just offshore holds breeding auks and Gannets. From here, a path continues S and eventually leads to the beach on the W side of the island. Following the path N brings you back to the Martello Tower. Ringed Plovers and Oystercatchers nest on the beach so *care should be taken to avoid nests when walking the beach.*

It is worth asking the boatman to bring the boat around the island on the return journey. This provides excellent views of the breeding seabird cliffs and the Gannet colony. It should be noted that the paths on Ireland's Eye are frequently overgrown by bracken in summer and that *in wet weather, great care needs to be taken along the cliff paths.*

Species
All year Fulmar, Cormorant, Shag.

Autumn, winter & spring Greylag Goose (winter), Barnacle Goose (R), Brent Goose, Wigeon, Red-breasted Merganser (O), Red-throated Diver, Great Northern Diver, Hen Harrier (R winter), Merlin, Buzzard (R winter), Snipe, Mediterranean Gull (R autumn & winter), Iceland Gull (R winter), Glaucous Gull (R winter), Short-eared Owl (winter), Black Redstart (R winter), Whinchat (R autumn), Ring Ouzel (R spring & autumn), Grasshopper Warbler (O spring), Chiffchaff (spring & autumn), Willow Warbler (spring & autumn), Pied Flycatcher (R autumn).

Summer Manx Shearwater, Gannet (100s nest), Lesser Black-backed Gull, Herring Gull, Great Black-backed Gull, Kittiwake, Sandwich Tern, Common Tern, Arctic Tern, Guillemot, Razorbill, Black Guillemot, Puffin, Sedge Warbler, Whitethroat.

Rarities Canada Goose, Dark-bellied Brent, Turtle Dove, Wryneck, Lesser Whitethroat, Carrion Crow.

East

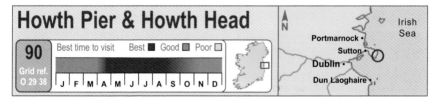

Howth Pier & Howth Head

90 Best time to visit   Best ■ Good ■ Poor □

Grid ref.
O 29 38 | J | F | M | A | M | J | J | A | S | O | N | D |

Irish Sea
Portmarnock •
Sutton •
Dublin •
Dun Laoghaire •

Howth is a small fishing village with several piers and a small sheltered harbour. Black Guillemots breed inside the harbour. To the south and above the village is Howth Head which has cliff walks. The steep cliffs attract large numbers of breeding seabirds each spring and summer, while the headland has proved to be good for migrants in spring and autumn.

Directions Map 59, next page. From Baldoyle, continue on the R106 for over 1km to the major crossroads (Sutton Crossroads) where the R106 meets the R105. Take a left and follow the R105 for 2.5km to Howth village.

At **Howth Village**, the first pier, the **West Pier**, has several fish processing plants and is good for

gulls in winter. Follow the pier out to the tip and check the inner harbour for Black Guillemots. Ireland's Eye can also be viewed from the tip of the West Pier.

At the **East Pier**, the inner harbour can be viewed from various points along the pier, while the small rocky beach just behind the public toilets often attract Black Redstarts in winter.

Howth Head From the East Pier in the village, follow the narrow coastal road uphill for 1km to the large carpark at Balscadden. From the carpark, follow the rough track uphill and follow the cliff walk. This narrow track runs for almost 3km around the headland from Balscadden carpark to the Bailey Lighthouse on the southern tip. In summer, the breeding seabird colonies can be

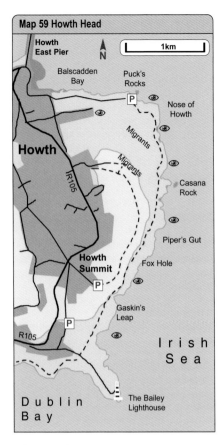

Map 59 Howth Head

Howth East Pier

N

1km

Balscadden Bay

Puck's Rocks

P

Nose of Howth

Howth

Migrants

R105

Migrants

Casana Rock

Piper's Gut

Howth Summit

Fox Hole

P

Gaskin's Leap

P

R105

Irish Sea

Dublin Bay

The Bailey Lighthouse

be good for migrants, while the stand of trees past the row of houses on the right are also good. Follow the road past the side of houses and follow the small track that runs uphill to the left. *It should be noted that access to many parts of the head is restricted.*

Howth Summit also has a good pathway. To reach the summit carpark, return to the R105, and follow the road uphill from Howth for approximately 1.8km. Follow the road left into the carpark. A path runs N from the carpark for over 1km. The hedges and short grass along this path are good for Wheatears in spring and autumn, as well as pipits.

Species
All year Fulmar, Cormorant, Shag, Peregrine, Black Guillemot.

Autumn, winter & spring Red-throated Diver, Great Northern Diver, Hen Harrier (R winter), Merlin, Mediterranean Gull (winter), Iceland Gull (R winter), Glaucous Gull (R winter), Short-eared Owl (winter), Black Redstart (winter), Whinchat (R autumn), Wheatear (autumn & spring) Ring Ouzel (R spring & autumn), Grasshopper Warbler (O spring), Reed Warbler (O autumn), Garden Warbler (R spring, O autumn), Blackcap (R spring, O autumn, R winter), Chiffchaff (spring & autumn), Willow Warbler (spring & autumn), Spotted Flycatcher (autumn), Pied Flycatcher (R autumn), Brambling (R winter), Snow Bunting (R winter).

Summer Manx Shearwater, Gannet, Lesser Black-backed Gull, Herring Gull, Great Black-backed Gull, Kittiwake, Sandwich Tern, Common Tern, Arctic Tern, Guillemot, Razorbill, Black Guillemot, Puffin, Sedge Warbler, Whitethroat.

Rarities Velvet Scoter, Great Shearwater, Sooty Shearwater, Balearic Shearwater, Long-tailed Skua, Laughing Gull, Little Auk, Turtle Dove, Pallid Swift, Bee-eater, Hoopoe, Wryneck, Great Spotted Woodpecker, Shore Lark, Tree Pipit, Lesser Whitethroat, Pallas's Warbler, Yellow-browed Warbler, Radde's Warbler, Firecrest, Red-breasted Flycatcher, Woodchat Shrike, Carrion Crow, Crossbill, Lapland Bunting, Snow Bunting.

viewed from various places along the path, especially along the first 1.5km of its length.

In spring and autumn, migrants can be anywhere on the headland, most often after strong E, SE or S winds with rain. One of the better locations is close to the start of the cliff path. Just where the path runs past the Nose of Howth, and brings you up several steps, is a small track to the right. This leads you into a small overgrown valley. This track runs S. An overgrown area above the valley close to ruined houses is also a good area to check.

Another good area for migrants can be found by returning to the carpark and, following the coastal road back towards the village, take the first left turn. Continue up this road and, at the cross-roads, go left and drive to the end. There are several gardens at the end of this road which can

Dublin Bay

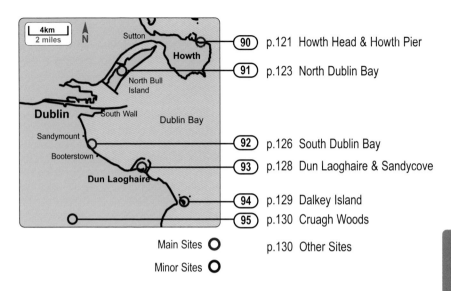

90	p.121 Howth Head & Howth Pier
91	p.123 North Dublin Bay
92	p.126 South Dublin Bay
93	p.128 Dun Laoghaire & Sandycove
94	p.129 Dalkey Island
95	p.130 Cruagh Woods
	p.130 Other Sites

Main Sites ○

Minor Sites ○

Dublin Bay is a large, shallow bay with intertidal sand and mudflats. The rivers Liffey, Tolka and Dodder feed into the bay and the entire area extends from Sutton south to Dun Laoghaire Pier. The bay holds internationally important numbers of wildfowl and waders each winter. It is also superb for gulls in winter and terns in summer. The bay is separated into two distinct sections, North Dublin Bay and South Dublin Bay.

North Dublin Bay includes Sutton, Dollymount Strand and the North Bull Island.

This is primarily intertidal mudflats. However, the beach on the North Bull Island consists of intertidal sandflats, while an extensive saltmarsh and sand dune system is also present.

South Dublin Bay extends from where the River Liffey enters the sea at the South Wall and encompasses the vast intertidal sandflats of Sandymount Strand which stretches south to Dun Laoghaire. The small marsh at Booterstown is also included in the South Dublin Bay area.

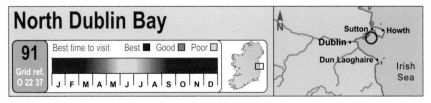

An extensive area of intertidal mudflats, sandflats and open sea which holds internationally important numbers of wildfowl and waders each winter.

The North Bull Island is over 5km long at low tide, and has a large saltmarsh and sand dune system. At high tide, most waders roost on the saltmarsh of the North Bull Island. The harbour to the S of the North Wall is good for grebes in winter and terns in summer. The area also holds large numbers of gulls in winter. The North Bull Island is best watched on a rising tide when birds are forced close to the road and causeway which runs from the main road onto the island.

Directions Map 60, below.

North Bull Island From Dublin, follow the R105 N out of Dublin, following signs for Fairview, Clontarf and Howth. At Fairview, at the point where the R105 swings left, continue straight and follow the coast road. Follow this road out through Clontarf for over 3km until you see the North Bull Island on the right. There are two access points onto the North Bull. The first is a narrow Wooden Bridge which runs onto the North Wall, also known as the Bull Wall. The second is a long causeway from the main road onto the island approximately 1.5km further N.

The mudflats from Clontarf to the Wooden Bridge can hold large numbers of Brent Geese, ducks, waders and gulls in winter. To reach the **Bull Wall** or **North Wall**, turn right off the coast road and cross the Wooden Bridge. The area to the left of the bridge is excellent for waders and gulls on the rising tide and can be viewed well from the parking area near the houses on the left. A small track runs from behind the houses out onto the saltmarsh.

To reach the beach at the SW end of **Dollymount Strand**, follow the road out and, where it ends, continue left down onto the beach. The beach is used by the public but the area where the beach meets the North Wall, and along the tideline, can be very good for waders and gulls in winter. The harbour on the right can be viewed from any point from the Wooden Bridge to the end of the road and is good for grebes and Goldeneye in winter. Terns can be seen well from this road in summer. The North Wall continues for 500m as a

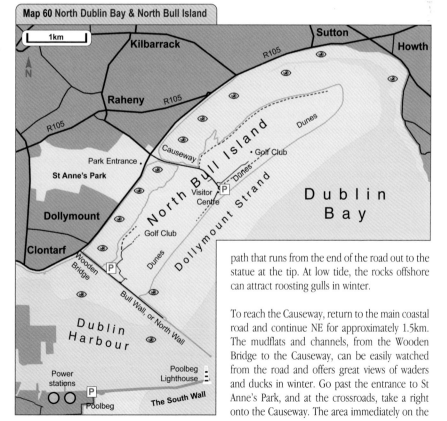

Map 60 North Dublin Bay & North Bull Island

path that runs from the end of the road out to the statue at the tip. At low tide, the rocks offshore can attract roosting gulls in winter.

To reach the Causeway, return to the main coastal road and continue NE for approximately 1.5km. The mudflats and channels, from the Wooden Bridge to the Causeway, can be easily watched from the road and offers great views of waders and ducks in winter. Go past the entrance to St Anne's Park, and at the crossroads, take a right onto the Causeway. The area immediately on the

Brent Goose

left (on the N side of the causeway) is a favoured roosting and washing site for gulls in the evening, while either side of the entire length of the Causeway gives excellent opportunities for viewing geese, ducks and waders in winter. On a rising tide, the last area of mud to be covered is on the far left side of the Causeway, where the mudflats and saltmarsh meet. The saltmarsh on either side can be accessed from the Causeway but on the left side of the Causeway, a small track runs NE along a wire fence beside the golf course. This continues out for over 2km to the tip of the North Bull. Past the golf course is an area of small trees and hedges which can be good for migrants in autumn. The small posts visible on the marsh on the N side of the Causeway are often used as perching posts by Merlins and Peregrines in winter. To reach the beach, continue to the end of the road and, at the roundabout, take the first exit to the beach. From here, you can walk the entire length of the beach to either end of the island. The North Bull Island also has an Interpretive Centre that is situated to the right side of the roundabout. This centre is open to the public.

To view the mudflats to the N of the Causeway, you can continue NE along the coastal road. The road rejoins the R105 and continues on to Sutton and Howth. A path runs alongside the mudflats for over 3km from the Causeway to Sutton and the channels and mudflats along this path hold large numbers of geese, ducks and waders in winter.

For **Sutton**, continue NE past the North Bull Island on the R105, and, at the major crossroads, take a right turn. Follow this road SE for almost 1km and take the first right turn. This small road

runs opposite the NE tip of the North Bull Island, and, at low tide, geese, ducks and waders can be easily seen from any point along here. Follow the road out and park at the large parking area on the right. The deep channels that run out past the North Bull Island can be good for grebes and Goldeneye in winter. Divers are usually present further out to sea from this point.

Species
Autumn, winter & spring Brent Goose (1000s), Wigeon (1000+), Gadwall, Teal (1000+), Pintail (400+), Shoveler (100s), Scaup (R winter), Eider (R winter), Goldeneye, Common Scoter, Red-breasted Merganser, Red-throated Diver, Great Northern Diver, Great Crested Grebe, Little Egret (autumn & winter), Hen Harrier (R autumn & winter), Merlin, Buzzard (R), Peregrine, Golden Plover (1000s), Grey Plover (1000+), Lapwing (100s), Knot (4000+), Little Stint (autumn), Curlew Sandpiper (autumn), Dunlin (9000+), Ruff (autumn), Jack Snipe (O winter), Snipe, Black-tailed Godwit, Bar-tailed Godwit, Whimbrel (spring & autumn), Spotted Redshank (R autumn & winter), Green Sandpiper (R autumn), Wood Sandpiper (R autumn), Grey Phalarope (R autumn), Mediterranean Gull (autumn & winter), Ring-billed Gull (winter), Iceland Gull (R winter), Glaucous Gull (R winter), Short-eared Owl (winter), Kingfisher (winter).

Summer Manx Shearwater (evenings, well offshore), Common Sandpiper, gulls, terns, Wheatear.

Rarities Dark-bellied Brent, Black Brant, American Wigeon, Green-winged Teal, American Black Duck, Garganey, Blue-winged Teal, Velvet Scoter, Red-necked Grebe, Slavonian Grebe, Black-necked Grebe, Leach's Petrel, Spoonbill, Quail, Osprey, Hobby, Gyr Falcon, Black-winged Stilt, Avocet, Little Ringed Plover, Killdeer, American Golden Plover, Semipalmated Sandpiper, Pectoral Sandpiper, Buff-breasted Sandpiper, Short-billed Dowitcher, Long-billed Dowitcher, Lesser Yellowlegs, Wilson's Phalarope, Laughing Gull, American Herring Gull, Yellow-legged Gull, Forster's Tern, Black Tern, White-winged Black Tern, Little Auk, Turtle Dove, Alpine Swift, Red-backed Shrike, Great Grey Shrike, Carrion Crow, Twite, Lapland Bunting, Snow Bunting.

East

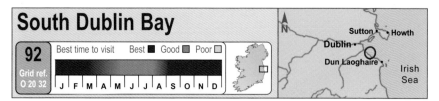

South Dublin Bay

92
Grid ref.
O 20 32

Best time to visit   Best ■ Good ■ Poor □

J F M A M J J A S O N D

Sutton • Howth
Dublin •
Dun Laoghaire •
Irish
Sea

An extensive area of intertidal sandflats and open sea which holds internationally important numbers of wildfowl and waders each winter. Sandymount Strand holds large numbers of gulls in winter, and is also an evening roosting site for terns in autumn.

The South Wall is over 2km long, and grebes, ducks and gulls can be seen well from any point from the base to the small lighthouse at the tip. Sandymount is best watched on a rising tide when birds are forced close inshore and one of the best locations is at the Merrion Gates. The small marsh at Booterstown lies just in from the coast and is used both as a roosting site for waders and gulls at high tide, but also by more freshwater species such as Snipe and Water Rail.

Directions Map 61, next page.

The South Wall From Dublin, follow E along the N side of the River Liffey for almost 2km following signs for 'The Point' theatre and the Eastlink Toll Bridge. At the end of the road is a roundabout. Go right, over the river and through the toll booths (Euro currency only accepted). You are now on the S side of the river. Follow this road, the R131, to the next roundabout and take the second exit (straight). Continue on this road for less than 200m and take the first left turn. This will bring you past container depots. Follow the road as it swings right and continue past the old sewerage treatment plant on the left and the new plant on the right. The road swings right past the entrance to the power station and then goes left before it runs along Sandymount Strand. At high tide, the area along this road offers good vantage points for seeing Brent Geese and waders. Continue along this road to the end, where it goes onto the South Wall. There is a parking area 200m along the wall. The inner harbour and the sea can be viewed from the entire length of the wall. The inner harbour at the base of the South Wall is excellent for gulls which feed just offshore in winter. Terns move upriver in summer and can be seen well

from anywhere along the South Wall. The sandflats on the coastal side of the South Wall are also good for waders at high tide in winter. It should be noted that during exceptionally high spring tides, part of the middle section of the wall can be submerged for short periods, leaving the tip of the South Wall cut off from the rest.

Sandymount Strand & Merrion Gates From the Eastlink Toll Bridge, follow the R131 along the S side of the river and at the roundabout, take the third exit, following signs for Dun Laoghaire. Follow this road for over 500m and, at the major junction, go left and follow the R131 SE. This road can also be reached from Dublin by following the road along the S side of the River Liffey, and taking a right just past the Ferryman pub. At the next crossroads, take a left and follow signs for Irishtown, Ringsend and Dun Laoghaire.

The R131 runs SE along Sandymount Strand and there are several carparks along this stretch of the road. A path also runs along the coast on this section. At high tide, anywhere along here is good for seeing geese, waders and gulls in winter. However, the best high tide vantage point is at the Merrion Gates. Continue SE past the Martello Tower. The strand is always visible on the left but towards the end of the road, the road runs slightly inland past a row of houses on the left. Just past these houses, the road crosses train tracks with large automatic railway gates. This is the area known as the **Merrion Gates**. Park close to the houses. Just at the gates is a small entrance to the strand. On a rising tide, this is one of the best areas for viewing waders and gulls in autumn and winter. Evening roosts of terns gather in this area in late summer/early autumn. 500m S of this area is a small river outflow. This can give a high vantage point over the area and it can sometimes be worthwhile positioning yourself at this point over one hour before high tide. Waders and gulls can give superb views as they wash and feed here. Further S again is a sand spit. Waders use this for a high tide roost and it can also be good for pipits

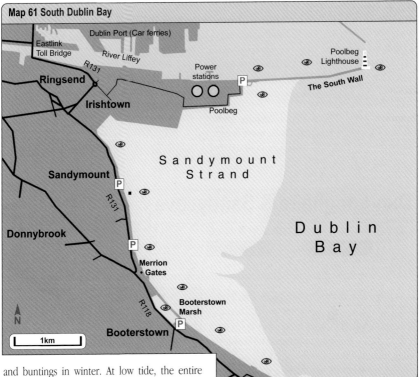

Map 61 South Dublin Bay

Dublin Port (Car ferries)

Eastlink
Toll Bridge
River Liffey

Poolbeg
Lighthouse

R131

Ringsend

Power
stations

The South Wall

Irishtown

Poolbeg

S a n d y m o u n t
S t r a n d

Sandymount

R131

Donnybrook

D u b l i n
B a y

Merrion
• Gates

R118

Booterstown
Marsh

N

1km

Booterstown

Blackrock

N31

Dun Laoghaire
(Site 93)

and buntings in winter. At low tide, the entire length of Sandymount Strand can be walked.

Alternatively, return to the R131 and continue over the railway tracks and follow the road left (SE), onto the R118, following signs for Blackrock and Dun Laoghaire. As you see Booterstown Marsh on the left, turn left at the lights into the railway station carpark. Waders and gulls on Sandymount Strand can be viewed by walking over the footbridge above the railway tracks and watching from the seawall. The R118 continues into Blackrock where it joins the N31. Follow the N31, signposted for the car ferry. The N31 continues along the coast to Dun Laoghaire. There are several vantage points along this road which overlook the S end of Sandymount Strand.

Booterstown Marsh From the Merrion Gates, continue left onto the R118, following signs for Blackrock and Dun Laoghaire. Continue SE on the R118 and, just past the office buildings on the left you will see an open area of wetland which is Booterstown Marsh. At the next set of traffic lights, go left into the railway station carpark. The S end of the marsh can be watched from the

carpark, although recent work has restricted the number of vantage points here. A channel runs along the entire length of the seaward side of the marsh, and this can be good for Kingfisher in winter. Better views of the marsh can be had from the path along the main road. The small reedbed directly below the main road has Water Rail throughout the year and the small channels and pools are good for Snipe in winter.

Species

Autumn, winter & spring Brent Goose (1000s), Scaup (R winter), Eider (R winter), Goldeneye, Common Scoter, Red-breasted Merganser, Red-throated Diver, Great Northern Diver, Great Crested Grebe, Little Egret (autumn & winter), Merlin, Peregrine, Water Rail, Grey Plover, Knot, Little Stint (autumn), Curlew Sandpiper (autumn), Dunlin, Ruff (autumn), Jack Snipe (O winter), Snipe, Black-tailed Godwit, Bar-tailed

127

Godwit, Whimbrel (spring & autumn), Spotted Redshank (R autumn & winter), Green Sandpiper (R autumn), Mediterranean Gull (autumn, winter & spring), Ring-billed Gull (winter & spring), Iceland Gull (R winter), Glaucous Gull (R winter), Kingfisher (winter), Black Redstart (O winter) Wheatear (autumn & spring).

Summer Manx Shearwater (evenings, well offshore), Common Sandpiper, gulls, terns, Sedge Warbler.

Rarities Dark-bellied Brent, Red-necked Grebe, Black-necked Grebe, Osprey, Crane, Semipalmated Sandpiper, Pectoral Sandpiper, Short-billed Dowitcher, Laughing Gull, Sabine's Gull, Bonaparte's Gull, Yellow-legged Gull, Forster's Tern, Black Tern, American Black Tern, White-winged Black Tern, Little Auk, Turtle Dove, Carrion Crow, Twite, Snow Bunting.

Dun Laoghaire & Sandycove

93

Grid ref.
O 24 29

Best time to visit   Best ■ Good ■ Poor □

| J | F | M | A | M | J | J | A | S | O | N | D |

Dublin · Sutton · Howth · Dun Laoghire · Irish Sea

Dun Laoghaire has two main piers, the West and East Piers, which shelter a marina and ferry terminal. The inner harbour is good for divers, grebes and auks in winter. The seaward sides of both piers can be good for gulls in winter and terns in summer. To the south of the East Pier lies the rocky coastline of Scotsman's Bay that runs to the small sheltered bathing area at Sandycove. This area is especially attractive for Mediterranean Gulls from early autumn to late spring.

Further south are the small piers at Bullock Harbour, another good area for gulls in winter.

Directions Map 62, next page.

Dun Laoghaire West Pier From Blackrock, follow the N31 SE for almost 2km along the coast road, following the signs for the car ferry and Dun Laoghaire. The road swings slightly inland and passes apartment blocks, a pub and a garage on the left. Just past the garage is a footbridge which brings you to the base of the West Pier. Alternatively, continue on the N31 and take the left turn for the car ferry terminal. Then take an immediate left turn and follow the road to the base of the pier.

From here you can walk from the back of the pier to Blackrock, along the S end of Sandymount

Black Redstart

Strand. The area around the immediate back of the pier can occasionally hold Black Redstart in winter. The West Pier runs out into Dublin Bay and is over 1.5km in length. The bay and the inner harbour can be viewed from anywhere along its entire length. The small pier of the inner harbour, directly opposite the start of the West Pier, has a small fish processing shop and this can attract gulls in winter. Grebes, divers and auks can be seen in winter on both the seaward side and on the inner harbour. There are two turns on the pier, known locally as 'elbows'. At the second elbow, you can take a path along the seaward side and this stretch of pier frequently holds Snow Buntings in winter. In summer, feeding terns can be seen well from this path.

Dun Laoghaire East Pier On the N31, go past the West Pier and do not take the left turn for the car ferry terminal. The road brings you past the

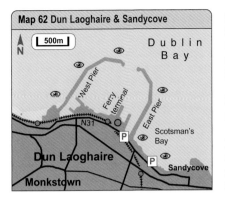

Map 62 Dun Laoghaire & Sandycove

this stretch of coastline to the beach at Sandycove is one of the best areas for finding Mediterranean Gulls in Ireland, from late summer to spring. In summer, terns can be seen feeding in shallow bays offshore.

Bullock Harbour From Scotman's Bay, follow the coast road and, at the T-junction, go right for 100m and, at the crossroads go left onto the R119. Follow this road E and take the second left turn, signposted for Bullock Harbour. This narrow road runs downhill and past two small piers. This area is also good for Mediterranean Gulls in winter.

Species
All year Cormorant, Shag, Black Guillemot, Kittiwake.

Autumn, winter & spring Brent Goose, Long-tailed Duck (R winter), Red-breasted Merganser, Goldeneye, Red-throated Diver, Great Northern Diver, Great Crested Grebe, Dunlin, Purple Sandpiper (winter), Grey Phalarope (R autumn), Guillemot, Razorbill, Mediterranean Gull, Iceland Gull (R winter), Glaucous Gull (R winter), Wheatear (spring), Black Redstart (O winter), Redstart (R spring), Redpoll (O winter) Snow Bunting (O winter).

Summer Gulls, terns.

Rarities Velvet Scoter, Black-throated Diver, White-billed Diver, Red-necked Grebe, Slavonian Grebe, Black-necked Grebe, Grey Phalarope, Kumlien's Gull, Ross's Gull, Little Auk.

railway station on the left and, at the crossroads, continue straight. Follow this road for over 400m and park just past the entrance to the East Pier. This pier runs for over 1km into the bay and is more widely used by the public than the West Pier. Grebes, divers and auks can be seen from both sides of the pier, with Black Guillemots preferring the inner harbour near the base. Purple Sandpipers are also common along the seaward side of the pier. To the right of the base of the pier is an old bathing area and this is excellent for gulls in winter. Black Redstarts are also frequently found here in winter. Terns can be seen well from the pier in summer.

Scotsman's Bay/Sandycove From the East Pier, follow the coast road E for over 1km. The rocky coastline to the left is Scotsman's Bay. A footpath also runs from the East Pier and follows the coast E to the sheltered beach at Sandycove. There are various parking areas along the road. In winter,

94 Dalkey Island Grid ref. O 27 26

A small, grass-covered island, good for nesting terns in summer, and a good selection of other species all year.

Dalkey Island is approximately 2km SE of Sandycove on the S coast of Dublin. The smaller islands of Maiden Rock and Lamb Island are rocky and bare. All can be viewed from Coliemore Harbour, which overlooks Dalkey Sound. In winter, this area can attract small numbers of gulls, while Peregrine and Short-eared Owl are frequently found on Dalkey Island.

In summer, the small rocky islands have small numbers of breeding Black Guillemot and Common and Arctic Tern, with Roseate Tern present each year. In late summer, larger numbers of roosting terns often attract skuas into the area, with Long-tailed Skua being recorded on several occasions. A juvenile Sabine's Gull has also been recorded in autumn in Dalkey Sound, while Little Gulls are seen in winter following easterly winds. Black Guillemots also breed in the seawalls above the small piers in the harbour.

A small ferry runs from Coliemore Harbour to Dalkey Island in summer.

East

95 Cruagh Woods Grid ref. O 13 22

A large coniferous woodland lying in the foothills of the Dublin Mountains, good for coniferous woodland species, notably Crossbill and Woodcock.

From Rathfarnham, follow the R115 S for just over 2km, and then take the R116 for Rockbrook. Go through Rockbrook and follow the road for over 2km into the area known locally as 'The Pine Forest'. Just where the main road swings sharply to the left, take the minor road to the right and follow for almost 1km to the carpark on the left. There are several paths into the woodlands from here. The whole area is good for Woodcock, Siskin, Redpoll and other common woodland species. However, when conditions cause Crossbills to invade from Europe, Cruagh Woods, and the area surrounding Cruagh Mountain, is one of the best areas in Dublin to find this species. **Three Rock Mountain** (O 17 23) 4km to the W, above Stepaside, is also noted for attracting Crossbills during such invasions.

Other sites

Rockabill Island (O 32 62) is located offshore from Skerries in N County Dublin and has one of the largest tern colonies in the country, including the largest Roseate Tern colony in NW Europe. The island is wardened by BirdWatch Ireland, and landing is usually not permitted, though views of the terns are possible. See also Skerries (Site 85).

Lambay Island (O 31 50) is a large, privately owned island 4km E of Portrane in N County Dublin. Although landing is usually not permitted, by enquiring locally it is possible to organise short boat trips from nearby Rush and Malahide. Many seabirds are present, nesting in large numbers on the E and N side of the island, including Puffin. Some boat trips from Malahide bring tourists around Lambay and Ireland's Eye on high speed, noisy boats. These have been known to scare seabirds from the breeding colonies and are best avoided.

Knocksedan (O 15 45), 2km W of Swords, is a woodland walk along a sheltered river valley floor. A wide selection of woodland species occur, including Treecreeper and Long-tailed Tit, while Kingfisher is present along the river.

The **Phoenix Park** (O 10 35) is a large open parkland over 3.5km long and 2km wide lying just 2km to the W of Dublin city centre. The Phoenix Park hosts Dublin Zoo, Áras an Uachtaráin (the official residence of the Irish President) and the Ordnance Survey offices.

The park has several broad roads and walkways and consists of open areas of grasslands, playing pitches, coniferous and deciduous woodlands, and small ponds. In winter, Fieldfare and Redwing are found on the pitches, while in summer, most of the common woodland species are found throughout the park.

The predominently deciduous woodlands of the 'Furry Glen' near the Knockmaroon Gate at the W end of the park are the best for breeding Blackcaps, while the small pool at the centre of the walks usually holds breeding Little Grebe. Jay is also found in the Phoenix Park throughout the year, but are most active at dawn. Long-eared Owl also breeds in the park, though the Phoenix Park is considered an unsafe place to visit at night.

Situated in Glasnevin, just 3km N of Dublin city centre, the **Botanic Gardens** (O 14 37) is a large, well-managed gardens with open grassland and a wide variety of trees. It is bordered by Glasnevin Cemetery and the Tolka River. In summer, common town and woodland species are found throughout the gardens, while Kingfisher, Grey Wagtail and, occasionally, Dipper can be found along the river. In winter, Redwing and Fieldfare are found, while wintering finches and Blackcap are also present. Waxwing has been seen on several occasions in winter and early spring.

Tymon Park (O 10 28) is a large parkland situated between Tallaght, Templeogue and Greenhills in the western suburbs of Dublin city. The area has extensive football pitches which attract large numbers of gulls in winter, with Ring-billed Gull recorded several times. The park also has several decorative ponds that are good for common duck species but which have also hosted Smew. The small areas of deciduous woods and scrub are also good for common finches and Reed Bunting in winter, while Yellow-browed Warbler has also been recorded once in winter.

Brittas Ponds (O 03 22) is a small, freshwater lake lying approximately 10km SW of Tallaght. From Tallaght, take the N81 following signs for Blessington and just before the small village of Brittas, you will see a small lake, approximately 800m long, on the left side of the road. This narrow road is quite busy and parking can be a problem. It is best to continue past the lake and park at the pub on the right. The lake can be viewed from several points along the road or by crossing over the fence and viewing from the lakeshore. In winter, the lake holds small numbers of Little Grebe, Teal, Pochard, Tufted Duck, Goldeneye, Lapwing and Snipe. Rarities seen include Green-winged Teal and Goosander.

By walking the relatively flat, heather covered moorlands of **Glendoo Mountain** (O 14 21) on the Dublin/Wicklow border, you have a good chance of seeing Red Grouse throughout the year. Raven and Wheatear are also present, the latter from late April to late August. Take the R115 from Ballyboden to Glencree/Sally Gap and explore the heather moorland along the highest stretches of this road, 6km to 7km S of Ballyboden.

County Kildare

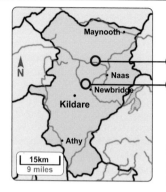

Minor Sites ○

Kildare lies to the west of Dublin and is a relatively low-lying county. The Grand Canal, as well as the rivers Liffey and Barrow, provide suitable habitats for species such as Kingfisher and Dipper, while small wetlands like

Pollardstown Fen and Ballinafagh Lake are good for wildfowl and waders in winter, and breeding species such as Sedge and Grasshopper Warblers in summer. The open grasslands of The Curragh attract large numbers of Golden Plover in winter. Small woodlands such as that of Donadea Forest Park are good for resident species like Treecreeper and Jay.

96 Ballinafagh Lake (Prosperous Reservoir) Grid ref. N 81 29

A small wetland, good for wildfowl and some waders in winter, and a good variety of breeding species in summer.

Lying approximately 2km NE of the village of Prosperous, Ballinafagh Lake is a shallow lake edged by reedbeds, heath and grassland. From Clane, follow the R403 W into Prosperous. At the main crossroads in the village, take a right and follow this road out until you meet the fork in the road. At this point, continue left and follow this road for almost 2km before taking a left turn. Follow this road for almost 1km, going past the graveyard and, just at the point where the road swings sharp right, take the small road to the left. The lake is just to the E of this road and there are small access tracks to the lake from this road.

In winter it attracts small numbers of Whooper Swans, ducks and waders.

Resident species include Kingfisher and Water Rail, while Cuckoo, Whinchat, Sedge Warbler and

Grasshopper Warbler are seen in summer. White-winged Black Tern has occurred here.

Whinchat

132

97 Pollardstown Fen <small>Grid ref. N 77 15</small>

Pools, scrub and reedbed, good for wetland and reedbed species throughout the year.

Directions Map 63, right. Located NW of the town of Newbridge. From Newbridge town centre, take the R445 SW for over 1km and, at Moorfield Crossroads just past Tesco's, go right, following signs for Church. At the next main crossroads go left, again following signs for Church. Continue on this road for 1.5km and take a right turn following signs for Pollardstown Fen. Continue over a narrow bridge over a railway track and follow this road as it swings left, then right (ignoring a left turn). 1.4km from the bridge, just as the road starts downhill is a small gate on the right which leads into the fen.

The area holds Teal, Shoveler, Golden Plover and Lapwing in winter, while Cuckoo, Whinchat, Sedge Warbler and Grasshopper Warbler are present in summer. Resident species include Water Rail and Kingfisher.

Map 63 Pollardstown Fen

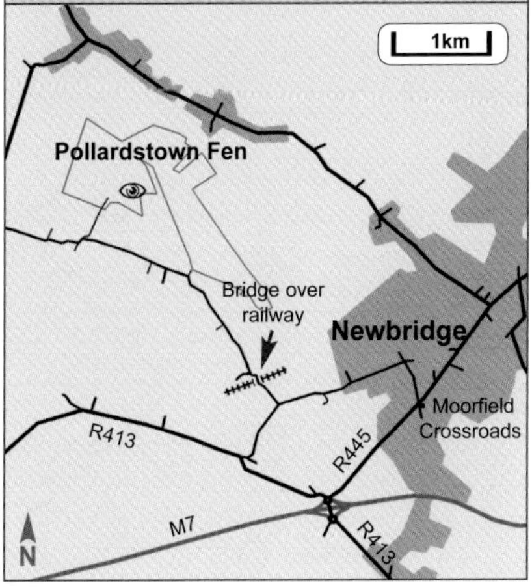

Rare species that have occurred here include Osprey, Marsh Harrier, Savi's Warbler and Reed Warbler.

Other sites

Donadea Forest Park (N 83 32) lying 5km N of Prosperous, is a large area of mixed deciduous and coniferous woodlands, excellent for resident woodland species such as Treecreeper and Jay. Woodcock and Long-eared Owl are also present, while large flocks of Siskins and Redpolls occur in winter. In summer, Blackcap, Willow Warbler and Chiffchaff are common.

From Clane, follow the R403 W into Prosperous. At the main crossroads in the village, take a right and follow this road until you meet the fork in the road. At this point, continue right and follow this road for almost 4km. At the crossroads, go straight and, at the next fork in the road, follow right. At the next junction, go right. The main entrance to the park is on the right, 600m from the junction. From the carpark, there are many tracks that lead into the woodlands as well as out to the fringes of the surrounding heath where Grasshopper Warbler can be found in summer. Great Spotted Woodpecker has been recorded here and Crossbills are sometimes seen in winter.

The Curragh (N 77 13) is a large area of flat grassland lying to the E of Kildare. It is bisected by the M7 and the main Dublin-Cork railway line. The area is noted for the large flocks of Golden Plover that occur each winter, with smaller numbers of Lapwing also present. The whole area stretches for over 10km and is almost 5km at its widest. It can be viewed from many points along the R413 and R415 that lead out of Kildare, as well as from the old N7 road into Kildare town.

County Wicklow

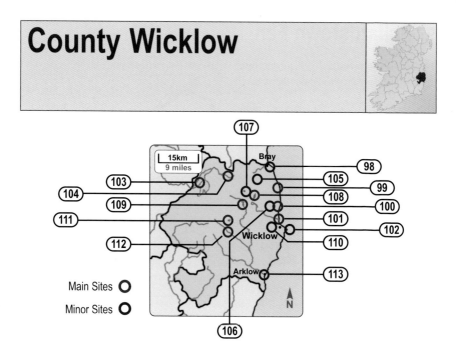

Wicklow lies to the south of Dublin, and is often referred to as 'the Garden of Ireland'. It has a rich variety of habitats, ranging from the steep granite and slate valleys of the mountains, to the upland blanket bog, upland lakes and coniferous woodlands that form the Wicklow Mountains National Park. Wicklow also hosts some of the best deciduous woodlands in Ireland. To the west lie the deep reservoirs around Blessington, while the coast includes the breeding seabird cliffs of Bray and Wicklow Heads, and the shingle beaches from Greystones to Wicklow. The coastal wetlands from Kilcoole to Broad Lough are superb for wildfowl and waders from autumn to early spring, while the reedbeds are excellent for breeding warblers in summer.

A small harbour, good for gulls in winter, and a large headland, good for seabirds in summer.

Lying off the N11, Bray is a coastal resort town situated on the Dublin/Wicklow border. The town has a long promenade that overlooks the main harbour. This harbour can attract good numbers of gulls in winter, with Little and Iceland Gull regularly recorded. Ireland's fourth Pallid Swift was also seen over the promenade in 2006.

Just to the S of the town is Bray Head. The cliffs along the southern side of the headland are excellent for breeding seabirds. There are two walks along the head. The first is reached from the southern end of the promenade. Follow the path uphill. This will lead both around the cliffs and up to the top of the hill. The area on the slope is good for migrant warblers in spring, while the area around the cross can also attract migrants. Ring Ouzel and Alpine Swift have been recorded here.

The southern cliff walk can be reached by taking the R766 from the promenade. At the main T-junction, go left onto the R761. Follow the R761 S for Greystones for over 2.5km and, just after the brow of the hill, take a minor left turn for Windgate. At the end of this road, a track runs to the left. This path brings you onto the southern section of the cliff walk. Breeding seabirds such as Fulmar, Kittiwake, Guillemot, Black Guillemot and Razorbill are present in summer.

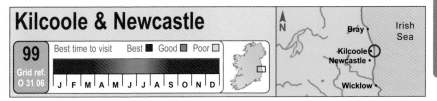

Kilcoole & Newcastle

99	Best time to visit	Best ■ Good ■ Poor □
Grid ref. O 31 06	J F M A M J J A S O N D	

Irish Sea

Bray
Kilcoole
Newcastle
Wicklow

East

A large coastal wetland and shingle beach, excellent for waders and wildfowl in winter, migrants in spring and autumn, and a variety of breeding species throughout summer.

Directions Map 64, next page. Located just S of Greystones, the wetland, comprising of tidal channels, lagoons and farmland, stretches for over 4km from Kilcoole Railway Station to Six Mile Point at Newcastle. It is separated from the coast by a high shingle ridge that has a breeding colony of Little Terns in summer. The main Dublin-Wexford railway line runs along the shingle bank. A small railway bridge over a drainage channel, half way between Kilcoole and Newcastle railway stations, is known as 'The Breaches', and is an excellent location for waders in autumn.

From Dublin, follow the main Dublin-Wexford road (M11/N11). The road passes through Kilmacanogue and then enters the wooded valley of the Glen of the Downs (Site 106). Approximately 4.8km from Kilmacanogue, and at the end of the Glen of the Downs, is a left turn onto the R762, signposted for Greystones and Delgany. Continue on the R762 through the village of Delgany and, approximately 700m after the village, is a small roundabout. Take the right exit and, at the next small roundabout, take the second exit uphill onto the R761, signposted for Kilcoole, Newcastle and Wicklow. Follow the R761 for 3km until you reach the village of Kilcoole. Continue into the village and follow the road downhill. At the bottom of the hill is a left turn for Sea Road. Take this left turn and follow for over 1.5km to the carpark at the end of the road.

At the N end of the carpark is an extensive reedbed that is excellent for Swifts, Swallows and martins, as well as breeding Sedge Warbler in summer. The small stands of trees along the lane at the back of the carpark can also hold migrant warblers in spring. At the S end of the carpark is a small gate that brings you onto the railway tracks. At this point, you can go left to view the reedbeds at the N end of the carpark. The railway tracks continue N for 3.5km to Greystones. However, the most productive areas lie to the S of Kilcoole

135

Railway Station so, at the tracks, go right. There is a path that runs along the top of the shingle beach but many people prefer to walk the actual railway tracks. For the entire 4km S to Newcastle, there are white markers indicating quarter miles. *Please note that this can be a busy railway track so caution is always required when walking this area.*

Immediately S of Kilcoole Railway Station is the BirdWatch Ireland Reserve and the wetlands here are superb for Teal and Snipe in winter. Water Rail is also found here, while Sedge Warblers are present in summer. The reserve can be viewed very well from the tracks. Further S is a large open area of farmland and channels. This is known as Webb's Field. In autumn, waders feed in the channels but can be quite difficult to see. In winter, the field attracts large numbers of Brent Geese, ducks and waders, while Whooper Swan is regularly found feeding on the farmlands immediately inland from this area.

Webb's Field continues S for almost 1km, and is separated from 'The Breaches' by a large ditch. Just N of 'The Breaches', and just S of the 20 mile marker, is a large stand of buckthorn that runs along the left side of the tracks. This can be very good for warblers in spring and autumn. Little Terns nest on the shingle beach in summer. They are usually found in an area stretching from the buckthorn down to 'The Breaches', although this can vary from year to year. The nest sites are protected and BirdWatch Ireland wardens are on duty each summer.

In winter, species such as Red-throated Diver are common on the sea from Kilcoole down to 'The Breaches', while Little Gulls are regularly seen in winter following strong easterly gales. The shingle beach also occasionally attracts Snow Bunting in winter. In autumn, seawatching can be productive in onshore winds, with Manx Shearwater frequently noted in large numbers.

Continuing S past the buckthorn will bring you to 'The Breaches'. Here the railway tracks cross over an intertidal channel. This is the best area for watching waders in autumn. The channels run inland, and many areas can be difficult to see well. From here, you can continue to walk the 2km S to Newcastle (Six Mile Point). The area inland from

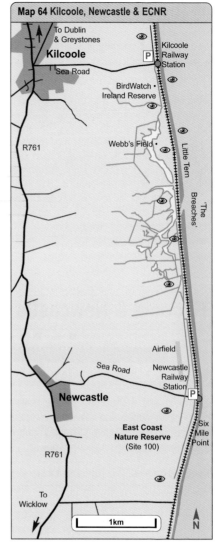

the beach is not as productive as that N of 'The Breaches', although a small stand of reedbeds at the back of the channels can attract Hen Harrier in winter, and occasionally Marsh Harrier in spring and summer. Just N of Newcastle Railway Station is an airstrip which is a favoured area for Short-eared Owl in winter. Alternatively, you can walk N to 'The Breaches' from Newcastle by returning to the village of Kilcoole and take the R761 S for 4km to Newcastle. At the village of Newcastle, take the left turn immediately after the small bridge. Follow this, the Sea Road, down to the end. From here, walk N along the tracks.

Species

All year Cormorant, Little Egret, Water Rail and Kingfisher.

Autumn, winter & spring Whooper Swan, Greylag Goose, Pink-footed Goose (R), White-fronted Goose (R), Barnacle Goose (R), Brent Goose (1000+), Wigeon, Gadwall (R), Teal, Shoveler (O), Common Scoter (O), Red-breasted Merganser (O), Red-throated Diver, Great Northern Diver, Hen Harrier, Merlin, Buzzard, Golden Plover (1000s), Grey Plover, Lapwing (1000s), Knot, Little Stint (autumn), Curlew Sandpiper (autumn), Dunlin, Ruff (autumn), Jack Snipe (R winter), Snipe, Black-tailed Godwit, Whimbrel (common May), Spotted Redshank (R autumn & winter), Green Sandpiper (R autumn), Wood Sandpiper (R autumn), Grey Phalarope (R autumn), Little Gull (O winter), Mediterranean Gull (R autumn & winter), Ring-billed Gull (R winter), Iceland Gull (R winter), Glaucous Gull (R winter), Short-eared Owl (winter), Black Redstart (R winter), Whinchat (R spring & autumn), Blackcap (R spring, O autumn, R winter), Whitethroat (spring), Reed Warbler (R spring), Brambling (R winter), Siskin, (O autumn & winter), Redpoll (O autumn).

Summer Common Sandpiper, gulls, Little Tern, Grasshopper Warbler (O), Sedge Warbler, Reed Warbler, Chiffchaff, Willow Warbler, Wheatear.

Rarities Dark-bellied Brent, Black Brant, American Wigeon, Green-winged Teal, Garganey, Blue-winged Teal, Velvet Scoter, Smew, Goosander, Black-throated Diver, Black-necked Grebe, Cory's Shearwater, Balearic Shearwater, Night Heron, Squacco Heron, Great White Egret, Purple Heron, Spoonbill, Marsh Harrier, Montagu's Harrier, Osprey, Red-footed Falcon, Hobby, Gyr Falcon, Little Ringed Plover, American Golden Plover, Semipalmated Sandpiper, Temminck's Stint, White-rumped Sandpiper, Baird's Sandpiper, Pectoral Sandpiper, Buff-breasted Sandpiper, Long-billed Dowitcher, Lesser Yellowlegs, Wilson's Phalarope, Red-necked Phalarope, Long-tailed Skua, Franklin's Gull, Sabine's Gull, Black Tern, White-winged Black Tern, Little Auk, Turtle Dove, Alpine Swift, Chimney Swift, Red-rumped Swallow, Water Pipit, Yellow Wagtail, Wood Warbler, Firecrest, Bearded Tit, Golden Oriole, Carrion Crow, Rose-coloured Starling, Twite, Crossbill, Lapland Bunting, Snow Bunting, Corn Bunting.

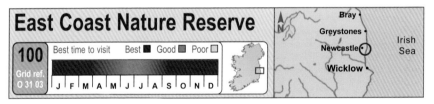

The BirdWatch Ireland East Coast Nature Reserve at Blackditch Wood, also known as Blackditch, is an area of wetlands, meadows, fen and woodlands with hides and walkways, and is excellent for Greylag Goose, duck, Hen Harrier and Short-eared Owl in winter, while Sedge and Grasshopper Warblers are found in summer. Marsh Harrier is an annual spring visitor.

Directions Map 65, next page. From the village of Kilcoole, take the R761 S for 4km to Newcastle. At the village of Newcastle, take the left turn immediately after the small bridge, down Sea Road. Follow this road to the end. The main entrance to the reserve is on the right side, approximately

500m before the end of the road. At the entrance, follow the short circular path that leads to two hides overlooking the scrapes, an open wetland that is good for geese and ducks in winter, and waders in autumn. This small path also passes tillage fields that are superb for finches and buntings in winter. Bramblings are frequently recorded here in winter.

Alternatively, you can take the long North-South pathway just to the right of the house at Six Mile Point. This path runs S along the E side of the reserve, giving more distant views of the scrapes. The path then swings inland, past an area of wet woodland, tillage fields and coniferous woodlands. These areas are excellent for breeding Sedge Warbler and Grasshopper Warbler in

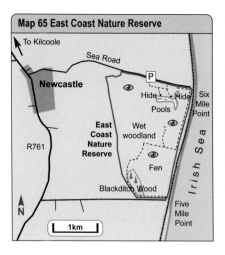

Map 65 East Coast Nature Reserve

To Kilcoole

Sea Road

Newcastle

P

Hide • Hide

Six
Mile
Point

Pools

East
Coast
Nature
Reserve

Wet
woodland

R761

Fen

Blackditch Wood

Irish Sea

Five
Mile
Point

N

1km

Species

All year Little Egret, Water Rail, Kingfisher.

Autumn, winter & spring Whooper Swan, Greylag Goose, Pink-footed Goose (R), White-fronted Goose (R), Barnacle Goose (R), Brent Goose, Wigeon, Gadwall (R), Teal, Shoveler (O), Hen Harrier, Merlin, Buzzard, Golden Plover, Lapwing, Little Stint (autumn), Curlew Sandpiper (autumn), Dunlin, Ruff (autumn), Jack Snipe (R winter), Snipe, Black-tailed Godwit, Whimbrel (common May), Spotted Redshank (R autumn & winter), Green Sandpiper (R autumn), Wood Sandpiper (R autumn), Grey Phalarope (R autumn), Little Gull (O winter), Mediterranean Gull (R autumn & winter), Short-eared Owl (winter), Black Redstart (R winter), Whinchat (R spring & autumn), Blackcap (spring) Whitethroat (spring), Reed Warbler (R spring), Brambling (winter), Siskin, (O autumn & winter), Redpoll (O autumn).

Summer Common Sandpiper, gulls, Little Tern, Grasshopper Warbler (O), Sedge Warbler, Reed Warbler, Chiffchaff, Willow Warbler, Wheatear.

Rarities Garganey, Great White Egret, Purple Heron, Spoonbill, Marsh Harrier, Montagu's Harrier, Osprey, Hobby, Corncrake, Alpine Swift, Red-rumped Swallow, Water Pipit, Yellow Wagtail, Firecrest, Crossbill.

summer, and finches in winter. Common woodland species also occur here. The path then runs past an area of open fen before bringing you back to the coast at Five Mile Point. The S end of Blackditch, at Five Mile Point, can be reached by taking the R761 S from the village of Newcastle. Continue for 1.5km and take the small left turn just after the row of houses on the left. This brings you onto a very narrow road. Follow this road for 1.3km to the end. Parking is very restricted in this area. From here, you can either enter the reserve or walk the railway tracks N to Six Mile Point. Alternatively, you can walk S along the tracks to Killoughter (Site 101, below).

Killoughter & Broad Lough

Bray
Greystones
Newcastle
Wicklow

Irish
Sea

N

101	Best time to visit	Best ■ Good ▣ Poor □	

**Grid ref.
T 30 97**

| J | F | M | A | M | J | J | A | S | O | N | D |

Marsh, lake and wetland, good for waterbirds throughout the year and breeding birds in summer.

Directions Map 66, next page.

Killoughter (T 30 98) is an area of reedbeds, scrubland, lagoons and channels, excellent for warblers in summer, as well as Little Egret all year round. The reedbed here is also good for raptors in summer and autumn.

Killoughter is just S of Blackditch Wood (Site 100). From the village of Newcastle, continue S on the R761 for 4.7km until you meet a small crossroads. At this crossroads take the left turn. The road is smooth for the first 600m but after that turns into a very rough track. This track can be flooded in autumn and winter, so care should be taken when driving it. The rough track continues for almost 1km to the old Killoughter Railway Station (which is now a private house).

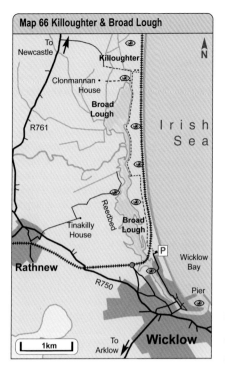

Map 66 Killoughter & Broad Lough

To Newcastle

Killoughter

Clonmannan House

Broad Lough

R761

I r i s h   S e a

Tinakilly House

Reedbed

Broad Lough

Rathnew

P

Wicklow Bay

R750

Pier

1km

To Arklow

Wicklow

N

East

From Killoughter Station, the reedbeds and lagoons to the N can be seen well but better views can be obtained by walking onto the railway tracks and continuing N for up to 1.5km. The open water and reedbeds can hold small numbers of duck in winter, while the scrubland at the N end of Killoughter is very good for Grasshopper Warbler and Whitethroat in summer. The tracks can be walked N for over 3.5km to Five Mile Point.

Broad Lough (T 30 97) is a large tidal lagoon, fed from the W by the Vartry River. The N end of Broad Lough is an intertidal mudflat and is excellent for ducks and waders in autumn and winter. An extensive reedbed on the western side is superb for breeding Reed and Sedge Warblers in summer. The S end of Broad Lough consists mostly of tidal channels and is not as productive, although small numbers of waders and duck are found in winter.

Broad Lough is located S of Killoughter, and N of Wicklow town. From Killoughter Station, walk S for almost 1km until you see the railway gate on the right side near an old derelict building. The area of reeds between Killoughter and the N end of Broad Lough is excellent for Reed, Sedge and

Grasshopper Warblers in summer, while Whitethroat is also common along this stretch in summer. At this point, climb over the gates. The N end of Broad Lough can be viewed from here. Just past the old house, you will see a track straight ahead which dissects the reedbed and leads to a large gate and then onto the private roads and grounds of Clonmannan House. The track to the right can give good views over the reedbeds but it is also private property. To view Broad Lough, go left at the old house and walk to the end of the gravel area before climbing up to view over the lough. Alternatively, follow the rough track along the top of the ridge above the gravel area to view the reeds at the N end of Broad Lough. A rough track follows S along the shore for almost 800m and eventually gives excellent views across towards Broad Lough House, on the W side. The mudflats in front of Broad Lough House are excellent for waders in autumn. This shoreline track runs all the way to the S end of Broad Lough and into Wicklow Harbour.

The W side of Broad Lough can be viewed by returning to the R761 from Killoughter and continuing S for almost 4km to the village of Rathnew. At Rathnew, continue left on the R750, following signs for Wicklow town. Approximately 400m out this road is a small left turn into Tinakilly House. Follow the long driveway up and continue left past the entrance. Then follow this narrow road to the end. This brings you to the W side of the lough, and closer to the reedbeds. A small bridge marks the point where you get clear views of the lough, and the channel inland from this bridge is good for Kingfisher. Viewing over the mudflats is, however, quite restricted from this side and the lands around the area are private.

Alternatively, to view the S side of Broad Lough you can continue from Rathnew on the R750 into Wicklow town. In the centre of the town is a small left turn which brings you to a bridge over the Leitrim River. After the bridge, follow left for almost 800m, past the industrial areas on the left. Park at the end of the road and continue N onto the rough track. This eventually leads to a small, tree-lined track which brings you onto the shoreline of the S end of Broad Lough. Continue N along the shore to reach the area opposite Broad Lough House.

Species

All year Cormorant, Little Egret, Water Rail, Kingfisher.

Autumn, winter & spring Bewick's Swan (R), Whooper Swan, Pink-footed Goose (R), White-fronted Goose (R), Greylag Goose, Barnacle Goose (R), Brent Goose, Wigeon, Gadwall, Teal, Shoveler, Scaup (R), Red-breasted Merganser (O), Red-throated Diver, Great Northern Diver, Hen Harrier (winter), Merlin, Buzzard, Golden Plover, Grey Plover, Lapwing, Knot, Little Stint (autumn), Curlew Sandpiper (autumn), Dunlin, Ruff (autumn), Jack Snipe (R winter), Snipe, Black-tailed Godwit, Bar-tailed Godwit, Whimbrel (O, common May), Spotted Redshank (R autumn & winter), Green Sandpiper (R autumn), Wood Sandpiper (R autumn), Grey Phalarope (R autumn), Little Gull (R), Mediterranean Gull (R autumn & winter), Ring-billed Gull (R winter), Iceland Gull (R winter), Glaucous Gull (R winter), Short-eared Owl (winter), Black Redstart (R winter), Whinchat (R autumn), Blackcap, Whitethroat, Brambling (R winter), Siskin, (O autumn & winter), Redpoll (O autumn).

Summer Common Sandpiper, gulls, terns, Cuckoo, Grasshopper Warbler (O), Sedge Warbler, Reed Warbler, Chiffchaff, Willow Warbler, Wheatear.

Rarities Dark-bellied Brent, Green-winged Teal, Garganey, Blue-winged Teal, Smew, Goosander, Cory's Shearwater, Night Heron, Great White Egret, Purple Heron, Glossy Ibis, Spoonbill, Black Kite, Marsh Harrier, Montagu's Harrier, Osprey, Hobby, Crane, Black-winged Stilt, American Golden Plover, Semipalmated Sandpiper, White-rumped Sandpiper, Baird's Sandpiper, Pectoral Sandpiper, Broad-billed Sandpiper, Buff-breasted Sandpiper, Long-billed Dowitcher, Lesser Yellowlegs, Wilson's Phalarope, Yellow-legged Gull, Black Tern, White-winged Black Tern, Turtle Dove, Alpine Swift, Hoopoe, Great Spotted Woodpecker, Water Pipit, Yellow Wagtail, Cetti's Warbler, Bearded Tit, Carrion Crow, Rose-coloured Starling, Lapland Bunting.

102 Wicklow Head Grid ref. T 34 92

A prominent headland, good for seabirds in summer and autumn, and small numbers of migrants, mainly in autumn.

See map 67, right. Lying just S of Wicklow town, this headland has steep seacliffs that hold good numbers of breeding seabirds in summer. Species found include Fulmar, Shag, Kittiwake, Black Guillemot, Guillemot and Razorbill. Peregrine also occurs. The area also has small gardens and dense cover, and is good for warblers such as Whitethroat in summer. Rarer species recorded here include Pied Flycatcher, Yellow-browed Warbler and Black-headed Bunting.

From Wicklow town, follow the R750 SE for approximately 1.5km. The road passes a small golf course on the left. After the golf course, you will meet a minor road on the left that leads to the lighthouse on Wicklow Head. Follow this narrow road out to the end. The cliffs below the light-house are where the main breeding seabird colonies are found. Seawatching in E or SE winds in autumn can result in good movements of Manx Shearwater, while Great, Arctic, Pomarine and Long-tailed Skua have also been recorded (See SEAWATCHING, p.356).

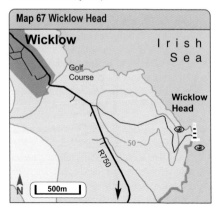

Map 67 Wicklow Head

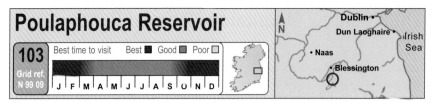

Poulaphouca Reservoir

103
Grid ref.
N 99 09

Best time to visit   Best ■ Good ■ Poor □

| J | F | M | A | M | J | J | A | S | O | N | D |

Dublin •
Dun Laoghaire • Irish
Sea
• Naas
• Blessington

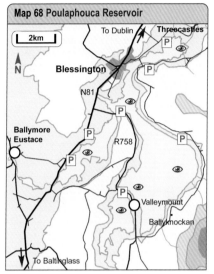

Map 68 Poulaphouca Reservoir

2km

N

To Dublin   Threecastles
P

Blessington
P

N81
P

Ballymore
Eustace
P   R758   P

P

P
Valleymount
Ballyknockan

To Baltinglass

Also known as Blessington Reservoir. A series of large lakes which are good for duck and good numbers of Greylag Geese in winter. The Threecastles area is good for waders in autumn.

The reservoir was created in 1938 by damming the River Liffey, which flows into the northern end of the reservoir.

Directions Map 68, above. Located to the E of the towns of Blessington and Ballymore Eustace in NW Wicklow. From Dublin, take the N81 SW to the village of Blessington. From Blessington, there are several circular routes which will bring you around the entire series of reservoirs. One of the better routes is to continue past Blessington village for 2km and take the left turn onto the R758. Over the next 7km, this road brings you along the reservoirs and over two bridges. There are many parking areas along the way which afford good views over the lakes. The road then brings you into the small village of Valleymount. Just over 1km S of Valleymount is a left turn that brings you onto a minor road. Take this turn and

follow the road that brings you along the S and E sides of the reservoir. Again, there are many parking areas along this route that allow good views over the lake.

The road continues through the small village of Ballyknockan and follows N and NW for almost 10km along the reservoir shore. The road then reaches Blessington Bridge. Go left over the bridge and, to return to Blessington village, go left at the T-junction. To check the Threecastles area, go left over the bridge and go right at the T-junction. Follow this road for almost 2km until you see a parking area on the right. The shoreline along this whole area is good for waders in autumn and winter, while the fields in this area are the best sites for Greylag Geese in winter.

Species
Autumn, winter & spring Bewick's Swan (R winter), Whooper Swan, Pink-footed Goose (R), White-fronted Goose (R), Barnacle Goose (R), Wigeon, Teal, Shoveler (O), Pochard, Tufted Duck, Scaup (R), Goldeneye, Little Egret (R winter), Hen Harrier (O), Merlin, Buzzard (R), Peregrine (O), Golden Plover, Lapwing, Little Stint (R autumn), Curlew Sandpiper (R autumn), Dunlin, Ruff (R autumn), Jack Snipe (R winter), Snipe, Black-tailed Godwit (R), Whimbrel (O autumn & spring), Green Sandpiper (R autumn & winter), Wood Sandpiper (R autumn), Mediterranean Gull (R winter), Short-eared Owl (R winter), Blackcap (O winter), Brambling (R winter), Crossbill (O winter), Siskin, (O autumn & winter), Redpoll (O autumn).

Summer Common Sandpiper, Blackcap, Grasshopper Warbler (O), Sedge Warbler, Chiffchaff, Willow Warbler, Wheatear, Spotted Flycatcher (O).

Rarities Green-winged Teal, Smew, Goosander, Osprey, Little Ringed Plover, Pectoral Sandpiper, Yellow-legged Gull, Carrion Crow.

East

The Wicklow Mountains National Park

The Wicklow Mountains National Park covers much of upland Wicklow. It contains an area of approximately 20,000 hectares and includes large areas of upland blanket bog, coniferous and deciduous woodlands, the river systems and many of the high mountain valleys and peaks. This entire area is excellent for species such as Red Grouse and for common woodland species such as Treecreeper and Jay. In summer, Wheatears are found on the high slopes, while common summer visitors include Chiffchaff and Willow Warbler. The valleys are also good for breeding Merlin and Peregrine, while the rivers hold Dipper and Grey Wagtail.

Some of the best areas are found in a region that stretches from Roundwood (Sites 108 & 109), to the Sally Gap and Coronation Plantation (Site 104), south to Glendalough (Site 111), Derrybawn and into Glenmalure (Site 112).

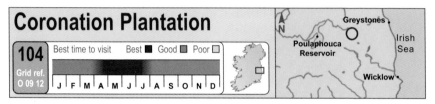

Coronation Plantation

104

Grid ref. O 09 12

| Best time to visit | Best ■ Good ▨ Poor ☐ |

J F M A M J J A S O N D

The Sally Gap is a high mountain pass set in upland blanket bog. This whole area is excellent for Red Grouse. To the north-west of the Sally Gap is Coronation Plantation that holds one of the last stands of mature Scots Pine in Wicklow. This area is excellent for Crossbill, as well as Whinchat and Merlin in summer.

Directions Map 69, below. From the N11, at Kilmacanogue take the R755 signposted for Roundwood and Glendalough. Follow this road for almost 11km and take the right turn onto the R759, signposted for the Sally Gap.

For **Sally Gap**, continue on the R759 for over 10km. This very narrow road runs uphill over open upland bog. The Sally Gap is a small cross-roads where the R759 meets the R115 which runs

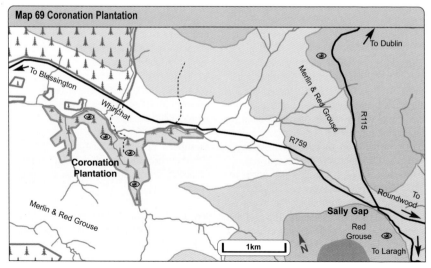

Map 69 Coronation Plantation

S into Laragh. This entire area holds good numbers of Red Grouse. They are hard to find and finding them often requires walking out across the blanket bog. However, they can occasionally be seen from the road and the best area lies just S of the Sally Gap. At the crossroads, take a left and head towards Laragh. Continue for almost 2.5km until you pass a small carpark on the right. Approximately 1km past this carpark is an open area of upland bog where Red Grouse are frequently seen. They prefer areas that have recently been burnt and where there is new growth of heather (young heather shoots are a favourite food of Red Grouse). Anywhere along the R115 between the Sally Gap and Glenmacnass Waterfall is suitable for Red Grouse. The area just N of Glenmacnass is also good for Wheatear and Skylark in summer.

For the **Coronation Plantation**, from the Sally Gap, continue NW on the R759 for approximately 4km until you see the Scots Pine plantation on the left side. Park near the gate, just past the house on the left, and follow the small path that runs downhill towards the plantation. This path then runs along the river which is excellent for Dipper, while the scrubland above the path before the river is good for Whinchat in summer. The path then crosses the river and brings you to an old ruined building. The Scots Pines behind this building are excellent for Crossbill, as well as resident woodland species. Merlin is frequently found in this area in summer.

Species
All year Red Grouse, Dipper, Raven, Crossbill, Siskin, Redpoll.

Summer Hen Harrier (R), Merlin, Peregrine, Common Sandpiper, Grasshopper Warbler (O), Whinchat, Wheatear.

Rarities Honey Buzzard.

105 Powerscourt Grid ref. O 21 16

Good for all the regular woodland species, particularly in spring.

The Powerscourt Estate lies just south of the town of Enniskerry and is a well-known tourist destination. The gardens of the old mansion have mature trees that are good for resident woodland species such as Treecreeper, while common warblers like Blackcap and Chiffchaff occur in summer. However, the estate also includes good stands of deciduous and coniferous woodlands, rivers, cliffs and a waterfall. These areas are good for species such as Dipper and Jay, while in summer, Blackcap and Grasshopper Warbler occur. Rarer species such as Wood Warbler and Redstart have also been recorded.

From the N11, take the R117 W, signposted for Enniskerry. Follow the R117 for 2km into the town and then take a left onto the R760. The entrance to the gardens is just over 500m S of Enniskerry. However, to get into the better area of the estate, follow the R117 for a further 1km and enter the estate through the gates on the right. There are many excellent birding areas throughout the entire estate. There is an entrance charge into the Powerscourt Estate.

106 Glen of the Downs Grid ref. O 26 11

Good for all the regular woodland species, particularly in spring.

The Glen of the Downs is an area of mature deciduous woodlands lying on the N11 which is the main Dublin-Wexford road. The road passes right through the woodlands. From Kilmacanogue, continue S on the N11 for 3.5km. On the right is the Glenview Hotel. The area of woodland on the right side of the road can be accessed by taking the flyover for the hotel, and driving to the far end of the hotel carpark. A path runs from the carpark into the woodlands at this point. Alternatively, you can continue S for a further 500m and take the left turn into the small parking area. There are several paths along this side of the woodlands and the river can also be seen well from this side.

The area is excellent for resident woodland species such as Treecreeper and Jay, while Woodcock are also present. In summer, warblers here include Blackcap, Chiffchaff and Willow Warbler, with Wood Warbler also recorded on occasions. The river can hold Dipper and Grey Wagtail.

107 Lough Tay Grid ref. O 16 07

A deep mountain lake in a steep, wooded valley which has woodland species throughout the year, and the possibility of Goosander in summer.

The Lough lies just to the NW of Roundwood village. From the N11, at Kilmacanogue take the R755 signposted for Roundwood and Glendalough. Follow this road for almost 11km and take the right turn onto the R759, signposted for the Sally Gap. Follow the R759 uphill for over 5km. There are several parking areas along this road. Opposite the last parking area is a small walk which gives you a good view over the entire lake. Goosander are regularly recorded here, while the fast-flowing rivers in the area are good for Dipper. Peregrine is also seen here in summer.

Other species seen here in summer include Blackcap, Chiffchaff, Willow Warbler, Wood Warbler (R), Redstart (R).

The slope above Lough Tay has superb woodland but the entire area is on private property.

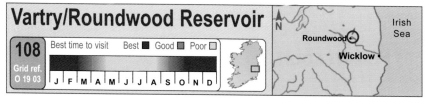

Vartry/Roundwood Reservoir

108   Best time to visit   Best ■ Good ▨ Poor □

Grid ref. O 19 03

J F M A M J J A S O N D

A large reservoir, attracting small numbers of diving duck in winter.

Directions Map 70, right. The Reservoir lies just E of the village of Roundwood, in the Wicklow Mountains. This large area of water can be viewed at several locations and is good for diving duck in winter. It has also attracted some rare species such as Great White Egret and Stone Curlew.

From the N11, at Kilmacanogue take the R755 signposted for Roundwood and Glendalough. Follow this road for almost 10km and take the left turn just at Sally's Bridge. Follow this narrow road down for over 600m until you come to a causeway over the reservoir. Both sides of the reservoir can be viewed from this point. The area of grassland and mud at the top end of the N side is where the Great White Egret and Stone Curlew were found. The coniferous trees close to the bridge are also good for Crossbill in winter. The shoreline can be walked by following the small track on the left at the far (SE) end of the bridge. Another section of the reservoir can be viewed by returning to the

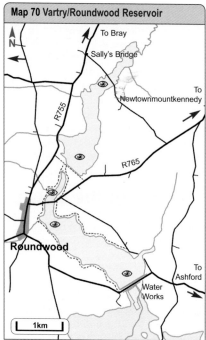

Map 70 Vartry/Roundwood Reservoir

Jay

R755, and continuing SW to Roundwood for 2km. The reservoir can be seen from the main road. The S end of the reservoir can also be seen by taking the left turn just before Roundwood village

onto the R765 and following signs for Newtownmountkennedy.

Species

All year Greylag Goose (feral birds), Dipper, Long-tailed Tit, Jay, Siskin, Redpoll.

Autumn & winter Whooper Swan (O), Goosander (O), Hen Harrier, Merlin, Brambling (R winter), Crossbill (O).

Spring & summer Goosander, Merlin, Peregrine, Common Sandpiper, Cuckoo, Wheatear, Redstart (R), Whinchat (O), Ring Ouzel (R), Garden Warbler (O), Blackcap, Chiffchaff, Willow Warbler, Wood Warbler (R), Spotted Flycatcher, Pied Flycatcher (R).

Rarities Great White Egret, Stone Curlew.

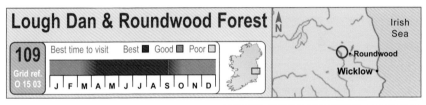

Lough Dan & Roundwood Forest

109

Grid ref.
O 15 03

Best time to visit   Best ■ Good ■ Poor □

J F M A M J J A S O N D

Irish Sea

Roundwood

Wicklow

East

Lough Dan is a deep mountain lake where Goosander can occasionally be found. The Lough is surrounded by extensive woodland, and nearby Roundwood Forest is an excellent broadleaved woodland for all the regular woodland species and a good chance of Wood Warbler in early summer.

Directions Map 71, right. Lough Dan lies 3km W of Roundwood, just off the R755 to Glendalough from Dublin. The best area of deciduous forest is just to the S of the Lough.

For **Roundwood Forest** (O 16 01), from Roundwood, heading S, take the small right turn just past the pub, signposted for Lough Dan. Continue on this road for over 600m, and continue left at the small fork in the road. Follow this road until the next small fork and follow left always following signs for Lough Dan. Shortly after this, the road begins to run downhill past deciduous woodland. There are good parking areas on the left half way down the hill and also at the bottom of the hill before the bridge. This area

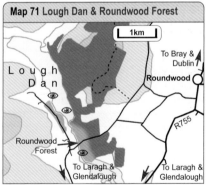
Map 71 Lough Dan & Roundwood Forest

1km

Lough Dan

To Bray & Dublin

Roundwood

R755

Roundwood Forest

To Laragh & Glendalough

To Laragh & Glendalough

is excellent for common woodland species such as Treecreeper and Jay, while in summer, Blackcap, Willow Warbler and Chiffchaff are common. Rarer species such as Wood Warbler also occur here on occasions.

For **Lough Dan** (O 15 03) from Roundwood Forest, continue over the bridge at the bottom of the hill and, at the junction, go right to view the SE edge of Lough Dan (left at this junction will bring you to Laragh). Follow this road (marked cul-de-sac) past the 'Scout Campsite' on the right and park on the left just after the entrance to the campsite. The road narrows just past this point and parking is prohibited. The woodlands along the road are good for common species, while Crossbill is often found in the coniferous plantations here. This area is also a good site for Cuckoo in summer. Lough Dan can be viewed from this road and, in summer, Goosander can occur. *It should be noted that many areas around Lough Dan are private working farms, so access is restricted.*

Species

All year Dipper, Long-tailed Tit, Jay, Siskin, Redpoll.

Autumn & winter Hen Harrier, Merlin, Brambling (R winter), Crossbill (O).

Spring & summer Goosander, Merlin, Peregrine, Common Sandpiper, Cuckoo, Wheatear, Redstart (R), Whinchat (O), Ring Ouzel (R), Garden Warbler (O), Blackcap, Chiffchaff, Willow Warbler, Wood Warbler (R), Spotted Flycatcher, Pied Flycatcher (R).

110 The Devil's Glen Grid ref. T 24 99

Good for all the regular woodland species, particularly in spring.

The Devil's Glen is an area of deciduous woodland, lying just W of the town of Ashford. From the N11, take the exit for Ashford and follow the road into the town. Just at the beginning of the town is a small roundabout. Take the second exit onto the R763, signposted for Annamoe. Follow this road W, continuing left (straight) at the fork. Follow this road for over 1km until it crosses over a small bridge. Approximately 300m past this bridge is a small parking area. There are several paths from here which lead into the woodland and along the river.

Common resident woodland species are found here, including Treecreeper and Jay, while Dipper and Grey Wagtail can be found along the river. In summer, warblers include Blackcap, Willow Warbler and Chiffchaff. Rarer species such as Wood Warbler have also been seen here, while Crossbill has also occurred.

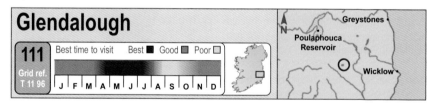

Excellent deciduous woodlands that attract many common species as well as some rarer ones like Wood Warbler and Redstart in summer. The two lakes (the Upper and Lower Lakes) in the valley can attract Goosander in winter, while the fast-flowing rivers are also good for Dipper.

With its monastic ruins and spectacular scenery, Glendalough is a famous tourist destination so, if visiting in spring and summer, it is best to get there as early as possible before there is too much disturbance.

Directions Map 72, next page. From Roundwood, take the R755 following signs for Laragh and Glendalough. After almost 4km, the road swings sharp right over a narrow bridge crossing the Avonmore River at Annamoe. This area can be very good for species such as Dipper and Grey Wagtail. Continue on the R755 towards Laragh and, in the village, continue straight (right) onto the R756, signposted for Glendalough. Follow the R756 for over 1.5km and, at the fork in the road, continue straight (left) onto the R757. This road passes the hotel on the left and there are parking facilities close to a Visitors Centre

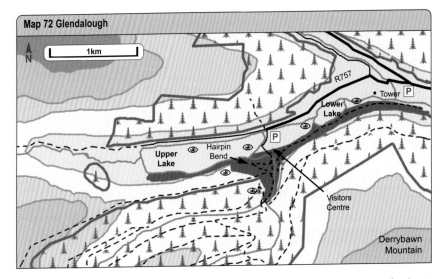

Map 72 Glendalough

1km

N

R757

Tower P

Lower Lake

P

Hairpin Bend

Upper Lake

Visitors Centre

Derrybawn Mountain

here. From the carpark, a path runs by the river and leads to a path along the S side of the **Lower Lake**. The woodland on the left along this path is good for common woodland species but occasionally Wood Warbler can be found along this stretch. This path leads to the area around the **Upper Lake**. You can also reach the Upper Lake by continuing past the Visitors Centre/hotel carpark and following the R757 over the narrow bridge and driving to the carpark at the end. There is a parking fee at this carpark.

From this carpark there are several options. You can return from the carpark onto the R757 and walk left. This walk will bring you past good woodland, another favoured area for many woodland species. The fast-flowing river below this path is also excellent for Dipper. This path will bring you along the N side of the Upper Lake and eventually will lead you up the Vale of Glendalough. However, a more productive walk is to head S out of the carpark and follow the main path past the small Visitors Centre. Follow the path over the bridge and continue right past the steps that lead up along the waterfalls. This wide path goes uphill and then swings sharply left. This left turn is known as 'The Hairpin Bend' and the woodland directly above the bend, and for the next 600m, is one of the best areas for common species such as Treecreeper, Spotted Flycatcher and Jay in summer. The path continues gradually uphill. Continue past the top of the steps near the waterfalls and you will then come to a more open

area where there is a small crossroads of paths. At this point, go left over the two small bridges and then take the small track that runs left off the main path. This will bring you down along the opposite side of the river and past some dense undergrowth. This area is a favoured site for Blackcap and Willow Warbler, while rarer species such as Garden Warbler have been seen frequently towards the end of this track. The track runs downhill, over a stile and eventually leads you on to the main path that runs from the Lower to the Upper Lake. Go left and this will bring you back to the small Visitors Centre. The area directly

Coal Tit

147

in front and opposite the Centre is also worth watching for species such as Blackcap. In winter, flocks of Redpolls and Siskins can be found in the trees close to the Visitors Centre.

Species
All year Greylag Goose (feral birds), Dipper, Long-tailed Tit, Jay, Siskin, Redpoll.

Autumn & winter Whooper Swan (O), Goosander (O), Hen Harrier, Merlin, Buzzard (R),

Brambling (R winter), Crossbill (O), Snow Bunting (R winter).

Spring & summer Goosander, Merlin, Peregrine, Buzzard (R), Common Sandpiper, Cuckoo, Wheatear, Redstart (R), Whinchat (O), Ring Ouzel (R), Garden Warbler (O), Blackcap, Chiffchaff, Willow Warbler, Wood Warbler (R), Spotted Flycatcher, Pied Flycatcher (R).

Rarities Osprey, Golden Oriole.

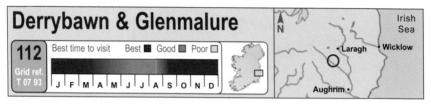

Derrybawn Woods (Clara Valley) is excellent for common woodland species in summer, while rarer species such as Wood Warbler frequently occur. Glenmalure Valley is a deep river valley with good upland woodlands which hold common woodland species.

The scree slopes at the far end of the Glenmalure Valley were once a regular site for Ring Ouzel. The species still occurs on occasions at this site but has become rarer and harder to find in recent years.

Directions Map 73, next page.

Derrybawn Woods is a deciduous woodland that lies to the S of the village of Laragh. From Laragh, take the R755 S, following signs for Rathdrum. The road goes over a narrow bridge and approximately 800m past the bridge is a sharp uphill turn to the right. This is the turn for Glenmalure. Go past this turn and continue on the R755 until you see the turn-off into a small picnic area on the left. Park at the picnic area and from here walk to the river where species such as Dipper and Grey Wagtail are frequently found. Goosander have also been seen along this river. The woodland here, and directly across the road from the picnic area, is excellent for resident species such as Treecreeper and Jay, while Spotted Flycatcher, Blackcap and occasionally, Wood Warbler, can be found in summer. The upper part of the woodland can be viewed by

returning onto the R755, and, from the picnic area taking a right turn back towards Laragh, and taking the sharp, uphill turn for Glenmalure. Park along the straight part of this road. By walking along the road, the woodlands can be viewed well above and below you. Approximately 700m along this road is a track on the right that brings you up into the woodland above the road.

Treecreeper

148

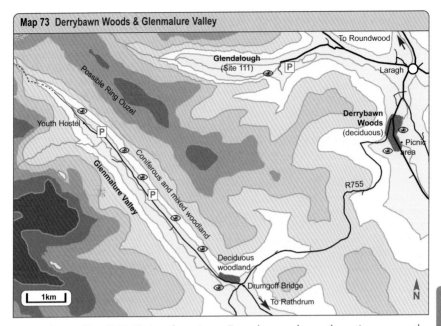

Map 73 Derrybawn Woods & Glenmalure Valley

To Roundwood

Glendalough
(Site 111)

P

Laragh

Youth Hostel

P

Possible Ring Ouzel

Glenmalure Valley

Coniferous and mixed woodland

P

Derrybawn Woods
(deciduous)

Picnic area

R755

Deciduous woodland

Drumgoff Bridge

To Rathdrum

1km

N

East

Glenmalure Valley (T 07 93) is a deep river valley to the SW of Derrybawn and Laragh. From Laragh, take the R755 S, following signs for Rathdrum. The road goes over a narrow bridge and approximately 800m past the bridge is a sharp uphill turn to the right signposted for Glenmalure. Take this narrow road and continue past the upper part of Derrybawn Woods. This is an old military road and brings you onto open farmland and upland bog. Follow this narrow road for over 6km until the road runs downhill to a small crossroads near Drumgoff Bridge. At the crossroads, take the right turn into the Glenmalure Valley. The deciduous woodland above the road on the right at the beginning of the valley is excellent for resident species as well as Blackcap, Chiffchaff and Willow Warbler in summer. Rarer species such as Redstart and Wood Warbler have also been recorded along this first stretch of road.

The road continues NW for almost 6km and there are several good stands of woodland along the entire length of the road. At the end of the road is a small carpark. From here, the high scree slopes can be viewed for nesting species such as Wheatear. Peregrine and Merlin are frequently seen along the high slopes. This was the main area for seeing Ring Ouzel, but in recent years this species has become extremely rare in Wicklow.

From the carpark, a path continues across the river and past the Youth Hostel. The woodlands along here hold Siskin, Repoll and occasionally Crossbill. In summer, Blackcap and Chiffchaff occur, while rarer species such as Redstart have been recorded. The river here is also good for Dipper and Grey Wagtail. The path continues past the hostel and divides. At this point, you can go left to climb higher above the tree line or go right to walk further up the valley. The track to the right affords better views of the scree slopes further up the valley.

Species
All year Dipper, Long-tailed Tit, Jay, Siskin, Redpoll.

Autumn & winter Goosander (O), Hen Harrier, Merlin, Brambling (R winter), Crossbill (O), Snow Bunting (R winter).

Spring & summer Goosander, Merlin, Peregrine, Common Sandpiper, Cuckoo, Wheatear, Redstart (R), Whinchat (O), Ring Ouzel (R), Garden Warbler (O), Blackcap, Chiffchaff, Willow Warbler, Wood Warbler (R), Spotted Flycatcher, Pied Flycatcher (R), Crossbill (O).

113 Arklow Ponds & Arklow Bridge

A freshwater pond and reedbed area, good for small numbers of duck in the winter and breeding species in summer.

The coastal town of Arklow lies towards the southern end of the Wicklow coastline. From the N11, take the signs for Arklow. This was the old N11 and brings you into the town of Arklow. The road follows downhill and swings right. Approximately 200m after this point is a left turn which brings you down to Arklow Ponds, a small park with ponds and reedbeds. Follow this road to the end and continue left into the park. The ponds can hold small numbers of Pochard, Tufted Duck and Coot in winter, while the reedbeds are good for Sedge Warbler and, occasionally, Reed Warbler in summer. Almost directly opposite the left turn for Arklow Ponds is a small track on the right which brings you into a larger stand of reeds that again holds Sedge and Reed Warblers in summer along with Grasshopper Warbler. The area is excellent for Swallows, martins and Swifts in summer. This reedbed area is under threat from development.

To view the area around Arklow Bridge, continue past the left turn for the ponds and follow the main road over the Avoca River. There is a small parking area to the right at the end of the bridge. In winter, gulls tend to roost in this area and species such as Iceland Gull, Glaucous Gull, Ring-billed Gull, Mediterranean Gull and Laughing Gull have all been recorded here.

Other sites

Wicklow Harbour (T 32 94). Lying in Wicklow town, the open harbour can be very good for gulls in winter. From the N11, take the exit for Rathnew. At the village of Rathnew, continue on the R750 into Wicklow town. In the centre of the town is a small left turn which brings you to a bridge over the Leitrim River. Just after the bridge, follow the small road straight. This leads to a small parking area overlooking the lifeboat station and pier to the right, and the harbour on the left. The area is especially good for Little Gull following strong easterly winds but species such as Iceland, Glaucous and Mediterranean Gull are regularly recorded. Franklin's Gull has also been seen here.

Coolattin/Tomnafinnoge Woods (T 00 68) is a small area of mixed deciduous woodlands lying just N of the Wicklow/Wexford border. From the village of Shillelagh, follow signs for Tinahely and take the R749 NW for over 4km. At the small crossroads, take the right turn signposted for Coolboy. Follow this narrow road and, just after the first small bridge, turn right in through the wooden gates to the carpark at the woodlands. From here, follow the boardwalk into the woods. The main track follows the river but there are several paths off this which lead to other parts of the woodland.

The area is excellent for common resident woodland species such as Treecreeper and Jay. In summer, Willow Warbler, Spotted Flycatcher and Blackcap are common. This area also attracts rarer species such as Wood Warbler on occasions.

County Carlow

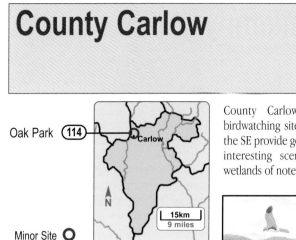

Oak Park (114)

Minor Site ⭘

County Carlow lacks any outstanding birdwatching sites, though the mountains to the SE provide good spring birdwatching with interesting scenery. The county has no wetlands of note and limited forest cover.

Hen Harrier

114 Oak Park Grid ref. S 74 80

The only lake in County Carlow.

Oak Park is a series of small, artificial ponds in the grounds of Teagasc, the Agricultural & Food Development Authority, 3km N of Carlow town, off the R417 road to Athy. Species recorded in winter include Whooper Swan, Teal, Wigeon, Mallard, Tufted Duck, Pintail (O), Shoveler (O), Pochard (O), Golden Plover, Lapwing and Snipe (O). The mixed forest around the ponds has Long-tailed Tit, Treecreeper and Jay all year. There have been access restrictions recently, so permission may have to be sought to enter the grounds.

Other sites

The rolling hills of the **Mount Leinster** (S 82 52) area, on the Carlow/Wexford border, have breeding Hen Harrier and Red Grouse (although both are at low densities). For Red Grouse, try more level upland areas with good heather cover, such as the ridge S of Mount Leinster, to Knockroe Mountain. Also try any high, level areas of heather which have been burnt within the previous year. Hen Harriers are best looked for in spring above and adjacent to young conifer plantations. Crossbill may be found occasionally in mature conifer forests.

The **River Barrow**, which runs through Carlow town, sometimes floods adjacent fields in winter, attracting Lapwing and Golden Plover. Small numbers of Wigeon and Teal can also be found. There are walks along the river banks, immediately N and S of the town.

South-east

151

County Kilkenny

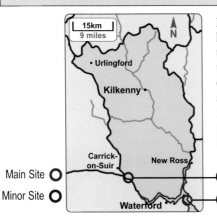

Kilkenny is a large county with good general hedgerow and farmland birdwatching throughout, but with few sites with concentrations of birds. The southern edge of the county, bordering County Waterford, has some good estuary birdwatching in Waterford Harbour (Site 136), and Tibberoughney Bog is particularly good for wildfowl and waterbirds in winter.

Main Site ◯

Minor Site ◯

115 Tibberoughney Bog Grid ref. S 43 21

A winter haunt of Whooper Swan and other wildfowl when it floods in winter.

See Map 74, right. The area lies between Fiddown and Carrick-on-Suir, on the N side of the River Suir. Bird numbers are highest when water levels are high, and are occasionally supplemented by birds from other similar sites along the River Suir.

When flooded, the grassland area adjacent to the River Suir attracts Whooper Swan, Greylag Goose, Wigeon (small numbers), Teal, Lapwing, Golden Plover and Snipe, gulls, and perhaps the occasional Shoveler, Tufted Duck or Pochard. This is only one of a series of wetlands along the River Suir and birds move freely between sites,

largely depending on disturbance. See also Site 150, Coolfin and Portnascully and Site 151, Blackwater Callows.

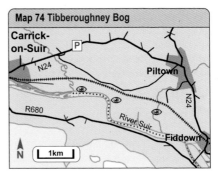

Map 74 Tibberoughney Bog

Other sites

Bishop's Lough (S 58 48) is 8km SE of Kilkenny city and 3km SE of Bennetsbridge, and is an area of grassland which attracts wildfowl when it occasionally floods in winter. Lapwing and Golden Plover are then usually present in some numbers, and some Wigeon, Teal and small numbers of

Pintail and Shoveler can be found, with Snipe, Black-tailed Godwit and Curlew along the wet margins.

Small numbers of similar species can be found at the **Avonmore Ponds** (S 43 71), 6km S of Durrow and 2km NW of Ballyragget, off the N77.

County Wexford

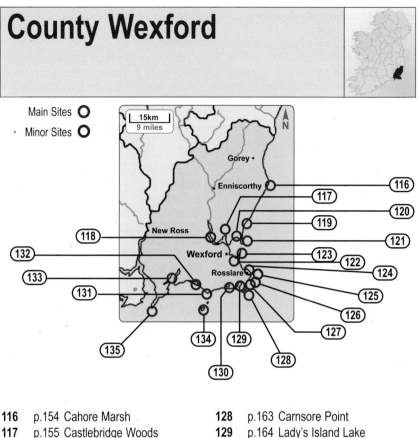

Main Sites ⭕
· Minor Sites ⭕

15km
9 miles

N

Gorey •

Enniscorthy ⭕ — (116)
(117)
(120)
(119)
New Ross — (118)
(121)
(132)
Wexford • — (123)
(133)
Rosslare — (122)
(124)
(131)
(125)
(126)
(127)
(135)
(134) (129)
(128)
(130)

South-east

Wexford is one of the best counties in Ireland for birdwatching, with a wide range and a high concentration of outstanding coastal and wetland habitats which together hold some of the largest bird concentrations in Ireland each winter.

A day visit in summer to the Saltee Islands offers outstanding opportunities to see most of Ireland's breeding seabird species, while in spring and autumn, the islands are a magnet for many common and some rare migrant species. Hook Head and several sites around Carnsore Point also offer opportunities for finding migrants, and this area, and Greenore Point, are also very good for seawatching in spring and autumn.

Wexford also has a deserved reputation for rare American waders, and Tacumshin Lake and

Lady's Island Lake in particular are magnets for such rarities each autumn.

Above all, Wexford is known as the winter haunt of the majority of the world's population of Greenland White-fronted Goose. The Wexford Wildfowl Reserve and the South Slob are the main winter quarters for this species, but between them, they also host thousands of other wildfowl and waders, as well as grebes, birds of prey, gulls and more.

Wexford is also one of the best counties for seeing terns in summer, with all five species nesting, along with many gulls, particularly at Lady's Island Lake.

Cahore Marsh

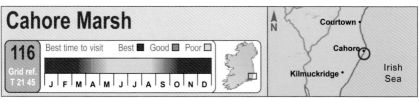

116	Best time to visit	Best ■ Good ■ Poor □											
Grid ref. T 21 45	J	F	M	A	M	J	J	A	S	O	N	D

Flooded fields, channels and marshland which attract waders and wildfowl in autumn and winter.

Directions Map 75, right. Cahore is located 10km SSE of Courtown and 8km NNE of Kilmuckridge. There are two access points to the marsh. Approaching from the N on the R742, approximately 2km S of the village of Ballygarret, take a left turn at Clonevin Crossroads, signposted for Old Bawn, and continue E towards the coast. After 2km, there is a bridge over a drainage channel which has views over the N part of the marsh. The surrounding fields are often flooded in winter and can hold many wildfowl. There is a carpark approximately 200m past the bridge which provides access to the coastline.

For the S part of the marsh, return to Clonevin Crossroads and turn left onto the R742 for approximately 2.5km. A windfarm is visible to the left. After 2.5km, turn left and continue E toward the coast for approximately 2.5km. (Approaching from the S, turn right approximately 3km N of Kilmuckridge on the R742). The road ends at a carpark where there is a gate and a signpost for Ballywater Farms. The S part of the marsh can be accessed by walking N beyond the gate along a dirt track between the dunes and the marsh. Access to the coastline is possible from the carpark.

Species
Autumn, winter & spring Whooper Swan, Bewick's Swan (O), Pink-footed Goose (O), White-fronted Goose, Greylag Goose (feral birds),

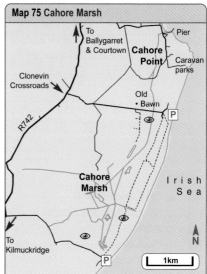

Map 75 Cahore Marsh

Wigeon (often 100s), Gadwall (O), Teal, Pintail, Shoveler, Pochard, Common Scoter (O), Goldeneye (O), Little Egret, Cormorant, Buzzard (R), Golden Plover (often 1000s), Lapwing, Little Stint (R autumn), Dunlin, Ruff (O autumn), Snipe, Jack Snipe (O), Black-tailed Godwit, Whimbrel (O spring), Curlew, Wood Sandpiper (R autumn), gulls, Kingfisher (O).

Summer Little Tern, Cuckoo, Sedge Warbler, Reed Warbler.

Rarities Marsh Harrier, Montagu's Harrier, Pectoral Sandpiper, Buff-breasted Sandpiper, Little Gull, Black Tern, Short-eared Owl, Hoopoe, Yellow Wagtail.

154

117 Castlebridge Woods Grid ref. T 04 27

Excellent woodland for a wide variety of typical woodland species throughout the year.

Map 76, right. 1km W of Castlebridge, 5km N of Wexford town. Leave Wexford town by taking the R741 to Gorey. After 5km you reach Castlebridge. Take the left fork and the next left after just 250m. 600m further, the road takes a sharp left. The woodland is on the right. Park here and walk along the river valley through broadleaved woodland.

Woodcock can be seen roding here in the late evenings between late March and July, particularly on calm evenings. The fast-flowing River Sow holds Dipper, while the broadleaved woodland holds all the regular woodland species, including Long-tailed Tit, Redpoll, Siskin, Jay.

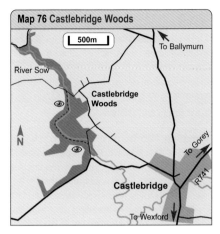

118 River Slaney Grid ref. S 98 31

A broad river with much intertidal mud, good for some wildfowl and waders in winter, and large numbers of Little Egret all year.

Map 77, right. The Slaney River runs through Enniscorthy, S to Wexford town, and into Wexford Harbour. Several minor roads lead to the shore at various points, with access generally easiest on the W side, where a railway runs parallel to the W shore. The broader stretches close to Wexford town are easily viewed from adjacent roads.

In winter, there are usually Wigeon, Teal and Red-breasted Merganser on the lower reaches, with small numbers of Shoveler, Pintail, Pochard and Goldeneye usually present, and good numbers of Tufted Duck. On the tidal areas, some waders can be found, including Lapwing, Dunlin, Snipe, Black-tailed Godwit and Curlew. Lesser Black-backed Gull and Black-headed Gull numbers can be substantial, and Green Sandpiper and Mediterranean Gull have been recorded.

Throughout the year, this is an excellent site for Little Egret, and many nest nearby in summer. Kingfisher can also be seen at any time of year, though they are always elusive.

In summer, Sedge Warbler and Reed Warbler can be found in the larger expanses of reedbed.

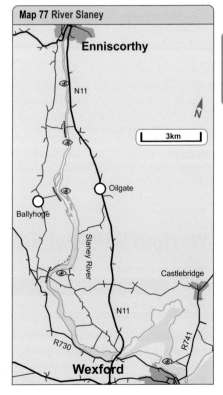

South-east

155

Curracloe

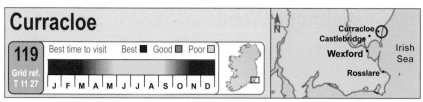

119

Best time to visit   Best ■ Good ■ Poor ☐

Grid ref.
T 11 27   J F M A M J J A S O N D

A long stretch of sandy beach, the winter haunt of large flocks of Common Scoter, and many divers and seaduck.

Directions Map 79, p.158. Curracloe village is 8km NE of Wexford town. From Wexford, leave N on the R741 (across the bridge), heading for Castlebridge and Gorey. 3km after the bridge, take a right onto the R742, signposted for Curracloe. Arriving into the village after 5km, the road forks. Taking a right onto the R743 will bring you to the extensive sand dunes which run parallel to the coast, and a minor road which runs behind these dunes for 2.5 km.

By continuing straight on through Curracloe village and taking a right after 2km, you will be at the opposite end of this coastal road, an area known as **Ballinesker**.

Common Scoter and Velvet Scoter

The best approach for finding birds is to stop along this road at several points, and climb the dunes to scan the sea for scoter flocks and other birds. The Ballinesker end of the coastal road in particular offers extensive views from a nearby hill. High tide brings birds a little closer and calm weather is best. A telescope is recommended.

Species
Autumn, winter & spring Wigeon, Teal, Eider (R), Long-tailed Duck (O), Common Scoter (often 100s, occasionally 1000s), Velvet Scoter (O), Red-breasted Merganser, Red-throated Diver, Black-throated Diver (R), Great Northern Diver, Great Crested Grebe, Slavonian Grebe, Red-necked Grebe (R), Fulmar, Cormorant, Hen Harrier (O), Golden Plover, Lapwing, Snipe, Little Gull (O), Sandwich Tern (R).

Rarities Surf Scoter, Black-necked Grebe, Glaucous Gull, Little Auk, Hoopoe.

Wexford Wildfowl Reserve

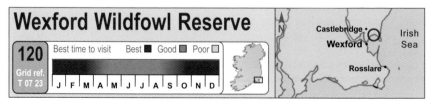

120

Best time to visit   Best ■ Good ■ Poor ☐

Grid ref.
T 07 23   J F M A M J J A S O N D

A winter haunt of half the world population of of Greenland White-fronted Geese, as well as 1000s of other wildfowl, waders and other species. A well-equipped and maintained reserve, with an impressive list of unusual species, all of which make a winter visit one of the outstanding birdwatching experiences in Ireland.

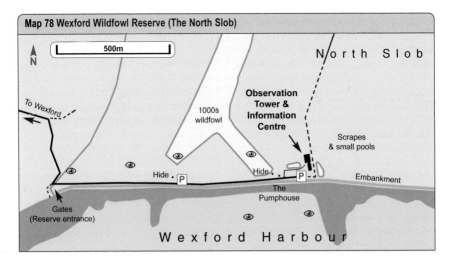

Map 78 Wexford Wildfowl Reserve (The North Slob)

The Wexford Wildfowl Reserve is part of **The North Slob**, an area of reclaimed land. Although the Reserve has easy access, most of the remainder of 'The Slobs' are private farmland, and cannot be entered without permission.

Directions Map 78, above. For a general map of the North Slob area, see Map 79, p.158. Leave Wexford town N, over the bridge, on the R741 to Gorey. There is a signpost for Wexford Wildfowl Reserve after 3km. Take the right and follow this narrow road for 2km until you come to the gates of the Reserve.

400m into the Reserve, the first hide (The Pat Walsh Hide) and a carpark are on your left, from where thousands of wildfowl and waders can be seen in and around the freshwater channel. Continue on another 500m to the main carpark. A tower hide overlooks another part of the channel, and the upper floor provides excellent views out over Wexford Harbour for waders, divers and grebes. A telescope is recomended for both these hides.

The Pumphouse, beside the main carpark, houses occasional exhibitions, but otherwise, enter the Reserve Centre through the metal gates beside the carpark. There are paths through a series of pools with a wildfowl collection where many of the typical species seen on the Reserve can be studied. The main Reserve Centre and Observation Tower are open from 9am to 5pm daily throughout the year. Closed on Christmas Day. An information board highlights recent sightings, and the tower is equipped with identification charts and telescopes. There is also a small display of the ornithological history of the area. Admission is free.

Species

All year Mute Swan (150+), Greylag Goose (feral birds), Cormorant, Little Egret, Peregrine, Water Rail (O), Kingfisher, Stock Dove (O), Barn Owl (O), Grey Wagtail (O) Tree Sparrow.

Autumn & winter Bewick's Swan (now O, declining), Whooper Swan, Pink-footed Goose (O), White-fronted Goose (1000s), Russian White-fronted Goose (a few most winters), Greylag Goose (small numbers), Barnacle Goose (O), Brent Goose (100s), Dark-bellied Brent (R), Wigeon (1000s), Gadwall, Teal (100s), Green-winged Teal (R), Pintail, Garganey (R autumn & spring), Shoveler, Pochard, Tufted Duck, Scaup, Long-tailed Duck (R), Common Scoter (R Wexford Harbour), Velvet Scoter (R Wexford Harbour), Goldeneye, Red-breasted Merganser, Ruddy Duck (R), Red-throated Diver (Wexford Harbour), Black-throated Diver (R Wexford Harbour), Great Northern Diver (Wexford Harbour), Little Grebe, Great Crested Grebe, Red-necked Grebe (R Wexford Harbour), Slavonian Grebe (O Wexford Harbour), Black-necked Grebe (R Wexford Harbour), Gannet (O Wexford Harbour), Hen Harrier, Buzzard (R), Merlin (O), Oystercatcher (100s), Golden Plover (100s), Grey Plover (Wexford Harbour), Lapwing (1000s), Knot

(Wexford Harbour), Little Stint (R), Pectoral Sandpiper (R), Curlew Sandpiper (O), Purple Sandpiper (O), Dunlin, Ruff (O autumn), Jack Snipe (O), Snipe, Woodcock (O), Black-tailed Godwit (100s), Bar-tailed Godwit, Whimbrel (O), Curlew (100s), Spotted Redshank (O), Green Sandpiper (R autumn), Wood Sandpiper (R autumn), Common Sandpiper (R), Mediterranean Gull (R), Little Gull (R), gulls, Black Tern (R autumn), Short-eared Owl (R), Black Redstart, Chiffchaff (O), Long-tailed Tit (O), Carrion Crow (R), Raven, Brambling (O), Snow Bunting (R), Lapland Bunting (R), Yellowhammer.

Spring & summer Cuckoo, Wheatear, Grasshopper Warbler, Sedge Warbler, Reed Warbler (R), Willow Warbler.

Rarities The list of species recorded in the area is one of the highest for any in Ireland.

First Irish records of Lesser White-fronted Goose, Paddyfield Warbler, Western Sandpiper, Isabelline Shrike and Pine Bunting have been seen here.

Other rarities recorded here include Bean Goose, Snow Goose, Canada Goose, Black Brant, American Wigeon, Blue-winged Teal, Ring-necked Duck, Lesser Scaup, Red-crested Pochard, Ferruginous Duck, Smew, Goosander, Spoonbill, Red Kite, Marsh Harrier, Montagu's Harrier, Osprey, Hobby, Gyr Falcon, Crane, Wood Sandpiper, Long-billed Dowitcher, Ring-billed Gull, Turtle Dove, Alpine Swift, Yellow Wagtail, Redstart and Ring Ouzel.

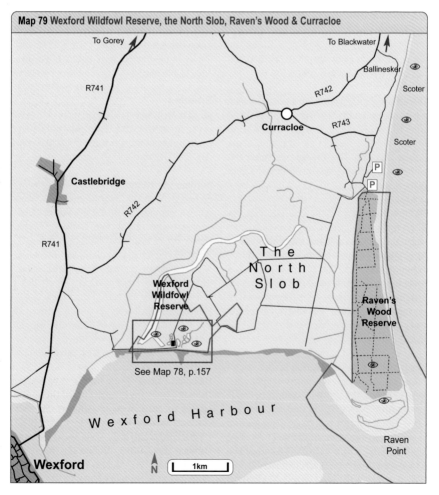

Map 79 Wexford Wildfowl Reserve, the North Slob, Raven's Wood & Curracloe

To Gorey

To Blackwater

Ballinesker

Scoter

R741

R742

Curracloe

R743

Scoter

P

P

Castlebridge

R742

R741

The North Slob

Wexford Wildfowl Reserve

Raven's Wood Reserve

See Map 78, p.157

Wexford Harbour

Raven Point

Wexford

N

1km

121 Raven's Wood Reserve Grid ref. T 11 25

A large, coastal coniferous forest, with many typical woodland species throughout the year, and which can be attractive to migrants in spring and autumn.

See Map 79, previous page. The Reserve is reached from Curracloe by taking the R743 for 2km to the coast, then, at the T-junction, taking the road to the right, parallel to the sand dunes. The forest becomes visible directly ahead after 1km. It is possible to park at the entrance. Access is on foot, either along the paths through the forest, or along the seaward side of the dunes.

Many of the regular woodland species can be found throughout the year, including Chiffchaff (summer), Spotted Flycatcher (summer),

Treecreeper, Siskin and Redpoll. **Raven Point** is the site of a large roost of White-fronted Geese, and watching their arrival on a winter's evening is an unforgettable experience. Passerine migrants have been found at the S tip of the forest, in spring and autumn, with Redstart and Wood Warbler recorded, though undoubtedly there is potential for more discoveries.

The forest is one of the better areas in Wexford to see Crossbill, usually from late summer into winter, and Woodcock can usually be seen during display flights at dusk from April to late June. Long-eared Owl is present, but only likely to be seen at last light, sometimes flying out over the North Slob to the W.

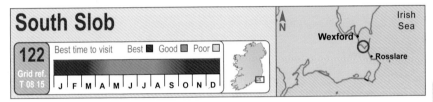

South Slob

| 122 | Best time to visit | Best ■ Good ■ Poor □ |
| Grid ref. T 08 15 | J F M A M J J A S O N D | |

N

Wexford

Irish Sea

Rosslare

Broad freshwater channels and reedbeds on vast, open expanses of reclaimed land, excellent for swans, geese and other wildfowl in winter, and good numbers of waders. Also an excellent site for raptors in winter.

The South Slob is private farmland, and permission must be sought from farm workers before venturing onto the Slob. At all times, do not block the road or venture from the car, and give way to any farm machinery. Access may be denied on winter days when shooting is being conducted.

Many of the geese and swans move between the South Slob and North Slob (the Wexford Wildfowl Reserve, Site 120), depending on disturbance.

Directions Map 80, next page. From Wexford, leave the town on the R730 to Rosslare. After 2km, take the left turn at the Farmer's Kitchen pub. After 1km take a left, and after another 1km the road crosses a canal and railway line, sometimes

necessitating opening and closing the gates at the level crossing. To reach the S side of the South Slob, ignore the left turn 1km from the Farmer's Kitchen and continue on this road for over 1.2km. Just where the road swings sharp right, go straight and follow this narrow road to the end and over the small bridge.

Please note that this is private farmland and permission should be sought before venturing further.

Species
All year Tufted Duck, Great Crested Grebe, Little Grebe, Cormorant, Little Egret, Buzzard, Water Rail, Kingfisher, Stock Dove, Tree Sparrow.

Autumn, winter & spring Whooper Swan, Bewick's Swan, White-fronted Goose (100s), Wigeon, Gadwall, Teal, Pintail, Shoveler, Pochard, Scaup, Long-tailed Duck (R), Goldeneye, Hen Harrier, Merlin, Peregrine, Golden Plover, Lapwing, Snipe, Jack Snipe (O), Woodcock (O),

Curlew, gulls, Little Gull (O), Short-eared Owl (R), Grey Wagtail, Chiffchaff, Willow Warbler, Brambling (R), Siskin, Redpoll.

Summer Gadwall (O), Pochard (O), Scaup (O), Marsh Harrier (R), Cuckoo (O), Reed Warbler, Sedge Warbler. Swallows, martins and swifts can occasionally number into the 100s over the main channel.

Rarities Pink-footed Goose, Barnacle Goose, Dark-bellied Brent Goose, Black Brant, Green-winged Teal, Garganey, Red-crested Pochard, Ring-necked Duck, Smew, Goosander, Ruddy Duck, Black-necked Grebe, Night Heron, Great White Egret, Red Kite, Osprey, Black Tern, Turtle Dove, Chimney Swift, Golden Oriole, Carrion Crow.

The Grey Partridges in this area are all feral birds, released for shooting.

Greenland White-fronted Geese

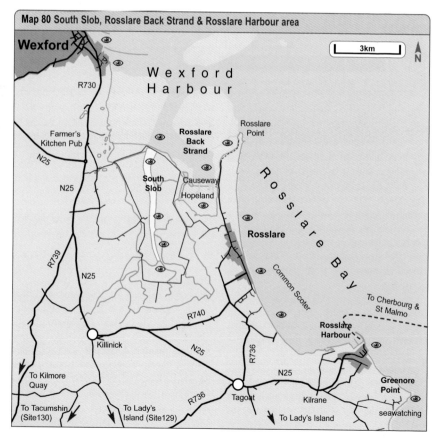

Map 80 South Slob, Rosslare Back Strand & Rosslare Harbour area

Rosslare Back Strand

123

Grid ref. T 08 17

Best time to visit   Best ■ Good ■ Poor □

J F M A M J J A S O N D

N

Wexford

Rosslare

Irish Sea

A vast intertidal mudflat, attracting large numbers of waders and some wildfowl in autumn, winter and early spring.

Directions Map 80, previous page. Located just N of Rosslare village. From Wexford town, take the N25 to Rosslare Harbour. 2km after passing through Killinick village take the left fork, onto the R740, signposted for Rosslare. At the roundabout, follow signs for Rosslare and at the T-junction in Rosslare village, go left and continue N until the large expanse of Rosslare Back Strand becomes visible on your left. The best views and largest number of birds occur from here (the area known as Hopeland), N to Rosslare Point, and the causeway across part of the bay is often used as a high tide roost by waders. Low tide should be avoided as many birds will be very distant.

Species
Autumn, winter & spring Brent Goose, Wigeon, Teal, Pintail (O), Red-breasted Merganser, Red-throated Diver, Great Northern Diver, Slavonian Grebe, Cormorant, Little Egret, Hen Harrier (O), Buzzard (O), Merlin (O), Peregrine, Golden Plover, Grey Plover, Lapwing, Little Stint (R autumn), Curlew Sandpiper (O autumn), Dunlin, Ruff (O autumn), Snipe, Black-tailed Godwit, Bar-tailed Godwit, Whimbrel (mainly spring), Curlew, Spotted Redshank (R), Common Sandpiper (spring), Mediterranean Gull (O), gulls, Short-eared Owl (R winter), Kingfisher (O).

Summer Sandwich Tern, Common Tern, Arctic Tern, Cuckoo, Wheatear.

Some non-breeding waders are usually present throughout summer, such as Knot, Bar-tailed Godwit and Turnstone.

Rarities Black Brant, Great White Egret, Spoonbill, American Golden Plover, Semipalmated Sandpiper, White-rumped Sandpiper, Terek Sandpiper, Gull-billed Tern, Great Spotted Woodpecker.

South-east

124 Rosslare Harbour area Grid ref. T 13 12

An open sandy bay and docks area, good for Common Scoter, divers and Black Redstart in winter.

See Map 80, previous page. The port of Rosslare is well signposted from Wexford and the surrounding area. From Wexford town, take the N25 all the way to the harbour area. It is possible to park near the last roundabout close to the port (in the area of sand dunes). Black Redstart is usually recorded each winter in and around the harbour walls and rocky shoreline.

In strong NE winds in autumn, seabirds shelter either in the harbour or just offshore, and Sabine's Gull has been seen in such circumstances. Offshore, Manx Shearwater and occasional skuas can pass, but if seabird passage looks promising, it might be better to go to nearby Greenore Point (Site 125). Fea's/Zino's Petrel, Mediterranean Gull, Little Auk, Hoopoe, Lesser Whitethroat and Rose-coloured Starling have been seen from the Rosslare Harbour area.

To view **Rosslare Bay**, return along the N25 for 5km toward Wexford and turn right onto the R736 at Tagoat. Any right turn along this road will lead to the shoreline, with elevated viewpoints along the coast. If travelling from Wexford, take the left fork off the N25 onto the R740, 10km from Wexford, signposted for Rosslare.

The best area for scoter is just S of Rosslare village. Smaller numbers occur N of Rosslare to Rosslare Point. Locating the scoter flocks is easier in calm weather, and as they are often distant, a telescope is recommended. Offshore, large numbers of Common Scoter, Red-throated Diver, Great Northern Diver and Red-breasted Merganser are present throughout winter, with occasional Velvet Scoter. Rarer birds recorded here include Dark-bellied Brent Goose, Surf Scoter, Red-necked Grebe, Slavonian Grebe, Black-necked Grebe and Desert Wheatear.

125 Greenore Point Grid ref. T 15 11

A good seawatching site in autumn in E or NE winds.

This seawatching site is only really worth visiting in strong E or NE winds, preferably with rain or overcast conditions, from July to November (Dec to Feb might prove worthwhile). If the wind is strong from the SE, S or SW, Carnsore Point (Site 128) is usually the better option. A telescope is recommended. See also SEAWATCHING p.356.

See Map 80, p.160 From Wexford, take the N25 to Rosslare Harbour. 3.5km before reaching the harbour, the road passes through Tagoat, and 2km further, just 1km before Rosslare Harbour, is the small village of Kilrane. Pass through the minor crossroads and continue for 100m, then take the minor road to the right. Travel straight for 1km before turning left and continue on this road to the end, and follow the small rise just before the sea cliff. Walk across the field to the small hut and view from there, or just below it.

In the right conditions, seabird numbers can be very high, with hundreds or even thousands of Manx Shearwaters passing, along with other common species such as Fulmar, Gannet and Kittiwake. There is likely to be a few Sooty Shearwater, Mediterranean Shearwater (O), Storm Petrel, terns, auks and gulls. Of the skuas, Arctic, Pomarine and Great are all regular in a good movement of seabirds, and this is one of the most likely sites on the E or SE coast to see Long-tailed Skua.

In recent years, rare birds seen here include Eider, Fea's/Zino's Petrel, Leach's Petrel, Great Shearwater, Grey Phalarope and Sabine's Gull.

126 Churchtown area Grid ref. T 12 05

Coastal gardens and hedgerow which attract migrants, particularly after SE winds in autumn (fewer birds in spring).

Map 81, p.165 Leaving Lady's Island for Carnsore Point, go about 1.5 km, then take a left at the Lobster Pot pub. Continue for 1km, then take a right. Anywhere from this turn, all the way to the small graveyard at Churchtown is good for migrants. After 1km, you reach the cluster of houses, walls and hedgerows of Churchtown. Many areas of foliage can be searched from the road, but be sure to ask permission before entering fields or gardens.

For much of the year, the gardens and hedgerows around Churchtown are unremarkable for birds (though Stock Dove is present all year). But following E, SE or S winds in autumn, especially if there has been accompanying rain, the area can host a good selection of grounded migrants. Chiffchaff, Willow Warbler, Blackcap and Spotted Flycatcher are often present under such conditions, and Black Redstart and Pied Flycatcher are occasionally found, but there is always the chance of something more unusual.

Rare birds seen here include Corncrake, Short-eared Owl, Chimney Swift, Whinchat, Pied Flycatcher, Ring Ouzel, Melodious Warbler, Icterine Warbler, Pallas's Warbler and Yellow-browed Warbler.

Nethertown & Carne Beach

127

Grid ref.
T 12 04

Best time to visit   Best ■ Good ■ Poor □

J F M A M J J A S O N D

Wexford
Rosslare
Kilmore Quay
Carnsore Point
Irish Sea

A loafing area for hundreds of terns in summer, and particularly early autumn, with good views of Roseate Terns possible.

Directions Map 81, p.165. For **Nethertown**, leave Lady's Island E, following the road for 1.2km and continue straight close to the Lobster Pot pub. Continue for 2km and take the left turn down towards the wind turbines. After 1km, the beach and rocky shoreline are visible. The main tern roosting and loafing areas are the rocks to the right, and the rocky headland along the beach to the left, 500m to the N.

For **Carne Beach**, leave Lady's Island E, following the road for 1.2km and take the left turn at the junction close to the Lobster Pot pub. Continue straight for 1.5km and go right near the caravan park until the beach and pier are visible. Explore the adjacent coast for terns and waders.

Seabirds can sometimes be seen passing offshore, but if conditions are good, nearby Carnsore Point (Site 128, below) provides the best opportunities for seawatching.

Species
Summer & autumn Divers, seabirds (see above), Dunlin (autumn), Golden Plover (autumn), Little Stint (O autumn), Pectoral Sandpiper (R autumn), Curlew Sandpiper (O autumn), skuas (regular autumn), Mediterranean Gull (O), Little Gull (O), Sandwich Tern, Roseate Tern, Common Tern, Arctic Tern, Little Tern (O), Black Tern (O autumn), auks, Black Redstart (R autumn & winter), Wheatear, Whitethroat (O).

Rarities Red Kite, Hobby, Baird's Sandpiper, Spotted Sandpiper, Bee-eater, Woodchat Shrike, Carrion Crow.

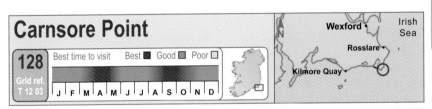

Carnsore Point

128

Grid ref.
T 12 03

Best time to visit   Best ■ Good ■ Poor □

J F M A M J J A S O N D

Wexford
Rosslare
Kilmore Quay
Irish Sea

A good site for migrants, and a good seawatching headland, best for both in spring and autumn.

Directions Map 81, p.165. From Lady's Island (Site 129), travel E for 1.5km and continue straight at the Lobster Pot pub. Continue for 2km and turn left onto an unsurfaced gravel track just at the point where the road swings sharp right. The thick hedgerows and overgrown fields here hold occasional migrants in spring and autumn. After 800m, this track turns sharp left, and from here becomes progressively rougher and may not be suitable for all vehicles. If in doubt, park at the side of the road and continue to Carnsore Point on foot. Migrants can be found anywhere in this

Sabine's Gull

South-east

163

general area in suitable conditions – a SE wind in spring or autumn is best.

Species

Seawatching is best from just seaward (to the SE) of the windfarm, behind some small, bare ditches and walls on the low clifftop, and is best in S or SE winds, though SW, E and NE winds can also be good. See also SEAWATCHING, p.356.

Spring & summer Manx Shearwater, Fulmar, Storm Petrel (O), Gannet, Shag, Kittiwake, Guillemot, Razorbill, Puffin (small numbers), skuas (R), Turtle Dove (R), Cuckoo (O), Wheatear.

Autumn Red-throated Diver, Great Northern Diver, Fulmar, Great Shearwater (R), Sooty Shearwater (O), Manx Shearwater, Balearic Shearwater (O), Storm Petrel, Leach's Petrel (mainly Sept & Oct), Gannet, Shag, Cormorant, Grey Phalarope (R), Pomarine Skua (O), Arctic

Skua, Great Skua, Little Gull (R), Sabine's Gull (R), Kittiwake, Sandwich Tern, Roseate Tern (O), Common Tern (O), Arctic Tern, Black Tern (R), Guillemot, Razorbill, Black Guillemot (R), Puffin (O), Whitethroat (O).

Winter Red-throated Diver, Great Northern Diver, Fulmar, Manx Shearwater (O), Gannet, Shag, Cormorant, Kittiwake, Great Skua (R), Guillemot, Razorbill, Black Guillemot (R), Little Auk (R), Puffin (O).

Rarities 'Blue' Fulmar, Cory's Shearwater, Little Bittern, Grey Phalarope, Honey Buzzard, Osprey, Hobby, Little Ringed Plover, Long-tailed Skua, Great Spotted Cuckoo, Short-eared Owl, Bee-eater, Hoopoe, Tree Pipit, Water Pipit, Yellow Wagtail, Whinchat, Black Redstart, Redstart, Ring Ouzel, Desert Wheatear, Lesser Whitethroat, Yellow-browed Warbler, Firecrest, Pied Flycatcher, Woodchat Shrike, Carrion Crow, Common Rosefinch, Lapland Bunting.

Lady's Island Lake

129	Best time to visit	Best ■ Good ■ Poor □
Grid ref. T 10 06	J F M A M J J A S O N D	

A large, shallow, brackish lagoon, with some reedbed. Good at all times of the year, with a wide variety of wildfowl and waders in winter and an accessible site for Roseate and other terns in summer.

In summer, Inish Island, the main island on the lake, holds one of the largest tern colonies in the country, with around 1000 pairs of Sandwich Tern, 100 of Roseate, 200+ Arctic and 400+ pairs of Common Tern, with a number of wader and gull species.

In autumn and winter, the lake holds good numbers of Gadwall, and other wildfowl and waders, particularly Whooper Swan, Wigeon, Scaup, Lapwing and Black-tailed Godwit. Autumn is the peak time for waders, but the numbers vary, declining with rising water levels as winter progresses. August and September are the best for waders (including rare American waders), and many terns frequent the area into September.

Directions Map 81, next page. 3 km W of Carnsore Point, in the SE corner of Ireland. There are three main areas of interest to birdwatchers.

Lady's Island village and island (actually a promontory) are on the N side of the lake and are reached by leaving Wexford on the main N25 to Rosslare. After about 14km (4km before Rosslare Harbour), the road passes through Tagoat. Take a right, clearly signposted for Lady's Island, and continue for another 4km to reach the village of Lady's Island and the lake. This whole lake area, reed patches and the small, flat island (Scarageen Island) to the W of the pilgrimage site, in front of and around the ruined tower, is very good for a variety of birds at all times of year. It is particularly good with lower water levels in early autumn, with numerous terns, waders and wildfowl. Many rare birds have been found in this area. There is a path either side of the pilgrimage altar which follows the shoreline in a full circle, about a 2km walk. This will take you to a small grotto overlooking

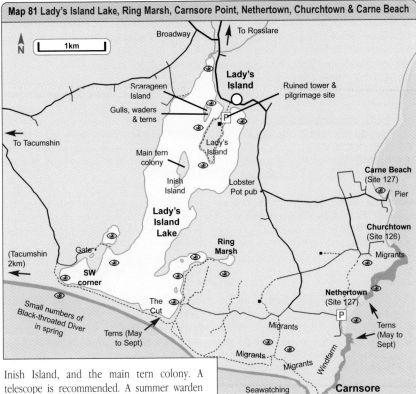

Map 81 Lady's Island Lake, Ring Marsh, Carnsore Point, Nethertown, Churchtown & Carne Beach

Inish Island, and the main tern colony. A telescope is recommended. A summer warden may be on hand to help identify the birds.

Ring Marsh Leave Lady's Island E, following the road for 1.2km and continue straight at the junction with at Lobster Pot pub. Continue for 3.5km until the road becomes a dirt track. It is possible to park carefully here and explore on foot. This area is good for Cuckoo, Whitethroat and occasional Whinchat in spring, and is a loafing area for terns in summer and autumn, especially along the dunes near The Cut. The indented, boulder-strewn shoreline often has many wildfowl and waders, particularly in autumn when the water levels are low. Walking N along this shoreline eventually leads to Ring Marsh on the right. This is a small, shallow pool surrounded by a large reedbed, and is good for duck and Reed and Sedge Warbler, though views of the pool are restricted and some wading may be necessary.

The **SW corner** is reached by leaving Lady's Island N (as if returning to Wexford), but taking the first left after 500m. Take another left after 250m (just at Broadway) and continue for 4km,

going through Tacumshin village, until you come to a large staggered crossroads where the main road continues sharp right. Take the left here and continue until the lake becomes visible ahead. The shoreline has waders, while some wildfowl and grebes are on the lake. The road continues straight but you can take the small road to the left. This road eventually stops at a gate, and while the small pool beyond is good for wildfowl and waders, it is best to enquire locally about access, and be sure to close the gate after you. Alternatively, continue straight and park near the dunes to scan the seaward side of the dunes. Black-throated Diver is often seen here in April and May, while Gannet, Cormorant, Fulmar and Kittiwake are usually present offshore throughout the year.

Species
Spring & summer Teal, Garganey (O), Ruddy Duck (O spring), Grey Plover (O), Lapwing, Dunlin, Snipe, Black-tailed Godwit, Cormorant,

Little Egret, Marsh Harrier (O Ring Marsh), Hen Harrier (O), Buzzard (R), Hobby (R), Water Rail, Ruff (O), Snipe, Whimbrel (especially May), Curlew, Spotted Redshank (R), Mediterranean Gull (O), Black-headed Gull (100s), Little Gull (O), gulls, Sandwich Tern, Roseate Tern, Common Tern, Arctic Tern, Black Tern (O spring), Cuckoo (O), Yellow Wagtail (R), Whinchat(O), Wheatear, Grasshopper Warbler (O), Sedge Warbler, Reed Warbler (Ring Marsh), Whitethroat, Willow Warbler, Spotted Flycatcher (trees S of pilgrimage site), Tree Sparrow (nests in the ruined tower and nearby farm buildings).

Autumn & winter Bewick's Swan (O small numbers), Whooper Swan (winter), Pink-footed Goose (R), White-fronted Goose (O), Greylag Goose (feral), Brent Goose (O), Wigeon (1000+), Gadwall (150+), Teal (100s), Green-winged Teal (R), Pintail, Shoveler, Pochard (100+), Tufted Duck, Scaup (winter), Goldeneye (winter), Red-breasted Merganser (winter), Ruddy Duck (O), Red-throated Diver (R), Great Crested Grebe (winter), Cormorant, Little Egret, Marsh Harrier (O autumn), Hen Harrier (O), Merlin, Water Rail, Golden Plover, Lapwing (1000+), Knot (O), Little Stint (autumn), Pectoral Sandpiper (O), Curlew Sandpiper (autumn), Dunlin (100s, autumn), Ruff (autumn), Jack Snipe (O), Snipe, Black-tailed Godwit, Bar-tailed Godwit (small numbers), Whimbrel (autumn), Curlew (often 200+), Spotted Redshank (O), Green Sandpiper (O Aug

& Sept), Wood Sandpiper (O Aug & Sept), Grey Phalarope (R), Mediterranean Gull, Little Gull (O), Short-eared Owl, Yellow Wagtail (R autumn), Grey Wagtail (O), Whinchat (O autumn), Tree Sparrow (O).

Black-throated Diver are regular in spring in small numbers, on the sea off the SW side of the lake.

Rarities Like Tacumshin, Lady's Island Lake is particularly well known for attracting rare American waders, particularly in August and September.

American Wigeon, Blue-winged Teal, Ring-necked Duck, Pied-billed Grebe, Slavonian Grebe, Black-necked Grebe, Great White Egret, Spoonbill, Montagu's Harrier, Osprey, Crane, Black-winged Stilt, Avocet, Stone Curlew, Little Ringed Plover, American Golden Plover, Pacific Golden Plover, Semipalmated Sandpiper, Temminck's Stint, White-rumped Sandpiper, Baird's Sandpiper, Short-billed Dowitcher, Long-billed Dowitcher, Lesser Yellowlegs, Wilson's Phalarope, Bonaparte's Gull, Ring-billed Gull, Yellow-legged Gull, Iceland Gull, Glaucous Gull, Gull-billed Tern, Forster's Tern, Elegant Tern, American Black Tern, White-winged Black Tern, Turtle Dove, Hoopoe, Wryneck, Short-toed Lark, Richard's Pipit, Black Redstart, Barred Warbler, Yellow-browed Warbler, Bearded Tit, Rose-coloured Starling, Lapland Bunting.

Tacumshin Lake

130
Grid ref.
T 05 06

Best time to visit   Best ■ Good ■ Poor □

| J | F | M | A | M | J | J | A | S | O | N | D |

N — Wexford • — Irish Sea — Rosslare — Kilmore Quay • — Carnsore Point

A large, shallow coastal lagoon, surrounded by open mud, sand, grassland and reedbeds. One of the best sites in Ireland for waders, including many rarities. Large numbers of wildfowl, waders and gulls occur throughout the year, but autumn and early winter are particularly good. In summer, a good variety of reed and wetland birds breed.

In autumn and winter, the lake holds internationally important numbers of Mute and Whooper

Swans and Black-tailed Godwit. Also in winter, there are nationally important numbers of a further 10 species: Wigeon, Gadwall, Teal, Pintail, Shoveler, Little Grebe, Coot, Golden Plover, Grey Plover and Lapwing.

In late summer, Tacumshin is one of the best sites in Ireland for seeing 'winter' waders, with Grey Plover, Knot and Black-tailed Godwits present. In early autumn, gatherings of Lesser Black-backed Gull can number over 600+.

Tacumshin is worth exploring extensively on foot. A pair of wellingtons and a telescope are recommended.

Directions Map 82, next page. Roughly mid-way between Carnsore Point and Kilmore Quay on the S Wexford coast. The four main access points, from E to W, are as follows:

East End From the N25 Wexford to Rosslare road take the right at Killinick, signposted for Lady's Island. Continue for 200m and take the right (the main road continues left) in the village. Follow the road and continue left. After 1.4km, go left at the T-junction. From here, go 4km, ignoring all turns and continuing left at one very sharp hairpin bend, until you reach a large staggered crossroads where the main road continues left, signposted for Lady's Island. Go right and follow this narrow road for 1.5km until you see a ruined castle to the left. Take this left and pass the castle on the right. The small pond beyond the castle is worth checking, with Night Heron found there in 2006. Take the left turn just past the castle and 500m down this road is a carpark overlooking the East End channels and lake. Explore from here on foot.

The pool to the left is good for Gadwall and other duck, and Garganey, harriers, Little Egret and Little Gulls are often present. Reed Warbler breeds here in the larger patches of *Phragmites* reeds. To the right, the main lake holds many hundreds or even thousands of waders and wildfowl throughout the year. It is possible to wade across the channel here to explore the large expanse of sandy shoreline.

The **Forgotten Corner** is reached by continuing straight past the ruined castle and the left turn for the East End, and following this road to the end where the lake is again visible ahead. Park at the end of the road and explore on foot. The Forgotten Corner is the small bay on your right, the main lake is in front and to your left. This sheltered bay can be excellent for waders, and is a very good spot for seeing Water Rail when water levels are low, as they feed along the edge of the sedges. The small bay between the Forgotten Corner and the East End is also worth checking.

The **Lingstown End** is best reached by taking a left turn just past the Post Office in the village of Tomhaggard. Continue past the pub on the left and follow this winding narrow road for 700m before taking the first turn on the right. Within 300m, a large area of reedbed is visible on your right. A little further on, it is possible to park and explore on foot. This large reedbed is one of the best areas for Reed Warbler and Marsh Harrier in spring and summer. It is possible to wade through the sedges to the central part of the lake and 'The Patches' (see below), while all around here, various small pools and muddy areas can hold a wide variety of waders, wildfowl, pipits, wagtails and others.

The **White Hole** can be reached by taking the road from Tomhaggard toward Kilmore Quay. After 1km, take a left onto a narrow winding road, and after 1km, left for Ballagh Shore, signposted 'Fishing'. This ends after 1km at a small bridge and it is possible to park here and explore the large open expanse of wetland. From here, follow the rough track left to view the W end of Tacumshin. There is good marsh and reedbed habitat here, but fewer waders.

Another area, known as **'The Patches'**, can be reached by a long walk from either the East End, the Forgotten Corner or the Lingstown End. It is a flat, open, sandy saltmarsh area on the W side of the lake with widely fluctuating water levels. Regardless of route taken, you will need wellingtons to cross channels. This is one of the most consistent spots in Europe to see Buff-breasted Sandpiper in September, along with many other waders, often 1000+ of Dunlin.

Species

Spring & summer Teal, Garganey (O), Grey Plover, Lapwing, Dunlin, Snipe, Black-tailed Godwit, Marsh Harrier (O), Hen Harrier (O), Montagu's Harrier (R), Buzzard (R), Water Rail, Ruff, Snipe, Whimbrel (autumn), Curlew, Spotted Redshank (O), Little Gull (O), gulls, Sandwich Tern (O spring), Black Tern (O spring), Cuckoo (O), Yellow Wagtail (R), Whinchat (O), Wheatear, Grasshopper Warbler, Sedge Warbler, Reed Warbler (E End & Lingstown), Whitethroat, Willow Warbler.

Autumn & winter (Water levels are often very high in winter and it may not be possible to walk around the main lake.) Mute Swan (200+),

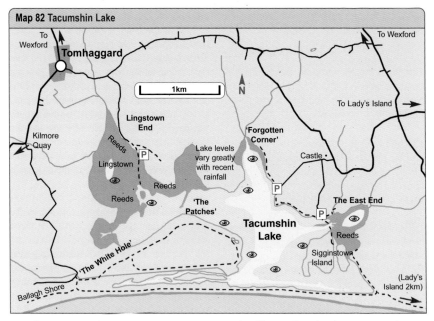

Map 82 Tacumshin Lake

To Wexford

Tomhaggard

1km

N

To Wexford

To Lady's Island

Lingstown End

Kilmore Quay

Reeds

P

Lingstown

Reeds

Reeds

'The Patches'

Lake levels vary greatly with recent rainfall

Reeds

'Forgotten Corner'

Castle

P

Tacumshin Lake

The East End

P

Reeds

Sigginstown Island

'The White Hole'

Ballagh Shore

(Lady's Island 2km)

Bewick's Swan (O), Whooper Swan (100s, winter), Pink-footed Goose (R), White-fronted Goose (O), Greylag Goose (feral), Brent Goose, Shelduck (50+), Wigeon (1000s), Gadwall (100+), Teal (1000+), Green-winged Teal (R), Pintail (200+), Shoveler (50+), Pochard, Tufted Duck, Scaup (winter), Goldeneye (winter), Red-breasted Merganser (winter), Little Grebe (100+), Great Crested Grebe (winter), Cormorant, Little Egret, Coot (100s), Marsh Harrier (O autumn, R winter), Hen Harrier, Merlin, Water Rail, Golden Plover (100s, mainly winter), Grey Plover, Lapwing (100s), Knot, Semipalmated Sandpiper (R Sept), Little Stint (autumn), White-rumped Sandpiper (R Sept), Baird's Sandpiper (R Sept), Pectoral Sandpiper (O), Curlew Sandpiper (autumn), Dunlin (100s, autumn), Buff-breasted Sandpiper (O Sept, 'The Patches'), Ruff (autumn), Jack Snipe (O), Snipe, Black-tailed Godwit (1000+), Bar-tailed Godwit (O), Whimbrel (autumn), Curlew (often 400+), Spotted Redshank, Green Sandpiper (Aug & Sept), Wood Sandpiper (O Aug & Sept), Little Gull (O), gulls, Sandwich Tern (O autumn), Short-eared Owl (O), Yellow Wagtail (R), Grey Wagtail (O), Whinchat (O autumn).

Rarities Tacumshin is particularly well known for attracting rare American waders. Of these, Semipalmated Sandpiper, White-rumped Sandpiper, Baird's Sandpiper, Pectoral Sandpiper and Buff-breasted Sandpiper are seen nearly every year in August and September. Others, seen every year or two in autumn, include Long-billed Dowitcher and Lesser Yellowlegs.

American Wigeon, American Black Duck, Blue-winged Teal, Ring-necked Duck, Pied-billed Grebe, Black-necked Grebe, Bittern, Night Heron, Great White Egret, Purple Heron, White Stork, Glossy Ibis, Spoonbill, Osprey, Montagu's Harrier, Hobby, Red-footed Falcon, Spotted Crake, Sora, Corncrake, Common Crane, Black-winged Stilt, Avocet, Killdeer, Kentish Plover, Dotterel, Little Ringed Plover, American Golden Plover, Pacific Golden Plover, Temminck's Stint, Sharp-tailed Sandpiper, Broad-billed Sandpiper, Stilt Sandpiper, Short-billed Dowitcher, Long-billed Dowitcher, Marsh Sandpiper, Lesser Yellowlegs, Spotted Sandpiper, Wilson's Phalarope, Red-necked Phalarope, Mediterranean Gull, Bonaparte's Gull, Ring-billed Gull, Yellow-legged Gull, Iceland Gull, Glaucous Gull, Gull-billed Tern, Whiskered Tern, White-winged Black Tern, Turtle Dove, Alpine Swift, Hoopoe, Short-toed Lark, Red-rumped Swallow, Richard's Pipit, Tawny Pipit, Tree Pipit, Red-throated Pipit, Water Pipit, Citrine Wagtail, Bluethroat, Savi's Warbler, Marsh Warbler, Dartford Warbler, Bearded Tit, Red-backed Shrike, Lapland Bunting.

In autumn and winter, a good area for seabirds, gulls and small numbers of waders.

See Map 83, next page. Leave Wexford on the N 25 Wexford to Rosslare road, and about 4km S of the town, take the R739 right, signposted for Kilmore Quay.

The main bird interest in the area is centred on and around the pier. Gulls gather here, depending on trawler activity, and can include Iceland (O) and Glaucous Gull (O) in winter, and Mediterranean, Little, Yellow-legged and Ring-billed Gull are seen most years. From the pier, it is possible to see numerous seabirds offshore, particularly Gannet, Fulmar, Cormorant, Shag, Kittiwake, Guillemot, Razorbill, Black Guillemot and Puffin (O). These can be seen throughout the

year, but are commonest from April to October. Terns are also usually present from May to late September, and Pomarine, Arctic and Great Skua have been seen in small numbers in spring and autumn. Storm Petrel is sometimes seen in late summer.

Small numbers of the regular waders can be seen on the beach to the E of the pier, particularly at low tide. Terns are also frequent this area in the summer months.

Rarities seen here include Velvet Scoter, Black-throated Diver, Hobby, Grey Phalarope, Ross's Gull, Little Auk, Black Redstart, and Ireland's first record of Brünnich's Guillemot.

The pier is where you board the boat to Great Saltee Island (Site 134).

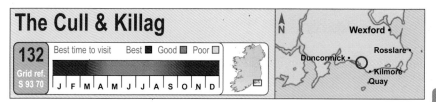

The Cull & Killag

132	Best time to visit	Best ■ Good ■ Poor □
Grid ref. S 93 70	J F M A M J J A S O N D	

A large estuary complex, with dunes and polder, very good in winter for waders and wildfowl, particularly Brent Goose and Black-tailed Godwit, and now one of the best sites in Ireland for Bewick's Swan.

Directions Map 83, next page For **The Cull**, from Kilmore Quay, drive NW on the minor road to Baldwinstown for 3km and take a left. Drive this straight road (heading for Duncormick) for 2.5km and take the left onto a track just as the road turns sharp right. There is a gate across the road – be sure to close it again after you. This track leads to the Cull Bank, where the highest concentrations of birds occur, with extensive views over the estuary, best two hours either side of high tide. The small pool to the E of the Bank has hosted a number of unusual waders. Walk across the causeway to reach the sand dunes. Divers and grebes can be seen from the seaward side of the dunes

There are a number of other minor roads either side of Duncormick (see Map 83) which offer

more views over the W end of the estuary. Red-breasted Merganser is more regular here and terns occasionally occur in summer.

For **Killag**, leave Kimore Quay NW on the minor road to Baldwinstown and take the second left after 2km. Explore this track for roughly 2km. Bewick's Swan, Lapwing and Golden Plover can be here in winter in considerable numbers. *This area is privately owned farmland, so avoid obstructing any farm activities.*

Species
All year Cormorant, Little Egret, Hen Harrier (O), Peregrine, Water Rail, Curlew (100s in autumn & winter, small numbers at other times), Kingfisher (O), Tree Sparrow (O).

Spring & summer Teal, Garganey (R), Little Grebe, Lapwing, Snipe, Whimbrel (especially May), Spotted Redshank (R), Mediterranean Gull (R), gulls, Sandwich Tern, Little Tern (O), Cuckoo (O), Wheatear, Grasshopper Warbler (R), Sedge Warbler, Whitethroat, Willow Warbler.

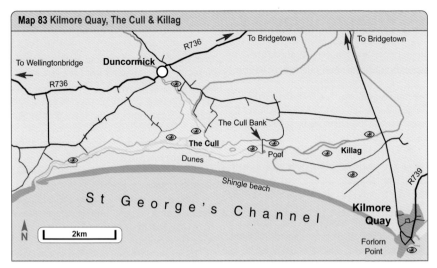

Map 83 Kilmore Quay, The Cull & Killag

Autumn & winter Bewick's Swan (Killag), Whooper Swan (small numbers), Pink-footed Goose (R), White-fronted Goose (O), Greylag Goose (feral birds), Brent Goose, Wigeon, Gadwall (R), Teal, Green-winged Teal (R), Pintail, Shoveler (O), Goldeneye, Red-breasted Merganser (W end of estuary), Red-throated Diver (offshore), Great Northern Diver (offshore), Merlin, Golden Plover (often 1000+), Grey Plover, Lapwing (2000+), Knot (O), Little Stint (O autumn), Pectoral Sandpiper (R autumn), Curlew Sandpiper (O autumn), Dunlin (often 100s), Ruff (O autumn), Jack Snipe (O), Snipe, Black-tailed Godwit, Bar-tailed Godwit, Whimbrel (autumn), Spotted Redshank (O), Green Sandpiper (O Aug & Sept), Wood Sandpiper (O Aug & Sept), Mediterranean Gull (O), Little Gull (R), gulls, Short-eared Owl (O), Yellow Wagtail (R autumn), Grey Wagtail (O), Whinchat (O autumn).

Rarities Dark-bellied Brent Goose, Blue-winged Teal, Black-throated Diver, Red-necked Grebe, Marsh Harrier, Hobby, Avocet, Dotterel, Western Sandpiper, White-rumped Sandpiper, Pectoral Sandpiper, Long-billed Dowitcher, Temminck's Stint, Little Gull, Water Pipit, Ring Ouzel, Melodious Warbler, Pied Flycatcher, Corn Bunting.

Bannow Bay

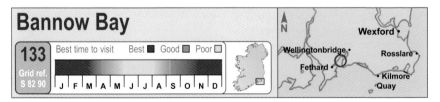

133

Grid ref. S 82 90

Best time to visit   Best ■ Good ■ Poor □

J F M A M J J A S O N D

A large estuary with many wintering wildfowl and waders, including internationally important numbers of Brent Goose and Black-tailed Godwit, and nationally important numbers of a further 11 species.

Directions Map 84, next page. The estuary is located to the SW of Wellingtonbridge. Timing is crucial, as many birds are very distant at low tide. Two hours either side of high tide is ideal.

The best area is the small bridge (Tintern Bridge) at Saltmills on the NW side of the estuary, about midway between Wellingtonbridge and Fethard. Little Egrets are numerous here, with many waders, Wigeon and Teal usually present in the small salt marsh here (fewer at low tide). Kingfisher is occasionally seen upriver from the bridge.

Another good area is Clonmines, where many waders roost at high tide. It is reached by leaving

170

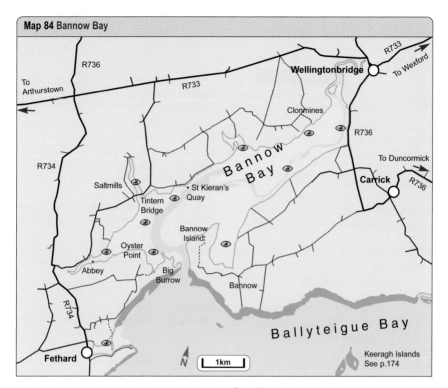

Map 84 Bannow Bay

To Arthurstown

R736

R733

Wellingtonbridge

To Wexford

R733

Clonmines

R736

Bannow Bay

To Duncormick

R734

Saltmills

St Kieran's Quay

Tintern Bridge

Carrick

R736

Bannow Island

Oyster Point

Abbey

Big Burrow

Bannow

R734

Ballyteigue Bay

Fethard

N

1km

Keeragh Islands
See p.174

Wellingtonbridge W on the R733 and taking a left after 3km. There are actually two left turns here, either of which will bring you to the shore, although these areas are private, so permission should be sought before crossing land. Two hours either side of high tide is much the best time to visit.

Other areas along the SE shore can be explored by taking the R736 to Carrick. Just 1.5km S of Wellingtonbridge, the estuary is easily viewed on the right, and by taking the next right another 1km further on, side roads to the shore can be explored. These narrow roads eventually lead to Bannow, where the bay to the E of Bannow Island is the main area for Brent Geese and many waders.

The W side of the estuary entrance, and the salt marshes at Oyster Point and Big Burrow, are another high tide roost for waders and wildfowl. Leaving Fethard N on the R734, take a right after 1.25km and continue to the end of the road. The shoreline can be explored on foot from here.

Species

All year Cormorant, Little Egret, Water Rail, Kingfisher.

Autumn, winter & spring Whooper Swan (O), Brent Goose (often 100s), Shelduck (100s), Wigeon, Teal, Tufted Duck (O), Pintail, Shoveler (O), Scaup (O), Goldeneye, Red-breasted Merganser, Red-throated Diver, Great Northern Diver, Great Crested Grebe (O), Hen Harrier (O), Buzzard (R), Merlin (O), Peregrine, Golden Plover, Grey Plover, Lapwing (1000s), Curlew Sandpiper (O autumn), Dunlin (1000s), Ruff (R autumn), Snipe, Jack Snipe (O), Black-tailed Godwit (usually 600+), Bar-tailed Godwit (100s), Whimbrel (mainly spring), Curlew (1000+), Spotted Redshank (R), Common Sandpiper (spring), gulls, Iceland Gull (O winter), Sandwich Tern (O spring & autumn, otherwise R), Short-eared Owl (R).

Summer Terns (estuary mouth), Cuckoo (O).

Rarities Marsh Harrier, Avocet, American Golden Plover, Mediterranean Gull, Hoopoe.

Great Saltee Island

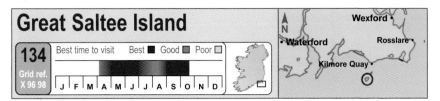

A large island with an important and accessible seabird colony, and excellent for migrants in spring and autumn.

Directions Map 85, below. The boat leaves from Kilmore Quay and runs between April and September, though there are no set times and all sailings are weather-dependent. Phone the boatman Declan Bates for details (+353 53 9129684). The island is privately owned, and landing is only permitted when the owner is absent. Camping is possible, with permission.

The main seabirds colonies are along the S and E side, with two sizeable Gannet colonies, on the S tip and the pinnacle of rock just SE of 'The Throne'. The coast between these two points holds most of the cliff-nesting birds, which are easily viewable from the clifftop.

Great Saltee is possibly the best spring migration site in Ireland. With light S, E or SE winds, it would not be unusual to see hundreds of migrants. The best areas are the trees and bushes around the main house, the avenue of small palm trees which runs S from the house 'The Royal Mile' and the line of small sycamores running NE from the

house. 'The Throne' area is good for pipits, wagtails and more 'open-country' species, as well as having some dense hedgerows. Much of the centre of the island is dense bramble thickets, which also hide numerous migrants.

Little Saltee Island is smaller, closer to the mainland, privately owned and more difficult to land on, has many fewer nesting species and is less attractive to migrants. The large Cormorant colony is an exception, and is absent as a nesting species on Great Saltee.

Species
Seabirds in spring & summer Fulmar (100s), Storm Petrel (O), Manx Shearwater, Gannet (1000s), Cormorant, Shag, Lesser Black-backed Gull (100s), Herring Gull (100s), Great Black-backed Gull (small numbers), Kittiwake (1000s), Guillemot (1000s), Razorbill (1000s), Black Guillemot (small numbers), Puffin (1000s).

Storm Petrel and Manx Shearwater are often seen from the boat between Kilmore Quay and Great Saltee Island, and skuas (O) and Black Tern (R) have also been seen.

Spring Whimbrel (O), terns (O), Turtle Dove (O), Cuckoo (O), Tree Pipit (O), Yellow Wagtail (O), Black Redstart (O), Redstart (O), Whinchat (O), Wheatear, Ring Ouzel (R), Grasshopper Warbler (O), Reed Warbler (O), Sedge Warbler, Whitethroat, Garden Warbler (O), Blackcap (O), Chiffchaff, Willow Warbler, Spotted Flycatcher, Pied Flycatcher (R), Wheatear.

Autumn Most of the seabirds listed above can be seen on and around the island into autumn. Sooty Shearwater (R), divers (O), Hen Harrier (O), Merlin, Golden Plover (O), Whimbrel (O), Pomarine Skua (O), Arctic Skua (O), Great Skua (O), Turtle Dove (O), Short-eared Owl (R), Black Redstart (O mainly Oct), Redstart (O), Whinchat (O), Wheatear, Grasshopper Warbler (O), Sedge Warbler, Reed Warbler (R), Lesser Whitethroat

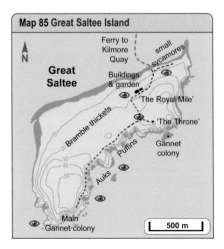

Map 85 Great Saltee Island

Great Saltee

Ferry to Kilmore Quay
small sycamores
Buildings & garden
'The Royal Mile'
'The Throne'
Bramble thickets
Puffins
Gannet colony
Auks
Main Gannet colony

500 m

(O), Whitethroat, Garden Warbler (O), Blackcap, Chiffchaff, Willow Warbler, Firecrest (R), Spotted Flycatcher, Pied Flycatcher (O), Brambling (R), Siskin (O), Lapland Bunting (R), Snow Bunting (O),

Rarities Leach's Petrel, Quail, Marsh Harrier, Buzzard, Hobby, Osprey, Stone Curlew, Dotterel, Grey Phalarope, Little Gull, Sabine's Gull, Hoopoe, Nightjar, Little Swift, Wryneck, Woodlark, Olive-backed Pipit, Richard's Pipit, Golden Oriole, Black-eared Wheatear, Icterine Warbler, Western Bonelli's Warbler, Wood Warbler, Subalpine Warbler, Yellow-browed Warbler, Woodchat Shrike, Red-backed Shrike, Red-breasted Flycatcher, Ortolan Bunting.

Hook Head

135	Best time to visit	Best ■ Good ▨ Poor □
Grid ref. X 73 97	J F M A M J J A S O N D	

An excellent site for passerine migrants in spring and autumn, with good seawatching.

Directions Map 86, right. At Fethard-on-Sea, go right and follow the road SW. Having passed a church on the right after 3.5km, continue for another 2km until you see the trees at the entrance to Loftus Hall. These are excellent for migrants. Continue S and at the T-junction, go either left or right.

Left will bring you to Slade Harbour. Just before the road swings right is Fortune's Lane on the left. This is another excellent area for migrants in spring and autumn. Continue down the road and follow the laneway to the right of the castle. This is Slade Lane and the hedges and gardens along its length are also excellent for migrants.

Right at the T-junction will bring you to Honey Pot Garden, Lupin Cottage and Lark Cottage, all on the left side of the road, and all excellent for migrants in spring and autumn. *Each of these gardens is private property so permission should always be sought to enter them.*

Just past Lark Cottage is a lane on the left. This is another good area for migrants while the lane to the right, by the ruined church, also has a good area of hedgerow and fields. The line of trees along the main road past (to the W of) the church is also good. Follow this road S and the stubble fields on both sides at the point where the road swings left are excellent for pipits and buntings in autumn. Finally, continue to the lighthouse.

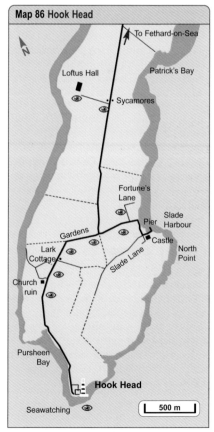

Map 86 Hook Head

Seawatching is best done from the small carpark, and SW to S winds are the best. See also SEAWATCHING, p.356.

Species

All year Cormorant, Shag, Water Rail (O), Guillemot, Razorbill, Black Guillemot (O), Puffin (O), Chough (formerly bred, now R).

Spring Purple Sandpiper, Dunlin (O), Whimbrel, Common Sandpiper (R), Pomarine Skua, Arctic Skua, Great Skua, Sandwich Tern, Roseate Tern (R), Common Tern (O), Arctic Tern, Little Tern (R), Turtle Dove (O), Cuckoo (O), Black Redstart (O), Redstart (O), Whinchat (O), Wheatear, Ring Ouzel (R), Grasshopper Warbler (O), Sedge Warbler, Whitethroat, Garden Warbler (O), Blackcap (O), Chiffchaff, Willow Warbler, Spotted Flycatcher.

Autumn White-fronted Goose (R), Wigeon (O), Teal, Pintail (R), Hen Harrier (O), Merlin, Peregrine, Golden Plover, Grey Plover (R), Knot (O), Dunlin, Ruff (R), Jack Snipe (R), Woodcock (R winter), Bar-tailed Godwit (R), Whimbrel (O), Mediterranean Gull (R), Iceland Gull (R), Glaucous Gull (R), Turtle Dove (O), Short-eared Owl (R), Grey Wagtail, Black Redstart (O mainly Oct & Nov), Redstart (O), Whinchat (O), Wheatear, Grasshopper Warbler (O), Sedge Warbler, Reed Warbler (R), Lesser Whitethroat (O), Whitethroat, Garden Warbler (O), Blackcap, Chiffchaff, Willow Warbler, Firecrest (R), Spotted Flycatcher, Pied Flycatcher (O), Brambling (R), Siskin (O), Lapland Bunting (R), Snow Bunting (O).

Seawatching, autumn Common Scoter (O), Red-breasted Merganser (R), Red-throated Diver, Great Northern Diver, Fulmar (scarce late autumn), Sooty Shearwater, Manx Shearwater (often 100s), Storm Petrel, Leach's Petrel (O), Grey Phalarope (O), Pomarine Skua, Arctic Skua, Great Skua, Little Gull (R), Sabine's Gull (R), Kittiwake, Sandwich Tern, Roseate Tern (R), Common Tern (O), Arctic Tern, Little Tern (R), Black Tern (R).

Rarities Bewick's Swan, Eider, Black-throated Diver, Cory's Shearwater, Great Shearwater, Hobby, Corncrake, Dotterel, Little Stint, Curlew Sandpiper, Buff-breasted Sandpiper, Spotted Redshank, Yellow-legged Gull, Little Auk, Long-eared Owl, Nightjar, Hoopoe (spring), Red-rumped Swallow, Wryneck, Richard's Pipit, Tree Pipit, Tawny Pipit, Red-throated Pipit, Yellow Wagtail, Icterine Warbler, Melodious Warbler, Subalpine Warbler, Barred Warbler, Greenish Warbler, Pallas's Warbler, Yellow-browed Warbler, Western Bonelli's Warbler, Radde's Warbler, Wood Warbler, Red-breasted Flycatcher, Golden Oriole (spring), Lesser Grey Shrike, Red-backed Shrike, Woodchat Shrike, Rose-coloured Starling, Red-eyed Vireo, Blackpoll Warbler, Twite, Common Rosefinch, Hawfinch, Ortolan Bunting, Corn Bunting, Bobolink.

Other sites

Courtown (T 20 56) is 4.5km SE of Gorey, on the R742. The coastal areas at, and N and S of the town, are good for Red-throated Diver, Great Northern Diver, small numbers of Common Scoter, and a small variety of coastal waders in winter. It also hold variable numbers of gulls in winter, with Black-headed Gull and Common Gull sometimes numbering in the 1000s.

The **Keeragh Islands** (S 86 05) lie 1.5 km offshore, close to the mouth of Bannow Bay (Site 133). It is perhaps best known for the substantial numbers of nesting Cormorant, with 200+ pairs, but other nesting species may include Shag, Herring Gull, Great Black-backed Gull and Arctic Tern.

Access is problematic, and boats trips must be arranged privately from Blackhall, Cullenstown or Kilmore Quay. Landing is only possible in calm weather.

County Waterford

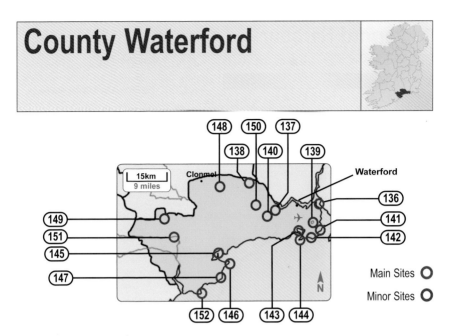

15km
9 miles

Clonmel

Waterford

Main Sites O
Minor Sites O

N

South-east

Situated on the south coast between Wexford and Cork, Waterford is one of the most productive birding locations in the country. Habitats vary from estuaries like Tramore and Dungarvan, to coastal headlands like Brownstown and Helvick Head. The low-lying flood plains of the River Blackwater attract large numbers of wildfowl in winter, while the Comeragh, Monavullagh and Knockmealdown Mountains provide an opportunity to see species such as Red Grouse. There are also numerous small lakes and reservoirs that are excellent for diving duck in winter. In summer, species such as Little Egret and Reed Warbler are found, while the rugged cliffs along the coast attract large numbers of seabirds. In autumn, seabird passage is excellent off headlands like Helvick Head and Brownstown Head, while common and rare migrants are found each year in autumn at these locations.

Waterford Harbour

Best time to visit   Best ■ Good ▨ Poor ☐

J F M A M J J A S O N D

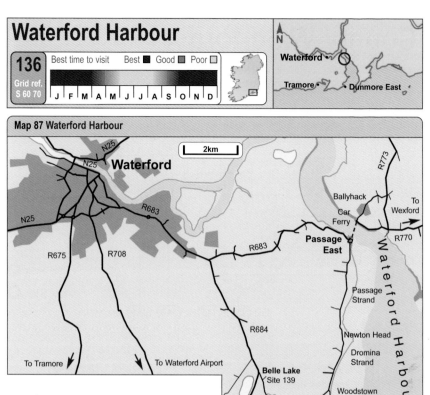

Map 87 Waterford Harbour

Waterford Harbour is a long, deep estuary and a very busy shipping port. The outer part of the western side of the estuary has intertidal mudflats that attract good numbers of wildfowl and waders in winter.

These mudflats are best viewed from areas between Passage East south to Creadan Head.

Directions Map 87, above. In Waterford city, follow the N25 along the seafront following the signs for Cork. The N25 turns sharp right as it leaves the seafront. Just 100m after this are traffic lights, with a left turn onto the R683, signposted for Passage East. Take this left turn and follow the R683 for almost 11km to the small, scenic village of Passage East. There is a small car ferry that operates throughout the year linking Passage East with Ballyhack in Wexford.

From Passage East, continue S on the minor Passage East-Dunmore East road to Woodstown Strand. This stretch of coastline can be watched from various viewing points and parking areas along its 5km length. Creadan (or Fornaght)

Strand lies S of Woodstown Strand and can be reached by continuing on the Passage-Dunmore road from Woodstown Strand for over 1.5km and taking the first left turn. Follow this road down to a T-junction and take a left. This road continues for just over 1km until it meets the strand.

Species

All year Fulmar, Cormorant, Shag, Little Egret, Water Rail, Kittiwake.

Autumn, winter & spring Brent Goose, Wigeon, Pintail (R winter), Teal, Scaup (R winter), Eider (R winter), Red-breasted Merganser, Great Northern Diver, Merlin, Golden Plover, Grey

Plover, Lapwing (1000s), Knot, Little Stint (R autumn), Curlew Sandpiper (R autumn), Dunlin, Ruff (R autumn), Jack Snipe (R winter), Snipe, Black-tailed Godwit, Bar-tailed Godwit, Whimbrel (O May), Little Gull (R winter), Mediterranean Gull (R autumn & winter), Iceland Gull (R winter), Glaucous Gull (R winter), Short-eared Owl (winter), Redstart (R autumn), Garden Warbler (R autumn),Whitethroat (O autumn).

Summer Common Sandpiper, gulls, terns, Grasshopper Warbler (O), Sedge Warbler, Reed Warbler (R), Chiffchaff, Willow Warbler, Wheatear.

Rarities Balearic Shearwater, Dark-bellied Brent Goose, Honey Buzzard, Sabine's Gull, Black Tern, Turtle Dove, Hoopoe, Lesser Whitethroat, Golden Oriole.

137 Kilmeaden Ponds Grid ref. S 51 08

Settling pools which in autumn and winter can attract small numbers of duck and waders. A good site for Water Pipit in winter.

Kilmeaden Ponds are a series of settling pools to the W of Waterford city and are designed to treat effluent from the local creamery. Some of the pools can be flooded while others can have low levels of water and exposed mud. The area is very good for Water Rail and small numbers of duck in winter. Green Sandpiper occurs in autumn, with some birds seen from late summer into winter. In autumn, a small passage of waders takes place, with occasional records of Ruff and Wood Sandpiper, while Garganey has also occurred

here. In recent years, the ponds have attracted several Water Pipits in winter.

From Waterford city, take the N25 W on the main Cork road for approximately 10km until you reach Kilmeaden village. On the right is The Sweep pub. Take a left turn at the Sweep junction (just past and almost opposite the pub). Follow this road down for less than 500m and take the first right turn. Continue straight and uphill until you reach the point where power-lines cross the road. Immediately to the right is a small access road that leads to the settling ponds. There are paths around the ponds but birds can easily be disturbed.

South-east

138 Knockaderry Reservoir Grid ref. S 49 06

A small lake which attracts diving duck and small numbers of waders in autumn and winter.

This small, natural lake and reservoir is located west from Waterford city. It also has small wetlands and woodlands around its margins. In winter, it attracts small numbers of diving duck such as Tufted Duck and Pochard. It also holds Whooper Swan, Wigeon, and Teal in winter, while Green Sandpiper occurs in autumn.

Access is restricted but the area can be seen well from the road. From Waterford city, take the N25 W on the main Cork road for approximately 10km until you reach Kilmeaden village. On the right is The Sweep pub. Take a left turn at the Sweep junction (just past and almost opposite the

pub). Follow this road down for less than 500m and take the first right turn. Continue straight and uphill for 1.1km past the access road to the Kilmeaden Ponds and, at the top of the hill, go left at the fork following signs for Knockaderry Reservoir. Continue for 1.3 km and take the right turn, signed for Knockaderry Reservoir. Then follow the road left and downhill to the causeway across the reservoir. This causeway is very narrow but there is a small parking area half way along on the right.

Rarities seen here include Red-necked Grebe, Green-winged Teal, Lesser Scaup, Smew, Ruddy Duck, Pectoral Sandpiper, Baird's Sandpiper, Ruff and Firecrest. Dipper and Grey Wagtail also breed along the stream at the NE side of the lake.

139 Belle Lake Grid ref. S 66 04

A lake which attracts waterfowl in winter and a good selection of breeding reedbed and woodland species nearby.

Lying between Waterford city and Dunmore East, Belle Lake is a freshwater lake with extensive reedbeds and with good deciduous woodland along its edge. From Waterford city, take the left turn onto the R683 and continue on the R683 for over 5km before going right onto the R684, following signs for Dunmore East. Continue on the R684 for almost 5km until the lake is visible on the right. It can be viewed from several points from the road. In winter, it attracts diving and dabbling ducks as well as Whooper Swan occasionally.

In spring and summer, the reedbeds attract breeding Reed Warbler and Sedge Warbler while Water Rail is present all year. The woodlands at the NE end of the lake attract common resident species such as Treecreeper, while in summer, Blackcap, Chiffchaff and Willow Warbler are found.

Rarer birds recorded here include Little Egret, Ruddy Duck, Long-tailed Duck, Marsh Harrier, Green Sandpiper, Ring-billed Gull and Black Tern.

140 Ballyshunnock Reservoir Grid ref. S 45 09

A reservoir which is good for waterfowl and waders in winter.

This man-made lake lies W of Waterford city. From Waterford, follow the N25 W for approximately 18km and take a right at Carroll's Cross. Continue on this minor road for almost 1.5km to the reservoir, where parking is available on either side of the causeway that runs across the lake.

In winter, diving ducks such as Tufted Duck and Pochard are found. Dabbling ducks include Teal and occasionally Gadwall, Shoveler and Pintail.

In winter, Whooper Swan is often seen, while the wet fields can attract Golden Plover, Lapwing and Curlew. In autumn, if water levels are low, waders such as Ruff, Greenshank, Common Sandpiper and Green Sandpiper are regularly seen.

In summer, the reservoir holds breeding Little Grebes, while breeding summer migrants include Whitethroat, Willow Warbler, Grasshopper Warbler and Sedge Warbler. Water Rail also occur around the lake fringes.

Rare species that have occurred here include Red-throated Diver, Bewick's Swan, Lesser Scaup, Ring-necked Duck, Long-tailed Duck, Buff-breasted Sandpiper, Little Stint, Jack Snipe, Wood Sandpiper and Black Redstart.

141 Dunmore East Grid ref. S S 68 01

A port which attracts gulls in winter and migrants in spring and autumn. A Kittiwake colony is present at the harbour.

Dunmore East lies to the S of Waterford city, at the mouth of Waterford Harbour. It is a fishery port and, in winter, can attract large numbers of gulls. The harbour also holds breeding colonies of Kittiwakes that can be easily viewed from the harbour from late spring into summer. The gardens and hedgerows in the area attract migrants in spring and autumn.

From Waterford city, take the left turn onto the R683 and continue on the R683 for over 5km before going right onto the R684, following signs for Dunmore East. In winter, the rocky shoreline nearby is good for Purple Sandpiper. Iceland, Glaucous and Little Gull have occurred in winter, while rarer species seen from, and around, Dunmore East include Balearic Shearwater, Velvet Scoter, Quail, Pomarine Skua, Sabine's Gull, Mediterranean Gull, Black Tern, Turtle Dove, Hoopoe, Wryneck, Black Redstart, Golden Oriole, Carrion Crow and Lapland Bunting.

Europe's first Indian House Crow, a ship-assisted vagrant from SE Asia, was found here in 1974, and remained until 1979.

142 Ballymacaw <small>Grid ref. X 64 98</small>

A good area for migrants in spring and autumn.

Lying to the W of Dunmore East, the well vegetated and wooded glens and gardens around Ballymacaw attract migrants in spring and autumn. From Dunmore East, follow the small coastal road W to the village of Ballymacaw. Two streams run down into Ballymacaw Cove, each with steep, well wooded glens. In summer, breeding warblers found here include Willow Warbler and Chiffchaff. In autumn, these glens attract common migrants, with the glen to the E being the easiest to view well from the road. Gardens in the village are also good for migrants.

Scarce and rare species recorded here include Turtle Dove, Black Redstart, Melodious Warbler, Garden Warbler, Yellow-browed Warbler, Firecrest, Pied Flycatcher and Brambling. Quail have also occurred in this area, while Green Sandpiper and Mediterranean Gull have also been recorded.

An area of a tidal estuary, saltmarsh and open bay with a good sand-dune system. It attracts internationally important numbers of Brent Geese and nationally important numbers of waders in winter, as well as holding a resident population of Little Egret. Small numbers of breeding seabirds and Chough are found at Great Newtown Head at the south-west end of the bay.

Directions Map 88, next page. Tramore Backstrand and Bay lie to the SW of Waterford city. From Waterford city, follow the N25 W and take the left turn onto the R675, signposted for Tramore. Follow the R675 all the way into Tramore town.

To view the S end of **The Back Strand**, go into Tramore, and, at the promenade (known locally as 'The Prom'), follow E to the carpark at the end. This carpark is close to the dump and the mudflats where good numbers of waders can be seen. The area is also good for gulls in winter. The extensive mudflat of the inner bay is known as the Back Strand, and is sheltered by an extensive dune system. There are two embankments crossing the mudflats just E of the dump, separated by a channel even at low tide. From the carpark, you can follow a path that brings you to

the tip of the dune system ('The Sandhills'). The path brings you in a circle around the dunes. Brent Geese, Red-breasted Merganser and waders are all present on the channels and on the mudflats in this area. A small, muddy area at the western corner of the dune system is also good for waders on a falling tide.

The N end of the Back Strand is best viewed from the road at Ballinattin. On the R675 from Waterford, take the left turn onto the R685, just after the village of Pickardstown, following signs for Dunmore East. Approximately 1km along this road there is a small turn off to the left. Park here and follow the lane directly opposite to view the Back Strand. Do not cross the gate at the end of the lane but walk right, just before it. The area can also be viewed from the road a little further NE of this lane. This area is very good for seeing Little Egret.

The E side of the Back Strand is best viewed from Saleen which lies on the SE side of Tramore. From Ballinattin, follow the R685 along the coast for almost 7km and then take the right turn onto the minor road for Kilmacleague. Follow this road over the bridge and, just over 1km from the bridge, take the right turn down to the carpark. This offers a good vantage point over the

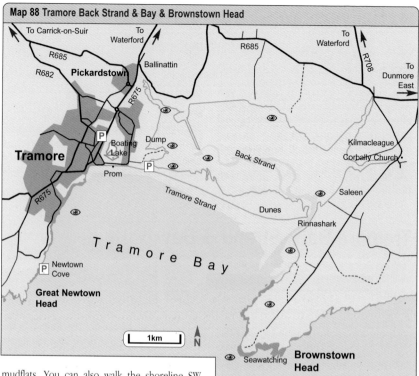

Map 88 Tramore Back Strand & Bay & Brownstown Head

mudflats. You can also walk the shoreline SW from here to Rinnashark. In winter, the mudflats and open channels along this walk are good for grebes and divers, as well as waders.

In Tramore, the small **Boating Lake** opposite 'The Prom' regularly attracts waders and gulls in winter, with Ring-billed and Mediterranean Gull regularly reported.

The E side of **Tramore Bay** can be viewed from several points along the road from Rinnashark to Brownstown Head (Site 144). The W side of the bay is best viewed from many vantage points from the pier in Tramore out to Newtown Cove to the SW. In winter, divers, grebes and Common Scoter are found in the bay. Black Redstarts are frequently seen in winter close to the pier. **Great Newtown Head** lies in SW corner of the bay and can be good for seawatching in SW winds (see SEAWATCHING, p.356). The headland can be reached by a path that runs from the parking area at Newtown Cove. The headland is also good for breeding seabirds such as Fulmar and Black Guillemot, while Chough are also found in this area.

Species

All year Fulmar, Cormorant, Shag, Little Egret, Water Rail, Kittiwake, Kingfisher, Chough.

Autumn, winter & spring Whooper Swan (O), White-fronted Goose (R), Barnacle Goose (R), Brent Goose, Wigeon, Teal, Shoveler (O), Scaup (O), Eider (R winter), Long-tailed Duck (R winter), Red-breasted Merganser, Red-throated Diver, Great Northern Diver, Hen Harrier, Merlin, Buzzard (R), Golden Plover (1000s), Grey Plover, Lapwing (1000s), Knot, Little Stint (autumn), Curlew Sandpiper (autumn), Dunlin, Ruff (autumn), Jack Snipe (R winter), Snipe, Black-tailed Godwit, Bar-tailed Godwit, Whimbrel (autumn & spring), Spotted Redshank (R autumn & winter), Green Sandpiper (R autumn), Wood Sandpiper (R autumn), Grey Phalarope (R autumn), Little Gull, Mediterranean Gull (R autumn & winter), Ring-billed Gull (R winter), Iceland Gull (R winter), Glaucous Gull (R winter), Short-eared Owl (winter), Black Redstart (winter), Redstart (R autumn), Whinchat (R autumn), Reed Warbler (O autumn), Spotted Flycatcher (autumn), Pied Flycatcher (R autumn), Brambling (R winter), Siskin, (O autumn & winter), Redpoll (O autumn).

Summer Common Sandpiper, gulls, terns, Grasshopper Warbler (O), Sedge Warbler, Reed Warbler (R), Chiffchaff, Willow Warbler, Wheatear.

Rarities Snow Goose, Dark-bellied Brent, Black Brant, Velvet Scoter, Black-throated Diver, Slavonian Grebe, Cory's Shearwater, Spoonbill, Red Kite, Osprey, Black-winged Stilt, Avocet, Yellow-legged Gull, Black Tern, Little Auk, Hoopoe, Snow Bunting.

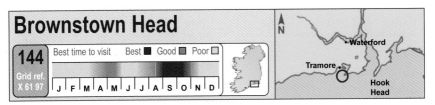

Brownstown Head

144
Grid ref.
X 61 97

Best time to visit   Best ■ Good ▨ Poor ☐

J F M A M J J A S O N D

Waterford
Tramore
Hook Head

An extensive area of sea-cliffs, farmland, gardens and scrub, noted for attracting rare migrants in spring and autumn (including Ireland's first Yellow Warbler). It is also a very good seawatching point in suitable conditions and Chough are also found here all year.

Directions Map 88, previous page. Brownstown Head lies to the SE of Tramore Bay, and W of Waterford Bay. From Waterford city, follow the N25 W and take the left turn onto the R675, signposted for Tramore. On the R675 from Waterford, take the left turn onto the R685, just after the village of Pickardstown, following signs for Dunmore East. Follow the R685 along the coast for almost 7km and then take the right turn onto the minor road for Kilmacleague. Follow this road over the bridge and take the right just beyond Corbally church. Continue on the straight road to the Head. The road ends near the 'main garden' on Brownstown Head. Park in this area. A small dirt track leads from here down to the Head. The garden at this point provides dense cover for migrants and is one of the most productive sites on the headland. The area can be watched well from the road.

The hedgerows along the track from here to the headland also provide excellent cover for migrants in spring and autumn. There are several small tracks that bring you across and along the edges of many of the fields and these are also worth walking when searching for migrants.

At the E side Brownstown Head, a stream runs through a steep, densely covered glen and down

Coolum Cove. This glen can be viewed from above at several locations and is also an excellent place for migrants in spring and autumn. The glen can be accessed by taking the small track to the left over 1km before the 'main garden' on the straight road out to the headland. At the end of the track, follow the glen around and view the areas from above. It can also be reached by taking the walk along the clifftop W of Brazen Head.

It is worth noting that gardens and scrub anywhere along the straight road out to the headland can be good for migrants.

Seawatching is best from August to Sept in S and SW winds with rain (see SEAWATCHING, p.356). The best viewing point is at the tip of the headland. From the 'main garden' walk the dirt track to the end. A small observation hut on the tip can give some shelter in bad weather.

Species
All year Fulmar, Cormorant, Chough.

Autumn, winter & spring Red-throated Diver, Great Northern Diver, Hen Harrier, Merlin, Buzzard (R), Green Sandpiper (R autumn), Short-eared Owl (winter), Wheatear (autumn & spring), Black Redstart (R autumn & winter), Redstart (R autumn), Whinchat (R autumn), Ring Ouzel (R autumn), Garden Warbler (O autumn), Blackcap (autumn), Whitethroat (autumn & spring), Reed Warbler (O autumn), Spotted Flycatcher (autumn), Pied Flycatcher (autumn), Brambling (R autumn & winter), Siskin, (O autumn & winter), Redpoll (O autumn).

181

Seawatching Red-throated Diver (O), Great Northern Diver (O), Fulmar, Great Shearwater (R Sept), Sooty Shearwater, Manx Shearwater, Balearic Shearwater (R), Storm Petrel, Leach's Petrel (R), Gannet, Cormorant, Shag, Grey Phalarope (O), Pomarine Skua, Arctic Skua, Great Skua, Little Gull (R), Sabine's Gull (R Sept), Sandwich Tern (O), Common Tern, Arctic Tern, Black Tern (O), Guillemot, Razorbill, Black Guillemot (small numbers), Little Auk (R Oct onward), Puffin (small numbers).

Rarities Great Shearwater, Balearic Shearwater, Leach's Petrel, Sociable Plover, Sabine's Gull, Black Tern, Little Auk, Turtle Dove, Scop's Owl, Hoopoe, Wryneck, Tree Pipit, Icterine Warbler, Melodious Warbler, Barred Warbler, Lesser Whitethroat, Greenish Warbler, Pallas's Warbler, Yellow-browed Warbler, Western Bonelli's Warbler, Wood Warbler, Firecrest, Red-breasted Flycatcher, Bearded Tit, Golden Oriole, Rose-coloured Starling, Red-backed Shrike, Woodchat Shrike, Red-eyed Vireo, Northern Parula, Yellow Warbler, Blackpoll Warbler, Lapland Bunting, Snow Bunting.

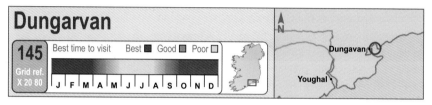

Dungarvan

145
Grid ref.
X 20 80

Best time to visit   Best ■ Good ▨ Poor ☐

J F M A M J J A S O N D

Dungarvan

Youghal

A large, semicircular bay enclosed by a long sand-spit which holds large numbers of Brent Geese and waders in winter and has attracted many rare waders and passerines in spring and autumn.

Directions Map 89, next page. Dungarvan lies on the S coast of County Waterford and is a large semicircular bay, partly enclosed on one side by a long sand-spit called the Cunnigar. The area has a mixed habitat, varying from the beach at Clonea to the east, an open bay and an extensive inter-tidal mudflat with large saltmarsh areas to the west of the Cunnigar.

From Waterford, take the N25 W for over 45km, following signs for Cork. The N25 bypasses Dungarvan. From the N25, follow the left turn into Dungarvan. There are many good areas within the

Dungarvan area for seeing wildfowl and waders in winter, as well as for searching for migrants in spring and autumn.

Clonea Strand lies to the E of Dungarvan and the beach at Clonea runs for over 3 km SW from Ballyvoyle Bridge to Ballinacourty Point at the NE corner of Dungarvan Bay. To reach Clonea Strand, take the left turn onto the R675 in Dungarvan town, and continue E, following signs for Clonea. Follow this road over Kilminnin (Barnawee) Bridge and 1.5km from here is the first right turn that brings you down to the strand. There are several other access roads to the strand along this 4km stretch of road, including that leading to the Clonea Strand Hotel. You can follow the R675 NE as far as Ballyvoyle Bridge. Ballyvoyle Glen as well as the gardens and scrub around Ballyvoyle Bridge can also be good for migrants in spring and autumn. At the S end of Clonea is an area known as **Ballinard** which lies on the E side of Ballinacourty Point. This area is rocky and is good for Purple Sandpipers in winter.

For **Kilminnin (Barnawee) Bridge & Ballynacourty**, from Dungarvan, take the R675 E out of the town, following signs for Clonea. This road crosses Kilminnin Bridge and, at high tide, waders can be seen well from the bridge and along the road between here and the old railway bridge.

Curlew

Map 89 Dungarvan area & Helvick Head

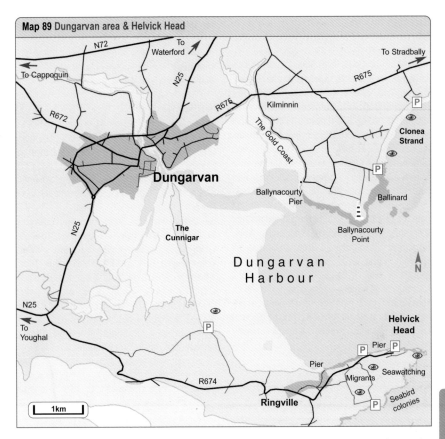

The coastline from Kilminnin Bridge out to **Ballynacourty Pier** is known as The Gold Coast. Take the right immediately after the bridge and follow this narrow road S for over 2km along the E side of Dungarvan Bay. This road can offer good views over the mudflats but parking can be difficult. To reach Ballynacourty, take a turn left just before the golf course. At the next junction, take a right and follow this narrow road to the end. Ballynacourty Pier is at the end of a road to the right and is good for divers and grebes in winter. Alternatively, at the junction after the golf course, take a left turn and then take the next right which brings you down to a carpark at Ballinclamper. This is a good area for waders and terns in autumn.

In **Dungarvan town**, divers, grebes and seaduck can be seen in winter. Follow the path from the Sports Centre past the old swimming baths and continue around the quays. Brent Geese are also found along this route. From Dungarvan you can continue W out of the town. This road meets the N25 (the Cork Road). The mudflats can be seen well to the left along this road and also along the N25 for further 500m.

The Cunnigar is one of the best areas in Dungarvan Bay and the entire 3km can be walked. Allow at least three hours to do it properly, and it is best during high tide when birds roost along the spit. It is excellent for waders and terns with many rare vagrants found there in autumn. From Dungarvan, take the N25 W for over 2.5km and take the left turn onto the R674, signposted for Helvick Head. Follow the R674 for over 1.5km, and take the minor left. Follow this narrow, winding road for approximately 2km and, at the farmhouse, take a sharp left to reach the parking area at the base of the Cunnigar. From here you can walk out along the spit. It should be remembered that at high tides, this spit is used by roosting birds, so *care should be taken to cause no disturbance.*

Species

All year Cormorant, Shag, Little Egret, Kingfisher, Chough.

Autumn, winter & spring Brent Goose, Wigeon, Teal, Shoveler (O), Scaup (O), Eider (R), Long-tailed Duck (0), Goldeneye, Red-breasted Merganser (O), Red-throated Diver, Great Northern Diver, Hen Harrier (winter), Merlin, Buzzard (R), Golden Plover (1000s), Grey Plover, Lapwing (1000s), Knot, Little Stint (autumn), Curlew Sandpiper (autumn), Dunlin, Ruff (autumn), Jack Snipe (R winter), Snipe, Black-tailed Godwit, Bar-tailed Godwit, Whimbrel (autumn & spring), Spotted Redshank (R autumn & winter), Green Sandpiper (R autumn), Wood Sandpiper (R autumn), Grey Phalarope (R autumn), Little Gull, Mediterranean Gull (R autumn & winter), Ring-billed Gull (R winter), Iceland Gull (R winter), Glaucous Gull (R winter), Short-eared Owl (winter), Black Redstart (R winter), Wheatear (autumn & spring), Spotted Flycatcher (autumn), Pied Flycatcher (R autumn),

Brambling (R winter), Siskin, (O autumn & winter), Redpoll (O autumn).

Summer Common Sandpiper, gulls, terns, Sedge Warbler, Chiffchaff, Willow Warbler.

Rarities Dark-bellied Brent, Black Brant, Garganey, Velvet Scoter, Goosander, Black-throated Diver, Red-necked Grebe, Slavonian Grebe, Black-necked Grebe, Cory's Shearwater, Balearic Shearwater, Night Heron, Squacco Heron, Great White Egret, Red Kite, Osprey, Hobby, Little Ringed Plover, American Golden Plover, Semipalmated Sandpiper, Baird's Sandpiper, Pectoral Sandpiper, Buff-breasted Sandpiper, Long-billed Dowitcher, Lesser Yellowlegs, Sabine's Gull, Bonaparte's Gull, Yellow-legged Gull, Ivory Gull, Forster's Tern, Whiskered Tern, Black Tern, White-winged Black Tern, Little Auk, Turtle Dove, Alpine Swift, Chimney Swift, Hoopoe, Tree Pipit, Waxwing, Booted Warbler, Golden Oriole, Red-backed Shrike, Lesser Grey Shrike, Woodchat Shrike, Carrion Crow, Twite, Snow Bunting.

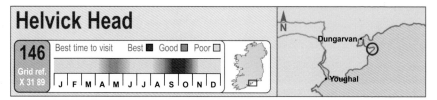

Helvick Head

146	Best time to visit	Best ■ Good ▨ Poor ☐
Grid ref. X 31 89	J F M A M J J A S O N D	

This headland has a breeding seabird colony in summer and, in autumn, the many gardens and areas of scrub are excellent for migrants. The headland is also very good for seawatching in autumn, while Chough are to be found throughout the year.

Directions Map 89, previous page. Helvick Head lies to the SE of Dungarvan, just at the mouth of Dungarvan Bay. From Dungarvan, follow the N25 W, following signs for Cork. Then take the left turn E onto the R674, signposted for Helvick. Continue on the R674 for over 7km to reach the carpark at Helvick Pier.

From the carpark, the trees, gardens and areas of scrub can hold migrants in autumn and spring. Back from the pier, any of the gardens along the

road can also be productive for finding migrants. The area around the pier is also good for gulls in winter.

Seawatching is best done from August to mid-October in S or SSW winds with rain. Seawatching can be done from either the pier carpark or the small cove nearby. However, the best views of seabirds are obtained by going onto the cliffs on the S side of the head (see SEAWATCHING, p.356).

In summer, the seabird colonies can be viewed by taking the road back from the pier and taking either the first or second left turn which both bring you to a carpark on the SW side of Helvick Head. *These cliffs are steep and quite dangerous* but hold species such as Kittiwake, Razorbill, Guillemot and Black Guillemot.

Species
All year Fulmar, Cormorant, Shag, Chough.

Summer Fulmar, Kittiwake, Razorbill, Guillemot, Black Guillemot, Chiffchaff, Wheatear.

Autumn, winter & spring Hen Harrier, Merlin, Grey Phalarope (R autumn), Little Gull, Mediterranean Gull (R autumn & winter), Iceland Gull (R winter), Glaucous Gull (R winter), Short-eared Owl (autumn), Black Redstart (R autumn & winter), Redstart (R autumn), Whinchat (autumn), Ring Ouzel (R autumn), Garden Warbler (O autumn), Blackcap (autumn), Whitethroat (O autumn), Reed Warbler (R autumn), Spotted Flycatcher (autumn), Pied Flycatcher (autumn), Brambling (R autumn & winter), Siskin, (O autumn), Redpoll (O autumn).

Seawatching Red-throated Diver (O), Great Northern Diver (O), Fulmar, 'Blue' Fulmar (R late autumn), Cory's Shearwater (R autumn), Great Shearwater (R autumn), Sooty Shearwater, Manx Shearwater, Balearic Shearwater, Storm Petrel, Leach's Petrel (R), Gannet, Cormorant, Shag, Grey Phalarope (O), Pomarine Skua, Arctic Skua, Long-tailed Skua (R), Great Skua, Little Gull (R), Sabine's Gull (O Sept), Sandwich Tern (O), Common Tern (O), Arctic Tern, Roseate Tern (R), Black Tern (O), Guillemot, Razorbill, Black Guillemot (small numbers), Little Auk (R Oct onward), Puffin (small numbers).

Rarities Black-throated Diver, Fea's/Zino's Petrel, Red-footed Falcon, Hobby, Yellow-legged Gull, Quail, Turtle Dove, Alpine Swift, Hoopoe, Tree Pipit, Icterine Warbler, Melodious Warbler, Lesser Whitethroat, Pallas's Warbler, Yellow-browed Warbler, Radde's Warbler, Firecrest, Red-breasted Flycatcher, Red-backed Shrike, Snow Bunting.

147 **Mine Head** Grid ref. X 28 82

A headland with many breeding seabirds in summer, migrants in autumn and Chough all year.

See Map 90, right. Mine Head lies to the S of Helvick Head (Site 146) and, in summer, the seacliffs are good for breeding seabirds. Chough is also found throughout the year around the headland. However, the vegetated valleys of Hacketstown and Ballymacart just to the SW of Mine Head have excellent potential for attracting migrants in spring and autumn.

From Dungarvan, follow the N25 W, following signs for Cork. Then take the left turn E onto the R674, signposted for Helvick. Continue on the R674 until you reach the village of Ring (Ringville). Take the right turn at Ring and follow this minor road SW for over 3km and take a left at the T-junction. From here continue SW.

To view the seabird cliffs at Mine Head, take the left turn at the crossroads approximately 2km along this road (near the Post Office). Follow the road down, and at the small junction, go right and then take the first left. A track leads you down to

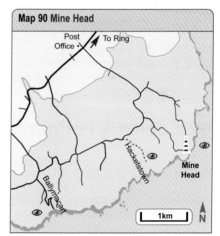

Map 90 Mine Head

the lighthouse. In summer, species such as Fulmar and Kittiwake are found.

The good areas for migrants lie just to the SW. Continue past the left turn for Mine Head and continue to Hacketstown Bridge where the valley can be checked and accessed from the road. Ballymacart Bridge is a further 2km down this road. A left turn, just past Ballymacart Bridge, also brings you down to the coast.

Rare species such as Honey Buzzard, Marsh Harrier, Little Auk, Turtle Dove, Garden Warbler, Yellow-browed Warbler, Firecrest, Pied Flycatcher and Red-eyed Vireo have been recorded in this area. Quail has also been recorded along the cliff tops near Mine Head in spring.

148 Comeragh & Monavullagh Mountains Grid ref. S 34 06

Upland moorland and forest species.

Lying to the W of Waterford city and to the NW of Dungarvan, the Comeragh & Monavullagh Mountains is a large area of upland moorlands, lakes and coniferous plantations. From Waterford, take the N25 W. Approximately 4km SW of Kilmacthomas, take the right turn just past the railway crossing. Follow this narrow road up for almost 3km until the road meets with the R676 near Mahon Bridge. There are several roads and pathways into the mountains from Mahon Bridge.

Red Grouse can be found on open moorland anywhere in the area, while the woodlands are excellent for Siskin and Crossbill. In summer, Wheatear is also found along the more rocky slopes.

Some of the rarer species recorded include Goshawk, Hobby, Dotterel, Long-tailed Skua, Nightjar, Black Redstart and Ring Ouzel.

149 Knockmealdown Mountains Grid ref. S 03 10

Upland moorland and forest species.

Lying in the NW corner of the county, the Knockmealdown Mountains is an area of upland moorlands, lakes and coniferous plantations. From Waterford city, follow the N25 W and then take the N72. The mountains can be reached by taking right turns at Cappoquin (R669) or at Lismore (R668). These roads meet near a bridge over a stream and then continue N as one road (R668) into the mountains and over into Tipperary. Along this road, the open moorland is excellent for Red Grouse, while the extensive conifer plantations can hold Siskin and Crossbill. There are many parking areas along this road. In summer, Hen Harrier can occur, while Wheatear is found on the more rocky slopes.

150 Coolfin & Portnascully Grid ref. S 41 51 to S 50 12

A good area for wildfowl, especially Greylag Geese, and waders in winter.

Lying to the NW of Waterford, Coolfin and Portnascully are marshes and pasture close to the River Suir near the Waterford/Kilkenny border. In winter, it attracts large numbers of wildfowl and waders. However, it is noted for the large numbers of Greylag Geese found feeding on the pastures.

From Waterford, take the N25 W for approximately 11km. Then take a right turn onto the R680, signed for Portlaw and Carrick-on-Suir. Approximately 5km out this road, continue right at Derrigal crossroads for Carrick-on-Suir. From here, the first fields used by geese at Coolfin can be seen from the road in an area just past the bridge. Another good site is from the farmgate approximately 1.5km further on, where the fields at Portnascully on the Kilkenny side can be seen well. Birds can also be found close to Derrigal crossroads, E of Coolfin.

Other species regularly recorded include Whooper Swan, Little Egret, White-fronted Goose, Teal, Golden Plover, Lapwing, Snipe and Green Sandpiper, while scarcer species include Barnacle Goose, Pink-footed Goose and Green-winged Teal.

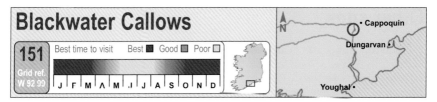

Blackwater Callows

151

Grid ref.
W 92 99

Best time to visit   Best ■ Good ■ Poor □

J F M A M J J A S O N D

Cappoquin
Dungarvan
Youghal

An area of low-lying fields along the Blackwater River which regularly floods in winter and attracts large numbers of wildfowl and waders.

Directions Map 91, below. The Blackwater Callows are located along the Blackwater River between Lismore in W Waterford and the Cork border. From the town of Cappoquin, follow the N72 W to Lismore. Just before the N72 crosses Lismore Bridge, take the right turn onto the R666, signposted for Ballyduff. Dipper and Grey Wagtail are often seen close to Lismore Bridge. Continue on the R666 and the wetlands can be seen well from the road just past the golf course. The road from the golf course to just before the village of Ballyduff is where the main concentrations of wildfowl occur. Continue on into Ballyduff, and to view the N side of the callows, continue on the

R666. To view the S side, go left at Ballyduff, cross over the small bridge and take an immediate right. This minor road gives good views over the callows and this is the favoured feeding area for Whooper Swans.

Species
All year Kingfisher.

Autumn, winter & spring Bewick's Swan(R), Whooper Swan, Greylag Goose (feral birds), White-fronted Goose (R), Barnacle Goose (R), Wigeon (4000+), Teal (1500+), Shoveler (O), Hen Harrier, Merlin, Peregrine, Golden Plover, Lapwing (1000+), Dunlin (R), Jack Snipe (R winter), Snipe, Black-tailed Godwit (1000+), Green Sandpiper (R autumn), Siskin, (O autumn & winter), Redpoll (O winter).

Summer Chiffchaff, Willow Warbler.

Rarities Green-winged Teal, Blue-winged Teal.

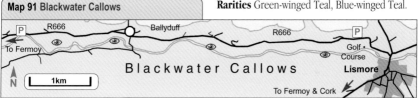

Map 91 Blackwater Callows

P R666 Ballyduff R666 P
To Fermoy Golf Course Lismore
B l a c k w a t e r   C a l l o w s
N 1km To Fermoy & Cork

South-east

152 Ardmore Head & Bay Grid ref. X 20 76

A headland with breeding seabirds in summer, migrants in autumn and Chough all year.

Ardmore Head and Bay lie to the E of Youghal on the Waterford/Cork border. The headland is good for breeding seabirds such as Fulmar, Shag, Kittiwake, Guillemot and Razorbill in summer. In winter, the bay can hold divers, while Chough are present throughout the year. In autumn, the gardens and areas of scrub around the village out to the Round Tower and onto Ardmore Head itself, can attract migrants.

From Dungarvan, follow the N25 SW for almost 7km and take a left turn onto the R673 at

Kiely's Crossroads. Follow the R673 into the village of Ardmore. The best migrant areas and the sea cliffs can be accessed near the Cliff House Hotel at the SW corner of Ardmore Bay. The main seabird breeding cliffs are just S of Ardmore Head at Ram Head. *These cliffs can be dangerous and care should always be taken when visiting this area.*

Scarce or rare birds recorded in this area include Black-throated Diver, Red-necked Phalarope, Black Tern, Turtle Dove, Hoopoe, Tawny Pipit, Black Redstart, Icterine Warbler, Lesser Whitethroat, Yellow-browed Warbler, Firecrest, Pied Flycatcher and Red-eyed Vireo.

187

Other sites

Ballyscanlan Lakes & Carrigavrantry Reservoir (S 54 03 &, S 54 02) lie to the W of Tramore. These two small lakes in the Ballyscanlan Hills attract small numbers of diving ducks in winter. Both are set within conifer plantations and species regularly recorded include Siskin and Crossbill. In summer, breeding Little Grebes are found, while common summer migrants include Sedge Warbler, Willow Warbler and Chiffchaff. Water Rail is also recorded on a regular basis, while Red Grouse and Hen Harrier have been seen in the area.

From Tramore, follow the R675 W towards Fennor. In Fennor, turn right at the church and at the next junction, continue left. Approximately 500m on you meet a fork in the road. To visit Ballyscanlan Lake, go left at this point. To visit Carrigavrantry Reservoir, go right and follow to the top of the hill and park. The reservoir is reached by following the path through the woodlands near the waterworks.

Annestown Bog (X59-S50) is located 10km W of Tramore on the R675, and is an area of reedbed, scrub and small freshwater pools.

In summer, Sedge Warbler and Willow Warbler are found, while Little Egret and Water Rail are present throughout the year. Chough are also found in the area, while Hoopoe has also been recorded in spring.

The area can be viewed from the road that runs along the west side of the main river as it flows into the sea near Annestown village. A number of pathways provide limited access to the bog but note that there are deep pools or marshy areas in this area.

Ballyvooney Cove (X382973), lying to the E of Dungarvan, is an area of open sea and cliffs that attracts good numbers of Red-throated Divers and Common Scoter in winter. In recent years, Surf Scoters have been seen with the scoter flocks, while Chough are found in this area throughout the year.

From Dungarvan, take the R675 E past Clonea to Ballyvoyle village. Then take the minor road on the right signposted for Stradbally. Follow this road to Stradbally village, and in the village take the right turn which brings you down to the parking area at the cove. The scoter flocks can usually be seen well from this point, or from the cliff just to the east.

In summer, cliff-nesting Sand Martins are present, while Black Redstart has occurred here in winter.

County Monaghan

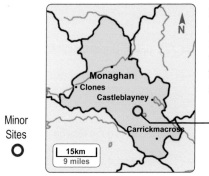

Monaghan is a small inland county with a large number of small, scattered lakes set in a rolling drumlin landscape. These lakes and wetlands attract small numbers of wintering wildfowl and waders. There is a good movement of birds between sites.

Minor
Sites

O

(153) p.189 Dromore Lakes

p.189 Other sites

153 **Dromore Lakes** Grid ref. H 62 17

A series of lakes, good for wildfowl and other waterbirds in winter.

The Dromore Lakes are a series of small inter-drumlin lakes and ponds along the Dromore River. The lakes attract wildfowl such as Whooper Swan, Wigeon, Teal, Pochard, Tufted Duck and Goldeneye in winter, as well as a small population of Lapwing. Resident species include Water Rail and Kingfisher. Pink-footed Goose has been recorded.

The lakes lie between Ballybay and Cootehill and can be viewed from several points along the R190. See also **Dromore River**, below.

Other sites

Lough Ross (H 88 16) is a large lake located on the Monaghan/Armagh border. It holds some wildfowl in winter, including Great Crested Grebe, small numbers of Whooper Swan, Wigeon, Pochard, Tufted Duck and Goldeneye.

The Dromore River (H 69 19), which flows from Ballybay south-west towards Lough Oughter in Cavan, provides river, lake and wetland habitats that attract good numbers of wildfowl and waders each winter. Wildfowl such as Whooper Swan, Wigeon (1000s), Gadwall, Teal, Pintail and Shoveler are regularly seen, while Golden Plover, Lapwing and Snipe also occur. Water Rail and Kingfisher are resident species.

Monalty Lough (H 866 02) is a small lake and marshland that attracts small numbers of wildfowl such as Whooper Swan, Wigeon, Teal, Pochard and Tufted Duck in winter. Small numbers of Golden Plover, Lapwing and Snipe are also found in winter. Monalty Lough lies approximately 2 km SW of Carrickmackross near the Monaghan/Louth border.

Lough Egish (H 79 14) is a large lake that attracts small numbers of wildfowl and waders in winter. Lying SW of Castleblaney close to where the R181 meets the R180, the lake holds Whooper Swan, Wigeon, Teal, Pochard, Tufted Duck and Goldeneye in winter. Small numbers of Golden Plover, Lapwing and Snipe also occur.

County Cavan

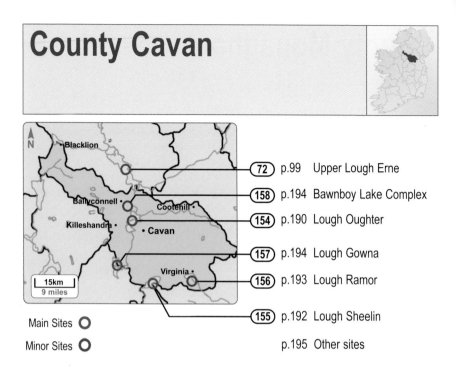

(72)	p.99	Upper Lough Erne
(158)	p.194	Bawnboy Lake Complex
(154)	p.190	Lough Oughter
(157)	p.194	Lough Gowna
(156)	p.193	Lough Ramor
(155)	p.192	Lough Sheelin
	p.195	Other sites

Main Sites O

Minor Sites O

Cavan is an inland county with scattered lakes set in a rolling drumlin landscape. Areas such as Lough Sheelin and the lake complex of Lough Oughter attract large numbers of wintering wildfowl and waders. However, many sites are difficult to view well and there is a good movement of birds between sites. There are also good woodlands around many of the lake systems that are excellent for resident woodland species as well as breeding migrants like Garden Warbler.

Lough Oughter

154

Grid ref. H 35 07

Best time to visit   Best ■ Good ■ Poor □

J F M A M J J A S O N D

An extensive area of lakes which attracts important numbers of wildfowl in winter. In summer, the woodlands along the southern areas are also good for breeding migrants, including Garden Warbler.

Lough Oughter is a series of small lakes, islands and channels often described as a lake system rather than a true lake. It is set in a belt of drumlins in the N of the county and is located within the course of the River Erne.

Directions Map 92, next page. There are many vantage points around the entire series of lakes, islands and channels. Taking the R199 SE from Killeshandra, follow for approximately 1.7km and take the minor road to the left. At the T-junction, go right and follow this minor road for over 1km and take the next left turn and follow to the end. This will bring you to **Lower Derries**, which has the best stand of reedbeds in the area. In autumn, this area is among the best locations for waders, especially when water levels are low.

190

Map 92 Lough Oughter

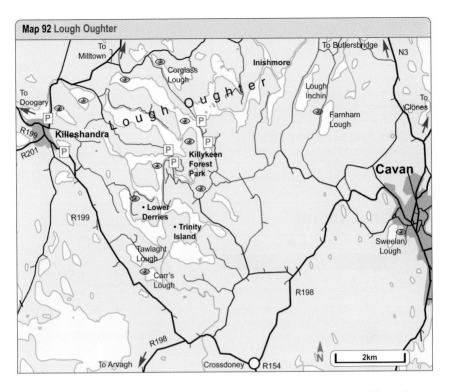

Waders are also found at **Trinity Island** and Killywally, just to the SE of Lower Derries. From here, return back to the R199 and continue SE for approximately 7.5km. Then take the left turn after the bridge approximately 1km from the point where you move from the R199 onto the R198. Follow this road out for approximately 2.5km and take a left following signs for the forest park. Follow this road NW for almost 3km and take the left into **Killykeen Forest Park**. There are many parking points around the park that give good views over the lakes, while the woodlands are excellent for common woodland species such as Treecreeper and Jay. In summer, Garden Warbler and Spotted Flycatcher also occur. A footbridge at the N end of this side of the park brings you over to the lakes and woodlands close to Killashandra.

From the forest park, return to the road and go left. There are many small roads leading to the lakeshore along the entire length of this minor road but some good views of the lake can be achieved by following left for Butlersbridge over 3km along this road. The **Inishmore** area, close

to Butlersbridge, can be very good for wildfowl in winter. Follow this minor road NE for Butlersbridge and, from there, take the N3 NW towards Belturbet. There are many points along the N3 where the small lakes can be viewed. From Belturbet, take the N37 W for 2km before taking a left onto the R201, following signs for Killeshandra. There are many roads leading from the R201 to the lakeshore, including a left turn just at the village of Milltown. This narrow road runs SE for over 3km and gives views of several parts of the lake complex.

Another left turn, approximately 6km from Milltown along the R201, brings you to the woodlands directly opposite Killykeen Forest Park. By following the track to the end, you will meet the footbridge which joins the two sections.

Birds from Lough Oughter often move to the many nearby smaller satellite lakes such as Derrybrick Lake, Drumgorry Lake, Lough Inchin, Carr's Lough, Town Lake, Ardan Lake, Parisee Lake and Round Lake.

Species

All year Greylag Goose (feral birds), Canada Goose (feral birds), Water Rail, Kingfisher, Treecreeper, Jay.

Autumn, winter & spring Bewick's Swan (R), Whooper Swan, White-fronted Goose, Wigeon (1000+), Teal (500+), Shoveler (O), Pochard, Tufted Duck, Scaup (O), Goldeneye, Hen Harrier (O), Merlin, Golden Plover (O), Lapwing, Little Stint (R autumn), Ruff (R autumn), Green Sandpiper (R autumn & winter), Wood Sandpiper (R autumn), Jack Snipe (R winter), Snipe, Woodcock, Brambling (R winter), Crossbill (R winter), Siskin, Redpoll.

Summer Common Sandpiper, gulls, Grasshopper Warbler (O), Sedge Warbler, Garden Warbler, Blackcap, Chiffchaff, Willow Warbler, Spotted Flycatcher, Siskin, Redpoll.

Rarities Ring-necked Duck, Smew, Goosander, Ruddy Duck, Pectoral Sandpiper.

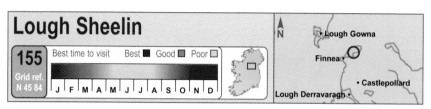

Lough Sheelin

155
Grid ref.
N 45 84

Best time to visit   Best ■ Good ▣ Poor □

J F M A M J J A S O N D

A large lake which attracts nationally important numbers of wildfowl, especially diving duck, in winter.

Directions Map 93, below. Lough Sheelin can be viewed from many vantage points along its entire shoreline, although the W side has more restricted access. From the town of Ballyjamesduff, follow the R194 SW for 6km and, at the crossroads, go left onto the R154. Continue SE for 1km and take the first right turn. Follow this road down for 1km to the parking area at the

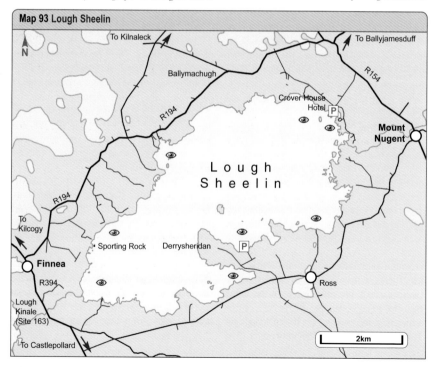

Map 93 Lough Sheelin

Crover House Hotel. The N and NE end of the lake can be seen well from this point. To view the SE end, follow the R154 SW to the village of Mount Nugent and take a right turn at the crossroads. Follow this minor road for approximately, 3km and take the small track on the right that leads to a slipway overlooking the lake. Alternatively, continue to the small village of Ross and, approximately 1km past the village, take the right turn. Follow this road to the woodlands at Derrysheridan. A parking area at the shore gives good views of the S end of the lake.

The SW corner is best seen by returning to the road from here and continuing SW for 4km. At the crossroads, go right and, after almost 1km, take the small road on the right that brings you to the lakeshore.

The W side of the lake has limited access with many small roads leading onto private ground along the shore. From the village of Finnea, follow the R394 N and then go NE on the R194. In autumn, waders have been found at the shore adjacent to Sporting Rock in the SW corner. Take the small right turn off approximately 1.5km out the R194 and take the first right turn and follow to the end.

To view other sections of the W side, return to the R194 and continue NE for almost 5km to a point where the road comes close to the lakeshore. A small right turn at a minor crossroads brings you down to a point close to the W side. Approximately 1km further along the R194, the last in a series of small private roads also brings you to the lakeshore. From here, continue through the village of Ballymachugh and, 2km later, take the right turn at the small crossroads. Follow this road to the end to park once again at the Crover House Hotel.

Species
All year Cormorant, Water Rail, Kingfisher.

Autumn, winter & spring Whooper Swan (O), Wigeon, Teal, Pochard, Tufted Duck, Scaup (O), Goldeneye, Great Northern Diver (R winter), Hen Harrier (winter), Buzzard (O), Merlin, Lapwing, Ruff (R autumn), Jack Snipe (R winter), Snipe, Whimbrel (O spring), Common Sandpiper (R winter), Siskin (O autumn & winter), Redpoll (O autumn).

Summer Common Sandpiper, gulls, Common Tern, Grasshopper Warbler (O), Sedge Warbler, Chiffchaff, Willow Warbler. Goldeneye has successfully bred here.

Rarities Ring-necked Duck, Smew, Red-necked Grebe, Slavonian Grebe, Manx Shearwater, Bittern, Osprey, Black Tern.

156 Lough Ramor Grid ref. N 50 60

A long, narrow, shallow lake which attracts good numbers of wildfowl and waders such as Golden Plover and Lapwing in winter.

The lake can be viewed well from many points along the N3 just to the SE of Virginia. There are also pathways around the lake in the town, while the park and golf course to the W of the town, also offer good vantage points over the lake. The W and S ends of the lake can be seen by following the R194 out of Virginia and taking a left onto the R195. The W side of the lake can be seen from several points along this route. To view the S side, take a left turn after the village of Eighter. Follow this narrow road for approximately 3km and take a left to go to the lakeshore at the S end. Waders are best looked for at Carrakeelty More and Islandboy in the SE corner. There can be some movement of birds between here and Lough Sheelin (Site 155, previous page). Species recorded here each winter include Whooper Swan, Wigeon, Teal, Pochard, Tufted Duck, Goldeneye, Golden Plover, Lapwing and Snipe. Resident species include Water Rail and Kingfisher. Ruff has been recorded in autumn, while Slavonian Grebe and Smew have been seen in winter.

In summer, Sedge Warbler, Grasshopper Warbler, Chiffchaff, Willow Warbler and Whinchat are found, with Garden Warbler present in small numbers at Deerpark in Virginia. Other notable records from here include Black Redstart and Crossbill, while a Great Spotted Woodpecker was recorded in September 2005.

157 Lough Gowna Grid ref. N 30 90

This large lake and associated smaller satellite lakes lie just N of the town of Granard and is on the Cavan/Longford border. In winter it attracts small numbers of wildfowl and waders.

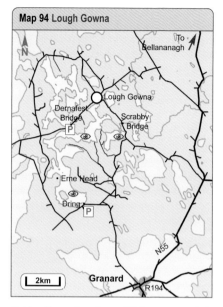

Map 94 Lough Gowna

Map 94, right. The S side of the lake can be viewed well from the parking area close to the small village of Dring, approximately 5km NE of Granard. Follow the road SW out of Dring and go right at the main crossroads. There are several small right turns off this road between 1.5km and 2.5km from the crossroads that lead down to Erne Head where a good stand of deciduous woodlands holds common woodland species such as Treecreeper and Jay. Continue on this road and go right at the next major turn and then right at the major crossroads. This will bring you across Dernafest Bridge. There is a parking area here and the lake and small rocky islets offshore are easily viewed. From here, continue NE into the village of Lough Gowna and take a right turn. This road brings you over Scrabby Bridge where Turtle Dove has been recorded.

In winter, small numbers of Whooper Swan, Wigeon, Teal, Pochard, Tufted Duck, Goldeneye,

Golden Plover, Lapwing and Snipe are recorded. Shoveler and Red-breasted Mergansers are also seen in some winters, while rarer species that have occurred in this area include American Wigeon, Goosander, Marsh Harrier and Black Tern.

158 Bawnboy Lake Complex Grid ref. H 21 16

A series of large lakes that attract wildfowl and waders in winter.

The lakes can be viewed from various points from the N87, E from Bawnboy towards Ballyconnell and NW to the junction with the R202. The areas can also be visited by taking minor roads off the R202 as well as the R205 S of Ballyconnell.

Among the better lakes are Brackley Lake, Bunerky Lake, Lakefield Lake, Bellaboy Lake, Templeport Lake, Killywillin Lake, Gortnaleck Lake, Ballymagauran Lake and Derrycassin Lake.

In winter, species such as Whooper Swan, Wigeon, Teal, Tufted Duck, Goldeneye, Lapwing and Snipe occur in small numbers, while Water Rail and Kingfisher are resident.

In summer, Garden and Grasshopper Warbler occur, while Woodcock and Common Sandpiper breed in the area.

In autumn, small numbers of Dunlin occur, with Green Sandpiper seen occasionally. Buzzard and Hen Harrier are regularly seen in autumn and winter. Osprey has also been recorded from this area.

Woodcock

Other sites

The **Woodford River Lakes** (H 30 20) are a series of small lakes just S of where the Woodford River approaches Upper Lough Erne on the border between Fermanagh and Cavan. The lakes lie just between Ballyconnell and Belturbet and attract good numbers of wintering wildfowl and waders, including Whooper Swan, Wigeon, Teal, Pochard, Tufted Duck, Goldeneye, Lapwing and Snipe. Water Rail and Kingfisher are resident, while Smew has occurred.

The best areas for viewing these small lakes lie off the N87 between the small villages of Ballyhugh and Ballyconnell. Take a right turn just past Ballyhugh and follow the road left at a T-junction to get views of the lakes close to Ballyconnell. Alternatively, go right at the T-junction and take the first and/or the second left turns to view the smaller lakes just N of Ballyhugh.

Ballinamore Lakes See Site 22, p.43.

Lough Macnean Upper (H 08 38) lies on the border of Cavan and Fermanagh. Lough MacNean Upper is 2km W of Blacklion on the N16. A lakeshore carpark provides good views over the area. In summer, Common Sandpiper is found here, while the lake also holds a small breeding colony of Common Gull. Garden Warbler is also found in the woodlands in the immediate area. In winter, small numbers of duck are present, while Whooper Swans are found close to the nearby golf course.

Burren district (H 07 34). From Blacklion, take the R206 SW for almost 2km and take the minor road to the left that runs S to Moneycashel. This minor road goes over a small area of upland bog with small coniferous plantations. These can hold common woodland species such as Jay, Crossbill and Siskin, while Hen Harrier and Cuckoo are found in this area in summer. Water Rail is also found at Lough Garvagh, a small lake near Moneycashel.

Commas/Cuilcagh Plateau (H 14 28) lies to the W of the small village of Swanlinbar and on the border of Cavan and Fermanagh. This is an area of mature upland blanket bog. Red Grouse and Golden Plover are occasionally found here, while Merlin and Hen Harrier are recorded in summer. Dotterel has occurred here on one occasion. See also Site 75.

Slieve Rusheen (H 23 22) lies on the Cavan/Fermanagh border, and just N of the village of Bawnboy between Ballyconnell and Swanlinbar on the N87. Slieve Rusheen is an area of upland blanket bog and small coniferous plantations. Red Grouse is resident in small numbers, while the woodlands hold species such as Woodcock, Jay, Siskin and Redpoll, and Grasshopper Warbler occurs in summer. The River Blackwater on the W side of the mountain is good for Dipper. Buzzard has been recorded in the area.

Castlesaunderson Demesne (H 42 19) lies just E of Belturbet and has an area of mixed coniferous and deciduous woodlands. Common woodland species such as Treecreeper, Jay and Siskin are present all year, while Garden Warbler and Spotted Flycatchers are found in summer. A small lake on the N side of the demesne has resident Water Rail. Buzzard has been recorded here in spring.

Bellamont Forest Park (H 60 14), just N of Cootehill on the R188, has good mixed woodlands and is excellent for common woodland species such as Woodcock, Long-eared Owl, Treecreeper, Jay, Siskin and Redpoll. In summer, common migrants include Blackcap, Chiffchaff and Willow Warbler, while Garden Warbler breed in small numbers. The small lakes (Coragh and Killyvaghan), just to the E, also attract small numbers of Whooper Swan and duck in winter.

Shercock Lake Complex (H 70). There are a number of small lakes, including Lough Sillan, Barnagrow Lake and Tacker Lake, that lie to the W and NW of the village of Shercock. These can be viewed from the R162, heading NW from Shercock and the R178 heading S, as well as several minor roads off both. In winter, small numbers of wildfowl and waders are found, including Whooper Swan, Wigeon, Teal, Pochard, Tufted Duck, Goldeneye, Lapwing and Snipe. Water Rail and Kingfisher are resident, while Smew and Green Sandpiper have occurred.

County Roscommon

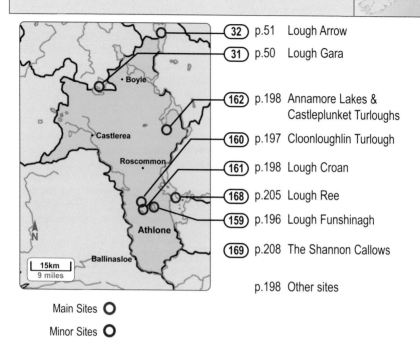

Main Sites **O**

Minor Sites **O**

Roscommon is a large inland, low-lying county. Throughout the county are a series of large and small lakes, as well as many turloughs that flood each winter. The county attracts large numbers of wintering wildfowl and waders such as Golden Plover and Lapwing, and holds breeding wildfowl in summer. The areas close to the River Shannon, near Athlone, are also good for Corncrake in summer.

Lough Funshinagh

159

Grid ref. **M 93 52**

Best time to visit   Best ■ Good ■ Poor □

J F M A M J J A S O N D

A large lake and turlough with fluctuating water levels, excellent for wintering wildfowl, while the reedbeds attracts species such as Sedge Warbler in summer.

Directions Map 95, next page. There are several ways to approach Lough Funshinagh from Athlone. To view the E and N side, follow the R362 NW from Athlone for over 12km going through the small village of Milltown Pass. Approximately 2km after Milltown Pass, take a right turn. Continue straight through the crossroads and continue for over 2km until you meet the SE corner of the lake.

To view the E side, continue along this road for 1.5km and take a left turn onto a minor road. The road narrows after 600m and continues on as a track along the E side of Lough Funshinagh for over 1km, before widening to a minor road again. This road continues along the E and NE side for another 1km before running inland and away from the lakeshore until it meets a T-junction. At this point you can go right to get onto the N61.

To view the W side of the lake, go left at the T-junction and then, 600m later, take the left turn. Follow this road for over 2.5km until you meet a major T-junction. At this point, go left back onto the R362. Continue SE for 2.3km and take the left turn onto a minor road. Follow this road to the end to view the W side of the lake. Another left turn off the R362, 300m further on, will bring you onto a very narrow road that leads down to the SW corner.

Species
All year Water Rail, Kingfisher.

Autumn, winter & spring Bewick's Swan (O), Whooper Swan, Pink-footed Goose (R), White-fronted Goose (R), Wigeon, Gadwall, Teal (1000+), Pintail, Shoveler, Pochard, Tufted Duck, Red-breasted Merganser (R), Hen Harrier (O winter), Merlin, Buzzard (R), Golden Plover

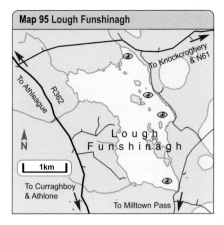

Map 95 Lough Funshinagh

(1000s), Lapwing (1000s), Knot (R), Little Stint (R autumn), Curlew Sandpiper (R autumn), Dunlin (O), Ruff (R autumn), Jack Snipe (R winter), Snipe, Black-tailed Godwit (R), Green Sandpiper (R autumn),

Summer Teal, Gadwall, Pintail, Shoveler, Tufted Duck, Pochard, Red-breasted Merganser, Snipe, Common Sandpiper, gulls, Grasshopper Warbler, Sedge Warbler, Chiffchaff, Willow Warbler.

Rarities Garganey, Black-necked Grebe (formerly bred), White Stork.

160 Cloonloughlin Turlough Grid ref. M 84 52

Cloonloughlin Turlough is an open, shallow lake that is formed by flooding in winter when it attracts good numbers of wildfowl and waders. However, by early spring, the area dries out.

See Map 96, right. From Athlone, follow the R362 W for 8km and then follow the R363. Continue on the R363 for approximately 11km and, at the crossroads, follow right onto the R357. Follow the R357 N for 8km until you reach the village of Four Roads. Follow right at the crossroads and the turlough is just on the left but can be difficult to see from the road.

Species such as Bewick's Swan, Whooper Swan, White-fronted Goose, Wigeon, Teal, Pintail,

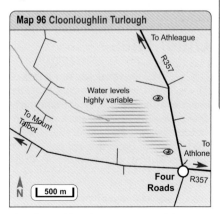

Map 96 Cloonloughlin Turlough

Shoveler, Golden Plover, Lapwing and Snipe are seen regularly.

161 Lough Croan Grid ref. M 88 48

Lough Croan is a small lake that attracts wildfowl and small numbers of waders in winter. It can dry out considerably in summer but still holds breeding Great Crested Grebes, Teal and occasionally Shoveler.

From Athlone, follow the R362 W for 8km and then follow the R363. Continue on the R363 for approximately 11km and, at the crossroads, follow right onto the R357. Follow the R357 N for approximately 4.5km and take a right onto the minor road. Continue on this minor road for just over 3km and, at the crossroads, take a left. The lake can be seen from this road.

In winter, species such as Wigeon, Teal, Pintail, Shoveler, Golden Plover, Lapwing and Snipe are regularly seen. Garganey has occurred in summer, while Black-necked Grebe has bred here in the past.

162 Annaghmore Lakes & Castleplunket Turloughs Grid ref. M 89 85

A series of freshwater lakes and turloughs, good for wildfowl and some waders in winter.

The Annaghmore Lakes complex is a series of small lakes and turloughs found along both sides of the 10km stretch of the R368 between the towns of Strokestown and Elphin in the N of Roscommon. Close by, to the SW, are the Castleplunket Turloughs which are also a series of lakes and turloughs that are on the W side of the N61 from Roscommon to Tulsk.

These areas attract large numbers of wildfowl and species such as Lapwing in winter. There is considerable movement of birds between all of these areas.

The area around Annamore Lough is the most productive and can be reached by taking the R368 from Strokestown, following signs for Elphin. Follow the R368 for approximately 4km and take a left turn. Follow this minor road for just over 1km until Annaghmore Lough is visible on the left. It can be viewed from the road.

Species recorded in these areas each winter include Whooper Swan, Wigeon, Teal, Pintail, Shoveler, Pochard, Tufted Duck, Goldeneye, Golden Plover and Lapwing.

Species such as Water Rail and Kingfisher are resident, while Common Sandpiper occurs in summer.

Other sites

Lying just N of Boyle, **Lough Key Forest Park** (G 83 05) is 350 hectares of mixed woodland overlooking Lough Key. It is a popular tourist destination with hotels, lodges and water sports facilities. The woodlands hold many resident species such as Treecreeper and Jay, while in summer, warblers such as Blackcap, Willow Warbler and Chiffchaff occur, with Spotted Flycatcher also found. In winter, Siskin and Redpoll are found. The park has an extensive series of pathways. The lake is large but very deep and does not support large numbers of wildfowl in winter.

County Longford

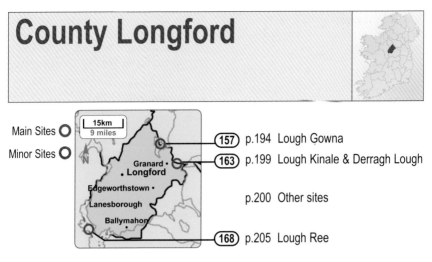

Main Sites ◯
Minor Sites ◯

15km
9 miles

Granard •
• Longford

Edgeworthstown •

Lanesborough

Ballymahon •

(157) p.194 Lough Gowna

(163) p.199 Lough Kinale & Derragh Lough

p.200 Other sites

(168) p.205 Lough Ree

County Longford is generally low-lying with a scattering of lakes and turloughs, and a winter visit to these habitats provides the main birdwatching interest. Lough Ree (Site 168), bordering the SW, and Lough Gowna (Site 157) are treated elsewhere in the book, but there is a host of other productive lakes scattered throughout the county. The 'Other sites' (next page) offer a flavour of the rewards awaiting anyone willing to take the time to explore the Longford wetlands in winter in this much underwatched locality.

Lough Kinale & Derragh Lough

163
Grid ref.
N 39 81

Best time to visit   Best ■ Good ■ Poor □

| J | F | M | A | M | J | J | A | S | O | N | D |

N

• Lough Sheelin

Granard •

• Castlepollard

Lough •
Derravaragh

Two lakes, good for wildfowl in winter, particularly Pochard and Tufted Duck.

The majority of birds occur on and around Derragh Lough, but both lakes suffer from frequent disturbance from shooting throughout winter, causing temporary abandonment of the area by many birds.

Directions Map 97, right. **Lough Kinale** can be explored from a number of vantage points and short side roads along the road between Abbeylara and Finnea. Views of the lake can be distant, so a telescope is recommended. For **Derragh Lough**, travel 1.5km SE of Abbeylara, on the road to Castlepollard, and take a left. After 2km, take another left. The lake is visible on the left, and the road approaches the lake edge, allowing for much better views.

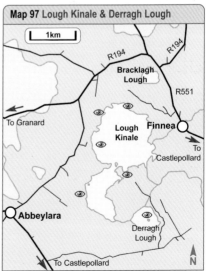

Map 97 Lough Kinale & Derragh Lough

1km

R194   R194

Bracklagh
Lough

R551

To Granard

Lough
Kinale   **Finnea**

To
Castlepollard

Abbeylara

Derragh
Lough

To Castlepollard   N

Midlands

199

Bracklagh Lough, 1km NW of Finnea, and visible from the R551, also attracts small numbers of wildfowl in winter.

Species
Winter Mute Swan (often 150+), Whooper Swan (O), Wigeon (small numbers), Teal (small numbers), Pochard (usually 700+), Tufted Duck (usually 500+), Goldeneye, Little Grebe, Great Crested Grebe, Cormorant, Water Rail (O), Merlin (R), Hen Harrier (O), Peregrine, Golden Plover, Lapwing, Snipe, gulls, Kingfisher, Short-eared Owl (R).

Rarities Ring-necked Duck, Great Northern Diver.

Other sites

Gorteen Lake (N 22 79) is located just S of Ballinalee, 7km NNW of Edgeworthstown, in the centre of County Longford. The lake and surrounding grassland and wetland become visible just after leaving the outskirts of Ballinalee, and can be explored from the surrounding roads. A telescope is recommended.

Golden Plover and Lapwing are noteworthy winter species, and Whooper Swan, Wigeon, Teal, Pochard, Tufted Duck and Goldeneye are usually present in small numbers from October to March.

Doogary Lough (N 20 95) is one of a series of small lakes in this general area that, together, can host quite large numbers of birds throughout winter. Doogary is one of the best of these and is located 4km W of Moyne, in the N of County Longford. Leave Moyne SW on the main R198 to Drumlish. After 1.5km, take a right fork and continue straight for 2km, then take a right, along a narrow winding road for another 2km. Doogary Lough is visible to your left and can be explored from the road, or on foot.

The lake holds good numbers of wintering wildfowl, inlcuding Teal, Wigeon, Pochard, Tufted Duck and Goldeneye, and a small flock of Whooper Swans. Golden Plover and large numbers of Lapwing are also present throughout winter. The chance of finding rarer species is quite high as this is a much underwatched area.

Turreen Lough (N 01 65), **Fortwillian Turlough** (N 01 63) and **Cordara Turlough** (N 03 63) are located within 6km S of Lanesborough just to the E of Lough Ree (Site 168). These turloughs regularly flood in winter and at such times can be very good for wetland birds. Several thousand Golden Plover and Lapwing are usually present, and depending on water levels, diving and dabbling duck are present in high numbers. Other species seen here include Whooper Swan, Wigeon, Teal, Shoveler (O), Pochard, Tufted Duck, Snipe, Black-tailed Godwit and gulls.

Great Crested Grebe, Dunlin and Kingfisher are sometimes seen, and scarcer winter visitors include Bewick's Swan, Little Egret, Merlin, Hen Harrier and Short-eared Owl.

County Westmeath

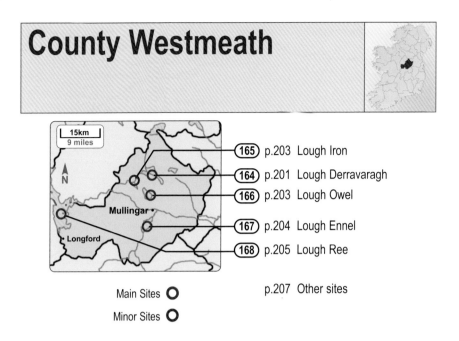

(165)	p.203	Lough Iron
(164)	p.201	Lough Derravaragh
(166)	p.203	Lough Owel
(167)	p.204	Lough Ennel
(168)	p.205	Lough Ree

p.207 Other sites

Main Sites O

Minor Sites O

Westmeath is a low-lying inland county with many lakes, including the south-western and western sides of the largest lake in this region, Lough Ree. Other important lakes for birds include Loughs Ennell, Derravaragh and Owel, all of which are excellent for wildfowl and waders in winter. There is considerable movement of birds between these sites.

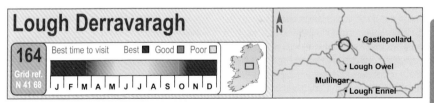

Lough Derravaragh

164

Grid ref.
N 41 68

Best time to visit   Best ■ Good ■ Poor □

J F M A M J J A S O N D

A large, shallow, limestone lake which attracts large numbers of wildfowl in winter. Woodlands on the southern shore are excellent for resident woodland species as well as finches and thrushes in winter, while the western side holds reedbed and marshland species.

Directions Map 98, next page. Lough Derravaragh lies to the N of Mullingar. On the main N4 Dublin to Sligo road, continue past the turn-offs for Mullingar and Lough Owel on the left

until you reach Bunbrosna. At Bunbrosna, take a right turn, following signs for Multyfarnham. As you come into the village, take a right and continue downhill. To view the W and N side of the lake, take the left turn just before the bridge at the bottom of the village and follow this narrow road N for over 3km until you cross the River Inny. Approximately 1km past this small bridge is a small right turn that brings you down to the lakeshore. The N end of the lake can be viewed by continuing along this road until you cross the River Inny a second time. Continue on until you meet a T-junction. Go right at the junction and

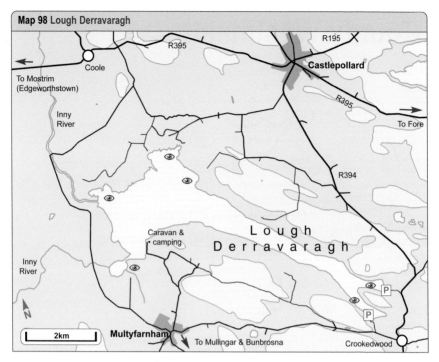

Map 98 Lough Derravaragh

To Mostrim (Edgeworthstown)
Coole
R395
R195
Castlepollard
R395
To Fore
Inny River
R394
Caravan & camping
Lough Derravaragh
Inny River
P
P
N
2km
Multyfarnham
To Mullingar & Bunbrosna
Crookedwood

then take the first right turn. As the road swings sharp right, a small track on the left leads to the shore. Alternatively, take the second right turn off the main road and, at the end of this narrow road, follow the track to the left.

To view the S side, continue over the small bridge at the bottom of Multyfarnham village and take an immediate left turn. Follow this narrow road for over 1km and continue left at the fork in the road. Continue along this road for almost 1km and take the next left turn. This road brings you through the woodlands and onto the lakeshore. There are many pathways along here and the lake can be viewed well from many points. It should be noted that this area is also used as a camping site and a caravan park.

Species

All year Cormorant, Water Rail, Kingfisher.

Autumn, winter & spring Whooper Swan, Wigeon, Teal, Shoveler (O), Scaup (O), Pochard, Tufted Duck, Common Scoter (R winter), Goldeneye, Hen Harrier (O winter), Golden Plover, Lapwing, Little Stint (R autumn), Curlew Sandpiper (R autumn), Dunlin (O autumn), Ruff (R autumn), Jack Snipe (R winter), Snipe, Green Sandpiper (R autumn), Brambling (R winter), Siskin, (autumn & winter), Redpoll (autumn & winter).

Summer Common Sandpiper, gulls, terns, Grasshopper Warbler (O), Sedge Warbler, Blackcap, Garden Warbler (R), Chiffchaff, Willow Warbler.

Rarities Red-crested Pochard, Ring-necked Duck, Smew, Slavonian Grebe, Wood Sandpiper, Sabine's Gull.

Cormorant

165 Lough Iron · Grid ref. N 34 63

A small, narrow lake just to the north-west of Lough Owel (Site 166) which holds large numbers of wildfowl in winter, including White-fronted Goose and Whooper Swan.

Map 99, right. Also present in winter are Wigeon, Gadwall, Teal, Shoveler, Pochard, Tufted Duck, Goldeneye, Red-breasted Merganser, Golden Plover and Lapwing. The lake is fringed by a reedbed that holds a resident population of Water Rail and also attracts Sedge Warbler in summer.

There are no direct access roads to the lakeshore, and lands immediately surrounding it are private. Lough Iron lies on the W side of the main N4 Dublin to Sligo road, just past the village of Bunbrosna. A small conifer plantation on the NW side of the lake is good for Siskin and Redpoll.

Rarities that have been seen here include Canada Goose, Barnacle Goose, Red-crested Pochard and Little Egret.

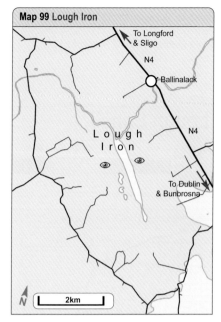

Map 99 Lough Iron

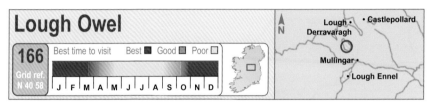

Lough Owel

166	Best time to visit	Best ■ Good ■ Poor ☐
Grid ref. N 40 58	J F M A M J J A S O N D	

A shallow limestone lake holding good numbers of diving ducks in winter. An area of reedbeds on the western side of the lake is good for Sedge Warbler in summer.

Directions Map 100, next page. Lough Owel lies close to the town of Mullingar on the N4 Dublin to Sligo road. The N4 bypasses the town of Mullingar and, approximately 4km past the turn-off for Mullingar, you will see the lake on the left side. The best area to view the lake is from the parking and picnic area a further 1km further on. This area provides elevated views over the lake. To get to the lakeshore, follow the path down from the car park, cross over the railway bridge and follow the steps down to the small piers. Diving ducks are usually concentrated on the side of the lake. The SE corner of the lake can be viewed by taking a left turn at the point where the lake comes into view. **Church Island** can be viewed from the road or by taking the small track to the right approxi-

mately 700m along this road. Follow the track over the railway line and view from the lakeshore.

The W side is best viewed by continuing NW on the N4, passing the picnic and parking area on the left, and at the village of Bunbrosna, take a left and follow this minor road S for just over 5km and take a left turn. Follow this road for over 1km, continuing straight (right) at the minor fork. This brings you to the lakeshore.

Species
All year Cormorant, Water Rail, Kingfisher.

Autumn, winter & spring Whooper Swan (O), Wigeon, Teal, Shoveler, Scaup (R winter), Pochard, Tufted Duck, Goldeneye, Long-tailed Duck (R winter), Red-breasted Merganser (O), Great Northern Diver (O), Hen Harrier (O), Peregrine, Golden Plover, Lapwing, Jack Snipe (R winter), Snipe.

Summer Common Sandpiper, gulls, Common Tern, Garden Warbler, Grasshopper Warbler (O), Sedge Warbler, Chiffchaff, Willow Warbler.

Rarities Red-crested Pochard, Ring-necked Duck, Smew, Goosander, Red-necked Grebe, Slavonian Grebe, Little Gull, Sabine's Gull, Black Tern, White-winged Black Tern.

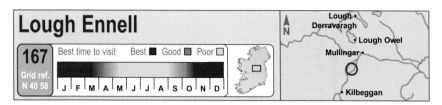

Lough Ennell

167

Grid ref.
N 40 58

Best time to visit   Best ■ Good ▨ Poor ☐

J F M A M J J A S O N D

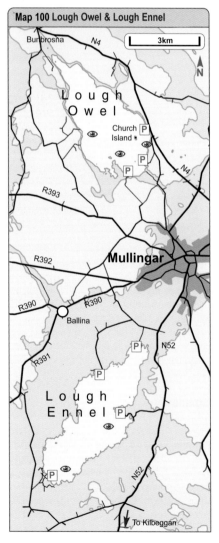

Map 100 Lough Owel & Lough Ennel

A shallow limestone lake which attracts good numbers of diving ducks in winter. The woodlands around the lake are also good for resident species and warblers in summer.

Directions Map 100, left. Lough Ennell lies just S of Mullingar town. The best areas for viewing it are from the E side and the SW corner. To view the E side, take the N52 S from Mullingar following signs for Tyrrellspass. Continue on the N52 for approximately 6km and take a right turn. Follow this minor road for over 1.1km to reach the lakeshore. This road runs along the shore to a parking area. To view the SW corner, from Mullingar, follow the R390 SW for 6km to the village of Ballina and then follow left onto the R391. Continue for just over 4km and take a left onto the minor road. Follow this road S for approximately 4km and take the left turn onto the narrow road which brings you to the lakeshore.

Species
All year Cormorant, Kingfisher.

Autumn, winter & spring Whooper Swan (O), Wigeon, Teal, Shoveler (R), Scaup (R winter), Pochard (1000s), Tufted Duck (1000s), Goldeneye, Long-tailed Duck (R winter), Red-breasted Merganser (O), Great Northern Diver (O), Hen Harrier (O), Golden Plover, Lapwing, Jack Snipe (R winter), Snipe,

Summer Common Sandpiper, gulls, Common Tern, Grasshopper Warbler (O), Sedge Warbler, Chiffchaff, Willow Warbler.

Rarities Ring-necked Duck, Smew, Goosander, Slavonian Grebe, Goshawk, Crossbill.

204

Lough Ree

• Lanesborough
• Roscommon

• Athlone

A large lake, with large numbers of wildfowl and waders in winter, and some interesting summer visitors.

Lough Ree is one of the largest lakes on the River Shannon system and is bordered by counties Longford, Roscommon and Westmeath. It has many sheltered bays and stands of reedbeds along its entire shoreline which make large areas of the lake hard to see well from the shore. In winter, it attracts large numbers of wildfowl and waders such as Golden Plover and Lapwing. In summer, common migrants are found, including Garden Warbler. Common Terns also nest in summer.

Directions Map 101, next page. There are many vantage points over Lough Ree. The S end can be seen from Coosan Point which looks out to Hare Island and is just N of Athlone. From the Athlone bypass (N6), take the exit for the N55 for Ballymahon. Having gone under the N6, take the first left turn and, after 1km, close to the church, take the right. Follow this road N for over 3km to the parking and viewing point.

The SE and E sides can be seen by turning off the N55 at several points heading NE for Ballymahon. The first area to check lies approximately 5km out the N55. At Ballykeeran, take the left turn and follow the minor road N along the lake shore for

over 1.2km before it swings back onto the N55. 3.5km further NE along the N55 is Auburn Crossroads. Take a left at this point and follow this narrow road NW taking a left at the first fork. Continue for over 1.5km and, at the staggered crossroads, continue straight. At the next fork almost 500m further on, go right and continue for 1km and take a left at the next fork in the road. Continue straight on this road to the end to view the lake, or take the first left turn, go past Creggan Lough, and follow to the end. The NE and N ends of the lake can be seen from several points along the R392 that runs NW from Ballymahon to Lanesborough. Approximately 14km NW along the R392 from Ballymahon is Derraghan Crossroads (where the R398 meets the R392). Take a left at this point and follow the minor road SW for over 3.5km and take a left at the T-junction. Continue for 1km and take a right turn before, 500m on, following the road left into and through the village of Newtown Cashel. Continue on this main road to the small harbour at Collum Point. The N end can be seen where the river enters Lough Ree at Lanesborough.

The W side of the lake can be seen from many points along the N61 from Athlone to Roscommon. The SW side is best seen by taking a right turn 4km from Athlone and following the road for almost 2km to the parking area at Hodson's Bay. The W side can be viewed by following the N61 NW for over 15km and taking a right turn for Lecarrow. Follow the road E out of the village for over 3km and, at the T-junction, park, and follow the track towards the church. This leads to Warren Point.

The NW end is best viewed by taking a right turn, 1km NE of Knockcroghery village, approximately 5km before the town of Roscommon. Continue on this road for almost 1.5km, turn right at the crossroads, and follow for over 3km to reach the small harbour overlooking Portrunny Bay. The road runs along the shore for over 700m at this point.

Golden Plover

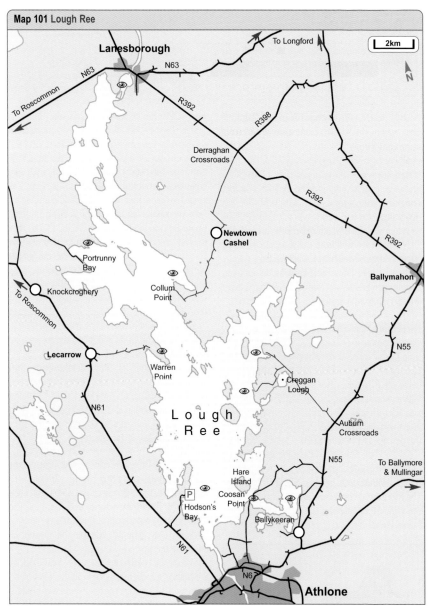

Map 101 Lough Ree

To Longford

2km

N

Lanesborough

N63

N63

To Roscommon

R392

R398

Derraghan
Crossroads

R392

R392

Newtown
Cashel

Portrunny
Bay

Collum
Point

Ballymahon

To Roscommon

Knockcroghery

N55

Lecarrow

Warren
Point

Creggan
Lough

N61

L o u g h
R e e

Auburn
Crossroads

N55

To Ballymore
& Mullingar

Hare
Island

P

Coosan
Point

Hodson's
Bay

Ballykeeran

N61

N6

Athlone

Species
All year Canada Goose (feral birds), Cormorant, Water Rail, Kingfisher.

Autumn, winter & spring Bewick's Swan (R), Whooper Swan (O), White-fronted Goose (R), Wigeon (1000s), Teal (1000s), Pintail, Shoveler, Tufted Duck (1000+), Pochard, Scaup (O), Red-breasted Merganser (O), Hen Harrier (O), Merlin (O), Golden Plover (1000s), Lapwing (1000s), Green Sandpiper (R autumn), Siskin, (O autumn & winter), Redpoll (O autumn).

Summer Common Sandpiper, gulls, Common Tern, Grasshopper Warbler (O), Sedge Warbler, Garden Warbler, Chiffchaff, Willow Warbler.

Rarities Pink-footed Goose, Marsh Harrier.

206

Other sites

Lough Lene (N 51 68) is a deep limestone lake that attracts good numbers of diving duck in winter.

The best areas for viewing lie at the E end of the lake. From Castlepollard, take the R395 SW for over 6.5km until you reach the village of Collinstown. In the village, take a left at the crossroads and continue NE for 2km before taking the small left turn. This narrow road brings you to a parking area overlooking the E side of the lake.

Species seen here in winter include Wigeon, Teal, Shoveler, Pochard, Tufted Duck and Goldeneye. Water Rail is also resident, while Red-crested Pochard has been recorded.

Glen Lough (N 28 67) is a small lake approximately 5 km south of Edgeworthstown on the Westmeath/Longford border. Water levels fluctuate at this site depending on rainfall.

In winter, it attracts internationally important numbers of Whooper Swans and small numbers of other wildfowl and waders, including White-fronted Goose, Wigeon, Teal, Pintail, Shoveler, Lapwing and Snipe. The area also has extensive reedbeds which hold Sedge Warbler in summer, while Water Rail and Kingfisher are resident. A small conifer plantation at the NW end of the lake is good for common woodland species such as Siskin.

Glen Lough is reached by taking the N4 SE from Edgeworthstown for almost 2km and turning right. Follow this minor road SW for approximately 2.5km and at Bohernacross, go left and follow the road to the end.

Swallows

County Offaly

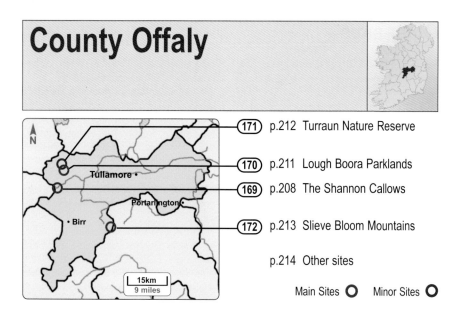

171   p.212 Turraun Nature Reserve

170   p.211 Lough Boora Parklands

169   p.208 The Shannon Callows

172   p.213 Slieve Bloom Mountains

       p.214 Other sites

       Main Sites ⭕   Minor Sites ⭕

Offaly is a low-lying inland county. The western edge of the county is bordered by the River Shannon, and the annual winter flooding of the river has created the Shannon Callows, a narrow band of grass meadows that stretch from Athlone in County Westmeath to Portumna in County Galway. The Callows attract large numbers of wildfowl and waders in winter and are excellent for Corncrakes in summer. The county also has numerous lowland blanket bog sites that are good for breeding species such as Lapwing. The Lough Boora Parklands situated in the centre of the county is now the last stronghold of the wild population of Grey Partridge in Ireland.

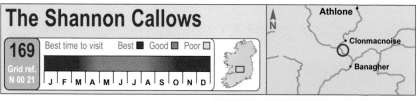

The Shannon Callows

169

Grid ref.
N 00 21

Best time to visit   Best ■ Good ▤ Poor ☐

J F M A M J J A S O N D

The Shannon Callows is a narrow band of grass meadows on the floodplains of the River Shannon. The callows stretch from Athlone in Westmeath to Portumna in Galway. It attracts large numbers of wildfowl and waders in winter, and is one of the best sites in Ireland for Corncrakes in summer.

The best locations include the areas between Bullock Island/Shannon Harbour, Banagher and Clonfert. See Map 102, next page, for the main areas.

Corncrake

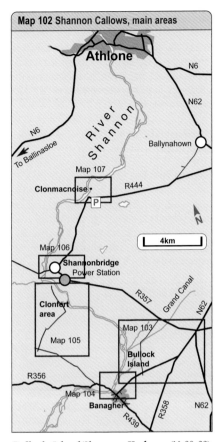

Map 102 Shannon Callows, main areas

Map 103, bottom left. From Ferbane, follow the N62 SW into Cloghan. At Cloghan, take the R356 SW for Banagher. Continue for 3km and follow the R356 right for a further 3km and take a right at the minor crossroads following signs for Shannon Harbour. Follow this minor road N for over 1km and, just as you have crossed over the railway bridge, there is a small area on the right where you can park. A gate directly opposite leads to a path onto Bullock Island. *It should be noted that much of the land in this area is private property.* From this point, continue N to Shannon Harbour. The road leading up to Shannon Harbour affords good views over the callows. Just at Shannon Harbour, take the left turn and continue past the old buildings on the left. This leads onto the old towpath along the canal and continues for almost 1km. The N end of Bullock Island can be viewed from here and Corncrakes can be heard from this path. Just past the last canal lock, a narrow path leads to a gate at the far corner of the field on the left. This brings you onto Bullock Island. Bee-eater has been seen along this path, while Spotted Crake and Quail have been recorded singing on Bullock Island.

Banagher (N 00 16) is a small town built on the River Shannon. The grasslands on the Galway side of the town are excellent for Corncrakes and Whinchat in summer.

Bullock Island/Shannon Harbour (M 99 22) Bullock Island is a large area of grass meadows that floods in winter. The fields here are excellent for Corncrake in summer and attract wildfowl and waders in winter. Shannon Harbour is a small village built beside the canal. A towpath runs along the canal and overlooks the north side of Bullock Island.

Map 104, below. From Shannon Harbour, return back onto the R356 and take a right turn following signs for Banagher. Follow this road for 3km and, at Banagher, take a right at the T-junction, following the R356. Continue through the town and over the bridge. Just at the end of the bridge

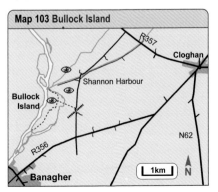

Map 103 Bullock Island

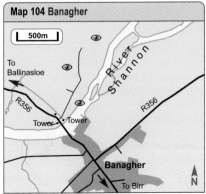

Map 104 Banagher

is a Martello Tower on the left. Go left into the parking area at this point. From here, return to the main road, walk left and take the small pathway on the right close to the next Martello Tower (on the right side of the road). Follow this narrow pathway which runs through grass meadows on both sides. After 600m, the path swings left and finishes a further 400m on. The meadows on either side of this path are excellent for Corncrakes and Whinchat in summer. Snipe and Cuckoo are also present in summer, while Quail has been recorded. Corncrakes can be heard from the bridge at Banagher.

Clonfert area (M 97 22) An excellent area of floodplains on the Galway side of the callows that attracts wildfowl in winter and is good for Corncrake in summer.

See Map 105, below. From Banagher, continue over the bridge and follow the R356 W for 2km and take the right turn signposted for Clonfert. Follow this road for almost 5km and take a right turn just at the B&B, following signs for Clonfert Cathedral. Go past the cathedral on the left and continue straight onto the minor road (the main road swings sharp left just past the cathedral). Follow this minor road over the narrow but steep humpback bridge. In summer, roding Woodcock can be seen from this bridge at dusk. Continue on

this narrow road for approximately 800m and follow the road as it turns sharp left. This road brings you to the power station but anywhere from 500m along this road to the station is good for Corncrake and Whinchat in summer. The small wetland areas on the right are also good for wildfowl in winter.

Shannonbridge (M 96 25) A good area of floodplains that attracts Corncrakes in summer.

See Map 106, below. From Cloghan, take the R357 NW for 12km until you reach Shannonbridge. Follow the R357 through the village. All areas on both sides of the bridge over the river are good habitat for Corncrake in summer. Whinchats also occur here in summer, while a Hoopoe was present in this area in November 1995.

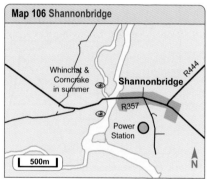

Map 106 Shannonbridge

Clonmacnoise (N 05 35) is an old monastic site overlooking the floodplains of the River Shannon. This area is excellent for Corncrakes and Whinchats in summer.

See Map 107, below. From Shannonbridge, take the R444 N, following signs for Clonmacnoise.

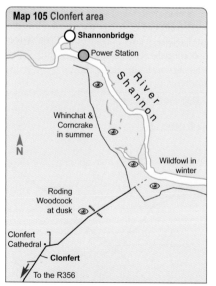

Map 105 Clonfert area

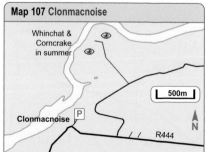

Map 107 Clonmacnoise

Continue on the R444 for just over 6km and follow the road as it swings right past the monastic ruins and visitors centre. Take the left turn approximately 700m along this road and follow this narrow road for almost 1.5km until you see a path on the left that runs down to the river. The grasslands on both sides of this path are excellent for Corncrake and Whinchat. The old graveyard at the back of the monastic ruins is also good for Spotted Flycatcher in summer.

Species
All year Water Rail, Kingfisher.

Autumn, winter & spring Bewick's Swan (R winter), Whooper Swan, Pink-footed Goose (R), White-fronted Goose (O), Wigeon (1000s), Teal (500+), Shoveler (O), Golden Plover (1000s), Lapwing (1000s), Dunlin, Ruff (R autumn), Jack Snipe (R winter), Snipe, Black-tailed Godwit, Green Sandpiper (R autumn), Short-eared Owl (O winter), Brambling (R winter), Siskin, (O autumn & winter), Redpoll (O autumn).

Summer Corncrake, Common Sandpiper, gulls, terns, Whinchat, Grasshopper Warbler, Sedge Warbler, Chiffchaff, Willow Warbler.

Rarities Canada Goose, Garganey, Quail, Marsh Harrier, Osprey, Spotted Crake, Sociable Plover, Bee-eater, Hoopoe.

Corncrakes frequent the flood meadows along the fringes of the River Shannon, and occasionally on adjacent, drier fields with long grass. They are fully protected by law, *so you must not try to flush birds by walking through fields*. In any case, you are far more likely to see a Corncrake by sitting patiently in an area overlooking several fields from which birds are calling, and waiting. Birds will often fly short distances and occasionally perch on walls, or in the open, if left alone. Trying to flush a bird usually drives it deeper into cover. *Do not use tape lures*.

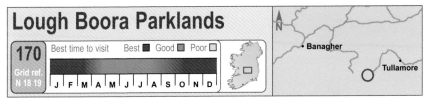

Lough Boora Parklands

170
Grid ref.
N 18 19

Best time to visit   Best ■ Good ■ Poor □

J F M A M J J A S O N D

N

• Banagher

○ Tullamore

Lough Boora Parklands, known also as **Boora Bog**, is a large, open area of regenerating lowland blanket bog with pastures, small forestry plantations, grasslands, wetlands and lakes. The area is excellent for wildfowl and waders in winter and is the last stronghold of wild Grey Partridge in Ireland. It is also excellent for breeding waders such as Lapwing in summer.

Directions Map 108, next page. From Tullamore, follow the N52 SW, signposted for Birr, for 10km and, at Blue Ball, turn right onto the R357, following signs for Cloghan and Shannonbridge. Continue on the R357 for over 7km until you see the first entrance to Boora on the left. Small lakes on the left side can hold small numbers of ducks in winter. Continue on the road to the right.

The best area for Grey Partridge is the crop fields on the right immediately after the point where the road swings left and right before straightening out. The road then goes sharp right and continues for almost 2km until you reach a T-junction. At this point, go left and you will see 'Tumduff Mór', a lake that attracts small numbers of wildfowl each winter. There is a bird hide here that is reached by walking the path out from the road. Boora Lake is reached by continuing past Tumduff Mór and following the road right and right again. There are several parking areas at the end of the road and the bird hide at the lake is reached from the second carpark. The wetlands to the W of the lake are good for Snipe, and occasionally Jack Snipe, in winter. The area can also be viewed along the 'Cycle Path/Offaly Way' that runs across the parklands from the entrance near Boora church which is further W along the R357. See also www.loughbooraparklands.com.

Midlands

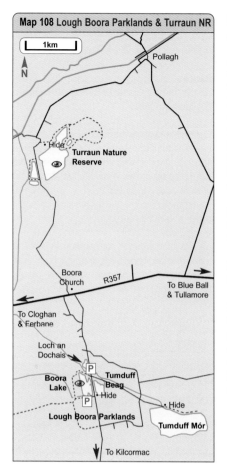

Map 108 Lough Boora Parklands & Turraun NR

1km

N

Pollagh

Hide
Turraun Nature Reserve

Boora Church

R357

To Blue Ball & Tullamore

To Cloghan & Ferbane

Loch an Dochais

P

Boora Lake

Tumduff Beag

Hide

P

Hide

Lough Boora Parklands

Tumduff Mór

To Kilcormac

Species

All year Grey Partridge, Water Rail, Kingfisher.

Autumn, winter & spring Bewick's Swan (R winter), Whooper Swan, Pink-footed Goose (R), White-fronted Goose, Wigeon, Teal, Shoveler (O), Red-throated Diver (R winter), Hen Harrier (winter), Merlin, Buzzard (R), Golden Plover (1000s), Lapwing (1000s), Dunlin (R), Ruff (R autumn), Jack Snipe (winter), Snipe, Black-tailed Godwit (O), Green Sandpiper (R autumn), Brambling (R winter), Siskin, (O autumn & winter), Redpoll (O autumn).

Summer Shoveler (R), Pochard (R), Lapwing, Common Sandpiper, Grasshopper Warbler, Sedge Warbler, Chiffchaff, Willow Warbler.

Rarities Garganey, Smew, Marsh Harrier, Osprey, Crane.

Lough Boora Parklands is the last stronghold of the Grey Partridge in Ireland. The species suffered serious decline due to habitat loss. A reintroduction project was launched at this site using eastern European birds. This, coupled with habitat management, has proved successful, with numbers increasing slowly each year.

171 Turraun Nature Reserve Grid ref. N 17 23

Turraun is an area of regenerated lowland blanket bog with wetlands, trees and a small lake. It is a good site for wildfowl and waders in winter.

See Map 108, above. From Tullamore, follow the N52 SW signposted Birr for 10km and, at Blue Ball, turn right onto R357 following signs for Cloghan and Shannonbridge. Continue on the R357 for over 8km until you reach Boora Church on the right. Turraun is reached by turning right (N) onto the gravel road beside Boora Church. This road continues on through Turraun and into Pollagh village. Do not cross the canal. There are

two carparks in the reserve, one at the S end and another at the N end, nearest to Pollagh village.

The bird hide is located 300m from the N carpark and is reached by continuing down the road towards Pollagh for approximately 150m and turning right down the gravel path. The hide provides a good vantage point from which to see the lake.

Species present all year include Water Rail and Kingfisher. In autumn, winter & spring, species present include Bewick's Swan (R winter), Whooper Swan, Pink-footed Goose (R), White-fronted Goose, Wigeon, Gadwall (R), Teal, Shoveler (O), Hen Harrier (winter), Merlin,

Golden Plover, Lapwing (1000+), Knot (R winter), Sanderling (R winter), Dunlin (R), Ruff (R autumn), Spotted Redshank (R winter), Jack Snipe (winter), Snipe, Siskin, (O autumn & winter) and Redpoll (O autumn).

In summer there are breeding Lapwing, Common Sandpiper, Grasshopper Warbler, Sedge Warbler, Chiffchaff, Willow Warbler. Temminck's Stint has also been recorded at this site.

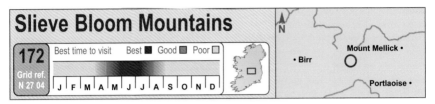

Slieve Bloom Mountains

172

Grid ref. N 27 04

Best time to visit   Best ■ Good ■ Poor □

J F M A M J J A S O N D

Mount Mellick •

• Birr   ○

Portlaoise •

Upland, moorland and woodland species.

The Slieve Bloom Mountains straddle the Laois/Offaly border and offer a selection of upland habitats, from coniferous plantations, rivers, mixed woodlands and upland blanket bog. This whole area is excellent for Hen Harrier in summer, while the blanket bog holds good numbers of Red Grouse. The woodlands are also excellent for resident species such as Jay, while species such as Grasshopper Warbler occur in summer. The coniferous plantations can occasionally hold good numbers of Crossbill.

Directions Map 109, below. From Tullamore, take the N52 SW for Birr. Less than 2km from Tullamore, take the left turn onto the R421, signed for Kinnitty and the Slieve Bloom Mountains. Follow this narrow road for approximately 13km and, at the T-junction, continue right

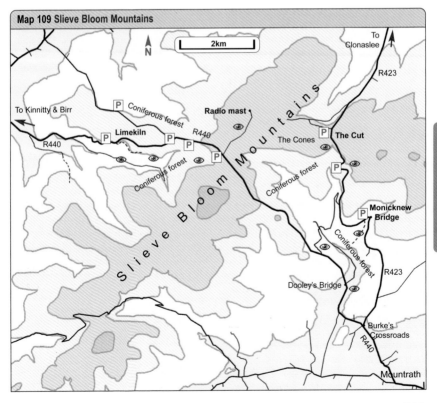

Map 109 Slieve Bloom Mountains

2km

To Clonaslee

R423

To Kinnitty & Birr

Coniferous forest

Radio mast

Limekiln

R440

R440

Coniferous forest

Slieve Bloom Mountains

The Cones   The Cut

Coniferous forest

Monicknew Bridge

Coniferous forest

R423

Dooley's Bridge

Burke's Crossroads

R440

Mountrath

Midlands

213

on the R421 following signs for Kinnitty. Continue on the R421 for almost 10km into the village of Kinnitty. Just as you get into the village, take the sharp left turn which brings you onto the R440. Follow the R440 as it goes uphill and above the valley on the right side. There are several parking areas along this very narrow road that give good views over the woodlands below. The best viewing area is across from the old **limekiln**. From this point, a small track runs downhill into the valley. Hen Harrier is often seen in this area, especially males doing flight displays in spring. There are several good areas along the track where Grasshopper Warbler are found, while common woodland birds such as Willow Warbler are present in summer.

From the limekiln, continue uphill and, at the T-junction, follow right on the R440. Less than 1km along this road you will see a track that leads up to the **radio mast** on the hill to the left. The upland blanket bog in this area is excellent for Red Grouse. They can be seen occasionally from the road and track to the mast. Hen Harrier are also frequently seen in this area in summer. From this point, continue SE on the R440. There are several viewing points along the road before it moves downhill. Again, these points are good for seeing displaying Hen Harrier in spring. Approximately 4.3km past the 'mast track' is a small turn off on the left. Follow this narrow road to the end and from here, take one of the tracks that run into the mixed woodland. Common woodland species are found here, with Crossbill occasionally recorded. From this small track, return to the R440 and continue SW for approximately 2.8km and take a left turn at Burke's Crossroads (800m past the school). Follow this narrow road for over 3.5km and park just past where the road swings sharp left over the **Monicknew Bridge**. From the carpark, follow the small track down to the left of the bridge. The river here is good for Dipper and the woodlands around the bridge are good for common woodland species in summer as well as resident species such as Jay. From here, continue N on the road through a narrow section of road called **The Cut**. The woodlands from the bridge to The Cut are good for common woodland species, while the viewpoint just beyond The Cut can also be a good site to watch for displaying Hen Harrier in spring.

Species

All year Red Grouse, Dipper, Raven, Crossbill, Siskin, Redpoll.

Summer Hen Harrier, Merlin, Peregrine, Common Sandpiper, Grasshopper Warbler, Blackcap, Chiffchaff, Willow Warbler, Whinchat.

Other sites

Little Brosna Callows see Site 174, Little Brosna & Ashton's Callows.

The **Blackwater Railway Lakes** (N 00 26) are situated on an exhausted Bord Na Móna site, approximately 5km SE of Shannonbridge. From Shannonbridge, follow the R357 SE for Cloghan and take a left into the Bord Na Móna 'Rail Tours' site. The small lakes around the site are good for wildfowl in winter, holding nationally important numbers of Pintail, Teal and Whooper Swan.

The **Cloghan Wetlands** (N 10 19) consist of a small lake called Cloghan Lake and an area of cutaway bog known as Drinagh Bog. The wetlands are situated in an area approximately 3km E and 4 km SE of Cloghan village and attracts almost 200 Whooper Swans each winter. Access to the wetlands is difficult but minor roads off the R357, over 2km E of Cloghan, will bring you onto the main area of blanket bog close to the wetlands.

County Laois

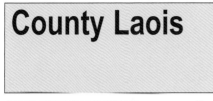

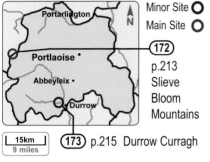

Minor Site ⭕	
Main Site ⭕	
(172)	
p.213	
Slieve	
Bloom	
Mountains	
(173) p.215 Durrow Curragh	

Laois is a small, relatively flat county, apart from the Slieve Bloom mountains (Site 172) to the west, with few wetlands and limited forest cover. Other than offering good general farmland and hedgerow bird species, there are few noteworthy sites for the birdwatcher. Durrow Curragh is the best site whenever it floods in winter, and Grantstown Lake nearby offers good general lake and woodland birdwatching.

173 Durrow Curragh Grid ref. S 37 78

An open grassland area that occasionally floods in winter, when it holds Whooper Swan and other wildfowl and waders.

Leave Durrow on the R434 to Borris in Ossory, turning left after 2km. A further 3km along this road, take a left and explore the flat grassland to locate flocks of wildfowl. Numbers of birds are variable, highest when water levels are high.

Species in winter include Whooper Swan, Wigeon, Golden Plover (1000+), Lapwing, Snipe, Curlew and gulls. Green Sandpiper has also been recorded in winter, and although White-fronted Goose and Bewick's Swan formerly wintered in the area, they are now rarely seen.

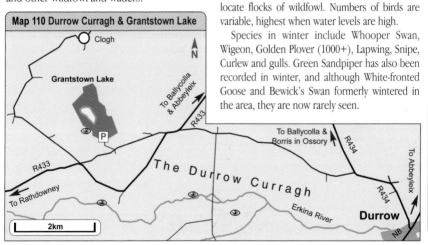

Map 110 Durrow Curragh & Grantstown Lake

Other sites

For **Grantstown Lake** (S 33 80), leave Durrow on the R434 to Borris in Ossory, turning left after 2km. Continue for 4km, ignoring the right which would take you to Ballycolla and Abbeyleix, and take a right just 200m past this turn. Grantstown Lake is signposted on the right after 1km. There is a carpark and trails through the woodland to the lake.

The lake is surrounded by mainly native broadleaved woodland and has good general woodland birdwatching, including Treecreeper, Long-tailed Tit, Siskin and Redpoll.

County Tipperary

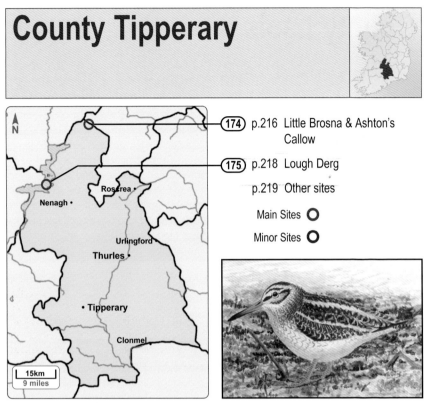

(174) p.216 Little Brosna & Ashton's Callow

(175) p.218 Lough Derg

p.219 Other sites

Main Sites O

Minor Sites O

Jack Snipe

Tipperary is a very large, inland county with notable wetlands in the north-west of the county which are particularly good for wintering wildfowl and waders.

The largest lake is Lough Derg which forms the north-west border, and this lake attracts many duck, particularly Tufted Duck, in winter, with breeding gulls and terns in summer.

The Little Brosna River forms the northern border of the county and is home to high numbers and a wide variety of wildfowl and waders in winter, and a good selection of breeding wetland birds in summer.

Little Brosna & Ashton's Callow

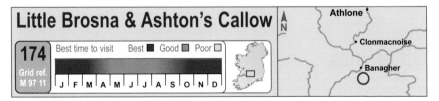

174

Grid ref.
M 97 11

Best time to visit   Best ■ Good ■ Poor □

J F M A M J J A S O N D

A floodplain which attracts large numbers of wildfowl and waders when it floods in winter, and a selection of breeding wetland birds in summer.

The Little Brosna is a narrow river that runs from Shinrone in Offaly to where it meets the River Shannon at Meelick. It runs along the border of Offaly and Tipperary and, each winter, floods to

216

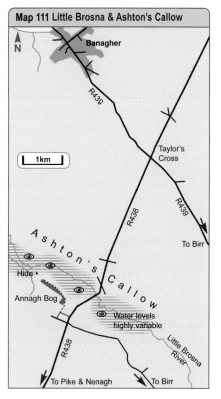

Map 111 Little Brosna & Ashton's Callow

Banagher

N

1km

R439

Taylor's Cross

R438

R439

To Birr

Ashton's Callow

Hide

Annagh Bog

Water levels highly variable

Little Brosna River

R438

To Pike & Nenagh

To Birr

Ruff

Annagh Bog. Follow the track for almost 1km until you reach the copse of trees. Go over the boardwalk and follow the track to the left before going over another boardwalk over the channels. The bird hide is just past this last boardwalk. In summer, the tall vegetation makes thc channels and the pools difficult to view.

Species
All year Water Rail, Kingfisher.

form a unique wetland that attracts large numbers of ducks and waders. Access to most parts of the floodplain is difficult, with the best site being at Ashton's Callow.

Directions Map 111, above. From the town of Banagher, take the R439 SE, following signs for Birr. Continue on the R439 for almost 4km and, at Taylor's Crossroads, take a right turn onto the R438 signposted for Nenagh. Continue on the R438 over the narrow bridge over the Little Brosna and, 800m past the bridge, take the small turn onto the track beside the white bungalow. Park close to the bungalow. From here, walk the track past the next bungalow and, just at the point where it swings right, go through the gate straight ahead of you. This is the track that leads out to the bird hide at Ashton's Callow. It should be noted that this track is usually quite muddy (even in summer) so wellington boots are advisable. Continue on this track, passing through the next gate. The track leads out onto the open area of

Autumn, winter & spring Bewick's Swan (R), Whooper Swan, Pink-footed Goose (R), White-fronted Goose, Barnacle Goose (R), Wigeon, Gadwall, Teal, Shoveler, Pochard, Tufted Duck, Scaup (R), Hen Harrier, Merlin, Peregrine, Golden Plover, Lapwing, Little Stint (R autumn), Curlew Sandpiper (R autumn), Dunlin, Ruff (O autumn), Jack Snipe (R winter), Snipe, Black-tailed Godwit, Spotted Redshank (R autumn & winter), Green Sandpiper (R autumn), Wood Sandpiper (R autumn), Short-eared Owl (R winter), Siskin, (O autumn & winter), Redpoll (O autumn).

Summer Common Sandpiper, gulls, Blackcap, Grasshopper Warbler, Sedge Warbler, Chiffchaff, Willow Warbler.

Rarities American Wigeon, Green-winged Teal, Garganey, Little Egret (winter), American Golden Plover, Long-billed Dowitcher, Red-necked Phalarope, Hobby, Crane.

Midlands

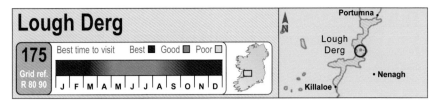

Lough Derg

175

Grid ref.
R 80 90

Best time to visit   Best ■ Good ■ Poor □

| J | F | M | A | M | J | J | A | S | O | N | D |

A large, relatively shallow lake which attracts large numbers of wildfowl in winter, while the numerous small islands attract breeding gulls and terns in summer.

Directions Map 112, below. Lough Derg forms part of the county boundaries between Tipperary, Galway and Clare. In winter, most of the wildfowl concentrate in the many bays along the entire length of the lake. These can be viewed from many points.

Youghal Bay in the SE corner is best accessed by taking the R494 W from Nenagh and taking a right turn approximately 4km past the village of Newtown. This small road leads to the lakeshore. The E side is viewed from many points off the R493, which is a left turn off from the N52 heading

out of Nenagh towards Portumna. **Goat Island**, which has a breeding Common Tern colony, is reached by taking a left turn just over 2km past the village of Coolbaun at a point where there is a large oak tree by the road. Follow this road to the end and park at the gate. By crossing the field you can reach the lakeshore and view the island from there.

The N end can be viewed from an area close to the village of Terryglass on the R493 and also from several points along the N52 between the villages of Carrigahorrig and Portumna. On the Galway side, large numbers of duck can be found on the flooded fields on the NW shore, especially at the **Portumna Estate**. The W side can be accessed at several locations along the R352 from Portumna to Scarriff in Clare. The SW end of the lake is not as productive but can be viewed from several points along the R463, heading N from Killaloe. There are also numerous conifer plantations along the W and NW sides of the lake that are good for common woodland species.

Species
All year Greylag Goose (feral birds), Cormorant, Water Rail, Kingfisher.

Autumn, winter & spring Bewick's Swan (R), Whooper Swan (O), White-fronted Goose (R), Wigeon, Gadwall, Teal, Shoveler (O), Pochard, Tufted Duck (1000s), Goldeneye, Red-breasted Merganser (O), Hen Harrier (O), Merlin, Golden Plover, Lapwing (1000s), Jack Snipe (R winter), Snipe, Black-tailed Godwit, Short-eared Owl (O winter), Siskin, (O autumn & winter), Redpoll (O autumn).

Summer Common Sandpiper, gulls, Common Tern, Grasshopper Warbler (O), Sedge Warbler, Chiffchaff, Willow Warbler.

Rarities Ring-necked Duck, Mediterranean Gull, Whiskered Tern, Black Tern, White-winged Black Tern.

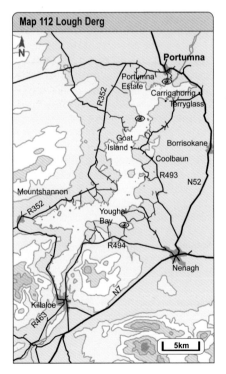

Map 112 Lough Derg

5km

Other sites

Firville Lake (M 95 02) is a small turlough that attracts small numbers of ducks and waders in winter. From the town of Banagher, take the R439 SE following signs for Birr. Continue on the R439 for almost 4km and, at Taylor's Crossroads, take a right turn onto the R438 signposted for Nenagh. Continue for almost 8km and, at the T-junction, go right onto the R489 and then take an immediate left back onto R438, following signs for Borrisokane and Nenagh. Continue for over 5km until you see a small pub on the left. Continue past the pub for another 200m and take the small left turn. Follow this narrow road down for 500m until you see a gate on the left and the beginning of Firville Lake on the left. Park here and walk to the end.

The lake can be viewed well from the road. Rarities found here include Garganey and Blue-winged Teal.

Pat Reddan's Lake (R 89 96) is a small, permanent lake that attracts grebes, ducks and waders in winter. In summer, a small population of Tufted Duck is present.

From the town of Borrisokane, take the turn signposted for Ballinderry. Continue out this road for 1.8km and take a right turn at the crossroads. Continue for almost 1km and take a left turn. Follow this road for less than 400m and you will see Pat Reddan's Lake on the left side. The lake can be viewed well from the road and there is a small area to park on the right side of the road halfway along the lake.

Rarities seen here include Red-crested Pochard, Ring-necked Duck, Ruddy Duck, Green Sandpiper, Wood Sandpiper, Mediterranean Gull and Little Gull.

Lough Eorna (R 88 86) is a small lake that attracts ducks in winter. There is a small breeding population of Tufted Ducks and Black-headed Gulls in summer. From Borrisokane, take the N52 SW, following signs for Nenagh. Continue on the N52 for almost 9.3km and take the right turn into the driveway of the B&B. There is a small area to park on the left just 100m down the driveway. From here, walk down the driveway and the lake can be seen well on the left side.

Rarities seen here include Garganey, Ring-necked Duck, Ruddy Duck and Mediterranean Gull. Please note that the area is private but birders are welcome. *Please park carefully.* Do not block the driveway and only view the lake from the driveway.

Lough Avan (R 85 94) is a small lake that attracts small numbers of Whooper Swans and White-fronted Geese in winter. From the town of Borrisokane, take the turn signposted for Ballinderry. Continue out this road for almost 6km and take the left turn. Go over the bridge and continue on this small road for almost 3km until you see Lough Avan on the left.

Midlands

County Limerick

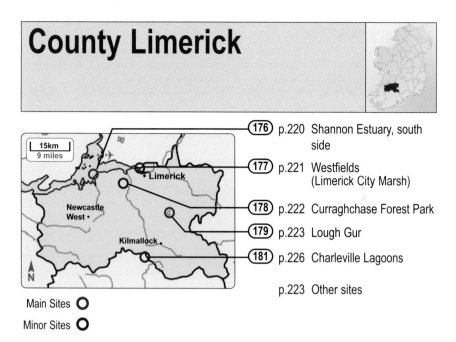

Main Sites O

Minor Sites O

The inner Shannon Estuary borders the north side of County Limerick, and is the main ornithological attraction. This vast area, the largest estuary in Ireland, is also one of the most important for wildfowl and waders in Ireland. Although the size of the estuary can be intimidating there are, fortunately, several areas where some of the main flocks are easily observed.

Two inland wetland sites – Lough Gur and Charleville Lagoons – attract a good diversity of waterbirds and waders, not least because the surrounding areas are low-lying agricultural land with few other waterbodies (Charleville Lagoons straddle the Limerick/Cork border, and are included in the County Cork section, p.226).

The sites above are best in winter, but one outstanding woodland site, Curraghchase Forest Park, is included, and a spring visit is well worthwhile for all the regular woodland species, and perhaps some rarer breeding species.

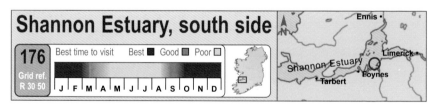

Shannon Estuary, south side

176

Grid ref.
R 30 50

Best time to visit   Best ■ Good ■ Poor □

| J | F | M | A | M | J | J | A | S | O | N | D |

Part of the Shannon Estuary, the largest estuary complex in Ireland, holding large numbers of wildfowl and waders in winter.

Directions Map 113, next page.

Another site on the S side of the Shannon Estuary is Site 216, Tarbert Area. For sites on the N side of the Shannon Estuary, in County Clare, see Site

269, Shannon Airport Lagoon; Site 270, Fergus Estuary; Site 272, Clonderalaw Bay; and Site 271, Poulnasherry Bay.

Most of the wetlands mentioned below are remote and vast. A telescope and plenty of time are needed to get the best from the area. Bird densities are particularly high here, though few birdwatchers visit the area.

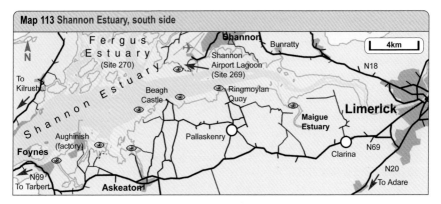

Map 113 Shannon Estuary, south side

From Limerick, the first area is the **Maigue Estuary**, reached by turning right at Clarina, off the N69 Limerick to Askeaton road. Take a right after 1km, then a left and another left and continue to the end of the road. This expanse of wetland and grassland is good for wildfowl, particularly Greylag Goose, and waders.

Ringmoylan Quay is another area with good views over the mudflats. Two hours either side of high tide is best. To get there, leaving Limerick for Askeaton on the N69, turn off for Pallaskenry after 16km. Go straight through the village of Pallaskenry and turn left 400m later. After 1.5km take a right then a left to the shore.

Return to Pallaskenry and turn right and drive straight for 5km and turn right after passing Ballysteen Post Office. This road leads to the shoreline at **Beagh Castle**, with further extensive views over the mudflats.

Another productive area for birds is in the vicinity of the enormous alumina plant at **Aughinish** Island. Robertstown Creek to the S of it is especially good for wildfowl and waders and is best approached from the Foynes side. Several side roads to the E of the plant, off the N69, are worth exploring for further views over the mudflats.

Species
All year Greylag Goose (mainly the Maigue Estuary), Cormorant, Little Egret, Water Rail, Kingfisher (R).

Autumn, winter & spring Whooper Swan, White-fronted Goose (O), Brent Goose, Wigeon (1000s), Gadwall, Teal (1000+), Pintail, Shoveler, Tufted Duck, Scaup, Goldeneye, Long-tailed Duck (O Foynes), Red-throated Diver (O), Black-throated Diver (R), Great Northern Diver, Great Crested Grebe, Red-necked Grebe (R), Slavonian Grebe (R), Little Egret, Hen Harrier (O), Merlin (O), Peregrine, Oystercatcher (100s), Golden Plover (1000s), Grey Plover (100s), Lapwing (1000s), Knot (100s), Little Stint (O autumn), Curlew Sandpiper (O autumn), Dunlin (1000s), Ruff (O autumn), Jack Snipe (R), Snipe, Black-tailed Godwit (100s), Bar-tailed Godwit, Whimbrel (small numbers, mainly spring), Curlew (100s), Spotted Redshank (O autumn & winter), Redshank (100s), Green Sandpiper (O autumn), Mediterranean Gull (O), Little Gull (R), Ring-billed Gull (R), Iceland Gull (O), Glaucous Gull (O).

Summer Sandwich Tern, Common Tern, Arctic Tern, Cuckoo (O), Sedge Warbler.

Rarities Bewick's Swan, Pink-footed Goose, Black-throated Diver, Red-necked Grebe, Slavonian Grebe

177 Westfields (Limerick City Marsh) Grid ref. R 56 57

A small, easily accessible freshwater lake on the outskirts of Limerick city, with good views of the waterbirds present.

See Map 114, next page. Leaving Limerick city centre by the N18 (the main road to Ennis and Shannon Airport), you cross a wide bridge, after

221

which the road veers left. 100m after the bridge, take a right, and then a left at a roundabout onto the North Circular Road, and another left after 500m, parking in front of the houses overlooking the marsh. Parking on the hard shoulder of the N18 is also possible. This site is only a ten-minute walk from Limerick city centre.

There is a path along the W and S sides, information boards and a viewing platform.

A selection of waterfowl is present throughout the year, but this site is best in winter. Species include Mute Swan, Little Grebe, Wigeon (O), Teal, Pochard, Tufted Duck, Coot, Lapwing, Snipe and Water Rail on and around the lake, and small numbers of the commoner waders and gulls are usually present. Long-tailed Tit and a variety of finches and thrushes are usually present in winter. Willow Warbler, Sedge Warbler, and Reed Bunting

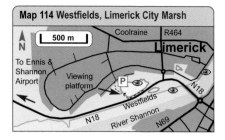

breed in the scrubby margins, and Sand Martin and House Martin are regular in summer.

Ring-billed Gull has been seen several times here, and Red-crested Pochard has been recorded. Iceland Gull, Mediterranean Gull and Yellow-legged Gull have been seen on the River Shannon nearby.

178 Curraghchase Forest Park Grid ref. R 41 49

A large area of mature deciduous and mixed woodland, excellent throughout the year for all the regular woodland species.

See Map 115, right. Located 8km NW of Adare and 8km E of Askeaton, to the SW of Limerick city. From Limerick, take the N69 to Askeaton, and 4.5km after passing through Kildimo New, turn left. Follow this road for almost 1.5km and go straight, through the signposted entrance of the Park. Continue along this forested, winding road to the carpark by the lake. Numerous trails emanate from this point throughout the woodland. There is an information board and picnic site, though no Visitor Centre. Admission is free and the park is open all year, at all times.

All the typical woodland species are present, including Woodcock, Long-eared Owl, Long-tailed Tit and Treecreeper. Early summer is the best time to visit, when the resident woodland birds are joined by summer visitors such as Blackcap, Chiffchaff, Willow Warbler and Spotted Flycatcher.

Hawfinch has been recorded at this site a number of times in winter, including a flock of up to 95 in the winter of 1988/89. They were usually found feeding on the hornbeam trees, which are common in the park, but particularly numerous in the area around the carpark and playground.

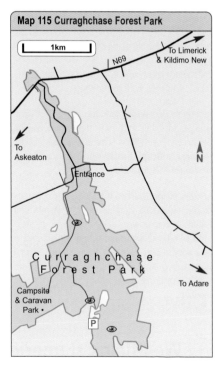

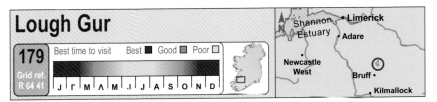

Lough Gur

179
Grid ref.
R 64 41

Best time to visit   Best ■ Good ▨ Poor □

J F M A M J J A S O N D

Shannon Estuary · Limerick · Adare

Newcastle West · Bruff ·

· Kilmallock

Good numbers of wildfowl in winter, particularly Wigeon, Mallard and Teal, with regular small numbers of Gadwall and Shoveler.

Directions Map 116, below. Lough Gur is a medium-sized, shallow, freshwater lake located 3km N of Bruff, about halfway between Limerick city and Kilmallock. The main part of the lake is open, with short grassy edges. The smaller lake is fringed by extensive reedbeds and scrub. From Bruff, take the main R512 N to Limerick. After 3km, take a right, at a junction with a garage and Reardon's pub. 1km along this narrow road, the lake is visible to your left. There are several laybys where it is possible to park and scan the lake. A telescope is recommended.

By continuing on and taking the next left, then after 1km, left again, you arrive at the Visitor Centre, carpark and picnic area, where further views of the NE corner of the lake are possible. There are several walks around parts of the lake from here, and mature woodland holds many of the regular woodland species.

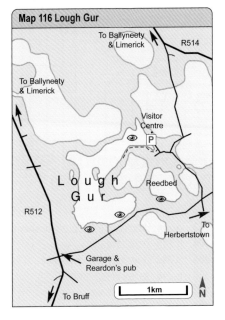

Map 116 Lough Gur

To Ballyneety & Limerick
R514
To Ballyneety & Limerick
Visitor Centre P
L o u g h
G u r
Reedbed
R512
To Herbertstown
Garage & Reardon's pub
1km
N
To Bruff

Species

Autumn, winter & spring Whooper Swan (see below), Pink-footed Goose (R), Greylag Goose, Shelduck (R), Wigeon, Gadwall, Teal, Pintail (O), Shoveler, Pochard, Tufted Duck, Scaup (O), Long-tailed Duck (R), Goldeneye, Ruddy Duck (R), Great Crested Grebe, Water Rail (O), Peregrine (O), Golden Plover, Lapwing, Curlew, Kingfisher (O), Long-tailed Tit.

The Whooper Swans can sometimes be found in the surrounding fields, but if not present near the lake, may be found 3km to the W, just NW of Herbertstown, on the fields bordering the Camoge River. They often use the lake for roosting at night.

Rarities American Wigeon, Green-winged Teal, Great Northern Diver.

Other sites

South-west

Raheenagh Lagoons (R 28 25) are 8km S of Newcastle West. These small lagoons often hold small numbers of waterbirds in the winter months. Species include Teal, Tufted Duck, Goldeneye, Lapwing, Jack Snipe (O), Snipe, Woodcock (O), Curlew, Green Sandpiper (O), Kingfisher (O).

County Cork

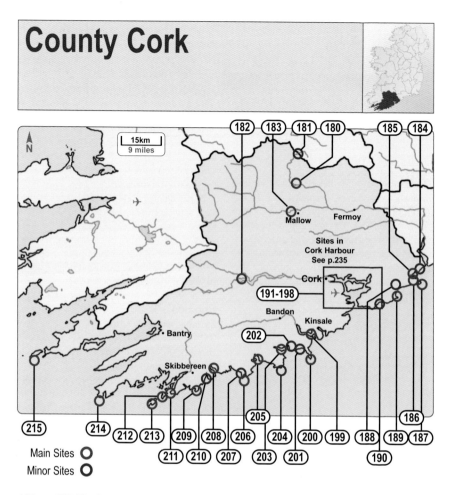

15km
9 miles

N

182 183 181 180   185 184

Mallow   Fermoy

Sites in
Cork Harbour
See p.235

Cork

191-198

Bandon

Kinsale

Bantry

202

Skibbereen

205

215   214 212 213 209 208 206   204 200 199 188 189 187

186

Main Sites O   211 210 207 203 201   190

Minor Sites O

Situated in the south-west, Cork is Ireland's largest county and one of the most productive birding locations in the country. Habitats vary from headlands and islands, coastal estuaries and lagoons, to inland lakes and reservoirs. The autumn passage of seabirds off Cape Clear Island, the Old Head of Kinsale, Galley Head and Mizen Head is among the best in Europe, while the estuaries produce many rare waders each year. Cork's many headlands and islands also provide excellent opportunities for finding rare Nearctic and Siberian passerines, while the inland lakes and reservoirs hold large numbers of wildfowl each winter.

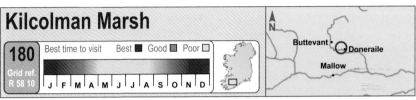

Kilcolman Marsh

180	Best time to visit	Best ■ Good ■ Poor ☐
Grid ref. R 58 10	J F M A M J J A S O N D	

A small marsh, lake and fields which flood in winter, when it attracts White-fronted Geese, Whooper Swans, ducks and waders.

The marsh, also known as Kilcolman Wildfowl Refuge, is privately owned and access is only by prior arrangement. Contact 022 24200.

Directions Map 117, right. From Mallow, head N on the N20, signposted for Limerick. 4km from Mallow is the village of New Twopothouse. At this village, take a right turn onto the R581, following signs for Doneraile. Go through the village, and continue straight for approximately 1.5km to a crossroads. At this point, go left, following signs for Rathluirc and continue for approximately 2.5km until you meet a small crossroads, signed Heatherside Hospital to the right. At this point, take a left turn and follow this narrow road to the gate that marks the entrance to Kilcolman. There is a comfortable hide on site and the flooded fields and small lake are easy to see from here.

Species
All year Greylag Geese (feral birds), Water Rail.

Autumn, winter & spring Bewick's Swan (R winter), Whooper Swan, White-fronted Goose (R winter), Wigeon (100s), Gadwall, Teal (100s), Pintail (R winter), Shoveler, Pochard, Tufted Duck, Goldeneye (R winter), Hen Harrier, Merlin, Peregrine, Golden Plover (1000s), Lapwing (1000s), Dunlin, Jack Snipe (R winter), Snipe, Green Sandpiper (R autumn & winter), Short-

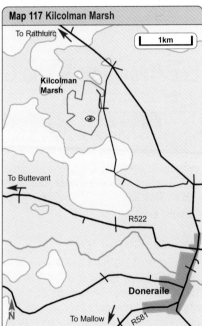

Map 117 Kilcolman Marsh

eared Owl (O winter), Siskin (winter), Redpoll (winter).

Summer Shoveler, gulls.

Rarities Bean Goose, American Wigeon, Green-winged Teal, Black Duck, Garganey, Ferruginous Duck, Ring-necked Duck, Ruddy Duck, Bittern/American Bittern, Marsh Harrier, Buzzard, Hobby, Bluethroat.

181 Charleville Lagoons Grid ref. R 54 26

A series of man-made lagoons on the grounds of the Golden Vale dairy plant, holding a good number of wildfowl, some waders and gulls in autumn and winter.

The lagoons are 2km N of Charleville, on the Cork/Limerick border. From Charleville, take the N20 N to Limerick (this is the main Cork to Limerick road). The Golden Vale plant and lagoons are located down a narrow road to the left, and the lagoons are actually signposted for a calf-rearing research station. Access is restricted to working hours, and you will have to seek permission to visit the lagoons, but staff are interested and enthusiastic. Exploring the various lagoons is on foot only.

The lagoons are particularly good for Teal and Shoveler, and species diversity at this site is high, with for example, 14 species of wader recorded.

Species, in autumn and winter, include Whooper Swan (R), Greylag Goose (R, feral), Shelduck (R), Wigeon, Gadwall (O), Teal, Pintail (O), Shoveler, Pochard, Tufted Duck, Scaup (O), Goldeneye (O), Water Rail (O), Golden Plover, Lapwing, Knot (R), Little Stint (R), Dunlin, Ruff (O), Snipe, Black-tailed Godwit (O), Bar-tailed Godwit (R), Curlew, Green Sandpiper (autumn, O winter), Wood Sandpiper (R autumn), Common Sandpiper (O autumn), gulls, Chiffchaff (O winter).

Rarer visitors include Buzzard, American Wigeon, Green-winged Teal, Ruddy Duck, Crane, Pectoral Sandpiper and Iceland Gull.

Lee Reservoir & The Gearagh

182 Best time to visit Best ■ Good ■ Poor □

Grid ref. Q 73 17 J F M A M J J A S O N D

Macroom • Coachford

A series of freshwater reservoirs which attracts good numbers of wildfowl and waders in winter (Lee Reservoir is also known as Inishcarra Reservoir).

Directions Map 118, next page. For **Dunisky,** from Cork take the N22 to Macroom. Go through the village of Lissarda and continue for 1.7 km until you see the first lagoon on the left. This area can be easily checked from the small carpark on the left side of the road. 200m past the first lagoon, the road swings sharply left over a bridge. Just before the bridge, take the right turn signposted for Cannovee. At the small T-junction, go left and follow the road for 600m, checking the reservoir on the left side. Viewing is restricted to just a few locations along the wire fence and access to the reservoir shore at this point is not possible.

The same area can also be checked by returning to the N22 and continuing N to Macroom for a further 800m to where there is a small parking spot near a farm gate on the left. The reservoir can

be viewed on the right from the farm gate opposite. Please note that the N22 at this point is a busy, narrow road and care should be taken when parking.

The reservoir shore can be accessed by continuing towards Macroom from the gate for 1.5km until you see two bungalows on the right side. Just beside the first bungalow, a small lane leads to the shore.

The Gearagh From the bungalows, continue for 4.3km towards Macroom and take a left onto the R584, signposted for Bantry. Continue on this road for 1km and take the left signposted for Toames. Continue down this road and park just before the bridge. On the right side is a metal stile that gives access to the shore. The area to the left of the bridge is also worth checking for duck and waders. The reservoir can also be checked by returning to the R584, and continuing W for 1km to the parking area on the left. From here, walk through the wooded pathways and view reservoir from various locations.

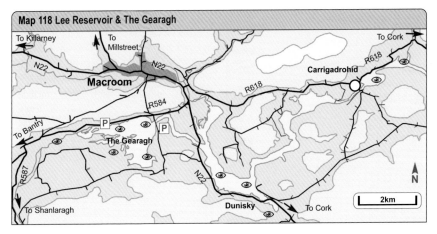

Map 118 Lee Reservoir & The Gearagh

Carrigadrohid From The Gearagh, return to the N22 and turn left for Macroom. Take the next right, signposted R618, Coachford. Follow the R618 for 6.8km until you reach the village of Carrigadrohid. 200m past the village, the reservoir can be seen on the right side. The area can be checked from various points for a further 1km along the road.

Although the reservoir extends for another 10km to the E of the map, there are few birds and access and views are restricted.

Species
All year Greylag Goose (feral birds), Kingfisher.

Autumn, winter & spring Whooper Swan, White-fronted Goose (R winter), Wigeon (1000s), Gadwall, Teal (1000s), Shoveler, Pochard, Scaup

(R winter), Long-tailed Duck (R winter), Great Northern Diver (R winter), Hen Harrier, Merlin, Peregrine, Golden Plover (1000s), Lapwing (1000s), Dunlin, Ruff (R autumn), Jack Snipe (R winter), Snipe, Whimbrel (spring), Spotted Redshank (R autumn & winter), Green Sandpiper (R autumn & winter), Ring-billed Gull (R autumn & winter), Iceland Gull (R winter), Short-eared Owl (O winter), Siskin (winter), Redpoll (winter).

Summer Common Sandpiper, gulls.

Rarities Bean Goose, Pink-footed Goose, American Wigeon, Green-winged Teal, Ring-necked Duck, Lesser Scaup, Smew, Goosander, Bufflehead, Red-necked Grebe, Slavonian Grebe, Black-necked Grebe, Goshawk, Osprey, Pectoral Sandpiper, Lesser Yellowlegs.

Mallow Sugar Factory Lagoons

183

Grid ref. W 50 97

Best time to visit   Best ■ Good ■ Poor □

J	F	M	A	M	J	J	A	S	O	N	D

A series of settling ponds which attract small numbers of waders and wildfowl each autumn and winter. An excellent location for Green Sandpiper from mid-summer into winter.

It should be noted that at the time of writing, access to the ponds is restricted by high gates and a wire fence. Access may change (indeed the

ponds themselves may change) following the closure of the factory in May 2006.

Directions Map 119, next page. From Mallow, travel W on the N72 for 3.5km, passing the Mallow Racetrack. Take a left turn onto the R621, signposted for Coachford and Sugar Factory. Follow the R621 for 500m until you meet a small

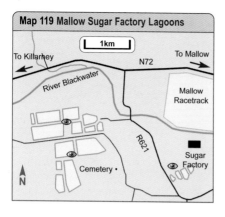

Map 119 Mallow Sugar Factory Lagoons

1km

To Killarney
N72
To Mallow

River Blackwater

Mallow Racetrack

R621

Cemetery •

Sugar Factory

N

Green Sandpiper

bridge over the River Blackwater. Immediately after this bridge is a small track on the right. Take this track and continue for 200m until you reach the barrier. The ponds closest to the river can be accessed by walking up the small slope ahead and viewing from the various tracks around the ponds.

To view the next set of ponds, return to the R621 and turn right. Follow the R621 for almost 1km and take the right turn signposted for Glantane. Follow this road for 500m and take the small road on the right marked cul-de-sac, just where the main road swings sharply to the left. Continue along this narrow road and follow right past Kilshannig Cemetery. Continue for 800m until you reach a long, straight stretch of narrow road with hedgerows on either side. Access to the ponds can be gained at various points on the left side of this road. To view the ponds, follow the various tracks around the area.

Species

Autumn, winter & spring Pochard, Tufted Duck, Little Stint (R autumn), Curlew Sandpiper (R Sept), Ruff (O Sept), Green Sandpiper (July to Oct, O winter), Wood Sandpiper (R autumn), Common Sandpiper (common spring, summer & autumn, O winter).

Rarities Garganey, Ring-necked Duck, Little Ringed Plover, Pectoral Sandpiper, Bonaparte's Gull.

184 Youghal Grid ref. X 10 77

A small town, located where the River Blackwater enters the sea, which has extensive mudflats and several small lagoons nearby which attract waders and gulls in autumn and winter. Little Egrets are particularly common in this area.

See Map 120, next page. Travelling W on the N25 from Waterford to Cork, continue W over the Youghal Bridge and take a left onto the R634, signposted for Youghal. Approximately 300m along the road into Youghal is a flooded field on the left known as 'Foxhole'. This can be viewed

from the road and attracts waders and gulls, as well as being a favourite roosting site for Little Egret. Further into the town of Youghal, the more open, deeper water of Youghal Bay can be viewed from several locations along the town and at the lighthouse.

Cormorant, Shag and Little Egret can be seen all year, while in autumn, winter and early spring, typical species include Wigeon, Teal, Red-throated Diver, Great Northern Diver, Lapwing, Dunlin, Green Sandpiper (R autumn) and Common Sandpiper (O spring & autumn). Ring-necked Duck has been recorded here.

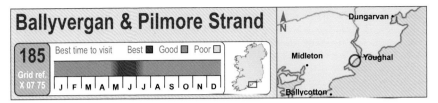

Ballyvergan & Pilmore Strand

185	Best time to visit	Best ■ Good ■ Poor □
Grid ref. X 07 75	J F M A M J J A S O N D	

Ballyvergan is an extensive area of reedbed which attracts breeding Reed Warbler in summer and raptors in spring, autumn and winter. Pilmore Strand is a nearby tidal sandflat which attracts waders and gulls in autumn.

Directions Map 120, below. From Youghal, follow the main road W towards Cork (this was the old N25 before Youghal was by-passed). Approximately 2km from Youghal, the eastern side of the reedbed can be viewed to your left. Better views can be obtained by taking a left turn

onto the R633. Approximately 300m down this road is a viewing platform on the left that gives elevated views over the reedbed. The road goes over a disused railway track and just at this point, go left and follow the track through the reedbed. The small trees on either side can attract migrants in spring and autumn. This rough track continues for over 1km.

The western side of the reedbed is not as accessible and is best viewed from the main road.

For **Pilmore Strand**, return to the R633 and from the point where the disused railway tracks cross

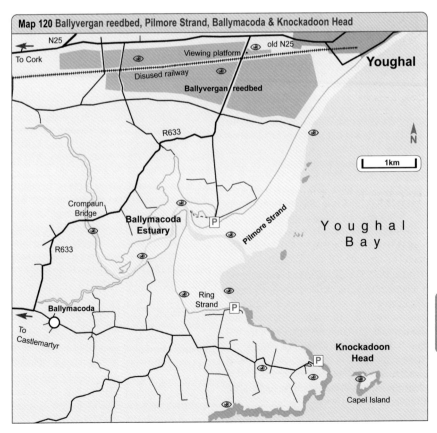

Map 120 Ballyvergan reedbed, Pilmore Strand, Ballymacoda & Knockadoon Head

the road, continue for 1km and take a left at the first crossroads. Continue on this road for over 1.5km until you reach the strand. Another viewpoint can be reached by returning to the R633 and continue SW for 500m and, just where the R633 swings sharp right, take the minor road on the left. Follow this minor road for 1.5km to reach a parking point overlooking the strand.

Species
All year Water Rail.

Autumn, winter & spring Hen Harrier, Merlin, Little Stint (O autumn), Jack Snipe (R winter), Snipe, Pomarine Skua (O autumn), Black Tern (O autumn), Short-eared Owl (O winter), Yellow Wagtail (O autumn), Blackcap (R spring, O autumn, R winter), Whitethroat (O autumn), Reed Warbler (O autumn), Spotted Flycatcher (autumn), Brambling (R winter), Siskin, (O autumn & winter), Redpoll (autumn & winter).

Summer Grasshopper Warbler (O), Sedge Warbler, Reed Warbler, Chiffchaff, Willow Warbler.

Rarities Bittern, Marsh Harrier, Osprey, Red-footed Falcon, Hobby, Ring-billed Gull, Caspian Gull, Gull-billed Tern, Forster's Tern, Turtle Dove, Wryneck, Savi's Warbler, Marsh Warbler, Golden Oriole.

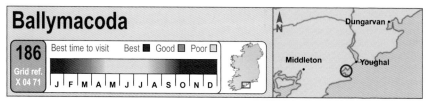

Ballymacoda

186 | Best time to visit   Best ■ Good ■ Poor □
Grid ref. X 04 71 | J F M A M J J A S O N D

A tidal mudflat and wetlands that attract wildfowl, waders and gulls in autumn and winter.

Directions Map 120, previous page. From the point where the disused railway tracks cross the road at Ballyvergan reedbed, continue SW on the R633 for 3.5km and take a left turn for Clonpriest Graveyard. Park at the graveyard and follow the track for 100m down to the estuary. The inner section of the estuary can also be viewed by returning to the R633 and continuing SW for a further 1.1km to where the road crosses the Womanagh River at Crompaun Bridge. From here, walk S along the riverbank until you meet the estuary.

To view the S side of the estuary, continue from Crompaun Bridge on the R633 for approximately 2km and, where the R633 swings right, take the minor road to the left, signposted for Ballymacoda. Continue through the village and take a third left which brings you down to the estuary. Easier access to the S side of the outer estuary is reached by taking either the third or fourth left turn after the village, both roads bringing you to Ring Strand.

Species
All year Canada Goose (feral birds), Little Egret, Water Rail, Kingfisher.

Autumn, winter & spring Bewick's Swan, Whooper Swan (O), White-fronted Goose (O), Brent Goose, Wigeon (1000+) Gadwall, Teal (1000+), Shoveler (O), Red-breasted Merganser (O), Hen Harrier (O winter), Merlin, Golden Plover (1000s), Grey Plover, Lapwing (1000s), Knot, Little Stint (O autumn), Curlew Sandpiper (O autumn), Dunlin, Ruff (O autumn), Jack Snipe (R winter), Snipe, Black-tailed Godwit (1000s), Bar-tailed Godwit, Whimbrel (spring), Spotted Redshank (R autumn & winter), Green Sandpiper (R autumn), Wood Sandpiper (R autumn), Mediterranean Gull (R autumn & winter), Ring-billed Gull (R winter), Glaucous Gull (R winter), Short-eared Owl (O winter).

Summer Common Sandpiper, gulls, terns, Sedge Warbler, Chiffchaff, Willow Warbler.

Rarities American Wigeon, Green-winged Teal, Garganey, Blue-winged Teal, Osprey, Killdeer, American Golden Plover, Baird's Sandpiper, Pectoral Sandpiper, Long-billed Dowitcher, Spotted Sandpiper, Gull-billed Tern, Caspian Tern, Elegant Tern, Cetti's Warbler.

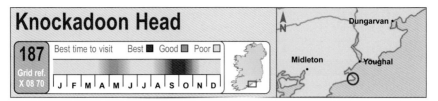

Knockadoon Head

187
Grid ref.
X 08 70

Best time to visit   Best ■ Good ■ Poor □

J F M A M J J A S O N D

Dungarvan
N
Midleton   Youghal

A coastal headland with a small, rocky beach, gardens and extensive hedgerows, good for migrants in spring and autumn.

Directions Map 120, p.229. From the village of Ballymacoda, follow the road E for approximately 5km, following the signs for Knockadoon Head. The road ends at a small harbour and the gardens around this area often hold migrants. This harbour has played host to Ireland's first Pied Wheatear, while the small beach is a regular site for Black Redstart in autumn. A small track runs above the beach and around the headland. The dense cover along here is also worth checking for migrants. Also, from the harbour, walk the road W, where all the gardens and roadside hedges can hold migrant warblers and flycatchers, especially after S, SE or E winds in autumn.

Approximately 1km W of the harbour is a cross-roads, marked by the caravan signpost. Take a left here and follow the narrow road down to the coast. The gardens along here have had many rare species, including Ireland's first Hume's Warbler.

Species
Autumn, winter & spring Glaucous Gull (R

winter), Short-eared Owl (O winter), Black Redstart (O autumn), Redstart (R autumn & spring), Whinchat (R autumn), Ring Ouzel (R autumn), Garden Warbler (O autumn), Blackcap (R spring, O autumn), Whitethroat (O autumn), Reed Warbler (O autumn), Spotted Flycatcher (autumn), Pied Flycatcher (O autumn), Brambling (R autumn), Siskin (O autumn & winter), Redpoll (O autumn).

Seawatching can be productive in autumn, though Capel Island offshore prevents many seabirds venturing close to the headland. Nearby Ballycotton (Site 189) is a better option, in S or SW winds. Arctic and Great Skuas and Manx Shearwater can be present in Youghal Bay in small numbers, in August and September. See also SEAWATCHING, p.356.

Rarities Eider, Great Shearwater, Osprey, Sabine's Gull, Turtle Dove, Hoopoe, Pied Wheatear, Melodious Warbler, Lesser Whitethroat, Sardinian Warbler, Pallas's Warbler, Hume's Warbler, Yellow-browed Warbler, Firecrest, Red-breasted Flycatcher, Golden Oriole, Red-backed Shrike, Woodchat Shrike, Red-eyed Vireo.

188 Ballyhonock Lake   Grid ref. W 99 73

A small, reed-fringed, freshwater lake, good for duck in autumn and winter.

The lake is located 3km E of Castlemartyr. At the village of Castlemartyr, take the turn onto the R632, signposted for Ladysbridge. Follow this road for approximately 1km, and take the first major turn on the left, 800m before Ladysbridge. Follow this narrow road NE for almost 3km and take a right turn. Follow this road for 500m until you see the lake. At the lake, take the small track to the left which runs along the N side of the lake.

This offers a good vantage point from which all the birds on the lake can be seen.

Water Rail and Kingfisher are present throughout the year, and in autumn and winter, typical species include Whooper Swan (O winter), Wigeon, Gadwall, Teal, Pintail (R winter), Shoveler, Pochard, Tufted Duck, Goldeneye (R winter), Little Grebe, Cormorant, Lapwing (100s), Snipe, Green Sandpiper (R autumn), and a number of gulls are usually present.

Rarer species seen here include Garganey, Blue-winged Teal, Red-crested Pochard and Ring-necked Duck.

South-west

231

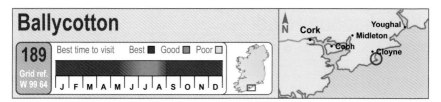

Ballycotton

189
Grid ref.
W 99 64

Best time to visit   Best ■ Good ▨ Poor □

J F M A M J J A S O N D

N Cork   Youghal
• Midleton
• Cobh   • Cloyne

A superb tidal beach with pools and reedbeds which attracts large numbers of waders and wildfowl in autumn and winter. The town is also a migrant hotspot in spring, and autumn.

The lighthouse on Ballycotton Island attracts passerine migrants in autumn, and as a result, the beaches, gardens and cliff walks of Ballycotton have produced many rarities. Seawatching in suitable conditions in autumn can produce a good passage of Manx Shearwaters and other seabirds.

This is also one of the better seawatching sites for Cory's Shearwaters in autumn. Rare American waders are seen every autumn, and many gulls and terns frequent the beach and pools. The reedbeds have breeding Reed Warbler.

Directions Map 121, below. From the village of Cloyne, follow the R629 E for approximately 7km and take a right turn, signposted for Ballycotton, at the petrol station/shop just before Shanagarry village. Continue on this road (which is still the

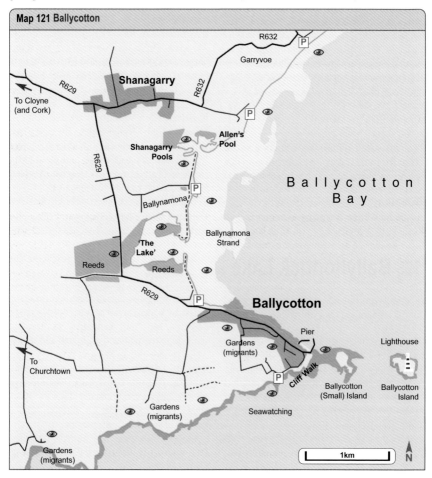

Map 121 Ballycotton

R632

P

Garryvoe

R629   **Shanagarry**   R632

To Cloyne
(and Cork)

P

Allen's
Pool

**Shanagarry
Pools**

R629

Ballynamona

P

**Ballycotton
Bay**

Ballynamona
Strand

'The
Lake'

Reeds   Reeds

Ballynamona

R629

P

Ballycotton

Pier

Gardens
(migrants)

Lighthouse

To
Churchtown

P   Cliff Walk

Ballycotton
(Small) Island

Ballycotton
Island

Gardens
(migrants)

Seawatching

Gardens
(migrants)

1km   N

R629) for 1km and, at the crossroads, take a left turn to Ballynamona Strand. Follow this narrow road for 1km until you reach the carpark overlooking the beach.

On a rising tide, the waders feeding on the beach can be pushed close to the carpark. To view **Shanagarry Pools**, walk along the rough track to the left (north) of the carpark, following the wire fence on the left until the pools are visible. To the right, a small stream enters the sea and this area can be very productive for waders, pipits and wagtails. The pools can be checked from this position but some areas are out of sight and can only be viewed well by walking through the channels to the back of the pools.

Another excellent pool can be reached by walking across the stream which, at high tide, can only be achieved by wearing wellington boots or by using the 'stepping stones'. Having crossed the stream, the open water and reed-fringed edges of **Allen's Pool** are immediately obvious. This area is best checked by walking the seaward side of the pools, checking the reed edges and open area for waders. The tall grass along the dunes above the beach is good for pipits.

To check '**The Lake**', return to the carpark, follow the path to the right, and head S along the top of the beach for 500m. The lake is a wide, open, muddy lagoon which attracts waders and gulls and is separated from the sea by a large shingle bank. The area can be viewed from various locations by following the edge of the lake along the wire fence. At low tide, the beach and seaweed-covered rocks below the shingle bank can attract large numbers of waders and gulls. These waders and gulls tend to move onto 'The Lake' at high tide.

Reedbeds at the western end of 'The Lake' can best be viewed by returning to the R629 and taking a left at the crossroads. Continue for almost 1km until the road dissects the reedbed which can be viewed from the road to the left and right. To view 'The Lake' from the road, continue past the reedbed, follow the road as it swings sharply left and stop at the gate on the left.

Ballycotton Village is reached by continuing on the R629 from the gate and past the church on the

right. In the village, several well-vegetated gardens have good cover for migrant passerines, which occur most often after S, SE or E winds. A track above the village is also worth checking for autumn migrants and is reached by taking the right turn in the village close to the Garda barracks and school. Continue up this small road past the Catholic church. At the point where the road swings left, take the track on the right beside the house on the corner. This track has hedges on both sides and leads to several productive gardens. Eventually this track reaches the Cliff Walk. The garden close to the house on the corner is also worth checking as it is a good area for migrant flycatchers and warblers that may have worked their way down the track.

To get to the **Cliff Walk**, from the R629, continue to the end of the village where there is a fork in the road. Take a right at this point and follow the road for 500m until you come to the carpark. From there, follow the path right. The area below the carpark is also a good site for **seawatching** in S or SW winds (see next page). The low shrubs and bushes along the cliff can have migrant passerines in autumn.

To view the **pier** area, return to the fork in the road and take a right turn. In winter, the pier frequently holds small numbers of gulls while, in late summer and autumn, the small island offshore attracts roosting terns and gulls.

The beach and pools E of **Shanagarry** village also hold many birds. From the village of Cloyne, continue E on the R629 to the point where you turn right at the petrol station/shop for Ballycotton. Do not take this right but continue straight, onto the R632. Continue on through the village for 1.2km and stop at the point where the road swings sharp left. The beach here can hold small numbers of waders. Continue SW along the top of beach and check the series of pools which eventually leads to Allen's Pool. The beach can also be checked by taking the small road on the right where the R632 swings left. Follow this small road for 400m to reach a parking area behind the beach.

Species
All year Canada Goose (feral birds), Fulmar, Cormorant, Shag, Little Egret, Peregrine, Water

Rail, Kittiwake, Kingfisher, Chough (along Cliff Walk).

Autumn, winter & spring Bewick's Swan (O), Whooper Swan (O), Pink-footed Goose (R), White-fronted Goose (R), Barnacle Goose (R), Brent Goose, Wigeon, Gadwall, Teal (500+), Shoveler (O), Scaup (O), Eider (O), Red-breasted Merganser (O), Red-throated Diver, Great Northern Diver, Hen Harrier, Merlin, Buzzard (R), Golden Plover (1000s), Grey Plover, Lapwing (1000s), Knot, Little Stint (autumn), Curlew Sandpiper (autumn), Dunlin, Ruff (autumn), Jack Snipe (R winter), Snipe, Black-tailed Godwit, Bar-tailed Godwit, Whimbrel (O, common May), Spotted Redshank (R autumn & winter), Green Sandpiper (R autumn), Wood Sandpiper (R autumn), Grey Phalarope (R autumn), Mediterranean Gull (R autumn & winter), Ring-billed Gull (R winter), Iceland Gull (R winter), Glaucous Gull (R winter), Short-eared Owl (winter), Black Redstart (R winter), Redstart (R autumn), Whinchat (R autumn), Ring Ouzel (R autumn), Garden Warbler (R spring, O autumn), Blackcap (R spring, O autumn, R winter), Whitethroat (O autumn), Reed Warbler (O autumn), Spotted Flycatcher (autumn), Pied Flycatcher (O autumn), Brambling (R winter), Siskin, (O autumn & winter), Redpoll (O autumn).

Summer Common Sandpiper, gulls, terns, Grasshopper Warbler (O), Sedge Warbler, Reed Warbler, Chiffchaff, Willow Warbler, Wheatear.

Rarities Ballycotton is famous for attracting many rare birds, particularly American waders in autumn. Rarities recorded include Dark-bellied Brent Goose, Black Brant, American Wigeon, Green-winged Teal, Garganey, Blue-winged Teal, Red-necked Grebe, Slavonian Grebe, Cory's Shearwater, Great Shearwater, Balearic Shearwater, Little Bittern, Night Heron, Purple Heron, White Stork, Glossy Ibis, Spoonbill, Black Kite, Marsh Harrier, Osprey, Red-footed Falcon, Hobby, American Coot, Spotted Crake, Stone-

Curlew, Little Ringed Plover, Killdeer, Kentish Plover, Dotterel, American Golden Plover, Semipalmated Sandpiper, Temminck's Stint, Least Sandpiper, Red-necked Stint, Long-toed Stint, White-rumped Sandpiper, Baird's Sandpiper, Pectoral Sandpiper, Sharp-tailed Sandpiper, Broad-billed Sandpiper, Stilt Sandpiper, Buff-breasted Sandpiper, Long-billed Dowitcher, Greater Yellowlegs, Lesser Yellowlegs, Wilson's Phalarope, Red-necked Phalarope, Long-tailed Skua, Sabine's Gull, American Herring Gull, Yellow-legged Gull, Kumlien's Gull, Ivory Gull, Gull-billed Tern, Caspian Tern, Lesser Crested Tern, Forster's Tern, Whiskered Tern, Black Tern, White-winged Black Tern, Little Auk, Turtle Dove, Alpine Swift, Hoopoe, Wryneck, Short-toed Lark, Richard's Pipit, Tawny Pipit, Tree Pipit, Red-throated Pipit, Yellow Wagtail, Citrine Wagtail, Nightingale, Bluethroat, Desert Wheatear, Savi's Warbler, Booted Warbler, Icterine Warbler, Melodious Warbler, Lesser Whitethroat, Greenish Warbler, Wood Warbler, Yellow-browed Warbler, Firecrest, Red-breasted Flycatcher, Bearded Tit, Golden Oriole, Red-backed Shrike, Lesser Grey Shrike, Woodchat Shrike, Carrion Crow, Rose-coloured Starling, Common Rosefinch, Hawfinch, Lapland Bunting, Snow Bunting.

Seawatching Best from late July to late October. Seabirds pass rather distantly at this site, so a telescope is recommended. Some shearwaters and skuas occasionally venture into Ballycotton Bay, following trawlers (see also SEAWATCHING, p.356).

Red-throated Diver (O), Great Northern Diver (O), Fulmar, 'Blue' Fulmar (R winter), Cory's Shearwater (R), Great Shearwater (R), Sooty Shearwater (O), Manx Shearwater (occasionally 1000s), Balearic Shearwater (O), Storm Petrel, Gannet, Pomarine Skua (O), Arctic Skua (O), Great Skua, Long-tailed Skua (R), Sabines's Gull (R), Kittiwake, Sandwich Tern, Common Tern, Arctic Tern, Black Tern (R), Guillemot, Razorbill, Black Guillemot, Puffin (O).

190 Inch Strand Grid ref. W 91 61

An area of dense hedgerows and gardens, lying west of Ballycotton, which is good for migrants in autumn.

Located 10km W of Ballycotton and about 7km S of Cloyne. From Midleton, follow the R630 signposted for Whitegate. Continue on the R630 for approximately 6.5km and take the minor turn to the left. Continue for almost 1km and, at the Y-junction, go right. Continue on this main road for over 4.5km and, at the T-junction (actually this is a staggered crossroads with a minor road straight ahead), go left, following the signs for Inch. At the village go right, following the road S to the strand. There is a parking area close to the strand. From here, any of the gardens and hedgerows can hold migrants in autumn, both back along the road, and down the track that runs right and S of the carpark. This is the W side of the valley and is the better side for migrants. Alternatively, continue past the carpark, and follow the road to the end.

The track beyond this point gives access to the E side. Both tracks bring you on to Power Head.

This site is best in autumn, especially after S or SE winds, when migrants can be expected. Species include Black Redstart (R), Redstart (R), Whinchat (R), Ring Ouzel (R), Blackcap (O), Whitethroat (O autumn), Reed Warbler (R), Spotted Flycatcher (O), Pied Flycatcher (R).

Some rare birds seen here include Purple Heron, Hobby, Red-throated Pipit, Yellow Wagtail, Melodious Warbler, Lesser Whitethroat, Yellow-browed Warbler, Pallas's Warbler, Firecrest and Red-eyed Vireo.

Cork Harbour

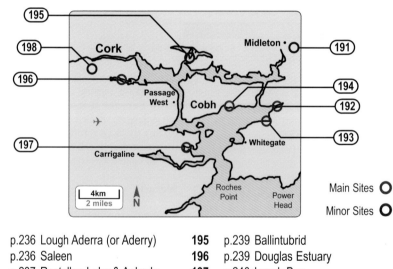

191 p.236 Lough Aderra (or Aderry)	**195** p.239 Ballintubrid
192 p.236 Saleen	**196** p.239 Douglas Estuary
193 p.237 Rostellon Lake & Aghada	**197** p.240 Lough Beg
194 p.237 Cobh area	**198** p.241 The Lough (or Cork Lough)

Cork Harbour is one of the most extensive series of tidal estuaries and channels in Ireland, and stretches south from the two main estuaries of the River Lee near Cork city at the north-west and from the Owennacurra River near Midleton at the north-east. Each winter, up to 5,000 wildfowl and almost 30,000 waders occur. The outer harbour encom-passes Great Island, Saleen, Rostellon and Whitegate to the east, Lough Beg to the west and then runs in to Cork city with the extensive mudflats surrounding the Douglas Estuary. There are numerous superb locations throughout this entire estuary complex which also attract rare ducks, waders and gulls each autumn and winter.

South-west

191 Lough Aderra (or Aderry) Grid ref. W 94 73

A roadside freshwater lake which attracts ducks and gulls in winter. A good location for Gadwall in winter.

See Map 122, p.238. Located about 5km E of Midleton and 2.5km W of Castlemartyr. From Cork, take the N25 E for 23km and, at the Midleton Roundabout, take the second exit, staying on the N25 to Youghal. Continue on the N25 for 5.6km until the lake is visible on the right. The lake can be viewed from the two parking areas.

Cormorant, Water Rail and Kingfisher (O) are present all year. In autumn, winter and early spring, it is good for Wigeon, Gadwall, Teal, Mediterranean Gull (R autumn & winter), Ring-billed Gull (O winter), Siskin, (O autumn & winter) and Redpoll (O autumn).

In summer, there are usually good numbers of gulls present, while Sedge Warbler is common in the surrounding reeds and scrub.

Rare birds seen here include Green-winged Teal, Garganey, Ring-necked Duck and Pied-billed Grebe. Hybrid Whooper x Mute Swan have been seen here.

Saleen

192 Best time to visit   Best ■ Good ■ Poor ☐

Grid ref. W 87 67

J F M A M J J A S O N D

A tidal estuary which attracts good numbers of duck, waders and gulls in winter. Little Egrets are also very common along the river.

Directions Map 122, p.238. From Cork, take the N25 E for 23km and, at the Midleton Roundabout, go right, onto the R630 signposted for Whitegate. Continue on the R630 for 4.8km until you reach the village of Saleen. Take a right turn signposted for East Ferry. Follow the road for 400m, where the road swings sharply right. Then, follow the main road left and continue downhill until the estuary is visible on the left. The river enters the estuary at this point and the river valley and the trees on the river banks are good for Little Egrets. The area can be viewed from many points along the road for a further 1.6km. The fields on the right can have large numbers of gulls, while the open water, which looks across to Whitegate and Aghada (Site 193), usually has grebes and scoters.

Species
All year Little Egret, Kingfisher.

Autumn, winter & spring Brent Goose, Wigeon, Teal, Red-breasted Merganser, Common Scoter, Red-throated Diver, Great Northern Diver,

Hen Harrier, Merlin, Buzzard (R), Peregrine, Golden Plover, Lapwing, Little Stint (R autumn), Curlew Sandpiper (R autumn), Dunlin, Ruff (R autumn), Snipe, Black-tailed Godwit, Whimbrel (spring), Spotted Redshank (R autumn & winter), Green Sandpiper (R autumn), Mediterranean Gull (regular winter), Ring-billed Gull (R winter).

Summer Common Sandpiper, gulls.

Rarities Green-winged Teal, Red-necked Grebe, Slavonian Grebe, Black-necked Grebe, Killdeer.

Dunlin

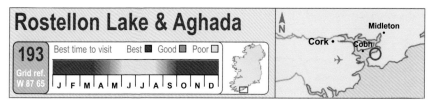

Rostellon Lake & Aghada

193

Grid ref. W 87 65

Best time to visit   Best ■ Good ■ Poor ☐

J F M A M J J A S O N D

A reed-fringed freshwater lake which is good for ducks, grebes and gulls in winter. The nearby woodland also attracts finches and tits in winter and common warblers in summer. West of Rostellon Lake is Aghada which is a tidal estuary and harbour which attracts scoter and grebes in winter.

Directions Map 122, next page.

Rostellon Lake From the Midleton Roundabout, take the R630 signposted for Whitegate. Continue SW on the R630 for 8km until you reach the village of Rostellon. The freshwater lake is on the right side and can best be viewed by entering the small hide on the right side of the road. Alternatively, continue on the R630 and take the right turn over the small bridge and park in the small carpark on the right close to the display sign. There is an entrance to the woodland just past the parking area and a small path runs parallel to the lake.

Aghada From Rostellon, continue W and check the open water on the right side. This area is well known for attracting Black-necked Grebe and Slavonian Grebe in winter and can be checked from any point between Rostellon and the small pier which is 1.3km further on.

Species

All year Greylag Goose (feral birds), Little Egret, Water Rail, Kingfisher.

Autumn, winter & spring Bewick's Swan (R winter), Whooper Swan (O), Brent Goose, Wigeon, Gadwall, Teal, Shoveler, Scaup (O), Long-tailed Duck (R winter), Goldeneye, Red-breasted Merganser (O), Red-throated Diver, Great Northern Diver, Golden Plover (1000s), Grey Plover, Lapwing (1000s), Knot, Little Stint (O autumn), Curlew Sandpiper (O autumn), Dunlin, Ruff (R autumn), Jack Snipe (R winter), Snipe, Black-tailed Godwit, Bar-tailed Godwit, Whimbrel (spring), Spotted Redshank (R autumn & winter), Green Sandpiper (R autumn), Common Sandpiper (R winter), Mediterranean Gull (R autumn & winter), Ring-billed Gull (R winter), Iceland Gull (R winter), Blackcap (R spring, O autumn, R winter), Siskin (O autumn & winter), Redpoll (O autumn).

Summer Common Sandpiper, gulls, terns, Sedge Warbler, Chiffchaff, Willow Warbler.

Rarities American Wigeon, Green-winged Teal, Red-crested Pochard, Ring-necked Duck, Surf Scoter, Velvet Scoter, Black-throated Diver, Pied-billed Grebe, Red-necked Grebe, Slavonian Grebe, Black-necked Grebe, Laughing Gull, Black Tern.

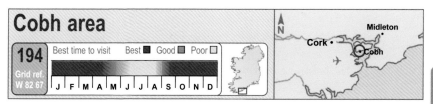

Cobh area

194

Grid ref. W 82 67

Best time to visit   Best ■ Good ■ Poor ☐

J F M A M J J A S O N D

(Includes Slatty's Bridge, Belvelly, Cobh, Cuskinny Marsh and Rossleague.) Cobh is a large tidal estuary and deep-water harbour which attracts ducks, waders and gulls in autumn and winter. To the east of the town is Cuskinny Marsh, which is a small, reed-fringed, brackish lagoon, good for ducks and gulls in autumn and winter. The woodland around the marsh is also good for common migrants in summer. To the north of Cobh lie several good vantage points which include Rossleague, Belvelly and Slatty's Bridge, all of

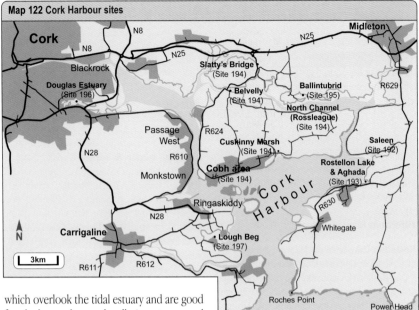

Map 122 Cork Harbour sites

which overlook the tidal estuary and are good for ducks, waders and gulls in autumn and winter. Little Egrets are also common on the estuaries in this area.

Directions Map 122, above. From Cork, take the N25 E and take the exit for the R624, signposted for Cobh and Fota.

Slatty's Bridge Follow the signs for Cobh and Fota Island and, having crossed the N25, the road passes a small tidal lagoon on the right. This area is known as Slatty's Bridge and is good for ducks, waders and gulls in autumn and winter.

Belvelly Continue on the R624 and, just after the entrance to Fota Wildlife Park on the right, the road crosses a narrow bridge over a tidal estuary. This is Belvelly, and the areas on either side of the bridge are good for ducks, waders and gulls in autumn and winter.

Cobh Just past the bridge, the R624 swings sharply right and continues into Cobh. Follow this road and, just as you reach the town of Cobh, there is a large tidal estuary and deep channels on the right which attract large numbers of waders and gulls in autumn and winter.

To look for gulls along the quays, the first area to check is Kennedy Pier. Continue into the town of Cobh and follow the main road downhill. Just at

the bottom of the hill, take a sharp right, following the signs for 'Tourist Information'. Park at the Cobh Heritage Centre and check the harbour and quayside. The piers that lie E from the Heritage Centre are also good areas, while one of the best gull locations is known locally as 'The Holy Ground'. Return to the main road and continue through the town. Just at the bottom of East Hill is a small right turn marked 'Cul-de-sac' which brings you to 'The Holy Ground'. A small parking area at the end of this road overlooks a small fishing pier and attracts good numbers of gulls in winter.

Cuskinny Marsh From 'The Holy Ground', go up East Hill out of the town of Cobh and continue on until you reach a roundabout. Go right, following the signs for Ballymore, and continue for 1km until you reach a small bridge. Just before the bridge is a parking area on the right. The small beach directly in front of the carpark is often good for gulls in winter. To view Cuskinny Marsh, walk left out of the carpark, and take the right turn signed for Rossleague. This road offers several vantage points over the marsh and open water. At the N end of the lake, there is a walkway into the woodlands which is good for common species in summer and winter.

238

North Channel (Rossleague) From the carpark near Cuskinny Marsh, go left and take an immediate right turn signposted for Rossleague. Continue past Cuskinny Marsh and follow the road for 1km and take a right, following the signposts for Rossleague. At the T-junction, take a left and then an immediate right, again following the signs for Rossleague. At the next T-junction, take a right turn and follow this road down to where the estuary meets the wall. This area, known locally as 'The North Channel', holds large numbers of waders and gulls in autumn and winter. By following the road W along the estuary from this point, you will arrive back at Belvelly.

Species
All year Cormorant, Shag, Little Egret, Water Rail, Peregrine, Kittiwake, Kingfisher.

Autumn, winter & spring Wigeon, Teal, Red-throated Diver, Great Northern Diver, Golden Plover (1000s), Grey Plover, Lapwing (1000s), Knot, Little Stint (O autumn), Curlew Sandpiper (O autumn), Dunlin, Ruff (O autumn), Jack Snipe (R winter), Snipe, Black-tailed Godwit (1000s), Bar-tailed Godwit, Whimbrel (spring, R winter), Spotted Redshank (R autumn & winter), Green Sandpiper (R autumn), Common Sandpiper (R winter, regular spring & autumn), Little Gull (R winter), Mediterranean Gull (O autumn & winter), Ring-billed Gull (O winter), Iceland Gull (O winter), Glaucous Gull (O winter), Short-eared Owl (R winter), Black Redstart (O winter), Blackcap.

Summer gulls, Sedge Warbler, Chiffchaff, Willow Warbler.

Rarities Velvet Scoter, Black-throated Diver, Red-necked Grebe, Slavonian Grebe, Black-necked Grebe, Osprey, Laughing Gull, Sabine's Gull, Bonaparte's Gull, American Herring Gull, Yellow-legged Gull, Thayer's Gull.

195 Ballintubrid   Grid ref. W 83 70

A small tidal lagoon and wetland, lying on the opposite side of Rossleague (site 194), good for a variety of wintering wetland birds.

From Slatty's Bridge (Site 194, Map 122, see previous page), follow the R624 to Fota Island and Cobh. Take the first left turn, signposted for Rossmore, and following the signs for the 'East Cork Trail'. Take this road for approximately 2.5km and at the small crossroads, go right. Follow this narrow road and, at the T-junction, go right. Follow this road to the end to view the lagoon.

Cormorant, Little Egret and Kingfisher are present all year at this site. The best time to visit is from autumn to early spring when typical wintering species include Wigeon, Teal, Golden Plover, Grey Plover, Lapwing, Curlew Sandpiper (R autumn), Dunlin, Jack Snipe (R winter), Snipe, Black-tailed Godwit, Bar-tailed Godwit, Whimbrel (spring, R winter), Common Sandpiper (R winter, common spring & autumn), Mediterranean Gull (R autumn & winter), Ring-billed Gull (R winter).

Rare birds recorded include American Wigeon and Green-winged Teal.

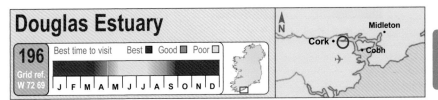

Douglas Estuary

196
Grid ref. W 72 69

Best time to visit   Best ■ Good ▨ Poor □

| J | F | M | A | M | J | J | A | S | O | N | D |

N
Cork • ✈   Midleton
Cobh

South-west

A large tidal estuary close to Cork city which attracts large numbers of ducks, waders and gulls in autumn and winter.

Directions Map 122, p.238. From Cork city, take the N27 out to the South Ring Road. Then take the N25 E. From the N25, the first part of the estuary can be checked on the left just before the

239

exit for Rochestown and Carrigaline. From here, take the Rochestown and Carrigaline exit and continue on the R610, the Douglas/Rochestown road. At the first roundabout, take a left and continue on the R610, signposted for Passage West. 200m after the roundabout, there is a small left turn through a small housing estate. Follow this road down to the end where there is a good vantage point over the estuary. From here, return to the R610, take a left and continue E for approximately 1.1km until you see a block of apartments on the left side. The carpark in front of these apartments gives good views over the estuary.

Alternatively, follow the pathway from the carpark which runs W along the route of the old railway line. This pathway continues along the estuary and provides excellent vantage points overlooking many good areas of mudflat. Just before the footbridge over the road, the path goes right over a small footbridge and continues along the opposite side of the estuary. This pathway will bring you to Blackrock Castle, a good area for waders and roosting gulls.

To reach Blackrock Castle by road, take the N25 (South Ring Road) E and take the left exit signposted Blackrock and Mahon. At the traffic lights, take a left and, at the next set of traffic lights, continue straight, following signs for Mahon and Blackrock. At the next set of lights, take a left turn. From here, take a right turn at the second set of traffic lights and continue past the playing pitch. At the T-junction, take a right following the signs for Blackrock. At the end of the road, the main road swings sharply right with

a minor road going straight and uphill. Follow this minor road uphill with the river below on the left and continue past Blackrock Castle. Just beyond the castle is a carpark with a pathway that runs along the estuary (the end of the pathway from the apartment block on the opposite side of the Douglas Estuary). In autumn and winter, the estuary directly below the castle is excellent on an incoming tide for waders and is a good area for roosting gulls.

Species
All year Cormorant, Little Egret, Kingfisher.

Autumn, winter & spring Wigeon, Teal, Golden Plover (1000s), Grey Plover, Lapwing (1000s), Knot, Little Stint (O autumn), Curlew Sandpiper (O autumn), Dunlin, Ruff (O autumn), Jack Snipe (R winter), Snipe, Black-tailed Godwit (1000s), Bar-tailed Godwit, Whimbrel (spring, R winter), Spotted Redshank (R autumn & winter), Green Sandpiper (R autumn), Common Sandpiper (spring & autumn, R winter), Little Gull (R winter), Mediterranean Gull (O autumn & winter), Ring-billed Gull (O winter), Iceland Gull (O winter), Glaucous Gull (O winter), Short-eared Owl (R winter), Black Redstart (O winter).

Summer Common Sandpiper, gulls, terns, Sedge Warbler, Chiffchaff, Willow Warbler.

Rarities American Wigeon, Green-winged Teal, Avocet, American Golden Plover, Pectoral Sandpiper, Lesser Yellowlegs, Laughing Gull, Franklin's Gull, Bonaparte's Gull.

Lough Beg

197

Grid ref. W 78 63

Best time to visit   Best ■ Good ▨ Poor ☐

J F M A M J J A S O N D

A small brackish, reed-fringed lagoon and tidal estuary, good for ducks, waders and gulls in autumn and winter. The small, rocky islands offshore attract small numbers of breeding Common Terns in summer.

Directions Map 122, p.238. From Cork, follow the N28 for over 10km, following the signs for

Ringaskiddy. At the roundabout, follow the N28 left, again following the signs for Ringaskiddy. Continue for 3.2km to the next roundabout and go straight on. From here, after just over 1.5km, take the right turn onto the R613, signposted for Ballinhassig. Take the left turn signposted for Currabinny after 1.1km and continue on this road for 1.5km, until you reach Lough Beg, directly ahead of you. Follow the road straight into the carpark near the chemical plants. There is a hide on the reserve and the key is kept at the security hut at the entrance to the chemical plant. The estuary can be seen on the left side.

Species
All year Cormorant, Little Egret, Water Rail, Kingfisher.

Autumn, winter & spring Wigeon, Teal, Golden Plover (1000s), Grey Plover, Lapwing (1000s), Knot, Little Stint (O autumn), Curlew Sandpiper (O autumn), Dunlin, Ruff (O autumn), Jack Snipe (R winter), Snipe, Black-tailed Godwit (1000s), Bar-tailed Godwit, Whimbrel (spring, R winter), Spotted Redshank (R autumn & winter), Green Sandpiper (R autumn), Wood Sandpiper (R autumn), Common Sandpiper (regular spring & autumn, R winter), Mediterranean Gull (O autumn & winter), Ring-billed Gull (O winter), Iceland Gull (O winter), Glaucous Gull (O winter), Short-eared Owl (R winter).

Summer Common Sandpiper, gulls, Common Tern, Sedge Warbler, Chiffchaff, Willow Warbler.

Rarities Stilt Sandpiper, Long-billed Dowitcher, Lesser Yellowlegs.

198 The Lough (or Cork Lough) Grid ref. W 66 70

A small, freshwater reservoir on the south-eastern side of Cork city, attracting ducks and gulls in winter.

The Lough is situated in the Glasheen area of Cork city, just 1.5km from the city centre. From the S side of the city, follow the R608 for Ballincollig. At the major Y-junction, continue left for Bishopstown. There are several lefts turns along this road and each one will bring you to The Lough. However, the best road to take is the fourth left turn at the crossroads. Follow this road down to reach the S end of the reservoir. There are many parking areas at this point. A path runs around the entire length of The Lough, and all the birds are easy to see from any point. People regularly feed the ducks here and, because of this, many gulls are very approachable as they try to take advantage of a free feed. Gulls also use this area for bathing and there is a constant movement of birds to and from the reservoir all day.

The Lough is at its best from autumn to spring, when species present include Teal (R), Pochard, and Tufted Duck, along with many of the common waterbirds, while many of the common gull species share The Lough, with Mediterranean Gull (O autumn & winter), Ring-billed Gull (O winter), Iceland Gull (O winter) and Glaucous Gull (R winter).

Rarer species recorded here include Ring-necked Duck, Laughing Gull, Bonaparte's Gull, American Herring Gull, Yellow-legged Gull, Kumlien's Gull and Thayer's Gull.

The Greylag and Canada Geese present here all year are feral birds.

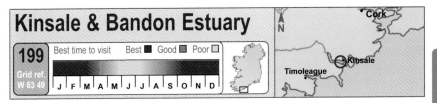

Kinsale & Bandon Estuary

| 199 | Best time to visit | Best ■ Good ■ Poor □ |

Grid ref. W 63 49

| J | F | M | A | M | J | J | A | S | O | N | D |

Kinsale is a small coastal town with an inter-tidal harbour which attracts gulls in winter. Kinsale Marsh (known locally as Commoge Marsh) is a small lagoon on the outskirts of the town and is good for waders in autumn. Across from the Marsh, the intertidal mudflats, where the Bandon River flows into Kinsale Harbour, are good for waders and gulls in autumn and winter.

Directions Map 123, right. From Cork, follow the R600, signposted for **Kinsale**. Go through the small village of **Belgooly** where, just on the southern side, the tidal channel of the Belgooly River is visible on the right. This area is very good for Green Sandpiper in autumn, and large concentrations of gulls and godwits also occur here. To reach Kinsale town, continue on the R600 and, at the town, follow the R600 left to reach the W side of the town. 500m along the road are a slipway and pier on the left where, at low tide, gulls can easily be checked.

To reach **Kinsale (Commoge) Marsh**, follow the R600 out of Kinsale and, just where it swings left over the bridge, take a right onto the R606. Continue on the R606 for 800m, until the marsh is visible on the right. The Marsh and **Bandon Estuary** can be viewed well from the road or from the disused factory a further 200m on.

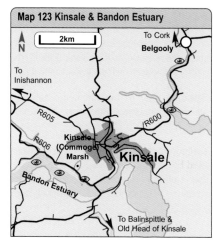

Map 123 Kinsale & Bandon Estuary

Species

All year Little Egret, Water Rail, Kingfisher.

Autumn, winter & spring Wigeon, Teal, Red-breasted Merganser (O), Buzzard (R winter), Golden Plover (1000s), Lapwing (1000s), Little Stint (autumn), Curlew Sandpiper (autumn), Dunlin, Ruff (autumn), Snipe, Black-tailed Godwit, Bar-tailed Godwit, Whimbrel (spring), Spotted Redshank (R autumn & winter), Green Sandpiper (R autumn), Wood Sandpiper (R autumn), Mediterranean Gull (R autumn & winter), Ring-billed Gull (R winter), Iceland Gull (R winter), Glaucous Gull (R winter).

Summer Common Sandpiper, gulls, terns, Sedge Warbler, Chiffchaff, Willow Warbler.

Rarities Green-winged Teal, Garganey, Blue-winged Teal, Spoonbill, Osprey, American Golden Plover, Semipalmated Sandpiper, White-rumped Sandpiper, Baird's Sandpiper, Pectoral Sandpiper, Long-billed Dowitcher, Lesser Yellowlegs, Franklin's Gull, Yellow-legged Gull, Ivory Gull, Turtle Dove, Yellow Wagtail.

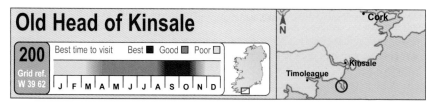

Old Head of Kinsale

200	Best time to visit	Best ■ Good ■ Poor □
Grid ref. W 39 62	J F M A M J J A S O N D	

A headland which holds breeding seabirds in summer, offers good seawatching in autumn, and is renowned for attracting rare migrants in spring and autumn.

Directions Map 124, next page. From the town of Kinsale, take the R600 and continue over the bridge following the R600. From the bridge, continue for 3.7km and take a left turn onto the R604, signposted for Garrettstown, Ballinspittle and 'Scenic Route'. Follow this road for approxi-

mately 5km. At the point where the R604 swings sharply to the right (opposite the Speckled Door pub), continue straight to go to the Old Head of Kinsale. From the Speckled Door, continue S for 600m. On the right is a small laneway which leads into a stand of trees known as '**The Plantation**'.

A further 1km along the road on the left side is another good area for migrants. A farmhouse with two large pillars marks the entrance to the lane. Follow the lane past the house and through the farmyard. *Please close all gates behind you.* This laneway follows downhill to a small valley and then continues over the hill to meet the coast. The hedgerows and fields along this laneway attract good numbers of migrants in autumn and spring. Any of the fields and gardens from the Speckled Door to this farmhouse are worth checking for migrants in spring and autumn, especially after S, SE or E winds.

2.4km from the Speckled Door is the entrance to 'Old Head Golf Links'. This golf course is private but access may be gained at the security hut at the entrance. The best seawatching is done in SW winds from a point below the lighthouse. The cliffs below the lighthouse also hold large numbers of breeding seabirds in summer.

Species
All year Fulmar, Cormorant, Shag, Chough.

Autumn, winter & spring Red-throated Diver (autumn), Great Northern Diver, Hen Harrier (R autumn), Merlin, Peregrine, Whimbrel (autumn & spring), Grey Phalarope (R autumn), Mediterranean Gull (R autumn & winter), Short-eared Owl (R autumn), Black Redstart (R autumn), Redstart (R autumn & spring), Whinchat (R autumn), Wheatear (autumn & spring), Ring Ouzel (R autumn), Garden Warbler (R autumn), Blackcap (autumn), Reed Warbler (O autumn), Spotted Flycatcher (autumn), Pied Flycatcher (autumn), Brambling (R autumn), Siskin, (O autumn & winter), Redpoll (O autumn).

Summer Manx Shearwater, Kittiwake, Razorbill, Guillemot.

Seawatching, autumn Red-throated Diver (O), Great Northern Diver (O), Fulmar, Cory's Shearwater (R), Great Shearwater (R), Sooty Shearwater (autumn, R winter), Manx Shearwater (often 1000s), Balearic Shearwater (O), Storm Petrel (O), Grey Phalarope (O), Pomarine Skua (O), Arctic Skua, Great Skua, gulls.

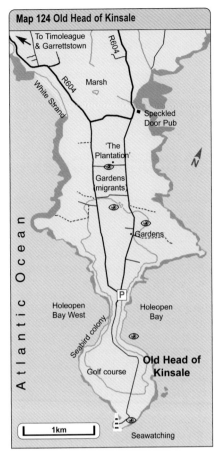

Map 124 Old Head of Kinsale

Rarities Surf Scoter, Fea's/Zino's Petrel, Wilson's Petrel, American Golden Plover, American Herring Gull, Turtle Dove, Hoopoe, Wryneck, Yellow Wagtail, Grey-cheeked Thrush, Icterine Warbler, Melodious Warbler, Barred Warbler, Lesser Whitethroat, Yellow-browed Warbler, Western/Eastern Bonelli's Warbler, Wood Warbler, Firecrest, Red-breasted Flycatcher, Red-backed Shrike, Woodchat Shrike, Isabelline Shrike, Carrion Crow, Rose-coloured Starling, Common Rosefinch, Hawfinch, Lapland Bunting, Snow Bunting.

South-west

201 Garrettstown Grid ref. W 59 43

A small marshland and reedbed good for spring and autumn migrants. The beach has waders and gulls in autumn and winter.

Located at the W side of The Old Head of Kinsale. See Site 200, above. From the Speckled Door Pub, continue right, or W, on the R604 for 800m until you see the beach (White Strand) on the left,

243

good for waders and gulls in autumn and winter. Continue on this road for 1.6km, and, just past the public toilets on the right, are the reedbeds and marsh of Garrettstown. The beach on the left usually has good numbers of gulls and waders.

Water Rail and Kingfisher are present all year, while in autumn, winter and early spring, typical species include Hen Harrier, Merlin, Peregrine,

Snipe, Whimbrel (autumn & spring), Mediterranean Gull (R autumn & winter), Ring-billed Gull (R winter), Iceland Gull (R winter) and Short-eared Owl (R winter).

In summer, Common Sandpiper, and Sedge Warbler are usually present, while rarer species recorded here include Purple Heron, Marsh Harrier and Spotted Crake.

202 Kilbrittain Creek Grid ref. W 53 45

A small tidal estuary, good for waders and gulls in autumn and winter.

See Map 125, next page. From Garrettstown (Site 201, above), continue W for 2.3km on the R604, following signs for Ballinspittle. Just after the sign for Ballinspittle village and opposite the school, take a left turn onto the R600, signposted Kilbrittain and Clonakilty. Follow the R600 for approximately 6km and just where the road swings left over a small causeway, signposted Timolegaue and Clonakilty, you will see a small lagoon on the right. This is Kilbrittain Creek. Immediately after the small causeway is a right turn. Take this turn and follow for 500m. This

road offers good vantage points over the creek. Directly opposite is Garraneteen Strand which often has various species of waders and gulls in autumn and winter.

Little Egret is present at the Creek in small numbers throughout the year, and Kingfisher can occasionally be seen.

This site is best in autumn, winter and spring when species might include Buzzard (R autumn & winter), Little Stint (O autumn), Curlew Sandpiper (O autumn), Dunlin, Snipe, Whimbrel (autumn), Spotted Redshank (R autumn & winter), Green Sandpiper (R autumn), Wood Sandpiper (R autumn). Osprey has also been recorded here.

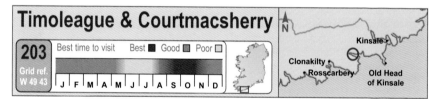

Timoleague and Courtmacsherry overlook a tidal estuary which holds large numbers of ducks, waders and gulls in autumn and winter. Broadstrand is a nearby small, sandy beach which attracts waders and gulls in autumn and winter.

Directions Map 125, next page.

Timoleague From Kilbrittain Creek (Site 202, above), continue on the R600, with the tidal estuary on the left. Anywhere along the 8.8km stretch to the village of Timoleague is worth checking for waders and gulls, including a small picnic area on the left just 1.7km from Kilbrittain

Creek. As you approach the village of Timoleague, take a left at the T-junction, keeping to the R600 and signposted for Clonakilty. This road brings you into Timoleague. As you enter the village, continue left onto the R601, following the signs for Courtmacsherry. The estuary directly opposite the old abbey is worth checking for ducks and gulls. Just past the abbey, take a left over the bridge and follow the coast road to Courtmacsherry.

Courtmacsherry From Timoleague, follow the R601 for 3.5km to Courtmacsherry. There are many vantage points over the estuary on the left along this road. At the end of Courtmacsherry

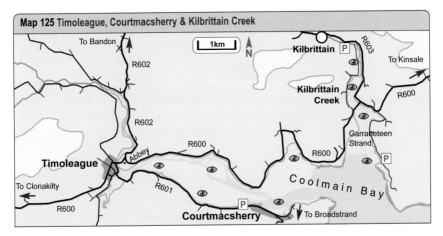

Map 125 Timoleague, Courtmacsherry & Kilbrittain Creek

village, the main road swings right and uphill. The small road to the left leads to a vantage point overlooking the bay. This can be a good area for gulls in winter.

Broadstrand From the end of Courtmacsherry village, follow the main road right and uphill signposted for Clonakilty. 1km out this road, take the left turn signposted for Broadstrand. Follow this road down for 1km to reach the beach.

Species
All year Little Egret, Kingfisher.

Autumn, winter & spring Brent Goose, Wigeon (1000s), Gadwall, Teal (500+), Long-tailed Duck (R winter), Red-breasted Merganser, Red-throated Diver, Great Northern Diver, Merlin, Buzzard (R), Peregrine, Golden Plover (1000s), Grey Plover,

Lapwing (1000s), Knot, Little Stint (autumn), Curlew Sandpiper (autumn), Dunlin, Ruff (autumn), Jack Snipe (R winter), Snipe, Black-tailed Godwit, Bar-tailed Godwit, Whimbrel (spring), Spotted Redshank (R autumn & winter), Green Sandpiper (R autumn), Wood Sandpiper (R autumn), Grey Phalarope (R autumn), Mediterranean Gull (R autumn & winter), Glaucous Gull (R winter), Short-eared Owl (winter), Wheatear (spring & autumn), Black Redstart (R autumn & winter).

Summer Common Sandpiper, gulls, terns, Chiffchaff, Willow Warbler.

Rarities American Wigeon, Black-throated Diver, Spoonbill, Osprey, American Golden Plover, Yellow-legged Gull, Gull-billed Tern, Chimney Swift.

204 **Seven Heads** Grid ref. W 49 35

A low-lying headland located between The Old Head of Kinsale to the east and Galley Head to the west. This is probably one of the most under-watched seawatching points on the south coast.

The headland has no lighthouse to attract passerine migrants, though the location of the headland makes it good for seawatching in autumn.

Several roads go from Butlerstown and lead to a Signal Tower and various coves. There are hollows and sheltered areas near the tower from

which to seawatch. *If crossing lands in this area, please seek permission from the local farmers.*

Seawatching in autumn in SW to S winds can produce Red-throated Diver (O), Great Northern Diver (O), Fulmar, Cory's Shearwater (R), Great Shearwater (R), Sooty Shearwater (autumn, R winter), Manx Shearwater (often 1000s), Balearic Shearwater (O), Storm Petrel (O), Grey Phalarope (O), Pomarine Skua (O), Arctic Skua, Great Skua, gulls, Common Tern (O), Arctic Tern, Sandwich Tern, Guillemot, Razorbill, Black Guillemot, Little Auk (Oct onward), Puffin (O). See also SEAWATCHING, p.356.

245

Clonakilty & Inchydoney

205

Grid ref.
W 40 38

Best time to visit   Best ■ Good ■ Poor ☐

J F M A M J J A S O N D

N

Kinsale

Clonakilty

Galley Head

Old Head
of Kinsale

A large expanse of tidal sandflats and mudflats with a series of lagoons, ponds and pools, attracting large numbers of waders in the autumn and winter, as well as a large resident population of Little Egrets. Rare vagrants have been found, mainly in spring and autumn.

The estuary is particularly important for Shelduck, Black-tailed Godwit, Curlew and Greenshank. Many birds move between both areas, depending on tides and the levels of disturbance at the respective sites.

Directions Map 126, next page.

Clonakilty From Bandon, travel SW on the N71 until you reach the small roundabout at Clonakilty town. The main estuary can be viewed from several vantage points.

To view the **eastern side**, at the roundabout, take a left, signposted for Ring. This road runs along the estuary for over 1.5km until you reach the small pier where the road turns inland. Anywhere along this road is good for seeing waders, egrets and gulls. At the very start of this road, close to the roundabout, a small lagoon inside the wall on the right often holds good numbers of gulls at high tide in winter. This road frequently floods on spring tides.

Grey Plover

246

To view the **upper end** of the estuary, at the roundabout, take the second exit (the N71 and the town by-pass). Less than 100m along this road are several seats on the left which look onto the upper estuary. The channel directly below the seats is worth checking for gulls and waders.

The **western side** of the estuary is reached by continuing on the N71 (past the seats) for 300m. The N71 swings sharp left and then sharp right. At the point where the N71 swings right, continue straight, following signs for Model Railway Village. Follow this road until the estuary is visible on the left. It is possible to check the estuary at various points for the next 2km.

At the end of this road is a right turn for Inchydoney. To view the large pond at the end of the road, the **Cul-de-Sac Pond**, ignore the turn for Inchydoney and continue straight down the small road marked cul-de-sac. At the end of this road, the large pond is clearly visible from the small causeway that runs to the left between estuary and the pond. The pools at the back of the pond can best be seen by taking the track to the right of the pond. The trees at the back of the pond have roosting Little Egrets each evening.

Inchydoney From Clonakilty, follow the road which runs along the western side of the Clonakilty estuary almost to the end and take the right turn signposted for Inchydoney (instead of going straight down to the Cul-de-Sac Pond). Continue along this road for less than 1km, and take a sharp right turn just when the estuary (Muckruss Strand) becomes visible. This right turn leads to a narrow, 400m long causeway from which there are excellent views of the estuary to the left and **White's Marsh** on the right. Due to farm machinery using the narrow causeway road, signs request that drivers do not park on the causeway. Park on the wider roads at either end. The pools of White's Marsh can be good for waders, Little Egret and Water Rail. The line of small trees at the top end of the marsh is also

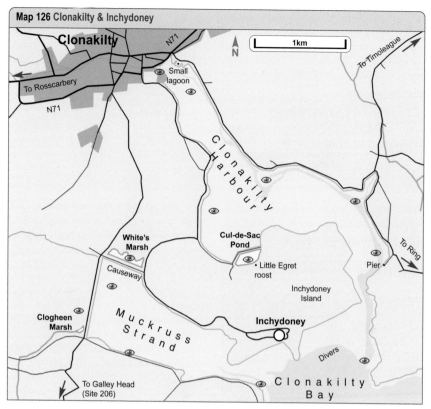

Map 126 Clonakilty & Inchydoney

Clonakilty

To Timoleague

N71

1km

N

To Rosscarbery

N71

Small lagoon

C l o n a k i l t y   H a r b o u r

White's Marsh

Cul-de-Sac Pond

To Ring

Pier

Causeway

Little Egret roost

Inchydoney Island

Clogheen Marsh

M u c k r u s s   S t r a n d

Inchydoney

To Galley Head (Site 206)

Divers

C l o n a k i l t y   B a y

worth checking for roosting herons. At low tide, many waders feed on the open estuary, although deep channels there can make viewing difficult. Waders tend to use the marsh at high tide.

To view **Clogheen Marsh** continue to the end of the causeway and, at the staggered crossroads, take a left turn. This long, straight stretch of road runs for approximately 800m with the estuary on the left and Clogheen Marsh on the right. A channel runs alongside the road hidden by the wall on the right. The best and most viewable area of the marsh can be found towards the end of the road less than 100m before the next crossroads. On the right side is a reed-fringed pool which attracts roosting waders and ducks. At the cross-roads, a river enters the estuary on the left and can attract ducks and gulls at low tide.

To check the S side of the estuary, take a left at the crossroads after Clogheen Marsh and follow this road for 1km. Views of the estuary are more limited from this road.

Species

Autumn, winter & spring Brent Goose (small numbers), Shelduck (100+), Wigeon, Teal, Pintail (O), Shoveler (R), Long-tailed Duck (R), Red-breasted Merganser, Red-throated Diver (Clonakilty Bay), Great Northern Diver (Clonakilty Bay), Cormorant, Little Egret, Water Rail, Golden Plover (1000+), Grey Plover, Lapwing (1000s), Knot, Little Stint (autumn), Curlew Sandpiper (autumn), Dunlin (1000+), Ruff (autumn), Snipe, Black-tailed Godwit (1000+), Bar-tailed Godwit, Whimbrel (especially May), Curlew (1000+), Spotted Redshank (O autumn & winter), Greenshank (often 40+), Wood Sandpiper (R autumn), Mediterranean Gull (R autumn & winter), Ring-billed Gull (R winter), Iceland Gull (R winter), Glaucous Gull (R winter), Sandwich Tern (O, R winter), Kingfisher.

Summer Sandwich Tern, auks (Clonakilty Bay), Cuckoo (O), Wheatear (O), Willow Warbler.

Rarities Dark-bellied Brent, American Wigeon, Green-winged Teal, Garganey, Cattle Egret, Night

South-west

247

Heron, Purple Heron, Spoonbill, Marsh Harrier, Hobby, Osprey, Spotted Crake, Black-winged Stilt, American Golden Plover, Little Ringed Plover, Semipalmated Sandpiper, White-rumped Sandpiper, Baird's Sandpiper, Pectoral Sandpiper, Stilt Sandpiper, Long-billed Dowitcher, Lesser Yellowlegs, Wilson's Phalarope, Laughing Gull, American Herring Gull, Yellow-legged Gull, Gull-billed Tern, Black Tern, Little Auk, Turtle Dove, Scop's Owl, Yellow Wagtail, Pied Flycatcher.

Galley Head area

206
Grid ref. W 34 32

Best time to visit   Best ■ Good ▧ Poor ☐

J F M A M J J A S O N D

Courtmacsherry
Clonakilty
Rosscarbery

Galley Head is a headland which offers good seawatching in autumn and is renowned for attracting rare migrants in spring and autumn.

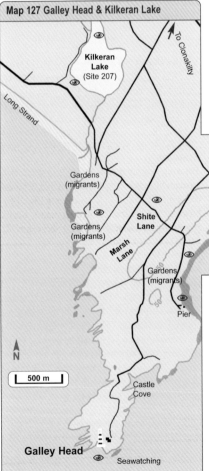

Map 127 Galley Head & Kilkeran Lake

Kilkeran Lake (Site 207)

To Clonakilty

Long Strand

Gardens (migrants)

Gardens (migrants)

Shite Lane

Marsh Lane

Gardens (migrants)

Pier

N

500 m

Castle Cove

Galley Head
Seawatching

There are several coves and gardens just before the headland which also attract migrants. Red Strand, a nearby beach, is good for waders and migrants in autumn, and gulls in winter.

Directions Map 127, this page. From Clonakilty, follow the road which runs along the W side of the Clonakilty estuary almost to the end and take the right turn signposted for Inchydoney. Continue for less than 1km, and take a sharp right turn just when the estuary becomes visible. This right turn leads to a narrow causeway which overlooks the

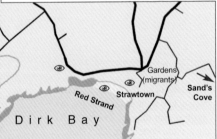

Gardens (migrants)
Strawtown
Sand's Cove
Red Strand
D i r k   B a y

estuary to the left and White's Marsh on the right (this route is shown on Map 126).

Continue to the end of the causeway and, at the staggered crossroads, take a left turn. This long, straight stretch of road runs for approximately 800m with the estuary on the left and Clogheen Marsh (Site 205) on the right. At the end of the road is a crossroads. At this point, take the right turn signposted for Galley Head. As the road swings uphill, follow the signs for Red Strand and Galley Head. 6.2km out this road is a left turn signposted for **Sand's Cove**. Follow this road downhill for 1km and park at the small harbour.

The area from the small harbour back up the road offers excellent cover on both sides for migrants in autumn. Several gardens closer to the main road are also worth checking for migrants.

Return to the main road and continue for 1.3km to Red Strand. Just as the road runs downhill towards the strand, take the small left turn which leads to an area of houses and gardens known as **Strawtown**. These gardens are also worth checking for migrants in autumn.

The beach at **Red Strand** often has waders, gulls and migrants. Continue W past Red Strand and as the road goes uphill, you will see the first garden on the left which has good cover. This garden is also worth checking for migrants in autumn.

Continue NW and take the first left turn signposted for Galley Head. Less than 1km out this road is a crossroads. At this point you can take a left turn signposted 'cul-de-sac'. This brings you down to **Dirk Bay**. Follow the road down to the small pier at the end of the road. The gardens and trees along this road have hosted many rare migrants in autumn, including Europe's first Philadelphia Vireo. Alternatively, at the crossroads, you can go right and follow the road down for 500m until you reach the large garden at the end of the road which provides excellent cover for migrants. The road down from the crossroads to the garden is known as **Shite Lane**. Just past this garden is a small crossroads. Go left and follow the road for 400m until you meet a dirt track. Park here and follow the dirt track down to the beach. A small stream runs just inside the ditch on the right and the slope above offers shelter and good cover for migrants. This lane is known as **Marsh Lane**. At the small crossroads near the garden, you can also go straight, where hedges and gardens close to the cement fencing offer more cover for migrants.

Seawatching off Galley Head is best done from below the lighthouse in S or SW winds. Having taken the left turn signposted for Galley Head, follow the road for 3km, ignoring the turns for Dirk Bay and 'Shite Lane'. The road narrows as you approach the lighthouse and access into the lighthouse compound is through the main gate. *Please note that the land immediately before the lighthouse is private property.* Park at the light-

house cottages. To gain the best vantage points for seawatching, it is best to climb down to the cliffs below the lighthouse wall. *The cliffs here can be quite slippery in wet conditions and extreme care should always be taken.*

Species
All year Fulmar, Peregrine, Chough.

Autumn, winter & spring Eider (R winter), Grey Phalarope (R autumn), Mediterranean Gull (R autumn & winter), Iceland Gull (R winter), Short-eared Owl (O winter), Wheatear (autumn & spring), Black Redstart (R autumn & winter), Redstart (R autumn & spring), Whinchat (autumn), Ring Ouzel (R autumn), Garden Warbler (R spring, O autumn), Blackcap (R spring, O autumn, R winter), Whitethroat (autumn), Reed Warbler (O autumn), Spotted Flycatcher (autumn), Pied Flycatcher (autumn), Brambling (R autumn), Siskin (O autumn & winter).

Rarities Goshawk, Turtle Dove, Wryneck, Desert Wheatear, Hermit Thrush, Marsh Warbler, Icterine Warbler, Melodious Warbler, Lesser Whitethroat, Pallas's Warbler, Yellow-browed Warbler, Radde's Warbler, Wood Warbler, Firecrest, Red-breasted Flycatcher, Philadelphia Vireo, American Redstart, Lapland Bunting, Snow Bunting, Little Bunting.

Seawatching Best from late July to mid October. Red-throated Diver (O), Great Nortern Diver (O), Fulmar, 'Blue' Fulmar (O late autumn), Cory's Shearwater (O mainly Sept), Great Shearwater (O

Manx Shearwater and Fea's/Zino's Petrel

mainly Sept), Sooty Shearwater (occasionally 100s), Manx Shearwater (often 1000s), Balearic Shearwater (small numbers), Storm Petrel, Leach's Petrel (R), Gannet (often 1000s), Cormorant, Shag, Grey Phalarope (O), Pomarine Skua, Arctic Skua, Long-tailed Skua (R), Great Skua, Little Gull (R), Sabine's Gull (O Sept), Sandwich Tern (O), Common Tern (O), Arctic Tern, Black Tern (O), Guillemot (often 100s), Razorbill (often 100s), Black Guillemot (small numbers), Little Auk (R Oct onward), Puffin (small numbers).

Rarer seabirds include Fea's/Zino's Petrel, Little Shearwater and Wilson's Petrel.

207 Kilkeran Lake Grid ref. W 33 34

A shallow, reed-fringed freshwater lake which attracts ducks and waders in spring, autumn and winter.

Located just to the N of Galley Head (Site 206). See Map 127, p.248. From Red Strand, follow the road NW, and go past the turn for Galley Head. Take the next left turn and go through the first small crossroads. Continue for over 500m until you meet the next small crossroads (which is at the garden at the end of 'Shite Lane') and take a right. From the crossroads, continue W for 800m and go over a small bridge. 300m past the bridge is a small right turn which brings you onto a narrow track along the lakeshore. This small track continues around the lake.

Water Rail and Kingfisher are present all year, while in autumn, winter and spring, species include Wigeon, Gadwall, Teal, Hen Harrier (O winter), Merlin, Peregrine, Little Stint (R autumn), Curlew Sandpiper (R autumn), Dunlin, Ruff (O autumn), Jack Snipe (R winter), Snipe, Black-tailed Godwit, Green Sandpiper (R autumn), Wood Sandpiper (R autumn), Mediterranean Gull (R autumn & winter) and Short-eared Owl (R autumn & winter).

Common Sandpiper, Sedge Warbler, Chiffchaff and Willow Warbler are present in summer, while rarer species seen here include Green-winged Teal, Black-necked Grebe, Black-winged Stilt, Long-billed Dowitcher and Little Auk.

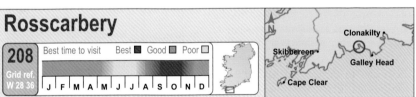

Rosscarbery

208

Grid ref.
W 28 36

Best time to visit   Best ■ Good ■ Poor □

J F M A M J J A S O N D

Clonakilty
Skibbereen
Galley Head
Cape Clear

A large, tidal mudflat attracting waders and gulls in autumn and winter.

Directions Map 128, next page. From Clonakilty, travel SW on the N71. Pass through the village of Lissavard and continue on for 6km. Approaching Rosscarbery, the causeway which separates the tidal mudflat to the left and the open water to the right is obvious as the road sweeps downhill. The E side of the estuary can be viewed by taking the left turn at the beginning of the causeway. Birds can be seen well from any point along this road. Follow this road down for 500m to reach a small pool on the left that attracts small numbers of waders.

The W side is reached by returning to the causeway, continuing W and taking a left turn at the end of the causeway opposite the hotel. A small, reed-fringed pool on the right can hold waders, ducks and occasionally Kingfisher. This road continues for almost 2km, and the mudflats can be viewed from many points. At the end of the road is a small pier from which divers and auks can be seen in winter.

Species
Autumn, winter & spring Brent Goose (O), Wigeon, Teal, Shoveler (R), Goldeneye, Red-breasted Merganser, Red-throated Diver, Great Northern Diver, Cormorant, Shag, Little Egret, Merlin (R), Peregrine, Water Rail, Golden Plover

(1000s), Grey Plover, Little Stint (O autumn), Curlew Sandpiper (O autumn), Purple Sandpiper, Dunlin, Ruff (O autumn), Black-tailed Godwit, Bar-tailed Godwit, Whimbrel (spring & autumn), Spotted Redshank (O autumn & winter), Common Sandpiper, Mediterranean Gull (R winter), Ring-billed Gull (O autumn & winter), gulls, auks, Kingfisher, Grey Wagtail (O).

Arctic Skua and terns can occasionally be seen at the mouth of the estuary in Aug and early Sept.

Summer Wheatear, Sedge Warbler, Willow Warbler.

Rarities American Wigeon, Green-winged Teal, Black-throated Diver, White Stork, Spoonbill, Osprey, American Golden Plover, Semipalmated Sandpiper, White-rumped Sandpiper, Baird's Sandpiper, Pectoral Sandpiper, Stilt Sandpiper, Buff-breasted Sandpiper, Long-billed Dowitcher, Lesser Yellowlegs, Long-tailed Skua, Franklin's Gull, Laughing Gull, Yellow-legged Gull.

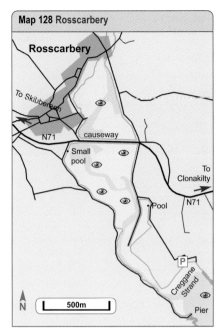

Toe Head

209	Best time to visit	Best ■ Good ▨ Poor □

Grid ref. W 14 26

J F M A M J J A S O N D

A large headland, lying to the west of Galley Head and to the east of Baltimore. The gardens and fields on the headland attract migrants in autumn.

Directions Map 129, next page. From Skibbereen, follow the R595 SE, following signs for Castletownshend. Approximately 5km from Skibbereen is a main crossroads (Raheen Crossroads). At this point, take a right and follow this road for approximately 5km until you come to a minor crossroads (Baunishall Crossroads). Go left at this point and follow this road S for 1km where you take the right turn. This small road brings you out to Toe Head. The gardens along this road often hold migrant passerines in spring and autumn but the main area is found 500m along this road where you meet a Y-junction. It is worth parking at this point and walking the road on either side of the junction. The gardens,

hedges and laneways along this narrow road can be very productive for migrants. The road continues in a loop around this area and eventually brings you back to the parking area.

Species
All Year Chough.

Autumn, winter & spring Black Redstart (R autumn), Whinchat (R autumn), Ring Ouzel (R autumn), Blackcap (O autumn), Whitethroat (O autumn), Spotted Flycatcher (autumn), Pied Flycatcher (O autumn), Siskin, (O autumn & winter), Redpoll (O autumn).

Seawatching, autumn in SW to S winds can produce Red-throated Diver (O), Great Northern Diver (O), Fulmar, Cory's Shearwater (R), Great Shearwater (R), Sooty Shearwater (autumn, R winter), Manx Shearwater (often 1000s), Balearic

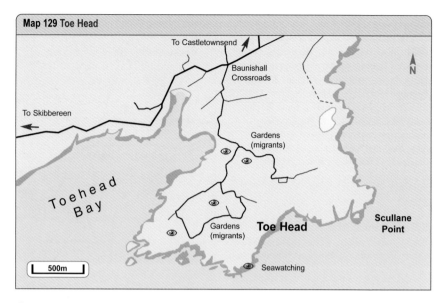

Map 129 Toe Head

To Castletownsend

Baunishall
Crossroads

N

To Skibbereen

Gardens
(migrants)

Toehead
Bay

Gardens
(migrants) **Toe Head**

Scullane
Point

500m

Seawatching

Shearwater (O), Storm Petrel (O), Grey Phalarope (O), Pomarine Skua (O), Arctic Skua, Great Skua, Sabine's Gull, gulls, Common Tern (O), Arctic Tern, Sandwich Tern, Guillemot, Razorbill, Black Guillemot, Little Auk (Oct onward), Puffin (O). See also SEAWATCHING, p.356.

Rarities Cory's Shearwater, Great Shearwater, Wryneck, Hoopoe, Subalpine Warbler, Lesser Whitethroat, Icterine Warbler, Arctic Warbler, Yellow-browed Warbler, Firecrest, Red-eyed Vireo, Rustic Bunting.

210 Union Hall Grid ref. W 20 34

Union Hall is a landing port for local trawlers and attracts gulls in autumn and winter. Just to the south-west is the small freshwater lake of Lough Cluhir which is good for ducks in autumn and winter. Further south is Blind Harbour, a tidal lagoon which is good for waders in autumn.

For **Union Hall**, from Rosscarbery, travel W towards Leap. Approximately 2km after the village of Leap, take a left signposted for Union Hall and follow that road for approximately 3km into the village. When the fishing fleet is in port, the whole area around Union Hall is worth checking for gulls.

From Union Hall, continue S for 2km to the staggered crossroads (where three minor roads converge). Continue left at this point and **Lough Cluhir** will be visible on the right. The lake can be viewed from the road.

Continue down the road along the E side of Lough Cluhir, and after 1km, the road swings sharply left. The lagoon of **Blind Harbour** is on the left and runs the entire length of the road. The road leads to **Squince Harbour** which is also good for waders.

Water Rail and Kingfisher can be found all year. Species in autumn, winter and spring include Whooper Swan, Wigeon, Teal, Shoveler, Pochard (R winter), Tufted Duck, Scaup (R winter), Goldeneye, Golden Plover, Lapwing, Snipe, Bar-tailed Godwit, Whimbrel (O autumn & spring, R winter), Curlew and variable numbers of gulls, depending on trawler activity.

Rare species seen in this area include Garganey, Ring-necked Duck, Marsh Harrier and Wilson's Phalarope. Recent offshore boat trips from Union Hall have recorded Cory's Shearwater, Great Shearwater, Balearic Shearwater and Wilson's Petrel.

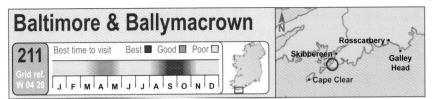

Baltimore & Ballymacrown

211	Best time to visit	Best ■ Good ■ Poor ☐
Grid ref. W 04 26	J F M A M J J A S O N D	

A small coastal village with extensive gardens that attract migrants each autumn. Most people visit Baltimore en-route to Cape Clear Island, but the village and surrounding area has produced many rare birds, including Ireland's first Baltimore Oriole.

Directions Map 130, right. From Skibbereen, follow the R595 SW for 13km, following the signs for Baltimore. Go through the village and follow the road SW above the harbour. The road then drops down to the right and into a sheltered cove. The gardens from the harbour to the cove can all hold migrants in autumn, while the small cove itself offers shelter and good cover. At the W side of the cove is a left turn which brings you uphill and out to the beacon which overlooks the sound between Baltimore and Sherkin. The fields and ditches along this road can also be worth checking for migrants.

Another area in the Baltimore vicinity which has proved productive for migrants in recent years is **Ballymacrown**. 1km before Baltimore on the R595, the main road swings very sharply right. At this point is a minor road on the left. Take this road and take a left after approximately 400m. Continue for 2.5km and take a right turn onto a narrow road. Continue for 2km until you meet a derelict building at the end of the road. The trees and hedgerows around this building are excellent for warblers and other migrants in autumn.

Map 130 Baltimore & Ballymacrown

Species

Autumn, winter & spring Grey Phalarope (R autumn), Mediterranean Gull (R autumn & winter), Iceland Gull (R winter), Glaucous Gull (R winter), Black Redstart (R autumn & winter), Redstart (R autumn), Whinchat (R autumn), Ring Ouzel (R autumn), Garden Warbler (R autumn), Blackcap (O autumn), Whitethroat (O autumn), Reed Warbler (O autumn), Spotted Flycatcher (autumn), Pied Flycatcher (O autumn), Siskin, (O autumn & winter).

Rarities Leach's Petrel, Chimney Swift, Red-rumped Swallow, Lesser Whitethroat, Yellow-browed Warbler, Radde's Warbler, Firecrest, Red-breasted Flycatcher, Woodchat Shrike, Red-eyed Vireo, Crossbill, Baltimore Oriole.

Sherkin Island

212	Best time to visit	Best ■ Good ■ Poor ☐
Grid ref. W 02 25	J F M A M J J A S O N D	

A large, narrow, L-shaped island, just under 5km long and situated between Baltimore and Cape Clear Island off south-west Cork. The numerous gardens and hedge-covered valleys attract many common and rare migrants in spring and autumn.

South-west

Map 131 Baltimore & Sherkin Island

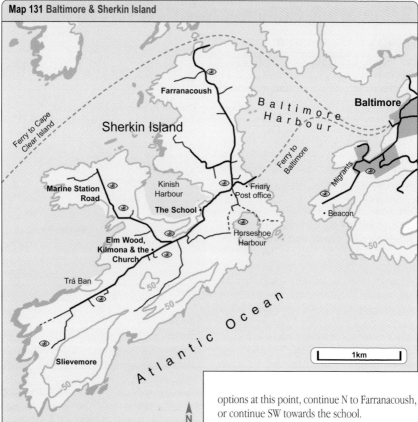

Farranacoush

Baltimore Harbour

Baltimore

Ferry to Cape Clear Island

Sherkin Island

Marine Station Road

Kinish Harbour

Ferry to Baltimore

Migrants

Friary
Post office

The School

Beacon

Elm Wood, Kilmona & the Church

Horseshoe Harbour

Trá Ban

50

50

Atlantic Ocean

50

50

Slievemore

1km

N

options at this point, continue N to Farranacoush, or continue SW towards the school.

The many small, intertidal inlets and beaches can be good for waders and gulls in autumn and winter. With Cape Clear Island so close, this island is often overlooked by birders in autumn but has superb potential. There are B&Bs, a pub, hotel, shop and Post Office. See www.sherkinisland.ie for more information

Directions Map 131, above. Sherkin Island is reached by regular ferry from Baltimore. Enquire locally for departure times, but there are usually several sailings a day, fewer in winter. The ferry is generally not affected by bad weather. It lands at the small harbour on the E side of the island. From the harbour, go uphill towards the abbey/friary. There are tall conifer trees along here that are good for migrants, as are the gardens on either side from the abbey to the first crossroads near the post office. There are two

Farranacoush Go right at the post office crossroads and follow the road N to the hotel. At the back of, and just below, the hotel is an old castle with ivy-covered walls. This area is superb for warblers in autumn, while the rocky beach below is worth checking for species such as Black Redstart in autumn. Continue N past the hotel for over 1km to reach the last bungalows at Farranacoush. There are open fields and areas of conifer trees along this road which may hold migrants, while the tillage fields around the last bungalow are excellent for finches and buntings.

The School At the post office crossroads, go straight. Behind the post office is a small track that brings you along the cliffs overlooking Horseshoe Harbour. The area along the track can be good for pipits in autumn. Continue along the main road and just before the school, the first bay is obvious on the right. This small estuary is good for waders and gulls and can be viewed well from the road.

The gardens and hedgerows from here to the school offer good cover for migrants.

Elm Wood, Kilmona & The Church Continue past the school, and just where the bay on the right ends, you will enter an extensive growth of elm trees on either side of the road. A small track on the left runs up from the road to a good garden at Kilmona. This garden seems to attract good numbers of warblers in autumn. Continue along the main road, and go straight past the right turn and uphill to reach the church. The hedges around the church offer good cover, while the area to the back of the church gives an excellent vantage point over the valley.

The Marine Station Road At the elm wood, take the right turn, just past the track for Kilmona. The road continues for over 1km to the station. There are many gardens along this route that offer great potential for finding migrants. The bay on the right is also good for waders and gulls in the autumn, while the two beaches on the left are good for Wheatears in spring and autumn. The Marine Station is at the end of this road.

Slievemore Area From the church, continue SW for over 1.3km to where the road comes to an end. The open fields along the road are good for finches and pipits, while an area of reeds at the back of the beach on the right (Trá Ban) is also a good area for warblers in spring and autumn. At the end of the road, a small track to the left brings you to a derelict farmhouse with a good stand of sycamores. This area, lying directly opposite Cape

Clear Island, is potentially one of the best spots for migrants in autumn.

Species
All year Fulmar, Cormorant, Shag, Peregrine, Black Guillemot, Chough.

Autumn, winter & spring Sooty Shearwater (autumn), Hen Harrier (R autumn), Merlin, Snipe, Whimbrel (regular autumn & spring), Grey Phalarope (R autumn), Mediterranean Gull (R autumn & winter), Glaucous Gull (R autumn & winter), Short-eared Owl (R autumn), Black Redstart (O autumn), Redstart (R autumn & spring), Whinchat (O autumn), Ring Ouzel (R autumn), Garden Warbler (R autumn), Blackcap (R spring, O autumn), Whitethroat (O autumn), Reed Warbler (R autumn), Spotted Flycatcher (autumn), Pied Flycatcher (O autumn), Brambling (O autumn), Siskin (O autumn & winter), Redpoll (O autumn).

Summer Common Sandpiper, gulls, terns, Sedge Warbler, Whitethroat, Wheatear.

Rarities White-billed Diver, Cory's Shearwater, Great Shearwater, Marsh Harrier, Baird's Sandpiper, Laughing Gull, Black Tern, Turtle Dove, Chimney Swift, Tree Pipit, Yellow Wagtail, Melodious Warbler, Barred Warbler, Lesser Whitethroat, Pallas's Warbler, Yellow-browed Warbler, Wood Warbler, Firecrest, Red-breasted Flycatcher, Carrion Crow, Serin, Crossbill, Common Rosefinch, Hawfinch, Lapland Bunting, Snow Bunting.

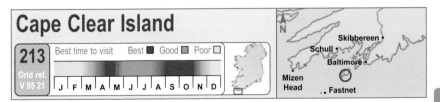

Cape Clear Island

213
Grid ref.
V 95 21

Best time to visit   Best ■ Good ■ Poor □

J F M A M J J A S O N D

N
Skibbereen •
Schull •
Baltimore •
Mizen Head
• Fastnet

South-west

A large island, just under 5km long and over 1.5km wide, which lies off south-west Cork. One of the best migration and seawatching sites in Europe.

Apart from the Fastnet Rock, Cape Clear is the most southerly point of Ireland. The many gardens and hedge-covered valleys play host to

many common and rare migrants in spring and autumn. The rugged cliffs of Pointabullaun (Bullaun) and Pointanbullig (Bullig) on the southern edges of the island provide good seawatching points. The southern tip of Blanan (Blananarragaun) is possibly one of the best seawatching spots in Europe in autumn. The island has a Bird Observatory, established in

Pallas's Warbler

August 1959, and a warden is usually on duty from March to November.

Directions Map 132, p.257. Access to Cape Clear is by a scheduled ferry service from Baltimore and, during the summer, from Schull (see www.capeclearferry.info for ferry times). All ferries arrive into the North Harbour on the island where the Bird Observatory is located. It is always worth paying a visit to the Observatory as the warden can advise you on the most recent sightings, access to lands (which can change from year to year) and areas where livestock such as free-roaming bulls might be encountered.

The island is separated into two distinct sections, the W and S side known as Ballyieragh, and the E and N side, with 'The Waist' being the middle section between the North and South Harbours.

From the North Harbour, follow the road straight uphill, ignoring the very steep road to the left, known as the A1. The first garden on the right as you approach the hill is **Cotter's Garden** and is famous for the number of rare Nearctic, Siberian and European species which have been found there in autumn. This garden has also played host to many rare European species in spring. The garden has several viewing points. The tall trees beside the pub can be watched from the area immediately in front of the pub entrance. However, to get a view of the whole garden, continue uphill and, at the top, enter through the

gate on the right. By standing on the slope, a very good view can be had of the whole area and bird activity is easily monitored from here.

From Cotter's Garden, take the right turn and continue straight along this road, ignoring the turn on the right which runs uphill and is known as the High Road (see p.258). The **Low Road** passes several good gardens on the left along the lower section, overlooking the South Harbour. These gardens are worth checking for migrants, as are the hedgerows on the right. After approximately 500m, the road swings right and uphill. Follow the road for a further 500m to the point where the road becomes a rough track. The **East Bog** can be viewed on the left at various points along this track. The area has a thick covering of reeds and open water is hard to see.

Blanan (or Blananarragaun) is one of the best seawatching vantage points in Ireland, but also *one of the most dangerous, especially in wet weather when the rocks becoming extremely slippery.* From the East Bog, continue on the rough track which runs left and continue through the gate. At the point where the track ends, continue left and follow the narrow grass track that runs above the western side of South Harbour. Continue over the small stile and follow this track for almost 1km to where the grass track runs out. At this point, a rough, rocky track goes for a short distance and, where it ends, you will see a large flat stone. This is the preferred seawatching location for some people but it is well back from the point, so seabirds are more distant than from the tip of Blanan itself. However, there is no marked track out to the tip and it is recommended that if you are visiting for the first time, to go with a person who knows the way. The route can be quite dangerous and requires you to go under 'the blowhole', a large gaping hole in the cliff face. Once out on the tip, some shelter can be gained behind some of the sloped rock faces. Seawatching is best in strong SW winds, though S can also be good. Some of the best seawatches occur during the foulest weather, so rain gear is essential at such times. See also SEAWATCHING, p.356.

To get to **Bullaun (or Pointabullaun)**, go uphill from the point where the track at the East Bog runs out and passes through the gate. Continue

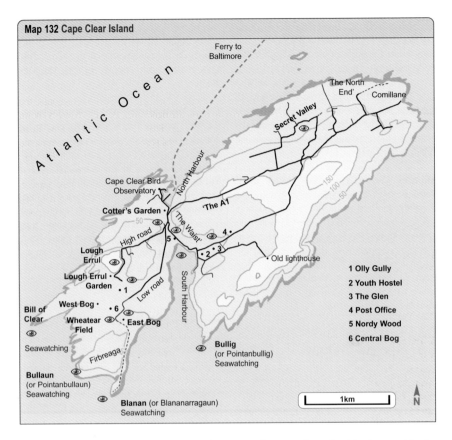

Map 132 Cape Clear Island

Ferry to
Baltimore

Atlantic Ocean

'The North
End'

Comillane

Secret Valley

North Harbour

Cape Clear Bird
Observatory

'The A1'

Cotter's Garden

'The Waist'

High road

4

5

50

Lough
Errul

2 · 3

Old lighthouse

Lough Errul
Garden

1

Low road

South Harbour

1 Olly Gully

2 Youth Hostel

3 The Glen

4 Post Office

5 Nordy Wood

6 Central Bog

West Bog

6

Bill of
Clear

Wheatear
Field

East Bog

Seawatching

Firbreaga

Bullig
(or Pointanbullig)
Seawatching

Bullaun
(or Pointanbullaun)
Seawatching

1km

N

Blanan (or Blananarragaun)
Seawatching

uphill and follow the line of the cliff around to the point where Blanan is visible on the left. Seawatching from close to the 'beehive huts' provides good but distant views and can often give an indication of seabird movements.

From the East Bog, continue on the rough track that runs left and continue through the gate. At the point where the track ends, go right for over 500m to the open area. This area, **The Wheatear Field**, is especially good for pipits, larks and buntings as well as species such as Dotterel. As the name suggests, it is also a favoured area for Wheatears. The Wheatear Field sweeps downhill towards the West Bog.

The **Central Bog** has been considerably reduced in recent years but the drainage channel and the hedges above Central Bog are a magnet for migrants. From the point where the Low Road meets the East Bog and runs into a grassy track, continue to where the track swings left. At this

point there is a stile on the right. Go over this stile and follow the track along the drainage ditch, where the slope on the opposite side can hold migrants. A track runs over the drainage ditch and continues uphill.

For the **West Bog**, continue straight from this point to where you meet the bottom of the Wheatear Field. There are several easy access points over the dividing wall but please replace any stones knocked when crossing. A track runs around the whole of the West Bog and the overgrown slope on the N side is worth checking thoroughly for migrants, as is the small channel on the W side. The walls on the S side seem to be a favoured location for Wryneck each autumn.

To get to the **Bill of Clear**, continue W from the West Bog to the furthest point, which offers some good seawatching possibilities in SW or S winds. The grassy slopes around the Bill are also good for pipits and buntings.

The **'Olly' Gully** is named after an Olivaceous Warbler that was found here, which subsequently turned out to be Ireland's first Syke's Warbler! It is an area of small, stunted conifers and hedgerows that runs uphill from the eastern end of the West Bog. The area that runs up from the bog is worth spending time on, checking the trees, hedges and the grass fields for migrants. Olly Gully can also be checked from the path that runs up from the drainage ditch in Central Bog.

Michael Vincent's and the **Lough Errul Garden** are two gardens close together above the West Bog and next to Lough Errul. By following the track from Central Bog, above Olly Gully, you come to Michael Vincent's. If you have followed the track up from West Bog, you go past the Lough Errul garden. This can also be watched from the road. Both gardens attract migrants which have been funnelled up Olly Gully from West Bog.

Lough Errul is a small lake with a grassy shore, ideal for larks, wagtails and pipits. At the far end of the SW side of the lake is an area of trees on the slope above. This area can be productive for migrants and runs over the hill to the slope above West Bog. At the far end of the lake, the marshy area close to the small wall can hold some waders in autumn, while the lake itself can hold ducks and gulls. Ireland's first Redhead was found here. From the Lough Errul garden, follow the road along the lake and continue right and uphill on the **High Road**. The fields and gardens on the right provide good cover for migrants. This road continues to meet the junction of the Low Road.

The Waist & 'Nordy Wood' From the top of the hill at Cotter's Garden, continue straight and follow the road down past the pub on the right. Just past the first house on the left is an open area that sweeps uphill. This is **The Waist,** and from the small stone wall on either side of the road, the area can be scanned for migrants. On the right is a small plantation of trees known by birders as '**The Nordy Wood'**. The area can be viewed from the road or from the patio area beside the pub. Just past the Waist is a small track on the right which runs down to the stone beach of the South Harbour. The gully that runs along this track and opposite the tennis courts provides excellent cover for migrants. A track also runs up along the side of the Waist and onto the hill above. This track continues over the hill and runs to the church on the eastern side of the island. This track is particularly favoured by Ring Ouzel in autumn.

For the **Youth Hostel**, from the Waist, continue downhill towards the South Harbour. At the bottom of the hill is the priest's house on the left. Just past this house, the road goes left. Follow left and the garden on the immediate right is the **Youth Hostel Garden**. It is worth watching this garden from the road or, from the priest's house, continue straight past the Youth Hostel and follow the road left and uphill onto the **Lighthouse Road** and view from there. From here, follow the road uphill and check the various gardens on the right. This road continues for over 1km and eventually brings you to the old lighthouse.

For **Pointanbullig (or Bullig)**, as you go uphill on the Lighthouse Road, you pass a small hall and, immediately before the first house on the right is a track to the right. Follow this track up and just opposite the next house is a path on the right signposted for hikers. Take this path and follow it out to the end. The best seawatching is from the lowest point of Bullig.

For the **Post Office**, from the priest's house, go left and continue uphill past the school. Continue on for less than 1km to the track that runs from the road to the Post Office, which is slightly elevated. The fields on both sides of the road to the Post Office are worth checking for migrants, while the garden and hedgerows around the Post Office itself are particularly good for migrants. The garden can be viewed from an area below and to the E of the Post Office. The hedgerows of the fields surrounding the area are also worth checking for migrants.

50m past the Post Office turn, there is a small stile on the left. This is a 'mass track' and leads to the church on the far side of the island. The hedges and fields along this track can also hold migrants in autumn.

The 'North End' is reached by walking uphill from the Post Office for 1.2km and, at the crossroads, going right. This road continues NW for over 1km, and there are several gardens and fields along this road which can hold migrants in autumn. One of the best areas can be found by taking the last right turn, approximately 1km from the crossroads. Follow this road to the gardens at the end.

The Alder Wood/Mary Timsey's & The Secret Valley. From the Post Office road, at the crossroads, continue straight and downhill. 600m down this road on the right was an area of alder trees that gave this location its name. The hedgerows and the remaining trees are always worth a look, as are the garden and trees close to the house. Just as the road swings left, go right over the stile, and the trees in front of the house can be viewed from several locations.

Alternatively, continue along the road for over 600m to where it swings sharply left and uphill. The area to the right is known as the **Secret Valley**. The hedges and gullies around this area can hold skulking migrants in autumn, but developments have made the area less attractive for birds in recent years. The road continues uphill and meets the **A1**, close to the church and Heritage Centre. To go to the North Harbour, go right and follow the road downhill. Again, fields on either side of the A1, from the church to the harbour, can hold migrants.

Species

All year Fulmar, Cormorant, Shag, Peregrine, Black Guillemot, Chough.

May, September and October are the peak times for migration, with August and September the best months for seawatching.

Autumn & spring Hen Harrier (O autumn), Merlin, Buzzard (R), Golden Plover (O autumn), Little Stint (R autumn), Curlew Sandpiper (R autumn), Ruff (R autumn), Jack Snipe (R autumn), Snipe, Whimbrel (autumn & spring), Spotted Redshank (R autumn), Green Sandpiper (R autumn), Wood Sandpiper (R autumn), Dotterel (R), Grey Phalarope (O autumn), Mediterranean Gull (R autumn), Glaucous Gull (R autumn), Short-eared Owl (O autumn), Turtle Dove (R spring, O autumn), Wryneck (R autumn), Tree Pipit (R autumn), Yellow Wagtail (R autumn), Black Redstart (autumn, R spring), Redstart (R),

Whinchat (O autumn), Ring Ouzel (O autumn), Icterine Warbler (R autumn), Melodious Warbler (R autumn), Garden Warbler (R spring, O autumn), Blackcap (R spring, O autumn), Whitethroat (autumn), Subalpine Warbler (R autumn), Barred Warbler (R autumn), Lesser Whitethroat (O autumn), Yellow-browed Warbler (O autumn), Wood Warbler (R), Reed Warbler (O autumn), Firecrest (O autumn), Red-breasted Flycatcher (R autumn), Spotted Flycatcher, Pied Flycatcher (O autumn), Golden Oriole (R spring), Red-backed Shrike (R autumn), Brambling (O autumn), Common Rosefinch (R autumn), Siskin (O autumn), Redpoll (O autumn) Lapland Bunting (R autumn), Snow Bunting (O autumn), Ortolan Bunting (R autumn).

Winter The island is seldom visited by birdwatchers in winter, though several interesting species have been seen: Mediterranean Gull (R), Glaucous Gull (R), Little Auk (O), Chiffchaff (O), Firecrest (R), Siskin.

Summer Common Sandpiper, gulls, Sedge Warbler, Wheatear.

Seawatching, autumn Cape Clear is famed for large movements of seabirds in autumn. Many tens of thousands of birds pass the S tip of the island during the largest movements, usually in August and September during strong SW to S winds with rain. In spring and summer there is less variety, with many shearwater and petrel species absent, but there are often huge movements of birds such as Gannet and Manx Shearwater, particularly in the evenings when tens of thousands return to their breeding grounds on offshore islands to the W of Cape Clear.

Red-throated Diver (O), Great Northern Diver (O), Fulmar, 'Blue' Fulmar (O late autumn), Cory's Shearwater (O mainly Sept), Great Shearwater (O mainly Sept), Sooty Shearwater (occasionally 100s), Manx Shearwater (often 1000s), Balearic Shearwater (small numbers), Wilson's Petrel (R Aug & early Sept), Storm Petrel, Leach's Petrel (R), Gannet (often 1000s), Cormorant, Shag, Grey Phalarope (O), Pomarine Skua, Arctic Skua, Long-tailed Skua (R), Great Skua, Little Gull (R), Sabine's Gull (O Sept), Sandwich Tern (O), Common Tern (O), Arctic Tern, Black Tern (O), Guillemot (often 100s),

Razorbill (often 100s), Black Guillemot (small numbers), Little Auk (R Oct onward), Puffin (small numbers).

Rarer seabird records include Black-browed Albatross, Magnificent Frigatebird, Fea's/Zino's Petrel, Little Shearwater, Bulwer's Petrel, White-winged Black Tern. See also SEAWATCHING, p.356.

Rarities Garganey, Blue-winged Teal, Redhead, Velvet Scoter, White-billed Diver, Quail, Little Bittern, Great White Egret, Purple Heron, Honey Buzzard, Red Kite, Marsh Harrier, Montagu's Harrier, Goshawk, Rough-legged Buzzard, Osprey, Red-footed Falcon, Hobby, Stone Curlew, Avocet, Killdeer, American Golden Plover, White-rumped Sandpiper, Pectoral Sandpiper, Buff-breasted Sandpiper, Lesser Yellowlegs, Solitary Sandpiper, Spotted Sandpiper, Yellow-billed Cuckoo, Scop's Owl, Nightjar, Little Swift, Alpine Swift, Needle-tailed Swift, Chimney Swift, Bee-eater, Hoopoe, Yellow-bellied Sapsucker, Short-toed Lark, Woodlark, Red-rumped Swallow, Richard's Pipit, Tawny Pipit, Red-throated Pipit, Olive-backed Pipit, Thrush Nightingale, Nightingale, Bluethroat, Siberian Stonechat, Black-eared Wheatear, Siberian Thrush, Swainson's Thrush, Grey-cheeked Thrush, Hermit Thrush, Fan-tailed Warbler, Pallas's Grasshopper Warbler, Aquatic Warbler, Eastern Olivaceous Warbler, Syke's Warbler, Dartford Warbler, Sardinian Warbler, Greenish Warbler, Arctic Warbler, Pallas's Warbler, Radde's Warbler, Dusky Warbler, Western Bonelli's Warbler, Lesser Grey Shrike, Woodchat Shrike, Carrion Crow, Rose-coloured Starling, Red-eyed Vireo, Serin, Twite, Crossbill, Hawfinch, Black and White Warbler, Yellow-rumped Warbler, Blackpoll Warbler, Blue-winged Warbler, American Redstart, Northern Waterthrush, White-throated Sparrow, Rustic Bunting, Little Bunting, Yellow-breasted Bunting, Corn Bunting, Rose-breasted Grosbeak, Indigo Bunting, Bobolink, Baltimore Oriole.

Mizen Head & Lissagriffin

214

Grid ref.
V 73 23

Best time to visit   Best ■   Good ▣   Poor □

J F M A M J J A S O N D

Bantry •

Ballydehob •

• Crookhaven

There are four main sites in this area which are particularly good for migrants in autumn. Mizen Head is also an excellent seawatching location in autumn.

Crookhaven is a small village in the SW of Cork and close to Brow Head. The village and the surrounding area have several excellent locations which attract migrants in autumn. Brow Head is a headland with good cover, also good for migrants in autumn. Lissagriffin Lake is a shallow, brackish lake that attracts waders and ducks in autumn and winter. The area between Lissagriffin and Mizen Head has many gardens and hedgerows which provide excellent cover for migrants in autumn. Mizen Head is Ireland's most south-westerly point and is an excellent location for seawatching in SW winds. The laneways, gardens and the headland itself also attract many migrants in autumn.

Directions Map 132, next page.

Crookhaven & Brow Head From the village of Goleen, follow the R591 for Barleycove and Crookhaven. After approximately 8km, the main road swings left for Crookhaven while a minor road on the right is signposted for Barleycove. Less than 100m before the Barleycove turn is a small road on the right. The hill provides shelter for migrants in E winds and it is worth parking at the bottom of the road, and walking to the top.

From here continue left on the main road to Crookhaven, past White Strand on the left. To visit Brow Head, take the first right turn after White Strand and drive to the end. Park at the top and check the lanes along here for migrants. There is a dense covering of gorse in this area and migrants can be difficult to locate.

To get to Crookhaven, go past the turn for Brow Head and continue on the R591 into the village. Park in the village and check the gardens. It is

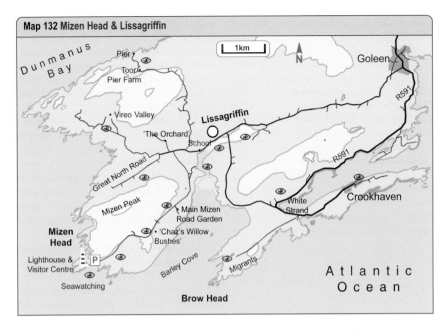

Map 132 Mizen Head & Lissagriffin

worth taking the road up behind the Yacht Centre (Rock Street) which leads to an area around a small pond. Just beyond the pond are tall trees which attract flycatchers and warblers in autumn. When in Crookhaven, it may be worth enquiring at Sullivan's Bar. The owner, Dermot O'Sullivan, may know if other birders are in the area and advise on any recent sightings.

Lissagriffin Lake From the point where the R591 swings left for Crookhaven, take the minor road on the right signposted for Barleycove and continue past the caravan park. Less than 2km along this road is Lissagriffin Lake which is bisected by a causeway. The area can be viewed from the causeway or alternatively, park in the visitors' carpark and walk the S shore. The adjoining sand dunes are good for pipits and wheatears.

Continue N to the end of the causeway and take a left at the T-junction. Continue for approximately 1km to **Lissagriffin School** which has large coniferous trees that can attract migrants.

From Lissagriffin School, follow W and take the next right turn. Follow this narrow road for over 3km, keeping right at the small fork in the road after approximately 1km. Continue to the pier and

park here. From the pier, walk back up the road to check the first garden around the house on the right which is **Toor Pier Farm**. This garden has good cover and attracts migrants every autumn. The bay in front of the pier is also worth scanning for skuas.

For **The Orchard**, from Lissagriffin School, continue past the right turn for Toor Pier and follow the road for 1km, taking the next right turn. Follow this road for 300m and park just at the sharp left bend before the farm. The road continues up through the farm, and the surrounding sycamore trees in this area are especially good for warblers in autumn. Just past the farm is a small orchard on the left which also provides good cover for migrants.

From the Orchard, return to the main road and take a right. Continue on this road and take the right at the small fork. Follow this small road for approximately 1.2km and park on the main road close to where a track goes up into a sheltered valley, known as **Vireo Valley**. This area is excellent for migrants after E winds. Birders are asked to view this area from the road and to please park carefully.

The 'Great North Road' At the small fork in the road where you take a right for Vireo Valley, go left and follow this narrow road out. The road continues for over 1km, but just over half way along this road is a garden on the right. This garden has attracted many migrants in the past, while the walls and ditches anywhere along this road can also be good for migrants.

The **Main Mizen Road Garden** is also reached from the Lissagriffin School. From the school, continue W for 800m and take the left turn signposted for Mizen Head. Follow the road out for approximately 1.4km and, close to the first small left turn, park near the small, grey house. The trees on either side of the road, and surrounding this house are considered to be one of the best sites for migrants in the area.

Continue SW from the Main Mizen Road Garden for approximately 500m to the small stand of willow bushes, known as **Chaz's Willow Bushes**. This is another excellent area for migrants and a small parking space is available close to this stand of trees which allows the area to be viewed from the road. Continue for another 600m and, again, park along the road to view the area above and below the road in the sheltered hollow around the farm sheds. This has proven to be a good area for migrants each autumn. *Access into this area is not permitted* but it can be viewed well from the road.

For **Mizen Head**, continue along the main road to the carpark at the Mizen Vision Interpretive Centre. Seawatching is possible from the watch-point but it is requested that birders check with staff at the Centre to ensure access to this area. The low grassy slope above the carpark can be reached by following the track to **Mizen Peak.** This area is excellent for pipits and larks, and attracted Ireland's first Isabelline Wheatear.

Species
All year Fulmar, Cormorant, Peregrine, Kittiwake, Kingfisher, Chough.

Autumn, winter & spring Wigeon, Teal, Red-breasted Merganser (O), Red-throated Diver, Merlin, Golden Plover, Lapwing, Little Stint (O autumn), Pectoral Sandpiper (R autumn), Curlew Sandpiper (O autumn), Dunlin, Ruff (O autumn), Snipe, Green Sandpiper (R autumn), Wood Sandpiper (R autumn), Common Sandpiper, Grey Phalarope (R autumn), Mediterranean Gull (R autumn & winter), Short-eared Owl (O autumn), Turtle Dove (O autumn), Yellow Wagtail (R autumn), Wheatear (spring & autumn), Black Redstart (O autumn), Redstart (O autumn), Whinchat (O autumn), Ring Ouzel (O autumn), Garden Warbler (O autumn), Blackcap (autumn), Whitethroat (O autumn), Reed Warbler (O autumn), Yellow-browed Warbler (O autumn), Wood Warbler (R autumn), Firecrest (R autumn), Spotted Flycatcher (autumn), Pied Flycatcher (O autumn), Brambling (R autumn), Siskin (O autumn & winter), Redpoll (O autumn), Lapland Bunting (R autumn), Snow Bunting (O autumn).

Rarities American Wigeon, Green-winged Teal, Blue-winged Teal, Quail, Red-necked Grebe, Slavonian Grebe, Black-necked Grebe, Night Heron, Spoonbill, Osprey, Hobby, Gyr Falcon, American Golden Plover, Semipalmated Sandpiper, White-rumped Sandpiper, Baird's Sandpiper, Buff-breasted Sandpiper, Long-billed Dowitcher, Alpine Swift, Wryneck, Isabelline Wheatear, Dartford Warbler, Subalpine Warbler, Booted Warbler, Barred Warbler, Lesser Whitethroat, Greenish Warbler, Radde's Warbler, Western Bonelli's Warbler, Golden Oriole, Red-backed Shrike, Woodchat Shrike, Red-breasted Flycatcher, Carrion Crow, Red-eyed Vireo, Cirl Bunting.

Seawatching, autumn Red-throated Diver (O), Great Northern Diver (O), Fulmar, 'Blue' Fulmar (O late autumn), Cory's Shearwater (O mainly Sept), Great Shearwater (O mainly Sept), Sooty Shearwater, Manx Shearwater (often 1000s), Balearic Shearwater (small numbers), Wilson's Petrel (R Aug & early Sept), Storm Petrel, Leach's Petrel (R), Gannet (often 1000s), Cormorant, Shag, Grey Phalarope (O), Pomarine Skua, Arctic Skua, Long-tailed Skua (R), Great Skua, Little Gull (R), Sabine's Gull (O Sept), Sandwich Tern (O), Common Tern (O), Arctic Tern, Black Tern (O), Guillemot (often 100s), Razorbill (often 100s), Black Guillemot (small numbers), Little Auk (R Oct onward), Puffin (small numbers).

Rare seabird records include Fea's/Zino's Petrel. See also SEAWATCHING, p.356.

Dursey Island & Firkeel

215

Best time to visit   Best ■ Good ■ Poor □

Grid ref.
V 50 41 | J | F | M | A | M | J | J | A | S | O | N | D |

Garinish, Firkeel and Dursey Island lie on the western end of the Beara peninsula, south-west of Castletownbere. Many gardens and hedgerows in the area play host to common and rare migrants in spring and autumn.

Dursey Island, a narrow, hilly island, is approximately 7km long and over 1.5km at its widest, and lies SW of Firkeel and Garinish. The many ditches, hedgerows and gardens on the island, combined with its south-westerly location, make Dursey Island superb for rare migrants in autumn. The best time for a visit is September and October, particularly after a spell of S or SE winds. American passerines have been recorded in most years, usually after prolonged SW gales, the peak time around early October. Access to the island is by cable car. Seawatching from the SW tip of Dursey is possible, and many of the species seen at Cape Clear (Site 213) can be seen here, though usually in smaller numbers and more distantly.

Directions Map 133, next page. All the areas listed below are on the SW tip of the Beara Peninsula.

For Allihies and Ballydonegan, from Castletownbere, take the R572 SW for 14.5km and then continue past the left turn for Dursey Island, going straight and then on to the R575 for 4km. The gardens and hedgerows around the village of

Ballydonegan are worth checking for migrants in autumn, and the village of **Allihies** offers many facilities such as pubs, B&Bs etc.

For **Lehanemore**, from Castletownbere, take the R572 SW for approximately 14.5km, and take the left turn following signs for Dursey Island, and continuing on the R572 W. Approximately 3km along the R572 from this turn is a small shop and community centre on the right side in the village of **Lehanemore (or Loughane More)**. About 500m before the shop is a garden with spruce trees on the seaward side. This garden can hold migrants in autumn.

For **Firkeel**, continue from Lehanemore on the R572 W for approximately 2km, and take the sharp left turn and follow the road for 100m and park carefully just as the road takes a sharp right. From here, you can enter Firkeel Glen by climbing over the wall at this point. Alternatively, continue to the end of the road and park at the small pier and walk up Firkeel Glen from there. Either side of the valley is excellent for migrants in autumn. Ireland's first Northern Parula was found in this valley. In recent years, access to some areas of Firkeel has been restricted. *It is advisable to seek permission from local farmers before crossing land around this valley.*

For **Garinish**, from the turnoff for Firkeel, follow the R572 NW for 500m. Just where the road swings sharp left is an area of brambles and willows below the road that is worth checking for migrants. Please note parking in this area can be difficult so it may be best to park further up the road and walk back to this area. Continue for a further 200m and, at the Y-junction, take the minor road on the right. The garden at the Y-junction (McNally's) can also hold migrants. This road continues for over 1km to Garinish Point, and the hedges and ditches anywhere along this road are good for migrants, especially those on the seaward side. Just past the second strand is a small, muddy lane on the left. The hedges and

Red-backed Shrike

South-west

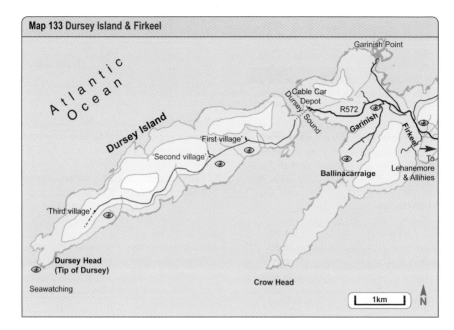

Map 133 Dursey Island & Firkeel

Garinish Point

Atlantic Ocean

Cable Car Depot

R572

Dursey Sound

Garinish

Firkeel

Dursey Island

'First village'

'Second village'

Ballinacarraige

To Lehanemore & Allihies

'Third village'

Dursey Head (Tip of Dursey)

Seawatching

Crow Head

1km

N

fields along this lane are another top migrant location. Seawatching can be good off Garinish Point in strong S to SW winds.

For **Ballinacarraige**, from the Y-junction, continue NW on the R572 for less than 500m, and at the carpark and 'standing stones', take a left and follow this narrow road down towards **Crow Head** for over 1.5km to the end. The garden which lies at the end of the road (Durrell's Garden) overlooks Dursey Sound, has excellent cover and is a superb area for migrants in autumn, and occasionally in spring. Ireland's first White-crowned Sparrow was found in this garden. Alternatively, you can park at the 'standing stones' and walk the entire length of the road. The ditches and fields along the road can be very good for migrants.

From the 'standing stones', continue W on the R572 for almost 2km to the **Cable Car Depot**. Anywhere along the road from the 'standing stones' is good for migrants, while the area around the depot can hold migrants coming off Dursey Island.

Access to **Dursey Island** is by cable car from the mainland. The cable car normally operates from 9.00am to 10.30am, and from 2.30pm to 4.30pm,

occasionally from 7.00pm to 7.30pm. Hours of operation can be extended during the summer but it is always worth checking with the depot for the up-to-date schedules. It is also worth noting that there are no facilities on Dursey (shops, B&Bs etc.), so it is advisable to bring all provisions (food, water etc.) with you when visiting the island.

Dursey has three distinct clusters of houses (villages) and the areas around each are all worth checking for migrants, while the SW tip of Dursey is good for pipits, buntings and for seawatching. It takes on average one hour 30 minutes to walk from the cable car landing point to the tip of Dursey.

From the cable car landing point, follow the road for almost 1.3km to the **first village**. The road goes uphill into the village. At this point, look for a house on the left named 'Zuma'. The garden around this house is the best in this village for migrants, but anywhere along the ditches, or in the laneways and the fields of the village has the capacity to hold migrants.

From the first village, continue on the road for 800m to the **second village**. Just before the second village is a well-vegetated gully to the left

264

which is worth checking. However, both sides above and below the road are good areas for migrants. Again, all the fields, laneways and gardens around the second village can be superb for rare migrants in autumn, but the last garden on the right is considered to be the best area for holding birds.

From here, continue SW to the **third village**. The one garden in this village, being the farthest SW on the island, can often be one of the best gardens for migrants. Again, the fields, hedges and valleys from the second to the third village are worth checking.

The road runs out just after the last village and there is no track from this point. To reach **The Tip of Dursey** (also known as **Dursey Head**), continue SW from the last village for over 1km. The short grass at the tip is good for larks, pipits and buntings, while species such as Buff-breasted Sandpiper have also been seen here. Seawatching is best done just back from the tip, although the small offshore islands can deflect seabirds away, and are thus often somewhat distant. A telescope is recommended.

Fulmar

Species
All year Chough.

Autumn, winter & spring Whooper Swan (R), Barnacle Goose (O autumn), Hen Harrier (R), Merlin, Golden Plover (autumn), Little Stint (R autumn), Curlew Sandpiper (R autumn), Dunlin (R autumn), Ruff (R autumn), Jack Snipe (autumn), Snipe, Whimbrel (O autumn & spring), Green Sandpiper (R autumn), Wood Sandpiper (R autumn), Grey Phalarope (O autumn), Mediterranean Gull (R autumn & winter), Ring-billed Gull (R winter), Iceland Gull (R winter), Glaucous Gull (R winter), Short-eared Owl (O autumn & winter), Black Redstart (O autumn & winter), Redstart (R autumn), Whinchat (O autumn), Ring Ouzel (O autumn), Garden Warbler (O autumn), Blackcap (O spring, regular autumn), Whitethroat (autumn), Reed Warbler (O autumn), Spotted Flycatcher (O autumn), Pied Flycatcher (O autumn), Brambling (O autumn), Siskin (O autumn & winter), Redpoll (O autumn).

Summer Gulls, terns, Wheatear.

Rarities Pink-footed Goose, Garganey, Quail, Black-browed Albatross, Cory's Shearwater, Great Shearwater, Balearic Shearwater, Leach's Petrel, Marsh Harrier, Montagu's Harrier, Goshawk, Osprey, Hobby, Dotterel, White-rumped Sandpiper, Pectoral Sandpiper, Buff-breasted Sandpiper, Upland Sandpiper, Great Snipe, Long-tailed Skua, Sabine's Gull, Black Tern, Little Auk, Turtle Dove, Common Nighthawk, Alpine Swift, Chimney Swift, Bee-eater, Hoopoe, Wryneck, Short-toed Lark, Red-rumped Swallow, Richard's Pipit, Tawny Pipit, Olive-backed Pipit, Tree Pipit, Red-throated Pipit, Pechora Pipit, Yellow Wagtail, Waxwing, Nightingale, Bluethroat, Swainson's Thrush, Paddyfield Warbler, Eastern Olivaceous Warbler, Icterine Warbler, Melodious Warbler, Dartford Warbler, Subalpine Warbler, Barred Warbler, Lesser Whitethroat, Greenish Warbler, Yellow-browed Warbler, Wood Warbler, Firecrest, Red-breasted Flycatcher, Golden Oriole, Red-backed Shrike, Woodchat Shrike, Carrion Crow, Rose-coloured Starling, Red-eyed Vireo, Twite, Arctic Redpoll, Crossbill, Common Rosefinch, Hawfinch, Northern Parula, Blackpoll Warbler, Ovenbird, Scarlet Tanager, White-crowned Sparrow, Lapland Bunting, Snow Bunting, Ortolan Bunting, Rustic Bunting, Little Bunting, Corn Bunting, Rose-breasted Grosbeak.

South-west

Other sites

Curraghlickey Lake (W 23 46) is a narrow, 1km long lake, lying NW of Clonakilty and S of Dunmanway. It attracts ducks in winter.

From Clonakilty, take the R599 to Dunmanway. Approximately 8km before Dunmanway, take the left turn onto the R637. Follow this road SW until the lake is visible on the left side. There are parking and picnic areas along the road and good views of the lake can be had from these.

Water Rail is present all year, but can be difficult to see. From October to March, Whooper Swan, Wigeon, Teal and Lapwing are usually present, along with small numbers of the commoner waders and gulls.

Bantry Bay (V 98 50) is a long, narrow bay running SW from the town of Bantry and contains several large islands, including Whiddy Island and Bear Island. The estuaries on the inner part of Bantry Bay attract ducks, waders and gulls in winter.

From the town of Bantry, follow the N71 N towards Ballylickey. The small estuaries, inlets and open sea along this 5km stretch from Bantry to Ballylickey hold the largest numbers of birds. Cormorant, Shag, Little Egret and Kingfisher are present all year. From early autumn to early spring, typical species include Wigeon, Scaup (O), Red-breasted Merganser, Great Northern Diver, Dunlin, Snipe, Black-tailed Godwit (R), Bar-tailed Godwit (R) and Glaucous Gull (R winter).

The small town of **Glengarrif** (V 92 56) lies on the N side of Bantry Bay, and has the best example of native oak woodland in Cork. Resident species such as Treecreeper and Jay are commonly seen, while the older forestry plantations hold Crossbills during invasion years. Species such as Siskin and Redpoll are quite common, while in summer, common migrants include Blackcap, Willow Warbler and Chiffchaff.

Castletown Bearhaven (V 67 45) is a small fishing village on the R572 on the Beara Peninsula, lying on the N side of Bantry Bay. In winter, the area can attract good numbers of gulls when the fishing fleets are in harbour. Species such as Iceland and Glaucous Gull are annual visitors.

Ballydehob (V 99 34) is an intertidal mudflat which attracts small numbers of waders and gulls in autumn and winter.

From Skibbereen, follow the N71 W, following signs for Ballydehob. At the village, take the R592, following the signs for Schull. Just past the harbour in the village is a small left turn which brings you onto a small road which runs along the W side of the harbour. 400m along this road is a viewing point which gives a good vantage point over the mudflats at low tide.

This area is generally best from Sept to March, when you should see Wigeon, Teal, Red-breasted Merganser, Great Northern Diver, Lapwing and Dunlin, along with other common waders and duck. Less usual sightings include Little Stint (O autumn), Curlew Sandpiper (O autumn) and Kingfisher. Western Sandpiper, Laughing Gull and Hawfinch have been recorded here.

The **Ballyhouras Mountains** (R 60 15), near Doneraile on the Cork/Limerick border, are good for upland woodland species such as Crossbill, Siskin and Redpoll. On the more open areas, Hen Harrier and Merlin occur in summer.

County Kerry

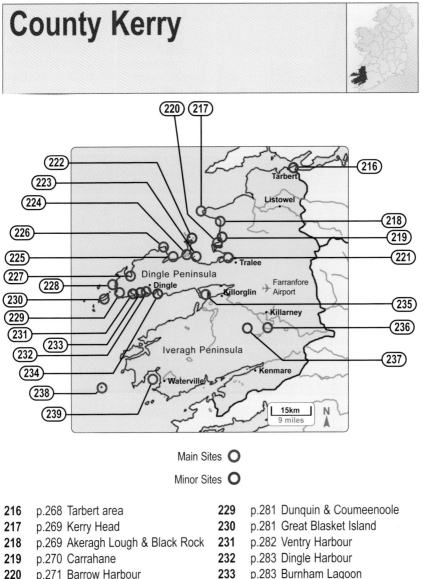

Dingle Peninsula

Tralee

Dingle

Killorglin

Farranfore Airport

Killarney

Iveragh Peninsula

Kenmare

Waterville

Tarbert

Listowel

220 217

222

223

224

226

225

227

228

230

229

231

233

232

234

238

239

216

218

219

221

235

236

237

15km
9 miles

N

Main Sites ○
Minor Sites ○

South-west

Manx Shearwaters passing Cathedral Rocks

Kerry is a large and ornithologically diverse county, with the full range of habitats, from the highest peaks in Ireland to numerous large wetlands, estuaries, headlands and islands. The Killarney National Park also has some of the best upland and woodland habitat in the country,

Tralee Bay, Blennerville, and the outlying estuaries of Barrow Harbour, Carrahane and Akeragh Lough contain one of the largest waterbird communities in the country – an outstanding area for birdwatching, particularly in autumn and winter.

The Dingle Peninsula has a great variety of habitats, with several excellent estuaries, bays,

lakes and seawatching headlands, with the added interest of the busy port of Dingle which attracts many gulls in winter. Unusual migrants also occur in autumn, around Dunquin on the western tip.

The Ivearagh Peninsula also has a series of estuaries and headlands with the potential to produce many interesting birds, particularly in autumn, but it remains one of the least known birdwatching areas in Ireland.

Offshore islands, most notably the Blaskets and the Skelligs, together hold some of the largest and most spectacular seabird colonies in Europe, and a summer visit to these bird-rich areas is always memorable.

216 Tarbert area Grid ref. R 06 47

In winter, estuary birds, mainly Wigeon, Teal and other wildfowl, and good numbers of the regular waders.

See Map 134, right. The mudflats at Tarbert are easily viewed from the road between Tarbert town and the ferry terminal. **Ballylongford Bay** and **Carrig Island** provide other convenient viewpoints. Take the main R551 road W from Tarbert to Ballybunion, turning right 500m after leaving Ballylongford.

The main species are Wigeon (100s), Teal (100s) and Red-breasted Merganser, while there are usually a few Pintail, Shoveler and Scaup. Little Egret is regular in the creeks immediately N of Tarbert and in Ballylongford Bay. Waders include

good numbers of Lapwing, Golden Plover (100s), Grey Plover and Bar-tailed Godwit. Rarities have included Green-winged Teal, Red-necked Grebe, Slavonian Grebe, Ring-billed Gull, Yellow Wagtail and Black Redstart.

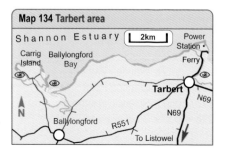

268

Kerry Head

217
Grid ref.
Q 68 30

Best time to visit   Best ■ Good ■ Poor □

J F M A M J J A S O N D

N

•Ballyheige

• Tralee

A good seawatching headland in autumn in NW or W winds.

Directions Driving W from Ballyheigue along the coast road, ignoring all turn-offs, follow the road as it climbs. At the highest point, take a left turn in front of a modern house with a red-roofed barn beside it. Park 1km down this track. Several tracks (not motorable) lead W to the cliffs, where there is an area of rocky ground near an offshore stack. Here it is possible to climb down to about 20m above the sea. *Take great care near cliffs.* Little seawatching has been done outside of autumn but is likely to be similar to Brandon Point (Site 226) at all times of the year.

Species

An onshore wind is most important at any time of year for seawatching, to drive the birds close to the headland. The best conditions are a strong NW wind, with showers or overcast, but any onshore wind can produce many birds. See also SEAWATCHING, p.356.

Autumn, seawatching Red-throated Diver, Great Northern Diver, Fulmar, Sooty Shearwater, Manx Shearwater, Balearic Shearwater (O), Storm Petrel (O), Leach's Petrel (mainly Sept & Oct), Gannet, Shag, Grey Phalarope (O), Pomarine Skua (O), Arctic Skua, Great Skua, Kittiwake, Common Tern (O), Arctic Tern, Black Tern (R), Guillemot, Razorbill, Black Guillemot, Puffin (O).

Rarities Cory's Shearwater, Great Shearwater, Fea's/Zino's Petrel, Sabine's Gull, Long-tailed Skua, Quail, Lapland Bunting.

Other species Peregrine (O all year), Golden Plover (spring & autumn), Purple Sandpiper (spring), Wheatear (spring & summer), Chough (all year), Snow Bunting (R, autumn to spring).

Akeragh Lough & Black Rock

218
Grid ref.
Q 75 26

Best time to visit   Best ■ Good ■ Poor □

J F M A M J J A S O N D

N

•Ballyheigue
• Ardfert
• Tralee

A large reedbed with small freshwater pools and channels, sand dune, saltmarsh and sheltered shoreline with large numbers of waders and gulls and some waterfowl in autumn and winter.

Akeragh Lough was famous in the past for the extraordinary number of American ducks and waders which were attracted to the pools and marsh. Unfortunately the area has been drained, polluted and shot over for the past 20 years to the point where there is hardly any open water and few waterbirds. It is hoped that the opening of the new sewerage treatment plant in Ballyheigue will help the wetland recover. The nearby beach at Black Rock still attracts large numbers of waders and gulls.

Directions Map 135, next page. For **Black Rock**, 10km N of Tralee, take the R551 from Tralee to Ballyheigue and take a left turn, signposted for Black Rock, 4km after passing through Ardfert. A small area for parking is 1km down this road, next to farm buildings (good for finches and Tree Sparrow in winter). Park and cross the small bridge, following the sandy path to the shore. This whole area of beach is worth a thorough search, best at mid to high tide.

South-west

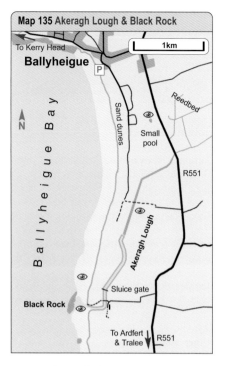

Map 135 Akeragh Lough & Black Rock

To Kerry Head
Ballyheigue
Ballyheigue Bay
N
Sand dunes
Reedbed
Small pool
R551
Akeragh Lough
Sluice gate
Black Rock
To Ardfert & Tralee
R551
1km

where you can park and explore the marsh further. The sand dunes offer good views.

Species

Autumn, winter & spring Greylag Goose (O), Brent Goose, Wigeon, Shoveler (O), Teal, Garganey (R spring), Common Scoter, divers, Little Egret (O), Marsh Harrier (R spring), Hen Harrier (O), Peregrine, Merlin (O), Water Rail, Golden Plover, Lapwing, Little Stint (O autumn), Curlew Sandpiper (O autumn), Dunlin (often 100s), Purple Sandpiper (O), Ruff (O autumn), Jack Snipe (R), Snipe, Bar-tailed Godwit, Black-tailed Godwit (O), Curlew, Spotted Redshank (O), Green Sandpiper (O, mainly July & Aug), Wood Sandpiper (R autumn), Curlew, Whimbrel (May), Mediterranean Gull (O), Ring-billed Gull (O), Sandwich Tern (O winter), Tree Sparrow (O), Brambling (O), Twite (R), Chough.

Summer Cuckoo (O), Sand Martin, Wheatear, Yellow Wagtail (R), Sedge Warbler,

Rarities Black Brant, Garganey, Spoonbill, Gyr Falcon, Marsh Harrier, Spotted Crake, American Golden Plover, Semipalmated Sandpiper, Temminck's Stint, White-rumped Sandpiper, Baird's Sandpiper, Stilt Sandpiper, Pectoral Sandpiper, Lesser Yellowlegs, Franklin's Gull, Glaucous Gull, Iceland Gull, Caspian Tern, Water Pipit, Scandinavian Rock Pipit.

To view what is left of **Akeragh Lough**, continue toward Ballyheigue along the R551. Take the next left, park and explore the channels on foot. Another 300m along the R551, a small pool about 20m left of the road is worth checking. From Ballyheigue, take the road S along the dunes

219 Carrahane Grid ref. Q 74 20

Estuary birds, particularly good in autumn for Dunlin, plovers and other waders, but time your visit to within two hours either side of high tide or you will only see a fraction of the birds.

Map 136, next page. The N side of the estuary is much the best. From Tralee, take the R551 N to Ardfert. At Ardfert, take the left turn opposite the shop and continue for 500m, then take the right, signposted for Casement Fort. This narrow road twists for 3.5km and becomes increasingly rough. It eventually passes the NE side of the estuary. Park near the metal barrier over the rough track (barely motorable) which goes to the left, between the dunes and the mudflat. Walk out onto the large area of flat saltmarsh ahead and to

the left of this track. As the tide comes in, waders are pushed toward the edge of the saltmarsh. There are other access points on the S side of the estuary, but fewer birds.

Flocks of Dunlin, Ringed Plover, Golden Plover, Lapwing and Bar-tailed Godwit are the main species present from September to April, and in autumn, Little Stint and Curlew Sandpiper are sometimes recorded.

Rarities have included American Golden Plover, Dotterel, Semipalmated Sandpiper, White-rumped Sandpiper, Baird's Sandpiper, Pectoral Sandpiper, Red-necked Phalarope and Yellow-legged Gull. A careful search of the flat saltmarsh area in early September may produce Buff-breasted Sandpiper, almost annual at this spot.

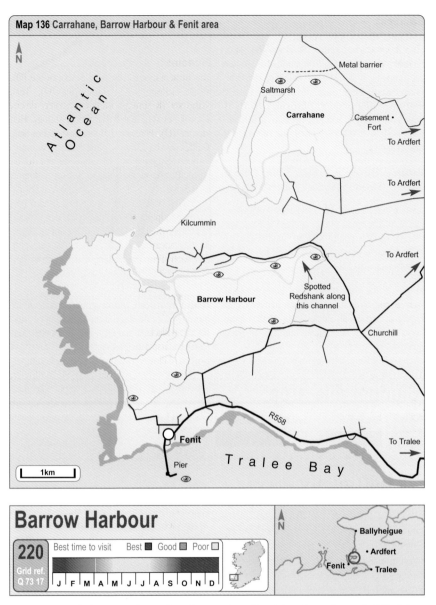

Map 136 Carrahane, Barrow Harbour & Fenit area

Atlantic Ocean

Metal barrier

Saltmarsh

Carrahane

Casement • Fort

To Ardfert

To Ardfert

Kilcummin

To Ardfert

Spotted Redshank along this channel

Barrow Harbour

Churchill

R558

To Tralee

Fenit

Pier

T r a l e e   B a y

1km

Barrow Harbour

220

Grid ref. Q 73 17

Best time to visit   Best ■ Good ■ Poor □

J F M A M J J A S O N D

Ballyheigue

Ardfert

Fenit

Tralee

An estuary with large numbers of waders, Brent Goose and Wigeon and one of the most reliable sites in County Kerry for Spotted Redshank in winter.

Directions Map 136, above. From Tralee, take the main R551 NW to Ardfert, then the R558 to Fenit at the roundabout just outside Tralee. Arriving at Fenit, take a right, signposted for Churchill. After 400m, a left turn brings you to the shore. Search here for waders and wildfowl, best at mid to high tide. Backtrack to the turn and continue to your left and after 1km, another viewpoint over the estuary is again visible on your left. Wigeon and Brent Geese are usually here in considerable numbers, particularly in early winter. Continue for 1km and turn left at the crossroads and after 1km the estuary is again visible to your left. The left turn after the small bridge offers more views of the estuary.

South-west

Species

Autumn, winter and spring Whooper Swan (O), Brent Goose, Pintail, Shoveler (O), Red-breasted Merganser (O), Common Scoter (outer bay), Little Egret (O), Merlin, Golden Plover, Grey Plover, Knot, Little Stint (R autumn), Curlew Sandpiper (R autumn), Bar-tailed Godwit, Whimbrel (May, R winter), Spotted Redshank, gulls, Kingfisher (O, river on E side of estuary), Brambling (O).

Rarities Dark-bellied Brent, Black Brant, American Wigeon, Black Duck, Forster's Tern.

Spotted Redshank can be found, from Nov to Mar, just W of the small bridge at the E end of the estuary, feeding along the main channel (except at high tide). One to three birds are usually present (see Map 136).

In winter, the back roads W of here, between Barrow and Ardfert, are full of Redwing and Fieldfare, occasional Stock Dove, Merlin, large flocks of finches and small numbers of Tree Sparrows.

Spotted Redshank

Fenit Pier is worth checking outside the summer months for divers, Purple Sandpiper and occasional Iceland and Glaucous Gulls. American Herring Gull has been seen here.

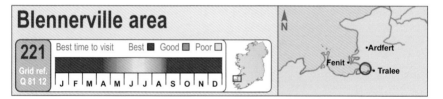

Blennerville area

221

Grid ref.
Q 81 12

Best time to visit   Best ■ Good ■ Poor □

| J | F | M | A | M | J | J | A | S | O | N | D |

Fenit •   •Ardfert
Tralee

An outstanding area for large numbers of waders and wildfowl in winter, with a long history for attracting rare birds, particularly rare North American waders in September. Golden Plover, Dunlin and Lapwing flocks often number over 1000, while Teal, Wigeon, Bar-tailed Godwit, Black-tailed Godwit, Knot, Redshank and Oystercatcher all number in the 100s.

Directions Maps 137 & 137a, next page. The N86 Tralee to Dingle road passes a very productive area, just 1km on the left past the last roundabout (with a fountain in the centre) in Tralee. Here, the saltmarsh and mudflats are easily watched from the roadside, as far as the hide beside the main bridge at Blennerville. More views of the saltmarsh can be had by continuing over the

bridge, turning left at the traffic lights, and walking the road along the S shore, next to the railway track.

The outer bay can be viewed from the rough road which passes behind the windmill at Blennerville. Take a right after about 50m along this rough track for views from an old pier wall. Continue along the grassy path behind the cottage for further views out into the bay. Another spot on the S side of the outer bay is 2km along the N86 to Dingle. Explore the track, signposted Annagh Burial Ground, to the shore.

Good views of the N side of the bay can be had by walking the old canal path, opposite the windmill, and from further W where the canal lock gates reach the sea. The walls projecting into the sea at the lock gates are a high tide roost for many waders and gulls. A further vantage point of the outer bay is at Spa, 4km NW of Tralee, on the R558

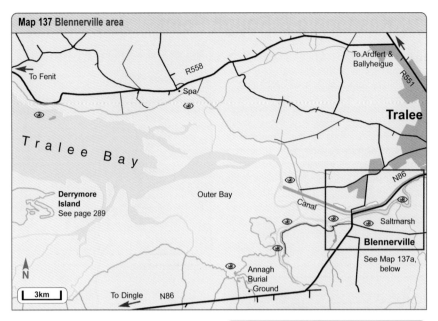

Map 137 Blennerville area

To Fenit

R558

Spa

To Ardfert &
Ballyheigue

R551

Tralee

T r a l e e B a y

Derrymore
Island
See page 289

Outer Bay

Canal

Saltmarsh

N86

Blennerville

See Map 137a,
below

N

3km

To Dingle   N86

Annagh
Burial
Ground

road to Fenit. A telescope is recommended for all these spots. Avoid low tide for searching the outer bay, as most birds will be too distant.

Birds are most numerous from September to February, dropping in spring, but the area is so rich and varied in birds it is worth a visit at any time. The majority of rare American waders are seen in September, with Pectoral Sandpiper, White-rumped Sandpiper and Semipalmated Sandpiper almost annual. Black-tailed Godwits sometimes summer in the area.

Species
Autumn, winter & spring Whooper Swan (O), Brent Goose, Wigeon, Teal, Shoveler, Goldeneye, Scaup, Red-breasted Merganser (outer bay), Great Crested Grebe (outer bay), Red-throated & Great Northern Diver (outer bay), Golden Plover

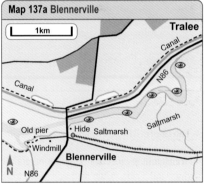

Map 137a Blennerville

1km

Tralee

Canal

N86

Canal

Old pier   Hide Saltmarsh

Saltmarsh

Windmill

Blennerville

N   N86

Lapwing

(1000s), Lapwing (1000s), Knot (100s), Little Stint (O autumn), Curlew Sandpiper (Sept, R winter), Dunlin (1000s), Ruff (O), Bar-tailed Godwit (100s, outer bay), Black-tailed Godwit (100s), Whimbrel, Spotted Redshank (O), Green Sandpiper (O autumn), Common Sandpiper (O winter), Mediterranean Gull (O), Little Gull (O), Ring-billed Gull (R), Twite (R).

Rarities Snow Goose, Dark-bellied Brent Goose, Black Brant, Gyr Falcon, Sociable Plover, Semipalmated Sandpiper, White-rumped Sandpiper, Baird's Sandpiper, Pectoral Sandpiper, Long-billed Dowitcher, Lesser Yellowlegs, Greater Yellowlegs, Terek Sandpiper, Bonaparte's Gull, Laughing Gull, Forster's Tern, Carrion Crow.

The peninsula north of Castlegregory can be good for waders in autumn and winter, and occasionally attracts large numbers of gulls.

See Map 138, this page, and Map 139, next page. Leave Castlegregory to the N, at the crossroads beside Fitzgerald's shop and pub, signposted for Fahamore/Magharees. After 3km, there is a junction. Straight on will take you to Fahamore and then on to Scraggane Pier. A right at the junction will bring you to a sandy beach on your left, and then to Kilshannig village, Rough Point and Kilshannig Point. All are worth searching for waders and gulls, and in the summer, Little, Common and Arctic Terns can be seen feeding offshore.

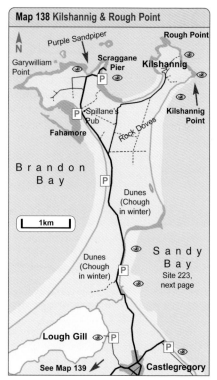

Map 138 Kilshannig & Rough Point

Purple Sandpiper

Fahamore Look opposite Spillane's Pub for waders and gulls. Best at low tide.

Scraggane Pier In winter, gulls occasionally frequent the pier, while Barnacle Geese can sometimes be seen on the Magharee Islands to the N (a telescope is recommended). Just 200m W of the pier, on the main road back to Castlegregory, a small shingle beach is visible below the road. This is a prime spot for Purple Sandpiper in winter, with other waders and gulls often in good numbers.

Kilshannig The beach to the SW of Kilshannig has waders and gulls, though numbers are highly variable. Best at mid to high tide.

Rough Point is reached by driving through Kilshannig village, bearing right, to the end of the road, and walking the grassy track to a small, rocky shoreline. Numbers of waders and gulls are highly variable. Little Tern, Sandwich Tern and Arctic Tern are often seen here in summer.

Kilshannig Point Just before reaching

Kilshannig village is an open expanse of close-cropped grass on your right. Park near the road, and check the beach to your right, to the E. Numbers of gulls and waders are highly variable, though this is a good spot for Chough all year and Wheatear in summer.

Throughout this area are crop fields which often have large flocks of Linnets, and many Goldfinches, Rock Doves and rarely, Twite. Chough are regular throughout in winter, and the gatherings in the sand dunes N of Castlegregory are the largest in NW Europe (100+ regularly recorded). In late May and June, this is also one of the best areas in SW Ireland to see 'winter' waders, with Grey Plover, Knot, Sanderling and Bar-tailed Godwit all regular, particularly from Rough Point to Kilshannig Point. Manx Shearwater and Storm Petrel can often be seen (distantly) offshore on summer evenings. Rarer birds recorded in this area include Eider, American Golden Plover, Broad-billed Sandpiper, Mediterranean Gull, Bonaparte's Gull, Iceland Gull, Glaucous Gull and Black Tern.

Sandy Bay

223

Grid ref.
Q 63 15

Best time to visit   Best ■ Good ▦ Poor □

J	F	M	A	M	J	J	A	S	O	N	D

Castlegregory • ○   • Tralee
• Dingle
N

Shallow coastal bay, very good outside the summer months for divers and wildfowl. A good site for Slavonian Grebe, and the most reliable site in Ireland for Red-necked Grebe.

Directions Map 139, below. At Fitzgerald's shop at the N end of Castlegregory village, take the road E, past the GAA grounds. Continue 300m to the carpark behind the beach. Further views can be had by returning to Castlegregory and turning right, taking the road signposted to Fahamore and Magharees. After 2km, the bay is again visible to your right and there is a small layby on the right offering extensive views over the bay. High tide with little or no swell is best, and afternoon and evening allow for better light conditions. A telescope is essential. 1 to 2 (occasionally 3 to 4) Red-necked Grebes are usually (not always) present from November to early April, and are often in summer plumage by March.

Species
All year Black Guillemot.

Autumn, winter & spring Brent Goose, Scaup, Eider (R), Common Scoter (small numbers), Velvet Scoter (R), Red-breasted Merganser, Black-throated Diver (R), Red-throated Diver, Great Northern Diver, Great Crested Grebe (R), Red-necked Grebe (especially Mar & early Apr), Slavonian Grebe, Curlew Sandpiper (O autumn), gulls, Guillemot, Razorbill.

Summer Little Tern, Arctic Tern, Common Tern, Sandwich Tern.

Rarities Dark-bellied Brent, Black Brant, Goosander, Black-necked Grebe, Grey Phalarope, Mediterranean Gull, American Herring Gull, Glaucous Gull, Ring-billed Gull, Little Auk.

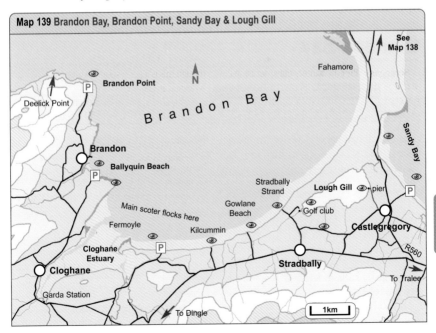

Map 139 Brandon Bay, Brandon Point, Sandy Bay & Lough Gill

South-west

Lough Gill

224
Grid ref.
Q 61 14

Best time to visit   Best ■ Good ■ Poor □

J F M A M J J A S O N D

A large freshwater lake and reedbed, good from late autumn to early spring for Whooper Swan, Scaup, Teal, Wigeon and other wildfowl.

Directions Map 139, previous page. Leaving Castlegregory W, 20m past the Natterjack Pub, take the right turn signposted 'Lough Gill 1km'. The open area and small pier at the end of this road will give views across the E and central part of the lake. Further views of the S side of the lake can be had by continuing W from the Natterjack Pub for 400m. The main road turns sharp left, but take the right, signposted for Stradbally Strand. Fields and reedbeds on the right can be scanned from the road. Continue on, taking a right, over a humpback bridge, and right again to Castlegregory Golf Club, where permission can be sought to view the W end of the lake. The path to the lake starts immediately behind the clubhouse. A telescope is recommended.

Species
All year Mute Swan (100+), Water Rail.

Autumn, winter & spring Whooper Swan, White-fronted Goose (R), Greylag Goose (O), Barnacle Goose (O), Wigeon (100s), Teal, Gadwall, Pintail (O), Shoveler, Pochard (O), Tufted Duck, Scaup (100s), Goldeneye (O), Long-tailed Duck (O), Common Scoter (R), Great Crested Grebe (O), Hen Harrier (O), Lapwing, Golden Plover (O), Dunlin (O), Curlew, Snipe, Green Sandpiper (O autumn), gulls.

Summer Gadwall, Little Grebe (O), Scaup (O May), Great Crested Grebe (O), Cuckoo (O), Sedge Warbler.

Rarities Bewick's Swan, Whistling Swan, Pink-footed Goose, Canada Goose, Snow Goose, Ring-necked Duck, Lesser Scaup, Ruddy Duck, Great Northern Diver, Grey Phalarope, Mediterranean Gull, Ring-billed Gull, Black Tern, Reed Warbler, Corn Bunting, Lapland Bunting.

Brandon Bay

225
Grid ref.
Q 56 14

Best time to visit   Best ■ Good ■ Poor □

J F M A M J J A S O N D

Large coastal bay, good in winter for divers, seabirds and scoter flocks, with over 700 Common Scoter usually present.

Directions Map 139, previous page. There are four access points to the shore, three of which are signposted from the main Castlegregory to Dingle road. They are, from E to W: 1) Stradbally, 2) Gowlane and 3) Kilcummin. For the 4th, Fermoyle, take the turn for Cloghane off the main Castlegregory to Dingle Road. All have parking areas just behind the beach. Stradbally, Gowlane and Fermoyle provide elevated views from nearby sand dunes, but birds are distributed widely

throughout the bay and are often distant, so a telescope is recommended. The scoter flocks favour the W side of the bay, at Fermoyle and Kilcummin, with usually only small numbers E of Kilcummin. High tide and days with little swell are best.

The **Cloghane Estuary** is relatively poor for birds, with only small numbers of waders and gulls. However, Red-breasted Merganser is usually present and a flock of Wigeon occurs from October to January. Little Egret, Yellow-legged Gull and Little Auk have been recorded. In August and early September, the mouth of the estuary is an excellent site for prolonged views of Pomarine (O), Arctic and Great Skuas, which enter the estuary to harass gatherings of Arctic and Sandwich Terns. The river beside the Garda Station at Cloghane is good for seeing Grey Wagtail and Dipper, while **Ballyquin Beach** and the pier at Brandon are worth checking for scoter, divers, gulls and auks.

Species

All year Fulmar, Gannet, Shag, Kittiwake, Razorbill, Guillemot (occasionally 1000+ Guillemot & Razorbill, Apr and autumn).

Autumn, winter & spring Scaup (2-300 on sea at Fermoyle, Oct to Apr), Eider (O), Long-tailed Duck (O), Common Scoter, Velvet Scoter (O), Red-throated Diver, Great Northern Diver, Black Guillemot, Pomarine Skua (O autumn), Arctic Skua (Aug & Sept), Great Skua (May & Aug to Oct), Chough (fields & dunes along shore).

Manx Shearwater gather in the bay in Apr and early May (more rarely in autumn) and can number 1000+.

Summer Common Scoter (small numbers), Red-throated Diver (R July), Great Northern Diver (several usually summer in the area), Manx Shearwater, Sandwich Tern, Arctic Tern (O).

Rarities Surf Scoter, Black-throated Diver, Black-necked Grebe, Little Gull, Yellow-legged Gull, Grey Phalarope, Little Auk, Snow Bunting.

Brandon Point

226 Best time to visit   Best ■ Good ▦ Poor □

Grid ref.
Q 52 17 | J | F | M | A | M | J | J | A | S | O | N | D |

Tralee •
Dingle Peninsula
• Dingle

With suitable winds, one of the finest seawatching locations in Europe. Also a reliable spot for Chough.

Directions Map 139, p.275. Well signposted, 8km N of Cloghane on the Dingle Peninsula. Follow the Cloghane to Brandon Point road to the carpark at the headland. Seawatching is possible from the carpark itself, though it is a little high and many prefer to walk lower down the slope to the E. A series of stone walls provides some shelter from the elements. *Take great care near cliffs.* For seawatching, a telescope is highly recommended.

At any time of year, an onshore wind is most important to drive birds into Brandon Bay and close to Brandon Point as they fly W out to open ocean. The best conditions are a strong NW wind, with showers or overcast, though N, W and even WSW wind can still produce spectacular numbers. Wind strength needs to be at least Force 3 to 4, ideally Force 5 to 7. Stronger winds can still be productive, though viewing conditions are often hampered by wind-shake and spray. The best seawatches often occur in the worst weather, so bring rain gear. See also SEAWATCHING, p.356.

Species

Spring & summer Evening passage of Manx Shearwaters can be dramatic, with hundreds, occasionally thousands, per hour (even in light offshore winds). Also Fulmar, Storm Petrel (O), Sooty Shearwater (O), Gannet, Shag, Kittiwake, Guillemot, Razorbill, Black Guillemot (R), Puffin (small numbers, often distant), skuas (R).

Autumn Red-throated Diver, Great Northern Diver, Fulmar, Cory's Shearwater (R), Great Shearwater (R), Sooty Shearwater, Manx Shearwater, Balearic Shearwater (O), Storm Petrel, Leach's Petrel (mainly Sept & Oct), Gannet (often 100s), Shag, Grey Phalarope (O), Pomarine Skua (O), Arctic Skua, Long-tailed Skua (R), Great Skua, Little Gull (R), Sabine's Gull (O), Kittiwake (often 100s), Common Tern (O), Arctic Tern, Black Tern (R), Guillemot, Razorbill, Black Guillemot (O), Puffin (O), Snow Bunting (R), Lapland Bunting (R).

Winter Red-throated Diver, Great Northern Diver, Fulmar, 'Blue' Fulmar (O), Manx Shearwater (O), Sooty Shearwater (O Nov, otherwise R), Leach's Petrel (O Nov), Gannet, Shag, Glaucous Gull (R), Kittiwake, Great Skua

(R). Guillemot, Razorbill, Black Guillemot (O), Little Auk (R), Puffin (O), Snow Bunting (R).

Other species Barnacle Goose (R), Chough (common all year except mid winter), Wheatear (spring, summer), Peregrine (O all year).

Rarities White-billed Diver, Black-browed Albatross, Fea's/Zino's Petrel, Little Shearwater and Wilson's Petrel. Although not an obvious headland for rare land migrants, Alpine Swift, Scandinavian Rock Pipit, Yellow Wagtail, Black Redstart, Lesser Whitethroat and Waxwing have been recorded. Small numbers of Whimbrel occur on passage, particularly in May.

Deelick Point (V 51 17) offers even better seawatching than Brandon Point – the same birds pass much closer – but requires a 20-minute hike over difficult terrain.

Directions Map 139, p.275. 1km W of the carpark at Brandon Point (Site 226). From the carpark at Brandon Point, go directly uphill, passing the old concrete coastguard hut. Cross the stile and continue to follow the clifftop ridge before passing a small ruined house. Contour along and slightly down for another five minutes before seeing Deelick Point below, a huge triangular black rock jutting into the sea. Descend after passing a deep gully on the right, aiming toward the tip of the black rock. The rock itself is inaccessible, but lower down the grassy slope are several sheltered spots to sit.

Take great care in descending and climbing the steep hillside.

Species
Same species (and conditions) as Brandon Point at all times of year.

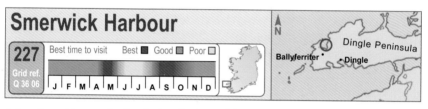

Smerwick Harbour

227

Grid ref.
Q 36 06

Best time to visit   Best ■ Good ▨ Poor □

J F M A M J J A S O N D

A large bay with a small saline lagoon, sandy beaches and large reedbed in the SE corner. Attracts small numbers of waders, gulls and duck throughout the year, but particularly good in autumn and winter, and with a growing reputation for attracting rare birds. The lagoon and reedbed area is also known as Baile an Reannaigh.

Directions Maps 140 & 140a, next page.

For **Baile an Reannaigh**, from Tig Bhric garage, pub and shop, 2km NE of Ballyferriter, take the sharp turn N, signposted for Wine Strand. After 200m take a right turn to the beach. Walk E along the beach, across the metal footbridge and up along the river channel for views of the lagoon and reedbed. The area with the small lagoon is prone to disturbance and is private property so *should not be entered without permission.* Water levels fluctuate with recent rainfall. Further views

of the reedbed can be had from the R559 road to Dingle, 1km E of the shop and garage.

Feohanagh, at the northern end of Smerwick Harbour, and the pier at Ballydavid, have occasional Iceland and Glaucous Gulls outside the summer months. In winter, divers and auks can usually be seen throughout Smerwick Harbour, and small numbers of Common Scoter are sometimes present. Skuas are occasionally seen, particularly in Aug and Sept.

Ferriter's Cove, just W of Smerwick Harbour, holds gulls and waders most of the year, and in autumn can attract rare American waders, some of which move between here and Baile an Reannaigh. In winter, Glaucous, Iceland and Kumlien's Gull have been found. From Ballyferriter, go W on the R559 toward Dunquin and take a right after 750m. Continue for 1.5km until the small beach becomes visible on the left.

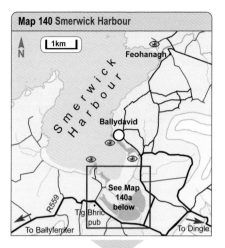

Map 140 Smerwick Harbour

Map 140a Baile an Reannaigh

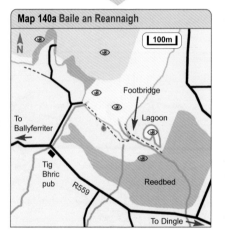

Species

Spring & summer Greylag Goose (R), Wigeon, Gadwall (O), Teal, Little Egret (O), Hen Harrier (O), Water Rail, Golden Plover (O), Lapwing (O), Curlew, Whimbrel (May), gulls, Cuckoo (O), Sand Martin, House Martin (O), Wheatear, Grasshopper Warbler, Sedge Warbler, Chough (O).

Autumn & winter Wigeon, Teal (often 100s), Shoveler (O), Gadwall (O), Tufted Duck (O), Little Egret (O), Hen Harrier, Peregrine (O), Merlin (O), Golden Plover, Lapwing, Little Stint (O autumn), Pectoral Sandpiper (R autumn), Curlew Sandpiper (O autumn), Dunlin, Ruff (O autumn), Snipe, Jack Snipe (R), Black-tailed Godwit (O autumn), Bar-tailed Godwit, Curlew, Spotted Redshank (O), Green Sandpiper (O, mainly July & Aug), Wood Sandpiper (R), gulls.

Other species Kingfisher (O all year). A large roost of several thousand Swallows and martins is present in the reedbed during Aug and early Sept.

Rarities Garganey, Blue-winged Teal, Green-winged Teal, American Wigeon, Ring-necked Duck, American Black Duck, Osprey, Marsh Harrier, American Golden Plover, Semipalmated Sandpiper, Buff-breasted Sandpiper, Lesser Yellowlegs, Wilson's Phalarope, American Black Tern, Yellow Wagtail, Citrine Wagtail, Rose-coloured Starling. Rare gulls (on the beach) have included Mediterranean, Glaucous, Iceland, Ring-billed, Laughing and American Herring Gull.

Clogher Head

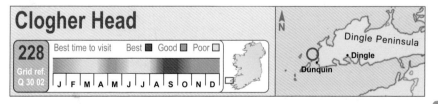

228

Grid ref. Q 30 02

Best time to visit   Best ■ Good ▨ Poor □

| J | F | M | A | M | J | J | A | S | O | N | D |

A good seawatching location in SW, W or NW winds in autumn.

Directions Map 141, next page. 3km NW of Dunquin. The main coast road leaving N from Dunquin to Ballyferriter takes a sharp right after about 2km. Clogher Head is the obvious headland immediately to the W. The scenery along this stretch is memorable. Parking is possible by the side of the road. There is a clear but rough path W along the ridge out to the tip where there are several sheltered spots to sit for seawatching. *Take great care near cliffs.* See SEAWATCHING, p.356.

For seawatching, a telescope is highly recommended, particularly at this site, where the birds tend to pass further out than at Brandon Point

(Site 226). An onshore wind is most important, with best conditions in a strong SW, W or NW wind, with showers or overcast, Wind strength needs to be at least Force 3 to 4, ideally Force 5 to 7. While Brandon Point provides better views and generally greater numbers of birds, Clogher Head can be a good option in a SW wind in autumn. Spring seawatching has produced little to date, though skua passage may occur under certain conditions.

Species

Autumn, seawatching Red-throated Diver, Great Northern Diver, Fulmar, Shag, Manx Shearwater, Sooty Shearwater, Balearic Shearwater (R), Gannet (sometimes 1000s), Leach's Petrel (O), Storm Petrel (R), Grey Phalarope (O), Pomarine Skua (O), Arctic Skua, Great Skua, Kittiwake, Common Tern (O), Arctic Tern, Guillemot, Razorbill, Black Guillemot (O).

Winter Red-throated Diver, Great Northern Diver, Fulmar, Gannet, Shag, Guillemot, Razorbill, Black Guillemot, Puffin (O), Kittiwake.

Spring & summer Evening passage of Manx Shearwaters can be dramatic, with hundreds per hour often seen. Also Fulmar, Sooty Shearwater (R), Gannet, Shag, Kittiwake, auks, skuas (R), Wheatear.

Other species Golden Plover (O autumn), Peregrine (O all year), Chough (all year), Snow Bunting (R autumn).

Rarities Great Shearwater, Long-tailed Skua, Sabine's Gull, Rose-coloured Starling.

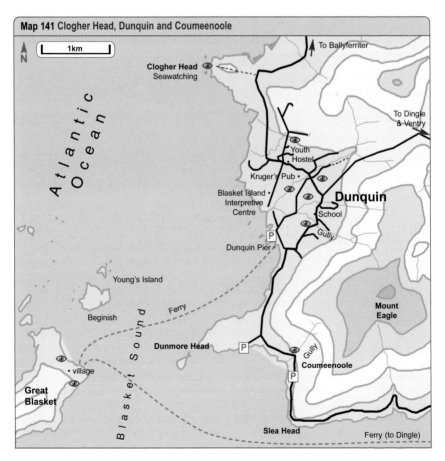

Map 141 Clogher Head, Dunquin and Coumeenoole

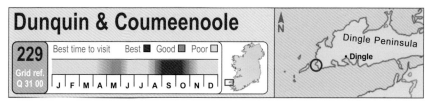

Dunquin & Coumeenoole

	Best time to visit	Best ■ Good ▨ Poor ☐
229		

Grid ref.
Q 31 00

J F M A M J J A S O N D

Dingle Peninsula
•Dingle

Two adjacent sites, good for migrants in autumn and a good area for Chough all year.

Directions Map 141, previous page. Although migrants can turn up anywhere in this area, the most productive spots in Dunquin are: trees and gardens around and to the NE of Kruger's Pub; the garden 50m N of the primary school; the vegetated gully 100m S of the primary school; and the garden with trees 200m S of the gully. All can be viewed from on, or near the main road which passes through Dunquin, though permission should always be sought for access to gardens or fields.

Coumeenoole is about 2km S of Dunquin and 1km N of Slea Head. The shelter offered by a single deep gully, stone walls, brambles and small fields provide cover for migrants in autumn (fewer in spring).

Reasonable seawatching can be had from Dunmore Head and Slea Head nearby, during W or NW winds in autumn, but you would be better advised to go to Clogher Head (Site 228), 3km NW of Dunquin, if conditions are suitable.

Species

All year Fulmar, Shag, Gannet, Peregrine, Dipper (rivers in Dunquin), Chough.

Spring Corncrake (R), Turtle Dove (R), Willow Warbler, Sedge Warbler, Blackcap (O).

Autumn Whooper Swan (R), Merlin (O), Water Rail, Snipe, Curlew, Turtle Dove (R), Whinchat (R), Garden Warbler (O), Reed Warbler (O), Whitethroat (R), Blackcap, Yellow-browed Warbler (R), Wood Warbler (R), Pied Flycatcher (O), Redstart (R), Black Redstart (O), Siskin, Redpoll (O), Brambling (O).

Rarities at Dunquin, Wood Sandpiper, Spotted Sandpiper, Red-backed Shrike, Tree Pipit, Red-throated Pipit, Waxwing, Lesser Whitethroat, Icterine Warbler, Melodious Warbler, Bonelli's Warbler, Golden Oriole, Red-eyed Vireo & Crossbill.

Rare birds seen at Coumeenoole include Red Kite, Glaucous Gull, Iceland Gull, Sabine's Gull, Long-tailed Skua, Nightingale, Brambling, Common Rosefinch & Snow Bunting. Ireland's first record of Cliff Swallow was seen at Dunmore Head in 1995.

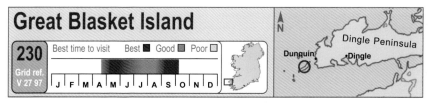

Great Blasket Island

	Best time to visit	Best ■ Good ▨ Poor ☐
230		

Grid ref.
V 27 97

J F M A M J J A S O N D

Dunquin
Dingle Peninsula
•Dingle

Seabirds throughout the summer, occasional migrants in spring and autumn and unforgettable scenery.

Directions Map 141, previous page. 1km S of Dunquin, there is a signpost for Dunquin pier, where boats leave for the island every few hours when the weather permits, from May to early October. Other boats leave several times a day from Dingle Harbour and all information relating

to ferries can be obtained from the Dingle Tourist Office, local hotels and B&Bs or Kruger's Pub in Dunquin. See also www.blasketisland.com. There is a hostel, café and campsite on the island, all operating throughout the summer, and an overnight stay is highly recommended. The other islands in the group are not served by a regular boat service and landings can only be attempted by local arrangement and in the calmest conditions.

South-west

281

Species

Spring & summer Fulmar, Storm Petrel (O well offshore), Sooty Shearwater (O Aug & Sept), Manx Shearwater, Gannet, Shag, Peregrine (O), Guillemot, Razorbill, Black Guillemot, Puffin (O), Great Skua (O May & autumn), Arctic Skua (O May & Sept), Arctic Tern, Common Tern (O), Sandwich Tern (O), Little Tern (O late summer), gulls, Wheatear, Chough.

The main auk colonies are at the far SW end of the island, at least a three-hour walk, round trip, from the pier at the NE end.

Autumn The island attracts migrants, though access can be a problem in early spring and late autumn when migrants are most likely. Most have been found around the ruins and gullies around the main village on the NE of the island.

Rarities Little Egret, Corncrake, Buff-breasted Sandpiper, Roseate Tern, Mediterranean Gull, Alpine Swift, Red-rumped Swallow, Yellow Wagtail, Wryneck, Icterine Warbler, Wood Warbler, Common Rosefinch, Twite (formerly bred), Yellow-rumped Warbler, Rose-breasted Grosbeak.

If staying overnight in spring and summer, there are opportunities to see large numbers of Manx Shearwater gather offshore at last light before returning to their nesting burrows. Although the islands are home to one of the largest Storm Petrel colonies in the world, they are rarely seen from or on Great Blasket, staying well offshore until dark. Try nearby Clogher Head (Site 228) or Brandon Point (Site 226) during onshore winds.

231 Ventry Harbour Grid ref. V 38 99

A large bay attracting small numbers of Brent Geese, divers, gulls and some waders, notably Golden Plover, in autumn and winter.

Map 142, below. The bay is 5km W of Dingle, on the R559 to Slea Head. Views can be had from the slipway below the post office at Ventry village, but the best area for birds is the beach and small lagoon on the S side of the bay. Driving W from Ventry village, after 2km take the turn left signposted for Cuan Pier. This left, or straight on at the same junction, will bring you to the beach. The small lagoon is midway between these two roads, behind the beach.

In winter, small numbers of Brent Goose, Wigeon, divers, Little Egret (O), waders and gulls are usually present. In autumn, Little Stint, Pectoral Sandpiper, Curlew Sandpiper and Green Sandpiper are recorded almost annually. From July to September this is a reliable spot for Water Rail, which can often be seen along the edges of the small pool on the S side. Kingfisher is occasionally seen here.

Rarities have included American Black Duck, Surf Scoter, Black-throated Diver, Red-necked Grebe, Black-necked Grebe, White-rumped Sandpiper, Baird's Sandpiper, Glaucous Gull and Mediterranean Gull.

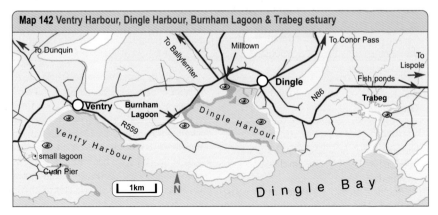

Map 142 Ventry Harbour, Dingle Harbour, Burnham Lagoon & Trabeg estuary

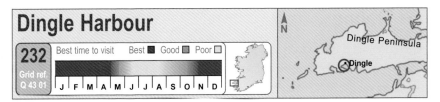

Dingle Harbour

232

Grid ref.
Q 43 01

Best time to visit   Best ■ Good ▦ Poor □

| J | F | M | A | M | J | J | A | S | O | N | D |

Dingle Peninsula

N

Dingle

Red-breasted Merganser

A very good site for gulls and small numbers of Brent Goose, Wigeon and waders throughout winter. Little Egret and Black Guillemot are present all year.

Directions Map 142, previous page. Note that Dingle is signposted locally as 'An Daingean'. The bay, port and marina at Dingle can be scanned from many spots along the waterfront of Dingle town. Viewing is straightforward from the road and bridge. All regular Irish species of gull can be

seen in reasonable numbers, often gathering at Milltown, around the main piers and on the nearby fish factory roof. Throwing bread from the main piers will quickly attract large numbers of gulls and is a useful method of obtaining close views. The E side of the bay can be scanned from the Coastguard boat house near the Dingle Skellig Hotel.

Species
All year Little Egret (Milltown, though scarce Apr to July), Black Guillemot, Barn Owl (R Milltown).

Spring, autumn & winter Brent Goose (small numbers), Wigeon (small numbers), Red-breasted Merganser, Eider (R), Shag, Whimbrel (May, R winter), Curlew, Spotted Redshank (R), Common Sandpiper (O, R winter), Mediterranean Gull (O), Ring-billed Gull (O), Iceland Gull (O), Glaucous Gull (O), Kittiwake (O), Sandwich Tern (spring, R winter), Twite (R winter).

Summer Sandwich Tern (O), occasionally some of the gulls mentioned above.

Rarities Black Brant, King Eider, Laughing Gull, American Herring Gull, Kumlien's Gull, Elegant Tern.

233 Burnham Lagoon   Grid ref. V 41 99

A good site for Little Egret and waders outside the summer months, and woodland birds, especially in May and June.

See Map 142, previous page. Located 3km SW of Dingle town on the R559 to Ventry. Pull off the main road and park on the left just as the road reaches an area of mature woodland on your left. Walk down the short, muddy path through the woodland to the shore. The small tidal lagoon is on your right.

In spring, autumn and winter, typical species present include Red-breasted Merganser, Little

Egret, Whimbrel (May, O in winter), Green Sandpiper (O Aug & Sept), Common Sandpiper (R in winter). Kingfisher (O low tide, perching on posts in the lagoon).

Most of the regular woodland species can be seen here, including Blackcap (O May to Aug), Spotted Flycatcher (May to Aug), Treecreeper (all year) and Long-tailed Tit (all year), although Jay is absent.

Rare species seen here include Eider, Surf Scoter, Spoonbill, Corncrake, White-rumped Sandpiper, Stilt Sandpiper, Mediterranean Gull, Ring-billed Gull and Brambling.

South-west

283

234 Trabeg Grid ref. Q 47 00

An estuary with a good variety of wildfowl, waders and gulls, especially in autumn.

Directions Map 142, p.282. The estuary is best viewed from the SE side, reached by taking the turn signposted for Cinn Aird, by the fish ponds, 6km E of Dingle on the N86 Dingle to Tralee road. Continue over the small bridge (occasional Kingfisher) and continue straight on at the next junction, where the main road turns sharp left, until the estuary becomes visible to your right. This stretch offers good views of most of the estuary. Access is possible from the W end but the road can be very muddy and views of the estuary are more limited.

Species

All year Red-breasted Merganser, Little Egret, Peregrine (O), Water Rail (O), Kingfisher (O).

Spring & summer Common Sandpiper, Cuckoo (O), Sedge Warbler.

Autumn & winter Wigeon, Teal, Golden Plover, Grey Plover (O), Cormorant, Lapwing, Knot (O), Dunlin, Ruff (R), Snipe, Jack Snipe (O), Black-tailed Godwit (mainly autumn), Bar-tailed Godwit, Whimbrel (May, R in winter), Curlew, Green Sandpiper (O, July to Sept), gulls.

Rarities Pink-footed Goose, Spoonbill, Osprey, Semipalmated Sandpiper, Little Stint, White-rumped Sandpiper, Pectoral Sandpiper, Curlew Sandpiper, Spotted Redshank, Lesser Yellowlegs, Ring-billed Gull, Yellow-legged Gull.

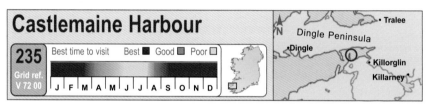

Castlemaine Harbour

235

Grid ref. V 72 00

Best time to visit   Best ■ Good ■ Poor □

J F M A M J J A S O N D

Dingle Peninsula

• Tralee

•Dingle

• Killorglin

Killarney •

A huge estuary with large numbers of wildfowl, especially Brent Geese and Wigeon, and high numbers of waders and gulls, in autumn and winter.

This whole area hosts up to 700 Brent Geese, some 3000+ Wigeon and 100+ Pintail each autumn and winter, along with many other wildfowl and waders, but the birds are often frustratingly distant. The key to getting the best out of the area is to time your visit to estuarine sites in Castlemaine Harbour to about two hours before high tide, especially Inch and Rossbehy. On the seaward side, tide is less important, and there can be hundreds of Common Scoter, and many divers and other sea duck present.

Directions Map 143, next page. Best areas are:

Inch On the seaward side, scoter, divers, waders gulls and auks can be seen, and Fulmar and Chough nest on the cliffs at the N end of the beach. The marsh and mudflats SE of Inch are the main area, on the N side of the estuary for Wigeon, Brent, Pintail and a host of waders. A major winter high tide roost of wildfowl and waders stretches for a full 4km along the E side of the dunes – an impressive sight. Views can be had opposite the small garage, or opposite the church. Another viewpoint is reached by taking the narrow, rough road uphill, behind a flat-topped modern house E of Inch. A telescope is recommended.

Caherfearlane Marsh is reached by leaving Castlemaine W on the R561 to Inch and taking the left after 5km, signposted for Old Keel Burial Ground. Continue for 2km and park at the pier. Walk to the right along the sea wall. Many wildfowl, waders and gulls can be seen here.

Cromane is a small fishing port which attracts Little Egret, Iceland Gull (O), divers, Red-breasted Merganser Long-tailed Duck (O) and Snow Bunting (R). Leaving Killorglin W on the N70, take a right after 2km. Continue for 5km and go right again at the church. Continue to the end of the road.

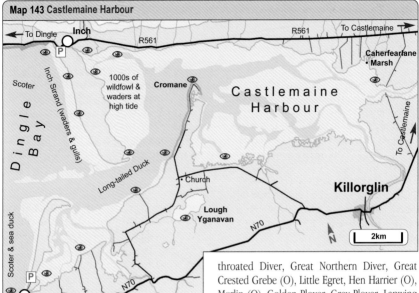

Map 143 Castlemaine Harbour

(Map labels: To Dingle, Inch, R561, To Castlemaine, Caherfearlane Marsh, Scoter, Inch Strand (waders & gulls), 1000s of wildfowl & waders at high tide, Cromane, Castlemaine Harbour, Dingle Bay, Long-tailed Duck, Church, Killorglin, Lough Yganavan, To Castlemaine, N70, Scoter & sea duck, 2km, Rossbehy, Glenbeigh, N70)

Lough Yganavan Tufted Duck.

Rossbehy On the seaward side, scoter, divers and seaduck. On the E side, Little Egret (O), some wildfowl and waders.

Species
All year Red-breasted Merganser, Little Egret (O), Peregrine (O), Water Rail (O), Kingfisher (O), Chough (dunes, nests on cliffs W of Inch).

Autumn & winter Whooper Swan (O), Brent Goose (100s), Wigeon (1000s), Teal (100s), Pintail (often 100+), Shoveler (O), Pochard (R), Tufted Duck (O), Scaup, Eider (O), Long-tailed Duck, Common Scoter, Goldeneye, Water Rail (R), Red-throated Diver, Great Northern Diver, Great Crested Grebe (O), Little Egret, Hen Harrier (O), Merlin (O), Golden Plover, Grey Plover, Lapwing (1000+), Knot, Curlew Sandpiper (O autumn), Dunlin, Jack Snipe (O), Ruff (O), Snipe, Black-tailed Godwit, Bar-tailed Godwit, Whimbrel (May, R in winter), Curlew, Green Sandpiper (O, July to Sept) gulls, auks, Kingfisher (R), Lapland Bunting (R), Snow Bunting (R).

Summer Fulmar, Cuckoo (O, dunes), Wheatear, Sedge Warbler.

Rarities Barnacle Goose, Dark-bellied Brent, American Wigeon, Ring-necked Duck, Surf Scoter, Velvet Scoter, Black-throated Diver, Spoonbill, Goshawk, Crane, Little Stint, White-rumped Sandpiper, Baird's Sandpiper, Pectoral Sandpiper, Buff-breasted Sandpiper, Spotted Redshank, Bonaparte's Gull, Ring-billed Gull, Yellow Wagtail.

Killarney National Park

236
Grid ref. V 90 85

| Best time to visit | Best ■ Good ■ Poor □ |

J F M A M J J A S O N D

(Map labels: Killorglin, Killarney, Kenmare)

South-west

Extensive broadleaved and mixed forest set among beautiful lakes and mountains. Particularly good in spring, with a wide range of typical Irish woodland and upland species, and wildfowl in winter.

Directions Map 144, next page. Located just to the S and W of Killarney, around Lough Leane.

The park covers some 10,000 ha, and several days would be needed to explore it fully. The National Park Visitor Centre at Muckross House provides

285

Map 144 Killarney National Park

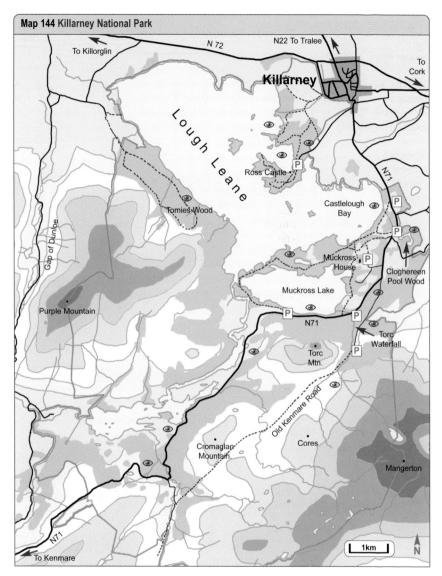

information on the wildlife and large-scale maps of the park. Particularly good areas for birds are as follows:

Ross Castle Best area for duck in winter and woodland species, including regular Treecreeper and Long-tailed Tit. For duck, scan from the castle. Another good area can be seen by taking the path to the right when facing the castle from the carpark. This leads through woodland, and after 1km, take a left, eventually to views of the lake to your left.

Castlelough Bay Duck in winter.

Muckross Lake Duck in winter.

Muckross House Good general woodland birds in the vicinity of the house.

Tomies Wood Good general woodland birds and spectacular scenery.

The mature woodland from **Cloghereen Pool Wood** to **Torc Waterfall** is the best area to check in spring and early summer for Redstart (R), Blackcap, Garden Warbler (R), Wood Warbler (R), Spotted Flycatcher and Jay.

The **Old Kenmare Road** has good woodland birds at its N end, and around **Cores** is very good for Cuckoo in May and June. Red Grouse can be found on the heathery plateaus above Cores.

Species

All year Little Grebe, Great Crested Grebe, Hen Harrier (R), Merlin (R), Peregrine, Red Grouse (O, above Cores, or Mangerton), Water Rail (R), Snipe (marshy areas), Woodcock, Long-eared Owl (R), Kingfisher (R), Grey Wagtail (rivers), Dipper (rivers), Long-tailed Tit, Treecreeper, Jay, Siskin (conifers), Redpoll (conifers), Crossbill (R, conifers)

Spring & summer Teal, Red-breasted Merganser (O), Golden Plover (Mangerton, spring), Redstart (R), Wheater (open, rocky areas), Ring Ouzel (R,

high peaks), Grasshopper Warbler (marshy scrub), Garden Warbler (R), Blackcap (O), Wood Warbler (R), Chiffchaff, Willow Warbler, Spotted Flycatcher.

Winter Whooper Swan (O), White-fronted Goose (O), Wigeon, Teal, Shoveler (O), Pochard, Tufted Duck, Goldeneye, Snipe, Woodcock (O, flooded woodland edges), Curlew (O), Brambling (R), Snow Bunting (O, Mangerton).

Rarities Garganey, Ring-necked Duck, Long-tailed Duck, Smew, Red-breasted Merganser, Goosander, Great Northern Diver, Gannet, Slavonian Grebe, Osprey, Nightjar, Icterine Warbler.

Unusual waders are occasionally seen on the shores of Lough Leane, including Little Stint, Pectoral Sandpiper, Ruff, Black-tailed Godwit and Green Sandpiper, with most of these recorded in autumn.

237 Magillicuddy Reeks Grid ref. V 80 85

The higest peaks in Ireland and one of only a handful of areas in Ireland where it is possible to see Ring Ouzel in summer.

Ring Ouzels prefer crags and scree slopes, generally over 750m. The species has been in decline in Ireland and many former haunts on lower slopes and peaks no longer hold breeding birds, though several pairs are still present on the highest Reeks. The best areas are the ridges between Beenkeeragh, Caher and Carrauntoohil, and the long, high ridge running for 5km to the E of Carrauntoohil. Birds are present on their breeding grounds from late April to September, though singing stops around the second half of June, making detection more difficult.

The Reeks also have a few pairs of inland nesting Chough. Snow Buntings are probably frequent in winter on high ridges, from November to late March, though weather often makes access difficult. *Take all suitable precautions when attempting to climb mountains, as weather conditions can change rapidly.*

Ring Ouzel

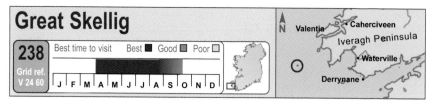

Great Skellig

238

Grid ref.
V 24 60

Best time to visit   Best ■ Good ■ Poor □

J F M A M J J A S O N D

A remote, rocky island with ancient monastic buildings and large numbers of seabirds, all of which make for a truly spectacular experience, not to be missed.

Directions Boats leave from Knightstown (Valentia), Portmagee, Caherciveen and Derrynane, weather permitting, usually between April and September, with only occasional sailings in good weather the rest of the year. Times and prices can be found easily throughout the region in guesthouses, hotels and tourist information centres. You are advised to book at least a day in advance if possible, as there is a daily limit to the number of people permitted to land. It is not unusual to have to wait several days for suffi-

ciently calm weather. Nevertheless, persevere – it's worth it!

Species
The boat passes Little Skellig island (landing is not permitted), home to some 30,000 pairs of Gannets. On Great Skellig, Fulmar, Shag, Kittiwake, Guillemot, Razorbill and Puffin are all easily found, and there is usually a pair or two of Chough present.

Manx Shearwater and Storm Petrel nest throughout the island and are often seen from the boat on the journey out. They can also be heard during the day, deep within rock crevices and some of the monastery walls.

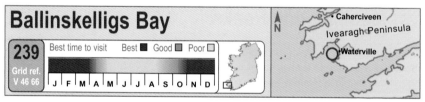

Ballinskelligs Bay

239

Grid ref.
V 46 66

Best time to visit   Best ■ Good ■ Poor □

J F M A M J J A S O N D

A large, shallow bay, good in winter for scoter, seaduck, divers and grebes.

Directions Map 145, right. This large bay is easily searched from a number of viewpoints, but most of the scoter and other sea duck are usually concentrated between Waterville town and the abandoned hotel 4km to the NW. Divers are distributed throughout the bay, often a hundred or more, and favour the E side of the bay. If time allows, a thorough search of the entire bay is worthwhile. As many birds will be far out in the bay, a telescope is recommended.

Lough Currane to the E of Waterville is not a particularly attractive lake for birds, but the **Inny estuary** to the NW of Waterville has some waders and duck, and might well produce American waders in autumn.

Map 145 Ballinskelligs Bay

288

Species

Autumn, winter & spring Whooper Swan (O), Brent Goose, Wigeon, Teal, Scaup (small numbers), Eider (a few each winter), Long-tailed Duck (O), Common Scoter, Surf Scoter (1 or 2, most winters), Velvet Scoter (O), Red-breasted Merganser, Red-throatcd Diver (up to 100), Great Northern Diver (often 50+), Black-throated Diver (R), Great Crested Grebe (O), Red-necked Grebe (O), Slavonian Grebe (a few each winter), Golden Plover, Grey Plover (O), Lapwing, Knot (O), Dunlin, Snipe, Curlew, gulls, Guillemot, Razorbill, Black Guillemot, Little Auk (R).

Other sites

Ballybunion (Q 86 41) has an enjoyable cliff walk just N of the town. Black Guillemot, Chough and other auks and seabirds can be seen, and there is a spectacular cliff roost of Starlings each winter, near the start of the walk, an hour before dark.

Cashen Estuary (Q 87 38) 3km S of Ballybunion. Whooper Swan is regular in winter (occasionally 100+), usually found SE of the main R551 road and bridge. In the estuary, to the W of the R551 road and bridge, there are also large flocks of Golden Plover and Lapwing. Other species (on the estuary) include Great Northern Diver, Wigeon, Teal, Red-breasted Merganser, Grey Plover, Knot, Dunlin, Bar-tailed Godwit and Curlew, with occasional Merlin and Peregrine. The estuary usually has one or two Little Egrets and has the potential to turn up a few rarer species.

Derrymore Island (actually a peninsula) (Q 75 13). A large, open area of shingle and saltmarsh, attracting most of the regular species listed for Blennerville (Site 221). In addition, Twite, Snow Bunting, Short-eared Owl and Merlin are possibilities in autumn and winter. Osprey, Pectoral Sandpiper, Yellow Wagtail and Citrine Wagtail have been recorded. About 8km from Tralee on the N86 to Dingle, the road goes over a small bridge. Just 10m further on, take the right turn, follow to the end of this road and walk out along the shore to the right.

The **Magharee Islands** (Q 62 21), N of Castlegregory, have breeding Shag, Little Tern, Common Tern, Arctic Tern, Common Gull, Chough and some waders in summer and occasional Roseate Tern. The main island, Illauntannig, has a single house which can be rented. E-mail jfcourtney@eircom.net or phone 066 9152420 for details. The islands may be reached by boat from Scraggane Pier (see Map 138). Enquire locally.

The estuary N and NE of **Caherciveen** (V 47 79) has small numbers of waders, waterfowl and gulls, and regular Little Egret. Can be scanned from a number of points along the N70 road and is best in autumn and winter.

Bolus Head (V 38 61) 15km W of Waterville and **Valentia island** (V 34 74) at the tip of the Iveragh Peninsula are underwatched and have potential in spring and autumn for rare migrants. White Stork, Bee-eater, Yellow-browed Warbler and Subalpine Warbler have all been recorded.

Derrynane (V 53 59) is a small, remote estuary 9km S of Waterville and 2km W of Caherdaniel which holds only small numbers of birds, but which has potential in autumn for rare American wildfowl and waders. Easily viewed from the coast road around Derrynane village. Common and Arctic Terns nest nearby and are often seen offshore in summer and early autumn.

Kenmare Bay (V 74 63) immediately SW of Kenmare town, is a large but relatively bird-poor estuary, though in winter, small numbers of Wigeon, Teal and occasional Shoveler can be found, while Little Egret is regular near the town. E of the bridge in Kenmare is a large reedbed area which can be good for wildfowl in winter. Large areas of woodland to the W of the town are worth exploring for typical woodland species, including Woodcock, Treecreeper, Long-tailed Tit and Jay.

Puffin Island (V 34 67), midway between Valentia Island and Bolus Head, is a BirdWatch Ireland Reserve, but landing is not permitted without their permission. The island has many nesting Puffins and it is possible to see them and other seabirds from the mainland, overlooking the channel, 7km S of Portmagee.

South-west

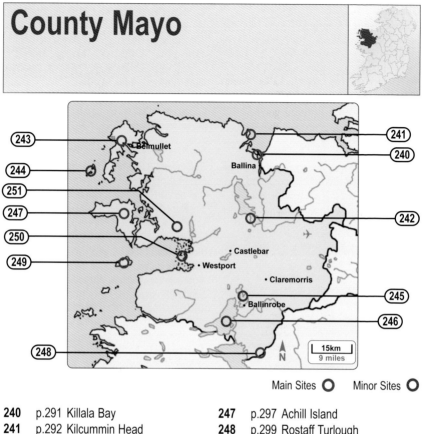

Main Sites ○   Minor Sites ○

County Mayo shares many geographical features with County Galway, low-lying in the east with high mountains on the western coastal fringe, and large numbers of lakes and turloughs. Lough Cullin is the outstanding freshwater lake, with large concentrations of diving duck in winter.

Mayo's coastline is indented, but is much more productive for birds than the relatively bird-poor south-west and west coast of County Galway. The Mullet Peninsula offers perhaps the best variety of habitats and birds, and has been relatively well studied in the past ten years, producing a wide variety of rare species.

Mayo also has three outstanding seawatch headlands: Annagh Head, Erris Head, and one of the best in Europe, Kilcummin. All three excel in autumn, with strong west or north-west winds. Sites on the extreme western fringe, such as the Inishkeas, Achill Island and the Mullet Peninsula, have attracted some very rare birds, especially in autumn, and with few birdwatchers in the area, the potential for new discoveries is great.

Killala Bay

240

Grid ref.
G 24 28

Best time to visit   Best ■ Good ■ Poor □

J F M A M J J A S O N D

A large, sandy estuary with a good mix of wildfowl and waders outside the summer months.

Directions Map 146, below. Most duck and waders frequent the inner bay of the **Moy Estuary**, particularly from August to October. Access to the E side of the inner bay involves walking W from Inishcrone.

Viewing of the upper Moy River is possible from the bridges and wier in Castlebar town centre, Belleek, Tom Ruane Park on the Sligo road, Crockets Town and Rathmoy. Red-breasted Merganser, Common Sandpiper (summer), Kingfisher and Dipper can be found.

The W side of the Inner Bay is easier to approach from several side roads off the main R314 Ballina to Killala road and at Killala itself. 1km N from Killala on the R314, take a right, to Ross Point, where good views can be had of the outer bay (scoter, divers, occasional Long-tailed Duck).

Species
Autumn, winter & spring Whooper Swan (O), Brent Goose, Wigeon, Teal, Long-tailed Duck (O, outer bay), Common Scoter (outer bay), Red-breasted Merganser, Great Northern Diver (outer bay), Great Crested Grebe (R), Little Egret (O), Hen Harrier (O), Merlin (O), Peregrine, Ringed Plover, Knot, Little Stint (R Sept), Curlew Sandpiper (O, autumn), Dunlin, Golden Plover, Grey Plover, Snipe, Lapwing, Bar-tailed Godwit, Black-tailed Godwit (autumn), Spotted Redshank (O, autumn & winter), Purple Sandpiper (rocky shores), gulls, Kingfisher, Dipper, Snow Bunting (R).

Rarities Wood Sandpiper, Laughing Gull, Ring-billed Gull, Iceland Gull, Glaucous Gull, Forster's Tern.

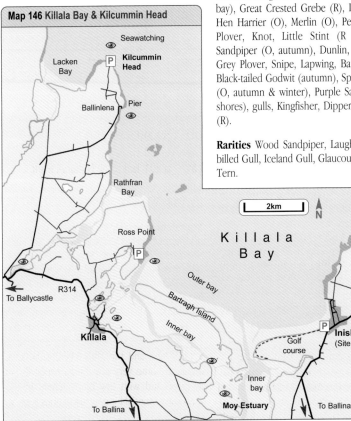

Map 146 Killala Bay & Kilcummin Head

Seawatching

Lacken Bay

Kilcummin Head

Ballinlena

Pier

Rathfran Bay

Ross Point

2km

N

To Sligo

K i l l a l a   B a y

R314
To Ballycastle

Outer bay

Bartragh Island

Inner bay

Killala

R297

Golf course

Inishcrone
(Site 30)

R298

Inner bay

To Ballina

Inner bay

Moy Estuary

To Ballina

West

291

Kilcummin Head

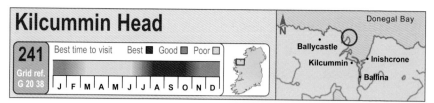

241

**Grid ref.
G 20 38**

Best time to visit   Best ■ Good ▨ Poor ☐

J F M A M J J A S O N D

Donegal Bay

Ballycastle
Kilcummin •   • Inishcrone
• Ballina

One of the best seawatching sites in Europe, best in a NW wind from August to November.

Directions Map 146, previous page. Take the R314 from Ballina to Killala, and continue for 4km beyond Killala. Here the road takes a sharp right across a narrow stone bridge (Dipper, occasional Kingfisher). Just across the river, take the right turn and continue, ignoring turnoffs until a further 4km, taking a right turn at this crossroads. After a further 3km, you will pass the pier and village of Ballinlena. Continue on uphill and take the first right. Continue straight, at a staggered crossroads, through a cluster of houses, and onto a rough track which takes you to a carpark just before the cliff. Seawatch from the carpark, or the clifftop nearby. *Take great care near cliffs.* For seawatching, a telescope is highly recommended.

At any time of year, a strong NW, W or WSW wind is most important to drive the birds into Killala Bay and close to Kilcummin Head as they fly NW out to open ocean. Birds can pass very close, particularly if there is rain or if it is overcast. Spring passage is often poor by comparison, though little systematic seawatching has been done to date.

The best seawatches often occur in the worst weather, so bring rain gear. See also SEAWATCHING, p.356.

Species

Seawatching, spring & summer Manx Shearwater, Fulmar, Storm Petrel (O), Gannet, Shag, Kittiwake, Guillemot, Razorbill, Black Guillemot (O), Puffin (O), skuas (R).

Seawatching, autumn Red-throated Diver, Great Northern Diver, Fulmar, Cory's Shearwater (R), Great Shearwater (R), Sooty Shearwater, Manx Shearwater, Balearic Shearwater (O), Storm Petrel, Leach's Petrel (mainly Sept & Oct), Gannet (often 100s), Shag, Grey Phalarope (O), Pomarine Skua (O), Arctic Skua, Long-tailed Skua (R), Great

Shag

Skua, Little Gull (R), Sabine's Gull (O), Kittiwake often 100s), Common Tern (O), Arctic Tern, Black Tern (R), Guillemot, Razorbill, Black Guillemot, Puffin (O),

Other species in autumn include Snow Bunting (R), Lapland Bunting (R).

Seawatching, winter Red-throated Diver, Great Northern Diver, Fulmar, 'Blue' Fulmar (O), Manx Shearwater (O), Sooty Shearwater (O Nov, otherwise R), Leach's Petrel (O Nov), Gannet, Shag, Kittiwake, Great Skua (R), Guillemot, Razorbill, Black Guillemot, Little Auk (R), Puffin (O).

Rarities Black-browed Albatross, Little Shearwater, Wilson's Petrel.

The pier at Ballinlena, 1km S of Kilcummin Head, is worth checking as skuas and Sabine's Gulls sometimes take shelter here before attempting to round the headland in bad weather.

Loughs Conn & Cullin

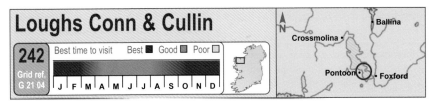

242
Grid ref.
G 21 04

Best time to visit   Best ■ Good ▦ Poor ☐

J F M A M J J A S O N D

A superb site for large numbers of wintering Pochard, Tufted Duck and Coot, with a variety of scarcer freshwater species.

Directions Map 147, below. Although combined the two lakes cover about 50km², the best areas for birds are around the junction of the two lakes near the village of Pontoon, and Gortnorabbey Pier in the NW corner of Lough Conn. Lough Cullin is the shallower of the two, and has far higher numbers of birds than the deeper Lough Conn, particularly the NW and N side of Lough Cullin in early winter. This is one of the best spots in the W of Ireland to see Goosander in winter.

There are a number of areas to park, especially along the R310 E of Pontoon, and all can be interesting. Late autumn sees the largest number of wildfowl (often 2000+ Pochard, 1500+ Coot, and 1000+ Tufted Duck), with reduced numbers and variety in spring. Water levels change frequently, but when low, it is possible to walk around sections of shoreline for further views, particularly the NE side of Lough Cullin.

For **Gortnorabbey Pier** (G 15 16), take the first left heading S on the R315 from Crossmolina. There are good views over the NW end of Lough Conn from the pier. In winter, the fields S of the pier hold a flock of White-fronted Geese (usually 50+), while good numbers of duck can be seen on the lake, and waders are present in the surrounding fields. Hen Harrier is occasionally seen here, and the surrounding woodland holds typical species.

Species

Summer Mute Swan, Whooper Swan (R), Common Scoter (O, particularly Massbrook Bay), Red-breasted Merganser, Ringed Plover, Common Sandpiper, Common Tern (O), Cuckoo, Grasshopper Warbler.

Autumn, winter & spring Whooper Swan (O), White-fronted Goose, Wigeon, Teal, Shoveler (O), Pochard, Ring-necked Duck (R), Tufted Duck, Scaup (O), Long-tailed Duck (O), Goldeneye, Red-breasted Merganser, Goosander (O), Great Northern Diver (particularly Massbrook Bay), Great Crested Grebe, Slavonian Grebe (R), Hen

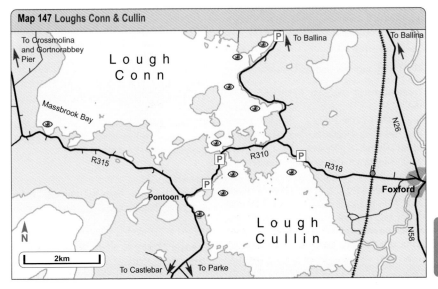

Map 147 Loughs Conn & Cullin

Harrier (O), Merlin (O), Peregrine (O), Golden Plover, Lapwing, Curlew, gulls.

Other species There are good tracts of coniferous and broadleaf woodland nearby, particularly N and W of Pontoon, where Treecreeper,

Blackcap and a variety of other woodland species can be found. Crossbill can occasionally be seen.

Rarities Ferruginous Duck, Smew, Buzzard, Osprey, Mediterranean Gull, Bonaparte's Gull.

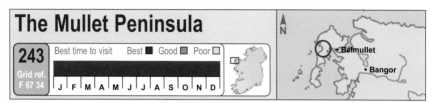

The Mullet Peninsula

243
Grid ref.
F 67 34

Best time to visit   Best ■ Good ■ Poor □

| J | F | M | A | M | J | J | A | S | O | N | D |

Belmullet

Bangor

An excellent site, full of variety throughout the year, with wintering swans, ducks and geese, breeding waders in summer, and excellent seawatching and unusual passerines during autumn migration.

Directions Map 148, next page. From Belmullet, access throughout the peninsula is straightforward. The R313 runs along the spine of the peninsula, and all sites S of Belmullet are on or just a short distance from this road. Best areas for birdwatching are:

Belmullet town Gulls and some waders can be found in the bays either side of town. An old churchyard to the W of the town can be good for migrants.

Erris Head N tip of Mullet Peninsula, 9km N of Belmullet and a 2km walk from the end of the road. Excellent seawatching in spring and autumn.

Blind Harbour Some gulls and waders in winter.

Termoncarragh Breeding Water Rail, waders and possible Corncrake. In winter, Whooper Swan, White-fronted Geese, Barnacle Geese, Twite and Chough can all be found. Wigeon, Teal, Tufted Duck and Scaup are regular in winter, and Snipe, Dunlin, Lapwing and Whinchat breed in summer. It is reached from Belmullet by taking the main road N out of town, toward Blacksod Point. After 100m, with mudflats on your left, take a right, and continue straight for 4km. The lake can be viewed distantly from the roads running to the N and S of the lake. A telescope is recommended. Termoncarragh is a BirdWatch Ireland Reserve.

Annagh Marsh is 1km SW of Termoncarragh Lake. Breeding birds include Snipe, Dunlin, Lapwing, Curlew and Chough. Whooper Swan and Twite are sometimes present in winter. Occasional Eider offshore. Viewing is from the road only. Managed by BirdWatch Ireland.

Annagh Head W tip of Mullet Peninsula. Excellent seawatching in spring and autumn.

Cross Lough Whooper Swan and wildfowl. The main area for Scaup. Some waders occur along the edges, while Barnacle Geese, Chough and Twite can be found in dunes and grassland nearby. Long-tailed Duck occur in winter just to the N at **Belderra Strand**.

Lough Leam Wildfowl and waders in autumn, winter and early spring.

Bays on E side of the Mullet All are worth checking in winter for divers and waders.

Portmore S tip of the Mullet Peninsula. In winter, check for waders and gulls on the beach, occasional Twite and Tree Sparrow in fields.

Blacksod Point Scanning the bay from here in winter may produce Long-tailed Duck, Eider, divers and Slavonian Grebe.

Species
All year Mute Swan, Water Rail, Lapwing, Dunlin, Rock Dove, Tree Sparrow (try around Portmore), Chough, Twite (O).

Summer Whooper Swan (R), Red-breasted Merganser, Merlin (O), Corncrake (try Termoncarragh or Fallmore), Ringed Plover,

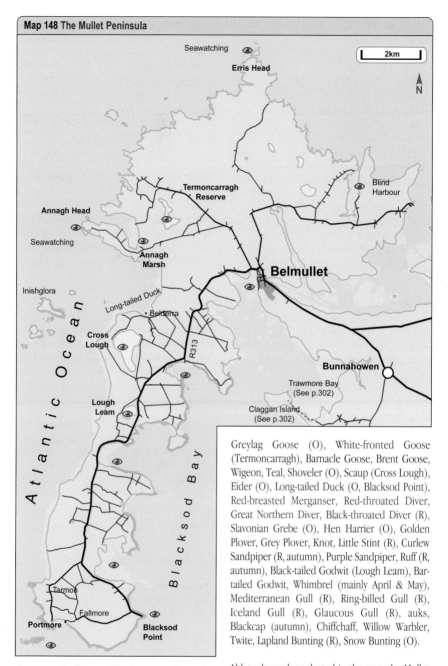

Map 148 The Mullet Peninsula

Seawatching

Erris Head

2km

N

Termoncarragh
Reserve

Blind
Harbour

Annagh Head

Seawatching

Annagh
Marsh

Belmullet

Inishglora

Atlantic Ocean

Long-tailed Duck

Belderra

Cross
Lough

R313

Bunnahowen

Trawmore Bay
(See p.302)

Lough
Leam

Claggan Island
(See p.302)

Blacksod Bay

Tarmon

Fallmore

Portmore

Blacksod
Point

Greylag Goose (O), White-fronted Goose (Termoncarragh), Barnacle Goose, Brent Goose, Wigeon, Teal, Shoveler (O), Scaup (Cross Lough), Eider (O), Long-tailed Duck (O, Blacksod Point), Red-breasted Merganser, Red-throated Diver, Great Northern Diver, Black-throated Diver (R), Slavonian Grebe (O), Hen Harrier (O), Golden Plover, Grey Plover, Knot, Little Stint (R), Curlew Sandpiper (R, autumn), Purple Sandpiper, Ruff (R, autumn), Black-tailed Godwit (Lough Leam), Bartailed Godwit, Whimbrel (mainly April & May), Mediterranean Gull (R), Ring-billed Gull (R), Iceland Gull (R), Glaucous Gull (R), auks, Blackcap (autumn), Chiffchaff, Willow Warbler, Twite, Lapland Bunting (R), Snow Bunting (O).

Common Sandpiper (O), Common Tern (O), Arctic Tern (O), Little Tern, Cuckoo, Wheatear, Grasshopper Warbler.

Autumn, winter & spring Whooper Swan (mainly at Cross Lough), Pink-footed Goose (O),

Although much neglected in the past, the Mullet Peninsula has received intensive coverage in the past few years from a small group of local observers. The long list of unusual species below shows the potential for further discoveries. Most rare passerine migrants have been found in autumn at the S tip, around Tarmon and at Blacksod Point. Erris Head and Annagh Head have also hosted several rare species.

Rarities Dark-bellied Brent Goose, Grey-bellied Brent Goose, Black Brant, Garganey, American Black Duck, Ring-necked Duck, Quail, Little Ringed Plover, American Golden Plover, Pectoral Sandpiper, White-rumped Sandpiper, Baird's Sandpiper, Buff-breasted Sandpiper, Lesser Yellowlegs, Wilson's Phalarope, Little Gull, Yellow-legged Gull, Caspian Gull, Forster's Tern, Turtle Dove, Snowy Owl, Bee-eater, Hoopoe, Short-toed Lark, Tree Pipit, Yellow Wagtail, Black Redstart, Reed Warbler, Yellow-browed Warbler, Wood Warbler, Booted Warbler, Lesser Whitethroat, Pied Flycatcher, Carrion Crow, Brambling, Crossbill, Common Rosefinch, Red-eyed Vireo.

Seawatching In spring, Annagh Head and Erris Head are the two best mainland sites in Ireland for Arctic, Pomarine and Long-tailed Skuas. Both are also excellent in autumn, with similar species (but smaller numbers) to Kilcummin Head (Site 241) See that account for likely species. In spring and autumn, a strong NW or W wind is best, though some birds can also be seen in a strong SW wind. See also SEAWATCHING, p.356.

Other species The Corn Bunting's last stronghold was the Mullet, but it is now believed extinct in Ireland and there have been no records for many years. Red-necked Phalaropes formerly bred at Annagh Marsh, for many years the only such site in Ireland, and attempts are being made by BirdWatch Ireland to re-create suitable habitat to encourage their return.

244 The Inishkea Islands Grid ref. F 60 30

A remote, uninhabited island group with large flocks of Barnacle Geese in winter, a wide variety of breeding seabirds in summer, and skua passage in spring.

See Map 149, right. The two main islands are 4km W of the Mullet Peninsula (Site 243). Access is difficult as there are no regular ferries to the islands, so private arrangements must be made, and all food and water taken for an overnight stay. In winter, one of the largest flocks of Barnacle Geese in the country occurs, with counts of up to 2800, although many of these commute to the nearby Mullet Peninsula and are far easier to see there. Single Canada Geese have been noted with the flock.

In summer, there are good numbers of seabirds, with small numbers of nesting Storm Petrel on Inishkea North. Gannet, Fulmar, Cormorant, Shag, and Kittiwake can all be seen, while there are nesting gulls and colonies of Common Tern, Arctic Tern, and Little Tern. Guillemot and Razorbill (occasionally Puffin) can be seen offshore, while Black Guillemot nest in small numbers. Eider sometimes occur, and this is the only breeding site for Great Skua in Ireland.

The Inishkeas are a good site in May for Pomarine, Arctic, Long-tailed and Great Skua passage, shown to pass offshore in W or NW winds. Sooty Shearwater is regular in autumn.

Although little study of migration has been carried out, the islands could easily hold a few surprises, such as the Snowy Owl which was present for several months in 2002.

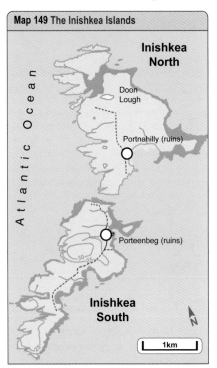

Map 149 The Inishkea Islands

Atlantic Ocean

Inishkea North

Doon Lough

Portnahilly (ruins)

Porteenbeg (ruins)

Inishkea South

1km

245 **Lough Carra** Grid ref. M 18 70

A large, shallow, freshwater lake, good for wildfowl in autumn and early winter.

See Map 150, right. Lough Carra is located between Castlebar and Ballinrobe, and several spots along the main N84 provide reasonable views over the W and S sides of the lake. Minor roads along the E side provide further views. A telescope is recommended as many birds will be distant.

Typical species in autumn and winter include Wigeon, Gadwall, Teal, Shoveler, Pochard, Tufted Duck, Scaup (R), Goldeneye, Red-breasted Merganser, Water Rail (O), Golden Plover, Great Northern Diver (O), Little Grebe, Great Crested Grebe, Cormorant, Lapwing, Snipe, Curlew, gulls, and Kingfisher (O).

In summer, Black-headed Gull, Common Gull, Lesser Black-backed Gull and Common Tern nest on some of the small rocky islands.

Rare species seen include Green-winged Teal, Smew, Long-tailed Duck, Goosander and Glaucous Gull.

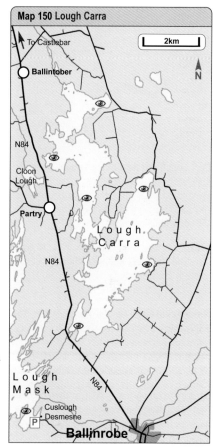

246 **Lough Mask** Grid ref. M 11 64

A large, deep lake, with many of the same species in lower numbers than at Lough Carra.

Access to most of the lake edge is difficult, but easiest on the NW side, though concentrations of birds are lacking and many of the better, shallower areas do not have ready access. Species are similar to Lough Carra (see above), but numbers are smaller and the birds more dispersed. However, Lough Mask can have Whooper Swan and White-fronted Geese (O), though they can be difficult to locate. Cuslough Desmesne, 3km W of Ballinrobe, has many typical woodland species and is best in May and June.

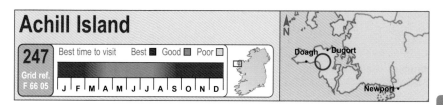

Achill Island

247 | Best time to visit | Best ■ Good ■ Poor □

Grid ref. F 66 05 | J F M A M J J A S O N D

A large island with a good variety of species throughout the year but particularly good in autumn and winter.

Directions Map 151, next page. There is one road onto the island, reached from Westport and Castlebar on the N59.

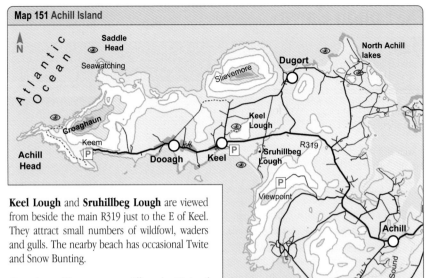

Map 151 Achill Island

Keel Lough and **Sruhillbeg Lough** are viewed from beside the main R319 just to the E of Keel. They attract small numbers of wildfowl, waders and gulls. The nearby beach has occasional Twite and Snow Bunting.

Croaghaun The enormous cliffs at the W tip of the island are spectacular, and although there are relatively few seabirds, Chough, Pergrine, Kestrel and occasional Twite can be found.

North Achill lakes A group of shallow lakes 3km E of Dugort attract swans, geese (O) and duck, with a small number of waders. This whole area is worth exploring fully in winter, including just offshore where diving duck and auks can be seen.

Achill has relatively few breeding seabirds, though Fulmar and Black Guillemot are regular. Auks and gulls are regular offshore throughout the year (particularly Keel Bay) and terns can occasionally be seen in summer.

Species

All year Mute Swan, Red-breasted Merganser, Cormorant, Peregrine, Rock Dove, Chough, Twite (O).

Summer Merlin (O), Ringed Plover, Common Sandpiper (O), Common Tern (O), Arctic Tern (O), Little Tern (O), Cuckoo, Wheatear, Sedge Warbler, Grasshopper Warbler, Willow Warbler.

Autumn, winter & spring Whooper Swan, Barnacle Goose (O), Wigeon, Teal, Long-tailed Duck (R), Red-breasted Merganser, Red-throated Diver, Great Northern Diver, Hen Harrier (O), Golden Plover, Grey Plover (O), Purple Sandpiper, Black-tailed Godwit (R), Bar-tailed Godwit, Whimbrel (mainly April & May), Ring-

billed Gull (R), Iceland Gull (R), Glaucous Gull (R), auks, Blackcap (autumn), Chiffchaff (autumn), Lapland Bunting (R), Snow Bunting (O).

Rarities Achill has potential in autumn to attract rare migrants, though it is seldom visited by birdwatchers at this time of year. Rarities seen include American Black Duck, Buzzard, Dotterel, Iceland Gull, Snowy Owl, Redstart, Pied Flycatcher, Raddes's Warbler, Carrion Crow, Tree Sparrow, Brambling and Corn Bunting.

Saddle Head is an excellent seawatching site in autumn in W or NW winds, though it involves a long, but spectacular, 5km walk through one of the wildest landscapes in Ireland. Achill Head is really too high, but seawatching is certainly possible. Park at Keem and follow the valley uphill to the NW. Arctic, Pomarine and Great Skuas have been seen from here in autumn, and Arctic Skua is regular offshore in August and September, including occasionally in Achill Sound. See also SEAWATCHING, p.356.

Rostaff Turlough

248

Grid ref.
M 25 49

Best time to visit   Best ■ Good ■ Poor □

J F M A M J J A S O N D

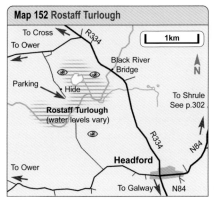

A small, shallow turlough, good for wildfowl and waders in winter.

As with all turloughs, water levels vary widely at this site, according to recent rainfall, but it is usually flooded in winter. When levels are high, the number and variety of birds increase.

Directions Map 152, right. Just N of the Galway/Mayo border, 2km NW of Headford and about 20km N of Galway city. Leave Headford N on the R334, signposted to Cross and Cong. After 2km, the turlough is visible on your left. Take the next left, 800m after Black River Bridge, and another left after 800m. There is parking at the end of this road, but backtrack 120m to the hide overlooking the turlough. Another viewpoint can be reached by heading W from Headford for 800m and taking a right to the end of the road.

Species

Autumn & winter Whooper Swan, Bewick's Swan (R), Pink-footed Goose (O), Greylag Goose (feral), White-fronted Goose (see below), Canada Goose (O feral), Brent Goose (R), Wigeon (often 750+), Gadwall, Teal, Pintail (O), Shoveler (often 50+), Pochard, Tufted Duck, Red-breasted Merganser (R), Great Crested Grebe (O), Cormorant, Little Egret (O), Hen Harrier (O),

Map 152 Rostaff Turlough

Merlin (O), Peregrine, Golden Plover (often 1000+), Dunlin, Little Stint (R autumn), Curlew Sandpiper (R autumn), Ruff (R autumn), Black-tailed Godwit, Snipe, Woodcock (O), gulls, Kingfisher.

There is a small flock of White-fronted Geese (usually 40+) which winters in the area, but if not present at Rostaff Turlough, it can be difficult to locate. Try Altore Lake to the S, or other nearby turloughs and lakes. The Whooper Swan flock occasionally feeds about 5km to the W, on fields adjacent to Lough Corrib (Site 255).

Rarities American Wigeon, Ruddy Duck.

Clare Island

249

Grid ref.
L 68 78

Best time to visit   Best ■ Good ■ Poor □

J F M A M J J A S O N D

A large, populated and easily accessible island, with a good variety of breeding seabirds.

Directions Map 153, next page. Ferries depart from Roonagh Quay, just W of Louisbergh, with six boats a day in summer, and daily sailings throughout the winter, weather permitting. There are buses from Westport which meet with the

ferries – enquire at the Westport Tourist Office, or local B&Bs and hotels for timetables. There is a hotel, bar, restuarant and several B&Bs on the island, located in the SE corner, near the pier.

Most seabirds nest on the N coast, with a small Gannet colony on an offshore stack. Small numbers of Puffin can also be found.

West

Species

All year Peregrine, Rock Dove, Chough, Twite (R).

Summer Fulmar, Gannet (see map), Cormorant, Shag, Corncrake (R), Ringed Plover, Common

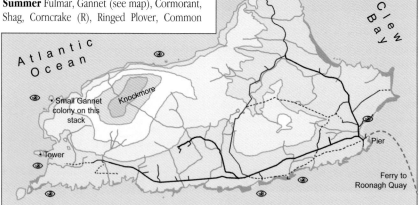

Map 153 Clare Island

Sandpiper (O), Kittiwake, gulls, Common Tern (O), Arctic Tern (O), Guillemot, Black Guillemot, Razorbill, Puffin, Cuckoo, Wheatear.

Autumn, winter & spring Little known, but Barnacle Goose (O), Eider (O), Red-throated Diver, Great Northern Diver, Golden Plover, Purple Sandpiper and auks can all be found. Skuas

and shearwaters are occasionally seen in autumn.

Rarities Glaucous Gull. No study of autumn migration has been carried out, but the island must surely attract unusual species. A white phase Gyr Falcon was found dead in 1994 and is now stuffed and on display in the hotel!

250 Clew Bay Grid ref. L 90 90

A large bay with many small islands, bays and inlets, good for wildfowl in autumn and early winter.

Clew Bay is a complex area to navigate, with numerous minor roads leading to small bays and inlets, each of which holds a number of wintering waders and some wildfowl, but there is no one outstanding area.

The N side of the bay, from just W of Malaranny, E to Newport, is generally the most productive, and offers a variety of views, including out over open water where divers and seaduck can be found. Mid to high tide is best for most spots.

There is a Barnacle Goose flock (usually 100+) which winters on the islands in the bay, though locating them can be difficult. Scan with a telescope from any high vantage point.

Other species, in winter, include Whooper Swan (O), Brent Goose, Wigeon, Teal, Common

Scoter, Red-breasted Merganser, Merlin (O), Peregrine, Golden Plover, Grey Plover (O), Dunlin, Snipe, Black-tailed Godwit (O), Bar-tailed Godwit, Common Sandpiper (R), gulls, Sandwich Tern (R), and Kingfisher.

Many of these species can also be found at **The Point, Westport.** From Westport, go to the Quays, passing the Westport House entrance on your right, before turning right at The Towers, and left at the intersection. The bay can be viewed from the road and the carpark.

Rarer species for Clew Bay include Black-throated Diver, Little Egret, Eider, Mediterranean Gull, Elegant Tern, Black Redstart and Snow Bunting.

Newport dump used to attract a variety of gulls in winter, including an impressive list of rare species (including Ivory Gull, Franklin's Gull and Thayer's Gull). The dump is now covered over and gulls no longer occur in any number.

251 Ballycroy National Park Grid ref. L 90 90

A huge wilderness area, very good for Red Grouse, Merlin and Golden Plover in summer

Map 154, below. Ballycroy National Park is an enormous, roadless, wilderness area of upland and lowland bog and mountains covering 250km². The Park and associated SPA (Special Protection Area) cover the area N of the Newport-Mulrany road, S of the Bangor-Crossmolina road, E of the Mulranny-Bangor road and W of a line between Newport and Crossmolina. The Park is relatively new, so trails and paths are not yet established. An Interpretive Centre is planned for Ballycroy.

Red Grouse breed in relatively high densities on the higher ground, particularly in the W half of the Park, and Golden Plover are present on all the higher plateaus and some of the lower bogs. Merlin are also relatively common throughout, and Peregrine nest on high cliffs. Good numbers of Common Sandpiper and Dipper also breed along the Owenduff River and other lowland rivers throughout the Park. Dotterel bred for the first time in Ircland, on Nephin More in 1975.

Snow Bunting winter on the high ridges and peaks, especially Nephin Beg and Slieve Carr (Corsleive). A flock of White-fronted Geese can be found in winter though they can be difficult to locate. Try around Ballycroy.

The Bangor Trail and the Western Way, both of which bisect the Park, offer the best access at present. These are shown in detail on Ordnance Survey Discovery maps, nos. 22 and 23.

The **Bangor Trail** starts in Bangor and goes SE to Furnace Lough across the middle of the Park. See www.mayoplus.com/Bangortrail.htm

The **Western Way** is a much longer trail and part of it skirts the E side of the Park. For further details, see www.mayoplus.com/Westernway.htm

Map 154 Ballycroy National Park

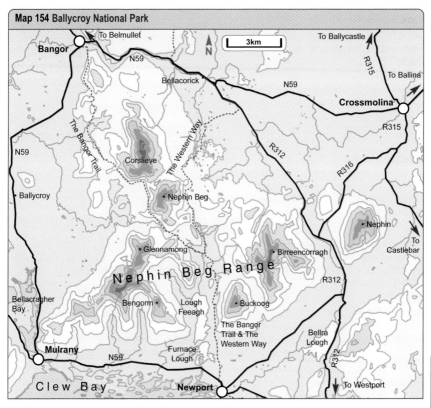

Other sites

Downpatrick Head (G 12 42) is well signposted N of Ballycastle and has numerous breeding Fulmars, Guillemots and Kittiwakes on the cliffs and stack. It is also a good seawatching vantage point in autumn, with similar species as Kilcummin (Site 241). Peregrine, Chough and Raven are present all year.

Illanmastir (F 93 43). An island with thousands of Puffins and other seabirds. There are also Peregrine, Chough and Twite in the area. Good views of the island can be obtained from the nearby mainland. Follow the clifftop along the coast for 5km, directly E from Porturlin.

Rossport (F 83 38), 6km S of Benwee Head, attracts some migrants in spring and autumn. Try the gardens and vegetated gullies around the town. Common Rosefinch and Red-backed Shrike have been seen.

Carrowmore Lake (F 8229), 3km NW of Bangor, is reached by leaving Bangor for Belmullet on the R313 and turning right after 2.5km. This road follows the S shore for 6km, from which various species can be seen. Pochard and Tufted Duck are present throughout winter, with smaller numbers of other waterbirds, gulls and waders. Black Duck, Goosander and Ring-necked Duck have been seen.

Claggan Island (F 71 27) (see Map 148), actually an isthmus, is accessed by turning S off the R313 in Bunnahowen (Glencastle) and taking the first right at the religious grotto. Follow the road to the end which opens to **Trawmore Bay** on your right. Typical species here, between September and April, include small numbers of Brent Goose, Lapwing, Grey Plover, Golden Plover (500+), Bar-tailed Godwit (500+), Dunlin (100s), Knot, and Curlew. On the S side of the isthmus is **Claggan Bay**. This is the main wintering area for Common Scoter (often 100s, late August to May), along with Red-throated and Great northern Divers and Red breasted Merganser. Black-throated Diver, Long-tailed Duck and Velvet Scoter have been recorded here. This is the most reliable spot for wintering Slavonian Grebes in County Mayo. A count of 64 in 2003 was exceptional, though more typically there are usually 10+ present.

Doolough (F 72 22), just S of Claggan Island (see above), on the E side of Blacksod Bay, is another area where large numbers of Common Scoter can be found offshore, with 500+ usually present throughout winter. Long-tailed Duck, Eider and Slavonian Grebe can occasionally be found.

Inishturk (L 60 74). A small island to the SW of Clare Island (Site 249). Ferries go from Roonagh Quay twice a day in summer, once daily in winter, weather permitting. Small numbers of seabirds nest on the W cliffs. Corncrake still occurs in some years, and though little birdwatching has been carried out during spring and autumn migration, it could prove rewarding.

One of the better broadleaved woodlands in Mayo is **Tourmakeady Forest** (M 09 68), adjacent to Tourmakeady on the NW shore of Lough Mask (Site 246). All the regular woodland species are present here, and Wood Warbler and Redstart have also been recorded in some summers. Another excellent area for woodland birds is around **Cong** (M 14 55) and **Ashford Castle** (M 14 54), where extensive stands of broadleaved, mixed and conifer forest hold all the regular woodland species.

Another excellent woodland is **Brackloon Woods** just off the N59 at Knappagh, 4km SW of Westport. The area is managed as a native forest and all non-native tree species have been removed. It has easy access and tracks thoughout. All typical woodland species are present, including Wood Warbler most summers. Blackcaps are particularly numerous at this site.

Shrule Turlough (M 27 52) is just 500m S of Shrule, about 8km NE of Headford on the N84. When flooded in winter, it can hold large numbers of waterbirds, including Whooper Swan, 100+ Pochard and 1000+ Golden Plover, along with a variety of other wintering waterbirds.

Cuilmore Lough (M 01 93) is a small lake which attracts Tufted Duck and small numbers of other waterfowl, and Ring-necked Duck has been recorded several times. Leave Newport on the R311 to Castlebar. The Lough is 3km along this road on the right, near Cuilmore village.

County Galway

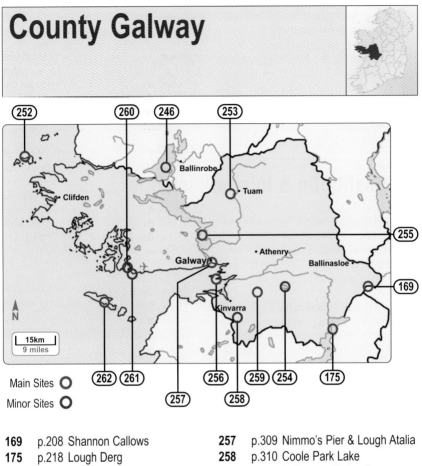

Main Sites ○
Minor Sites ○

The rugged west coast of County Galway is the quintessential Irish landscape of rolling moorland and bog, scattered lakes and high mountains. Turloughs are another characteristic Irish habitat, and Rahasane and Belclare Turloughs are two of the best in the country when they flood in winter, attracting thousands of wildfowl and waders.

Of the numerous islands to the west of the county, the Aran Islands are perhaps the most spectacular and most famous, although Inishbofin has its own special character, and both have a good selection of seabirds and other unusual nesting species in summer.

Lough Corrib is the second largest lake in Ireland, with high numbers of wintering and breeding waterbirds. Despite its size there are particular areas favoured by birds, making for a very rewarding visit at any time of year. Lough Rea and Coole Park Lake are much

West

smaller and easier to access, and both have high concentrations of waterbirds.

Glaway Bay is the only substantial area of estuary in the county, and the many sandy inlets and sheltered shores on its northern and eastern fringes support very large numbers of waders, along with numerous geese, duck, raptors and gulls. For the gull enthusiast, Nimmo's Pier, just south of Galway city centre, is alive with wintering gulls, more waders and duck, and the chance of something rarer. Glaucous Gull, Iceland Gull and Ring-billed Gull are usually present throughout winter, and two extremely rare species, Ross's Gull and American Herring Gull, have occurred almost every winter.

252 Inishbofin & Inishark Islands Grid ref. L 46 56

Inishbofin is a large inhabited island which still holds small numbers of Corncrakes each summer, while Inishark is much smaller and is uninhabited. Both islands have great potential for autumn migrants and seawatching.

See Map 155, below. **Inishbofin** is reached by ferry from Cleggan (which has a connecting bus from Clifden), and tickets can be purchased on the pier, or at the Clifden Tourist Office. There are two to five sailings per day from April to September, but much reduced sailings in winter, generally one or two per week. Ring Kings Ferries (095 44642, or *MV Galway Bay* ferry 095 45903). There are several hotels, B&Bs, a pub, hostel, post office and shop, and bikes can be rented on the island.

A few pairs of Corncrake can still be found each summer, usually around the fields on the south and east of the island. The small gardens and hedgerows around the main village and along the southern shore attract migrants and could produce a few surprises, particularly in autumn. A couple of pairs of Chough and Peregrine are present, but the birdlife of the two islands is not well known, and exciting discoveries undoubtedly await.

Rarities recorded include Gyr Falcon, Pacific Golden Plover, Golden Oriole, Waxwing and Common Rosefinch.

Inishark has no regular ferry, so arrangements would need to be made locally. The potential for rare migrants in autumn is very high, as is the seawatching in autumn and spring.

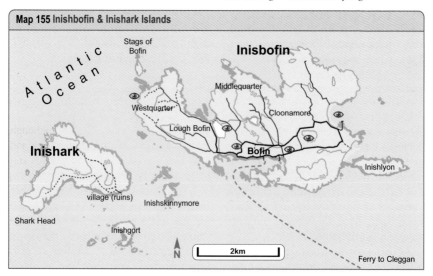

Map 155 Inishbofin & Inishark Islands

Belclare Turlough

253

Grid ref.
M 39 49

Best time to visit   Best ■ Good ▨ Poor ☐

J F M A M J J A S O N D

Lough Mask • Ballinrobe
N
Lough Corrib   • Tuam
• Headford

When flooded in winter, this turlough attracts high numbers of wildfowl and waders.

Directions Map 253, below. Located 5km west of Tuam. From Tuam, take the N17 to Galway. 3km after leaving Tuam take a right, onto the R333 for Headford. After 1.2km, take the right at Belclare village, signposted for Sylaun. After 800m there is parking and on the left, a small stone built hide with a brown door.

Species
All year Cormorant, Water Rail (O).

Autumn, winter & spring Whooper Swan, Bewick's Swan (O), White-fronted Goose, Wigeon, Gadwall (O), Teal, Pintail (O), Shoveler, Pochard, Tufted Duck, Hen Harrier (O), Merlin (O), Peregrine, Golden Plover (100s), Lapwing (100s), Dunlin, Ruff (R autumn), Jack Snipe, Snipe (R), Black-tailed Godwit (O), Curlew, gulls.

Rarities Pink-footed Goose, Green-winged Teal, Little Egret, Long-billed Dowitcher, Mediterranean Gull.

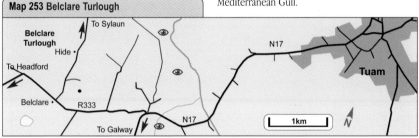

Map 253 Belclare Turlough

Belclare Turlough
To Sylaun
Hide •
To Headford
Belclare •   R333
To Galway
N17
N17
Tuam
1km   N

254 Lough Rea Grid ref. M 61 15

A reed-fringed, freshwater lake which holds high numbers of waterfowl in winter.

See Map 157, right. Located SW of Loughrea town, 32km SE of Galway city. The lake is easily accessible along its entire N and E shores, bordered by the N66 and R351, along which are many viewpoints and carparking areas.

The best time to visit is between September and April, when numbers of waterbirds are particularly high. Shoveler often number over 200 and Coot often exceed 1000 birds. Others include Whooper Swan (O), Wigeon, Teal, Pochard, Tufted Duck, Goldeneye, Golden Plover, Lapwing, Dunlin (O), Snipe, Jack Snipe (R), Curlew and gulls. Smew, Long-tailed Duck, Slavonian and Red-necked Grebe have been seen.

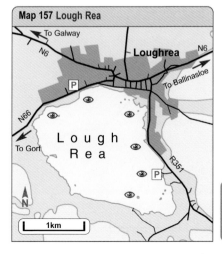

Map 157 Lough Rea

To Galway
N6   Loughrea   N6
P   To Ballinasloe
N66
To Gort   L o u g h
R e a   R351
P
N
1km

305

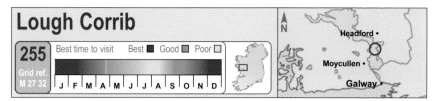

Lough Corrib

255

Grid ref.
M 27 32

Best time to visit   Best ■ Good ▨ Poor □

J F M A M J J A S O N D

Headford •

Moycullen •

Galway •

The second-largest lake in Ireland, good for wildfowl, particularly Pochard, Tufted Duck and Coot in winter and a good variety of breeding waterbirds in summer.

Directions Map 158, below. Much of the 180km² lake is difficult to access, other than by boat, but most of the wildfowl occur on the shallow S and SE end. A telescope is recommended.

The best viewing spot over the lake is at **Angliham Marble Quarries** (M 29 30), just N of Menlough, 5km N of Galway city centre. Here, large numbers of Tufted Duck, Pochard and other wildfowl gather in winter.

Curraghmore (M 32 33), 3km N of Ballindooly on the N84, is often referred to locally as the Curraghline. Just to the N and W of the bridge

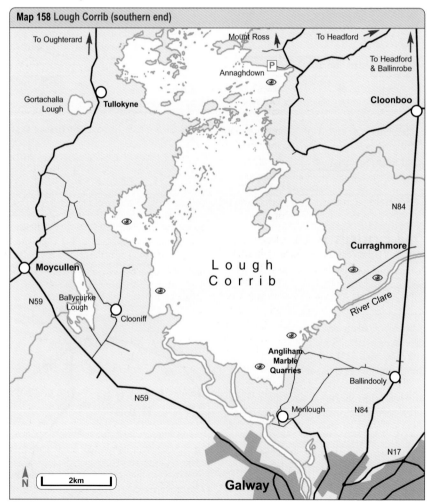

Map 158 Lough Corrib (southern end)

To Oughterard

Mount Ross

To Headford

P

Annaghdown

To Headford & Ballinrobe

Gortachalla Lough

Tullokyne

Cloonboo

N84

Curraghmore

Moycullen

Lough Corrib

River Clare

N59

Ballycuirke Lough

Clooniff

Angliham Marble Quarries

Ballindooly

N59

Menlough

N84

N17

2km

Galway

over the River Clare and W of the N84, there is a large expanse of open rough ground which holds Whooper Swan and White-fronted Goose in winter, along with a wide selection of raptors, such as Hen Harrier and Merlin.

Views over the W side of Lough Corrib are generally distant. Moycullen, Clooniff and Tullokyne are good areas from which to explore, with some good woodland habitat in the general vicinity. These are all accessed from the N59 Galway to Clifden road.

Species

Summer Gadwall (O), Tufted Duck, Pochard, Shoveler (O), Common Scoter, Red-breasted Merganser, Great-crested Grebe, Little Grebe, Lapwing, Common Sandpiper, Common Tern, Arctic Tern, gulls, Cuckoo (O), Sedge Warbler.

Autumn, winter & spring Whooper Swan (small numbers), White-fronted Goose (O), Wigeon, Gadwall, Teal, Pintail (O), Shoveler (small numbers), Tufted Duck (100s), Scaup, Pochard (1000+), Goldeneye (100s), Little Grebe, Great Crested Grebe, Hen Harrier (O), Merlin (O), Peregrine, Coot (1000+), Lapwing, Golden Plover, Snipe, Curlew, gulls.

Rarities Great Northern Diver, Velvet Scoter, Buzzard, Osprey, Bittern, Marsh Harrier, Little Stint, Pectoral Sandpiper, Spotted Sandpiper, Black Tern, Little Gull, Ring-billed Gull, Arctic Skua.

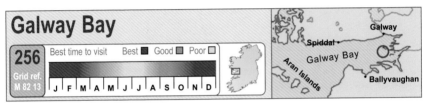

Galway Bay

256
Grid ref.
M 82 13

Best time to visit   Best ■ Good ■ Poor □

J F M A M J J A S O N D

The eastern and southern shores of Galway Bay are deeply indented with many rocky bays and inlets, holding a wide variety of wildfowl and waders outside the summer months.

Directions Map 159, next page. Sites are described clockwise around the bay.

Rusheen Bay is a Bird Sanctuary, located 4km to the W of Galway city centre, visible on the seaward side of the road on the main R336. The bay is a shallow, sheltered inlet with a narrow opening to the sea and extensive mudflats at low tide. Access is straightforward, with two carparks on the W side and easy access on three sides. A good variety of waders is present throughout autumn and winter, notably Greenshank, and Sandwich and Common Tern are often seen in late summer and autumn. Teal, Wigeon and Red-breasted Merganser are regular. Scarcer species recorded here include Curlew Sandpiper (regular September), Spotted Redshank, Little Gull and Black Redstart. On the NW side of the bay, BirdWatch Ireland's Small Wood Reserve offers good views over the bay, and has a variety of woodland birds. **Silver Strand** can be good for skuas in autumn.

For **Nimmo's Pier** & **Lough Atalia**, see Site 257.

Tawin Island is actually connected to the mainland by a bridge and projects far into the E end of Galway Bay. From Galway city, take the N18 to Limerick and turn right at Clarinbridge. After 4km, turn right at a T-junction and then left after a further 1.5km. There are good numbers of waders, wildfowl and gulls in the bays here in winter, and this is one of the better areas for Brent Goose, Snipe and Grey Plover. Offshore, Great Northern and Red-throated Divers are reasonably common, with Scaup and Little Egret regularly seen.

The bay at **Kinvarra**, SW of Kilcolgan on the N67, is worth exploring for further small numbers of wildfowl (notably Long-tailed Duck) and waders.

Traucht is reached by continuing on the N67 past Kinvarra and continuing for a further 3km W. Take the right turn, signposted for Durras Hostel. Follow this road for 1.5km and take the right turn at the junction, signposted for Beach. A few hundred metres further on, check the small inlet for wildfowl and waders. Spotted Redshank is occasionally seen here. Continue for another 1km

West

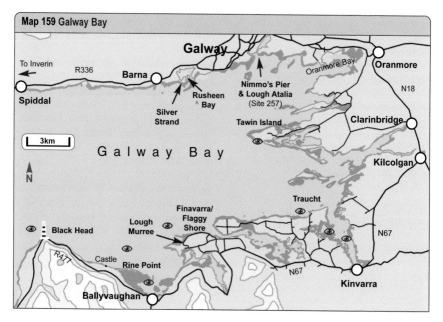

Map 159 Galway Bay

To Inverin
R336
Spiddal
Barna
Galway
Silver Strand
Rusheen Bay
Nimmo's Pier & Lough Atalia (Site 257)
Oranmore Bay
Oranmore
N18
Tawin Island
Clarinbridge
Kilcolgan

3km

N

Galway Bay

Traucht

Finavarra/ Flaggy Shore

Lough Murree

Black Head

Castle
Rine Point
R477

Ballyvaughan

N67

Kinvarra

N67

---

to the carpark at the beach. This stretch of coastline is worth a thorough search for species such as Velvet Scoter, Eider, Long-tailed Duck and Slavonian Grebe. Red-throated Diver and Great Northern Diver are regular, and this is also a good spot for Black-throated Diver.

10km W of Kinvarra, on the N67 to Ballyvaughan, the road takes a sharp left, just as a small lake appears on the right side of the road. Take the minor road to the right and then left after 2km and explore this area of shoreline, known as **Finavarra** or **Flaggy Shore**. Species offshore are similar to Truacht Beach above, but with a better chance of skuas in the autumn, often harassing small flocks of terns. Also here is a small shallow lake, obvious by the roadside, called **Lough Murree**, which has occasional Whooper Swan, and regular Brent Goose, Wigeon, Scaup and Goldeneye. Viewing the bay from the tower area (Finavarra) looking SW toward Ballyvaughan is worthwhile, with Black-throated Diver recorded here most winters.

Continue W on the main N67 to **Ballyvaughan**. The pier is famous among birdwatchers for hosting a Belted Kingfisher in 1984. It is also a good spot for small numbers of Brent Goose and Red-breasted Merganser, with Velvet Scoter, Slavonian Grebe and Ring-billed Gull occasionally

seen. This stretch of coast is one of the best in Ireland for seeing Black-throated Diver, with double figures sometimes seen in winter, and totals of over 50 on several occasions (though recently these numbers have decreased). A telescope is recommended and a calm day makes it much easier to locate them offshore.

Just 3km W of Ballyvaughan, on the R477 to Black Head, a long, rocky spit can be seen on the right, stretching out into Galway Bay for nearly 1km. This is **Rine Point** and is best reached by locating a stile on the right of the road, signposted 'Fishing', and walking down to the shore and along the stony beaches. This is one of the best areas in Galway Bay for Snow Bunting, and divers and grebes can be seen offshore in winter. Another 3km W of the stile, Gleninagh Castle is easily seen on the seaward side of the road. This is a regular haunt of Chough, and again, divers and grebes can be seen offshore. The road finally reaches **Black Head**, a good seawatching spot in W or NW winds from August to mid-October. Park at the layby overlooking the lighthouse. Numbers and variety are not as great as Loop Head to the S (Site 273), but this site can still produce spectacular seawatches in the right conditions. Likely species in autumn include Red-throated Diver, Great Northern Diver, Fulmar, Cory's Shearwater (R), Great Shearwater (R), Sooty

Shearwater, Manx Shearwater, Balearic Shearwater (R), Storm Petrel, Leach's Petrel (mainly Sept & Oct), Gannet, Shag, Grey Phalarope (O), Pomarine Skua, Arctic Skua, Long-tailed Skua (R), Great Skua, Sabine's Gull (R), Kittiwake, Common Tern (O), Arctic Tern, Guillemot, Razorbill, Black Guillemot, Puffin (O), and Snow Bunting (O winter).

Species

(The following list is for Galway Bay, excluding Nimmo's Pier and Lough Atalia, Site 257, and Black Head, see above.)

All year Fulmar, Gannet, Shag, Kittiwake, Razorbill, Guillemot, Chough, Twite (R).

Autumn & winter Whooper Swan (O), Brent Goose, Wigeon, Teal, Shoveler, Scaup, Eider (O), Long-tailed Duck (O), Common Scoter (small numbers), Velvet Scoter (O), Goldeneye, Red-

breasted Merganser, Red-throated Diver, Black-throated Diver (O), Great Northern Diver, Great Crested Grebe (O), Red-necked Grebe (R), Slavonian Grebe (O), Little Egret (O), Golden Plover, Lapwing, Knot, Little Stint (R autumn), Curlew Sandpiper (O Sept, R winter), Purple Sandpiper (O rocky coasts), Dunlin, Ruff (R), Bar-tailed Godwit, Black-tailed Godwit, Whimbrel, Spotted Redshank, Green Sandpiper (O autumn), Common Sandpiper (O winter), Little Gull (O), Pomarine Skua (R Aug & Sept), Arctic Skua (O Aug & Sept), Great Skua (O Aug & Sept), Mediterranean Gull (O), Ring-billed Gull (R), Iceland Gull (R), Glaucous Gull (R), Sandwich Tern (common to Sept, R winter), Snow Bunting.

Rarities Dark-bellied Brent Goose, Green-winged Teal, Surf Scoter, Bonaparte's Gull, Ross's Gull, Little Auk, Snowy Owl, Black Redstart, Carrion Crow. See also rarities recorded at Nimmo's Pier, Site 257, below.

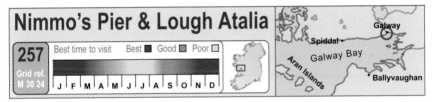

Nimmo's Pier & Lough Atalia

257

Best time to visit   Best ■ Good ■ Poor □

Grid ref.
M 30 24   J F M A M J J A S O N D

Two outstanding sites in the heart of Galway city, very good for wildfowl, some waders and lots of gulls, especially in the winter months.

Directions Map 160, right. Galway city centre.

Nimmo's Pier The River Corrib runs through the centre of Galway city, and Nimmo's Pier is located on the S shore (opposite The Spanish Arch), where it meets the sea. Simply walk the pier, searching the channel and river edges for wildfowl, waders and particularly, gulls. More wildfowl and waders can be seen in Galway Bay, to the S and SW. Best at low tide. Nimmo's Pier is the best spot in Ireland to see Ross's Gull, a much sought-after Arctic species. It occurs almost annually at this site. There are also usually several semi-resident Ring-billed Gulls present. Iceland Gull and Glaucous Gull are less predictable, but there are usually one or two of each present between here and the docks in winter. Recently, American Herring Gull has been shown to be

regular. The fields W of the pier occasionally hold Snow Bunting and rarely, Twite.

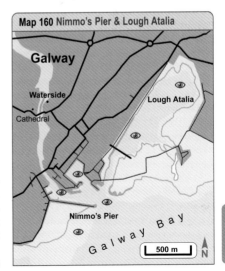

Map 160 Nimmo's Pier & Lough Atalia

Species

Autumn & winter Whooper Swan (R), Brent Goose, Wigeon, Teal, Red-breasted Merganser, Velvet Scoter (R), Red-throated Diver, Great Northern Diver, Shag, Little Egret (O), Merlin, Golden Plover, Lapwing, Knot, Dunlin, Bar-tailed Godwit (O), Whimbrel, Common Sandpiper (R winter), Little Gull (O), Arctic Skua (O Aug & Sept), Mediterranean Gull (O), Ring-billed Gull (1 to 3 usually present), Iceland Gull (O), Glaucous Gull (O), Sandwich Tern (common autumn, R winter), Guillemot, Razorbill, Black Guillemot (O), Snow Bunting (R), Twite (R).

Rarities Red-necked Grebe, Storm Petrel, Double-crested Cormorant, Bonaparte's Gull, Laughing Gull, Kumlien's Gull, American Herring Gull, Ross's Gull, Forster's Tern, Black Tern.

Lough Atalia (M 31 25) This narrow inlet in Galway Bay is just NE of Nimmo's Pier and access is straightforward, with roads on all sides allowing full views over the lough. It is adjacent to both Galway Railway Station and the main Galway-Dublin Road. Tidal ranges are small, but low tide may see a few more waders present.

In winter, Wigeon, Teal, Goldeneye and Red-breasted Merganser are usually present, and this is a particularly good site to see Scaup. Great Crested and Little Grebe are usually present in small numbers. Commoner waders like Redshank, Greenshank, Curlew, Oystercatcher and Lapwing are usually present, while Kingfisher is regular. Rarer sightings include Ring-necked Duck and Long-tailed Duck, and some of the more unusual gulls from Nimmo's Pier may be seen.

Another area where gulls congregate is **Waterside**, upriver from Nimmo's Pier. From St Nicholas's Cathedral, cross the bridge across the Corrib and turn left. The river widens N of the bridge and many gulls gather around the wier and the Rowing Club building.

258 Coole Park Lake Grid ref. M 41 04

A large park, consisting of a freshwater lake, turloughs and some excellent broadleaved woodland. A very good site for waterfowl in winter, and woodland species all year.

See Map 161, right. From Gort, go N on the N18 to Ardrahan and Galway. Coole Park is signposted on the left after 2km. There are carparks, toilets and two signposted Nature Trails. There is an admission charge to the Visitor Centre, which has some displays of the flora and fauna.

The main birdwatching interest outside the summer months is the lake to the W of the Visitor Centre, **Coole Lough**. Another area worth looking at in winter are the turloughs S of Coole Lough. The water levels at **Lough Nacarriga** and **Newtown Lough** vary with recent rainfall, but when flooded, this whole wetland area can attract high numbers of wildfowl and waders.

In winter, on the lake and turloughs, you can find Whooper Swan, Bewick's Swan (R), Greylag Goose (O), Wigeon (100s), Teal, Pintail, Shoveler, Pochard, Tufted Duck, Goldeneye, Golden Plover, Lapwing, Dunlin, Black-tailed Godwit (O), Curlew and gulls. Ruff, Garganey and Ferruginous Duck have been recorded.

The woodlands surrounding Coole Lough are particularly good, holding all the regular woodland species. The woodland paths emanating from the Visitor Centre are generally good, but there are plenty of longer walks through excellent broadleaved and mixed woodland. Bear in mind that the park is a popular amenity area and weekends are usually best avoided.

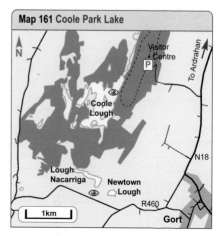

Map 161 Coole Park Lake

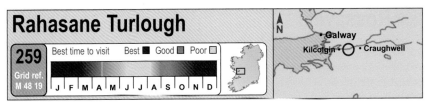

Rahasane Turlough

259
Grid ref.
M 48 19

Best time to visit   Best ■ Good ▨ Poor ☐

J F M A M J J A S O N D

A turlough which, when flooded in winter, can hold very large numbers of wildfowl and waders. Also attracts many scarcer species, particularly in autumn and winter.

In winter, the Dunkellin River floods, inundating the river banks on either side, and can form a large shallow lake 3km long and 1km wide. It is one of the best areas on the west coast for White-fronted Goose, and one of the better areas to find Pintail and Gadwall in County Galway. It also attracts a selection of scarce and rare waders each autumn and rare wildfowl each winter.

Directions Map 162, below. From Galway, take the N18 to Limerick. At Kilcolgin, 18km SE of Galway, take a right onto a minor road, for Craughwell. After 3km, the river (or lake, depending on water levels) will become visible on your right. There are several viewpoints from this road, and from laneways leading from it. If travelling on the N6 from Dublin to Galway, take a left 500m after passing through Craughwell.

Species

Autumn, winter & spring Whooper Swan (small numbers), Bewick's Swan (O), White-fronted Goose, Greylag Goose (feral birds), Wigeon (100s), Gadwall (O), Teal, Pintail (O), Shoveler, Tufted Duck, Pochard, Goldeneye (O), Little Grebe (O), Great Crested Grebe (O), Cormorant, Merlin (O), Peregrine, Golden Plover (sometimes 1000s), Lapwing (100s), Dunlin, Ruff (O autumn), Jack Snipe, Snipe, Black-tailed Godwit, Bar-tailed Godwit (O), Whimbrel (spring & autumn, R winter), Curlew, Spotted Redshank (R autumn & winter), Common Sandpiper, gulls, Kingfisher (O).

Rarities Pink-footed Goose, Barnacle Goose, American Wigeon, Garganey, Smew, Ruddy Duck, Great Northern Diver, Great White Egret, Osprey, Dotterel, Little Stint, Pectoral Sandpiper, Curlew Sandpiper, Long-billed Dowitcher, Lesser Yellowlegs, Wood Sandpiper, Mediterranean Gull, Ring-billed Gull, Black Tern, Yellow Wagtail.

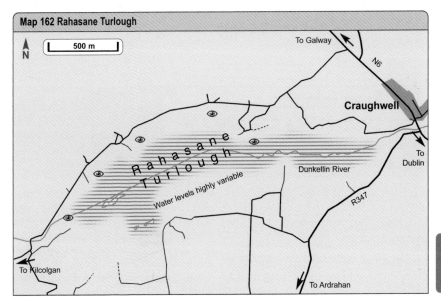

Map 162 Rahasane Turlough

260 Rossaveal Grid ref. L 96 25

For those travelling to the Aran Islands (site 262, below), it is worth allowing time to search around Rossaveal for gulls and Little Egret, especially in the winter months.

Rossaveal is well signposted off the main R336 between Galway city and Maam Cross. Take the R372 for Rossaveal. At the main junction in the village, a left turn will reveal views of Lough Ros, with a good chance of unusual gulls, Little Egret and occasional wildfowl in winter. Around the harbour there is an excellent chance of finding Iceland Gull, particularly in mid-winter.

A variety of rare birds have been seen in this area over recent years, including Green-winged Teal, Little Egret, Mediterranean Gull, Sabine's

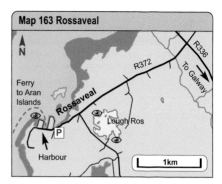

Gull, Little Gull, Ring-billed Gull, Franklin's Gull, American Herring Gull, Iceland Gull, Kumlien's Gull, Glaucous Gull, Roseate Tern and Little Auk.

261 Ballynahown Grid ref. L 98 20

A good seawatching area in westerly winds in autumn.

Located 3 km SW of Inverin. From Inverin, go W on the R336 to Rossaveal, going straight on at a crossroads where the main road veers right. After 400m, turn left and continue straight for 2.5km to the shore. In SW to W winds in autumn, migrating seabirds are pushed into the entrance of Galway Bay and many pass close to this point.

Likely species in autumn include Red-throated Diver, Great Northern Diver, Fulmar, Sooty Shearwater, Manx Shearwater, Storm Petrel, Leach's Petrel (mainly Sept & Oct), Gannet, Shag, Grey Phalarope (O), Pomarine Skua (O), Arctic Skua, Great Skua, Sabine's Gull (R), Kittiwake, Common Tern (O), Arctic Tern, Guillemot, Razorbill, Black Guillemot, Puffin.

This may well prove to be a good spot for seeing skuas on spring migration.

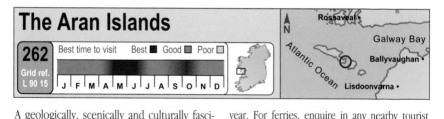

A geologically, scenically and culturally fascinating group of islands, with a variety of birds in summer, and the possibility of scarce migrants in autumn.

Directions Map 164, next page. 40km W of Galway city. Several ferries and one airline operate regular services to the islands throughout the

year. For ferries, enquire in any nearby tourist office, and most hotels, B&Bs, pubs and shops advertise services. The two main ports are Galway and Rossaveal. Aer Árann (www.aerarann.ie) offer daily flights to the three islands from Inverin, just south of Rossaveal. Ferries and flights are frequent during summer, but are less regular and more prone to weather-induced cancellations from

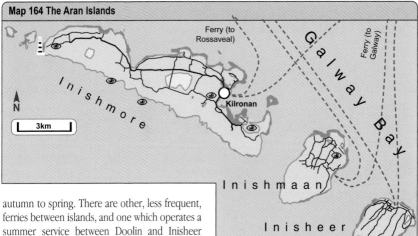

Map 164 The Aran Islands

Ferry (to Rossaveal)

Galway Bay

Ferry (to Galway)

Inishmore

Kilronan

N

3km

Inishmaan

Inisheer

autumn to spring. There are other, less frequent, ferries between islands, and one which operates a summer service between Doolin and Inisheer (www.doolinferries.com). Enquire locally. If travelling to the Aran Islands via Rossaveal, see Site 260, previous page.

Inishmore is much the largest island and caters well for the visitor, with six hostels, numerous B&Bs, pubs and a supermarket. Bicycle hire is possible at the pier in Kilronan. **Inishmaan** and **Inisheer** are much less visited by tourists (and birdwatchers), but both still boast a hotel, B&Bs and a pub. The bird list below is based on that of Inishmore, though many of these should occur on the two smaller islands.

Species

All year Fulmar, Peregrine, Cormorant, Shag, Curlew, Kittiwake, Guillemot, Black Guillemot, Razorbill, Rock Dove, Chough, Raven.

Spring & summer Lapwing, Common Sandpiper, Sandwich Tern, Arctic Tern, Little Tern, Cuckoo, Wheatear, Sedge Warbler (O), Whitethroat, Chiffchaff (O).

Winter Whooper Swan (O), Brent Goose (O), Red-breasted Merganser, Snipe. The birdlife is not well known at this time of year.

Recent study of autumn migration has been limited but has shown that passerine migrants such as Chiffchaff, Blackcap and Goldcrest are regular. Rarities have included Green Sandpiper, Iceland Gull, Black Redstart, Red-breasted Flycatcher, Reed Warbler, Barred Warbler, Yellow-browed Warbler, Wood Warbler, Red-eyed Vireo, Blackpoll Warbler and Lapland Bunting. Most of the rare passerines have been found on the NW end of Inishmore, in the bramble and ivy patches and stone walls to the east of the lighthouse.

Little seawatching has been carried out, though Arctic Skua, Pomarine Skua, Great Skua and Manx Shearwater are regularly seen from the ferries, particularly in autumn. Little is known about migration or seawatching possibilities on the smaller two islands.

Other sites

Slyne Head (L 39 41) is the best site in Ireland for the spring migration of skuas. Early May and W to NW winds have proved the most productive, and all four species of skua have been seen, sometimes in high numbers. Access to the outermost in the chain of islands making up Slyne Head is problematic and a boat would need to be arranged locally. See also SEAWATCHING, p.356.

The beaches, pools, lakes and shoreline just back from Slyne Head could prove to be good for migrants in autumn, though little systematic searching has ever been carried out in this area.

West

County Clare

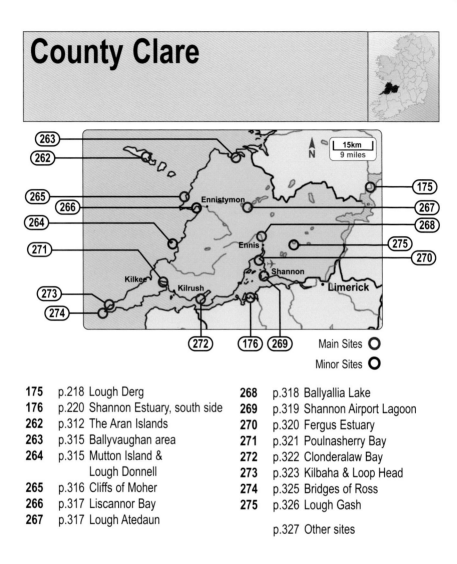

County Clare is flanked to the south by the largest estuary complex in Ireland, the Shannon, and one of the most important for waterbirds. At 80km long and 10km wide, the Fergus Estuary, and Poulnasherry and Clonderalaw Bays are intimidatingly large areas, though time spent searching these bird-rich areas should reap rewards. Up to 20,000 waterbirds spend the winter here. The Shannon Airport Lagoon, on the other hand, is a compact, easily viewed area, with many wildfowl, waders and reedbed species.

At the mouth of the Shannon Estuary lies Loop Head, an excellent area for autumn migrants, and nearby, the Bridges of Ross, perhaps one of the best seawatching locations in Europe. From August to October, strong onshore winds can drive thousands of seabirds past the headland in one of the great natural spectacles the country has to offer.

To the north, along the coast, the Cliffs of Moher offer dramatic scenery and close-up views of thousands of nesting seabirds, while the rocky coastal landscape around Ballyvaughan has a good variety of wintering species.

Inland there are many lakes holding a wide variety of wintering waterbirds, and densities of wildfowl can be particularly high at two of the best, Lough Atedaun and Ballyallia Lake.

263 Ballyvaughan area Grid ref. L 99 20

One of the best areas on the Irish west coast for wintering divers.

This area is shown on Map 159, p.308. The rocky coast around Ballyvaughan has small numbers of many of the commoner wintering wildfowl and waders, but is perhaps best known as an excellent site for divers. From September to April, Red-throated Diver and Great Northern Diver are common throughout the bay, and this is one of the better sites in Ireland for wintering Black-throated Diver. A calm day is best and, as many birds will be distant, a telescope is recommended.

Rine Point, 3km NW of Ballyvaughan, is a narrow, 1.5km long rocky headland and can be worthwhile for closer views of divers. It also offers a chance of wintering Snow Bunting on the shingle beaches along its length. Choughs nest on the castle tower just W of the start of this walk.

Black Head, 8km NW of Ballyvaughan on the R477, provides good opportunities for seawatching in autumn. See p.308 for details.

Rare species seen around Ballyvaughan include Eider, Red-necked Grebe, Ring-billed Gull, Mediterranean Gull, Glaucous Gull, Nightjar, Belted Kingfisher and Carrion Crow.

264 Mutton Island & Lough Donnell Grid ref. Q 97 74

The only regular wintering site for Barnacle Geese in County Clare, and one of the best spots on the west coast for Purple Sandpiper. There is a small number of wildfowl and waders on nearby Lough Donnell.

Map 165, below. **Mutton Island**, 2.5km W of Quilty, is uninhabited and there are no ferries, but reasonable views can be had of the large Barnacle Geese flock from Lurga Point, 2.5km W of Quilty on the coast road. There are generally 200+

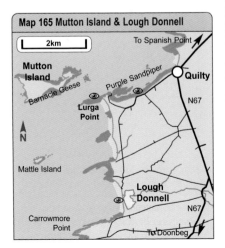

Map 165 Mutton Island & Lough Donnell

2km

To Spanish Point

Mutton Island

Purple Sandpiper

Barnacle Geese

Quilty

N67

Lurga Point

N

Mattle Island

Lough Donnell

N67

Carrowmore Point

To Doonbeg

present on the island between November and April, and they make occasional forays to the nearby mainland and to Mattle Island to the S. A telescope is recommended.

The whole stretch of rocky coastline from **Quilty** to **Lurga Point** is excellent for Purple Sandpiper (with regular counts of over 200) and other waders from late October to April. Sanderling, Turnstone and Grey Plover are common, and more unusual sightings include Leach's Petrel, Curlew Sandpiper, Spotted Redshank, Grey Phalarope, Pomarine Skua, Arctic Skua, Ring-billed Gull, Iceland Gull, Glaucous Gull, Black Redstart, Twite and Snow Bunting.

Lough Donnell is 3km S of Lurga Point, reached by continuing S on the coast road until the lough is visible directly ahead. The lake can be viewed from the beach. From September to March, small numbers of Wigeon are usually present, while Golden Plover, Grey Plover, Lapwing, Dunlin and Curlew are regular, and Whooper Swan has summered. Rarities include Purple Heron, Little Stint, Mediterranean Gull and Glaucous Gull, and though seldom visited, the Lough must surely attract some of the rarer waders and wildfowl, particularly in autumn.

West

315

Cliffs of Moher

265
Grid ref.
Q 04 91

Best time to visit   Best ■ Good ■ Poor □

J F M A M J J A S O N D

Spectacular cliff scenery, with large numbers of breeding seabirds in summer. A particularly good spot to see Puffin.

Directions Map 166, right. The cliffs are well signposted from the nearest main towns: Doolin to the N, Liscannor to the S, and Lahinch and Ennistymon to the SE.

The Visitor Centre provides parking and offers superb views over the cliffs. From here, most of the bird species listed below can be seen throughout spring and summer. Puffins nest on Goat Island, below the Visitor Centre, one of the most accessible sites in Ireland for this species.

The Burren Way is a waymarked trail of 30km, from Liscannor to Ballyvaughan. This path follows close to the clifftop for much of its length and provides further opportunities for exploring the cliffs. It passes close to the Visitor Centre and its full length is shown on Ordnance Survey map 51.

Razorbills

Map 166 Cliffs of Moher

Species
All year Chough, Rock Dove, Twite (R, possibly locally extinct).

Spring & summer Fulmar (1000s), Manx Shearwater (usually distant), Gannet, Cormorant, Shag, Peregrine, Kittiwake (1000s), Guillemot (1000s), Razorbill (1000s), Black Guillemot (small numbers), Puffin (100s), Rock Dove, Wheatear.

Some of these seabirds can be seen outside the breeding season, though Manx Shearwater and Puffin are usually absent in winter.

Liscannor Bay is a large sea bay to the S of the Cliffs of Moher (Site 265), good for Common Scoter and a regular site for Black-throated Diver in winter.

The bay is located 4km W of Ennistymon on the N67. There is a large estuary behind the main beach, midway between Liscannor and Lahinch, with saltmarsh and sand dunes, and open sandflats on the seaward side. These hold a variety of waders and wildfowl and are easily explored from the beach, or from the inland side of the main R478 road between the two villages.

Up to 600 Common Scoter and small numbers of Black-throated Diver occur in the main bay between Lahinch and Liscannor throughout winter, though a telescope is recommended.

Other species in winter include Whooper Swan, Greylag Goose (feral), Brent Goose, Wigeon, Teal, Pochard, Tufted Duck, Scaup (O), Eider (O), Long-tailed Duck (O), Velvet Scoter (O), Red-breasted Merganser, Red-throated Diver, Great Northern Diver, Oystercatcher (1000+), Golden Plover, Grey Plover, Lapwing, Purple Sandpiper, Dunlin, Jack Snipe (R), Snipe, Black-tailed Godwit (O), Bar-tailed Godwit, Curlew, Merlin, Chiffchaff (R).

Rarer species include Mediterranean Gull, Bonaparte's Gull, Ring-billed Gull, Yellow-legged Gull, Iceland Gull and Glaucous Gull.

Lough Atedaun

267	Best time to visit	Best ■ Good ▨ Poor ☐
Grid ref. R 29 89	J F M A M J J A S O N D	

A shallow, freshwater lake bordered by fen, cut-away bog and marsh, good in winter for wildfowl.

Directions Map 167, below. 1km E of Corrofin. A carpark and extensive views of the lake can be had by taking the first main right turn, just after leaving Corrofin on the R460 to Gort. After 300m, take a right and continue to the lake. More distant views can be obtained from the S side. Leaving

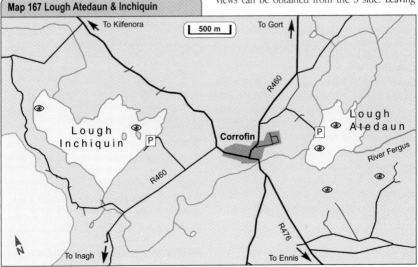

Map 167 Lough Atedaun & Inchiquin

Corrofin on the R476 to Ennis, take the first left after 2km. The first and second left turns will lead to views over the lake.

Lough Atedaun is a shallow lake, and water levels fluctuate widely, sometimes almost drying out in summer, though usually flooded in winter. In autumn, muddy margins may be attractive to waders, though little is known about the birds at this time of year. The grassy shores of the lake regularly flood in winter, providing feeding for numerous waterbirds, notably Mute Swan and Wigeon. Species density and diversity are particularly high at this site.

Inchiquin Lough is signposted, just 1km to the NW of Corrofin. See Map 167, previous page. While deeper and larger than Lough Atedaun, it has much the same wildfowl species but in smaller numbers. Birds most often frequent the N end of the lake, especially if there is disturbance at other nearby sites, including Atedaun. There is added interest with extensive woodlands on the W side of the lough.

Species
Autumn, winter & spring Mute Swan (200+), Bewick's Swan (R), Whooper Swan, White-fronted Goose (formerly regular, now O winter), Greylag Goose (O, feral birds), Wigeon (sometimes 1000+), Gadwall, Teal, Pintail, Shoveler, Pochard, Tufted Duck, Goldeneye, Great Crested Grebe, Merlin (O), Hen Harrier (O), Peregrine, Water Rail (O), Golden Plover, Lapwing, Dunlin, Ruff (O), Snipe, Black-tailed Godwit, Curlew, Spotted Redshank (R), Green Sandpiper (O), Common Sandpiper (O winter), gulls (small numbers).

Rarities Pink-footed Goose, Bufflehead, Ring-necked Duck, Long-tailed Duck, Slavonian Grebe, Great White Egret, Little Gull, Black Tern, Hoopoe.

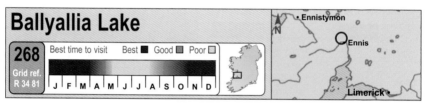

Ballyallia Lake

268

Grid ref. R 34 81

Best time to visit   Best ■ Good ▨ Poor □

J F M A M J J A S O N D

An excellent site for a good variety of wildfowl and Black-tailed Godwit in winter. This lake has one of the highest densities of wildfowl in the country and is the only internationally important wintering site for Shoveler in Ireland, with 200+ usually present.

Directions Map 168, right. 4km N of Ennis, on the old N18 Limerick to Galway, take a left turn for Ruan. This road leads to the E shore of the lake after 1km, where there is a carpark and picnic spot. Much of the lake can be scanned from here. Further views of other parts of the lake are from private land, so *permission must be sought if entering fields.* Distant views can be had from the road on the W and S sides, though a telescope is recommended. The road along the NE shoreline is private, though permission for access can be sought locally.

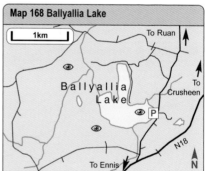

Map 168 Ballyallia Lake

1km

To Ruan

Ballyallia Lake

To Crusheen

P

N18

To Ennis

Species
Autumn, winter & spring Whooper Swan, Greylag Goose (feral), Wigeon (up to 2000), Gadwall, Teal (1000+), Pintail, Shoveler, Pochard, Tufted Duck, Coot (often 500+), Great Crested Grebe, Lapwing, Dunlin, Ruff (O), Black-tailed Godwit (often 750+), Curlew, gulls.

Rarities Ring-necked Duck, Ruddy Duck.

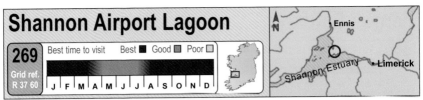

Shannon Airport Lagoon

269	Best time to visit	Best ■ Good ▦ Poor □
Grid ref. R 37 60		J F M A M J J A S O N D

Ennis

Shannon Estuary • Limerick

A shallow lagoon, with reedbed and nearby mudflats, very good for waders and duck mainly outside the summer months.

Directions Map 169, right. Shannon Airport is well signposted throughout the region. Follow the signs to the airport right up to the last 200m. As you approach, the terminal buildings appear on your right. Just before the car hire return depot is a track on the left. Park near the gate *(do not block it)* and walk along the causeway to get views of the lagoon on the right and the estuary on the left.

To view the opposite side of the lagoon, continue past the car hire depot and go left, following signs for the golf course and go past the oil depot. This tree-lined road leads to the carpark in front of the golf clubhouse. At the far end of the carpark is a gate which leads to a track along the edge of the lagoon. Climbing the embankment on the right gives good views of the outer estuary. The hide is no longer in use at this site.

Water levels at the lagoon vary throughout the year, but are often low in late summer and early autumn, attracting large numbers of waders.

Species

All year Cormorant, Tufted Duck, Water Rail, Kingfisher (O, channel near the hide), Redpoll.

Autumn, winter & spring Greylag Goose (R), White-fronted Goose (R), Whooper Swan (O), Bewick's Swan (R), Wigeon, Gadwall, Teal, Pintail (O), Garganey (R spring & autumn), Shoveler, Pochard, Scaup, Red-breasted Merganser (O), Little Grebe, Great Crested Grebe (River Shannon), Hen Harrier, Merlin, Peregrine, Golden Plover, Grey Plover, Lapwing, Knot, Little Stint (R spring, O autumn), Curlew Sandpiper (autumn), Dunlin, Ruff (autumn), Jack Snipe (R), Snipe, Woodcock (R), Black-tailed Godwit, Bar-tailed

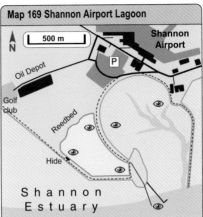

Map 169 Shannon Airport Lagoon

500 m

Shannon Airport

Oil Depot

Golf club

Reedbed

Hide

S h a n n o n
E s t u a r y

Godwit, Whimbrel (spring), Curlew, Spotted Redshank (O autumn), Green Sandpiper (O), Wood Sandpiper (R), Common Sandpiper, Mediterranean Gull (R), Short-eared Owl (R).

Summer Wigeon (R), Gadwall (O), Black-tailed Godwit, Sandwich Tern (River Shannon), Common Tern (River Shannon), Arctic Tern (River Shannon), Stock Dove (O), Cuckoo, Wheatear, Grasshopper Warbler, Sedge Warbler, Reed Warbler (O) Blackcap, Chiffchaff, Willow Warbler, Siskin.

Rarities American Wigeon, Green-winged Teal, Red-necked Grebe, Storm Petrel, Bittern, Spoonbill, Blue-winged Teal, Smew, Goosander, Ruddy Duck, Marsh Harrier, Hobby, Semipalmated Sandpiper, Least Sandpiper, Baird's Sandpiper, White-rumped Sandpiper, Pectoral Sandpiper, Broad-billed Sandpiper, Long-billed Dowitcher, Wilson's Phalarope, Long-tailed Skua, Great Skua, Laughing Gull, Little Gull, Iceland Gull, Glaucous Gull, White-winged Black Tern, Citrine Wagtail, Bluethroat, Black Redstart, Savi's Warbler, Brambling, Twite, Crossbill, Snow Bunting.

West

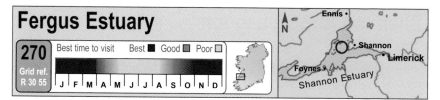

Fergus Estuary

270

Grid ref.
R 30 55

Best time to visit   Best ■ Good ■ Poor □

| J | F | M | A | M | J | J | A | S | O | N | D |

The main section of the largest estuary in Ireland, attracting enormous numbers of birds in winter. Holds internationally important numbers of Brent Goose, Black-tailed Godwit and Redshank and nationally important numbers of a further 19 species.

Directions Map 170, below. The Fergus and Shannon Estuary is 50,000 ha in extent, almost 80km in length and 10km at its widest point. It divides County Clare to the N and counties Limerick and Kerry to the S, and runs W from Limerick city. The habitats, including saltmarsh, reedbed, mudflats and marsh, cover a vast area to which access is often problematic. Few roads are adjacent to the shoreline, necessitating long detours to view only relatively small areas of the estuary.

The Fergus Estuary is the largest section of the Shannon Estuary and holds the bulk of the birds, though many are highly mobile. All sites need to be visited at high, or near-high tide, otherwise most birds will be very distant. Some of the best areas in the Fergus Estuary are as follows.

On the W side, **Islandavanna** (R 32 68) is reached from Ennis by taking the R473 S to Ballynacally and taking a left after 6km. The shore is reached after 1km and there are good views over mudflats and grassland. Continue along this road, exploring the grassland until you reach **Islandmagrath** (R 34 71). Both areas are good for Whooper Swan in winter, and numerous waterfowl and waders can be found on the grassland and estuary.

3km SW of Islandavanna, on the R473, distant views are possible of **Ballycorrick Creek** (R 39 66), with more wildfowl and waders.

At Ballynacally, take the minor road SE to the shore, for more views over the estuary and nearby **Ballynacally Creek** (R 28 63).

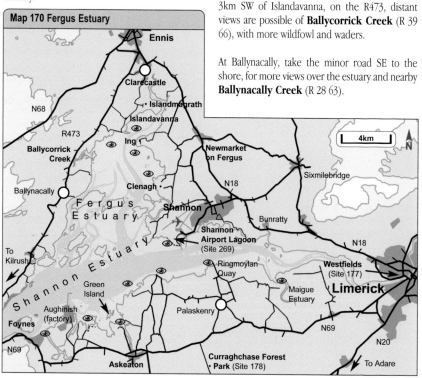

Map 170 Fergus Estuary

On the E side, one of the best viewpoints is the small hill at **Ing** (R 35 68), overlooking the N section of the estuary. From Ennis, take the N18 to Limerick. 3km after passing through Clarecastle, the road passes over Latoon Bridge. After 600m take a right and continue straight for 3km, then take a right. The hill is obvious ahead. Numerous flocks of wildfowl and waders can be seen from here.

From Ing, backtrack to the last turn and turn right. After 4km there is a fork in the road. Take the right and continue for 1km to the castle at **Clenagh** (R 36 65). The shoreline can be explored from this point and there are good views over the mudflats.

Other sites within the Shannon Estuary are: Site 176, Shannon Estuary south side; Site 216, Tarbert Area; Site 269, Shannon Airport Lagoon; Site 271, Poulnasherry Bay; and Site 272, Clonderalaw Bay.

Species
All year Greylag Goose (feral birds), Cormorant, Little Egret, Water Rail, Kingfisher (R).

Autumn, winter & spring Whooper Swan, White-fronted Goose (O), Brent Goose, Shelduck (100s), Wigeon (1000s), Gadwall, Teal (1000+), Pintail, Shoveler, Tufted Duck, Scaup, Goldeneye, Long-tailed Duck (R), Red-throated Diver (O), Black-throated Diver (R), Great Northern Diver, Great Crested Grebe, Red-necked Grebe (R), Slavonian Grebe (R), Little Egret, Hen Harrier (O), Merlin (O), Peregrine, Oystercatcher (100s), Golden Plover (1000s), Grey Plover (100s), Lapwing (often 10,000+), Knot (1000+), Little Stint (O autumn), Curlew Sandpiper (O autumn), Dunlin (1000s), Ruff (O autumn), Jack Snipe (R), Snipe, Black-tailed Godwit (100s), Bar-tailed Godwit (100s), Whimbrel (small numbers, mainly spring), Curlew (100s), Spotted Redshank (O autumn & winter), Redshank (1000+), Green Sandpiper (O autumn), Mediterranean Gull (O), Little Gull (R), Ring-billed Gull (R), Iceland Gull (O), Glaucous Gull (O).

Summer Sandwich Tern, Common Tern, Arctic Tern, Cuckoo (O), Sedge Warbler.

Rarities Bewick's Swan, Black-necked Grebe, Green-winged Teal.

Poulnasherry Bay

271 Grid ref. Q 94 58 | Best time to visit | Best ■ Good ■ Poor □

J F M A M J J A S O N D

A large, sheltered estuary with high numbers of waders and wildfowl throughout winter.

Directions Map 171, next page. Located 4km NW of Kilrush, at the N side of the mouth of the Shannon Estuary.

For the east side of the estuary, from Kilrush take the N67 to Kilkee, and 1km from the outskirts of Kilrush, take a left and then a right after 1.2km. This road leads to the shoreline at **Carrowncalla**, with extensive views over the outer reaches of the bay. Divers, Great Crested Grebe and Scaup can be seen here. By returning to the N67 and taking another left after 800m, you reach another section of the eastern shoreline after 1.3km.

Moyasta is particularly good for waders and wildfowl, and the shoreline and sheltered creek of the village are easily explored from the picnic area just to the N of the village.

The N side of the estuary can be explored by taking any of the left turns off the N67 between Moyasta and Lisdeen, all of which lead to the shore.

For the western side of the estuary, leave Moyasta for Kilkee on the N67 and take a left for Carrigaholt, after 3.5km. **Blackweir Bridge** is just 250m along this road, and the channels, reeds and creeks in this area hold many waders and wildfowl, and are potentially one of the best areas

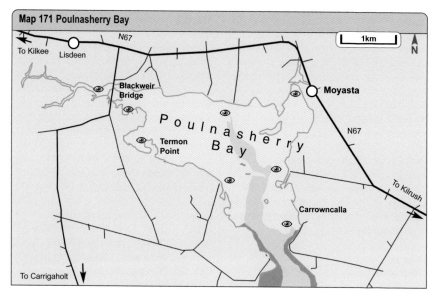

Map 171 Poulnasherry Bay

for rare waders in autumn. The shore S from here to **Termon Point** is an excellent area for more wildfowl and waders and is best two hours around high tide.

From Blackweir Bridge, continue S toward Carrigaholt but take the left after just 100m. This road passes close to Termon Point, but by continuing for 2.2km, taking a left and another immediate left, it is possible to reach the shoreline.

Species
All year Cormorant, Little Egret (O), Water Rail (O), Kingfisher (O).

Autumn, winter & spring Whooper Swan (O), (O), Brent Goose, Greylag Goose (O), Wigeon, Gadwall (O), Teal, Pintail (O), Shoveler (O), Tufted Duck (O), Scaup, Goldeneye (O), Long-

tailed Duck (R), Red-throated Diver (O), Great Northern Diver, Great Crested Grebe, Slavonian Grebe (R), Merlin (O), Peregrine, Oystercatcher, Golden Plover, Grey Plover, Lapwing (100s), Knot, Little Stint (O autumn, R winter), Curlew Sandpiper (O autumn), Dunlin, Ruff (O autumn), Jack Snipe (R), Snipe, Black-tailed Godwit, Bar-tailed Godwit, Whimbrel (small numbers, mainly spring), Curlew, Spotted Redshank (R autumn & winter), Green Sandpiper (O autumn), Mediterranean Gull (O), Little Gull (R), Ring-billed Gull (R), Iceland Gull, Glaucous Gull.

Summer Sandwich Tern, Common Tern, Arctic Tern, Sedge Warbler.

Rarities Bewick's Swan, White-fronted Goose, Green-winged Teal, Goosander, Spoonbill, Goshawk, Pectoral Sandpiper, Lesser Yellowlegs, Pomarine Skua, Yellow-legged Gull, Reed Warbler.

Clonderalaw Bay

272

Grid ref. R 11 53

Best time to visit   Best ■ Good ▣ Poor □

J F M A M J J A S O N D

A sheltered estuary with large numbers of waders and wildfowl, particularly Pintail, throughout winter.

Directions Map 172, next page. Located 5km E of Killimer, on the R473 between Ennis and Kilrush.

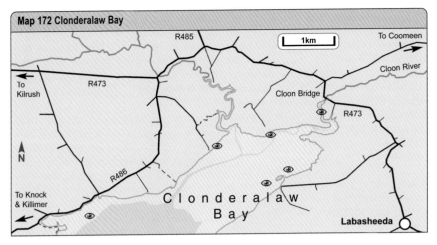

Map 172 Clonderalaw Bay

R485
To Coomeen
Cloon River
1km
To Kilrush
R473
Cloon Bridge
R473
N
R486
C l o n d e r a l a w
B a y
To Knock & Killimer
Labasheeda

The SE side of the estuary is best viewed by leaving Labasheeda N for Kilrush on the R473. After 1.5km, take the left turn immediately after the sharp left on the main road. This will lead to the shore after 2km, with extensive views over the mudflats.

Further views over the estuary can be had by returning to the R473 and going left, toward Kilrush. Take a left, 1km after passing the bridge over the Cloon River and another left after 1km. Views here are more distant. Another viewpoint can be reached by taking a left, 3.5km after passing Cloon Bridge toward Kilrush on the R473. Continue straight for 1.5km to the shoreline. Two hours either side of high tide is best for all these areas.

By continuing along the R473 toward Kilrush, the outer reaches of the estuary are visible to the left, and some duck can be usually be seen offshore.

Species
All year Cormorant, Little Egret (O), Water Rail (O), Kingfisher (R).

Autumn, winter & spring Whooper Swan (O), Brent Goose, Wigeon, Gadwall (R), Teal, Pintail, Shoveler (O), Scaup (O), Goldeneye (O), Red-throated Diver (O), Great Northern Diver, Great Crested Grebe, Merlin (O), Peregrine, Oystercatcher, Golden Plover, Grey Plover, Lapwing (100s), Knot, Dunlin, Ruff (R autumn), Jack Snipe (R), Snipe, Black-tailed Godwit, Bar-tailed Godwit, Whimbrel (small numbers, mainly spring), Curlew, Spotted Redshank (R autumn & winter), Redshank, Green Sandpiper (O autumn), Mediterranean Gull (O), Little Gull (R), Iceland Gull (O), Glaucous Gull (O).

Summer Sandwich Tern, Common Tern, Arctic Tern, Sedge Warbler.

Rarities Green-winged Teal, Slavonian Grebe, Ring-billed Gull.

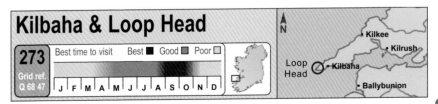

Kilbaha & Loop Head

273
Grid ref.
Q 68 47

Best time to visit   Best ■ Good ▨ Poor ☐

| J | F | M | A | M | J | J | A | S | O | N | D |

Kilkee
Kilrush
Loop Head · Kilbaha
Ballybunion

An excellent headland in spring and autumn for a good variety of scarce and rare migrants.

Directions Map 173, next page. Kilbaha and Loop Head are located at the extreme western tip of County Clare, about 30km W of Kilrush. The headland is signposted from Kilrush and Kilkee.

West

323

The lighthouse on Loop Head attracts occasional migrants in autumn, though the grounds are private property and *permission should be sought to enter the grounds*. The surrounding open moorland and fields have seen occasional rare birds, such as Hobby, Buff-breasted Sandpiper, Dotterel, Richard's Pipit and Short-toed Lark. Seawatching is possible from near the lighthouse but is a little high. If conditions are good for seawatching (strong W or NW wind), go to the nearby Bridges of Ross (Site 274).

Heading inland from the lighthouse, there is virtually no cover for 2km, until some hedges and garden, start to appear, about 1km before reaching Kilbaha. This straight stretch of road attracts many migrants in autumn. A large area of sallows is on your left, and approaching Kilbaha there is a sycamore grove and orchard, all with potential for holding migrants. *Note that gardens and farmyards should not be entered without permission*, but that in most cases, it is possible to view all these areas from the road.

There is a small pool in Kilbaha by the road junction which has occasional waterbirds, and the beach below the junction is worth checking for divers, waders and gulls. In addition, Cloghaun Lough, 2km E of Kilbaha, has regular small numbers of waterfowl and a few waders.

The best conditions for passerine migrants are any wind from the S or E, particularly if accompanied by rain or fog, from August to early November. A S or SW wind can also produce Continental migrants if the winds originate in the Bay of Biscay area.

American passerines are occasionally found, usually after a day or two of gale force W winds (which, unfortunately, usually means there are few other European migrants present). The peak time for these is the last week of September and the first two weeks of October.

In summer, there is a substantial seabird colony, on the cliffs just NE of the lighthouse. The main species are Fulmar, Kittiwake, Guillemot and Razorbill.

Species
All year Peregrine, Chough, Raven.

Spring & summer Fulmar, Shag, Peregrine (O all year), Arctic Tern (O), Kittiwake, Guillemot, Razorbill, Black Guillemot (O), Puffin (O), Cuckoo (O), Wheatear, Sedge Warbler, Willow Warbler.

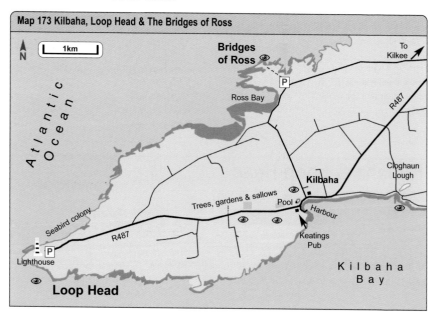

Map 173 Kilbaha, Loop Head & The Bridges of Ross

Pied Flycatcher

Autumn

For all seabirds, see Bridges of Ross (Site 274). Whooper Swan (O), Barnacle Goose (O especially October), Red-throated Diver, Great Northern Diver, Hen Harrier (O), Merlin, Golden Plover, Little Stint (O), Pectoral Sandpiper (O), Green Sandpiper (O), Curlew, Whimbrel, Mediterranean Gull (O), Sabine's Gull, Iceland Gull (R), Glaucous Gull (R), Turtle Dove (O), Redstart (R), Whinchat (R), Reed Warbler (R), Whitethroat (O), Lesser Whitethroat (R), Garden Warbler (O), Blackcap, Yellow-browed Warbler (R), Firecrest (R), Spotted Flycatcher (O), Pied Flycatcher (O), Brambling (R), Lapland Bunting (O), Snow Bunting (O).

Redwing and Fieldfare arrive on Loop Head, sometimes in considerable numbers each year, from late September and October, often during N or E winds.

Rarities Loop Head is famed for some particularly rare birds recorded over the years, with perhaps the most celebrated being Slate-coloured Junco in 1905, Rock Thrush and Yellow Warbler in 1995, Common Yellowthroat in October 2003 and Canada Warbler in 2006.

Other rarities include Buzzard, Spotted Crake, Hobby, Dotterel, American Golden Plover, Buff-breasted Sandpiper, Spotted Sandpiper, Wryneck, Short-toed Lark, Red-rumped Swallow, Richard's Pipit, Tree Pipit, Yellow Wagtail, Pied Wheatear, Red-breasted Flycatcher, Barred Warbler, Arctic Warbler, Carrion Crow, Red-eyed Vireo, Common Rosefinch, Crossbill, Ortolan Bunting, Rustic Bunting, Little Bunting, Black-headed Bunting.

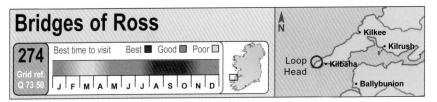

Bridges of Ross

274
Grid ref.
Q 73 50

Best time to visit   Best ■ Good ▨ Poor ☐

| J | F | M | A | M | J | J | A | S | O | N | D |

Loop Head   Kilkee   Kilrush   Kilbaha   Ballybunion

With suitable winds, one of the finest seawatching locations in Europe.

Directions Map 173, previous page. From Kilkee, take the R487 SW, and approximately 4km before Kilbaha, take the sharp right and follow this road until you see a small parking area on the right. Park here and walk out along the small headland. *Take great care near cliffs*. For seawatching, a telescope is highly recommended.

A note on conditions At any time of year, an onshore wind is most important to drive the birds against the coastline and close to 'The Bridges'. The best conditions are in autumn when a low pressure system to the N of Ireland moves swiftly E, between Scotland and Iceland. This typically produces strong SW winds, with an active weather front with rain, and then, as the front passes over, the wind swings W and then NW, with heavy rain giving way to showers. As this front clears, you are virtually guaranteed to see hundreds, or thousands, of seabirds passing the headland.

These ideal conditions usually only occur a few times each autumn, but any onshore wind is likely to produce good numbers of birds throughout the autumn. NNW and SW winds can also produce spectacular numbers. Strong winds are preferable, but it should be noted that, particularly at the height of seabird migration in August and September, it is possible to see a good variety of

West

birds even in calm conditions. Winter seawatching has only occasionally been carried out, but the same weather conditions apply. The very best seawatches often occur in the worst weather, so bring rain gear. See also SEAWATCHING, p.356.

Species

Spring & summer Evening passage of Manx Shearwaters can reach hundreds, occasionally thousands, per hour (even in light offshore winds). Also Fulmar, Storm Petrel (O), Sooty Shearwater (O), Gannet, Shag, Kittiwake, Guillemot, Razorbill, Black Guillemot (O), Puffin (small numbers, often distant), skuas (R).

Autumn Red-throated Diver, Great Northern Diver, Fulmar, Cory's Shearwater (R), Great Shearwater (R), Sooty Shearwater, Manx Shearwater (often 1000s), Balearic Shearwater (O), Storm Petrel, Leach's Petrel (mainly Sept & Oct), Gannet (often 100s), Shag, Grey Phalarope (O), Pomarine Skua, Arctic Skua, Long-tailed Skua (R), Great Skua, Little Gull (R), Sabine's Gull (O), Kittiwake (often 100s), Common Tern (O), Arctic Tern, Black Tern (R), Guillemot, Razorbill, Black

Guillemot (O), Puffin (O), Snow Bunting (R), Lapland Bunting (R).

Winter Red-throated Diver, Great Northern Diver, Fulmar, 'Blue' Fulmar (O), Manx Shearwater (O), Sooty Shearwater (O Nov, otherwise R), Leach's Petrel (O Nov), Gannet, Shag, Great Skua (R), Kittiwake, Glaucous Gull (R), Guillemot, Razorbill, Black Guillemot (O), Little Auk (R), Puffin (O), Snow Bunting (R).

Other species Chough, Wheatear (spring, summer), Peregrine (O all year), Rock Dove (O).

Rarities Since regular seawatching started at 'The Bridges' in 1977, an impressive list of rare birds has been recorded, including Goosander, Surf Scoter, Black-browed Albatross, White-billed Diver, Fea's/Zino's Petrel, Little Shearwater, Wilson's Petrel, Little Tern, Roseate Tern, Sooty Tern and White-winged Black Tern. Buff-breasted Sandpiper has been seen flying in from the sea.

See also Loop Head (Site 273).

275 Lough Gash Grid ref. R 46 72

A turlough which, when it floods in winter, attracts wildfowl, particularly Gadwall, and waders.

Map 173, right. Lough Gash is situated in a low-lying farmland area 6km NNW of Sixmilebridge, and 3km NW of of Kilmurray Post Office on the R469. Lough Gash Turlough is the best of many similar lakes and turloughs in this area when water levels are high. The extent of the lake varies throughout the year, but this is one of the last turloughs in this area to dry out each spring and sometimes retains water throughout the summer. It is also by far the best site for Gadwall in the area.

A number of waterbirds and some waders frequent the turlough and surrounding fields in winter, including Whooper Swan, Wigeon, Gadwall, Teal, Shoveler, Pochard, Tufted Duck, Goldeneye, Great Crested Grebe, Merlin (O), Peregrine, Water Rail (O), Golden Plover, Lapwing, Snipe, Woodcock (O), Black-tailed Godwit and Curlew.

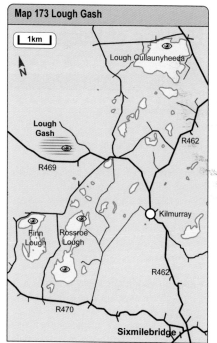

Map 173 Lough Gash

1km

Lough Cullaunyheeda

Lough Gash

R462

R469

Kilmurray

Finn Lough

Rossroe Lough

R462

R470

Sixmilebridge

Some of these species can also be found on nearby lakes, though densitites are often small. A thorough exploration of the area is well worthwhile. Of these lakes, **Lough Cullaunyheeda** 6km to the N of Kilmurray is good, and has extensive woodland around the W and SW shore, and two lakes 5km NW of Sixmilebridge, **Finn Lough** and **Rossroe Lough**, can also be good and all are best in winter.

Other sites

Kells (R 20 90) is an area of grassland which often floods in winter, attracting good numbers of wildfowl and some waders. It is 4km SE of Kilfenora in the flat, low-lying fields bordering the River Fergus, to the right of the R476 from Kilfenora to Corrofin.

Species include Bewick's Swan (R), Whooper Swan (100+), Greylag Goose (feral), Wigeon (up to 2000), Teal, Shoveler (O), Tufted Duck, Goldeneye (O), Great Crested Grebe (O), Merlin (O), Golden Plover (up to 2000), Lapwing, Dunlin, Snipe, Black-tailed Godwit and Curlew.

Lough O'Grady (R 61 84) is 3km west of Scarriff, and is best viewed from the main R461 Scarriff to Gort road. The lake is to the left, leaving Scarriff for Gort. A freshwater lake with patches of wet grassland and woodland around it, it attracts a number of birds in winter, including Great Crested Grebe (O), Whooper Swan, Pink-footed Goose (R), White-fronted Goose (O), Greylag Goose (feral), Wigeon, Teal, Shoveler (O), Pochard, Tufted Duck, Golden Plover, Lapwing, Little Stint (R), Dunlin (O), Snipe, Black-tailed Godwit (O), Curlew, gulls, Kingfisher (O).

Illaunonearaun (Q 83 57) is a large, flat-topped stack located approximately 6km SW of Kilkee, on the Loop Head Peninsula. It can be seen from the coast road, and is about 200m offshore. In winter, a flock of about 100 Branacle Geese is present.

Killimer (R 06 52). If taking the Killimer to Tarbert ferry, be sure to check the small inlet (not marked on Ordnance Survey maps) beside and W of the ferry terminal. It is immediately to your right as you descend the small hill into the terminal carpark. Good numbers of waders and gulls are often present at low tide, as well as occasional Little Egret, Mediterranean Gull and Kingfisher.

The Irish List

The **Species** column gives the English and Latin names. Alternative names are included in brackets, ie '(Northern) Gannet'.

The **Race**, or Subspecies, column includes the Latin name of any race or subspecies (the terms are interchangeable). '—' indicates where there are none, ie the species is monotypic. The symbol > indicates race/subspecies.

The **Category** column is represented by the following:

Category A Species that have been recorded in an apparently natural state in Ireland at least once since January 1950.

Category B Species that have been recorded in an apparently natural state in Ireland at least once up to 31st December 1949, but have not been recorded subsequently.

Category C1 Species that, although originally introduced by man, have established feral breeding populations in Ireland which apparently maintain themselves without necessary recourse to further introductions.

Category C2 Species that have occurred, but are considered to have originated from established naturalised populations outside Ireland.

Category D1 Species that would otherwise appear in Categories A or B, except that there is a reasonable doubt that they have ever occurred in a natural state.

Category D2 Species that have arrived through ship or other human assistance.

Category D3 Species that have only ever been found dead on the tideline.

Category D4 Species that would otherwise appear in Category C1, except that their feral populations may or may not be self-supporting.

Category E Species that have been recorded as introductions, transportees or escapes from captivity.

The **Breeding** column indicates the following:
b = breeds
rb = rare breeding
fb = formerly bred

The **Status** column gives a summary of the species' occurrence in Ireland and, where relevant, offers likely sites and habitats in which to find them. All very rare, rare and most scarce, or locally rare species will feature on the rare bird phone lines, when their presence is known. See p.5.

Species English & Latin name	Race	Category	Breeding	Status
❏ Mute Swan *Cygnus olor*	—	A,C1	b	Resident, common, widespread and conspicuous on most freshwater lakes. See p.8.
❏ Bewick's Swan *Cygnus columbianus*	*bewickii*	A	—	Winter visitor. Declining, with most birds now wintering at just two County Wexford sites: Site 122, South Slob and Site 132, The Cull & Killag. Infrequent at other wetlands.
> Whistling Swan	*columbianus*	—	—	Very rare.
❏ Whooper Swan *Cygnus cygnus*	—	A	rb	Common winter visitor to many large wetlands throughout Ireland.
❏ (Taiga) Bean Goose *Anser fabalis*	*fabalis*	A	—	Rare winter visitor.
> Tundra Bean Goose	*rossicus*	—	—	Very rare winter visitor.
❏ Pink-footed Goose *Anser brachyrhynchus*	—	A	—	Scarce winter visitor. Typically found among Greylag and other goose flocks.

English & Latin name	Race	Breeding Category	Status
❏ (Greenland) White-fronted Goose *Anser albifons*			
	flavirostris	A —	Local winter visitor. Most of the world population winters at Sites 120 and 122, Wexford Wildfowl Reserve and South Slob. See also Sites 8 & 36, Loughs Swilly and Foyle, and Sites 164–168 in County Westmeath.
> Russian White-fronted Goose	*albifrons*	— —	Rare.
❏ Lesser White-fronted Goose *Anser erythropus*		A —	Very rare.
❏ Greylag Goose *Anser anser*	*anser*	A,C1 —	Scarce local feral resident, notably at Site 129, Lady's Island Lake. Local winter visitor, mainly to wetlands in the N and E, though occurs in small numbers throughout the country. Notable sites include Site 8, Lough Swilly, Sites 77 and 78 in County Louth, and Sites 100, 101 and 103 in County Wicklow.
❏ (Lesser) Snow Goose *Anser caerulescens*	*caerulescens*	A —	Rare winter visitor. Almost annual at Site 120, Wexford Wildfowl Reserve.
> Greater Snow Goose	*atlanticus*	— —	Very rare.
❏ Canada Goose *Branta canadensis*	*canadensis*	A,C1 —	Scarce, local, feral resident, particularly in wetlands in Counties Cavan, Down and Fermanagh, and Site 189, Ballycotton. True vagrants almost annual, particularly with Barnacle Goose flocks in the NW, and at Site 120, Wexford Wildfowl Reserve.
> Taverner's Canada Goose	*taverneri*	— —	Very rare winter visitor.
> Richardson's Canada Goose	*hutchinsii*	— —	Very rare winter visitor.
> Todd's Canada Goose	*interior*	— —	Very rare winter visitor.
> Lesser Canada Goose	*parvipes*	— —	Very rare winter visitor.
❏ Barnacle Goose *Branta leucopis*	—	A,C1 —	Locally common winter visitor to coastal grasslands, mainly on islands, in Counties Donegal, Sligo, Mayo, Galway and Clare. Accessible mainland flock at Sites 25 and 26 in County Sligo. Small resident feral population, mainly in the NE.
❏ (Light-bellied) Brent Goose *Branta bernicla*			
	hrota	A —	Common winter visitor to almost every estuary of note throughout Ireland.
> Dark-bellied Brent Goose	*bernicla*	— —	Rare. Invariably seen with Brent Goose flocks.
> Grey-bellied Brent Goose	subspecies uncertain		Very rare.
		— —	Very rare.
> Black Brant	*nigricans*	— —	Very rare. Almost annual at Site 59, Strangford Lough.
❏ Red-breasted Goose *Branta ruficollis*	—	D1 —	Very rare.
❏ Ruddy Shelduck *Tadorna ferruginea*	—	B —	Very rare. May involve escapes.
❏ Shelduck *Tadorna tadorna*	—	A —	Common resident and winter visitor. See p.8.
❏ Mandarin Duck *Aix galericulata*	—	C1 —	Rare, local resident at Site 65, Tollymore Forest Park.
❏ Wigeon *Anas penelope*	—	A fb	Common winter visitor to all estuaries, and coastal and inland wetlands throughout Ireland.
❏ American Wigeon *Anas americana*	—	A —	Rare. Recorded mainly in autumn and winter, though has been seen in all months. Usually associates with Wigeon flocks.
❏ Gadwall *Anas strepera*	—	A b	Scarce local resident and uncommon winter

English & Latin name	Race	Breeding Category	Status
			visitor, mainly to the main County Wexford wetlands, Site 59; Strangford Lough, Lough Neagh (see p.71); and many turloughs and lakes in the W. Scarce or absent from much of the NW and far SW of Ireland.
❏ Baikal Teal *Anas formosa*	—	D1 —	Very rare.
❏ Teal *Anas crecca*	*crecca*	A b	Common winter visitor to all estuaries, and coastal and inland wetlands throughout Ireland. Breeds in small numbers on lakes and pools, often in open moorland and mountainous areas, mainly in the SW, W, NW and N.
❏ Green-winged Teal *Anas carolinensis*	—	A —	Rare, though small numbers occur at wetlands each winter, usually associating with Teal. Sightings feature on the bird information phone lines when their presence is known.
❏ Mallard *Anas platyrhynchos*	*platyrhynchos*	A b	Common resident and winter visitor. See p.8.
❏ American Black Duck *Anas rupripes*	—	A —	
❏ Pintail *Anas acuta*	*acuta*	A rb	Common winter visitor to most major lakes and estuaries and some inland turloughs, though scarce or absent from much of the extreme SW and NW.
❏ Garganey *Anas querquedula*	—	A rb	Scarce passage migrant and rare breeding species, seen mainly in spring at wetland sites in the SE, though can occur at wetlands throughout. One of the most reliable is Site 130, Tacumshin Lake. Sightings feature on the bird information phone lines when their presence is known.
❏ Blue-winged Teal *Anas discors*	—	A —	Very rare.
❏ Shoveler *Anas clypeata*	—	A b	Common winter visitor to most large estuaries and many inland lakes and turloughs, though scarce in the extreme SW and NW. Scarce breeding species, mainly on larger lakes in the NE and Midlands.
❏ Red-crested Pochard *Netta rufina*	—	A —	Very rare.
❏ Pochard *Aythya ferina*	—	A rb	Common winter visitor to freshwater lakes throughout. Particularly numerous at Lough Neagh (see p.71) and Site 255, Lough Corrib. Rare breeding species, mainly on larger lakes in the NE and Midlands.
❏ Redhead *Aythya americana*	—	A —	Very rare.
❏ Ring-necked Duck *Aythya collaris*	—	A —	Very rare. Between 5 and 15 occur most winters on freshwater lakes, usually associated with Pochard and Tufted Duck flocks. Sightings feature on the bird information phone lines when their presence is known.
❏ Ferruginous Duck *Aythya nyroca*	—	A —	Very rare.
❏ Tufted Duck *Aythya fuligula*	—	A b	Common winter visitor to most freshwater lakes throughout. Less common though widespread breeding species in all but the SE.
❏ (Greater) Scaup *Aythya marila*	*marila*	A —	Common but local winter visitor. Notable sites include Lough Neagh (see p.71); Site 51, Belfast Lough; Site 67, Carlingford Lough; the County

331

English & Latin name	Race	Breeding Category		Status

English & Latin name	Race			Status
				Wexford coastal sites; and Sites 223 and 224 in the Tralee Bay area. Very rare in summer.
❏ Lesser Scaup *Aythya affinis*	—	A	—	Very rare.
❏ Common Eider *Somateria mollissima*	*mollissima*	A	b	Common but local resident along rocky coasts in the N and NW, from Site 58, Outer Ards Coast, to Site 25, Raghly. Easily seen at e.g. Site 47, Rathlin Island. Slightly more widespread in winter with individuals or small numbers appearing elsewhere, often with flocks of Common Scoter.
> Northern Eider	*borealis*		—	Very rare.
❏ King Eider *Somateria spectabilis*	—	A	—	Very rare.
❏ Long-tailed Duck *Clangula hyemalis*	—	A	—	Local and uncommon winter visitor, notably at Sites 2, 12, 13 and 17 in County Donegal (see also p.40); Sites 23, 24 and 26 in County Sligo; Site 36, Lough Foyle; and Site 51, Belfast Lough. Individuals or small numbers appear irregularly elsewhere, often with flocks of Common Scoter. Rare inland.
❏ Common Scoter *Melanitta nigra*	*nigra*	A	rb	Common but local winter visitor (September to May), to large shallow bays and coasts, often some distance offshore.
❏ Surf Scoter *Melanitta perspicillata*	—	A	—	Very rare, though occurs annually, among flocks of Common Scoter (especially Sites 225 and 239 in County Kerry). Sightings feature on the bird information phone lines when their presence is known.
❏ Velvet Scoter *Melanitta fusca*	*fusca*	A	—	Scarce but regular winter visitor with individuals or small numbers occasionally present among flocks of Common Scoter, particularly on the E coast.
❏ Bufflehead *Bucephala albeola*	—	A	—	Very rare.
❏ Barrow's Goldeneye *Bucephala islandica*	—	A	—	Very rare.
❏ Goldeneye *Bucephala clangula*	*clangula*	A	rb	Common winter visitor to most freshwater lakes throughout, and some coastal sites.
❏ Hooded Merganser *Lophodytes cucullatus*	—	B	—	Very rare.
❏ Smew *Mergellus albellus*	—	A	—	Rare but regular winter visitor, mainly to freshwater lakes in the N half of Ireland. Sightings feature on the bird information phone lines when their presence is known.
❏ Red-breasted Merganser *Mergus serrator*	—	A	b	Uncommon but widespread winter visitor to most large bays and outer estuaries, though scarcer in the SW. In summer breeds in small numbers on coast and some inland lakes, N of a line from Galway to Dundalk.
❏ Goosander *Mergus merganser*	*merganser*	A	rb	Scarce winter visitor to freshwater lakes, mainly in the N, particularly around Lough Neagh (see p.71), and in County Wicklow at Sites 101, 107 and 111. Very rare breeding bird. Sightings feature on the bird information phone lines when their presence is known.
❏ Ruddy Duck *Oxyura jamaicensis*	*jamaicensis*	C1+2	b	Scarce and local resident, mainly at sites around Lough Neagh (see p.71) and a small population

English & Latin name	Race	Breeding Category	Status
			at Site 129, Lady's Island Lake. Rare elsewhere, though sightings often feature on the bird information phone lines when their presence is known.
❏ Red Grouse *Lagopus (lagopus) scotica*	—	A b	Local resident at low densities, mostly on high plateau with heather moorland. Best areas include Site 48, the Glens of Antrim; Sites 73, 74 and 75 in County Fermanagh; and Site 104 in County Wicklow. See also p.131, Glendoo Mountain.
❏ Grey Partridge *Perdix perdix*	*perdix*	A,C1 b	Rare local resident, only found at Site 170, Lough Boora Parklands.
❏ Quail *Coturnix coturnix*	*coturnix*	A b	Rare and local summer visitor and rare passage migrant. Sightings feature on the bird information phone lines when their presence is known.
❏ Pheasant *Phasianus colchicus*	*colchicus*	C1 b	Very common resident. See p.9.
❏ Red-throated Diver *Gavia stellata*	—	A rb	Very common winter visitor to shallow coastal waters throughout. Rare only in mid-summer.
❏ Black-throated Diver *Gavia arctica*	*arctica*	A —	Scarce winter visitor. Favoured areas include Sites 16 and 17 in County Donegal; Site 129, Lady's Island Lake, particularly in spring; and Site 256, Galway Bay. Occurs rarely at other sites, and these sightings feature on the bird information phone lines when their presence is known. Very rare inland.
❏ Great Northern Diver *Gavia immer*	—	A —	Very common winter visitor to all shallow coastal waters. Rare only in mid-summer.
❏ White-billed Diver *Gavia adamsii*	—	A —	Very rare.
❏ Pied-billed Grebe *Podilymbus podiceps*	*podiceps*	A —	Very rare.
❏ Little Grebe *Tachybaptus ruficollis*	*ruficollis*	A b	Common resident on most shallow, freshwater lakes and slow-moving or still waters.
❏ Great Crested Grebe *Podiceps cristatus*	*cristatus*	A b	Common in winter on shallow coastal bays and lakes, especially in the NE, Midlands and E. Scarce or absent in many W and SW areas. In summer, breeds mainly on the larger NE and Midland lakes.
❏ Red-necked Grebe *Podiceps grisegena*	*grisegena*	A —	Rare winter visitor. Usually seen each winter at Site 120, in Wexford Harbour; at Site 223, Sandy Bay; and Site 256, Galway Bay. Sightings feature on the bird information phone lines when their presence is known.
❏ Slavonian Grebe *Podiceps auritus*	*auritus*	A —	Scarce and local winter visitor to shallow coastal bays. Reliable sites include Sites 8 and 16 in County Donegal; Sites 35 and 36 in County Derry; Site 59, Strangford Lough; Site 223, Sandy Bay; and Site 256, Galway Bay and occasionally elsewhere. Sightings feature on the bird information phone lines when their presence is known.
❏ Black-necked Grebe *Podiceps nigricollis*	*nigricollis*	A fb	Rare winter visitor, usually occurring at coastal sites favoured by other grebes and divers. Sightings feature on the bird information phone lines when their presence is known.

English & Latin name	Race	Breeding Category		Status
❏ Black-browed Albatross *Diomedea melanophris*				
	melanophris	A	—	Very rare.
❏ Fulmar *Fulmarus glacialis*	*glacialis*	A	b	Common at coastal cliffs and common offshore throughout the year.
❏ Fea's/Zino's Petrel *Pterodroma Feae/madeira*		A	—	Very rare.
❏ Bulwer's Petrel *Bulweria bulwerii*	—	A	—	Very rare.
❏ Cory's Shearwater *Calonectris diomedea*	*borealis*	A	—	Rare to scarce passage migrant in autumn. See p.356.
❏ Great Shearwater *Puffinus gravis*	—	A	—	Rare to scarce passage migrant in autumn. See p356.
❏ Sooty Shearwater *Puffinus griseus*	—	A	—	Passage migrant. See p.356.
❏ Manx Shearwater *Puffinus puffinus*	—	A	b	Common offshore on all coasts from late April to early November. Rare in winter. See p.356.
❏ Balearic Shearwater *Puffinus mauretanicus*	—	A	—	Scarce passage migrant in autumn. See p.356.
❏ Little Shearwater *Puffinus assimilis*	*baroli*	A	—	Very rare. See p.356.
❏ Wilson's Petrel *Oceanites oceanicus*	*exasperatus*	A	—	Very rare passage migrant in autumn. See p.356.
❏ Storm Petrel *Hydrobates pelagicus*	—	A	b	Common well offshore, from May to late September. See p.356.
❏ Leach's Petrel *Oceanodroma leucorhoa*	*leucorhoa*	A	b	Scarce passage migrant mainly off N and W coasts in September and October. See p.356.
❏ Swinhoe's Petrel *Oceanodroma monorhis*	—	A	—	Very rare.
❏ Madeiran Petrel *Oceanodroma castro*	—	B	—	Very rare.
❏ (Northern) Gannet *Morus bassanus*	—	A	b	Common offshore throughout spring, summer and autumn, less frequent in winter. See p.8 and p.356.
❏ Cormorant *Phalacrocorax carbo*	*carbo*	A	b	Common resident on most large lakes and rivers throughout and present at most major seabird colonies in summer.
> Continental Cormorant	*sinensis*	—	—	Very rare.
❏ Double-crested Cormorant *Phalacrocorax auritus*				
	auritus	A	—	Very rare.
❏ Shag *Phalacrocorax aristotelis*	*aristotelis*	A	b	Common in all coastal areas throughout the year. Strictly coastal – virtually never seen inland.
❏ Frigatebird sp., probably.		A	—	Very rare.
Magnificent Frigatebird *Fregata magnificens*				
❏ (Common) Bittern *Botaurus stellaris*	*stellaris*	A	fb	Very rare.
❏ American Bittern *Botaurus lentiginosus*	—	A	—	Very rare.
❏ Little Bittern *Ixobrychus minutus*	*minutus*	A	—	Very rare.
❏ (Black-crowned) Night Heron *Nycticorax nycticorax*				
	nycticorax	A	—	Very rare.
❏ Squacco Heron *Ardeola ralloides*	—	A	—	Very rare.
❏ Green Heron *Butorides virescens*	—	A	—	Very rare.
❏ Cattle Egret *Bubulcus ibis*	*ibis*	A	—	Very rare.
❏ Little Egret *Egretta garzetta*	*garzetta*	A	b	Scarce to common (and increasing) at estuaries and coastal wetlands throughout the year, S of a line from Galway to Belfast, though small numbers increasingly appearing in the N.
❏ Great White Egret *Ardea alba*	*alba*	A	—	Very rare.
❏ Grey Heron *Ardea cinerea*	*cinerea*	A	b	Common resident. See p.9.
❏ Purple Heron *Ardea purpurea*	*purpurea*	A	—	Very rare.

English & Latin name	Race	Breeding Category		Status
❏ Black Stork *Ciconia nigra*	—	A	—	Very rare.
❏ White Stork *Ciconia ciconia*	*ciconia*	A	—	Very rare.
❏ Glossy Ibis *Plegadis falcinellus*	*falcinellus*	A	—	Very rare.
❏ Spoonbill *Platalea leucorodia*	*leucorodia*	A	—	Rare.
❏ Greater Flamingo *Phoenicopterus ruber*	*roseus*	D1	—	Very rare. Status uncertain.
❏ Honey Buzzard *Pernis apivorus*	—	A	—	Very rare.
❏ Black Kite *Milvus migrans*	*migrans*	A	—	Vagrant.
❏ Red Kite *Milvus milvus*	*milvus*	A,C2	—	Rare.
❏ White-tailed (Sea) Eagle *Haliaeetus albicilla*	—	A	fb	Very rare. Planned reintroduction project underway at Site 236, Killarney National Park.
❏ Bald Eagle *Haliaeetus leucocephalus*	*washingtonien*	A	—	Very rare.
❏ Griffon Vulture *Gyps fulvus*	*fulvus*	B	—	Very rare.
❏ (Western) Marsh Harrier *Circus aeruginosus aeruginosus*		A	fb	Scarce to rare, frequenting large reedbeds, mainly from May to September. Most reliable is Site 130, Tacumshin Lake.
❏ Hen Harrier *Circus cyaneus*	*cyaneus*	A	b	Rare local breeder in midlands and W, mainly in upland conifer plantations. More widespread but still uncommon in winter, usually at large wetlands.
❏ Montagu's Harrier *Circus pygargus*	—	A	fb	Rare.
❏ Goshawk *Accipiter gentilis*	*gentilis*	A	b	Rare.
> American Goshawk	*atricapillus*	—	—	Very rare.
❏ Sparrowhawk *Accipter nisus*	*nisus*	A	b	Common resident. See p.9.
❏ Buzzard *Buteo buteo*	*buteo*	A	b	Scarce to uncommon resident, mainly in N half of Ireland. Slowly increasing in the S and SW, though still rare in County Kerry. Particularly good sites include Site 1, Malin Head; Sites 44 to 48 in County Antrim; and Site 86, Rogerstown Estuary.
❏ Rough-legged Buzzard *Buteo lagopus*	*lagopus*	A	—	Very rare.
> Rough-legged Hawk	*sanctijohanni*	A	—	Very rare.
❏ Spotted Eagle *Aquila clanga*	—	B	—	Very rare.
❏ Golden Eagle *Aquila chrysaetos*	*chrysaetos*	A	fb	Very rare. Almost annual in summer at Site 47, Rathlin Island. Reintroduction project under way at Site 9, Glenveagh National Park.
❏ Booted Eagle *Hieraaetus pennatus*	—	D1	—	Very rare.
❏ Osprey *Pandion haliaetus*	*haliaetus*	A	—	Rare, in spring and autumn. Regular at Site Site 42, Lough Beg, in August and September.
❏ Lesser Kestrel *Falco naumanni*	—	B	—	Very rare.
❏ Kestrel *Falco tinnunculus*	*tinnunculus*	A	b	Common resident. See p.9.
❏ Red-footed Falcon *Falco vespertinus*	—	A	—	Very rare.
❏ Merlin *Falco columbarius*	*aesalon*	A	b	Scarce to rare in summer, breeding in open heather moorland mainly in the N, W and in County Wicklow. Uncommon migrant and winter visitor, most often seen at or near coastal wetlands.
> Iceland Merlin	*subaesalon*	—	—	Winter visitor.
> Taiga Merlin	*columbarius*	—	—	Very rare.
❏ Hobby *Falco subbuteo*	*subbuteo*	A	—	Rare.
❏ Gyr Falcon *Falco rusticolus*	—	A	—	Rare.
❏ Peregrine *Falco peregrinus*	*peregrinus*	A	b	Scarce resident at coastal and inland cliffs throughout Ireland. More widespread in winter,

English & Latin name	Race	Breeding Category		Status
				often at coastal wetlands and estuaries.
❏ Water Rail *Rallus aquaticus*	aquaticus	A	b	Common throughout the year in reedbeds and wetland scrub. Very vocal, though always difficult to see.
❏ Spotted Crake *Porzana porzana*	—	A	fb	Rare.
❏ Sora Rail *Porzana carolina*	—	A	—	Very rare.
❏ Little Crake *Porzana parva*	—	B	—	Very rare.
❏ Baillon's Crake *Porzana pusilla*	intermedia	B	—	Very rare.
❏ Corncrake *Crex crex*	—	A	b	Scarce to rare and local summer visitor. Site 3, Tory Island, and Site 169, The Shannon Callows, are reliable sites where they can often be heard, but are difficult to see.
❏ Moorhen *Gallinula chloropus*	chloropus	A	b	Common resident. See p.9.
❏ Coot *Fulica atra*	atra	A	b	Common resident. See p.9.
❏ American Coot *Fulica americana*	americana	A	—	Very rare.
❏ Common Crane *Grus grus*	grus	A	—	Rare.
❏ Sandhill Crane *Grus canadensis*	canadensis	B	—	Very rare.
❏ Little Bustard *Tetrax tetrax*	—	B	—	Very rare.
❏ Great Bustard *Otis tarda*	tarda	B	—	Very rare.
❏ Oystercatcher *Haematopus ostralegus*	ostralegus	A	b	Common throughout the year. See p.10.
❏ Black-winged Stilt *Himantopus himantopus*	himantopus	A	—	Rare.
❏ Avocet *Recurvirostra avosetta*	—	A	fb	Rare.
❏ Stone Curlew *Burhinnus oedicnemus*	oedicnemus	A	—	Very rare.
❏ Cream-coloured Courser *Cursorius cursor*	cursor	A	—	Very rare.
❏ Collared Pratincole *Glareola pratincola*	pratincola	A	—	Very rare.
❏ Black-winged Pratincole *Glareola nordmanni*	—	A	—	Very rare.
❏ Little Ringed Plover *Charadrius dubius*	curonicus	A	rb	Very rare.
❏ Ringed Plover *Charadrius hiaticula*	hiaticula	A	b	Common resident and winter visitor. See. p.10.
> Tundra Ringed Plover	tundrae	—	—	Uncommon passage migrant.
❏ Semipalmated Plover *Charadrius semipalmatus*	—	A	—	Very rare.
❏ Killdeer *Charadrius vociferus*	vociferus	A	—	Very rare.
❏ Kentish Plover *Charadrius alexandrinus*	alexandrinus	A	—	Very rare.
❏ Dotterel *Charadrius morinellus*	—	A	fb	Rare passage migrant.
❏ American Golden Plover *Pluvialis dominica*	—	A	—	Very rare.
❏ Pacific Golden Plover *Pluvialis fulva*	—	A	—	Very rare.
❏ Golden Plover *Pluvialis apricaria*	—	A	b	Scarce local breeder in upland moorland in the W and NW. Common winter visitor to most large estuaries, wetlands and wet grasslands.
❏ Grey Plover *Pluvialis squatarola*	—	A	—	Common winter visitor to most large estuaries and some coastal beaches. Rare in summer (though non-breeding birds often seen at Site 130, Tacumshin Lake).
❏ Sociable Plover *Vanellus gregaria*	—	A	—	Very rare.
❏ Lapwing *Vanellus vanellus*	—	A	b	Common winter visitor to all estuaries, wetlands and wet grasslands throughout Ireland. Scarce breeding bird, at shallow lakes mainly in the W and NW.
❏ (Red) Knot *Calidris canutus*	canutus	A	—	Common winter visitor to all large estuaries. Rare in summer (though non-breeding birds often seen at Site 130, Tacumshin Lake).
❏ Sanderling *Calidris alba*	—	A	—	Common winter visitor to most large sandy beaches and estuaries throughout Ireland. Rare in mid-summer. See p.10.

English & Latin name	Race	Breeding Category	Status
❑ Semipalmated Sandpiper *Calidris pusilla*	—	A —	Very rare.
❑ Western Sandpiper *Calidris mauri*	—	A —	Very rare.
❑ Red-necked Stint *Calidris ruficollis*	—	A —	Very rare.
❑ Little Stint *Calidris minuta*	—	A —	Uncommon passage migrant to coastal wetlands in September and October. Most often encountered wherever flocks of Dunin are present, particularly on the E, SE and S coast.
❑ Temminck's Stint *Calidris temminckii*	—	A —	Very rare.
❑ Long-toed Stint *Calidris subminuta*	—	A —	Very rare.
❑ Least Sandpiper *Calidris minutilla*	—	A —	Very rare.
❑ White-rumped Sandpiper *Calidris fuscicollis*	—	A —	Very rare. Annual in September/October at Site 130, Tacumshin Lake.
❑ Baird's Sandpiper *Calidris bairdii*	—	A —	Very rare. Annual in September/October at Site 130, Tacumshin Lake.
❑ Pectoral Sandpiper *Calidris melanotus*	—	A —	Rare, mainly on muddy or sparsely vegetated pools at coastal wetlands. Almost annual in September at Site 86, Rogerstown Estuary; Site 99, Kilcoole; Sites 127, 130 and 132 in County Wexford; Site 189, Ballycotton; and Site 227, Smerwick Harbour. Sightings feature on the bird information phone lines when their presence is known.
❑ Sharp-tailed Sandpiper *Calidris acuminata*	—	A —	Very rare.
❑ Curlew Sandpiper *Calidris ferruginea*	—	A —	Uncommon passage migrant from late August to early October at estuaries, mainly in the E and SE. Numbers vary annually, though Site 130, Tacumshin Lake, is particularly reliable in September. Sightings feature on bird information phone lines when their presence is known.
❑ Purple Sandpiper *Calidris maritima*	—	A —	Scarce, local winter visitor to rocky coasts, particularly in the W. On the E coast, good areas include Sites 85 and 93 in County Dublin. Highest numbers occur at Site 264 in County Clare.
❑ Dunlin *Calidris alpina*	alpina	A —	Common in spring, autumn and winter at all estuaries and muddy wetlands. Rare at these sites in early summer.
>	arctica	— —	Scarce passage migrant.
>	schinzii	— b	Scarce local breeder at shallow lakes and pools in the W and NW.
❑ Broad-billed Sandpiper *Limicola falcinellus falcinellus*		A —	Very rare.
❑ Stilt Sandpiper *Micropalama bimantopus*	—	A —	Very rare.
❑ Buff-breasted Sandpiper *Tryngites subruficollis*		A —	Very rare. Almost annual in September at Site 130, Tacumshin Lake and Site 219, Carrahane.
❑ Ruff *Philomachus pugnax*	—	A —	Uncommon passage migrant, mainly in August and September, and uncommon winter visitor to wetlands and estuaries. Most regular sites are Site 55, Belfast Harbour RSPB Reserve; the Wexford wetlands; and Site 189, Ballycotton, though small numbers can turn up at other wetland sites.
❑ Jack Snipe *Lymnocryptes minimus*	—	A —	Scarce, though widespread winter visitor to wetland fringes. Rarely seen, and usually flushes from almost underfoot.

337

English & Latin name	Race	Breeding Category		Status
❏ (Common) Snipe *Gallinago gallinago*	*gallinago*	A	b	Common and widespread. See p.10.
❏ Wilson's Snipe *Gallinago delicata*		A	—	Very rare.
❏ Great Snipe *Gallinago media*	—	A	—	Very rare.
❏ Short-billed Dowitcher *Limnodromus griseus griseus*		A	—	Very rare.
❏ Long-billed Dowitcher *Limnodromus scolopaceus*		A	—	Very rare.
❏ Woodcock *Scolopax rusticola*	—	A	b	Resident in open, mature woodland edges throughout Ireland, though scarce along W coastal fringes. Most easily seen during display flight at dusk, from April to June.
❏ Black-tailed Godwit *Limosa limosa islandica*		A	rb	Common from August to late April, on most large estuaries and wetlands, though scarce in the NW, W and extreme SW. Some non-breeding birds occur in summer, particularly at Site 130, Tacumshin Lake.
> Black-tailed Godwit	*limosa*	—	—	Very rare.
❏ Bar-tailed Godwit *Limosa lapponica*	*lapponica*	A	—	Common winter visitor to sandy shores and estuaries. Rare from May to August.
❏ Eskimo Curlew *Numenius borealis*	—	B	—	Very rare (species probably extinct).
❏ Whimbrel *Numenius phaeopus*	*phaeopus*	A	—	Common passage migrant in spring and autumn, particularly in May. Small numbers occur on rocky coasts, particularly on the W coast in mid-summer and winter.
> Hudsonian Whimbrel	*hudsonicus*	—	—	Very rare.
❏ Curlew *Numenius arquata*	*arquata*	A	b	Common throughout the year. See p.10.
❏ Upland Sandpiper *Bartramia longicauda*	—	A	—	Very rare.
❏ Spotted Redshank *Tringa erythropus*	—	A	—	Uncommon passage migrant and winter visitor. Regular sites include Site 120, Wexford Wildfowl Reserve; Site 208, Rosscarbery; and Site 220, Barrow Harbour.
❏ (Common) Redshank *Tringa totanus*	*totanus*	A	b	Common winter visitor and scarce breeding species. See p.11.
❏ Marsh Sandpiper *Tringa stagnatilis*	—	A	—	Very rare.
❏ Greenshank *Tringa nebularia*	—	A	fb	Common passage migrant and winter visitor. Rare between late May and mid-July. See p.11.
❏ Greater Yellowlegs *Tringa melanoleuca*	—	A	—	Very rare.
❏ Lesser Yellowlegs *Tringa flavipes*	—	A	—	Very rare.
❏ Solitary Sandpiper *Tringa solitaria*	*solitaria*	A	—	Very rare.
❏ Green Sandpiper *Tringa ochropus*	—	A	—	Uncommon passage migrant to upper reaches of estuaries and muddy pools, mainly in July and August. Rarer in September and through out winter. Most regular at E coast sites, especially Site 86, Rogerstown Estuary, though high numbers can occur at Site 183, Mallow Sugar Factory Lagoons.
❏ Wood Sandpiper *Tringa glareola*	—	A	—	Scarce autumn passage migrant, to shallow muddy pools, lagoons and upper reaches of estuaries. No regular sites, though any sightings feature on the bird information phone lines when their presence is known.
❏ Terek Sandpiper *Xenus cinereus*	—	A	—	Very rare.
❏ Common Sandpiper *Actitis hypoleucos*	—	A	b	Summer visitor, breeding on open mountain lake edges in the SW, W and NW. In spring and autumn often seen on upper reaches of estuaries and sheltered coastlines. Occasionally

English & Latin name	Race	Breeding Category		Status
				winters, on sheltered coasts or estuaries.
❏ Spotted Sandpiper *Actitis macularia*	—	A	—	Very rare.
❏ Turnstone *Arenaria interpres*	interpres	A	—	Common winter visitor and passage migrant to all rocky coasts. Small numbers of non-breeding birds present throughout summer. See p.11.
❏ Wilson's Phalarope *Phalaropus tricolor*	—	A	—	Very rare.
❏ Red-necked Phalarope *Phalaropus lobatus*	—	A	fb	Very rare.
❏ Grey Phalarope *Phalaropus fulicarius*	—	A	—	Uncommon offshore passage migrant (rarely on coastal wetlands), in September and October. See p.356. Rare in winter. Sightings feature on the bird information phone lines when their presence is known.
❏ Pomarine Skua *Stercorarius pomarinus*	—	A	—	Uncommon passage migrant, mainly in May and autumn. See p.356.
❏ Arctic Skua *Stercorarius parasiticus*	—	A	—	Common passage migrant mainly in May and autumn. See p.356.
❏ Long-tailed Skua *Stercorarius longicaudus*	longicaudus	A	—	Rare passage migrant. See p.356.
❏ Great Skua (Bonxie) *Catharacta skua*	—	A	rb	Common passage migrant, mainly in May and autumn. Rare in winter. See p.356.
❏ Mediterranean Gull *Larus melanocephalus*	—	A	rb	Uncommon, but slowly increasing, in autumn, winter and early spring, scarce in summer. Can occur on estuaries, beaches and harbours – wherever large numbers of gulls gather, notably Sites 91, 92 and 93 in County Dublin and Site 194, Cobh. Regular at E, SE and S coastal sites, scarcer to the NW and rare inland.
❏ Laughing Gull *Larus atricilla*	megalopterus	A	—	Very rare.
❏ Franklin's Gull *Larus pipixican*	—	A	—	Very rare.
❏ Little Gull *Larus minutus*	—	A	—	Scarce passage migrant and winter visitor, mainly to E and SE coastal sites, wherever gull flocks gather. Uncommon to rare on W coast, though small numbers winter at Site 256, Galway Bay. Can occur in 100s, particularly Sites 98 and 99 during E gales in winter.
❏ Sabine's Gull *Larus sabini*	—	A	—	Scarce passage migrant to offshore waters, mainly in September. See p.356.
❏ Bonaparte's Gull *Larus philadelphia*	—	A	—	Very rare.
❏ Black-headed Gull *Larus ridibundus*	—	A	b	Very common all year. See p.11.
❏ Ring-billed Gull *Larus delawarensis*	—	A	—	Rare but regular throughout the year, wherever large numbers of gulls gather. Notable sites include Site 257, Nimmo's Pier, and Sandymount Strand (see Site 92) where one or more are usually present throughout the year.
❏ Common Gull *Larus canus*	canus	A	b	Common throughout the year. See p.11.
❏ (Western) Lesser Black-backed Gull *Larus fuscus graellsii*		A	b	Common summer visitor, small numbers in winter. See p.12.
> Continental Lesser Black-backed Gull	intermedius	A	—	Rare.
❏ Herring Gull *Larus argentatus*	argenteus	A	b	Common throughout the year. See p.12.
> Scandinavian Herring Gull	argentatus	A	—	Scarce winter visitor.
❏ American Herring Gull *Larus smithsonianus*		A	—	Very rare winter visitor. Regular sightings at Site 257, Nimmo's Pier. Individuals often remain for long periods and sightings feature on the bird information phone lines when their presence is known.

English & Latin name	Race	Breeding Category		Status
❏ Yellow-legged Gull *Larus michahellis*	*michahellis*	A	—	Rare, mainly in winter, and most often at E and SE coastal sites, wherever gull flocks gather. Sightings feature on the bird information phone lines when their presence is known.
❏ Caspian Gull *Larus cachinnans*	*cachinnans*	A	—	Very rare.
❏ Iceland Gull *Larus glaucoides*	*glaucoides*	A	—	Uncommon winter visitor, particularly to coastal harbours, notably Site 15, Killybegs; Site 257, Nimmo's Pier; and Site 232, Dingle Harbour. Numbers vary each winter. Sightings feature on the bird information phone lines when their presence is known.
> Kumlien's Gull	*kumlieni*	A	—	Very rare.
❏ Thayer's Gull *Larus thayeri*	—	A	—	Very rare.
❏ Glaucous Gull *Larus hyperboreus*	*hyperboreus*	A	—	Uncommon winter visitor, particularly to coastal harbours, notably Site 15, Killybegs, and Site 257, Nimmo's Pier. Numbers vary each winter. Sightings feature on the bird information phone lines when their presence is known.
❏ Great Black-backed Gull *Larus marinus*	—	A	b	Common throughout the year. See p.12.
❏ Ross's Gull *Rhodostethia rosea*	—	A	—	Very rare. Most records from Site 257, Nimmo's Pier.
❏ (Black-legged) Kittiwake *Rissa tridactyla*	*tridactyla*	A	b	Common summer visitor and passage migrant to coastal waters. Breeds on vertical cliffs at nearly all coastal seabird colonies. Smaller numbers in winter in coastal areas, and can occur in very large numbers.
❏ Ivory Gull *Pagophila eburnea*	—	A	—	Very rare.
❏ Gull-billed Tern *Sterna nilotica*	*nilotica*	A	—	Very rare.
❏ Caspian Tern *Sterna caspia*	—	A	—	Very rare.
❏ Royal Tern *Sterna maxima*	*maxima*	D3	—	Very rare.
❏ Lesser Crested Tern *Sterna bengalensis*	*torresii*	A	—	Very rare.
❏ Sandwich Tern *Sterna sandvicensis*	*sandvicensis*	A	b	Common summer visitor and passage migrant. Best areas include Site 49, Larne Lough; Site 59, Strangford Lough; Site 67, Carlingford Lough; and Site 129, Lady's Island Lake. Common in small numbers on all coasts in spring and autumn. Rare in winter (though regular at Site 257, Nimmo's Pier).
❏ Elegant Tern *Sterna elegans*	*elegans*	A	—	Very rare.
❏ Roseate Tern *Sterna dougallii*	*dougallii*	A	b	Uncommon and local summer visitor. Can be seen in the vicinity of Site 49, Larne Lough; Site 85, Skerries; and Site 129, Lady's Island Lake. In August and September, evening roosts occur at Site 92 (Sandymount Strand) and Site 127, Nethertown Beach. Rare elsewhere.
❏ Common Tern *Sterna hirundo*	*hirundo*	A	b	Common, but local summer visitor, mainly to E and SE colonies (same as Sandwich Tern, above), though smaller numbers also breed at eg Sites 91 and 92, Dublin Bay; Site 197, Lough Beg; and Site 256, Galway Bay.
❏ Arctic Tern *Sterna paradisaea*	—	A	b	Common summer visitor and passage migrant. Occurs at sites listed for Sandwich and Common Tern above. Common in spring and

English & Latin name	Race	Breeding Category		Status
❏ Forster's Tern *Sterna forsteri*	—	A	—	Very rare.
❏ Bridled Tern *Sterna anaethetus*	*melanoptera*	D3	—	Very rare.
❏ Sooty Tern *Sterna fuscata*	*fuscata*	A	—	Very rare.
❏ Little Tern *Sterna albifrons*	*albifrons*	A	b	Scarce and local summer visitor. Accessible sites include Site 3, Tory Island; Site 116, Cahore; Site 99, Kilcoole; Site 222, Rough Point; and Site 243, The Mullet Peninsula. Rare elsewhere.
❏ Whiskered Tern *Chlidonias hybridus*	*hybridus*	A	—	Very rare.
❏ Black Tern *Chlidonias niger*	*niger*	A	fb	Scarce to rare passage migrant, particularly to coastal wetlands in the SE, and from headlands in the SW and W in autumn. Sightings feature on the bird information phone lines when their presence is known.
> American Black Tern	*surinamensis*	—	—	Very rare.
❏ White-winged Black Tern *Chlidonias leucopterus*		A	—	Rare passage migrant, mainly in autumn.
❏ (Southern) Guillemot *Uria aalge*	*albionis*	A	b	Common in coastal waters throughout the year. Breeds in large colonies on all coasts, the most spectacular at Site 47, Rathlin Island.
> Northern Guillemot	*aalge*	—	—	Common winter visitor.
❏ Brünnich's Guillemot *Uria lomvia*	*lomvia*	A	—	Very rare.
❏ Razorbill *Alca torda*	*islandica*	A	b	Common in coastal waters throughout the year. Breeds in large colonies on all coasts.
> Northern Razorbill	*torda*	—	—	Rare.
❏ Black Guillemot *Cepphus grylle*	*arcticus*	A	b	Widespread in small numbers on all rocky coasts, islands and some harbours throughout the year, though scarce on SE and S coasts. Accessible sites include Site 56, Bangor; Sites 85, 89 and 90 in County Dublin; and Site 232, Dingle Harbour. Common at Sites 212 and 213, Sherkin Island and Cape Clear Island.
❏ Little Auk *Alle alle*	*alle*	A	—	Scarce winter visitor, from early November to April, to offshore waters, rarely inshore. Sightings feature on the bird information phone lines when their presence is known.
❏ Puffin *Fratercula arctica*	*grabae*	A	b	Common but local summer visitor, breeding mainly on remote offshore islands. Most accessible sites include Site 47, Rathlin Island; Site 134, Great Saltee Island; Site 238, Great Skellig; and particularly Site 265, Cliffs of Moher. Scarce in winter, usually well offshore.
❏ Pallas's Sandgrouse *Syrrhaptes paradoxus*	—	B	—	Very rare.
❏ Rock Dove *Columba livia*	*livia*	A	b	Local resident in extreme SW, W and NW. Large feral population common in towns and cities. See p.12.
❏ Stock Dove *Columba oenas*	*oenas*	A	b	Uncommon resident, mainly on rich agricultural land and cereal growing areas in the E, SE and S. Largely absent from far SW, W and NW.
❏ Woodpigeon *Columba palumbus*	*palumbus*	A	b	Very common resident. See p.13.
❏ Collared Dove *Streptopelia decaocto*	*decaocto*	A	b	Common resident. See p.13.

English & Latin name	Race	Category	Breeding	Status
❏ Turtle Dove *Streptopelia turtur*	*turtur*	A	fb	Scarce passage migrant, mainly to headlands and islands on S and SE coasts, though can occur inland. Regular in May at Site 134, Great Saltee Island, and at Site 213, Cape Clear Island in autumn.
❏ Great Spotted Cuckoo *Clamator glandarius* —		A	—	Very rare.
❏ (Common) Cuckoo *Cuculus canorus*	*canorus*	A	b	Scarce and decreasing summer visitor, from May to early July. Occurs in a wide variety of habitats throughout, favouring scrub and wetland edges, but nowhere common. A good area is the Burren, in the vicinity of Site 263, Ballyvaughan.
❏ Black-billed Cuckoo *Coccyzus erythrophthalmus* —		B	—	Very rare.
❏ Yellow-billed Cuckoo *Coccyzus americanus* —		A	—	Very rare.
❏ Barn Owl *Tyto alba*	*alba*	A	b	Uncommon resident in low-lying agricultural areas.
> Dark-breasted Barn Owl	*guttata*	—	—	Very rare.
❏ Scops Owl *Otus scops*	*scops*	A	—	Very rare.
❏ Snowy Owl *Nyctea scandiaca*	—	A	rb	Very rare.
❏ Little Owl *Athene noctua*	*vidalli*	A	—	Very rare.
❏ Long-eared Owl *Asio otus*	*otus*	A	b	Scarce resident, in mature woodland. The commonest owl in Ireland, though always difficult to see.
❏ Short-eared Owl *Asio flammeus*	*flammeus*	A	fb	Uncommon winter visitor to wetland edges, coastal grasslands and sand dunes, mainly on E coasts, eg Site 86, Rogerstown Estuary; Sites 99, 100 and 101 in County Wicklow; and Site 130, Tacumshin Lake.
❏ (European) Nightjar *Caprimulgus europaeus europaeus*		A	rb	Very rare summer visitor. Rare passage migrant.
❏ Common Nighthawk *Chordeiles minor*	*minor*	A	—	Very rare.
❏ Chimney Swift *Chaetura pelagica*	—	A	—	Very rare.
❏ White-throated Needletail *Hirundapus caudacutus*	*caudacutus*	A	—	Very rare.
❏ (Common) Swift *Apus apus*	*apus*	A	b	Common summer visitor. See p.13.
❏ Pallid Swift *Apus pallidus*	*brehmorum*	A	—	Very rare.
❏ Alpine Swift *Apus melba*	*melba*	A	—	Very rare.
❏ Little Swift *Apus affinis*	*galilejensis*	A	—	Very rare.
❏ Kingfisher *Alcedo atthis*	*ispida*	A	b	Uncommon resident on most slow-moving rivers and lake edges, occasionally on higher reaches of estuaries.
❏ Belted Kingfisher *Ceryle alcyon*	—	A	—	Very rare.
❏ (European) Bee-eater *Merops apiaster*	—	A	—	Very rare.
❏ (European) Roller *Coracias garrulus*	*garrulus*	A	—	Very rare.
❏ Hoopoe *Upupa epops*	*epops*	A	—	Rare passage migrant.
❏ Wryneck *Jynx torquilla*	*torquilla*	A	—	Rare passage migrant.
❏ Yellow-shafted (Northern) Flicker *Colaptes auratus*		D2	—	Very rare.
❏ Green Woodpecker *Picus viridis*	*viridis*	B	—	Very rare.
❏ Yellow-bellied Sapsucker *Sphyrapicus varius*		A	—	Very rare.
❏ Great Spotted Woodpecker *Dendrocopos major*		A	fb	Rare.
❏ Short-toed Lark *Calandrella brachydactyla*	*brachydactyla*	A	—	Rare passage migrant.
❏ Woodlark *Lullula arborea*	*arborea*	A	fb	Very rare.
❏ Skylark *Alauda arvensis*	*arvensis*	A	b	Very common resident. See p.13.
❏ Shore Lark *Eremophila alpestris*	*flava*	A	—	Very rare.
> (Northern) Horned Lark	*alpestris*	—	—	Very rare.

English & Latin name	Race	Breeding Category	Status
❏ Sand Martin *Riparia riparia*	riparia	A b	Common summer visitor. See p.13.
❏ (European Barn) Swallow *Hirundo rustica*	rustica	A b	Very common summer visitor. See p.13.
❏ Red-rumped Swallow *Hirundo daurica*	rufula	A —	Rare passage migrant.
❏ (American) Cliff Swallow *Hirundo pyrrhonota pyrrhonota*		A —	Very rare.
❏ House Martin *Delichon urbica*	urbica	A b	Common summer visitor. See p.13.
❏ Richard's Pipit *Anthus novaeseelandiae*	richardi	A —	Rare passage migrant.
❏ Tawny Pipit *Anthus campestris*	campestris	A —	Rare passage migrant.
❏ Olive-backed Pipit *Anthus hodgsoni*	yunnanensis	A —	Very rare.
❏ Tree Pipit *Anthus trivialis*	trivialis	A —	Scarce passage migrant, mainly in May, to headlands and islands, particularly on S and SE coasts.
❏ Pechora Pipit *Anthus gustavi*	gustavi	A —	Very rare.
❏ Meadow Pipit *Anthus pratensis*	whistleri	A b	Very common resident. See p.14.
❏ Red-throated Pipit *Anthus cervinus*	—	A —	Very rare.
❏ Rock Pipit *Anthus petrosus*	petrosus	A b	Very common resident. See p.14.
> Scandinavian Rock Pipit	littoralis	— —	Very rare.
❏ Water Pipit *Anthus spinoletta*	spinoletta	A —	Rare passage migrant and winter visitor, particularly to Site 130, Tacumshin Lake.
❏ Buff-bellied Pipit *Anthus rubescens*	rubescens	A —	Very rare.
❏ Yellow Wagtail *Motacilla flava*	flavissima	A rb	Rare and sporadic summer visitor, occasionally breeding. Scarce passage migrant to headlands and islands, particularly on S and SE coasts. Sightings feature on the bird information phone lines when their presence is known. Scarce passage migrant.
> Blue-headed Wagtail	flava	— fb	Rare. Has bred.
> Ashy-headed Wagtail	cinereocapilla	— fb	Very rare. Has bred.
> Grey-headed Wagtail	thunbergi	— —	Very rare.
❏ Citrine Wagtail *Motacilla citreola*	citreola	A —	Very rare.
❏ Grey Wagtail *Motacilla cinerea*	cinerea	A b	Common resident throughout Ireland, frequenting fast-flowing rivers and stream edges, occasionally along sheltered coasts and in towns and cities.
❏ Pied Wagtail *Motacilla alba*	yarrellii	A b	Very common resident. See p.14.
> White Wagtail	alba	— —	Passage migrant.
❏ Waxwing *Bombycilla garrulus*	garrulus	A —	Scarce winter visitor. Numbers vary annually and sightings feature on the bird information phone lines when their presence is known.
❏ (Irish) Dipper *Cinclus cinclus*	hibernicus	A b	Uncommon resident on fast-flowing rivers and streams throughout Ireland.
> Black-bellied Dipper	cinclus	— —	Very rare.
❏ Wren *Troglodytes troglodytes*	indigenus	A b	Very common resident. See p.14.
❏ Grey Catbird *Dumetella carolinensis*	—	A —	Very rare.
❏ Dunnock (Hedge Sparrow) *Prunella modularis hebridium*		A b	Very common resident. See p.14.
❏ Rufous Bush Robin *Cercotrichas galactotes*	galactotes	A —	Very rare.
❏ Robin *Erithacus rubecula*	melophilus	A b	Very common resident. See p.14.
> Continental Robin	rubecula	— —	Passage migrant. Winter visitor.
❏ Thrush Nightingale *Luscinia luscinia*	—	A —	Very rare.
❏ Nightingale *Luscinia megarhynchos*	megarhynchos	A —	Very rare.
❏ (Red-spotted) Bluethroat *Luscinia svecica*	svecica	A —	Very rare.
> White-spotted Bluethroat	cyanecula	— —	Very rare.
❏ Black Redstart *Phoenicurus ochruros*	gibraltariens	A —	Uncommon passage migrant and winter visitor, mainly to rocky coasts and harbours on the E

343

English & Latin name	Race	Breeding Category	Status
			coast. Notable sites include Sites 90 and 93 in County Dublin.
❏ (Common) Redstart *Phoenicurus phoenicurus phoenicurus*	A	rb	Very rare summer visitor to mature deciduous woodland, especially Sites 48, Glens of Antrim; and Sites 105, 107, 109 and 111 in County Wicklow. More often seen during spring and autumn migration, on headlands and islands on SE, S and SW coasts.
❏ Whinchat *Saxicola rubetra* —	A	b	Scarce and local summer visitor, to eg Site 104, Coronation Plantation, and Site 169, The Shannon Callows. Occasionally seen during spring and autumn migration on headlands and islands on SE, S and SW coasts.
❏ Stonechat *Saxicola torquata*	*hibernans*	A b	Common resident. See p.14.
> Stonechat ssp, either/both *torquata* ssp.	*maura/stejnegeri* —	—	Very rare.
❏ Isabelline Wheatear *Oenanthe isabellina* —	A	—	Very rare.
❏ (Northern) Wheatear *Oenanthe oenanthe*	*oenanthe*	A b	Common summer visitor to open grassy and rocky areas on mountains, hillsides and coasts.
> Greenland Wheater	*leucorrhoa*	— —	Scarce passage migrant.
❏ Pied Wheatear *Oenanthe pleschanka* —	A	—	Very rare.
❏ (Western) Black-eared Wheatear *Oenanthe hispanica*			
	hispanica	A —	Very rare.
❏ Desert Wheatear *Oenanthe deserti*	*homochroa*	A —	Very rare.
❏ Black Wheatear sp.		A —	Very rare.
or White-crowned Black Wheatear *Oenanthe leucopyga/ leucura*			
❏ Rock Thrush *Monticola saxatilis* —	A	—	Very rare.
❏ White's Thrush *Zoothera dauma*	*aurea*	A —	Very rare.
❏ Siberian Thrush *Zoothera sibirica*	*sibirica*	A —	Very rare.
❏ Hermit Thrush *Catharus guttatus*	*faxoni*	A —	Very rare.
❏ Swainson's Thrush *Catharus ustulatus*	*swainsoni*	A —	Very rare.
❏ Grey-cheeked Thrush *Catharus minimus*	*minimus*	A —	Very rare.
❏ Ring Ouzel *Turdus torquatus*	*torquatus*	A rb	Rare local summer visitor, now largely confined to highest peaks and scree slopes, particularly Site 237, Magillicuddy Reeks, and the County Donegal mountains, eg Site 9, Glenveagh National Park. Occasionally seen during spring and autumn migration, on headlands and islands on SE, S and SW coasts.
❏ Blackbird *Turdus merula*	*merula*	A b	Very common resident. See p.15.
❏ Fieldfare *Turdus pilaris* —	A	—	Common winter visitor. See p.15.
❏ Song Thrush *Turdus philomelos*	*clarkei*	A b	Very common resident. See p.15.
❏ Redwing *Turdus iliacus*	*iliacus*	A —	Common winter visitor. See p.15.
> Icelandic Redwing	*coburni*	— —	Passage migrant. Winter visitor.
❏ Mistle Thrush *Turdus viscivorus*	*viscivorus*	A b	Common resident. See p.15.
❏ American Robin *Turdus migratorius*	*migratorius*	A —	Very rare.
❏ Cetti's Warbler *Cettia cetti*	*cetti*	A —	Very rare.
❏ Fan-tailed Warbler (Zitting Cisticola) *Cisticola juncidis*			
	cisticola	A —	Very rare.
❏ Pallas's Grasshopper Warbler *Locustella certhiola*			
	rubescens	A —	Very rare.
❏ Grasshopper Warbler *Locustella naevia*	*naevia*	A b	Common summer visitor to scrub and wetland edges, particularly in W half of Ireland. Very difficult to see.

English & Latin name	Race	Breeding Category		Status
❏ Savi's Warbler *Locustella luscinioides*	*luscinioides*	A	—	Very rare.
❏ Aquatic Warbler *Acrocephalus paludicola*	—	A	—	Very rare.
❏ Sedge Warbler *Acrocephalus schoenobaenus*	—	A	b	Common summer visitor to reedbeds and scrub. Often seen during spring and autumn migration, on headlands and islands on all coasts.
❏ Paddyfield Warbler *Acrocephalus agricola*	*capistrata*	A	—	Very rare.
❏ Marsh Warbler *Acrocephalus palustris*	—	A	—	Very rare.
❏ Reed Warbler *Acrocephalus scirpaceus*	*scirpaceus*	A	rb	Rare local summer visitor to large reedbeds, mainly in the E, SE and S. Notable sites include Site 101, Killoughter and Broad Lough; Sites 118, 122, 129 and 130 in County Wexford; and Sites 185 and 189 in County Cork. Scarce autumn passage migrant to headlands and islands on E, SE, S and SW coasts.
❏ Great Reed Warbler *Acrocephalus arundinaceus*	*arundinaceus*	A	—	Very rare.
❏ Eastern Olivaceous Warbler *Hippolais pallida elaeica*		A	—	Very rare.
❏ Booted Warbler *Hippolais caligata*	—	A	—	Very rare.
❏ Sykes's Warbler *Hippolais rama*	—	A	—	Very rare.
❏ Icterine Warbler *Hippolais icterina*	—	A	—	Rare.
❏ Melodious Warbler *Hippolais polyglotta*	—	A	—	Rare.
❏ Dartford Warbler *Sylvia undata*	*dartfordiensi*	A	—	Very rare.
❏ Subalpine Warbler *Slyvia cantillans*	*cantillans*	A	—	Very rare.
❏ Sardinian Warbler *Sylvia melanocephala*	*melanocephala*	A	—	Very rare.
❏ Barred Warbler *Sylvia nisoria*	*nisoria*	A	—	Very rare autumn passage migrant.
❏ Lesser Whitethroat *Sylvia curruca*	*curruca*	A	rb	Scarce passage migrant, mainly in autumn to headlands and islands on SE, S and SW coasts.
> Siberian Lesser Whitethroat	*blythi*	A	—	Very rare.
❏ Whitethroat *Sylvia communis*	*communis*	A	b	Common summer visitor to woodland edges and dense hedgerows, mainly in the E, Midlands and SE. Largely absent from the SW and extreme W, though occurs on many coastal headlands and islands in autumn.
❏ Garden Warbler *Sylvia borin*	*borin*	A	b	Scarce and local summer visitor, mainly to County Fermanagh (Sites 71 and 72. See also p.101), and County Cavan (Sites 154, 156 and 158. See also p.195). Uncommon passage migrant on coastal headlands and islands in autumn.
❏ Blackcap *Sylvia atricapilla*	*atricapilla*	A	b	Common summer visitor to broadleaved woodland throughout Ireland, and increasingly common winter visitor, often frequenting bird feeders. Common passage migrant on coastal headlands and islands in autumn.
❏ Greenish Warbler *Phylloscopus trochiloides*	*viridanus*	A	—	Very rare.
❏ Arctic Warbler *Phylloscopus borealis*	*borealis*	A	—	Very rare.
❏ Pallas's Warbler *Phylloscopus proregulus*	*proregulus*	A	—	Very rare.
❏ Yellow-browed Warbler *Phylloscopus inornatus*		A	—	Rare passage migrant on coastal headlands and islands in autumn.
❏ Hume's Leaf Warbler *Phylloscopus humei*	*humei*	A	—	Very rare.
❏ Radde's Warbler *Phylloscopus schwarzi*	—	A	—	Very rare.
❏ Dusky Warbler *Phylloscopus fuscatus*	*fuscatus*	A	—	Very rare.

English & Latin name	Race	Breeding Category		Status
Western Bonelli's Warbler *Phylloscopus bonelli*	—	A	—	Very rare.
Wood Warbler *Phylloscopus sibilatrix*	—	A	rb	Rare summer visitor to mature broadleaved woodland, notably Site 48, Glens of Antrim, and Sites 105, 107, 109, 111 and 112 in County Wicklow. Rare passage migrant on coastal headlands and islands in autumn.
Chiffchaff *Phylloscopus collybita*	collybita	A	b	Very common summer visitor to all areas of broadleaved woodland and mature hedgerows. Rare in winter.
> Scandinavian Chiffchaff	abietinus	—	—	Status uncertain.
> Siberian Chiffchaff	tristis	—	—	Rare autumn passage migrant. Status uncertain.
Willow Warbler *Phylloscopus trochilus*	trochilus	A	b	Very common summer visitor to scrub, woodland edges and hedgerows throughout Ireland.
Goldcrest *Regulus regulus*	regulus	A	b	Very common resident. See p.15.
Firecrest *Regulus ignicapillus*	ignicapillus	A	—	Scarce autumn passage migrant on coastal headlands and islands.
Spotted Flycatcher *Muscicapa striata*	striata	A	b	Common but inconspicuous summer visitor to mature woodland throughout Ireland.
Red-breasted Flycatcher *Ficedula parva*	parva	A	—	Rare passage migrant.
Pied Flycatcher *Ficedula hypoleuca*	hypoleuca	A	rb	Scarce passage migrant on coastal headlands and islands, especially Site 213, Cape Clear Island, where regular in autumn. Rare breeding bird in mature, broadleaved woodland.
Bearded Tit *Panurus biarmicus*	biarmicus	A	fb	Very rare.
Long-tailed Tit *Aegithalos caudatus*	rosaceus	A	b	Common resident throughout Ireland, wherever there is mature hedgerow and broad-leaved scrub and woodland.
Marsh Tit *Parus palustris*	palustris	A	—	Very rare.
(Irish) Coal Tit *Parus ater*	hibernicus	A	b	Very common resident. See p.15.
> British Coal Tit	britannicus	A	b	Very common resident, mainly in NE.
> Continental Coal Tit	ater	A	—	Very rare.
Blue Tit *Parus caeruleus*	obscurus	A	b	Very common resident. See p.16.
Great Tit *Parus major*	newtoni	A	b	Very common resident. See p.16.
Treecreeper *Certhia familiaris*	britannica	A	b	Common but inconspicuous resident in mature woodland throughout Ireland.
Golden Oriole *Oriolus oriolus*	oriolus	A	—	Rare.
Isabelline Shrike *Lanius isabellinus*		A	—	Very rare.
Brown Shrike *Lanius cristatus*	cristatus	A	—	Very rare.
Red-backed Shrike *Lanius collurio*	collurio	A	—	Rare passage migrant.
Lesser Grey Shrike *Lanius minor*		A	—	Very rare.
Great Grey Shrike *Lanius excubitor*	excubitor	A	—	Very rare.
Woodchat Shrike *Lanius senator*	senator	A	—	Rare passage migrant.
> Balearic Woodchat Shrike	badius	—	—	Very rare.
(Irish) Jay *Garrulus glandarius*	hibernicus	A	b	Common but shy and inconspicuous resident of mature broadleaved woodland throughout Ireland, except for far W coastal fringes.
Magpie *Pica pica*	pica	A	b	Very common resident. See p.16.
Chough *Pyrrhocorax pyrrhocorax*	pyrrhocorax	A	b	Locally common resident of S, SW, W and NW coastal cliffs and grasslands.
Jackdaw *Corvus monedula*	spermologus	A	b	Very common resident. See p.16.
> Eastern Jackdaw	soemmerringii	A	—	Very rare.
Indian House Crow *Corvus splendens*	splendens	D2	—	Very rare.

English & Latin name	Race	Breeding Category		Status
❏ Rook *Corvus frugilegus*	*frugilegus*	A	b	Very common resident. See p.16.
❏ Carrion Crow *Corvus corone*	*corone*	A	rb	Scarce, mainly occurring in E coastal counties.
❏ Hooded Crow *Corvus cornix*	*cornix*	A	b	Very common resident. See p.16.
❏ (Northern) Raven *Corvus corax*	*corax*	A	b	Common resident. See p.16.
❏ Starling *Sturnus vulgaris*	*vulgaris*	A	b	Very common resident. See p.16.
❏ Rose-coloured Starling *Sturnus roseus*	—	A	—	Rare.
❏ House Sparrow *Passer domesticus*	*domesticus*	A	b	Very common resident. See p.17.
❏ Tree Sparrow *Passer montanus*	*montanus*	A	b	Scarce and local resident. Only common at Site 3, Tory Island. Other reliable sites include Site 86, Rogerstown Estuary, and Site 120, Wexford Wildfowl Reserve.
❏ Philadelphia Vireo *Vireo philadelphicus*	—	A	—	Very rare.
❏ Red-eyed Vireo *Vireo olivaceus*	*olivaceus*	A	—	Very rare.
❏ Chaffinch *Fringilla coelebs*	*gengleri*	A	b	Very common resident. See p.17.
> Continental Chaffinch	*coelebs*	A	—	Passage migrant. Winter visitor.
❏ Brambling *Fringilla montifringilla*	—	A	—	Uncommon winter visitor. Erratic in locations and numbers each year, though reasonably regular at Site 120, Wexford Wildfowl Reserve. Rare passage migrant on coastal headlands and islands in autumn. Sightings feature on the bird information phone lines when their presence is known.
❏ Serin *Serinus serinus*	—	A	—	Very rare.
❏ Greenfinch *Carduelis chloris*	*chloris*	A	b	Common resident. See p.17.
❏ Goldfinch *Carduelis carduelis*	*britannica*	A	b	Common resident. See p.17.
❏ Siskin *Carduelis spinus*	—	A	b	Common resident and winter visitor, mainly in mature coniferous woodland, occasionally at feeders in gardens in winter. Scarce but regular passage migrant on coastal headlands and islands in autumn.
❏ Linnet *Carduelis cannabina*	*cannabina*	A	b	Common resident. See p.17.
❏ Twite *Carduelis flavirostris*	*pipilans*	A	b	Uncommon local resident, mainly at Site 243, The Mullet Peninsula. Now rare elsewhere, though small flocks may appear in winter at Site 36, Lough Foyle and elsewhere. Sightings feature on the bird information phone lines when their presence is known.
❏ (Lesser) Redpoll *Carduelis flammea*	*cabaret*	A	b	Common resident, mainly in the vicinity of mature coniferous woodland, though more widespread in most woodland habitats outside the breeding season.
> Mealy Redpoll	*flammea*	—	—	Rare.
> Greenland Redpoll	*rostrata*	—	—	Very rare.
❏ (Hornemann's) Arctic Redpoll *Carduelis hornemanni*	*bornemanni*	A	—	Very rare.
❏ Two-barred Crossbill *Loxia leucoptera*	*bifasciata*	B	—	Very rare.
❏ Crossbill *Loxia curvirostra*	*curvirostra*	A	rb	Rare to uncommon resident. Highly irruptive, with large flocks occurring in some years. Best sites include Site 48, Glens of Antrim, and Site 104, Coronation Plantation, though birds may appear at any coniferous forest in good years.
❏ Common Rosefinch *Carpodacus erythrinus*	*erythrinus*	A	—	Rare.
❏ Bullfinch *Pyrrhula pyrrhula*	*pileata*	A	b	Common resident. See p.17.

347

English & Latin name	Race	Breeding Category		Status
> Northern Bullfinch	pyrrhula	—	—	Very rare.
❏ Hawfinch *Coccothraustes coccothraustes*		A	—	Rare.
❏ Blue-winged Warbler *Vermivora pinus*	—	A	—	Very rare.
❏ Black & White Warbler *Mniotilta varia*	—	A	—	Very rare.
❏ Northern Parula *Parula americana*	—	A	—	Very rare.
❏ Yellow Warbler *Dendroica petechia*	—	A	—	Very rare.
❏ Myrtle (Yellow-rumped) Warbler *Dendroica coronata*				
	coronata	A	—	Very rare.
❏ Blackpoll Warbler *Dendroica striata*	—	A	—	Very rare.
❏ American Redstart *Setophaga ruticilla*	—	A	—	Very rare.
❏ Ovenbird *Seiurus aurocapillus*	aurocapillus	A	—	Very rare.
❏ Northern Waterthrush *Seiurus noveboracensis*		A	—	Very rare.
❏ Common Yellowthroat *Geothlypis trichas*		A	—	Very rare.
❏ Scarlet Tanager *Piranga olivacea*	—	A	—	Very rare.
❏ Red (Eastern) Fox Sparrow *Passerella iliaca iliaca*		A	—	Very rare.
❏ White-throated Sparrow *Zonotrichia albicollis*		A	—	Very rare.
❏ White-crowned Sparrow *Zonotrichia leucophrys*				
	leucophrys	A	—	Very rare.
❏ Slate-coloured (Dark-eyed) Junco *Junco hyemalis*				
	hyemalis	A	—	Very rare.
❏ Lapland Bunting *Calcarius lapponicus*	lapponicus	A	—	Scarce passage migrant and rare winter visitor. Regularly seen in autumn, at Sites 1, 3 and 14 in County Donegal, and Sites 213 and 215 in County Cork, though can appear on any headland. In winter, occasionally found at Site 36, Lough Foyle. Other sightings feature on the bird information phone lines when their presence is known.
❏ Snow Bunting *Plectrophenax nivalis*	nivalis	A	—	Scarce passage migrant and uncommon winter visitor, occurring at the same sites as Lapland Bunting above, though more often frequenting shingle beaches such as Site 99, Kilcoole, and Site 263, Ballyvaughan area. Small flocks occasionally found on high peaks in winter.
❏ Pine Bunting *Emberiza leucocephalos*	leucocephalos	A	—	Very rare.
❏ Yellowhammer *Emberiza citrinella*	—	A	b	Locally common resident, mainly in the E and SE, especially grain-growing regions. Regular at Site 86, Rogerstown Estuary.
❏ Cirl Bunting *Emberiza cirlus*	cirlus	A	—	Very rare.
❏ Ortolan Bunting *Emberiza hortulana*	—	A	—	Very rare.
❏ Rustic Bunting *Emberiza rustica*	rustica	A	—	Very rare.
❏ Little Bunting *Emberiza pusilla*	—	A	—	Very rare.
❏ Yellow-breasted Bunting *Emberiza aureola*	aureola	A	—	Very rare.
❏ Reed Bunting *Emberiza schoeniclus*	schoeniclus	A	b	Common resident. See p.17.
> Siberian Reed Bunting	pallidior	—	—	Very rare.
❏ Red-headed Bunting *Emberiza bruniceps*	—	D1	—	Very rare.
❏ Black-headed Bunting *Emberiza melanocephala*		A	—	Very rare.
❏ Corn Bunting *Miliaria calandra*	clanceyi	A	fb	Very rare. Formerly a widespread and common resident, now probably extinct in Ireland.
❏ Rose-breasted Grosbeak *Pheucticus ludovicianus*		A	—	Very rare.
❏ Indigo Bunting *Passerina cyanea*	—	A	—	Very rare.
❏ Bobolink *Dolichonyx oryzivorus*		A	—	Very rare.
❏ Baltimore (Northern) Oriole *Icterus (galbula) galbula*		A	—	Very rare.

Irish Bird Names

This list includes the official names of all the species in the Irish language as published by the Irish Rare Birds Committee (IRBC 1998). The names were standardised by An Coiste Téarmaíochta (the Terminology Committee) of the Department of Education in Ireland.

For well-known species, the names tend to reflect traditional usage; for the more inconspicuous and rarer species, they have been devised in conjunction with An Coiste Téarmaíochta.

Red-throated Diver **Lóma rua**
Black-throated Diver **Lóma Artach**
Great Northern Diver **Lóma mór**
White-billed Diver **Lóma gobgheal**
Pied-billed Grebe **Foitheach gob-alabhreac**
Little Grebe **Spágaire tonn**
Great Crested Grebe **Foitheach mór**
Red-necked Grebe **Foitheach píbrua**
Slavonian Grebe **Foitheach cluasach**
Black-necked Grebe **Foitheach píbdhubh**
Black-browed Albatross **Albatras dú-mhalach**
Fulmar **Fulmaire**
Bulwer's Petrel **Peadairín Bulwer**
Cory's Shearwater **Cánóg Cory**
Great Shearwater **Cánóg mhór**
Sooty Shearwater **Cánóg dhorcha**
Manx Shearwater **Cánóg dhubh**
Balearic Shearwater **Cánóg Bhailéarach**
Little Shearwater **Cánóg bheag**
Wilson's Petrel **Guairdeall Wilson**
Storm Petrel **Guairdeall**
Leach's Petrel **Guairdeall gabhlach**
Madeiran Petrel **Guairdeall Maidéarach**
Gannet **Gainéad**
Cormorant **Broigheall**
Double-crested Cormorant **Broigheall cluasach**
Shag **Seaga**
Bittern **Bonnán**
American Bittern **Bonnán Meiriceánach**
Little Bittern **Bonnán beag**
Night Heron **Corr oíche**
Squacco Heron **Corr scréachach**
Cattle Egret **Éigrit eallaigh**

Little Egret **Éigrit bheag**
Great White Egret **Éigrit mhór**
Grey Heron **Corr réisc**
Purple Heron **Corr chorcra**
Black Stork **Storc dubh**
White Stork **Storc bán**
Glossy Ibis **Íbis niamhrach**
Spoonbill **Leitheadach**
Mute Swan **Eala bhalbh**
Bewick's Swan **Eala Bewick**
Whooper Swan **Eala ghlórach**
Bean Goose **Síolghé**
Pink-footed Goose **Gé ghobghearr**
White-fronted Goose **Gé bhánéadanach**
Lesser White-fronted Goose
    Mionghé bhánéadanach
Greylag Goose **Gé ghlas**
Snow Goose **Gé shneachta**
Canada Goose **Gé Cheanadach**
Barnacle Goose **Gé ghiúrainn**
Brent Goose **Cadhan**
Ruddy Shelduck **Seil-lacha rua**
Shelduck **Seil-lacha**
Mandarin Duck **Lacha mhandrach**
Wigeon **Rualacha**
American Wigeon **Rualacha Mheiriceánach**
Gadwall **Gadual**
Teal **Praslacha**
Green-winged Teal **Praslacha ghlaseiteach**
Mallard **Mallard**
American Black Duck **Lacha chosrua**
Pintail **Biorearrach**
Garganey **Praslacha shamhraidh**

349

Blue-winged Teal **Praslacha ghormeiteach**
Shoveler **Spadalach**
Red-crested Pochard **Póiseard ciordhearg**
Pochard **Póiseard**
Ring-necked Duck **Lacha mhuinceach**
Ferruginous Duck **Póiseard súilbhán**
Tufted Duck **Lacha bhadánach**
Scaup **Lacha iascán**
Lesser Scaup **Mionlacha iascán**
Eider **Éadar**
King Eider **Éadar taibhseach**
Long-tailed Duck **Lacha earrfhada**
Common **Scoter Scótar**
Surf Scoter **Scótar toinne**
Velvet Scoter **Sceadach**
Goldeneye **Órshúileach**
Hooded Merganser **Síolta chochaill**
Smew **Síolta gheal**
Red-breasted Merganser **Síolta rua**
Goosander **Síolta mhór**
Ruddy Duck **Lacha rua**
Honey Buzzard **Clamhán riabhach**
Black Kite **Cúr dubh**
Red Kite **Cúr rua**
White-tailed Eagle **Iolar mara**
Bald Eagle **Iolar maol**
Griffon Vulture **Bultúr gríofa**
Marsh Harrier **Cromán móna**
Hen Harrier **Cromán na gcearc**
Montagu's Harrier **Cromán liath**
Goshawk **Spioróg mhór**
Sparrowhawk **Spioróg**
Buzzard **Clamhán**
Rough-legged Buzzard **Clamhán lópach**
Spotted Eagle **Iolar breac**
Golden Eagle **Iolar fíréan**
Osprey **Coirneach**
Lesser Kestrel **Mionphocaire gaoithe**
Kestrel **Pocaire gaoithe**
Red-footed Falcon **Fabhcún cosdearg**
Merlin **Meirliún**
Hobby **Fabhcún coille**
Gyr Falcon **Fabhcún mór**
Peregrine **Fabhcún gorm**
Red Grouse **Cearc fhraoigh**
Capercaillie **Capall coille**
Grey Partridge **Patraisc**

Quail **Gearg**
Pheasant **Piasún**
Water Rail **Rálóg uisce**
Spotted Crake **Gearr breac**
Sora **Gearr sora**
Little Crake **Gearr beag**
Baillon's Crake **Gearr Baillon**
Corncrake **Traonach**
Moorhen **Cearc uisce**
Coot **Cearc cheannann**
American Coot
    Cearc cheannann Mheiriceánach
Crane **Grús**
Sandhill Crane **Grús Ceanadach**
Little Bustard **Bustard beag**
Great Bustard **Bustard mór**
Oystercatcher **Roilleach**
Black-winged Stilt **Scodalach dubheiteach**
Avocet **Abhóiséad**
Stone Curlew **Crotach cloch**
Cream-coloured Courser **Rásaí bánbhuí**
Collared Pratincole **Pratancól muinceach**
Black-winged Pratincole **Pratancól dubheiteach**
Little Ringed Plover **Feadóigín chladaigh**
Ringed Plover **Feadóg chladaigh**
Killdeer **Feadóg ghlórach**
Kentish Plover **Feadóigín chosdubh**
Dotterel **Amadán móinteach**
American Golden Plover
    Feadóg bhuí Mheiriceánach
Pacific Golden Plover **Feadóg bhuí Áiseach**
Golden Plover **Feadóg bhuí**
Grey Plover **Feadóg ghlas**
Sociable Plover **Pilibín ealtúil**
Lapwing **Pilibín**
Knot **Cnota**
Sanderling **Luathrán**
Semipalmated Sandpiper
    Gobadáinín mionbhosach
Western Sandpiper **Gobadáinín iartharach**
Little Stint **Gobadáinín beag**
Temminck's Stint **Gobadáinín Temminck**
Long-toed Stint **Gobadáinín ladharfhada**
Least Sandpiper **Gobadáinín bídeach**
White-rumped Sandpiper
    Gobadán bánphrompach
Baird's Sandpiper **Gobadán Baird**

Pectoral Sandpiper **Gobadán uchtach**
Sharp-tailed Sandpiper **Gobadán earr-rinneach**
Curlew Sandpiper **Gobadán crotaigh**
Purple Sandpiper **Gobadán cosbhuí**
Dunlin **Breacóg**
Broad-billed Sandpiper **Gobadán gobleathan**
Stilt Sandpiper **Gobadán scodalach**
Buff-breasted Sandpiper
   Gobadán broinn-donnbhuí
Ruff **Rufachán**
Jack Snipe **Naoscach bhídeach**
Snipe **Naoscach**
Great Snipe **Naoscach mhór**
Short-billed Dowitcher **Guilbnín gobghearr**
Long-billed Dowitcher **Guilbnín gobfhada**
Woodcock **Creabhar**
Black-tailed Godwit **Guilbneach earrdhubh**
Bar-tailed Godwit **Guilbneach stríocearrach**
Eskimo Curlew **Crotach Artach**
Whimbrel **Crotach eanaigh**
Curlew **Crotach**
Upland Sandpiper **Gobadán sléibhe**
Spotted Redshank **Cosdeargán breac**
Redshank **Cosdeargán**
Marsh Sandpiper **Gobadán corraigh**
Greenshank **Laidhrín glas**
Greater Yellowlegs **Ladhrán buí**
Lesser Yellowlegs **Mionladhrán buí**
Solitary Sandpiper **Gobadán aonarach**
Green Sandpiper **Gobadán glas**
Wood Sandpiper **Gobadán coille**
Terek Sandpiper **Gobadán Terek**
Common Sandpiper **Gobadán coiteann**
Spotted Sandpiper **Gobadán breac**
Turnstone **Piardálaí trá**
Wilson's Phalarope **Falaróp Wilson**
Red-necked Phalarope **Falaróp gobchaol**
Grey Phalarope **Falaróp gobmhór**
Pomarine Skua **Meirleach pomairíneach**
Long-tailed Skua **Meirleach earrfhada**
Great Skua **Meirleach mór**
Mediterranean Gull **Sléibhín Meánmhuirí**
Laughing Gull **Sléibhín an gháire**
Franklin's Gull **Sléibhín Franklin**
Little Gull **Sléibhín beag**
Sabine's Gull **Sléibhín Sabine**
Bonaparte's Gull **Sléibhín Bonaparte**

Black-headed Gull **Sléibhín**
Ring-billed Gull **Faoileán bandghobach**
Common Gull **Faoileán bán**
Lesser Black-backed Gull **Droimneach beag**
Herring Gull **Faoileán scadán**
American Herring Gull **Faoileán Mheiriceánach**
Yellow-legged Gull **Faoileán Mheiriceánach**
Caspian Gull **Faoileán Chaispeach**
Iceland Gull **Faoileán Íoslannach**
Glaucous Gull **Faoileán glas**
Great Black-backed Gull **Droimneach mór**
Ross's Gull **Faoileán Ross**
Kittiwake **Saidhbhéar**
Ivory Gull **Faoileán eabhartha**
Gull-billed Tern **Geabhróg ghobdhubh**
Caspian Tern **Geabhróg Chaispeach**
Lesser Crested Tern **Miongheabhróg chíorach**
Sandwich Tern **Geabhróg scothdhubh**
Elegant Tern **Geabhróg ghalánta**
Roseate Tern **Geabhróg rósach**
Common Tern **Geabhróg**
Arctic Tern **Geabhróg Artach**
Forster's Tern **Geabhróg Forster**
Little Tern **Geabhróg bheag**
Whiskered Tern **Geabhróg bhroinndubh**
Black Tern **Geabhróg dhubh**
White-winged Black Tern
   Geabhróg bháneiteach
Guillemot **Foracha**
Brünnich's Guillemot **Foracha Brünnich**
Razorbill **Crosán**
Great Auk **Falcóg mhór**
Black Guillemot **Foracha dhubh**
Little Auk **Falcóg bheag**
Puffin **Puifín**
Pallas's Sandgrouse **Gaineamhchearc Pallas**
Rock Dove **Colm aille**
Stock Dove **Colm gorm**
Woodpigeon **Colm coille**
Collared Dove **Fearán baicdhubh**
Turtle Dove **Fearán**
Great Spotted Cuckoo **Mórchuach bhreac**
Cuckoo **Cuach**
Black-billed Cuckoo **Cuach ghobdhubh**
Yellow-billed Cuckoo **Cuach ghob-bhuí**
Barn Owl **Scréachóg reilige**
Scops Owl **Ulchabhán scopach**

Snowy Owl **Ulchabhán sneachtúil**
Little Owl **Ulchabhán beag**
Long-eared Owl **Ceann cait**
Short-eared Owl **Ulchabhán réisc**
Nightjar **Tuirne lín**
White-throated Needletail
Gabhlán earrspíonach
Swift **Gabhlán gaoithe**
Pallid Swift **Gabhlán bánlíoch**
Alpine Swift **Gabhlán Alpach**
Little Swift **Gabhlán beag**
Kingfisher **Cruidín**
Belted Kingfisher **Cruidín creasa**
Bee-eater **Beachadóir Eorpach**
Roller **Rollóir**
Hoopoe **Húpú**
Wryneck **Cam-mhuin**
Green Woodpecker **Cnagaire glas**
Yellow-bellied Sapsucker **Súdhiúlaí tarrbhuí**
Great Spotted Woodpecker
Mórchnagaire breac
Short-toed Lark **Fuiseog ladharghearr**
Woodlark **Fuiseog choille**
Skylark **Fuiseog**
Shore Lark **Fuiseog adharcach**
Sand Martin **Gabhlán gainimh**
Swallow **Fáinleog**
Red-rumped Swallow **Fáinleog ruaphrompach**
Cliff Swallow **Fáinleog aille**
House Martin **Gabhlán binne**
Richard's Pipit **Riabhóg Richard**
Tawny Pipit **Riabhóg dhonn**
Olive-backed Pipit **Riabhóg dhroimghlas**
Tree Pipit **Riabhóg choille**
Pechora Pipit **Riabhóg Pechora**
Meadow Pipit **Riabhóg mhóna**
Red-throated Pipit **Riabhóg phíbrua**
Rock Pipit **Riabhóg chladaigh**
Water Pipit **Riabhóg uisce**
Buff-bellied Pipit **Riabhóg tharr-dhonnbhuí**
Yellow Wagtail **Glasóg bhuí**
Citrine Wagtail **Glasóg chiotrónach**
Grey Wagtail **Glasóg liath**
Pied Wagtail **Glasóg shráide**
Waxwing **Síodeiteach**
Dipper **Gabha dubh**
Wren **Dreoilín**

Grey Catbird **Catéan liath**
Dunnock **Donnóg**
Rufous Bush Robin **Torspideog ruadhonn**
Robin **Spideog**
Thrush Nightingale **Filiméala smólaigh**
Nightingale **Filiméala**
Bluethroat **Gormphíb**
Black Redstart **Earrdheargán dubh**
Redstart **Earrdheargán**
Whinchat **Caislín aitinn**
Stonechat **Caislín cloch**
Isabelline Wheatear **Clochrán gainimh**
Wheatear **Clochrán**
Pied Wheatear **Clochrán alabhreac**
Black-eared Wheatear **Clochrán cluasdubh**
Desert Wheatear **Clochrán fásaigh**
Rock Thrush **Smólach aille**
White's Thrush **Smólach White**
Siberian Thrush **Smólach Sibéarach**
Swainson's Thrush **Smólach Swainson**
Grey-cheeked Thrush **Smólach glasleicneach**
Ring Ouzel **Lon creige**
Blackbird **Lon dubh**
Fieldfare **Sacán**
Song Thrush **Smólach ceoil**
Redwing **Deargán sneachta**
Mistle Thrush **Liatráisc**
American Robin **Smólach imirce**
Cetti's Warbler **Ceolaire Cetti**
Fan-tailed Warbler **Ceolaire earrfheanach**
Pallas's Grasshopper Warbler
Ceolaire casarnaí Pallas
Grasshopper Warbler **Ceolaire casarnaí**
Savi's Warbler **Ceolaire Savi**
Aquatic Warbler **Ceolaire uisce**
Sedge Warbler **Ceolaire cíbe**
Paddyfield Warbler **Ceolaire gort ríse**
Blyth's Reed Warbler **Ceolaire Blyth**
Marsh Warbler **Ceolaire corraigh**
Reed Warbler **Ceolaire giolcaí**
Great Reed Warbler **Mórcheolaire giolcaí**
Olivaceous Warbler **Ceolaire bánlíoch**
Icterine Warbler **Ceolaire ictireach**
Melodious Warbler **Ceolaire binn**
Dartford Warbler **Ceolaire fraoigh**
Subalpine Warbler **Ceolaire Fo-Alpach**
Sardinian Warbler **Ceolaire Sairdíneach**

Barred Warbler **Ceolaire barrach**
Lesser Whitethroat **Gilphíb bheag**
Whitethroat **Gilphíb**
Garden Warbler **Ceolaire garraí**
Blackcap **Caipín dubh**
Greenish Warbler **Ceolaire scothghlas**
Arctic Warbler **Ceolaire Artach**
Pallas's Warbler **Ceolaire Pallas**
Yellow-browed Warbler **Ceolaire buímhalach**
Radde's Warbler **Ceolaire Radde**
Dusky Warbler **Ceolaire breacdhorcha**
Bonelli's Warbler **Ceolaire Bonelli**
Wood Warbler **Ceolaire coille**
Chiffchaff **Tiuf-teaf**
Willow Warbler **Ceolaire sailí**
Goldcrest **Cíorbhuí**
Firecrest **Lasairchíor**
Spotted Flycatcher **Cuilire liath**
Red-breasted Flycatcher **Cuilire broinnrua**
Pied Flycatcher **Cuilire alabhreac**
Bearded Tit **Meantán croiméalach**
Long-tailed Tit **Meantán earrfhada**
Marsh Tit **Meantán lathaí**
Coal Tit **Meantán dubh**
Blue Tit **Meantán gorm**
Great Tit **Meantán mór**
Treecreeper **Snag**
Golden Oriole **Óiréal órga**
Red-backed Shrike **Scréachán droimrua**
Lesser Grey Shrike **Mionscréachán liath**
Great Grey Shrike **Mórscréachán liath**
Woodchat Shrike **Scréachán coille**
Jay **Scréachóg**
Magpie **Snag breac**
Chough **Cág cosdearg**
Jackdaw **Cág**
Rook **Rúcach**
Hooded Crow **Caróg liath**
Carrion Crow **Caróg dhubh**
Raven **Fiach dubh**
Starling **Druid**
Rose-coloured Starling **Druid rósach**
House Sparrow **Gealbhan binne**
Tree Sparrow **Gealbhan crainn**
Philadelphia Vireo **Glaséan Philadelphia**
Red-eyed Vireo **Glaséan súildearg**
Chaffinch **Rí rua**

Brambling **Breacán**
Serin **Seirín**
Greenfinch **Glasán darach**
Goldfinch **Lasair choille**
Siskin **Siscín**
Linnet **Gleoiseach**
Twite **Gleoiseach sléibhe**
Redpoll **Deargéadan**
Two-barred Crossbill **Crosghob báneiteach**
Crossbill **Crosghob**
Common Rosefinch **Rósghlasán coiteann**
Bullfinch **Corcrán coille**
Hawfinch **Glasán gobmhór**
Black-and-white Warbler **Ceolaire dubh is bán**
Northern Parula **Parúl tuaisceartach**
Yellow Warbler **Ceolaire buí**
Yellow-rumped Warbler
    Ceolaire buíphrompach
Blackpoll Warbler **Ceolaire dubhéadanach**
American Redstart **Earrdheargán Meiriceánach**
Ovenbird **Éan oighinn**
Northern Waterthrush
    Smólach uisce tuaisceartach
Scarlet Tanager **Tanagair scarlóideach**
Fox Sparrow **Gealbhan sionnaigh**
White-throated Sparrow **Gealbhan píbgheal**
Dark-eyed Junco **Luachairín shúildubh**
Lapland Bunting **Gealóg Laplannach**
Snow Bunting **Gealóg shneachta**
Pine Bunting **Gealóg phéine**
Yellowhammer **Buíóg**
Ortolan Bunting **Gealóg gharraí**
Rustic Bunting **Gealóg thuathúil**
Little Bunting **Gealóg bheag**
Yellow-breasted Bunting **Gealóg bhroinnbhuí**
Reed Bunting **Gealóg ghiolcaí**
Black-headed Bunting **Gealóg cheanndubh**
Corn Bunting **Gealóg bhuachair**
Rose-breasted Grosbeak
    Gobach mór broinnrósach
Indigo Bunting **Gealóg phlúiríneach**
Bobolink **Bobóilinc**

References & Bibliography

Archer E. 2004. Port of call. *BirdWatch*, no.141, March 2004.

Belfast RSPB Member's Group. 1981. *Birds around Belfast*. RSPB.

Bird D. 1991. Site Guide: Cape Clear Island, Co. Cork. *Irish Birding News*, 1:3.

Brennan P. 1990. Site Guide: Loop Head, Co. Clare. *Irish Birding News*, 1:1.

Carruthers T. 1993. *The birds of Killarney National Park*. Stationery Office, Dublin.

Carruthers T. 1998. *Kerry – a natural history*. The Collins Press.

Chapman B. 1990. Site Guide: Moy Valley, Co. Mayo. *Irish Birding News*, 1:2.

Colhoun K. 2001. *Irish Wetland Bird Survey, 1998—99. Results from the fifth winter of the Irish Wetland Bird Survey*. BirdWatch Ireland, Dublin.

Cork Bird Report Editorial Team. 2006. *Cork Bird Report 1996—2004*. Privately published.

Crowe O. 2005. *Ireland's Wetlands and their Waterbirds: Status and Distribution*. BirdWatch Ireland.

Dempsey E & McGeehan A. 1992. Long-tailed Skuas in Ireland – Autumn 1991. *Irish Birding News*, 2:2.

Dempsey E & O'Clery M. 1993. *The Complete Guide to Ireland's Birds*. Gill & Macmillan.

Ellis RJ. 1987. The wintering birds of Dundrum Inner Bay, Co. Down. *Irish Birds* 3: 395—404. Irish Wildbird Conservancy.

Gibbons DW, Reid JB & Chapman RA. 1993. *The New Atlas of breeding birds in Britain and Ireland*. T & AD Poyser.

Grace K & McGeehan A. 1993. Passage of Pomarine and Long-tailed Skuas off Inishkea South, Co. Mayo, May 19th—25th, 1984. *Irish Birding News*, 3:4.

Greenwood M, et al. 2003. *The Rough Guide to Ireland*. Rough Guides.

Griffin T. 1995. Galway. A personal view. Part 1. *Irish Birdwatching*, 4:2. Part 2. *Irish Birdwatching*, 4:3.

Griffin T, Breen B, O'Donaill A & Peppiatt C. 2004. Birds of Galway. A review of recent records and field studies 1991—2000. Galway Branch, BirdWatch Ireland.

Heery S. 1996. Birds in Central Ireland. BirdWatch Ireland.

Hutchinson C. 1986. *Watching Birds in Ireland*. County House.

Hutchinson C. 1989. *Birds in Ireland*. T&AD Poyser.

Hutchinson C. 1994. *Where to watch birds in Ireland*. Christopher Helm.

Irish Rare Birds Committee. 1998. *Checklist of the Birds of Ireland*. BirdWatch Ireland.

Kelly A. 2005. Tacumshin and Lady's Island Lakes, Co. Wexford. *Birdwatch* no.157, July 2005.

Lack P. 1986. *The Atlas of wintering birds in Britain and Ireland*. T & AD Poyser.

Lovatt JK. 1984. *Birds of Hook Head, Co. Wexford 1883—1983*. Irish Wildbird Conservancy.

Lovatt JK. 2006. *Birds in Cavan*. BirdWatch Ireland.

Lysaght LS. 1986. The birds of Westfields, Limerick City. *Irish Birds* 3: 255—266. Irish Wildbird Conservancy.

Lysaght L. 2002. *An Atlas of Breeding Birds of the Burren and the Aran Islands*. BirdWatch Ireland.

MacLochlainn C. 1984. Breeding and wintering bird communities of Glenveagh National Park, Co. Donegal. *Irish Birds* 2: 482—500.

MacLochlainn C. 2003. *Toraigh – Tory Island, a remote and historic outpost*. Comharchumann Thoraí Teoranta.

Magee E. 2005. A view from Donegal. *I-WeBS News*, Issue 9, August 2005. BirdWatch Ireland.

Marr BAE. 1992. Groomsport and its birds. *Northern Ireland Bird Report 1986—90*. Northern Ireland Birdwatchers' Association.

McDermott P. 1992. Site Guide: Akeragh Lough and Tralee Bay, Co. Kerry. *Irish Birding News* 2:4.

McElwaine JG. 1991. Wintering waterfowl on County Down lakes, 1986/87—1990/91. *Irish Birds* 4: 335—368.

McGeehan A. 2004. *A Checklist of the birds of Rocky Point, Donegal*. Unpublished report.

Merne OJ. 1974. *The birds of Wexford, Ireland*. English & Co., Wexford.

Merne OJ. 2004. Breeding Seabirds of Bray Head, County Wicklow, 1986—2004. *Irish Birds* 7:3.

Mitchell PI, Newton S, Ratcliffe N & Dunn TE. 2004. *Seabird populations of Britain and Ireland*. Christopher Helm.

Murphy C. 1992. Site Guide: Tory Island, Co. Donegal. *Irish Birding News*, 3:1.

Murphy J. 2003. The Shannon Airport Lagoon. *Wild Ireland*, July—August 2003.

Murphy J, Cooney A, Rattigan J & Lynch T. 2003. *The Shannon Airport Lagoon. A unique Irish Habitat.* Clare Branch, BirdWatch Ireland.

O'Clery M. 1991. Site guide: Dunquin, Co. Kerry. *Irish Birding News* 2: 29–36. Birds of Ireland News Service.

O'Clery M. 2002. *The Dingle Peninsula Bird Report 1999–2001.* Corca Dhuibhne Branch, BirdWatch Ireland.

O'Clery M. 2005. *The Dingle Peninsula Bird Report 2002–2004.* Corca Dhuibhne Branch, BirdWatch Ireland.

Pierce S. 1998. Birds of Shennick Island, Co. Dublin. *Irish Birds,* 6:2.

Ruttledge RF. 1989. *Birds in Counties Galway & Mayo.* BirdWatch Ireland.

Sharrock JTR. 1976. *The Atlas of breeding birds in Britain & Ireland.* T & AD Poyser.

Sheppard R. 1993. *Ireland's Wetland Wealth.* Irish Wildbird Conservancy.

Sheppard R. 2002. The wintering waterbirds of Lough Swilly, Co. Donegal. *Irish Birds* 7:1.

Smiddy P. 1992. The birds of Ballymacoda, Co. Cork. *Irish Birds* 4: 525–548. Irish Wildbird Conservancy.

Tierney TD, Hudson J & Casey C. 2002. Survey of breeding waders on the River Shannon Callows, 2002. *Irish Birds* 7:1.

Upton AJ. 2001. Breeding Seabirds on the Isle of Muck, Co. Antrim. *Northern Ireland Bird Report 2001.* Northern Ireland Birdwatchers Association.

Wallace DIM, McGeehan A & Allen D. Autumn migration in westernmost Donegal. *British Birds* 94:103–120.

Walsh A. 1992. Site Guide: North Sloblands, Co. Wexford. *Irish Birding News,* 2:3.

Walsh D. 2004. *Oileáin – A guide to the Irish islands.* Pesda Press.

Whilde T. 1980. *Birds of Galway – A review of recent records and field studies.* Galway Branch, Irish Wildbird Conservancy.

Wilson J. Discover the Birds of East Cork. East Cork Tourism Leaflet.

Annual or regular publications

Irish Bird Report. Published annually in *Irish Birds* by BirdWatch Ireland. See IRBC website on www.birdwatchireland.ie for summary and announcements.

Northern Ireland Bird Report. Published by The Northern Ireland Birdwatchers Association. Issues appear almost annually, though some have covered two or more years.

Irish East Coast Bird Report. Published annually since 1980, currently edited by Richard H. Coombes & Declan F. Murphy. Covers counties Louth, Meath, Dublin and Wicklow and is published by BirdWatch Ireland.

I-WeBS Reports. Annual summaries of Irish Wetland Bird Surveys, by Simon Delany (1996 & 1997) & Kendrew Colhoun (1999, 2000 & 2001). Published by BirdWatch Ireland.

Appendix 1
Seawatching

Each autumn, there are hundreds of thousands of seabirds in Irish offshore waters. Many are open ocean, or 'pelagic', species, such as Storm and Leach's Petrels, Sooty and Great Shearwaters and Sabine's Gull. They usually remain far out to sea, and can only be seen from land when driven against the coastline by strong onshore winds. The exact weather conditions which cause the phenomena can be difficult to predict, but there are very specific sites on exposed headlands and islands from which to observe this amazing spectacle (See illustration, next page).

For birdwatchers, so-called 'seawatching' can be an exciting experience, and offers the chance to see 30 or more species of seabird, occasionally in huge numbers. A typical two to three hour seawatch in the autumn on the SW coast, for example, might result in seeing 2-3000 Manx Shearwater, 1000 Gannet, 1000 or more of Kittiwake and Fulmar, 100s of Guillemot and Razorbill, a few Puffin, 50 Storm Petrel, 50 Sooty Shearwater, a few Arctic, Great and Pomarine Skuas, and maybe one or two Balearic Shearwaters. There are always small numbers of other associated coastal birds, gulls, a few divers, perhaps some terns. For the more serious birdwatcher, a particularly good movement of seabirds might include a few rarer birds – a Sabine's Gull, a Great or Cory's Shearwater, a Long-tailed Skua, and maybe, just maybe, that bird of a lifetime, a Fea's Petrel, a Little Shearwater or a Black-browed Albatross.

Where & When
North & West Coasts
In autumn, a frequent feature of the weather is a low pressure system, deepening in the mid-Atlantic and moving E, between Scotland and Iceland. In Ireland, this often produces S, then strengthening SW winds on its southern

Leach's Petrel, Manx Shearwater and Sooty Shearwaters

356

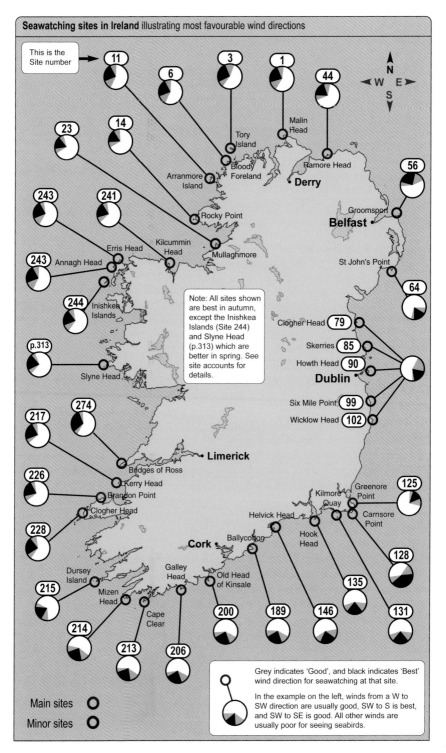

Seawatching sites in Ireland illustrating most favourable wind directions

This is the Site number

Tory Island
Malin Head
Bloody Foreland
Arranmore Island
Ramore Head
Derry
Rocky Point
Groomsport
Belfast
Erris Head
Kilcummin Head
Mullaghmore
St John's Point
Annagh Head
Inishkea Islands
Clogher Head
Skerries
Howth Head
Dublin
Slyne Head
Six Mile Point
Wicklow Head
Bridges of Ross
Limerick
Kerry Head
Brandon Point
Clogher Head
Kilmore Quay
Greenore Point
Carnsore Point
Helvick Head
Hook Head
Cork
Ballycotton
Dursey Island
Galley Head
Old Head of Kinsale
Mizen Head
Cape Clear

Note: All sites shown are best in autumn, except the Inishkea Islands (Site 244) and Slyne Head (p.313) which are better in spring. See site accounts for details.

Main sites ○
Minor sites ○

Grey indicates 'Good', and black indicates 'Best' wind direction for seawatching at that site.

In the example on the left, winds from a W to SW direction are usually good, SW to S is best, and SW to SE is good. All other winds are usually poor for seeing seabirds.

357

flank, and as the centre of the low passes Scotland, the winds will swing to the W and then the NW. There are often fronts, or rainbelts, associated with this change in wind direction, thus SW winds are generally accompanied by heavy rain and mist. As winds change to the NW, this rain usually gives way to scattered heavy showers. It is during this phase – NW winds with scattered showers – that numbers of seabirds passing headlands along the entire N and W coasts can be enormous. Thousands of seabirds have been pushed into large bays and close to the coast, and are struggling to fly back W, out to sea.

South-west & South Coasts Much the same conditions apply to the SW and S coasts, but the S and SW winds produced from a low pressure system approaching from the W or SW are best. Any S wind in autumn can be good.

East Coast Any wind from between S and E is best. A low pressure system centred off the S or SW coast of Ireland will produce SE winds for a time. Seawatching on the east coast usually involves smaller numbers and fewer species than other coasts, and suitable winds tend to last for a shorter period, but can still be very productive. NE winds can also produce seabird movements, especially at Greenore Point (Site 125), in the SE of Ireland.

There is a degree of unpredictability about seawatching, which itself makes it so exciting. The conditions described above are *usually* the best, but you can never tell what unusual birds might pass a headland at any given time, and some rare birds have passed headlands and islands in calm conditions. Watching weather forecasts and trying to predict the 'where' and 'when' is all part of the fun.

Time of year makes an enormous difference to the number and variety of species. By far the best time for nearly all seabird species is

from early August to late September, though July and October can also be very good. Winter can be productive with more northerly species such as auks more in evidence, but many other species can be scarce or absent. Spring can see large movements of Irish breeding seabirds such as Gannet, auks and Manx Shearwater.

Time of day can be important, and the first two or three hours of daylight are often the best. This varies however, with the timing of any increase, decrease or change of direction of the wind.

How

The right equipment Binoculars and rain gear are the two essential items. 7x and 8x magnification binoculars are best. While 10x might seem better, they are more difficult to keep steady, especially for prolonged periods. Though not essential, a telescope and tripod are recommended, as many birds will pass at medium or long range. A 25x to 35x magnification is ideal, and special wide-angle lenses are best. A notebook and pen can be useful to keep track of your sightings.

With particularly good conditions, a large passage of seabirds can continue all day (and even into the next day). Additional 'comfort' items for a long spell sitting on a clifftop might include a cushion or camp stool, an umbrella, flask and food, and tissues to wipe rain from lenses.

Height above the sea is important. If you sit too high up the cliff, many birds will pass outside (either above or below) your field of view. Sit too low, and many will 'disappear' for long periods in the wave troughs. This decision will vary with local access, and occasionally weather conditions. Each seawatching site described in this book gives suggestions for the ideal spots to sit for a prolonged seawatch.

Index